Lecture Notes in Computer S

Commenced Publication in 1973
Founding and Former Series Editors:
Gerhard Goos, Juris Hartmanis, and Jan van Leeuwen

T0238521

Ranjit Jhala   Atsushi Igarashi (Eds.)

Programming Languages and Systems

10th Asian Symposium, APLAS 2012
Kyoto, Japan, December 11-13, 2012
Proceedings

 Springer

Volume Editors

Ranjit Jhala
University of California, San Diego
Computer Science Department
9500 Gilman Drive, La Jolla, CA 92093-6237, USA
E-mail: jhala@cs.ucsd.edu

Atsushi Igarashi
Kyoto University
Graduate School of Informatics
Yoshida-Honmachi, Sakyo-ku, Kyoto 606-8501, Japan
E-mail: igarashi@kuis.kyoto-u.ac.jp

ISSN 0302-9743   e-ISSN 1611-3349
ISBN 978-3-642-35181-5   e-ISBN 978-3-642-35182-2
DOI 10.1007/978-3-642-35182-2
Springer Heidelberg Dordrecht London New York

Library of Congress Control Number: 2012952150

CR Subject Classification (1998): D.3, D.2, F.3, D.4, D.2.4, D.1, F.4.1, C.2

LNCS Sublibrary: SL 2 – Programming and Software Engineering

Typesetting: Camera-ready by author, data conversion by Scientific Publishing Services, Chennai, India

Printed on acid-free paper

Springer is part of Springer Science+Business Media (www.springer.com)

Preface

This volume contains the proceedings of the 10th Asian Symposium on Programming Languages and Systems (APLAS 2012), held in Kyoto, Japan during December 11–13, 2012. APLAS aims at stimulating programming language research by providing a forum for the presentation of the latest results and the exchange of ideas in topics concerned with programming languages and systems. APLAS is based in Asia, but is an international forum that serves the worldwide programming language community. The past APLAS symposia were successfully held in Kenting (2011), Shanghai (2010), Seoul (2009), Bangalore (2008), Singapore (2007), Sydney (2006), Tsukuba (2005), Taipei (2004), and Beijing (2003) after three informal workshops.

The topics covered in the conference include, but are not limited to, semantics, logics, and foundational theory; design of languages and foundational calculi; domain-specific languages; type systems; compilers, interpreters, and abstract machines; program derivation, synthesis, and transformation; program analysis, constraints, verification, and model-checking; software security; concurrency and parallelism; and tools for programming, verification, and implementation.

This year, 58 papers were submitted to APLAS. Each submission was reviewed by three or more program committee members. After thoroughly evaluating the relevance and quality of each paper, the committee chose to accept 24 papers for presentation at the conference.

This year's program also continues the APLAS tradition of invited talks by distinguished researchers:

- Jan Vitek (Purdue University) on *Planet Dynamic or: How I Learned to Stop Worrying and Love Reflection*
- Greg Morrisett (Harvard University) on *Scalable Formal Machine Models*, and,
- Xavier Leroy (INRIA) on *Mechanized Semantics for Compiler Verification*.

This program would not have been possible without the unstinting efforts of several people, whom we would like to thank. First, the program committee and subreviewers for the hard work put in towards ensuring the high quality of the proceedings. Our thanks also go to the Asian Association for Foundation of Software (AAFS), founded by Asian researchers in cooperation with many researchers from Europe and the USA, for sponsoring and supporting APLAS. We would like to warmly thank the steering committee in general and Jacques Garrigue and Kohei Suenaga for their support in the local organization and for organizing the poster session. Finally, we are grateful to Andrei Voronkov whose EasyChair system eased the processes of submission, paper selection, and proceedings compilation.

December 2012

Ranjit Jhala
Atsushi Igarashi

Conference Organization

General Chair

Atsushi Igarashi

Program Chair

Ranjit Jhala

Program Committee

Amal Ahmed	Northeastern University
Satish Chandra	IBM Research
Juan Chen	Microsoft Research
Jean-Christophe Filliatre	CNRS
Deepak Garg	Max Planck Institute for Software Systems
Aarti Gupta	NEC Laboratories America
Arie Gurfinkel	SEI, Carnegie Mellon University
Aquinas Hobor	National University of Singapore
Chung-Kil Hur	University of Cambridge
Atsushi Igarashi	Kyoto University
Thomas Jensen	INRIA
Ranjit Jhala	UC San Diego
Akash Lal	Microsoft Research
Keiko Nakata	Tallinn University of Technology
James Noble	Victoria University of Wellington
Luke Ong	University of Oxford
Sungwoo Park	Pohang University of Science and Technology
Zvonimir Rakamaric	Carnegie Mellon University
Tachio Terauchi	Nagoya University
Dimitrios Vytiniotis	Microsoft Research
Bow-Yaw Wang	Academia Sinica
Stephanie Weirich	University of Pennsylvania
Eran Yahav	Technion
Xiangyu Zhang	Purdue University
Jianjun Zhao	Shanghai Jiao Tong University

Additional Reviewers

Albarghouthi, Aws
Besson, Frederic
Blackshear, Sam
Bonfante, Guillaume
Chang, Xi
Danvy, Olivier
Downen, Paul
Drossopoulou, Sophia
Gaboardi, Marco
Ganty, Pierre
Garoche, Pierre-Loic
Golan Gueta, Guy
Gopan, Denis
Harris, William
Hasegawa, Masahito
Im, Hyeonseung
Jia, Limin
Johannsen, Jacob
Komuravelli, Anvesh
Kong, Soonho

Li, Yi
Madhavan, Ravichandhran
Meshman, Yuri
Park, Jonghyun
Pearce, David
Pichardie, David
Rinetzky, Noam
Rolf, Carl Christian
Sinha, Nishant
Sjöberg, Vilhelm
Staton, Sam
Stump, Aaron
Suenaga, Kohei
Sun, Qiang
Swamy, Nikhil
Xie, Feng
Yorsh, Greta
Zhang, Cheng
Zhang, Sai

Table of Contents

Session V: Static Analysis II

Session VI: Language Design

Session VII: Dynamic Analysis

Session VIII: Complexity and Semantics

Session IX: Invited Talk

Session X: Program Logics and Verification

Session XI: Invited Talk

Planet Dynamic or: How I Learned to Stop Worrying and Love Reflection

Jan Vitek

Purdue University
jv@cs.purdue.edu

Abstract. A fundamental belief underlying forty years of programming languages research, aptly captured by the slogan *"Well-typed programs can't go wrong"*, is that programs augmented with machine-checked annotations are more likely to be free of bugs. But of course, real programs do wrong and programmers are voting with their feet. Dynamic languages such as RUBY, PYTHON, LUA, JAVASCRIPT and R are unencumbered by redundant type annotations and are increasingly popular. JAVASCRIPT, the *lingua franca* of the web, is moving to the server with the success of Node.js. R, another dynamic language, is being used in statistics, biology and finance for data analysis and visualization. Not only are these languages devoid of types, but they utterly lack any static structure that could be used for program verification. This talk will draw examples from recent results on JAVASCRIPT and R to illustrate the extent of the problem and propose some directions for research.

R. Jhala and A. Igarashi (Eds.): APLAS 2012, LNCS 7705, p. 1, 2012.

JATO: Native Code Atomicity for Java

Siliang Li[1], Yu David Liu[2], and Gang Tan[1]

[1] Department of Computer Science & Engineering, Lehigh University
[2] Department of Computer Science, SUNY Binghamton

Abstract. Atomicity enforcement in a multi-threaded application can be critical to the application's safety. In this paper, we take the challenge of enforcing atomicity in a multilingual application, which is developed in multiple programming languages. Specifically, we describe the design and implementation of JATO, which enforces the atomicity of a native method when a Java application invokes the native method through the Java Native Interface (JNI). JATO relies on a constraint-based system, which generates constraints from both Java and native code based on how Java objects are accessed by threads. Constraints are then solved to infer a set of Java objects that need to be locked in native methods to enforce the atomicity of the native method invocation. We also propose a number of optimizations that soundly improve the performance. Evaluation through JATO's prototype implementation demonstrates it enforces native-method atomicity with reasonable run-time overhead.

1   Introduction

Atomicity in programming languages is a fundamental concurrency property: a program fragment is *atomic* if its execution sequence—regardless of how the latter interleaves with other concurrent execution sequences at run time—exhibits the same "serial" behavior (*i.e.*, as if no interleaving happened). Atomicity significantly simplifies the reasoning about concurrent programs because invariants held by the atomic region in a serial execution naturally holds for a concurrent execution. Thanks to the proliferation of multi-core and many-core architectures, there is a resurgence of interest in atomicity, with active research including type systems and program analyses for atomicity enforcement and violation identification (*e.g.*, [6,23,11,5]), efficient implementation techniques (*e.g.*, [10]) and alternative programming models (*e.g.*, [1,21,3]).

As we adopt these research ideas to serious production settings, one major hurdle to cross is to support atomicity across foreign function interfaces (FFIs). Almost all languages support an FFI for interoperating with modules in low-level languages (*e.g.*, [20,28,17]). For instance, numerous classes in java.lang.* and java.io.* packages in the Java Development Kit (JDK) use the Java Native Interface (JNI), the FFI for Java. Existing atomicity solutions rarely provide direct support for FFIs. More commonly, code accessed through FFIs—called *native code* in JNI—is treated as a "black box."

The "black box" assumption typically yields two implementations, either leading to severe performance penalty or unsoundness. In the first implementation, the behavior of the native code is over-approximated as "anything can happen," *i.e.*, any memory

R. Jhala and A. Igarashi (Eds.): APLAS 2012, LNCS 7705, pp. 2–17, 2012.

area may be accessed by the native code. In that scenario, a "stop-the-world" strategy is usually required to guarantee soundness when native code is being executed—all other threads must be blocked. In the second implementation, the run-time behavior of native code is ignored, an unsound under-approximation. Atomicity violations may occur when native code happens to access the same memory area that it interleaves with. Such systems, no matter how sophisticated their support for atomicity for non-native code, technically conform to weak atomicity [22] at best. The lack of atomicity support for native code further complicates the design of new parallel/concurrent programming models. For example, several recent languages [1,15,3] are designed to make programs atomic by default, promoting the robustness of multi-core software. Native code poses difficulties for these languages: the lack of atomicity support for it is often cited [1] as a key reason for these languages to design "opt-out" constructs from their otherwise elegant implicit atomicity models.

We present JATO for atomicity enforcement across the JNI. It is standard knowledge that atomicity enforcement requires a precise accounting of the relationship between threads and their accessed memory. JATO is built upon the simple observation that despite rather different syntax and semantics between Java and native code, the memory access of both languages can be statically abstracted in a uniform manner. JATO first performs a static analysis to abstract memory access from both non-native code and native code, and then uses a lock-based implementation to guarantee atomicity, judiciously adding protection locks to selected memory locations. With the ability to treat code on both sides of the JNI as "white boxes" and perform precise analysis over them, our solution is not only sound, but also practical in terms of performance as demonstrated by a prototype implementation. This paper makes the following contributions:

- We propose a novel static analysis to precisely identify the set of Java objects whose protection is necessary for atomicity enforcement. The analysis is constructed as a constraint-based inference, which uniformly extracts memory-access constraints from JNI programs.
- The paper reports a prototype implementation, demonstrating the effectiveness and the performance impact on both micro-benchmarks and real-world applications.
- We propose a number of optimizations to further soundly improve the performance, such as no locks on read-only objects.

2 Background and Assumptions

The JNI allows Java programs to interface with low-level native code written in C, C++, or assembly languages. It allows Java code to invoke and to be invoked by native methods. A native method is declared in a Java class by adding the **native** modifier to a method. For example, the following Node class declares a native method named add:

```
class Node {int i=10; native void add (Node n);}
```

Once declared, native methods are invoked in Java in the same way as how Java methods are invoked. Note that the Java side may have multiple Java threads running, each of which may invoke some native method.

The implementation of a native method receives a set of Java-object references from the Java side; for instance, the above add method receives a reference to this object and a reference to the n object. A native-method implementation can interact with Java through a set of JNI interface functions (called JNI functions hereafter) as well as using features provided by the native language. Through JNI functions, native methods can inspect/modify/create Java objects, invoke Java methods, and so on. As an example, it can invoke MonitorEnter to lock a Java object and MonitorExit to unlock a Java object.

Assumptions. In any language that supports atomicity, it is necessary to define the *atomic region*, a demarcation of the program to indicate where an atomic execution starts and where it ends. One approach is to introduce some special syntax and ask programmers to mark atomic regions – such as atomic blocks. JATO's assumption is that each native method forms an atomic region. This allows us to analyze unannotated JNI code directly. Furthermore, we believe that this assumption matches Java programmers' intuition nicely. Java programmers often view native methods as black boxes, avoiding the reasoning about interleaving between Java code and native code. Finally, the assumption does not affect expressiveness. For instance, an atomic region with two native method invocations can be encoded as creating a third native method whose body contains the two invocations. If there is Java code fragment in between the two invocations, the encoded version can model the Java code by inserting a Java callback between the two invocations. Overall, the core algorithm we propose stays the same regardless of the demarcation strategy of atomic regions.

When enforcing native-method atomicity, JATO focuses on those Java objects that cross the Java-native boundary. It ignores the memory regions owned by native methods. For instance, native code might have a global pointer to a memory buffer in the native heap and lack of protection of the buffer might cause atomicity violations. Enforcing this form of atomicity can be performed on the native-side alone (*e.g.*, [2]). Furthermore, native code cannot pass pointers that point to C buffers across the boundary because Java code does not understand C's type system; native code has to invoke JNI functions to create Java objects and pass references to those Java objects across the boundary. Because of these reasons, JATO focuses on language-interoperation issues and analyzes those cross-boundary Java objects.

3   The Formal Model

In this section, we use an idealized JNI language to describe the core of JATO: a constraint-based lock inference algorithm for ensuring the atomicity of native methods.

3.1   Abstract Syntax

The following BNF presents the abstract syntax of an idealized JNI language where notation $\overline{X}$ represents a sequence of X's. Its Java subset is similar to Featherweight Java (FJ) [13], but with explicit support for field update and let bindings. For simplicity, the language omits features such as type casting, constructors, field initializers, multi-argument methods on the Java side, and heap management on the native side.

$$
\begin{array}{llll}
P & ::= & \overline{\textbf{class } \textsf{c} \textbf{ extends } \textsf{c} \ \{F \ M \ N\}} & \textit{classes} \\
F & ::= & \overline{\textsf{c f}} & \textit{fields} \\
M & ::= & \overline{\textsf{c m}(\textsf{c } x)\{e\}} & \textit{Java methods} \\
N & ::= & \overline{\textbf{native } \textsf{c m}(\textsf{c } x)\{t\}} & \textit{native methods} \\
e & ::= & x \mid \textbf{null} \mid e.\textsf{f} \mid e.\textsf{f}:=e \mid e.\textsf{m}(e) \mid \textbf{new}_\ell \ \textsf{c} \mid \textbf{let } x = e \textbf{ in } e & \textit{Java terms} \\
t & ::= & x \mid \textbf{null} \mid \texttt{GetField}(t, fd) \mid \texttt{SetField}(t, fd, t) & \textit{native terms} \\
& & \mid \ \texttt{NewObject}_\ell(\textsf{c}) \mid \texttt{CallMethod}(t, md, t) \mid \textbf{let } x = t \textbf{ in } t & \\
bd & ::= & e \mid t & \textit{method body} \\
fd & ::= & \langle \textsf{c}, \textsf{f} \rangle & \textit{field ID} \\
md & ::= & \langle \textsf{c}, \textsf{m} \rangle & \textit{method ID}
\end{array}
$$

A program is composed of a sequence of classes, each of which in turn is composed of a sequence of fields F, a sequence of Java methods M, and a sequence of native methods N. In this JNI language, both Java and native code are within the definition of classes; real JNI programs have separate files for native code. As a convention, metavariable $\textsf{c}(\in \mathbb{CN})$ is used for class names, $\textsf{f}$ for field names, $\textsf{m}$ for method names, and x for variable names. The root class is $\texttt{Object}$. We use e for a Java term, and t for a native term. A native method uses a set of JNI functions for accessing Java objects. $\texttt{GetField}$ and $\texttt{SetField}$ access a field via a field ID, and $\texttt{CallMethod}$ invokes a method defined on a Java object, which could either be implemented in Java or in native code. Both the Java-side instantiation expression (**new**) and the native-side counterpart ($\texttt{NewObject}$) are annotated with labels $\ell(\in \mathbb{LAB})$ and we require distinctness of all ℓ's in the code. We use notation $\mathcal{L}_P : \mathbb{LAB} \mapsto \mathbb{CN}$ to represent the mapping function from labels to the names of the instantiated classes as exhibited in program P. We use $mbody(\textsf{m}, \textsf{c})$ to compute the method body of $\textsf{m}$ of class $\textsf{c}$, represented as $x.bd$ where x is the parameter and bd is the definition of the method body. The definition of this function is identical to FJ's namesake function when $\textsf{m}$ is a Java method. When $\textsf{m}$ is a native method, the only difference is that the method should be looked up in N instead of M. We omit this lengthy definition in this short presentation.

Throughout this section, we will use a toy example to illustrate ideas, presented in Fig. 1. We liberally use void and primitive types, constructors, and use "$x = e_1; e_2$" for **let** $x = e_1$ **in** e_2. Note that the $\texttt{Node}$ class contains a native method for adding integers of two $\texttt{Node}$ objects and updating the receiver object. The goal in our context is to insert appropriate locks to ensure the execution of this native method being atomic.

3.2 Constraint Generation: An Overview

Atomicity enforcement relies on a precise accounting of memory access, which in JATO is abstracted as constraints. Constraints are generated through a type inference algorithm, defined in two steps: (1) constraints are generated intraprocedurally, both for Java methods and native methods; (2) all constraints are combined together through a closure process, analogous to interprocedural type propagation. The two-step approach is not surprising for object-oriented type inference, because dynamic dispatch

```
class Node extends Object {                class Main extends Object {
  int i=10;                                  void main() {
  native void add (Node n) {                   n1=new Node_ℓ₁ ();
    x1=GetField(this,<Node,i>);                n2=new Node_ℓ₂ ();
    x2=GetField(n,<Node,i>);                   th=new Thread2_ℓ_th (n1,n2);
    SetField(this,<Node,i>,x1+x2);}}           th.start();
class Thread2 extends Thread {                 n1.add(n2);
  Node n1, n2;                               }
  Thread2(Node n1, Node n2) {              }
    this.n1=n1; this.n2=n2;}
  void run() {n2.add(n1);}}
```

Fig. 1. A running example

approximation and concrete class analysis are long known to be intertwined in the presence of interprocedural analysis [27]: approximating dynamic dispatch – *i.e.*, determine which methods would be used to enable interprocedural analysis – requires the knowledge of the *concrete classes* (*i.e.*, the class of the run-time object) of the receiver, but interprocedural analysis is usually required to compute the concrete classes of the receiver object. JATO performs step (1) to intraprocedurally generate constraints useful for dynamic dispatch approximation and concrete class analysis, and then relies on step (2) to perform the two tasks based on the constraints. The details of the two steps are described in Sec. 3.3 and Sec. 3.4, respectively.

One interesting aspect of JATO is that both Java code and native code will be abstracted into the same forms of constraints after step (1). JATO constraints are:

$$
\begin{array}{lll}
\mathcal{K} ::= \overline{\kappa} & \textit{constraint set} \\
\kappa ::= \alpha \xrightarrow{\theta} \alpha' \mid \alpha \leq \alpha' \mid [\alpha.\mathsf{m}]^{\alpha'} & \textit{constraint} \\
\theta ::= \mathsf{R} \mid \mathsf{W} & \textit{access mode} \\
\alpha ::= \ell \mid \phi \mid \mathsf{thisO} \mid \mathsf{thisT} & \textit{abstract object/thread} \\
\quad \mid \alpha.\mathsf{f} \mid \alpha.\mathsf{m}^+ \mid \alpha.\mathsf{m}^- &
\end{array}
$$

An *access constraint* $\alpha \xrightarrow{\theta} \alpha'$ says that an (abstract) object α accesses an (abstract) object α', and the access is either a read ($\theta = \mathsf{R}$) or a write ($\theta = \mathsf{W}$). Objects in JATO's static system are represented in several forms. The first form is an instantiation site label ℓ. Recall earlier, we have required all ℓ's associated with the instantiation expressions (**new** or NewObject) to be distinct. It is thus natural to represent abstract objects with instantiation site labels. Our formal system's precision is thus middle-of-the-road: we differentiate objects of the same class if they are instantiated from different sites, but reins in the complexity by leaving out more precise features such as nCFA [29] or n-object context-sensitivity [25]. The other forms of α are used by the type inference algorithm: label variables $\phi \in \mathbb{LVAR}$, thisO for the object enclosing the code being analyzed, thisT for the thread executing the code being analyzed, $\alpha.\mathsf{f}$ for an alias to field f of object α, and $\alpha.\mathsf{m}^+$ and $\alpha.\mathsf{m}^-$ for aliases to the return value and the formal parameter of a method invocation to method name m of α, respectively.

$$(\text{T-Read}) \quad \frac{\Gamma \vdash e : \alpha \backslash \mathcal{K}}{\Gamma \vdash e.f : \alpha.f \backslash \mathcal{K} \cup \{\text{thisT} \overset{R}{\rightarrow} \alpha\}}$$

$$(\text{T-Write}) \quad \frac{\Gamma \vdash e : \alpha \backslash \mathcal{K} \qquad \Gamma \vdash e' : \alpha' \backslash \mathcal{K}'}{\Gamma \vdash e.f := e' : \alpha' \backslash \mathcal{K} \cup \mathcal{K}' \cup \{\alpha' \leq \alpha.f, \text{thisT} \overset{W}{\rightarrow} \alpha\}}$$

$$(\text{T-Msg}) \quad \frac{\Gamma \vdash e : \alpha \backslash \mathcal{K} \qquad \Gamma \vdash e' : \alpha' \backslash \mathcal{K}'}{\Gamma \vdash e.m(e') : \alpha.m^+ \backslash \mathcal{K} \cup \mathcal{K}' \cup \{\alpha' \leq \alpha.m^-, [\alpha.m]^{\text{thisT}}\}}$$

$$(\text{T-Thread}) \quad \frac{\Gamma \vdash e : \alpha \backslash \mathcal{K} \qquad javaT(\Gamma, e) \text{ is of a thread class}}{\Gamma \vdash e.\text{start}() : \alpha \backslash \mathcal{K} \cup \{[\alpha.\text{run}]^\alpha\}}$$

$$(\text{T-New}) \ \Gamma \vdash \mathbf{new}_\ell \ c : \ell \backslash \emptyset \qquad (\text{T-NewThread}) \ \frac{c \text{ is of a thread class} \qquad \phi \text{ fresh}}{\Gamma \vdash \mathbf{new}_\ell \ c : \ell \backslash \{\ell \leq \phi, \ \phi \leq \ell\}}$$

$$(\text{T-Var}) \ \Gamma \vdash x : \Gamma(x) \backslash \emptyset \qquad\qquad (\text{T-Null}) \ \Gamma \vdash \mathbf{null} : \ell_{\text{null}} \backslash \emptyset$$

$$(\text{T-Let}) \quad \frac{\Gamma \vdash e : \alpha \backslash \mathcal{K} \qquad \Gamma \rhd [x \mapsto \alpha] \vdash e' : \alpha' \backslash \mathcal{K}'}{\Gamma \vdash \mathbf{let} \ x = e \ \mathbf{in} \ e' : \alpha' \backslash \mathcal{K} \cup \mathcal{K}'}$$

Fig. 2. Java-Side Intraprocedual Constraint Generation

The additional two forms of constraints, $\alpha \leq \alpha'$ and $[\alpha.m]^{\alpha'}$, are used for concrete class analysis and dynamic dispatch approximation, respectively. Constraint $\alpha \leq \alpha'$ says that α may flow into α'. At a high level, one can view this form of constraint as relating two aliases. (As we shall see, the transitive closure of the binary relation defined by $\leq$ is *de facto* a concrete class analysis.) Constraint $[\alpha.m]^{\alpha'}$ is a *dynamic dispatch placeholder*, denoting method m of object α is being invoked by thread α'.

3.3 Intraprocedural Constraint Generation

We now describe the constraint-generation rules for Step (1) described in Sec. 3.2. Fig. 2 and Fig. 3 are rules for Java code and native code, respectively. The class-level constraint-generation rules are defined in Fig. 4. *Environment* Γ is a mapping from x's to α's. *Constraint summary* $\mathcal{M}$ is a mapping from method names to constraint sets. Judgement $\Gamma \vdash e : \alpha \backslash \mathcal{K}$ says expression e has type α under environment Γ and constraints $\mathcal{K}$. Since no confusion can exist, we further use $\Gamma \vdash t : \alpha \backslash \mathcal{K}$ to represent the analogous judgement for native term t. Judgement $\vdash_{\text{cls}} \mathbf{class} \ c \ldots \backslash \mathcal{M}$ says the constraint summary of class c is $\mathcal{M}$. Operator $\rhd$ is a mapping update: given a mapping U, $U \rhd [u \mapsto v]$ is identical to U except element u maps to v in $U \rhd [u \mapsto v]$.

$$(\text{TN-Read}) \quad \frac{\Gamma \vdash t : \alpha \backslash \mathcal{K} \qquad fd = \langle \mathsf{c}, \mathsf{f} \rangle}{\Gamma \vdash \texttt{GetField}(t, fd) : \alpha.\mathsf{f} \backslash \mathcal{K} \cup \{\texttt{thisT} \xrightarrow{R} \alpha\}}$$

$$(\text{TN-Write}) \quad \frac{\Gamma \vdash t : \alpha \backslash \mathcal{K} \qquad \Gamma \vdash t' : \alpha' \backslash \mathcal{K}' \qquad fd = \langle \mathsf{c}, \mathsf{f} \rangle}{\Gamma \vdash \texttt{SetField}(t, fd, t') : \alpha' \backslash \mathcal{K} \cup \mathcal{K}' \cup \{\alpha' \leq \alpha.\mathsf{f}, \ \texttt{thisT} \xrightarrow{W} \alpha\}}$$

$$(\text{TN-Msg}) \quad \frac{\Gamma \vdash t : \alpha \backslash \mathcal{K} \qquad \Gamma \vdash t' : \alpha' \backslash \mathcal{K}' \qquad md = \langle \mathsf{c}, \mathsf{m} \rangle}{\Gamma \vdash \texttt{CallMethod}(t, md, t') : \alpha.\mathsf{m}^+ \backslash \mathcal{K} \cup \mathcal{K}' \cup \{\alpha' \leq \alpha.\mathsf{m}^-, \ [\alpha.\mathsf{m}]^{\texttt{thisT}}\}}$$

$$(\text{TN-Thread}) \quad \frac{\Gamma \vdash t : \alpha \backslash \mathcal{K} \qquad md = \langle \mathsf{c}, \texttt{start} \rangle \qquad \mathsf{c} \text{ is a thread class}}{\Gamma \vdash \texttt{CallMethod}(t, md) : \alpha \backslash \mathcal{K} \cup \{[\alpha.\texttt{run}]^\alpha\}}$$

$$(\text{TN-New}) \ \Gamma \vdash \mathbf{new}_\ell \ \mathsf{c} : \ell \backslash \emptyset$$

$$(\text{TN-NewThread}) \quad \frac{\mathsf{c} \text{ is a thread class} \qquad \phi \text{ fresh}}{\Gamma \vdash \texttt{NewObject}_\ell(\mathsf{c}) : \ell \backslash \{\ell \leq \phi, \ \phi \leq \ell\}}$$

$$(\text{TN-Var}) \ \Gamma \vdash x : \Gamma(x) \backslash \emptyset \qquad\qquad (\text{TN-Null}) \ \Gamma \vdash \mathbf{null} : \ell_{\texttt{null}} \backslash \emptyset$$

$$(\text{TN-Let}) \quad \frac{\Gamma \vdash t : \alpha \backslash \mathcal{K} \qquad \Gamma \triangleright [x \mapsto \alpha] \vdash t' : \alpha' \backslash \mathcal{K}'}{\Gamma \vdash \mathbf{let} \ x = t \ \mathbf{in} \ t' : \alpha' \backslash \mathcal{K} \cup \mathcal{K}'}$$

Fig. 3. Native-Side Intraprocedural Constraint Generation

Observe that types are abstract objects (represented by α's). Java nominal typing (class names as types) is largely orthogonal to our interest here, so our type system does not include it. Taking an alternative view, one can imagine we only analyze programs already typed through Java-style nominal typing. For that reason, we liberally use function $javaT(\Gamma, e)$ to compute the class names for expression e.

On the Java side, (T-Read) and (T-Write) generate constraints to represent the read-/write access from the current thread ($\texttt{thisT}$) to the object whose field is being read-/written (α in both rules). The constraint $\alpha' \leq \alpha.\mathsf{f}$ in (T-Write) abstracts the fact that e' flows into the field f of e, capturing the data flow. The flow constraint generated by (T-Msg) is for the flow from the argument to the parameter of the method. That rule in addition generates a dynamic dispatch placeholder. (T-Thread) models the somewhat stylistic way Java performs thread creation: when an object of a thread class is sent a $\texttt{start}$ message, the $\texttt{run}$ method of the same object will be wrapped up in a new thread and executed. (T-New) says that the label used to annotate the instantiation point will be used as the type of the instantiated object. (T-NewThread) creates one additional label variable to represent the thread object. The goal here is to compensate the loss of precision of static analysis, which in turn would have affected soundness: a thread object may very well be part of a recursive context (a loop for example) where one instantiation point may be mapped to multiple run-time instances. The static analysis

$$\vdash_{cls} \textbf{class } c_0 \ldots \backslash \mathcal{M}$$

$$[\texttt{this} \mapsto \texttt{thisO}, \; x \mapsto \texttt{thisO.m}^-] \vdash bd : \alpha \backslash \mathcal{K} \text{ for all } mbody(\texttt{m}, \texttt{c}) = x.bd$$

$$\mathcal{K}' = \mathcal{K} \cup \{\alpha \leq \texttt{thisO.m}^+\}$$

(T-Cls) $\dfrac{}{\vdash_{cls} \textbf{class } \texttt{c} \textbf{ extends } c_0 \; \{F \; M \; N\} \backslash (\mathcal{M} \triangleright \overline{\texttt{m} \mapsto \mathcal{K}'})}$

(T-ClsTop) $\vdash_{cls} \textbf{class } \texttt{Object} \backslash []$

Fig. 4. Class-Level Constraint Generation

needs to be aware if all such instances access one shared memory location – a soundness issue because exclusive access by one thread or shared access by multiple threads have drastically different implications in reasoning about multi-threaded programs. The solution here is called *doubling* [15,34], treating every instantiation point for thread objects as two threads. Observe that we do not perform doubling for non-thread objects in (T-New) because there is no soundness concern there. The rest of the three rules should be obvious, where $\ell_{\texttt{null}}$ is a predefined label for **null**. For the running example, the following constraints will be generated for the two classes written in Java:

$\texttt{Main} : \{\texttt{main} \mapsto \{\ell_{th} \leq \phi_2, \; \phi_2 \leq \ell_{th}, \; [\ell_{th}.\texttt{run}]^{\ell_{th}}, \; \ell_2 \leq \ell_1.\texttt{add}^-, \; [\ell_1.\texttt{add}]^{\texttt{thisT}}\}\}$
$\texttt{Thread2} : \{\texttt{run} \mapsto \{\ell_1 \leq \ell_2.\texttt{add}^-, \; [\ell_2.\texttt{add}]^{\texttt{thisT}}\}\}$

The native-side inference rules have a one-on-one correspondence with the Java-side rules – as related by names – and every pair of corresponding rules generate the same form of constraints. This is a crucial insight of JATO: by abstracting the two worlds of Java syntax and native code syntax into one unified constraint representation, the artificial boundary between Java and native code disappears. As a result, thorny problems such as callbacks (to Java) inside native code no longer exists – the two worlds, after constraints are generated, are effectively one. The constraints for the Node class in the running example are:

$\texttt{Node} : \{\texttt{add} \mapsto \{\texttt{thisT} \xrightarrow{R} \texttt{thisO}, \; \texttt{thisT} \xrightarrow{W} \texttt{thisO}, \; \texttt{thisT} \xrightarrow{R} \texttt{thisO.add}^-\}\}$

3.4 Constraint Closure

Now that the constraint summary has been generated on a per-class per-method basis, we can discuss how to combine them into one global set. This is defined by computing the *constraint closure*, defined as follows:

Definition 1 (Constraint Closure). *The closure of program P with entry method md, denoted as $[\![P, md]\!]$ is the smallest set that satisfies the following conditions:*

- *Flows: $\leq$ is reflexive and transitive in $[\![P, md]\!]$.*
- *Concrete Class Approaching: If $\{\alpha' \leq \alpha\} \cup \mathcal{K} \subseteq [\![P, md]\!]$, then $\mathcal{K}\{\alpha'/\alpha\} \subseteq [\![P, md]\!]$.*

- **Dynamic Dispatch:** If $[\ell.\mathsf{m}]^{\ell_0} \in [\![P, md]\!]$, then $\mathcal{M}(\mathsf{m})\{\ell/\mathtt{thisO}\}\{\ell_0/\mathtt{thisT}\} \subseteq [\![P, md]\!]$ where $\mathcal{L}_P(\ell) = \mathsf{c}$ and $\vdash_{\mathtt{cls}}$ **class** $\mathsf{c} \ldots \setminus \mathcal{M}$.
- **Bootstrapping:** $\{[\ell_{\mathsf{BO}}.\mathsf{m}]^{\ell_{\mathsf{BT}}}, \ell_{\mathsf{BP}} \le \ell_{\mathsf{BO}}.\mathsf{m}^{-}\} \subseteq [\![P, md]\!]$ where $md = \langle \mathsf{c}, \mathsf{m} \rangle$.

The combination of **Flows** and **Concrete Class Approaching** is *de facto* a concrete class analysis, where the "concrete class" in our case is the object instantiation sites (not Java nominal types): the **Flows** rule interprocedurally builds the data flow, and the **Concrete Class Approaching** rule substitutes a flow element with one "up stream" on the data flow. When the "source" of the data flow – an instantiation point label – is substituted in, concrete class analysis is achieved. Standard notation $\mathcal{K}\{\alpha'/\alpha\}$ substitutes every occurrence of α in $\mathcal{K}$ with α'. **Dynamic Dispatch** says that once the receiver object of an invocation resolves to a concrete class, dynamic dispatch can thus be resolved. The substitutions of $\mathtt{thisO}$ and $\mathtt{thisT}$ are not surprising from an interprocedural perspective. The last rule, **Bootstrapping**, bootstraps the closure. $\ell_{\mathsf{BO}}, \ell_{\mathsf{BT}}, \ell_{\mathsf{BP}}$ are pre-defined labels representing the bootstrapping object (the one with method md), the bootstrapping thread, and the parameter used for the bootstrapping invocation.

For instance, if P is the running example, the following constraints are among the ones in the closure from its main method, *i.e.*, $[\![P, \langle \mathsf{c_{main}}, \mathsf{m_{main}} \rangle]\!]$:

$$\ell_{\mathsf{BT}} \xrightarrow{\mathsf{R}} \ell_1 \qquad \ell_{\mathsf{BT}} \xrightarrow{\mathsf{W}} \ell_1 \qquad \ell_{\mathsf{BT}} \xrightarrow{\mathsf{R}} \ell_2$$
$$\ell_{th} \xrightarrow{\mathsf{R}} \ell_2 \qquad \ell_{th} \xrightarrow{\mathsf{W}} \ell_2 \qquad \ell_{th} \xrightarrow{\mathsf{R}} \ell_1$$

That is, the bootstrapping thread performs read and write access to object ℓ_1 and read access to object ℓ_2. The child thread performs read access to object ℓ_1 and read and write access to object ℓ_2. This matches our intuition about the program.

3.5   Atomicity Enforcement

Based on the generated constraints, JATO infers a set of Java objects that need to be locked in a native method to ensure its atomicity. JATO also takes several optimizing steps to remove unnecessary locks while still maintaining atomicity.

Lock-all. The simplest way to ensure atomicity is to insert locks for all objects that a native method may read from or write to. Suppose we need to enforce the atomicity of a native method md in a program P, the set of objects that need to be locked are:

$$Acc(P, md) \stackrel{\text{def}}{=} \{\, \alpha \mid (\alpha' \xrightarrow{\theta} \alpha) \in [\![P, md]\!] \wedge (\alpha \in \mathbb{LAB} \vee labs(\alpha) \subseteq \{\ell_{\mathsf{BO}}, \ell_{\mathsf{BP}}\}) \,\}$$

The first predicate $(\alpha' \xrightarrow{\theta} \alpha) \in [\![P, md]\!]$ says that α is indeed read or written. The α's that satisfy this predicate may be in a form that represents an alias to an object, such as $\ell.\mathsf{f}_1.\mathsf{f}_2.\mathsf{m}^{+}$, and it is clearly desirable to only inform the lock insertion procedure of the real instantiation point of theobject (the $\alpha \in \mathbb{LAB}$ predicate) – *e.g.*, "please lock the object instantiated at label ℓ_{33}." This, however, is not always possible because the instantiation site for the object enclosing the native method and that for the native method parameter are abstractly represented as ℓ_{BO} and ℓ_{BP}, respectively. It is thus impossible to concretize any abstract object whose representation is "built around them". For example, $\ell_{\mathsf{BO}}.\mathsf{f}_3$ means that the object is stored in field f_3 of the enclosing object ℓ_{BO}, and access to the stored object requires locking the enclosing object. This is the intuition behind predicate $labs(\alpha) \subseteq \{\ell_{BO}, \ell_{BP}\}$, where $labs(\alpha)$ enumerates all the labels in α.

For the running example, the set of objects to lock for the native add method – $Acc(P, \langle Node, add \rangle)$ – is $\{\ell_{BO}, \ell_{BP}\}$, meaning both the enclosing object and the parameter needs to be locked.

Locking all objects in $Acc(P, md)$ is sufficient to guarantee the atomicity of md. This comes as no surprise: every memory access by the native method is guarded by a lock. The baseline approach here is analogous to a purely dynamic approach: instead of statically computing the closure and the set of objects to be locked as we define here, one could indeed achieve the same effect by just locking at run time for every object access.

In the lock-all approach, JATO inserts code that acquires the lock for each object in the set as computed above and releases the lock at the end. The lock is acquired by JNI function `MonitorEnter` and released by `MonitorExit`.

Lock-on-write. In this strategy, we differentiate read and write access, and optimize based on the widely known fact that non-exclusive reads and exclusive writes are adequate to guarantee atomicity. The basic idea is simple: given a constraint set $\mathcal{K}$, only elements in the following set needs to be locked, where *size* computes the size of a set:

$$lockS(\mathcal{K}) \overset{\text{def}}{=} \{\ell \mid size(\{\ell' \mid \ell' \xrightarrow{W} \ell \in \mathcal{K}\}) \neq 0 \wedge size(\{\ell' \mid \ell' \xrightarrow{\theta} \ell \in \mathcal{K}\}) > 1\}$$

It would be tempting to compute the necessary locks for enforcing the atomicity of native method md of program P as $lockS(\llbracket P, md \rrbracket)$. This unfortunately would be unsound. Consider the running example. Even though the parameter object n is only read accessed in native method add, it is not safe to remove the lock due to two facts: (1) in the main thread, add receives object ℓ_1 as the argument; (2) in the child thread, object ℓ_1 is mutated. If the lock to the parameter object n were removed, atomicity of add could not be guaranteed since the integer value in the parameter object may be mutated in the middle of the method. Therefore, it is necessary to perform a global analysis to apply the optimization.

The next attempt would be to lock objects in $lockS(\llbracket P, \langle c_{main}, m_{main} \rangle \rrbracket)$. Clearly, this is sound, but it does not take into the account that native method md only accesses a subset of these objects. To compute the objects that are accessed by md, we define function $AccG(P, md)$ as the smallest set satisfying the following conditions, where $md = \langle c, m \rangle$ and $\mathcal{K}_0 = \llbracket P, \langle c_{main}, m_{main} \rangle \rrbracket$:

- If $\{[\ell.m]^{\ell_0}, \ell_1 \leq \ell.m^-\} \subseteq \mathcal{K}_0$ where $\mathcal{L}_P(\ell) = c$, then
  $Acc(P, md)\{\ell/\ell_{BO}\}\{\ell_0/\ell_{BT}\}\{\ell_1/\ell_{BP}\} \subseteq AccG(P, md)$.
- If $\ell \leq \alpha \in \mathcal{K}_0$ and $\alpha \in AccG(P, md)$, then $\ell \in AccG(P, md)$.

In other words, $Acc(P, md)$ almost fits our need, except that it contains placeholder labels such as ℓ_{BO}, ℓ_{BT}, and ℓ_{BP}. $AccG$ concretizes any abstract object whose representation is dependent on them. With this definition, we can now define our strategy: locks are needed for native method md of program P for any object in the following set:

$$AccG(P, md) \cap lockS(\llbracket P, \langle c_{main}, m_{main} \rangle \rrbracket).$$

Lock-at-write-site. Instead of acquiring the lock of an object at the beginning of a native method and releasing the lock at the end, this optimization inserts locking around the code region of the native method that accesses the object. If there are multiple accesses of the object, JATO finds the smallest code region that covers all accesses and acquires/releases the lock only once.

4   Prototype Implementation

We implemented a prototype system based on the constraint-based system described in the previous section. Java-side constraint generation in JATO is built upon Cypress [35], a static analysis framework focusing on memory access patterns. Native-side constraint generation is implemented in CIL [26], an infrastructure for analyzing and transforming C code. The rest of JATO is developed in around 5,000 lines of OCaml code.

One issue that we have ignored in the idealized JNI language is the necessity of performing Java-type analysis in native code. In the idealized language, native methods can directly use field IDs in the form of $\langle c, f \rangle$ (and similarly for method IDs). But in real JNI programs, native methods have to invoke certain JNI functions to construct those IDs. To read a field of a Java object, native method must take three steps: (1) use GetObjectClass to get a reference to the class object of the Java object; (2) use GetFieldID to get a field ID for a particular field by providing the field's name and type; (3) use the field ID to retrieve the value of the field in the object.

For instance, the following program first gets obj's field nd, which is a reference to another object of class Node. It then reads the field i of the Node object.

```
jclass cls = GetObjectClass(obj);
jfieldID fid = GetFieldID(cls, "nd", "Node");
jobject obj2 = GetField(obj, fid);
jclass cls2 = GetObjectClass(obj2);
jfieldID fid2 = GetFieldID(cls2, "i", "I");
int x1 = GetIntField(obj, fid2);
```

The above steps may not always be performed in consecutive steps; caching field and method IDs for future use is a common optimization. Furthermore, arguments provided to functions such as GetFieldID may not always be string constants. For better precision, JATO uses an inter-procedural, context-sensitive static analysis to track constants and infer types of Java references [19]. For the above program, it is able to decide that there is a read access to obj and there is a read access to obj.nd. To do this, it is necessary to infer what Java class cls represents and what field ID fid represents.

5   Preliminary Evaluation

We performed preliminary evaluation on a set of multithreaded JNI programs. Each program was analyzed to generate a set of constraints, as presented in Sec. 3. Based on the closure of the generated constraints, a set of objects were identified to ensure atomicity of a native method in these programs. Different locking schemes were evaluated to examine their performance.

All experiments were carried out on an iMac machine running Mac OS X (version 10.7.4) with Intel core i7 CPU of 4 cores clocked at 2.8GHz and with 8GB memory. The version of Java is OpenJDK 7. For each experiment, we took the average among ten runs.

We next summarize the JNI programs we have experimented with. The programs include: (1) a parallel matrix-multiplication (MM) program, constructed by ourselves; (2) a Fast-Fourier-Transform (FFT) program, adapted from JTransforms [33] by rewriting some Java routines in C; (3) the compress program, which is a module that performs multithreaded file compression provided by the MessAdmin [24] project; (4) the derby benchmark program is selected from SPECjvm2008 [30] and is a database program. Both compress and derby are pure Java programs, but they invoke standard Java classes in java.io and java.util.zip, which contain native methods.

The analysis time and LOC for both Java side and C side on each program are listed below. It is observed that majority of the time is spent on Java side analysis, particularly on Java-side constraint-generation.

Program	LOC (Java)	Time (Java)	LOC (C)	Time (C)
MM	275	3.34s	150	10μs
FFT	6,654	8.14s	3,169	0.01s
compress	3,197	27.8s	5,402	0.05s
derby	919,493	81.04s	5,402	0.05s

All programs are benchmarked under the three strategies we described in the previous section. L-ALL stands for the lock-all approach. L-W stands for the lock-on-write approach. L-WS stands for the case after applying the lock-on-write and lock-at-write-site optimizations.

Matrix multiplication. The programs takes in two input matrices, calculates the multiplication of the two and writes the result in an output matrix. It launches multiple threads and each thread is responsible for calculating the result of one element of the output matrix. The calculation of one element is through a native method. In this program, three two-dimensional arrays of double crosses the boundary from Java to the native code.

For this program, JATO identifies that the native method accesses the three cross-boundary objects. These objects are shared among threads. The input matrices and their arrays are read-accessed whereas the resulting matrix and its array are read- and write-accessed.

Fig. 5(a) presents the execution times of applying different locking schemes. The size of the matrices is 500 by 500 with array elements ranging between 0.0 and 1000.0. L-WS has the best performance overall.

FFT. The native method of this program takes in an array of double to be transformed and sets the transformed result in an output array. The input array is read-accessed whereas the output array is write-accessed. The arrays are shared among threads. Fig. 5(b) shows the results of FFT. Similar to the program of matrix multiplication, L-W improved upon L-ALL, and L-WS performs the best among the three.

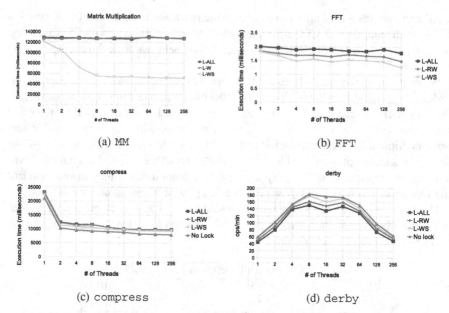

Fig. 5. Execution time of the benchmark programs under different locking schemes

compress. This program compresses an input file by dividing the file into smaller blocks and assigning one block to one thread for compression. The actual compression is performed in the native side using the `zlib` C library. JATO identifies that a number of objects such as `Deflater` are shared among threads and read/write accessed at the Java side. One exception is `FileInputStream`, where it is only read-accessed in Java but is write-accessed at the native side. In term of the number of locks inserted, there is little difference between lock-all and lock-on-write.

Fig. 5(c) presents the results of `compress`. The file size is about 700MB and the block size is 128K. The performance gain of L-W over L-ALL is negligible. We see there is some minor improvement using L-WS. This is because in the native code, write-access code regions to the locked objects are typically small.

derby. It is a multithreaded database. Some `byte` arrays and `FileInputStream` objects are passed into the native code. They are read-accessed between threads from the Java side. On the native side, both kinds of objects are write-accessed.

Fig. 5(d) shows the result of running derby. The experiment was run for 240 seconds with 60 seconds warm-up time. The peak ops/min occurs when the number of threads is between 8 to 32. We can see that in L-WS approach, the performance gains at its peak is about 35% over L-ALL.

For `compress` and `derby`, we also experimented with the no-lock scheme in which no locking is inserted in native methods. Although the uninstrumented programs run successfully, there is no guarantee of native-method atomicity as provided by JATO. The programs of matrix multiplication and `FFT` would generate wrong results when no locks were inserted for native-method atomicity. For the matrix-multiplication program, even though the native method of each thread calculates and updates only one element of the output matrix, it is necessary to acquire the lock of the output matrix before operating on it: native methods use JNI function `GetArrayElements` to get a pointer to the output matrix and `GetArrayElements` may copy the matrix and return a pointer to the copy [20].

6 Related Work

The benefits of static reasoning of atomicity in programming languages were demonstrated by Flanagan and Qadeer [6] through a type effect system. Since then, many static systems have been designed to automatically insert locks to enforce atomicity: some are type-based [23,15]; some are based on points-to graphs [11]; some reduce the problem to an ILP optimization problem [5]. Among them, JATO's approach is more related to [15]. Unlike that approach where the focus is on the interaction between language design and static analysis, JATO focuses on static analysis in a mixed language setting.

Atomicity can either be implemented via locks (*e.g.*, the related work above) or by transactional memory (TM) [10]. Related to our work are two concepts articulated in TM research: *weak atomicity* and *strong atomicity* [22]. In a system that supports weak atomicity, the execution of an atomic program fragment exhibits serial behaviors *only* when interleaving with that of other atomic program fragments; there is no guarantee when the former interleaves with *arbitrary* executions. To support the latter, *i.e.*, strong atomicity, has been a design goal of many later systems (*e.g.*, [4]). Most existing strong atomicity algorithms would disallow native methods to be invoked within atomic regions, an unrealistic assumption considering a significant number of Java libraries are written in native code for example. Should they allow for native methods but ignore their impact these approaches would revert back to what they were aimed at solving: weak atomicity.

In a software transactional memory setting where the atomicity region is defined as atomic blocks, *external actions* [9] are proposed as a language abstraction to allow code running within an atomic block to request that a given pre-registered operation (such as native method invocation) be executed outside the block. In the "atomicity-by-default" language AME [1], a `protected` block construct is introduced to allow the code within the block to opt out of the atomicity region. Native methods are cited as a motivation for this construct. Overall, these solutions focus on how to faithfully model the non-atomicity of native methods, not how to support their atomicity.

This work belongs to the general category of improving upon FFIs' safety, reliability, and security. FFI-based software is often error-prone; recent studies found a large number of software bugs in the interface code between modules of different languages based on static analysis [7,8,32,14,18,19] and dynamic analysis [31,16], and new interface languages for writing safer multilingual code (*e.g.*, [12]). JATO performs interlanguage analysis and lock insertion to ensure atomicity of native methods in JNI code. We are not aware of other work that addresses concurrency issues in FFI code.

7 Conclusion and Future Work

JATO is a system that enforces atomicity of native methods in multi-threaded JNI programs. Atomicity enforcement algorithms are generalized to programs developed in multiple languages by using an inter-language, constraint-based system. JATO takes care to enforce a small number of locks for efficiency.

As future work, we will investigate how to ensure locking inserted by JATO does not cause deadlocks (even though we didn't encounter such cases yet during our experiment), probably using the approach of a global lock order as in Autolocker [23]. Moreover, we believe that JATO's approach can be generalized to other FFIs such as the OCaml/C interface [17] and the Python/C interface [28].

Acknowledgements. The authors would like to thank Haitao Steve Zhu for his assistance with running experiments in Cypress. The authors would also like to thank the anonymous reviewers for their thorough and valuable comments. This research is supported by US NSF grants CCF-0915157, CCF-151149211, a research award from Google, and in part by National Natural Science Foundation of China grant 61170051.

References

1. Abadi, M., Birrell, A., Harris, T., Isard, M.: Semantics of transactional memory and automatic mutual exclusion. In: POPL 2008, pp. 63–74 (2008)
2. Berger, E.D., Yang, T., Liu, T., Novark, G.: Grace: safe multithreaded programming for c/c++. In: OOPSLA 2009, pp. 81–96 (2009)
3. Bocchino Jr., R.L., Heumann, S., Honarmand, N., Adve, S.V., Adve, V.S., Welc, A., Shpeisman, T.: Safe nondeterminism in a deterministic-by-default parallel language. In: POPL 2011, pp. 535–548 (2011)
4. CarlStrom, B., McDonald, A., Chafi, H., Chung, J., Minh, C., Kozyrakis, C., Olukotun, K.: The atomos transactional programming language. In: PLDI 2006 (June 2006)
5. Emmi, M., Fischer, J.S., Jhala, R., Majumdar, R.: Lock allocation. In: POPL 2007, pp. 291–296 (2007)
6. Flanagan, C., Qadeer, S.: A type and effect system for atomicity. In: PLDI 2003, pp. 338–349 (2003)
7. Furr, M., Foster, J.S.: Checking type safety of foreign function calls. In: ACM Conference on Programming Language Design and Implementation, PLDI, pp. 62–72 (2005)
8. Furr, M., Foster, J.S.: Polymorphic Type Inference for the JNI. In: Sestoft, P. (ed.) ESOP 2006. LNCS, vol. 3924, pp. 309–324. Springer, Heidelberg (2006)
9. Harris, T.: Exceptions and side-effects in atomic blocks. Sci. Comput. Program. 58(3), 325–343 (2005)
10. Harris, T., Fraser, K.: Language support for lightweight transactions. In: OOPSLA 2003, pp. 388–402 (2003)
11. Hicks, M., Foster, J.S., Prattikakis, P.: Lock inference for atomic sections. In: TRANSACT 2006 (June 2006)
12. Hirzel, M., Grimm, R.: Jeannie: Granting Java Native Interface developers their wishes. In: ACM Conference on Object-Oriented Programming, Systems, Languages, and Applications, OOPSLA, pp. 19–38 (2007)
13. Igarashi, A., Pierce, B., Wadler, P.: Featherweight java - a minimal core calculus for java and gj. ACM Transactions on Programming Languages and Systems, 132–146 (1999)
14. Kondoh, G., Onodera, T.: Finding bugs in Java Native Interface programs. In: ISSTA 2008: Proceedings of the 2008 International Symposium on Software Testing and Analysis, pp. 109–118. ACM, New York (2008)

15. Kulkarni, A., Liu, Y.D., Smith, S.F.: Task types for pervasive atomicity. In: OOPSLA 2010 (October 2010)
16. Lee, B., Hirzel, M., Grimm, R., Wiedermann, B., McKinley, K.S.: Jinn: Synthesizing a dynamic bug detector for foreign language interfaces. In: ACM Conference on Programming Language Design and Implementation, PLDI, pp. 36–49 (2010)
17. Leroy, X.: The Objective Caml system (2008), http://caml.inria.fr/pub/docs/manual-ocaml/index.html
18. Li, S., Tan, G.: Finding bugs in exceptional situations of JNI programs. In: 16th ACM Conference on Computer and Communications Security, CCS, pp. 442–452 (2009)
19. Li, S., Tan, G.: JET: Exception checking in the Java Native Interface. In: ACM Conference on Object-Oriented Programming, Systems, Languages, and Applications, OOPSLA, pp. 345–358 (2011)
20. Liang, S.: Java Native Interface: Programmer's Guide and Reference. Addison-Wesley Longman Publishing Co., Inc. (1999)
21. Liu, Y.D., Lu, X., Smith, S.F.: Coqa: Concurrent Objects with Quantized Atomicity. In: Hendren, L. (ed.) CC 2008. LNCS, vol. 4959, pp. 260–275. Springer, Heidelberg (2008)
22. Martin, M.M.K., Blundell, C., Lewis, E.: Subtleties of transactional memory atomicity semantics. Computer Architecture Letters 5(2) (2006)
23. McCloskey, B., Zhou, F., Gay, D., Brewer, E.: Autolocker: synchronization inference for atomic sections. In: POPL 2006, pp. 346–358 (2006)
24. messAdmin, http://messadmin.sourceforge.net/
25. Milanova, A., Rountev, A., Ryder, B.G.: Parameterized object sensitivity for points-to analysis for java. ACM Trans. Softw. Eng. Methodol. 14(1), 1–41 (2005)
26. Necula, G.C., McPeak, S., Rahul, S.P., Weimer, W.: CIL: Intermediate Language and Tools for Analysis and Transformation of C Programs. In: Horspool, R.N. (ed.) CC 2002. LNCS, vol. 2304, pp. 213–228. Springer, Heidelberg (2002)
27. Palsberg, J., Schwartzbach, M.I.: Object-oriented type inference. In: OOPSLA 1991, pp. 146–161 (1991)
28. Python/C API reference manual (April 2009), http://docs.python.org/c-api/index.html
29. Shivers, O.: Control-Flow Analysis of Higher-Order Languages. PhD thesis, Carnegie-Mellon University, Pittsburgh, PA (May 1991), CMU-CS-91-145
30. SPECjvm2008, http://www.spec.org/jvm2008/
31. Tan, G., Appel, A., Chakradhar, S., Raghunathan, A., Ravi, S., Wang, D.: Safe Java Native Interface. In: Proceedings of IEEE International Symposium on Secure Software Engineering, pp. 97–106 (2006)
32. Tan, G., Morrisett, G.: ILEA: Inter-language analysis across Java and C. In: ACM Conference on Object-Oriented Programming, Systems, Languages, and Applications, OOPSLA, pp. 39–56 (2007)
33. Wendykier, P., Nagy, J.G.: Parallel colt: A high-performance java library for scientific computing and image processing. ACM Trans. Math. Softw. 37(3), 31:1–31:22 (2010)
34. Whaley, J., Lam, M.S.: Cloning-based context-sensitive pointer alias analysis using binary decision diagrams. In: PLDI 2004, pp. 131–144 (2004)
35. Zhu, H.S., Liu, Y.D.: Scalable object locality analysis with cypress principle. Technical report, SUNY Binghamton (May 2012)

Ownership Types for Object Synchronisation

Yi Lu, John Potter, and Jingling Xue

Programming Languages and Compilers Group
School of Computer Science and Engineering
University of New South Wales
Sydney, NSW 2052, Australia
{ylu,potter,jingling}@cse.unsw.edu.au

Abstract. Shared-memory concurrent programming is difficult and error prone because memory accesses by concurrent threads need to be coordinated through synchronisation, which relies on programmer discipline and suffers from a lack of modularity and compile-time support. This paper exploits object structures, provided by ownership types, to enable a structured synchronisation scheme which guarantees safety and allows more concurrency within structured tasks.

1   Introduction

Shared-memory concurrent programming remains complex and error-prone, despite it having become essential in the multicore era. Most object-oriented (OO) languages adopt *unstructured parallelism*, where threads may be ubiquitously spawned with arbitrary lifetimes. It is notoriously difficult to catch concurrency errors, such as data-races, atomicity violations and deadlocks, because they are caused by unexpected thread interleaving. In practice, "most Java programs are so rife with concurrency bugs that they work only by accident" [15]. Lee argues that if we are to have any hope of simplifying parallel programming for the vast majority of programmers and applications, then parallel programming models must greatly constrain the possible interleaving of program executions [19].

Programming models with more disciplined parallelism have attracted recent interest. Based on hierarchical fork/join parallelism where tasks are managed lexically [14,18], a number of structured parallel programming models [2,10,31] are emerging. They are able to forbid task interference in type systems or program analysis, guaranteeing deterministic behaviour [2,31] or allowing the compiler to find implicit parallelism from sequential object-oriented programs [10]. While significantly simplifying concurrency, these models preclude task interference thereby having limited applicability to object-oriented programs with extensive sharing and mutation. Finally, by not allowing synchronisation, these models cannot allow task interference, which essentially reduces their application to immutable object applications; immutability makes concurrency easier, but there are undoubtedly applications that need to combine concurrency and mutability. In this paper, we use an ownership type and effect system to reason about *interference and synchronisation for parallel tasks*.

When there is potential interference between parallel tasks, we infer a *synchronisation requirement* which needs to be met by a suitable lock (or other

R. Jhala and A. Igarashi (Eds.): APLAS 2012, LNCS 7705, pp. 18–33, 2012.
© Springer-Verlag Berlin Heidelberg 2012

synchronisation technique) to prevent the interference. Our type system ensures atomicity for each task, thereby guaranteeing serialisability of all tasks. When there is no interference between tasks, no synchronisation is necessary.

Meeting synchronisation requirements involves choices. Too little synchronisation may not preserve program safety, while too much synchronisation compromises concurrency and increases the chances of deadlock. Moreover, there is a tradeoff between the choices of synchronisation granularity. Choosing a coarse granularity results in less overhead (synchronisation requires runtime resources) but may reduce concurrency. For example, when we enforce synchronisation with coarse-grained locks, objects protected by the same lock can never be accessed in parallel (e.g. SafeJava, see Section 3.3). On the other hand, using a fine granularity increases the overhead of synchronisation. The fundamental problem here is that synchronisation is a whole program requirement, which is hard to localise to a single class or module. All code that accesses a piece of shared state must know and obey the same synchronisation convention regardless of who developed the code or where it is deployed. Large object-oriented programs are typically developed and deployed in a modular way by different programmers. As each programmer may follow their own conventions on synchronisation (e.g. some use finer granularity, others use coarser granularity) which are not formally or precisely specified, understanding and writing synchronised code is difficult and error prone.

We support modular reasoning about parallel tasks using ownership types and effects. Ownership types [8,9] allow programmers to structure the object store hierarchically as an ownership tree; ownership-based effects [5,6,8] use ownership tree to reason about side effects in object-oriented programs and to capture potential conflict between tasks. A major contribution of the paper is the ability to automatically infer finer-grained synchronisation requirements for parallel tasks, sufficient to prevent any potential interference between them. Such implicit synchronisation eases the design and understanding of concurrent object-oriented programs by hiding lower level concurrency safety requirements. Code is less fragile.

Another key novelty comes from the combination of object ownership with structured task parallelism: when the two structures align well, we expect to see good concurrency. For example, a task synchronising on an object (coarser granularity) may be able to allow its subtasks to access the object's subobjects without explicit synchronisation, even though the sub-tasks may still be in conflict with external sub-tasks. Such structural refinement of granularity and interference-based on-demand synchronisation strategy can reduce overhead without needlessly sacrificing potential concurrency (as shown in the examples given in later sections). Moreover, with structured parallelism, it is simpler to achieve lock ordering so then there is no chance of deadlock from multiple locks.

This paper presents the basics of our model: Section 2 discusses ownership types, object aliasing and ownership-based effects; Section 3 introduces our structured parallel task model and discusses synchronisation requirements with an example; Section 4 formally presents static semantics and dynamic semantics of the type system; Section 5 provides more discussion and reviews related work, followed by a brief summary of our contributions in Section 6.

The complete formalism including rules and properties and synchronisation inference algorithms are included in an extended version of this paper [22].

2   Ownership Types and Effects in a Nutshell

Originally ownership types were proposed to provide object encapsulation [9,8,20,24]. Here we use ownership types to describe effects as structured sets of objects, similar to what has been done by others [5,8,23,6,10], without enforcing encapsulation. First we provide a quick overview of ownership types, and indicate how our model of structured objects allows us to statically reason about objects being disjoint, guaranteeing non-aliasing properties for program variables. Then we discuss how program effects can be succinctly summarised using ownership structure. Ultimately our concern is to provide a practical means for reasoning about conflicting effects of concurrent behaviours.

2.1   Ownership Types and Aliasing

In an ownership type system, every object has a fixed owner, either world, for root objects, or another object; we say that an object is strictly inside its owner. The ownership relation establishes a dynamic tree structure, rooted at world, with every object created as a child of its owner. Ownership types allow us to reason statically about hierarchical object structures.

Owners are often called *(ownership) contexts* in ownership type systems. Classes are parameterised by formal context parameters, possibly with constraints such as inside $\preceq$, strictly inside $\prec$ or disjoint $\#$. The first formal context parameter of a class determines the owner of this object within the class. Types are formed by binding actual contexts to their class parameters; the first context argument of a type determines the actual owner of objects of the type. Within a class definition, contexts can use formal class parameters, the root context world, the current context this and final expressions (see Section 4). Consider the following Java-style example:

```
class Customer {
    final Account<this> sav = new Account<this> ();
    final Account<this> chq = new Account<this> ();
    void transfer(int amt) <this> { sav.withdraw(amt); chq.deposit(amt); }
}
```

The context argument of the Account type for the read-only sav and chq fields specifies the owner for the objects referenced by those fields. In this case, it is the current object this of class Customer, meaning that a customer owns savings and cheque accounts. We omit formal parameters of a class when none are used in its definition, as for Customer. Ownership types are often used for object encapsulation by constraining references. For instance, accounts cannot be directly accessed unless through their owning customer. This enables object access control and localised reasoning on objects. However, in this paper, we do not enforce encapsulation or constrain references because our type system relies only on (ownership) effects: ownership determines object structure, and structured objects allow us to succinctly summarise effects. Encapsulation can still be enforced independently if desired.

Even without enforcing encapsulation, ownership types allow us to derive more distinctions for reasoning about object aliasing. We rely on this in two related ways: we can determine when effects are disjoint, and when synchronisation requirements are non-overlapping. For example, objects with different (i.e. non-aliased) owners must be non-aliased. Also, objects cannot alias their owners: $x \prec y$ implies $x \otimes y$ (we write this *must-not-alias* relation with $\otimes$). Beside ownership, there are a variety of type-based techniques for determining when reference variables must not alias the same object, such as uniqueness [17], linearity [32], regions [30], freshness and more. They can be used in our type system to enhance alias reasoning, but we do not consider all of them for the simplicity of the formalism. In the above code, we can determine that sav and chq refer to distinct objects, because they are initialised to fresh objects in their declaration, and are not permitted to be re-assigned. Alternatively, if we want sav and chq to be mutable fields, we can simply let them have different owners in order to distinguish the objects they refer to.

2.2 Ownership Effects

Effect systems [25] offer abstract views of program behaviours, identifying, for example, subsets of memory affected by read and write operations. The key idea for ownership effect systems is to specify memory effects on whole subtrees of objects. An effect on an object subsumes effects on objects that it owns. This allows effects to be abstracted to higher level contexts where the details of individual objects may be unknown.

For the Customer class above, the method **transfer** has effect **this**, which means the body of the method may access (read or write, directly or indirectly via calls) the fields of the current object and any object inside (transitively owned by) the current object. The body of the **transfer** method calls **sav.withdraw** to access the **balance** field in the savings account, defined by:

```
class Account {
  int balance = 0;
  void deposit(int amount) <this> { balance += amount; }
  void withdraw(int amount) <this> { balance -= amount; }
}
```

The effect of the call sav.withdraw is {sav}, found by substituting the target sav for the declared method effect {this} in class Account. Similarly the effect of chq.deposit is {chq}. The effect of the transfer is sound because the combined effect of its body, {sav, chq}, is subsumed by (that is, is a smaller effect than) the effect of the calling context (the Customer object): both the sav and chq objects are inside the Customer object in the ownership tree.

Such static knowledge of effects is needed in the type system of Section 4 to determine the effect of tasks and then infer synchronisation to protect them if they may interfere with each other. An effect, denoted as ε, is simply a set of objects indicating a read or write dependency on that object; semantically the effect includes any sub-objects of the specified set. *Disjointness* of effects $\varepsilon_1 \,\#\, \varepsilon_2$ says that the two effects do not overlap: this is interpreted semantically, so disjointness implies that there are no common sub-objects for the two given sets. If two program behaviours have disjoint effects then they are non-interfering. Because ownership is tree structured, disjointness of owners is inherited by their sub-objects; thus we can separate whole collections of objects just by separating their owners. In summary, ownership type systems model hierarchical object structures; each context in an effect specifies a tree of objects rooted at the context, thus allowing large effects to be summarised in a single context.

3   Structured Parallelism and Synchronisation

Fork-join frameworks [14,18] typically assume that subtasks do not interfere with one another; recent type systems enforce such non-interference [2,10]. We present a similar structured model for parallel tasks, but allow tasks to interfere.

3.1   Structured Parallelism with Effects

Since all possible sibling tasks can be identified lexically, the synchronisation requirement for a task need only prevent potential interference with its siblings, and not with any other tasks in the program, which are dealt with by the parent. Such a model relies on knowledge of the task structure and an effect system which can track all the effects of subtasks. Since the effects of subtasks are subsumed by the effect of their parents, subtasks may inherit their parents' protection. For instance, subtasks of a parent task are correctly synchronised with the subtasks of the parent's siblings through the synchronisation (if any) of the parent tasks.

We adopt a parallel-let form in which subtasks are forked, and may return a result which can only be used in the continuation after all subtasks complete:

$$\begin{aligned}
&\textbf{par } \{ \\
&\quad x_1 = \textbf{sync } (\pi_1) \; e_1, \\
&\quad \ldots , \\
&\quad x_n = \textbf{sync } (\pi_n) \; e_n \\
&\} \; e
\end{aligned}$$

Here, e is the continuation for the tasks e_i, which assign their return values to the local variables x_i which may be used in e. Each task is guarded by an inferred synchronisation requirement $\textbf{sync } (\pi_i)$ which depends on the overlap between the effect of e_i and the effects of all its siblings, as discussed below. We present a particular example of an effect system in Section 4. For now, we simply assume that an effect ε of an expression e is a set denoting all memory locations or objects which may be read or written in the computation of e; overlaps of such effects are used to define tasks' synchronisation requirements π which correspond to the sets of objects that the tasks must synchronise on. The notation $\varepsilon_1 \,\#\, \varepsilon_2$ means that the two effects are guaranteed to be disjoint (and the computations of e_1 and e_2 are non-interfering).

The intended operational behaviour for synchronisation is simple. Sibling tasks synchronising on the same object are mutually excluded within the same

par. A dynamic semantics for our type system is presented in Section 4, which ensures a task will only proceed if its sync requirement π does not overlap with those of the currently active sibling tasks.

Each synchronisation requirement for a **par** can be implemented as a lock-set. These lock-sets can be minimised to anti-chains in the ownership order. To ensure deadlock freedom it is only necessary to ensure that individual locks for the tasks of a par are acquired in a consistent order; there is no risk of deadlock from locking associated with different pars. It is possible to refine coarse-grain locks, pushing sync requirements onto subtasks, adapting techniques discussed elsewhere [29,16]. Such fine-grain approaches should increase concurrency at the cost of greater locking overhead. They will still preserve data-race freedom, but may allow interleaving of subtask behaviours, so program serialisability may not be preserved. The coarse grain approach adopted in this paper preserves atomicity, hence serialisability, of all tasks. Instead of using lock-sets, we could use other means, such as software transactions, to implement the synchronisation requirements, which then become static advice about which objects need to be checked for conflict and need for task roll-back. Our focus here is to combine object ownership types with effects of tasks to infer synchronisation requirements.

3.2   Ownership-Based Synchronisation Requirements

For two parallel tasks with effects ε_1 and ε_2, we consider two different kinds of constraints on their sync requirements π_1 and π_2. Each of the constraints are sufficient to prevent concurrent activation of potentially interfering tasks thus ensuring safety; we denote this safety condition as $(\pi_1)\,\varepsilon_1 \perp (\pi_2)\,\varepsilon_2$.

The first constraint says that a mutex, where the sync requirements overlap, is always good enough, irrespective of the effects:

$$\pi_1 \cap \pi_2 \neq \emptyset \tag{1}$$

In practice we often want to maximise concurrency, so we would only choose this form if we know that the effects definitely overlap. Then we can simply choose π_1 and π_2 to be an arbitrary singleton mutex. Because the sync requirements overlap, our dynamic model ensures that the two tasks can only be run in mutual exclusion—thus ensuring serialisability.

At runtime, the effects and sync requirements correspond to sets of objects. However, static effect systems only capture approximations of the runtime effects, and have to deal with possible aliasing amongst program variables. In the `transfer` method of the `Customer` example of Section 2, we might allow `sav.withdraw` and `chq.deposit` to run in parallel. If we could not guarantee that `sav` and `chq` were never aliased, then we would need to protect them with `sync(sav)` and `sync(chq)`. The second form of constraint copes with possible (rather than definite) overlap of effects, but attempts to allow maximal concurrency when the possible overlap is not actually manifested at runtime (e.g. if `sav` and `chq` referred to distinct accounts).

$$\pi_1 \otimes \pi_2 \implies \varepsilon_1 \# \varepsilon_2 \tag{2}$$

```
class Customer {
  final Account<this> sav = new Account;
  final Account<this> chq = new Account;
  void transfer(int amt) <this> {
    par {
      sync() sav.withdraw(amt),
      sync() chq.deposit(amt)
    };
  }
  int creditCheck() <this> {
    return par {
      s = sync() sav.balance(),
      c = sync() chq.balance()
    } (s + c);
}}

class Bank {
  ...
  void touch(Customer<this> cus1, Customer<this> cus2) {
    par {
      sync(cus1) cus1.transfer(10),
      sync(cus2) cus2.creditCheck()
    };
} }
```

Fig. 1. Customer with *Inferred Synchronisation*

This is a variation of the *conditional must-not-aliasing* safety requirement introduced in [26]. It allows us to write sync requirements, without knowing whether they will actually inhibit concurrent activation or not. The safety condition (2) says that if the sync requirements are not aliases (hence will not block concurrent activation) then the task side effects must not be aliased (that is, non-interfering). The converse statement may be easier to understand: whenever the tasks may interfere, then the sync requirements must also. This means that we can choose the sync requirements for potentially overlapping subtasks by restricting the sync requirement to just that part of the effect which may overlap with the other task. We give an example of this below.

3.3   An Example

We adopt the bank account example of [5] to discuss our inferred synchronisation (details of the algorithm are omitted in the short paper). In the listing of Figure 1 we provide a two-level ownership structure: a bank owns a list of customers while a customer may own a list of accounts, as illustrated for our model in Figure 2.

Instead of explicit synchronisation, we infer sync requirements to guarantee the task safety; these are shown in grey italic. In class Customer, subtasks are spawned (in the par block) to access the accounts in the transfer and creditCheck methods. In both of these methods, all the subtasks have inferred sync()—the empty parenthesis means no synchronisation is required. *Why is*

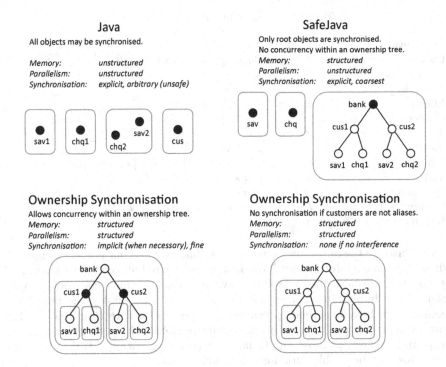

Fig. 2. Comparison of models: circles are objects; filled circles are synchronised; objects are in ownership trees; boxes are tasks; tasks contain objects they use and subtasks.

this safe? Let us look at the `transfer` method. The effect, as declared, of the `transfer` is the current object this. Such an effect is used by the type system as a safety contract between the tasks created inside the method body (subtasks) and the task that calls the method (parent task). When the method is called, the parent task guarantees that the call is safe—no other tasks may interfere with it. Within the method body of `transfer`, the calls on `sav.withdraw(amt)` and `chq.deposit(amt)` cannot interfere: the call on `sav.withdraw(amt)` will only access objects inside `sav` while `chq.deposit(amount)` will only access objects inside `chq`—being initialised with new account objects, the final fields `sav` and `chq` must refer to distinct objects. Since `sav` and `chq` can own no objects in common, there is no chance of interference. Therefore, no synchronisation is required for these tasks.

Consider the `touch` method in the `Bank`. The call `cus1.transfer(10)` has side-effect {`cus1`} and `cus2.creditCheck()` has {`cus2`}. But we cannot guarantee that `cus1` and `cus2` are not aliases, so those two calls may interfere. Synchronisation is required. By synchronising each call on different variables, `cus1` and `cus2`, we only block concurrent execution when they are actual run-time aliases. Our type system allows this conditional blocking by safety condition (2). To perform a safe inter-customer transfer (not in the example), a bank-level task would process transactions on two customers; our inference algorithm would add both customers into the sync requirement for the task.

Table 1. Syntax and Type Environment

Programs	P ::=	$\overline{L}\ e$
Classes	L ::=	class $c\langle\overline{p}\rangle\ [\lhd\ t]_{opt}$ where $\overline{p\ R\ p}$ $\{[\text{final}]_{opt}\ t\ f;\ \overline{M}\}$
Constraints	R ::=	$\prec\ \mid\ \preceq\ \mid\ \#$
Methods	M ::=	$t\ m(\overline{t\ x})\ \varepsilon\ \{e\}$
Effects	ε, π ::=	$\emptyset\ \mid\ \{k\}\ \mid\ \varepsilon\cup\varepsilon$
Contexts	k ::=	world $\mid\ p\ \mid\ e$
Types	t ::=	$c\langle\overline{k}\rangle$
Variables	z ::=	$x\ \mid$ this
Expressions	e ::=	$z\ \mid$ new $t\ \mid\ e.f\ \mid\ e.f = e\ \mid\ e.m(\overline{e})\ \mid\ \overline{a}; e$
Tasks	a ::=	$x = s\ \pi\ e$
Sync states	s ::=	sync
Environments	Γ ::=	$\emptyset\ \mid\ \Gamma, p\ \mid\ \Gamma, p\ R\ p\ \mid\ \Gamma, z : t\ \mid\ \Gamma, \pi\otimes\pi$
Identifiers	c, p, f, m, x	

We illustrate the difference between Java, SafeJava and our model in Figure 2, whose caption explains the notation. In Java, all shared objects may be accessed by any thread. Java allows arbitrary synchronisation which does not provide safety. The simplest mechanism for thread-safety is to employ the per-object monitor. SafeJava [5] extends previous type systems for data race freedom [12], with ownership types where objects are encapsulated within threads or on the heap. In SafeJava, at most one thread can be active within a tree at any one time; this may be problematic for some applications.

By way of contrast, Figure 2 highlights the ability for tasks in our model to concurrently access objects inside an ownership tree (i.e. protected by the same coarse-grained lock). Unlike in SafeJava, accounts can be both encapsulated and accessed concurrently. If potential interference is inferred (because the two customer variables may be aliases for the same object), then synchronisation may be needed, but not necessarily at the top of the hierarchy. The tasks may run in parallel if the two customers are different objects. If we can determine that the two customers are indeed distinct, then no synchronisation is required at all, as in the last diagram. The diagrams make it clear that our model provides a general structure of active objects and synchronisation patterns. This generality is achieved without explicit synchronisation.

4   A Type System for Ownership Synchronisation

Our type system focuses on static checking of ownership synchronisation requirements, ensuring that runtime computations cannot interfere with one another. In this section, we summarise key type rules and a small step dynamic semantics. The syntax of a core language with ownership types and effects is given in Table 1. We allow final expressions to be used as owner contexts (including final fields and read-only variables) since they cannot change [5]. Type environments Γ record context parameters, the assumed ordering between them, and the types of variables.

The parallel-let expression is the only construct for expressing parallelism in this simple language. In the examples, we have used essentially the same syntax,

Table 2. Expression Typing Rules

[VARIABLE]
$$\frac{z : t \in \Gamma}{\Gamma \vdash z : t \,!\, \emptyset}$$

[NEW]
$$\frac{\Gamma \vdash t}{\Gamma \vdash \mathsf{new}\ t : t \,!\, \emptyset}$$

[SELECT]
$$\frac{\Gamma \vdash e : t \,!\, \varepsilon \qquad (t'\ f) \in fields(t, e)}{\Gamma \vdash e.f : t' \,!\, \varepsilon \cup \{e\}}$$

[FINAL]
$$\frac{\Gamma \vdash e : t \,!\, \varepsilon \qquad (\mathsf{final}\ t'\ f) \in fields(t, e)}{\Gamma \vdash e.f : t' \,!\, \varepsilon}$$

[UPDATE]
$$\frac{\Gamma \vdash e : t \,!\, \varepsilon \qquad (t'\ f) \in fields(t, e) \qquad \Gamma \vdash e' : t' \,!\, \varepsilon'}{\Gamma \vdash e.f = e' : t' \,!\, \varepsilon \cup \varepsilon' \cup \{e\}}$$

[CALL]
$$\frac{method(m, t, e, \overline{e}) = t'\ \overline{t}\ \varepsilon' \ ... \qquad \Gamma \vdash e : t \,!\, \varepsilon \qquad \Gamma \vdash \overline{e : t \,!\, \varepsilon}}{\Gamma \vdash e.m(\overline{e}) : t' \,!\, \bigcup \overline{\varepsilon} \cup \varepsilon \cup \varepsilon'}$$

[PARALLEL]
$$\frac{\Gamma \vdash \overline{e : t \,!\, \varepsilon} \qquad \Gamma, \overline{x : t} \vdash e : t \,!\, \varepsilon \qquad \forall k \in \bigcup \overline{\pi} \cdot \Gamma \vdash k \qquad \forall i, j \in 1..|\overline{e}| \cdot i \neq j \implies \Gamma \vdash (\pi_i)\ \varepsilon_i \perp (\pi_j)\ \varepsilon_j}{\Gamma \vdash \overline{x = \mathsf{sync}\ \pi\ e}; e : t \,!\, \bigcup \overline{\varepsilon} \cup \varepsilon}$$

[SUBSUMPTION]
$$\frac{\Gamma \vdash e : t' \,!\, \varepsilon' \qquad \vdash t' \leq t \qquad \Gamma \vdash \varepsilon' \sqsubseteq \varepsilon}{\Gamma \vdash e : t \,!\, \varepsilon}$$

with the explicit keyword **par**, which we now omit in the abstract syntax. Like conventional let expressions, our parallel-let introduces local variables to be used in the expression after the semicolon. The semicolon serves as a join boundary; the expression after the semicolon will only be evaluated after all the concurrent expressions join. The sync requirements π may be declared by the programmer or inferred by the compiler. The type system considers π given and ensures they are sufficient for guaranteeing safety.

Table 2 defines expression types and effects, which are largely standard except [PARALLEL]. The *fields()* and *method()* functions look up types for fields and methods from the class definition. [FINAL] states that accessing final fields has no side effect, because they are read-only. Sync requirements are checked in the last premise of [PARALLEL]. The elements in a sync requirement must be valid contexts, such as final expressions.

In Table 3 the antecedent for [S-MUTEX] states that the sync requirements overlap, and thus will always ensure the tasks execute in mutual exclusion, which is safe. [S-COND] corresponds to safety condition (2) of Section 3. Details of these rules are left to [22].

Table 3. Synchronisation Rules

[S-MUTEX]
$$\frac{k \in \pi \qquad k \in \pi'}{\Gamma \vdash (\pi)\ \varepsilon \perp (\pi')\ \varepsilon'}$$

[S-COND]
$$\frac{\Gamma, \pi \otimes \pi' \vdash \varepsilon \,\#\, \varepsilon'}{\Gamma \vdash (\pi)\ \varepsilon \perp (\pi')\ \varepsilon'}$$

Table 4. Extended Syntax for Dynamic Semantics

Locations	l
Variables	$z ::= \ldots \mid l$
Sync states	$s ::= \ldots \mid \mathsf{synced} \mid \mathsf{rel}$
Objects	$o ::= \overline{f \mapsto l}$
Heaps	$H ::= \overline{l \mapsto o_t}$
Eval states	$S ::= H; e$
Eval contexts	$E ::= [\,] \mid E.f \mid E.f = e \mid l.f = E \mid E.m(\overline{e}) \mid l.m(E) \mid \overline{l}, E, \overline{e}$

Table 4 defines the extended syntax and features used in the dynamic semantics. In order to formalise the properties of the type system, we establish a connection between the static and dynamic semantics by including ownership in the dynamic semantics (preserved in the types of objects in the heap). But the ownership information does not affect how expressions are evaluated; ownership is only used for static type checking so it need not be available at runtime. We extend the syntax of variables with runtime locations l. Sync state synced indicates locks have been acquired and rel indicates locks have been released. A heap is a mapping from locations to objects with their types; an object maps its fields to locations. Evaluation states S contain a heap and an expression to be evaluated. The initial state is $(\emptyset; e)$ where e is the body of the main method and the heap is empty. We use standard evaluation contexts to reduce the number of evaluation rules.

Table 5 presents a small step operational semantics. The transition rules are mostly standard [12,11,2], where each single step is atomic and task interleaving is modelled as random choices (in [R-INT]). The label on the transition ε is the effect of the transition, which may either be empty ($\emptyset$) or a singleton location ($\{l\}$). For simplicity, we adopt the object creation semantics from [6] where all fields are initialised with new objects, hence [R-NEW] has no side effect.

The sync requirement of a task must be met in order for the task to be executed. The *synced* function tracks the total requirements for all the active (synced) tasks in its argument; it is used to ensure non-overlapping of sync requirements from different active tasks. This semantics is similar to [11], which abstracts away from a specific implementation as seen in [12]. The premise of [R-ACQ] blocks a task unless its sync requirement has no overlap with *synced*, the other active tasks' synchronisation, thus preventing any possible interference. (This premise just uses set intersection; there is no effect subsumption or context ordering as we do not depend on ownership information at runtime.) Once a task is active, it remains non-interfering with any other active task. This is the essence of the safety guarantee for serialisability. Note that [R-ACQ] is an atomic step no matter how many objects need to be synchronised in the sync requirement, hence is not prone to deadlock (see discussion in Section 3). [R-REL] removes a task from the active set, and releases its sync; its π no longer contributes to the active requirements *synced*. [R-JOI] ensures the order of sequential execution. The reduction rules for other expressions are mostly standard.

In database systems, serial means that transactions do not overlap in time and cannot interfere with each other, i.e., as if all transactions in the system had executed serially, one after another. Serialisability is usually proved by using

Table 5. Small Step Operational Semantics

[R-SEL]
$$\frac{H(l) = o_t \qquad (t'\ f) \in \mathit{fields}(t,l)}{H;l.f \xrightarrow{\{l\}} H;H(l)(f)}$$

[R-FIN]
$$\frac{H(l) = o_t \qquad (\mathsf{final}\ t'\ f) \in \mathit{fields}(t,l)}{H;l.f \xrightarrow{\emptyset} H;H(l)(f)}$$

[R-CAL]
$$\frac{H(l) = o_t \qquad \mathit{method}(m,t,l,\overline{l}) = ...\ e}{H;l.m(\overline{l}) \xrightarrow{\emptyset} H;e}$$

[R-NEW]
$$\frac{l \notin \mathit{dom}(H) \qquad H_1 = H, l \mapsto \emptyset_t \qquad (...\ t\ f) = \mathit{fields}(t,l)}{\dfrac{\forall i \in 1..|\overline{f}| \quad\cdot\quad H_i; \mathsf{new}\ t_i \xrightarrow{\emptyset} H_{i+1}; l_i}{H; \mathsf{new}\ t \xrightarrow{\emptyset} H_{|\overline{f}|+1}[l \mapsto (\overline{f \mapsto l})_t];l}}$$

[R-ASS]
$$H;l.f = l' \xrightarrow{\{l\}} H[l \mapsto H(l)[f \mapsto l']];l'$$

[R-SYN]
$$\frac{H;\overline{e} \xrightarrow{\emptyset} H';\overline{e'}}{H;\overline{a}, x = \mathsf{sync}\ \{\overline{e}\}\ e, \overline{a'};e' \xrightarrow{\emptyset} H;\overline{a}, x = \mathsf{sync}\ \{\overline{e'}\}\ e, \overline{a'};e'}$$

[R-ACQ]
$$\frac{\{\overline{l}\} \cap \mathit{synced}(\overline{a},\overline{a'}) = \emptyset}{H;\overline{a}, x = \mathsf{sync}\ \{\overline{l}\}\ e, \overline{a'};e' \xrightarrow{\emptyset} H;\overline{a}, x = \mathsf{synced}\ \{\overline{l}\}\ e, \overline{a'};e'}$$

[R-REL]
$$H;\overline{a}, x = \mathsf{synced}\ \pi\ l, \overline{a'};e \xrightarrow{\emptyset} H;\overline{a}, x = \mathsf{rel}\ \pi\ l, \overline{a'};e$$

[R-INT]
$$\frac{H;e \xrightarrow{\varepsilon} H';e'}{H;\overline{a}, x = \mathsf{synced}\ \pi\ e, \overline{a'};e'' \xrightarrow{\varepsilon} H';\overline{a}, x = \mathsf{synced}\ \pi\ e', \overline{a'};e''}$$

[R-JOI] $H;\overline{x = \mathsf{rel}\ \pi\ l};e \xrightarrow{\emptyset} H;[\overline{l/x}]e$ [R-CTX] $\dfrac{H;e \xrightarrow{\varepsilon} H';e'}{H;E[e] \xrightarrow{\varepsilon} H';E[e']}$

an *acyclic precedence graph* [27]. A precedence graph for a schedule contains a node for each transaction and an edge from transaction T_i to T_j if an action in T_i occurs before an action in T_j and they conflict. Serialisable means that the precedence graph for any possible schedule is acyclic. In our system, all tasks run in a completely isolated fashion, even though they may execute concurrently with other (non-interfering) tasks. To prove serialisability, we represent a schedule with an arbitrary number of transitions. For example, a schedule $S \xRightarrow{G} S_3$ is a sequence of transitions $S \xrightarrow[x_1]{\varepsilon_1} S_1 \xrightarrow[x_2]{\varepsilon_2} S_2 \xrightarrow[x_3]{\varepsilon_3} S_3$, where actions are denoted by their task names and effects. We only track actions in active (synced) tasks because [R-INT] is the only case where tasks may interfere. We write $G \vdash x_1\ \varepsilon_1 \vartriangleright x_3\ \varepsilon_3$ to denote that, in the schedule G, an action in task x_1 with effect ε_1 occurs before another action in task x_3 with effect ε_3.

Theorem 1 (Serialisability) states that tasks associated with conflicting actions must always appear in the same order in a schedule, so the precedence graph is indeed acyclic as required. Because tasks are lexically scoped and hierarchically defined, all parallel tasks are serialisable. We can therefore rely on conventional techniques for reasoning about state-based updates in a sequential style. Serialisability subsumes data race freedom such as that provided in [5,11].

Theorem 1 (Serialisability)

Given $H; (\overline{x = s\ \pi\ e}; e)$ *is a well-formed eval state and* $H; (\overline{x = s\ \pi\ e}; e) \overset{G}{\Longrightarrow} H'; (\overline{x = s'\ \pi\ e'}; e)$, *if* $G \vdash x\ \varepsilon \triangleright x'\ \varepsilon'$ *and* $\varepsilon \cap \varepsilon' \neq \emptyset$, *then* $G \nvdash x'\ \varepsilon''' \triangleright x\ \varepsilon''$.

5   Discussion and Related Work

This research attempts to combine concurrency and OO using ownership types and effects to reason about structured object synchronisation. Programmers can take the advantage of domain knowledge of object structures, specified via ownership types and effects, to design concurrency and synchronisation. In general, finer-grained object structures not only allow finer-grained reasoning on task effects and their overlapping, but also provide the opportunity for finding more allowable concurrency in structured parallelism, supported by our structured synchronisation scheme. With the ability to locally reason about tasks, programmers may control and possibly reduce interference between tasks to allow more tasks to run in parallel; they may also split tasks to achieve a finer granularity of execution and synchronisation.

We adopt a whole-task synchronisation approach for ensuring parallel tasks are executed in isolation, like previous type systems for atomicity [13]. By making all tasks serialisable and synchronisation implicit, we simplify concurrent programming and allow programmers to focus on their program logic as they would for sequential programs within any task. However, structured parallelism is not as flexible as a free-range threading model. Fortunately, it is possible to ensure threads do not interfere with serialisable tasks [22], so that programmers can choose to use threads or tasks as appropriate.

Our type and effect system supports modular, compile-time type checking, and relies only on effects for preventing task interference, but otherwise placing no restriction on references as seen in previous ownership types for encapsulation. For example, an owned object can be typed and referenced from outside its owner by naming the owner argument of the type with a read-only variable. But this may be somewhat limited due to the naming restriction of ownership types [5]. To completely remove naming restriction and provide for liberal reference to owned objects in ownership type systems, we have proposed ownership abstraction [21] and variances [20]. For simplicity we do not adopt these earlier schemes in this paper. In addition, like [5], our type system does not distinguish read and write effects as done in [8,6]. This is somewhat over-conservative in that it does not allow simultaneous reads of an object. We believe that adding a treatment of read-write effects to our type system should not be difficult, at the cost of extra effect annotations.

Reasoning about concurrent programs is difficult, in part because behaviour of code is rather informally and imprecisely specified. Effect annotations enhance program reasoning [6,4]. Our type system uses explicit and checkable type and effect annotations as a means of recording programmer intent. On the other hand, annotations add programming overhead. With sensible defaults we can reduce the annotation load so that not all type occurrences need explicit annotations. Different ownership inference techniques have been studied elsewhere, e.g. [28,5].

Much work has addressed the challenges of shared-memory concurrent programming. Here we restrict attention to directly related work. In JOE [8], Clarke and Drossopoulou introduced an ownership-based effect system. MOJO [6] developed these ideas further, focusing on the use of multiple ownership to increase the precision of effects. Ownership domains [1] provided a richer structure than ownership tree, which may be useful for more precise effect reasoning. In this paper, we only consider ownership trees for objects, but it should be feasible to extend the ideas to other object structures.

Previous attempts to utilise ownership types for object synchronisation are rather limited and structureless. In SafeJava [5], objects are encapsulated within threads or on the heap. Concurrent access to shared objects on the heap from different threads is guaranteed to be safe by synchronising on the root objects—an object can only be accessed when holding the lock on its root owner. Moreover, no external reference to non-root objects is allowed. Thus, within a root object, all behaviour is single-threaded; this is the coarsest-grained ownership synchronisation. In [11], data-races on objects are controlled by synchronisations on their direct owners; different levels of object access do not rely on higher-level synchronisations, and must be separately synchronised. It is finer-grained than SafeJava. Unlike these previous techniques which rely on a fixed granularity throughout system, we provide a more unified and structured ownership synchronisation discipline. Moreover, [5,11] and other type-based race detection techniques [12] only check for the sufficiency of synchronisation, called the *locking discipline*, requiring all accesses to shared data to be protected by a common lock regardless of thread interference. This can lead to excessive locking even when synchronisation is unnecessary, for example, there is no need to protect a location shared by different tasks but will never be accessed concurrently. In our model, we apply synchronisation only when there is potential interference, hence achieve a more precise interference-based discipline.

Java 7 provides library support for structured parallelism based on Lea's fork/join framework [18], which in turn, is based on Cilk [14]. Although able to access shared memory, parallel tasks are typically assumed to work with distinct subsets of memory, and consequently, should not interfere with one another. Deterministic Parallel Java (DPJ) [2] proposed a region-based effect system to enforce noninterference among tasks in the fork/join model, thus guaranteeing deterministic semantics. Synchronisation is never needed because tasks may never conflict with one other. Such determinism is useful for certain programs (e.g. scientific applications) where interference is limited, but too strong in realistic object-oriented programs with extensive sharing and mutation. The latest work on DPJ [3] recognises the necessity and challenge for nondeterminism, by allowing interference in some branches of the task tree. Programmers are required to explicitly declare atomic blocks and place every access to shared memory inside atomic blocks, so that data race freedom can be guaranteed by software transactional memory (STM). Beside the limitations of STM at this moment [7], it does not support threads because thread interference cannot be captured by their type and effect systems. Rather than regions, [10] uses an ownership-based effect system to reason about data dependencies and allow the compiler to parallelise code wherever task interference is not possible. These models are special cases of ours (except some special features, such as index-parameterised array types [2]), where the inferred sync requirements are empty. By scheduling parallel tasks whose sync requirements overlap to execute in sequential order, our behavioural model is reduced to theirs. With synchronisation, our model allows more concurrency than deterministic programming which requires all potentially interfering tasks to be executed in a specified order, though synchronisation may have runtime overhead.

6   Conclusion

In this paper we have proposed the use of ownership types to enforce a structured synchronisation discipline for safe execution of structured tasks. We use ownership effects to reason about interference between parallel tasks, and establish synchronisation requirements that guarantee serialisability. Synchronisation requirements can be inferred to simplify concurrent programming, thus lowering the bar for programmers—they are not responsible for choosing appropriate synchronisation. The strong serialisability property simplifies reasoning about concurrent programs by allowing every piece of code to be reasoned about separately without fear of interference. Although this paper has focused on structured parallelism, it can be extended to coexist with conventional unstructured threads. With this work, we hope to stimulate further exploration of how object and effect structure can facilitate safe and efficient concurrent programming.

References

1. Aldrich, J., Chambers, C.: Ownership Domains: Separating Aliasing Policy from Mechanism. In: Vetta, A. (ed.) ECOOP 2004. LNCS, vol. 3086, pp. 1–25. Springer, Heidelberg (2004)
2. Bocchino Jr., R.L., Adve, V.S., Dig, D., Adve, S.V., Heumann, S., Komuravelli, R., Overbey, J., Simmons, P., Sung, H., Vakilian, M.: A type and effect system for Deterministic Parallel Java. In: OOPSLA (2009)
3. Bocchino Jr., R.L., Heumann, S., Honarmand, N., Adve, S.V., Adve, V.S., Welc, A., Shpeisman, T.: Safe nondeterminism in a deterministic-by-default parallel language. In: POPL (2011)
4. Boyapati, C., Liskov, B., Shrira, L.: Ownership types for object encapsulation. In: POPL (2003)
5. Boyapati, C., Rinard, M.: A parameterized type system for race-free Java programs. In: OOPSLA (2001)
6. Cameron, N., Drossopoulou, S., Noble, J., Smith, M.: Multiple Ownership. In: OOPSLA (2007)
7. Cascaval, C., Blundell, C., Michael, M., Cain, H.W., Wu, P., Chiras, S., Chatterjee, S.: Software transactional memory: Why is it only a research toy? ACM Queue (2008)
8. Clarke, D., Drossopoulou, S.: Ownership, encapsulation and disjointness of type and effect. In: OOPSLA (2002)

9. Clarke, D., Potter, J., Noble, J.: Ownership types for flexible alias protection. In: OOPSLA (1998)
10. Craik, A., Kelly, W.: Using Ownership to Reason about Inherent Parallelism in Object-Oriented Programs. In: Gupta, R. (ed.) CC 2010. LNCS, vol. 6011, pp. 145–164. Springer, Heidelberg (2010)
11. Cunningham, D., Drossopoulou, S., Eisenbach, S.: Universe Types for Race Safety. In: VAMP (2007)
12. Flanagan, C., Abadi, M.: Types for Safe Locking. In: Swierstra, S.D. (ed.) ESOP 1999. LNCS, vol. 1576, pp. 91–108. Springer, Heidelberg (1999)
13. Flanagan, C., Freund, S.N., Lifshin, M., Qadeer, S.: Types for atomicity: Static checking and inference for Java. TOPLAS 30(4), 1–53 (2008)
14. Frigo, M., Leiserson, C.E., Randall, K.H.: The implementation of the Cilk-5 multithreaded language. In: PLDI (1998)
15. Goetz, B., Peierls, T., Bloch, J., Bowbeer, J., Holmes, D., Lea, D.: Java Concurrency in Practice. Addison-Wesley Professional (2005)
16. Golan-Gueta, G., Bronson, N.G., Aiken, A., Ramalingam, G., Sagiv, M., Yahav, E.: Automatic fine-grain locking using shape properties. In: OOPSLA (2011)
17. Hogg, J.: Islands: aliasing protection in object-oriented languages. In: OOPSLA (1991)
18. Lea, D.: A Java fork/join framework. Java Grande (2000)
19. Lee, E.A.: The problem with threads. IEEE Computer 39(5), 33–42 (2006)
20. Lu, Y.: On Ownership and Accessibility. In: Hu, Q. (ed.) ECOOP 2006. LNCS, vol. 4067, pp. 99–123. Springer, Heidelberg (2006)
21. Lu, Y., Potter, J.: Protecting representation with effect encapsulation. In: POPL (2006)
22. Lu, Y., Potter, J., Xue, J.: Ownership Types for Object Synchronisation. Extended version, available at http://www.cse.unsw.edu.au/~ylu/0813.pdf
23. Lu, Y., Potter, J., Xue, J.: Validity Invariants and Effects. In: Bateni, M. (ed.) ECOOP 2007. LNCS, vol. 4609, pp. 202–226. Springer, Heidelberg (2007)
24. Lu, Y., Potter, J., Xue, J.: Ownership Downgrading for Ownership Types. In: Hu, Z. (ed.) APLAS 2009. LNCS, vol. 5904, pp. 144–160. Springer, Heidelberg (2009)
25. Lucassen, J.M., Gifford, D.K.: Polymorphic effect systems. In: POPL (1988)
26. Naik, M., Aiken, A.: Conditional must not aliasing for static race detection. In: POPL (2007)
27. Papadimitriou, C.: The theory of database concurrency control. Computer Science Press, Inc., New York (1986)
28. Potanin, A., Noble, J., Clarke, D., Biddle, R.: Generic ownership for generic Java. In: OOPSLA (2006)
29. Potter, J., Shanneb, A.: Incremental lock selection for composite objects. Journal of Object Technology 6(9), 477–494 (2007)
30. Tofte, M., Talpin, J.-P.: Implementation of the typed call-by-value lambda-calculus using a stack of regions. In: POPL (1994)
31. Vechev, M., Yahav, E., Raman, R., Sarkar, V.: Automatic Verification of Determinism for Structured Parallel Programs. In: Cousot, R., Martel, M. (eds.) SAS 2010. LNCS, vol. 6337, pp. 455–471. Springer, Heidelberg (2010)
32. Wadler, P.: Is there a use for linear logic? In: PEPM (1991)

A Functional View
of Imperative Information Flow

Thomas H. Austin[1], Cormac Flanagan[1], and Martín Abadi[1,2]

[1] University of California, Santa Cruz
[2] Microsoft Research Silicon Valley

Abstract. We analyze dynamic information-flow control for imperative languages in terms of functional computation. Specifically, we translate an imperative language to a functional language, thus accounting for the main difficulties of information-flow control in the imperative language.

1 Introduction

Dynamic information-flow control appears to be increasingly popular, useful, but intricate. These characteristics partly stem from the treatment of realistic languages, in particular with imperative features. (Dynamic information-flow control for the pure lambda calculus seems considerably simpler and less practically relevant.) In this paper we aim to contribute to the understanding of dynamic information-flow control, by translating imperative features to a functional calculus. The translation accounts for difficulties of information-flow control in the source language; information-flow control in the target language is comparatively straightforward.

The rest of this introduction presents our goals and results in more detail, putting them in the context of a long line of prior work.

Information-Flow Security
In the classic information-flow model of security [6, 7, 9], data is associated with security levels, and then one aims to guarantee that information propagates consistently with those levels. For example, for confidentiality policies, the security levels may be "secret" and "public", and then one requires, for instance, that secret data is not disclosed on public output channels. For integrity policies, similarly, the security levels may be "tainted" and "trusted", and then trusted outputs should not be computed from tainted inputs.

More precisely, a frequent, principled requirement is *non-interference*, which basically means that events observable at certain security levels are not influenced by events at certain other security levels. The events often correspond to straightforward inputs and outputs. So, concretely, the non-interference property implies that secret inputs do not influence public outputs, and that tainted inputs do not influence trusted outputs. Note that the non-interference property precludes partial flows of information. For example, given a secret integer input,

R. Jhala and A. Igarashi (Eds.): APLAS 2012, LNCS 7705, pp. 34–49, 2012.

non-interference forbids revealing not only the entire integer but also its sign on a public output channel.

The enforcement of information-flow rules can rely on a variety of mechanisms. Since the early days of the subject, special architectures have been considered for this purpose. More commonly, the enforcement may be done in software, particularly in operating systems and in programming languages.

Static and Dynamic Language-Based Information-Flow Control

Working within a programming language enables fine-grained tracking of information flows. In this context, the enforcement may be done statically (e.g., at compile-time) or dynamically (at run-time). Static and dynamic techniques may also be combined. Sabelfeld and Myers [18] review the research on language-based information-flow control as of 2003.

Although dynamic techniques are far from new, until recently they were somewhat neglected in the programming-language research literature, because of concerns that they could not be both sound and precise enough. In contrast, flexible type systems were developed for static enforcement [13, 22], and led to realistic programming languages such as Jif [14, 16] and FlowCaml [10, 17].

Nevertheless, various forms of dynamic information-flow control may be attractive in practice, for instance in the context of widespread languages such as Perl and JavaScript (which are light on static guarantees). Language-level dynamic techniques also connect with dynamic tracking in operating systems, where they have been prominent in recent research artifacts (such as Asbestos [15] and HiStar [24]) and in deployed commercial systems (in SELinux and in aspects of Windows, in particular).

Accordingly, we have seen renewed interest and substantial progress in research on dynamic information-flow control in recent years [3, 11, 19, 20]. This research has aimed to develop, then to use, flexible and efficient systems that satisfy non-interference properties. For instance, this research effectively supports promising uses of dynamic information-flow control in Web browsers [5, 8, 12, 21]. This research is often clever and intricate—so we do not attempt to give a complete description here, but we focus on some of the intricacies below.

Imperative Systems and the Problem of Sensitive Upgrades

Whether static or dynamic, information-flow control accounts for a useful range of realistic language features and computational phenomena. Even straightforward imperative features can be challenging. The following classic example illustrates some of the difficulties:

Function f x	$x = \text{true}^H$	$x = \text{false}^H$
y := true;	$y = \text{true}^L$	$y = \text{true}^L$
z := true;	$z = \text{true}^L$	$z = \text{true}^L$
if (x) y := false;	y set to false^H	—
if (!y) z := false;	—	z set to false^L
!z;	returns true^L	returns false^L
Return value:	true^L	false^L

The superscript H marks private data; similarly, the superscript L marks public data. When (f $true^H$) is called, the value for the reference cell y must be updated. Since the update to y is conditional on the value of x, information about x's private value leaks to y. If the value for y is set to $false^H$ to capture the influence of private data, an attacker can use y in a second conditional assignment statement to leak the value of x. Since y is $false^H$, the value for z remains $true^L$, and therefore (f $true^H$) = $true^L$. When (f $false^H$) is called, the value of y remains $true^L$. Therefore, z is set to $false^L$ (since y is public), and (f $false^H$) = $false^L$. Thus, if allowed to run to completion, this piece of code leaks a secret input.

One sensible approach to preventing this leak is to forbid sensitive upgrades [3, 23]. Specifically, programs are not allowed to write to locations that contain low-security data within high-security contexts (e.g., after branching on some secret). This approach can be realized either statically or dynamically:

- Statically, it seems fairly natural to require that each location has a fixed security level, much like (in virtually all programming languages) it has a fixed type, and to combine the security level with the type.
- Dynamically, on the other hand, the various realizations of this approach introduce interesting twists, typically to enhance efficiency or flexibility.

Simple Functional Systems

Remarkably, these difficulties and the related complications do not seem to arise in the context of pure functional languages.

In the pure lambda calculus, in particular, a traditional system of labels, with extremely simple rules, suffices for sound information-flow tracking [2]. In this system, each subexpression of a program may have a label that indicates its sensitivity. Formally, if e is an expression and H is a label, then $H : e$ is an expression.

A basic rule permits lifting labels in order to permit function application:

$$(H : e_1)(e_2) \rightarrow H : (e_1 \; e_2)$$

Here, e_1 and e_2 are arbitrary expressions. When e_1 is a function of the form $(\lambda x.e)$, this rule enables the subsequent, straightforward application of the β rule (which returns the result of replacing x with e_2 in e, as usual), underneath the label H.

Analogously, for conditionals, labels may be lifted out of guards:

$$\text{if } (H : e_1) \text{ then } e_2 \text{ else } e_3 \rightarrow H : (\text{if } e_1 \text{ then } e_2 \text{ else } e_3)$$

If conditionals are primitive, then so is the rule. If conditionals are encoded as functions, then this rule is easily derived from the rule for application.

Functional vs. Imperative Systems

This contrast between functional and imperative systems suggests a number of questions:

- Are the difficulties really specific to imperative programming?
  If so, perhaps the lambda calculus is not an appropriate core language for understanding computational phenomena, at least not for security?
- On the other hand, since imperative programs can be translated to functional programs, by passing stores as values, could the difficulties be analyzed and resolved by translation? Perhaps more than one translation should be considered in order to account for some of the twists in information-flow control?

For static information-flow control, such questions seem relatively simple, and they have been at least partly resolved. In particular, one can translate various static information-flow systems for imperative languages to the Dependency Core Calculus (DCC) [1], which is a functional computational lambda calculus. The present paper aims to address such questions for dynamic information-flow control.

Contents of This Paper
For this purpose, the paper defines a simple imperative language and a simple functional language. Both have primitive rules for tracking flows of information.

- In the imperative language, the rules are analogous to those from the literature, and may be judged reasonably permissive.
- In the functional language, the rules amount to a mostly unsurprising management of labels, of the kind that we have shown for the lambda calculus.

Both sets of rules for tracking flows of information are sound, in the sense that they yield non-interference properties. The paper shows how to account for the imperative rules in terms of the functional rules, by translation.

There is a straightforward, naive translation from the imperative language to the functional language (by passing stores, as indicated above). Although sound, this translation is overly conservative. For instance, the translation of

$$\texttt{if } H\!:\!x \texttt{ then } y\!:=\!0 \texttt{ else } y\!:=\!0$$

is roughly the function

$$(\lambda\sigma.\ \texttt{if } H\!:\!x \texttt{ then } \langle 0, \sigma[y := 0]\rangle \texttt{ else } \langle 0, \sigma[y := 0]\rangle)$$

which, when applied to a store σ_0 yields

$$H : \langle 0, \sigma_0[y := 0]\rangle$$

where $\sigma_0[y := 0]$ is the store that agrees with σ_0 except that it maps y to 0. Note that the entire resulting store is under the label H, so it is all tainted. Reading the contents of some unrelated location z after executing this program will yield a result of the form $H\!:\!v$, always with a label H.

This paper defines a more sophisticated translation that addresses these difficulties. This translation includes a refined management of the store as a value. It dynamically separates and recombines the parts of a store that are updated or left unchanged in high-security contexts, without tainting the unchanged parts in the process, and without requiring static information for distinguishing those two parts of the store. Via this translation, the tracking for the imperative language can be replicated by the tracking in the functional language.

Both translations can be written in monadic style, if one wishes, and arguably the monadic style has certain benefits. However, we do not believe that monads are the answer: the straightforward use of monads, by itself, does little to resolve the problems that we tackle.

Variants and Further Work

Our languages have certain specific characteristics (often limitations), and considering other languages might be attractive in further work.

- For simplicity, our source language does not include dynamic allocation.
- Both our source language and our target language permit dynamic tests on labels. Such tests are attractive because they make it easy to write certain programs, and they preserve the main security properties of interest. On the other hand, their inclusion means that our target language is not the minimal labelled lambda calculus.
- We consider only two security levels, rather than a general lattice of security levels. Although the case of two levels is both instructive and common in practice, it seems interesting to generalize our results to arbitrary lattices.
- Finally, one may wonder about other language features, such as exceptions.

Our results are purely theoretical. However, analogous results might be of practical value. In scenarios where one language is compiled to another, refined translations such as ours may enable dynamic information-flow control to happen, soundly and flexibly, in the target language.

2   An Imperative Language with Information-Flow Control

We consider an imperative language ImpFlow that supports information-flow control. Its definition, which we give in this section, is along the lines of previous work [3]. The language (see Figure 1) extends the lambda calculus with mutable reference cells, a way of designating private expressions, and a way of testing for private labels. Terms include variables (x), functions ($\lambda x.m$), and function applications ($m_1\ m_2$). To support imperative updates and illustrate the challenges of implicit flows, ImpFlow includes terms for assignment ($i := m$) and dereferencing ($!i$). Here, i denotes an address in the range of $1, ..., n$. The term $H : m$ marks the result of evaluating m as private. The term $H?\ m$ tests if the result of evaluating m is private.

Syntax:

$$
\begin{array}{lll}
m ::= & & \textit{Term} \\
\quad x & & \text{variable} \\
\quad (\lambda x.m) & & \text{abstraction} \\
\quad m_1\ m_2 & & \text{application} \\
\quad i := m & & \text{assignment} \\
\quad !i & & \text{dereference} \\
\quad H : m & & \text{high expression} \\
\quad H?\ m & & \text{high test} \\
\quad w & & \text{values} \\
\\
\quad x, y, z & & \textit{Variable}
\end{array}
$$

Runtime Syntax:

$$
\begin{array}{llll}
w & \in & \textit{Value} & ::= \quad (\lambda x.m)^k \\
k, pc & \in & \textit{Label} & ::= \quad L \mid H \\
\Sigma & \in & \textit{Store} & = \quad \textit{Addr} \rightarrow w \\
i & \in & \textit{Addr} & = \quad \{1, ..., n\}
\end{array}
$$

Evaluation Rules: $\boxed{m, \Sigma \Downarrow_{pc} w, \Sigma'}$

$$\frac{}{w, \Sigma \Downarrow_{pc} w \sqcup pc, \Sigma} \quad \text{[M-VAL]}$$

$$\frac{}{!i, \Sigma \Downarrow_{pc} \Sigma(i) \sqcup pc, \Sigma} \quad \text{[M-DEREF]}$$

$$\frac{}{(\lambda x.m), \Sigma \Downarrow_{pc} (\lambda x.m)^{pc}, \Sigma} \quad \text{[M-FUN]}$$

$$\frac{\begin{array}{c} m, \Sigma \Downarrow_{pc} w, \Sigma' \\ pc \sqsubseteq label(\Sigma'(i)) \end{array}}{i := m, \Sigma \Downarrow_{pc} w, \Sigma'[i := w]} \quad \text{[M-ASSIGN]}$$

$$\frac{\begin{array}{c} m_1, \Sigma \Downarrow_{pc} (\lambda x.m)^k, \Sigma_1 \\ m_2, \Sigma_1 \Downarrow_{pc} w_2, \Sigma_2 \\ m[x := w_2], \Sigma_2 \Downarrow_{pc \sqcup k} w, \Sigma' \end{array}}{m_1\ m_2, \Sigma \Downarrow_{pc} w, \Sigma'} \quad \text{[M-APP]}$$

$$\frac{\begin{array}{c} m, \Sigma \Downarrow_{pc} (\lambda x.m')^k, \Sigma' \\ \text{If } pc = H \text{ or } k = H \\ \text{then } b = \textbf{true} \\ \text{else } b = \textbf{false} \end{array}}{H?\ m, \Sigma \Downarrow_{pc} b^{pc}, \Sigma'} \quad \text{[M-PRED]}$$

$$\frac{m, \Sigma \Downarrow_{pc} w, \Sigma'}{H : m, \Sigma \Downarrow_{pc} w \sqcup H, \Sigma'} \quad \text{[M-LABEL]}$$

Standard Encodings:

$$
\begin{array}{lll}
\textbf{true} & \stackrel{\text{def}}{=} & (\lambda x.(\lambda y.x)) \\
\textbf{false} & \stackrel{\text{def}}{=} & (\lambda x.(\lambda y.y)) \\
\textbf{if } e_1 \textbf{ then } e_2 \textbf{ else } e_3 & \stackrel{\text{def}}{=} & (e_1\ (\lambda d.e_2)\ (\lambda d.e_3))\ (\lambda x.x)
\end{array}
$$

Fig. 1. The Imperative Language ImpFlow

The semantics for ImpFlow is defined in Figure 1. A value $(\lambda x.m)^k$ combines an abstraction $(\lambda x.m)$ with a label k, where k may be either L for public data or H for private data. A program counter pc tracks the influences on the current execution. A store (Σ) maps addresses (i) to values (w).

We define the operational semantics of ImpFlow via the big-step relation:

$$m, \Sigma \Downarrow_{pc} w, \Sigma'$$

This relation evaluates an expression m in the context of a store Σ and the current label pc of the program counter, and it returns the resulting value w and the (possibly modified) store Σ'.

When a function is evaluated via the [M-FUN] rule, the program counter is attached as the label of the function. The evaluation of a value w is similar, via rule [M-VAL], and relies on an auxiliary operation to join a label onto a value:

$$(\lambda x.m)^k \sqcup pc \quad \overset{\text{def}}{=} \quad (\lambda x.m)^{k \sqcup pc}$$

The rule [M-APP] evaluates the body of the called function $(\lambda x.m)^k$ with upgraded program counter label $pc \sqcup k$, since the callee "knows" that that function was invoked. As usual, we assume $L \sqsubset H$, and so, for example, $L \sqcup H = H$.

The [M-LABEL] rule for $H : m$ evaluates the subexpression m and joins the label H to the resulting value, marking the result as private. The [M-PRED] rule evaluates an expression to a value and returns true (Church-encoded) if either the program counter or the value's label is private. Otherwise, it returns false.

Mutable reference cells must be handled carefully in order to guarantee non-interference. The [M-DEREF] rule reads a value from the store and returns it, joining the program counter to the value. The real complexity lies in handling updates to the store. Much as in several previous systems, the [M-ASSIGN] rule uses the no-sensitive-upgrade check [3, 23], which forbids updates to public reference cells when in a private block of code. Here the function *label* extracts the label from a value:

$$label(\ (\lambda x.m)^k\ ) \quad \overset{\text{def}}{=} \quad k$$

3   Non-interference in ImpFlow (Start)

We briefly consider information-flow guarantees satisfied by ImpFlow.

For this purpose, we consider two ImpFlow values to be *equivalent modulo under labels* if they only differ under H superscripts. More formally, the equivalent modulo under labels relation on ImpFlow values, terms, or stores is the congruence closure of the rule:

$$(\lambda x.m_1)^H \quad \sim_{ul} \quad (\lambda x.m_2)^H$$

The key property of the ImpFlow semantics is termination-insensitive non-interference: if two computations from equivalent initial states terminate, then they yield equivalent results.

Theorem 1 (Termination-insensitive non-interference for ImpFlow).
Suppose $m_1 \sim_{ul} m_2$ and

$$m_1, \Sigma \Downarrow_{pc} w_1, \Sigma_1$$
$$m_2, \Sigma \Downarrow_{pc} w_2, \Sigma_2$$

where w_1, w_2 are public Booleans ($\texttt{true}^L$ or $\texttt{false}^L$). Then $w_1 = w_2$.

As usual, the theorem could be refined to say that the final stores Σ_1 and Σ_2 are related, and it could also be generalized to allow different but related initial stores and to apply to non-Boolean results. Such changes are fairly routine, and we avoid them for simplicity.

Theorem 1 can be proved directly. (See for example Austin and Flanagan [3] for analogous results). Below, we study how to obtain non-interference for ImpFlow via a translation from ImpFlow into a functional language. We proceed in this manner not so much because the direct proof would be hard, but rather in order to give evidence that the translation is helpful and sensible. The resulting indirect proof is remarkably simple.

4   A Functional Language with Information-Flow Control

Next we consider a functional language called FunFlow with information-flow control. FunFlow is an extension of the lambda calculus (see Figure 2). It includes variables (x), functions ($\lambda x.e$), function applications ($e_1 \; e_2$), a mechanism for specifying high expressions ($H\!:\!e$), and label reflection ($H?\; e$). Unlike ImpFlow, this language is purely functional and does not include reference cells. It also leaves implicit the label for low-security data: H is the only label.

Though this language is minimal, additional constructs can be encoded, as usual. Figure 2 details the constructs employed in our translation. Boolean values ($\texttt{true}$ and $\texttt{false}$) and conditional evaluation ($\texttt{if}\; e_1 \;\texttt{then}\; e_2 \;\texttt{else}\; e_3$) are Church-encoded in the usual way. Tuples ($\langle e_1, ..., e_n \rangle$) contain a list of expressions (and are used when translating stores from ImpFlow to FunFlow, which we discuss in more depth in Section 6). There are operations for projecting the ith value from a tuple ($e.i$) and setting the value at the ith position ($e[i := e']$). The let construct includes a variant ($\texttt{let}\; \langle x_1, x_2 \rangle = e_1 \;\texttt{in}\; e_2$) that deconstructs pairs.

We formalize the operational semantics of FunFlow via the small-step relation:

$$e_1 \rightarrow e_2$$

This relation evaluates an expression e_1 and returns a new expression e_2. Instead of using a program counter to track the current influences on execution, the semantics for FunFlow divides evaluation contexts ($\mathcal{E}$) into private contexts ($Context_H$), which have an enclosing $H\!:$, and public contexts ($Context_L$). Values in FunFlow are either functions ($\lambda x.e$) or labeled values ($H\!:\!v$).

The rule [E-BETA] applies β-reduction, replacing occurrences of the specified variable with the given value. The rule [E-LIFT] handles the application of a private function $H\!:\!v$ to an argument v' by moving the entire application under the H, yielding $H\!:\!(v \; v')$.

Syntax:

$$e ::= \qquad\qquad\qquad\qquad Term$$

$$\begin{array}{ll} x & variable \\ (\lambda x.e) & abstraction \\ e_1\ e_2 & application \\ H\!:\!e & high\ expression \\ H?\ e & high\ test \end{array}$$

$$x, y, z \qquad\qquad\qquad Variable$$

Runtime Syntax:

$$\begin{array}{lll} v & \in & Value \quad ::= \quad (\lambda x.e) \mid H\!:\!v \\ \mathcal{E} & \in & Context \quad ::= \quad \mathcal{E}\ e \mid v\ \mathcal{E} \mid H\!:\!\mathcal{E} \mid H?\ \mathcal{E} \mid \bullet \end{array}$$

$$\begin{array}{ll} Context_H & = \quad \mathcal{E}_1[H\!:\!\mathcal{E}_2] \\ Context_L & = \quad Context\ /\ Context_H \end{array}$$

Evaluation Rules: $\boxed{e \to e'}$

$$\begin{array}{ll} \mathcal{E}[(\lambda x.e)\ v] \to \mathcal{E}[e[x := v]] & [\text{E-BETA}] \\ \mathcal{E}[(H\!:\!v)\ v'] \to \mathcal{E}[H\!:\!(v\ v')] & [\text{E-LIFT}] \\ \mathcal{E}[H?\ (H\!:\!v)] \to \mathcal{E}[\mathbf{true}] & [\text{E-PRED-TRUE1}] \\ \mathcal{E}[H?\ (\lambda x.e)] \to \mathcal{E}[\mathbf{true}] & [\text{E-PRED-TRUE2}] \\ \qquad \text{if } \mathcal{E} \in Context_H & \\ \mathcal{E}[H?\ (\lambda x.e)] \to \mathcal{E}[\mathbf{false}] & [\text{E-PRED-FALSE}] \\ \qquad \text{if } \mathcal{E} \in Context_L & \end{array}$$

Standard Encodings:

$$\begin{array}{rcl} \mathbf{true} & \stackrel{\text{def}}{=} & (\lambda x.(\lambda y.x)) \\ \mathbf{false} & \stackrel{\text{def}}{=} & (\lambda x.(\lambda y.y)) \\ \mathbf{if}\ e_1\ \mathbf{then}\ e_2\ \mathbf{else}\ e_3 & \stackrel{\text{def}}{=} & (e_1\ (\lambda d.e_2)\ (\lambda d.e_3))\ (\lambda x.x) \\ \langle e_1, ..., e_n \rangle & \stackrel{\text{def}}{=} & (\lambda f.(f\ e_1..e_n)) \\ e.i & \stackrel{\text{def}}{=} & e\ (\lambda x_1..x_n.x_i) \\ e[i := e'] & \stackrel{\text{def}}{=} & e\ (\lambda x_1..x_n.(\lambda f.f\ x_1..x_{i-1}\ e'\ x_{i+1}..x_n)) \\ \mathbf{let}\ x = e_1\ \mathbf{in}\ e_2 & \stackrel{\text{def}}{=} & (\lambda x.e_2)\ e_1 \\ \mathbf{let}\ \langle x_1, x_2 \rangle = e_1\ \mathbf{in}\ e_2 & \stackrel{\text{def}}{=} & \mathbf{let}\ x = e_1\ \mathbf{in} \\ & & \mathbf{let}\ x_1 = x.1\ \mathbf{in} \\ & & \mathbf{let}\ x_2 = x.2\ \mathbf{in}\ e_2\ \text{for}\ x \notin FV(e_2) \\ e_1\ ;\ e_2 & \stackrel{\text{def}}{=} & \mathbf{let}\ x = e_1\ \mathbf{in}\ e_2\ \text{for}\ x \notin FV(e_2) \end{array}$$

Fig. 2. FunFlow Language

Label reflection determines if a value is private, either by an explicit label (rule [E-PRED-TRUE1]) or if it is in a private context (rule [E-PRED-TRUE2]). When the value is not explicitly H-labeled and is in a public context, then the result is `false` (rule [E-PRED-FALSE]).

For consistency with prior work, there are significant differences in the formal semantics of ImpFlow and FunFlow. The semantics of ImpFlow follows that of Austin and Flanagan [3]; it is a big-step semantics with *universal labeling*, where every value has exactly one associated label. In contrast, the semantics of FunFlow follows that of prior work on labeled lambda calculus [2]; it is a small-step semantics with no pc label, and with *sparse-labeling*, where values may have zero or multiple enclosing labels.

5   Non-interference in FunFlow

We consider two FunFlow expressions to be *equivalent modulo under labels* if the only difference between the two expressions is in their private components. More formally, the relation $e_1 \sim_{ul} e_2$ is defined as the congruence closure of

$$H : e_1 \sim_{ul} H : e_2$$

If two expressions are equivalent modulo under labels, evaluating them produces values that are equivalent modulo under labels, assuming both evaluations terminate. It is possible that only one of the computations will diverge, thereby leaking one bit of information. This notion is formalized below:

Theorem 2 (Termination-insensitive non-interference for FunFlow).
If $e_1 \sim_{ul} e_2$ and $e_1 \to^* v_1$ and $e_2 \to^* v_2$, then $v_1 \sim_{ul} v_2$.

This non-interference proof follows from the following lemma that relates each evaluation step of e_1 to a corresponding computation (possibly divergent) of e_2:

Lemma 1. *If $e_1 \sim_{ul} e_2$ and $e_1 \to e_1'$, then either $e_2 \to^\infty$ or there exists e_2' such that $e_2 \to^* e_2'$ and $e_1' \sim_{ul} e_2'$.*

The proof of this lemma is via a case analysis of $e_1 \to e_1'$.

6   Translating Imperative Information-Flow Control to Functional Information-Flow Control

We next explain how to translate ImpFlow programs into FunFlow. Our translation preserves semantics (at least for properly terminating programs). It also preserves information-flow guarantees, as we show in the next section. Of course, other translations may be invented, possibly with somewhat different properties and making different trade-offs. For instance, it may be viable to define a translation that passes two stores, basically one for each level but with "low writes" modifying both stores. Our translation, instead, occasionally creates two stores but then combines them into a single one.

Term Translation Rules: $\quad \boxed{[\![\bullet]\!] : m \;\to\; e}$

$$
\begin{aligned}
[\![x]\!] &= \lambda\sigma.\langle x, \sigma\rangle & &[\text{TR-VAR}]\\
[\![(\lambda x.m)]\!] &= \lambda\sigma.\langle(\lambda x\sigma'.[\![m]\!]\;\sigma'), \sigma\rangle & &[\text{TR-LAM}]\\
[\![H\!:\!m]\!] &= \lambda\sigma.\texttt{let } \langle x, \sigma'\rangle = [\![m]\!]\;\sigma \texttt{ in } \langle H\!:\!x, \sigma'\rangle & &[\text{TR-HI}]\\
[\![H?\;m]\!] &= \lambda\sigma.\texttt{let } \langle x, \sigma'\rangle = [\![m]\!]\;\sigma & &[\text{TR-PRED}]\\
&\quad \texttt{in } \langle \texttt{if } H?\;x \texttt{ then } [\![\texttt{true}^L]\!]_{\text{val}} \texttt{ else } [\![\texttt{false}^L]\!]_{\text{val}}, \sigma'\rangle\\
[\![!i]\!] &= \lambda\sigma.\langle \sigma.i, \sigma\rangle & &[\text{TR-DEREF}]\\
[\![i\!:=\!m]\!] &= \lambda\sigma.\texttt{let } \langle x, \sigma'\rangle = [\![m]\!]\;\sigma & &[\text{TR-ASSIGN}]\\
&\quad \texttt{in } \langle x, \sigma'[i := x]\rangle\\
[\![w]\!] &= \lambda\sigma.\langle [\![w]\!]_{\text{val}}, \sigma\rangle & &[\text{TR-VAL}]\\
[\![m_1\;m_2]\!] &= \lambda\sigma.\texttt{let } \langle x_1, \sigma_1\rangle = [\![m_1]\!]\;\sigma \texttt{ in} & &[\text{TR-APPLY}]\\
&\qquad \texttt{let } \langle x_2, \sigma_2\rangle = [\![m_2]\!]\;\sigma_1 \texttt{ in}\\
&\qquad \texttt{let } \langle x, \sigma'\rangle = x_1\;x_2\;\sigma_2 \texttt{ in}\\
&\qquad \texttt{if } H?\;x_1\\
&\qquad \texttt{then } \langle x, merge\;\sigma_2\;\sigma'\rangle\\
&\qquad \texttt{else } \langle x, \sigma'\rangle
\end{aligned}
$$

Value Translation Rules: $\quad \boxed{[\![\bullet]\!]_{\text{val}} : w \;\to\; v}$

$$
\begin{aligned}
[\![(\lambda x.m)^L]\!]_{\text{val}} &= (\lambda x\sigma.[\![m]\!]\;\sigma) & &[\text{TR-LAM-LO}]\\
[\![(\lambda x.m)^H]\!]_{\text{val}} &= H\!:\!(\lambda x\sigma.[\![m]\!]\;\sigma) & &[\text{TR-LAM-HI}]
\end{aligned}
$$

Store Translation Rules: $\quad \boxed{[\![\bullet]\!]_{\text{st}} : w \;\to\; v}$

$$
[\![\Sigma]\!]_{\text{st}} = \langle [\![\Sigma(i)]\!]_{\text{val}}^{i\in 1..n}\rangle \qquad\qquad [\text{TR-STORE}]
$$

Auxiliary Definition:

$$
merge = (\lambda\sigma\sigma'.\langle(\texttt{if } H?\;(\sigma.i) \texttt{ then } \sigma'.i \texttt{ else } \sigma.i)^{i\in 1..n}\rangle)
$$

Fig. 3. Translation Rules

The translation is defined in Figure 3 by three mutually recursive functions, $[\![m]\!]$, $[\![w]\!]_{\text{val}}$, and $[\![\Sigma]\!]_{\text{st}}$, which translate ImpFlow terms (m), values (w), and stores (Σ) into FunFlow. The translation $[\![\Sigma]\!]_{\text{st}}$ converts an ImpFlow store Σ into a FunFlow n-tuple by translating each contained value. The value translation $[\![(\lambda x.m)^k]\!]_{\text{val}}$ maps an ImpFlow value to a FunFlow function that adds an additional parameter σ for the threaded store, as follows:

$$
(\lambda x\sigma.[\![m]\!]\;\sigma)
$$

The value translation in turn calls the expression translation function $[\![m]\!]$. If the ImpFlow value is H-labeled, then the translation wraps the above FunFlow value in an enclosing $H\!:$ via the rule [TR-LAM-HI].

The expression translation function $[\![m]\!]$ converts an ImpFlow expression m into a FunFlow expression of the form $(\lambda\sigma.e)$, where σ represents the encoding of a store. The result of applying this function $(\lambda\sigma.e)$ to an encoded store results in a pair $\langle v, \sigma'\rangle$ where v represents a value $(\lambda x\sigma.e')$ and σ' represents the possibly modified store.

The [TR-VAR] rule is one of the simplest translations and illustrates the design. The function $[\![x]\!] = (\lambda\sigma.\langle x, \sigma\rangle)$ takes the store σ and returns a pair of a variable x and the unmodified store σ. ImpFlow functions are translated by the rule [TR-LAM] in a similar manner. The resulting FunFlow function takes an encoded store σ and returns a pair of a function and the store σ. The returned function $(\lambda x\sigma'.[\![m]\!]\ \sigma')$ applies the translated function body to store σ'.

The translation of $H\!:\!m$, via the [TR-HI] rule, takes the expression m resulting in the pair $\langle x, \sigma'\rangle$, and then returns the pair $\langle H : x, \sigma'\rangle$ where x is labeled as private. Critically, the store σ' is *not* labeled as private. Likewise, the translation of $H?\ m$ converts the expression m to a function that returns the pair $\langle x, \sigma'\rangle$ via the [TR-PRED] rule. It performs label reflection on x and then either returns (appropriately translated versions of) **true** or **false**.

The translations for operations on mutable reference cells are fairly straightforward. The translated function for dereferencing i returns the ith element of the store tuple, as indicated by the rule [TR-DEREF]. The [TR-ASSIGN] rule for $i:=m$ translates the right-hand side m, resulting in a function that will return a pair $\langle x, \sigma\rangle$ when it is applied to store σ. This pair is returned, except that position i in σ' is replaced with x.

The translation of a function application $(m_1\ m_2)$ is subtle and requires some care. A naive approach is to thread the store through m_1, m_2, and the callee in the standard manner:

$$[\![m_1\ m_2]\!] = \lambda\sigma.\texttt{let}\ \langle x_1, \sigma_1\rangle = [\![m_1]\!]\ \sigma\ \texttt{in} \qquad \text{[TR-APPLY-NAIVE]}$$
$$\texttt{let}\ \langle x_2, \sigma_2\rangle = [\![m_2]\!]\ \sigma_1\ \texttt{in}$$
$$\texttt{let}\ \langle x, \sigma'\rangle = x_1\ x_2\ \sigma_2\ \texttt{in}$$
$$\langle x, \sigma'\rangle$$

Unfortunately, this translation results in making the entire store private whenever a private function is applied, as discussed in the introduction. For example, $[\![(\lambda x.x)^H\ w]\!]\ \sigma \to^* H\!:\!\langle[\![w]\!]_{\texttt{val}}, \sigma\rangle$.

The [TR-APPLY] rule applies a more intricate translation in cases where the target function x_1 is private (that is, when $H?\ x_1$ is true). This translation determines the stores σ_2 and σ' before and after the call to x_1, and then combines these two stores via the auxiliary function *merge* $\sigma_2\ \sigma'$. Any entry $\sigma_2.i$ that is public should not be updated during the call, according to the no-sensitive-upgrade rule, so in this case $(merge\ \sigma_2\ \sigma').i$ returns $\sigma_2.i$. Conversely, for private entries $\sigma_2.i$, $(merge\ \sigma_2\ \sigma').i$ can safely return the private value $\sigma'.i$.

Note that this transformation ignores updates to public entries in the store in a manner that is somewhat analogous to the no-sensitive-upgrade rule, which forbids such updates. Both approaches guarantee non-interference. We can formalize the same behavior for the ImpFlow semantics as follows:

$$\frac{m, \Sigma \Downarrow_{pc} w, \Sigma' \quad pc \not\sqsubseteq label(\Sigma'(i))}{i := m, \Sigma \Downarrow_{pc} w, \Sigma'} \text{ [M-ASSIGN-IGNORE]}$$

Critically, the translation preserves *equivalent modulo under labels*.

Lemma 2. *If $m_1 \sim_{ul} m_2$, then $[\![m_1]\!] \sim_{ul} [\![m_2]\!]$.*

Consequently, if $m_1 \sim_{ul} m_2$ and

$$[\![m_1]\!] \; [\![\Sigma]\!]_{\text{st}} \to^* \langle v_1, \sigma_1 \rangle$$
$$[\![m_2]\!] \; [\![\Sigma]\!]_{\text{st}} \to^* \langle v_2, \sigma_2 \rangle$$

then $v_1 \sim_{ul} v_2$. That is, implementing ImpFlow via our translation to FunFlow preserves termination-insensitive non-interference.

It is not obvious how the semantics via translation to FunFlow corresponds to the big-step operational semantics of ImpFlow from Figure 3, particularly given the difference between the two languages: imperative vs. functional, universal vs. sparse labeling, and the no-sensitive-upgrade check vs. the *merge* function.

We aim to establish that the translation preserves semantics. We might conjecture a correspondence property of the form:

If $m, \Sigma \Downarrow_L w, \Sigma'$ then $[\![m]\!][\![\Sigma]\!]_{\text{st}} \to^* \langle v, \sigma \rangle$ where $v = [\![w]\!]_{\text{val}}$ and $\sigma = [\![\Sigma']\!]_{\text{st}}$.

Unfortunately this correspondence does not hold, since v and $[\![w]\!]_{\text{val}}$ may have syntactic differences in labels that are not observable. That is, a label H that is nested under another label H is redundant. Therefore we define a $\sim_{lul}$ relation that determines if two expressions are *equivalent modulo labels under labels*. This relation relies on a $\sim_l$ relation, which compares two expressions and tests if they are *equivalent modulo labels*. The rules for both relations are given below.

$$\frac{}{x \sim_{lul} x} \text{ [BEQ-VAR]} \qquad\qquad \frac{}{x \sim_l x} \text{ [BEQ-H-VAR]}$$

$$\frac{e \sim_{lul} e'}{(\lambda x.e) \sim_{lul} (\lambda x.e')} \text{ [BEQ-FUN]} \qquad \frac{e \sim_l e'}{(\lambda x.e) \sim_l (\lambda x.e')} \text{ [BEQ-H-FUN]}$$

$$\frac{e \sim_{lul} e'}{H? \; e \sim_{lul} H? \; e'} \text{ [BEQ-PRED]} \qquad \frac{e \sim_l e'}{H? \; e \sim_l H? \; e'} \text{ [BEQ-H-PRED]}$$

$$\frac{e_1 \sim_{lul} e_1' \quad e_2 \sim_{lul} e_2'}{e_1 \; e_2 \sim_{lul} e_1' \; e_2'} \text{ [BEQ-APP]} \qquad \frac{e_1 \sim_l e_1' \quad e_2 \sim_l e_2'}{e_1 \; e_2 \sim_l e_1' \; e_2'} \text{ [BEQ-H-APP]}$$

$$\frac{e \sim_l e'}{H : e \sim_{lul} H : e'} \text{ [BEQ-LABEL]} \qquad \frac{e \sim_l e'}{e \sim_l H : e'} \text{ [BEQ-H-RIGHT]}$$

$$\frac{e \sim_l e'}{H : e \sim_l e'} \text{ [BEQ-H-LEFT]}$$

If two expressions in FunFlow are equivalent modulo labels under labels, then evaluation maintains this property, as formalized by the following lemma.

Lemma 3. *If $e_1 \sim_{lul} e_2 \to e_3$ then there exists e_4 such that $e_1 \to^* e_4 \sim_{lul} e_3$.*

The $\sim_{ul}$ relation includes strictly more terms than the $\sim_{lul}$ relation, since it accepts all terms that vary under H.

Lemma 4. $(\sim_{lul}) \subseteq (\sim_{ul})$

We define a new relation that combines the small-step evaluation relation for FunFlow with the equivalent modulo labels under labels relation. This relation $\Rightarrow$ enables us to add and remove redundant labels as necessary to obtain the desired correspondence sketched above.

$$(\Rightarrow) \;\overset{\text{def}}{=}\; (\to) \cup (\sim_{lul})$$

Lemma 5. *If $e_1 \Rightarrow^n e_2$ then there exists e_3 such that $e_1 \to^* e_3 \sim_{lul} e_2$.*

Evaluation in a high context does not affect public reference cells.

Lemma 6. *If $m, \Sigma \Downarrow_H w, \Sigma'$ then for all i such that $\Sigma(i) \neq \Sigma'(i)$, $\Sigma(i)$ and $\Sigma'(i)$ are both high.*

If a program does not modify public reference cells in private blocks of code, then the *merge* operation has no effect.

Lemma 7. *Suppose for all i with $\Sigma(i) \neq \Sigma'(i)$ we have that both $\Sigma(i)$ and $\Sigma'(i)$ are high. Then merge $[\![\Sigma]\!]_{\text{st}} \; H : [\![\Sigma']\!]_{\text{st}} \Rightarrow^* [\![\Sigma']\!]_{\text{st}}$.*

We now show the correctness of the translation. If a program of the source language executes successfully, then the translation also executes successfully and exhibits the same behavior.

Theorem 3. *If $m, \Sigma \Downarrow_{pc} w, \Sigma'$ then $\mathcal{E}[[\![m]\!] \; [\![\Sigma]\!]_{\text{st}}] \Rightarrow^* \mathcal{E}[\langle [\![w]\!]_{\text{val}}, [\![\Sigma']\!]_{\text{st}} \rangle]$ for all $\mathcal{E} \in Context_{pc}$.*

Proof. The proof is provided in a related technical report [4].

7 Non-interference in ImpFlow (Continued)

Showing the correctness of the translation and the non-interference property of FunFlow enables a short proof of non-interference for ImpFlow. This proof gives evidence that the translation is helpful and sensible. Albeit indirect, it is pleasingly simple. We now prove non-interference in the source language (Theorem 1). The proof relies on the correctness of the translation of ImpFlow programs that run to completion, and the non-interference property of the FunFlow semantics.

Proof (of Theorem 1). By Lemma 2, $[\![m_1]\!] \; [\![\Sigma]\!]_{\text{st}} \sim_{ul} [\![m_2]\!] \; [\![\Sigma]\!]_{\text{st}}$.
By Theorem 3, $[\![m_i]\!] \; [\![\Sigma]\!]_{\text{st}} \Rightarrow^* \langle [\![w_i]\!]_{\text{val}}, [\![\Sigma_i]\!]_{\text{st}} \rangle$ for all i.
Hence by Lemma 5, for all i there exists v_i such that
$[\![m_i]\!] \; [\![\Sigma]\!]_{\text{st}} \to^* v_i \sim_{lul} \langle [\![w_i]\!]_{\text{val}}, [\![\Sigma_i]\!]_{\text{st}} \rangle$.
By Theorem 2, $v_1 \sim_{ul} v_2$, so by Lemma 4, $[\![w_1]\!]_{\text{val}} \sim_{ul} [\![w_2]\!]_{\text{val}}$.
Note that $[\![\text{true}^L]\!]_{\text{val}} \not\sim_{ul} [\![\text{false}^L]\!]_{\text{val}}$, hence w_1 and w_2 are not distinct public Booleans, so $w_1 = w_2$. $\square$

8   Conclusion

This paper aims to further understanding of dynamic information flow in a language with imperative updates through translation to a purely functional core. A naive translation is unnecessarily restrictive, but through careful handling of stores, a translation can preserve the flexibility of the source language. Reasoning about the translation and the non-interference properties of the target language enables a simple proof of non-interference in the source language.

Both the source language and the target language embody fairly standard ideas present in the literature. We hope that our results thus shed some light on other languages. Nevertheless, we recognize that not all variants of the languages will necessarily lend themselves easily to analogous treatments. The detailed consideration of those variants may be a worthwhile subject for further research.

Acknowledgements. We would like to thank Gérard Boudol, Anindya Banerjee, Steve Zdancewicz, Andrew Myers, Greg Morrisett, Alejandro Russo, Jean-Jacques Lévy, Damien Doligez, and Cédric Fournet for helpful discussions. This work was supported by the NSF under grants CNS-0905650 and CCF-1116883.

References

1. Abadi, M., Banerjee, A., Heintze, N., Riecke, J.G.: A core calculus of dependency. In: Symposium on Principles of Programming Languages (1999)
2. Abadi, M., Lampson, B.W., Lévy, J.-J.: Analysis and caching of dependencies. In: International Conference on Functional Programming (1996)
3. Austin, T.H., Flanagan, C.: Efficient purely-dynamic information flow analysis. In: Workshop on Programming Languages and Analysis for Security (2009)
4. Austin, T.H., Flanagan, C., Abadi, M.: A functional view of imperative information flow, extended version. Technical Report UCSC-SOE-12-15, The University of California at Santa Cruz (2012)
5. Chugh, R., Meister, J.A., Jhala, R., Lerner, S.: Staged information flow for JavaScript. In: Conference on Programming Language Design and Implementation (2009)
6. Denning, D.E.: A lattice model of secure information flow. Communications of the ACM 19(5), 236–243 (1976)
7. Denning, D.E., Denning, P.J.: Certification of programs for secure information flow. Communications of the ACM 20(7), 504–513 (1977)
8. Dhawan, M., Ganapathy, V.: Analyzing information flow in JavaScript-based browser extensions. In: Annual Computer Security Applications Conference (2009)
9. Fenton, J.S.: Memoryless subsystems. The Computer Journal 17(2), 143–147 (1974)
10. FlowCaml homepage, http://pauillac.inria.fr/~simonet/soft/flowcaml/ (accessed May 2010)
11. Le Guernic, G., Banerjee, A., Jensen, T., Schmidt, D.A.: Automata-Based Confidentiality Monitoring. In: Okada, M., Satoh, I. (eds.) ASIAN 2006. LNCS, vol. 4435, pp. 75–89. Springer, Heidelberg (2008)
12. Hedin, D., Sabelfeld, A.: Information-flow security for a core of JavaScript. In: Computer Security Foundations Symposium (2012)

13. Heintze, N., Riecke, J.G.: The SLam calculus: Programming with secrecy and integrity. In: Symposium on Principles of Programming Languages (1998)
14. Jif homepage (2010), http://www.cs.cornell.edu/jif/ (accessed October 2010)
15. Krohn, M.N., Efstathopoulos, P., Frey, C., Frans Kaashoek, M., Kohler, E., Mazières, D., Morris, R., Osborne, M., Vandebogart, S., Ziegler, D.: Make least privilege a right (not a privilege). In: Workshop on Hot Topics in Operating Systems (2005)
16. Myers, A.C.: JFlow: Practical mostly-static information flow control. In: Symposium on Principles of Programming Languages (1999)
17. Pottier, F., Simonet, V.: Information flow inference for ML. Transactions on Programming Languages and Systems 25(1), 117–158 (2003)
18. Sabelfeld, A., Myers, A.C.: Language-based information-flow security. Journal on Selected Areas in Communications 21(1), 5–19 (2003)
19. Shroff, P., Smith, S.F., Thober, M.: Dynamic dependency monitoring to secure information flow. In: Computer Security Foundations Symposium (2007)
20. Stefan, D., Russo, A., Mitchell, J.C., Mazières, D.: Flexible dynamic information flow control in Haskell. In: Symposium on Haskell (2011)
21. Vogt, P., Nentwich, F., Jovanovic, N., Kirda, E., Krügel, C., Vigna, G.: Cross-site scripting prevention with dynamic data tainting and static analysis (2007)
22. Volpano, D., Irvine, C., Smith, G.: A sound type system for secure flow analysis. Journal of Computer Security 4(2-3), 167–187 (1996)
23. Zdancewic, S.A.: Programming languages for information security. PhD thesis, Cornell University (2002)
24. Zeldovich, N., Boyd-Wickizer, S., Kohler, E., Mazières, D.: Making information flow explicit in HiStar. Communications of the ACM 54(11), 93–101 (2011)

End-to-end Multilevel Hybrid Information Flow Control*

Lennart Beringer

Department of Computer Science, Princeton University,
35 Olden Street, Princeton NJ 08540
eberinge@cs.princeton.edu

Abstract. We present models and soundness results for hybrid information flow, i.e. for mechanisms that enforce noninterference-style security guarantees using a combination of static analysis and dynamic taint tracking. Our analysis has the following characteristics: (i) we formulate hybrid information flow as an end-to-end property, in contrast to disruptive monitors that prematurely terminate or otherwise alter an execution upon detecting a potentially illicit flow; (ii) our security notions capture the increased precision that is gained when static analysis is combined with dynamic enforcement; (iii) we introduce path tracking to incorporate a form of termination-sensitivity, and (iv) develop a novel variant of purely dynamic tracking that *ignores* indirect flows; (v) our work has been formally verified, by a comprehensive representation in the theorem prover Coq.

1 Introduction

Hybrid information flow techniques integrate static analyses with dynamic taint tracking or execution monitoring to ensure the absence of illicit flows. In the systems community, instrumentations that control *direct* data flows in assignments have been refined, using compile-time transformations or dynamic binary instrumentation, to capture *indirect* (or *implicit*) flows arising from the branching behavior or aliasing [29,23,14,19,18]. Typically, these systems focus on efficient implementability and are justified by informal arguments, but lack mathematically precise definitions of the intended security guarantee or formal soundness proofs.

The inverse observation applies to work on language-based security. Here, the traditional focus on static techniques has recently been complemented by studies of coupled or inlined monitors, with different mechanisms for detecting, preventing, or handling potentially illicit flows [30,28,27,13,24,20,3,4,22]. Typically, these analyses are illustrated with proof-of-concept implementations that are less comprehensive than those of the systems community but are backed up with (pencil-and-paper) soundness proofs based on precise definitions of operational models and the intended security guarantee.

Our long-term goal is to integrate flexible information flow enforcement into frameworks such as the Verified Software Toolchain [2]. As a stepping stone, and building on formalizations of type systems for noninterference [7,10,1], we present the first hybrid enforcement that is backed up by an implementation in a proof assistant, Coq [9].

---

* This work was funded in part by the Air Force Office of Scientific Research (FA9550-09-1-0138).

R. Jhala and A. Igarashi (Eds.): APLAS 2012, LNCS 7705, pp. 50–65, 2012.

Our analysis takes inspiration from RIFLE [29], one of the first hybrid systems with a precise treatment of indirect flows. In particular, we provide an analysis of one of RIFLE's core ideas, the use of separate taint registers for direct and indirect flows. Underpinning RIFLE's intuitive soundness argument with a formal guarantee, we show in which sense the tracking of indirect flows using dedicated **join** instructions improves precision when compared to a more naive system where only data taints are tracked dynamically. The latter system in turn is more precise than the standard static system, the flow-sensitive type system of Hunt and Sands [16,17].

The guarantees recently proposed for inlined [13] or non-inlined [27] monitors prematurely terminate or alter executions upon detecting a potentially illicit flow. Our analysis shows that dynamic enforcement may alternatively be understood as an *asymmetric* end-to-end indistinguishability notion that refines (multilevel) noninterference. Here, the asymmetry captures the difference between the actual (taint-instrumented) execution and hypothetical competitor executions (which may be taint-instrumented or not). The resulting notion captures the systems-oriented intuition that each value's final taint should carry fine-grained information regarding its (potential) origins.

Asymmetric interpretations have previously been considered by Le Guernic and Jensen [21,20], and also by Magazinius et al. [22]. These works limit their attention to two-level security and track direct and indirect flows jointly. In addition, Le Guernic and Jensen specify the set of observable (final) variables statically. Our analysis exposes additional fine-grained structure of taint tracking and highlights that the noninfluence between taints and the native execution actually refines to a ternary discipline: data taints (capturing direct flows) are unaffected by control taints (capturing indirect flows), and neither one affects the data plane (i.e. the native execution).

Finally, we introduce *path tracking*, by adding a further taint register that collects the taints of all branch conditions encountered. Path tracking propagates termination from tracked to untracked executions, and also provides a meaningful indistinguishability guarantee for pure data flow tracking. In particular, we outline in which sense control taints can be safely eliminated without detrimentally affecting the security guarantee.

Summarizing our contributions, we present an analysis of hybrid information flow enforcement that considers fine-grained taint-tracking with separated control and data taints. We develop appropriate notions of formal security, prove corresponding soundness results, and investigate the relative precision of different syntheses. We introduce path tracking as an extension of previous instrumentations, obtaining termination-aware tracking and an (to our knowledge: the first) extensional interpretation of data flow tracking. In contrast to all previous developments of hybrid information flow or dynamic flow tracking, our development is backed up by a formalization in Coq – see [9].

In contrast to RIFLE's assembly-level formulation, our analysis is carried out for the language of structured commands and loops. This setting suffices for studying the intended security notion and the core aspects of **join**-based taint instrumentation, but a study of additional aspects would certainly be profitable. Of particular interest in this regard would be RIFLE's treatment of memory, which combines a reaching-definitions analysis with external aliasing analyses. However, the exploitation of aliasing information in RIFLE's synthesis is such that use-sites of taint registers are not necessarily dominated by their def-sites, prohibiting a proof of soundness along the program structure. For this reason, our synthesis uses a different allocation policy for taint registers. A future integration of memory may allow us to study this aspect in more detail and may take additional inspiration from the recent work of Moore and Chong [24].

2   Static Flow-Sensitive Information Flow

We start by fixing some notation and revising aspects of Hunt & Sands' static analysis.

2.1   Native Language

For disjoint sets $\mathcal{X}$ of program variables and $\mathcal{V}$ of value constants, our language concerns expressions $\mathcal{E}$ and commands $\mathcal{C}$ according to the grammar

$$e \in \mathcal{E} ::= x \mid v \mid e \oplus e$$
$$C \in \mathcal{C} ::= \mathbf{skip} \mid x := e \mid C; C \mid \mathbf{if}\ e\ \mathbf{then}\ C\ \mathbf{else}\ C \mid \mathbf{while}\ e\ \mathbf{do}\ C$$

where $x, y, \ldots \in \mathcal{X}$, $v, w, \ldots \in \mathcal{V}$ and $\oplus$ ranges over binary operations. The set of program variables possibly modified (i.e. assigned to) in some command C is denoted by $\mathrm{MV}(C)$. Expression evaluation $s \vdash e \Downarrow v$ and (big-step) command execution $s \xrightarrow{C} t$ are formulated over stores $s, t, \ldots$ from the space $\mathcal{S} = \mathcal{X} \rightarrow \mathcal{V}$. Throughout the paper, update operations of various total or partial functions are written as $.[. \mapsto .]$, and lookups as $.(.)$ or simply juxtaposition. We denote empty lists (over various types) by ϵ, list append by @, and list prefixing by ::. The definition of these auxiliary notions, and of the operational judgements are entirely standard and hence omitted.

   We formulate our analysis generically over a semilattice $\mathcal{L}$ with partial order $\sqsubseteq: \mathcal{L} \rightarrow \mathcal{L} \rightarrow \mathrm{Prop}$, least upper bound $\sqcup : \mathcal{L} \rightarrow \mathcal{L} \rightarrow \mathcal{L}$, and bottom element $\bot$. We typically write the binary operators in infix position and extend $\sqcup$ to subsets of $\mathcal{L}$, with $\sqcup \emptyset = \bot$, and also to $\mathcal{L}^*$ (i.e. finite lists over $\mathcal{L}$), with $\sqcup \epsilon = \bot$. Example programs use the ternary semilattice $low \subsetneq mid \subsetneq high$ and silently name variables according to their typical *initial* taint: $l : low, m : mid, h : high$. Of course, the static level and the dynamic taint of a variable may differ from this at different program points.

2.2   Flow-Sensitive Type System in the Style of Hunt and Sands

The starting point of our analysis is the flow-sensitive type system for multilevel noninterference by Hunt & Sands [16,17]. Its algorithmic formulation (given in [17]) employs judgements $\vdash \{\Gamma\}C\{\Delta\}$ where the contexts Γ, Δ associate security elements to all program variables and also to a distinguished pseudo-variable $\mathbf{pc} \notin \mathcal{X}$. We denote the restriction of context Γ to the program variables by $|\Gamma|$ and let $G, H, \ldots$ range over such $\mathbf{pc}$-erased contexts. Lattice constants and operations are lifted to erased or unerased contexts in the standard pointwise fashion. Label evaluation $[\![e]\!]_G$ is given by

$$[\![x]\!]_G = G(x) \qquad [\![v]\!]_G = \bot \qquad [\![e_1 \oplus e_2]\!]_G = [\![e_1]\!]_G \sqcup [\![e_2]\!]_G$$

and is extended to non-erased contexts via $[\![e]\!]_\Gamma = [\![e]\!]_{|\Gamma|}$. The proof rules for $\vdash \{\Gamma\}C\{\Delta\}$ are summarized in Figure 1, with an explicit construction of the (least) fixed point context in rule HS-WHILE. We write $\mathcal{D} \vdash \{\Gamma\}C\{\Delta\}$ to refer to a particular derivation for $\vdash \{\Gamma\}C\{\Delta\}$. It is easy to see that $\vdash \{\Gamma\}C\{\Delta\}$ implies

$$\text{HS-COMP} \frac{\forall i \in \{1,2\}.\ \vdash \{\Gamma_i\}C_i\{\Gamma_{i+1}\}}{\vdash \{\Gamma_1\}C_1;C_2\{\Gamma_3\}} \qquad \text{HS-ASS} \frac{\Delta = \Gamma[x \mapsto \Gamma(\mathbf{pc}) \sqcup [\![e]\!]\Gamma]}{\vdash \{\Gamma\}x{:=}e\{\Delta\}}$$

$$\text{HS-SKIP} \frac{}{\vdash \{\Gamma\}\mathbf{skip}\{\Gamma\}} \qquad \text{HS-ITE} \frac{\begin{array}{c} p = \Gamma(\mathbf{pc}) \qquad \Gamma' = \Gamma[\mathbf{pc} \mapsto p \sqcup [\![e]\!]\Gamma] \\ \forall i \in \{1,2\}.\ \vdash \{\Gamma'\}C_i\{\Delta_i\} \end{array}}{\vdash \{\Gamma\}\mathbf{if}\ e\ \mathbf{then}\ C_1\ \mathbf{else}\ C_2\{(\Delta_1 \sqcup \Delta_2)[\mathbf{pc} \mapsto p]\}}$$

$$\text{HS-WHILE} \frac{\begin{array}{c} \forall i < n.\ \Gamma_i \neq \Gamma_{i+1} \qquad \forall i \geqslant n.\ \Gamma_i = \Gamma_{i+1} \qquad p = \Gamma(\mathbf{pc}) \\ \Gamma_0 = \Gamma[\mathbf{pc} \mapsto p \sqcup [\![e]\!]\Gamma] \qquad \forall i.\ \vdash \{\Gamma_i\}C\{\Delta_i\} \\ \forall i.\ \Gamma_{i+1} = (\Delta_i \sqcup \Gamma)[\mathbf{pc} \mapsto (\Delta_i \sqcup \Gamma)(\mathbf{pc}) \sqcup [\![e]\!]\Delta_i \sqcup \Gamma] \end{array}}{\vdash \{\Gamma\}\mathbf{while}\ e\ \mathbf{do}\ C\{\Gamma_n[\mathbf{pc} \mapsto p]\}}$$

Fig. 1. System $\vdash \{\Gamma\}C\{\Delta\}$ by Hunt & Sands with explicit (least) fixed point in rule HS-WHILE

- $\Gamma(\mathbf{pc}) = \Delta(\mathbf{pc})$
- $\Delta = \Delta'$ whenever $\vdash \{\Gamma\}C\{\Delta'\}$ (functionality of H. & S.-typing)
- $\Delta' \sqsubseteq \Delta$ whenever $\vdash \{\Gamma'\}C\{\Delta'\}$ and $\Gamma' \sqsubseteq \Gamma$ (monotonicity of H. & S.-typing)
- $\Delta(\mathbf{pc}) \sqsubseteq \Delta x$ for $x \in \mathrm{MV}(C)$, and $\Delta x = \Gamma x$ for $x \notin \mathrm{MV}(C)$.

Furthermore, we have the following:

Lemma 1. *For* $\vdash \{\Gamma\}C\{\Delta\}$ *and* $s \xrightarrow{C} t$, *any* $x \in \mathcal{X}$ *satisfies* $\Delta(\mathbf{pc}) \sqsubseteq \Delta x$ *or* $sx = tx \wedge \Gamma x \sqsubseteq \Delta x$.

Following common practice, our security notions are formulated using *indistinguishability* relations over stores, given some threshold $\kappa \in \mathcal{L}$:

Definition 1. *States* s *and* s' *are G-indistinguishable below* $\kappa \in \mathcal{L}$, *notation* $s =^G_{\sqsubseteq\kappa} s'$, *if all* x *with* $Gx \sqsubseteq \kappa$ *satisfy* $sx = s'x$. *Command* C *is* κ-*secure for* G *and* H, *notation* $\models_\kappa \{G\}C\{H\}$, *if* $s =^G_{\sqsubseteq\kappa} s'$ *implies* $t =^H_{\sqsubseteq\kappa} t'$ *whenever* $s \xrightarrow{C} t$ *and* $s' \xrightarrow{C} t'$.

We note that for $\kappa' \sqsubseteq \kappa$ and $G \sqsubseteq G'$, $s =^G_{\sqsubseteq\kappa} s'$ implies $s =^{G'}_{\sqsubseteq\kappa'} s'$ (monotonicity of indistinguishability). Soundness of $\vdash \{\Gamma\}C\{\Delta\}$ is then given by the following result.

Theorem 1. *If* $\vdash \{\Gamma\}C\{\Delta\}$ *then* $\models_\kappa \{|\Gamma|\}C\{|\Delta|\}$ *for any* κ.

3   Data Flow Tracking

The first step towards a more dynamic regime is a language where only direct flows (from e into x in assignments $x{:=}e$) are tracked. Indirect flows are treated by program annotations based on the static analysis, so that the taints of all affected assignments are incremented by the branch conditions' *static* security levels. While being less permissive than the system we will develop in Section 4, this language suffices for motivating our formulation of soundness and discussing some aspects of the program synthesis.

3.1 Language with Decorated Assignments

The category of taint-instrumented commands $\mathcal{T}$ (typically ranged over by T) agrees with that for native commands $\mathcal{C}$ except that assignments take the form $[\lambda]\, x{:=}e$ where $\lambda \in \mathcal{L}^*$. We denote the native command arising from recursively erasing all decorations from assignments by $|T|$.

Operationally, the taint-extended language manipulates states $\sigma, \tau, \ldots$ that are pairs of stores s and (erased) contexts[1] G. Command evaluation $\sigma \xrightarrow{T}_\mathsf{T} \tau$ is defined in parallel to the native $s \xrightarrow{C} t$, with the exception that an instrumented assignment $[\lambda]\, x{:=}e$ additionally updates the taint for x to the lub of λ and the taint of e (given by the lub of the taints associated with the variables in e):

$$\text{T-Ass} \quad \frac{s \vdash e \Downarrow v \qquad \llbracket e \rrbracket_G = a \qquad \sqcup \lambda = l}{(s, G) \xrightarrow{[\lambda]\, x{:=}e}_\mathsf{T} (s[x \mapsto v], G[x \mapsto (l \sqcup a)])}$$

As a consequence, the language satisfies the following simple erasure property: for any G, $s \xrightarrow{|T|} t$ is equivalent to $\exists H.\ (s, G) \xrightarrow{T}_\mathsf{T} (t, H)$.

3.2 Program Synthesis

Given a program C, the task of the program synthesis is to generate a program T that is suitably annotated for noninterference and is functionally equivalent to C. To this end, a synthesis must achieve two tasks: first, assignment annotations must be derived that correctly account for all implicit flows. Second, assignments in conditionally executed code regions must be counter-balanced so that no information leaks from the execution *or non-execution* of a particular program path. This is achieved by lifting the taints of all variables *potentially* modified in a piece of code to (at least) the taint of any branch condition enclosing the code fragment, using *compensation code*:

Definition 2. *For $\kappa \in \mathcal{L}$, command C, and an (arbitrary) enumeration $x_1, \ldots, x_n$ of* $\mathsf{MV}(C)$, *we define* $\mathsf{CompCd}_\kappa(C)$ *to be* $[\kappa]\, x_1{:=}x_1; \ldots; [\kappa]\, x_n{:=}x_n$.

Thus, $\mathsf{CompCd}_\kappa(C)$ lifts the taints of all x_i to at least κ without changing their data values. Taints already above κ are also unaffected. While the term *compensation code* appears to have been coined by Chudnow and Naumann [13], the concept itself is already present in RIFLE [29] and Venkatakrishnan et al.'s work [30], and represents an extensional, non-disruptive alternative to the policy of *no sensitive-upgrade* [3,5].

The synthesis of annotated code is now defined on the basis of a derivation $\mathcal{D} \vdash \{\Gamma\}C\{\Delta\}$. Figure 2 defines the synthesis of instrumented code $\theta(\mathcal{D}, C)$ by case distinction on C, with recursive reference to the subderivations of $\mathcal{D}$.

The annotation $[\Gamma(\mathbf{pc})]$ in assignments models the indirect flows from enclosing branch conditions into assigned variables, as statically approximated by context Γ. Direct flows from variables in e into x are dealt with (in a dynamically precise manner) by the second side condition of the operational rule T-Ass and thus need not be taken

---

[1] This treatment is equivalent to annotating values with their taint directly, i.e. to a model with stores that map registers to *tainted* values.

C	$\theta(\mathcal{D}, C)$	where ...
skip	**skip**	
$x:=e$	$[\Gamma(\mathbf{pc})]\,x:=e$	
$C_1;C_2$	$\theta(\mathcal{D}_1, C_1); \theta(\mathcal{D}_2, C_2)$	$\mathcal{D}_i \vdash \{\Gamma_i\}C_i\{\Gamma_{i+1}\},$ $(\Gamma, \Delta) = (\Gamma_1, \Gamma_3)$
if e **then** C_1 **else** C_2	**if** e **then** $\theta(\mathcal{D}_1, C_1)$ **else** $\theta(\mathcal{D}_2, C_2)$; $\mathsf{CompCd}_\kappa(C_1; C_2)$	$\mathcal{D}_i \vdash \{\Gamma'\}C_i\{\Delta_i\}$ $\kappa = \Gamma(\mathbf{pc}) \sqcup [\![e]\!]_\Gamma$
while e **do** C'	**while** e **do** $\theta(\mathcal{D}_n, C')$; $\mathsf{CompCd}_\kappa(C')$	$\mathcal{D}_n \vdash \{\Gamma_n\}C'\{\Delta_n\}$ $\kappa = \Gamma(\mathbf{pc}) \sqcup [\![e]\!]_{\Gamma_n}$

Fig. 2. Synthesis of taint-instrumented code given a derivation $\mathcal{D} \vdash \{\Gamma\}C\{\Delta\}$. Items are named in accordance with Figure 1: in the cases for composition and conditionals, the derivations $\mathcal{D}_i$ refer to the subderivations for the respective subphrases C_i ($i \in \{1, 2\}$). Similarly in the case for loops: n is the index where the fixed point iteration stabilizes (cf. Figure 1).

into consideration during program generation. The clauses for composition, conditionals, and loops assemble the recursively generated code fragments, adding compensation code in the latter two cases. In the case for loops, it suffices to add compensation code as a loop epilogue. We note that the given taint κ not only dominates $\Gamma(\mathbf{pc}) \sqcup [\![e]\!]_{\Gamma_n}$ but also all $[\![e]\!]_{\Gamma_i}$ ($i < n$), by the monotonicity of typing.

Taint-tracking respects the static analysis in the following sense:

Lemma 2. *For* $\mathcal{D} \vdash \{\Gamma\}C\{\Delta\}$ *and* $(s, G) \xrightarrow{\theta(\mathcal{D},C)}_\mathsf{T} (t, D)$, $G \sqsubseteq |\Gamma|$ *implies* $D \sqsubseteq |\Delta|$.

A typical case where the claim in Lemma 2 holds strictly is the (native) program **if** m **then** $x:=3$ **else** $x:=h$, where $\Gamma = [h : high, m : mid, \mathbf{pc} : low]$. For $G = |\Gamma|$ we have $Dx = mid \subsetneq high = \Delta x$ whenever s is such that $s \vdash m \Downarrow \mathbf{true}$.

Functional equivalence between $\theta(\mathcal{D}, C)$ and C follows from the above erasure property and the fact that compensation code does not affect the data plane. We now turn our attention to the noninterference guarantee of taint tracking.

3.3 Interpretation and Soundness

Intuitively, the tag associated with a value in a *final* state of a taint-enhanced execution indicates the *initial* values it may have been affected by. Thus, the guarantee is *execution*-oriented rather than *program*-classifying [21]. In contrast to monitor-based formulations that preemptively terminate executions in case of a potential security violation, this intuition treats taints in an end-to-end fashion, but is nontrivial only if at least the instrumented execution terminates. In order to clarify its relationship with noninterference, we give below (Definition 4) a formal reading of our intuition, capturing the asymmetry by designating the tainted (and terminating) execution as the *lead* or *major* execution, and considering the second (tainted or untainted) execution the *minor* or *competitor* execution. Typographically, we distinguish major from minor executions by consistently using primed entities for the latter. Part of the intuitive reading then is that the terminal tags of lead executions determine which minor executions need to be considered, separately for each final value.

As a preliminary step, let us first consider the following symmetric and static notion.

Definition 3. *Program* T *is* statically (G, H)-secure *if for* $(s, G) \xrightarrow{T}_\mathsf{T} (t, D)$ *and* $(s', G) \xrightarrow{T}_\mathsf{T} (t', D')$ *and for each* x, $s =^G_{\sqsubseteq Hx} s'$ *implies* $tx = t'x$.

By quantifying over x outside of the implication, this notion captures explicitly that final values in x could only be influenced by certain initial values, namely those held in variables y with $Gy \sqsubseteq Hx$ (note that the executions agree on their initial taint state G here). Indeed, the static type system ensures static security:

Theorem 2. *For* $\mathcal{D} \vdash \{\Gamma\}C\{\Delta\}$, $\theta(\mathcal{D}, C)$ *is statically* $(|\Gamma|, |\Delta|)$-secure.

Thus, indistinguishability of s and s' (w.r.t. $|\Gamma|$) below $|\Delta|(x)$ suffices for guaranteeing $tx = t'x$. In fact, it is easy to see that static security reformulates universal κ-security pointwise for each variable:

Lemma 3. *For any* G, H, s, s', t, t', *the following are equivalent:*

1. *for all* x, $s =^G_{\sqsubseteq Hx} s'$ *implies* $tx = t'x$ *(the clause in Definition 3)*
2. *for all* κ, $s =^G_{\sqsubseteq \kappa} s'$ *implies* $t =^H_{\sqsubseteq \kappa} t'$ *(the clause in Definition 1).*

Applying this lemma to the case where $s \xrightarrow{C} t$ and $s' \xrightarrow{C} t'$ for some C (and using erasure) yields that Theorems 2 and 1 are equivalent - the universal quantification over κ in the latter and the pointwise formulation in Definition 3 are equally powerful.

The effect of the dynamic taints is exploited (and the asymmetry emerges) if we refine Definition 3 as follows, i.e. instantiate H by the dynamic final taint map D:

Definition 4. T *is* dynamically G-secure *if for* $(s, G) \xrightarrow{T}_\mathsf{T} (t, D)$ *and* $(s', G) \xrightarrow{T}_\mathsf{T} (t', D')$ *and for each* x, $s =^G_{\sqsubseteq Dx} s'$ *implies* $tx = t'x$.

Now, the final dynamic taints of the major execution, held in D, determine whether s and s' are indistinguishable, instead of the static $|\Delta|$ as before. As $Dx \sqsubseteq |\Delta|(x)$ holds for each x, this change *relaxes* the condition on competitor states s' to s and hence admits more minor executions for consideration. Indeed, using Lemma 2 and the monotonicity of indistinguishability one may show that dynamic G-security strengthens (i.e. implies) static (G, H)-security, with strict inequality again holding for any variable x for which the type system performs a strictly approximate lub-operation at some control flow merge point (cf. the example at the end of Section 3.2).

For $x \in \mathsf{MV}(C)$, the final taint Dx necessarily dominates the taint of all those branch or loop conditions encountered during the lead execution whose body (whether executed or not) contains an assignment to a variable that (directly or indirectly) flows into x. Hence, these conditionals necessarily evaluate identically in the minor execution.

Like static security, dynamic security may also be expressed using universal quantification over security levels κ: by Lemma 3, Definition 4 is equivalent to the guarantee that for $(s, G) \xrightarrow{T}_\mathsf{T} (t, D)$ and $(s', G) \xrightarrow{T}_\mathsf{T} (t', D')$, $s =^G_{\sqsubseteq \kappa} s'$ implies $t =^D_{\sqsubseteq \kappa} t'$, for any κ. In this formulation, the formal asymmetry and the increased precision of dynamic tracking emerge in the final state indistinguishability relation, again via the use of D rather than D' or Δ. Similar comments apply to the results in the remainder of this article: we may always reformulate these results as κ-security for appropriate final-state-indistinguishability relations determined by the final taints of the major execution.

Again, dynamic security is satisfied by synthesized programs:

Theorem 3. $\mathcal{D} \vdash \{\Gamma\}C\{\Delta\}$, $\theta(\mathcal{D}, C)$ *is dynamically* $|\Gamma|$-*secure.*

For the proof of Theorem 3 (and similarly for a direct proof of Theorem 2 that avoids Theorem 1 and Lemma 3), one shows the following generalization, by induction on $\mathcal{D}$. The proofs for conditionals and loops involve case splits on $x \in \mathrm{MV}(C)$, and the proof for loops proceeds by induction on the operational judgement of the lead execution:

Lemma 4. *Suppose* $\mathcal{D} \vdash \{\Gamma\}C\{\Delta\}$ *and* $T = \theta(\mathcal{D}, C)$. *Let* $(s, G) \xrightarrow{T}_T (t, D)$ *and* $(s', G') \xrightarrow{T}_T (t', D')$, *where* $G \sqsubseteq |\Gamma|$ *and* $G' \sqsubseteq |\Gamma|$. *Then each* x *with* $\forall y.\ Gy \sqsubseteq Dx \to (sy = s'y \wedge Gy = G'y)$ *satisfies* $tx = t'x \wedge Dx = D'x$.

The indistinguishability conditions on the taint components guarantee that no information leaks via the taints themselves. The formulation of Lemma 4 extends the notions used by Magazinius et al. and Le Guernic and Jensen [21,20,22] to multilevel security, and avoids a static classification of variables according to their observation level.

A result similar to Lemma 4 may also be obtained for differently instrumented programs $T = \theta(\mathcal{D}, C)$ and $T' = \theta(\mathcal{D}', C)$ originating from the same native C, where $\mathcal{D} \vdash \{\Gamma\}C\{\Delta\}$, $\mathcal{D}' \vdash \{\Gamma'\}C\{\Delta'\}$, $\Gamma \sqsubseteq \Gamma'$, $G \sqsubseteq |\Gamma|$ and $G' \sqsubseteq |\Gamma'|$.

On the other hand, Theorem 3 and the erasure property yield the following relationship between taint-instrumented lead executions and native minor executions:

Corollary 1. *For* $\mathcal{D} \vdash \{\Gamma\}C\{\Delta\}$ *and* $G = |\Gamma|$ *let* $(s, G) \xrightarrow{\theta(\mathcal{D},C)}_T (t, D)$ *and* $s' \xrightarrow{C} t'$. *Then, each* x *with* $s =^G_{\sqsubseteq Dx} s'$ *satisfies* $tx = t'x$.

In the following section, we will derive a guarantee similar to Corollary 1 for a synthesis that also tracks implicit flows dynamically (Theorem 4).

4 Taint Tracking with Control Dependencies

As discussed above, lowering the pivot κ that governs the indistinguishability of initial states strengthens the guarantee enjoyed by a taint-instrumented program. RIFLE's instrumentation pushes this process further, by replacing the assignment-decorating taint *constants* obtained from typing derivations by taint *variables*, and by complementing them with additional *security registers* that can be explicitly manipulated using a novel instruction **join**. The gain in precision arises from inserting **join**-instructions in such a way that the taint variables are upper-bounded by the constants. In effect, indirect flows are statically converted into additional direct flows that are then tracked dynamically.

In this section we treat a **join**-extended language motivated by RIFLE's insight, but apply a synthesis that avoids assignment annotations. Treating RIFLE's taint variables as a subcategory of security registers, we obtain a slightly simpler model that is closer to the regime of Venkatakrishnan et al. [30]. In order to emphasize their slightly different roles, we track data taints operationally separately from control taints, combining them only when formulating the soundness results.

The development is motivated by the following example.

Example 1. For $\{\kappa, \kappa_y, \kappa_v\} \subseteq \mathcal{L}$ and $\Gamma_0(\mathbf{pc}) \sqsubseteq \kappa$ we have

$$\frac{\vdash \{\Gamma_0\}\text{if } e \text{ then } x{:=}m \text{ else } x{:=}h\{\Gamma_1\} \quad \vdash \{\Gamma_1\}\text{if } x \text{ then } y{:=}v \text{ else skip}\{\Gamma_2\}}{\vdash \{\Gamma_0\}(\text{if } e \text{ then } x{:=}m \text{ else } x{:=}h); \text{if } x \text{ then } y{:=}v \text{ else skip}\{\Gamma_2\}}$$

where $\Gamma_0 = [m : mid, h : high, e : \kappa, y : \kappa_y, v : \kappa_v]$, $\Gamma_1 = \Gamma_0[x \mapsto \kappa \sqcup mid \sqcup high]$, and $\Gamma_2 = \Gamma_1[y \mapsto \kappa \sqcup mid \sqcup high \sqcup \kappa_y \sqcup \kappa_v]$. Consequently, synthesis θ annotates the assignment $y{:=}v$ in the second conditional as $[\kappa \sqcup high] y{:=}v$, leading to taint level $\kappa_v \sqcup \kappa \sqcup high$ for y whenever this branch is taken. However, for runs from initial states s with $[\![e]\!]_s = \mathbf{true}$ the taint $\kappa \sqcup mid$ for x would suffice, as any competing initial state s' indistinguishable from s below $\kappa \sqcup mid$ necessarily follows the same execution path. Thus, instead of using the *static* level of the branch condition x when annotating $y{:=}v$, we'd prefer to use the *dynamic* one.

In order to replace the use of the *static* level of branch conditions with suitable *dynamic* taints, we introduce a fresh category of *security registers* $\mathcal{Z}$ (typically ranged over by z, with α ranging over $\mathcal{Z}^*$), and extend the category of commands via

$$J \in \mathcal{J} ::= C \mid z{:=}\mathbf{join} \ [e_1, \ldots, e_m] \ [z_1, \ldots, z_n].$$

The language operates over triples $\mu = (s, G, M)$ where $M \in \mathcal{Z} \to \mathcal{L}$ associates lattice elements to security registers. We define the judgement form $\mu \xrightarrow{J}_\mathsf{J} \nu$ by embedding the rules of $s \xrightarrow{C} t$ for all instruction forms other than assignments, and adding the rules

$$\text{J-Ass} \ \frac{s \vdash e \Downarrow v \qquad [\![e]\!]_G = a}{(s, G, M) \xrightarrow{x{:=}e}_\mathsf{J} (s[x \mapsto v], G[x \mapsto a], M)}$$

$$\text{J-Join} \ \frac{l = \sqcup_{i=1}^n M(z_i) \sqcup \sqcup_{i=1}^m [\![e_i]\!]_G \qquad N = M[z \mapsto l]}{(s, G, M) \xrightarrow{z{:=}\mathbf{join} \ [e_1,\ldots,e_m] \ [z_1,\ldots,z_n]}_\mathsf{J} (s, G, N)}$$

Assignments leave the control taints unaffected and update the data taints only based on other data taints. **join**-instructions combine data and control taints to modify the latter but leave the former unchanged. Indeed, it is easy to show formal noninterference results for $\mu \xrightarrow{J}_\mathsf{J} \nu$ which express that control taints do not affect data taints and that neither control nor data taints affect the data plane.

4.1 Synthesis

The synthesis of **join**-instrumented programs employs two kinds of security registers. First, for each $x \in \mathcal{X}$, we introduce a security register z^x, intended to hold the implicit flows into x, leaving G to track the direct flows. Second, in order to capture the effect of **pc**, we introduce security registers z^i ($i \in \mathcal{N}$), which will be allocated in a stack-based fashion according to the nesting of conditionals and loops. For program expression e we write $z(e)$ for the formal expression resulting from substituting each x in e with z^x. Similarly, for $F \in \mathcal{N}^*$, $F = [i_1, \ldots, i_n]$, we write $z(F)$ for the list $[z^{i_1}, \ldots, z^{i_n}]$.

A native command C is translated the into **join**-instrumented program $\iota(\epsilon, C)$ via the rules in Figure 3, where $F \in \mathcal{N}^*$ and $\mathbf{Join}(i, C)$ is given by

$$z^{x_1}{:=}\mathbf{join} \ \epsilon \ [z^i, z^{x_1}]; \ldots; z^{x_n}{:=}\mathbf{join} \ \epsilon \ [z^i, z^{x_n}]$$

C	$\iota(F,C)$	where ...
skip	**skip**	
$x:=e$	$x:=e;\ z^x:=\textbf{join}\ \epsilon\ (z(e)@z(F))$	
$C_1; C_2$	$\iota(F,C_1);\iota(F,C_2)$	
if e **then** C_1 **else** C_2	$z^i:=\textbf{join}\ [e]\ \alpha;$ **if** e **then** $\iota(i :: F, C_1); \textbf{Join}(i, C_2)$ **else** $\iota(i :: F, C_2); \textbf{Join}(i, C_1)$	$i \notin F$ $\alpha = z(F)@z(e)$
while e **do** C'	$z^i:=\textbf{join}\ [e]\ \alpha_1;$ **while** e **do** $\iota(i :: F, C'); \textbf{Join}(i, C');;$ $z^i:=\textbf{join}\ [e]\ \alpha_2$ $\textbf{Join}(i, C')$	$i \notin F$ $\alpha_1 = z(F)@z(e)$ $\alpha_2 = z^i :: \alpha_1$

Fig. 3. Synthesis of **join**-instrumented programs $\iota(F,C)$

where $x_1, \ldots, x_n$ is an (arbitrary) enumeration of $\mathsf{MV}(C)$.

Mirroring the effect of the annotations λ in the previous section, the translation of $x:=e$ updates z^x with the lub of the security registers associated with the variables in e and the dynamic taints of the enclosing branches as modeled by F. Composite statements $C_1; C_2$ are translated compositionally. Discarding any additions that may have been applied to F in $\iota(F,C_1)$, code $\iota(F,C_2)$ may well reuse some register z^i already in use in $\iota(F,C_1)$ (but not in F): the synthesis ensures that the liveness ranges of such z^i do not overlap, hence the variables in effect are distinct. Indeed, the translations of conditionals and loops initialize newly allocated z^i in their first instruction, by combining the data taint of the branch condition with its control taint $z(e)$ and the surrounding control flow taint $z(F)$, refining the use of $\Gamma(\textbf{pc})$ in Figure 2. Bodies of conditionals and loops are translated compositionally by pushing the register i onto F, and are extended with compensation code using **Join**. Optimizing the behavior slightly in comparison to Figure 2, compensation code in conditionals is only added for variables modified in the opposite branch (in principle, adding compensation code for $\mathsf{MV}(C_2)\backslash\mathsf{MV}(C_1)$ in C_1 suffices, and similarly for C_2). Additionally, a loop body updates the security register z^i, thus propagating the taints of loop-controlling variables to the next iteration. By including i in α_2, we ensure that z^i monotonically increases, i.e. that information is appropriately propagated to later iterations. Finally, we add compensation code in a loop epilogue, ensuring that no information leaks from loops that are never entered.

Some simple properties of $\iota(F,C)$ are as follows:

Lemma 5. *Let* $(s, G, M) \xrightarrow{\iota(F,C)}_J (t, D, N)$. *Then (i)* $M(z^x) = N(z^x)$ *for all* $x \notin \mathsf{MV}(C)$, *(ii)* $M(z^i) = N(z^i)$ *for all* $i \in F$, *and (iii)* $N(z^i) \sqsubseteq N(z^x)$ *for* $x \in \mathsf{MV}(C)$ *and* $i \in F$.

Example 2. Revisiting Example 1, we see that synthesis $\iota(F,C)$ generates code

$$z^0:=\textbf{join}\ [x]\ [z^x];$$
$$\text{if } x \text{ then } y:=v; z^y:=\textbf{join}\ \epsilon\ [z(v), z^0] \text{ else } z^y:=\textbf{join}\ \epsilon\ [z^0, z^y]$$

for the second conditional, where z^0 is a fresh taint register. The first instruction sets z^0 to the lub of the (dynamic) data and control taints of the branch condition x. In the positive branch, this taint is then propagated to the control taint of y (together with the control taint of v). The negative branch is equipped with compensation code, lifting z^y to at least z^0. The code generated for the first conditional amounts to

$$z^0:=\textbf{join}\ [e]\ (z(e));$$
$$\textbf{if}\ e\ \textbf{then}\ x:=m;\ z^x:=\textbf{join}\ \epsilon\ [z(m), z^0]\ \textbf{else}\ x:=h;\ z^x:=\textbf{join}\ \epsilon\ [z(h), z^0]$$

where we have silently eliminated the compensation code $z^x:=\textbf{join}\ \epsilon\ [z^0, z^x]$ that is formally appended to both branches, based on the observation that compensation code is redundant for variables modified in both branches. In particular, a run starting in (s, G, M) with $[\![e]\!]_s = \textbf{true}$ only lifts z^x to the data and control taints of e and m, and hence correctly guarantees final-state-indistinguishability w.r.t. variable y for any execution starting in some state s' with $s =^{\Gamma_0}_{\sqsubseteq \kappa \sqcup mid}\ s'$.

The interpretation of join-instrumented executions combines the taint components for direct and indirect flows. We write $G \bigtriangleup M$ for the map that sends each program variable x to $Gx \sqcup M(z^x)$. We have proven results similar to those in Section 3; details are available in our Coq development [9]. In particular, the following result shows the agreement between an instrumented and a native execution, in the style of Corollary 1.

Theorem 4. *Let* $(s, G, M) \xrightarrow{\iota(F,C)}_{\text{J}} (t, D, N)$ *and* $s' \xrightarrow{C} t'$. *For any* x, $s =^{G \bigtriangleup M}_{\sqsubseteq (D \bigtriangleup N)x}\ s'$ *implies* $tx = t'x$.

The proof proceeds by induction on C, again with case distinctions on $x \in \text{MV}(C)$ in the cases for conditionals and loops, and an induction on the (instrumented) operational judgement in the case for loops where $x \in \text{MV}(C)$.

Furthermore, the execution of $\iota(F, C)$ respects the static typing:

Lemma 6. *For* $\vdash \{\Gamma\}C\{\Delta\}$ *and* $(s, G, M) \xrightarrow{\iota(F,C)}_{\text{J}} (t, D, N)$ *let* $\sqcup_{i \in F} M(z^i) \sqsubseteq \Gamma(\textbf{pc})$ *and* $G \bigtriangleup M \sqsubseteq |\Gamma|$. *Then* $D \bigtriangleup N \sqsubseteq |\Delta|$.

In fact, $\iota(F, C)$ is more precise than $\theta(\mathcal{D}, C)$:

Theorem 5. *For* $\mathcal{D} \vdash \{\Gamma\}C\{\Delta\}$, $\sqcup_{i \in F} M(z^i) \sqsubseteq \Gamma(\textbf{pc})$, *and* $G \bigtriangleup M \sqsubseteq |\Gamma|$ *let* $(s, G, M) \xrightarrow{\iota(F,C)}_{\text{J}} (t, D, N)$ *and* $(s', G \bigtriangleup M) \xrightarrow{\theta(\mathcal{D},C)}_{\text{T}} (t', D')$. *Then each* x *with* $s =^{G \bigtriangleup M}_{\sqsubseteq (D \bigtriangleup N)x}\ s'$ *satisfies* $tx = t'x \wedge (D \bigtriangleup N)x \sqsubseteq D'x$.

Example 2 is a typical case where $\iota(F, C)$ is *strictly* more precise than $\theta(\mathcal{D}, C)$.

5   Path Tracking

The previous sections focused on termination-insensitive security, a notion that is trivially satisfied whenever either execution fails to terminate. We now extend the synthesis so that termination is instead *propagated* from lead to minor executions.

The extension rests on the observation made in Section 3.3 that the execution paths taken by minor executions are to a large extent determined by the major execution, via the relationships between the taints of dynamically encountered conditionals and the final taints of possibly-assigned variables. The exception to this rule are cases where the final value of a variable x in a major execution is independent from all assignments in a conditional, as in (**if** m **then** $y:=2$ **else** $y:=3$); $x:=5$, or indeed

$$(\textbf{if } m \textbf{ then } y:=2 \textbf{ else while true do skip}); x:=5.$$

In both cases, the final *low* taint of x does not constrain the value of $m : mid$ in a competitor initial state s'. Hence, competitor executions may follow different program paths. The same is true for cases where $x \notin MV(C)$.

We modify synthesis $\iota(F, C)$ by adding a further security register, z^{pc} that collects the taints of *all* control-flow affecting expressions encountered during a (lead) run, in effect *tracking the (decisions determining the choice of) execution path*. Figure 4 presents the resulting synthesis $\xi(F, C)$. At each branch point, the taint held in z^{pc} is incremented by the direct and indirect taints of the control-flow affecting expression.

C	$\xi(F,C)$	where ...
skip	skip	
$x:=e$	$x:=e;\ z^x:=\textbf{join } \epsilon\ (z(e)@z(F))$	
$C_1; C_2$	$\xi(F,C_1); \xi(F,C_2)$	
if e **then** C_1 **else** C_2	$\boxed{z^{pc}:=\textbf{join } [e]\ \alpha_t}\ ; z^i:=\textbf{join } [e]\ \alpha;$ **if** e **then** $\xi(i :: F, C_1); \textbf{Join}(i, C_2)$ **else** $\xi(i :: F, C_2); \textbf{Join}(i, C_1)$	$i \notin F$ $\alpha = z(F)@z(e)$ $\boxed{\alpha_t = z^{pc} :: z(e)}$
while e **do** C'	$\boxed{z^{pc}:=\textbf{join } [e]\ \alpha_t}\ ; z^i:=\textbf{join } [e]\ \alpha_1;$ **while** e **do** $\xi(i :: F, C'); \textbf{Join}(i, C');$ $\boxed{z^{pc}:=\textbf{join } [e]\ \alpha_t}\ ; z^i:=\textbf{join } [e]\ \alpha_2;$ $\textbf{Join}(i, C')$	$i \notin F$ $\alpha_1 = z(F)@z(e)$ $\alpha_2 = z^i :: \alpha_1$ $\boxed{\alpha_t = z^{pc} :: z(e)}$

Fig. 4. Path-tracking synthesis $\xi(F, C)$. Differences to Figure 3 are $\boxed{\text{marked}}$.

The following result combines the termination assurance with a claim similar to Theorem 4. Note that s and s' are still compared below $(D \vartriangle N)x$ rather than below the weaker $N(z^{pc}) \sqcup (D \vartriangle N)x$. Indeed, $(D \vartriangle N)x \subsetneqq N(z^{pc})$ typically holds whenever the most secret branch is encountered after the last assignment to x.

Theorem 6. *Let* $(s, G, M) \xrightarrow{\xi(F,C)}_{\text{J}} (t, D, N)$ *and* $s =^{G \vartriangle M}_{\subseteq N(z^{pc})} s'$. *Then, there is some* t' *with* $s' \xrightarrow{C} t'$, *and we have* $tx = t'x$ *for any* x *with* $s =^{G \vartriangle M}_{\subseteq (D \vartriangle N)x} s'$.

In the examples above, the lead executions for $s \vdash m \Downarrow$ **true** yield $N(z^{pc}) = (G \vartriangle M)m \sqcup M(z^{pc})$. Thus, minor executions starting in states s' with $s =^{G \vartriangle M}_{\subseteq N(z^{pc})} s'$ necessarily satisfy $s'(m) = s(m)$, follow the same execution paths and hence terminate.

Synthesis $\xi(F, C)$ agrees with $\iota(F, C)$ on all taints other than z^{pc}: writing $M \approx M'$ if $Mz = M'z$ for all $z \neq z^{pc}$, we have that for $(s, G, M) \xrightarrow{\xi(F,C)}_{\text{J}} (t, D, N)$ and

$$\text{TS-Ass} \frac{\Delta = \Gamma[x \mapsto \Gamma(\mathbf{pc}) \sqcup \llbracket e \rrbracket_\Gamma]}{\vdash_q \{\Gamma\} x{:=}e\{\Delta\}} \qquad \text{TS-Comp} \frac{\forall i \in \{1,2\}.\ \vdash_q \{\Gamma_i\} C_i \{\Gamma_{i+1}\}}{\vdash_q \{\Gamma_1\} C_1; C_2 \{\Gamma_3\}}$$

$$\text{TS-Skip} \frac{}{\vdash_q \{\Gamma\} \mathbf{skip} \{\Gamma\}} \qquad \text{TS-Ite} \frac{\begin{array}{c} p = \Gamma(\mathbf{pc}) \qquad \Gamma' = \Gamma[\mathbf{pc} \mapsto p \sqcup \llbracket e \rrbracket_\Gamma] \\ \forall i \in \{1,2\}.\ \vdash_q \{\Gamma'\} C_i \{\Delta_i\} \qquad \boxed{p \sqcup \llbracket e \rrbracket_\Gamma \sqsubseteq q} \end{array}}{\vdash_q \{\Gamma\} \mathbf{if}\ e\ \mathbf{then}\ C_1\ \mathbf{else}\ C_2 \{(\Delta_1 \sqcup \Delta_2)[\mathbf{pc} \mapsto p]\}}$$

$$\text{TS-While} \frac{\begin{array}{c} \forall i < n.\ \Gamma_i \neq \Gamma_{i+1} \qquad \forall i \geqslant n.\ \Gamma_i = \Gamma_{i+1} \qquad p = \Gamma(\mathbf{pc}) \\ \Gamma_0 = \Gamma[\mathbf{pc} \mapsto p \sqcup \llbracket e \rrbracket_\Gamma] \qquad \forall i.\ \vdash_q \{\Gamma_i\} C\{\Delta_i\} \qquad \boxed{\Gamma_n(\mathbf{pc}) \sqsubseteq q} \\ \forall i.\ \Gamma_{i+1} = (\Delta_i \sqcup \Gamma)[\mathbf{pc} \mapsto (\Delta_i \sqcup \Gamma)(\mathbf{pc}) \sqcup \llbracket e \rrbracket_{\Delta_i \sqcup \Gamma}] \end{array}}{\vdash_q \{\Gamma\} \mathbf{while}\ e\ \mathbf{do}\ C \{\Gamma_n[\mathbf{pc} \mapsto p]\}}$$

Fig. 5. System $\vdash_q \{\Gamma\} C \{\Delta\}$. Differences to system $\vdash \{\Gamma\} C \{\Delta\}$ are $\boxed{\text{marked}}$.

C	$\delta(C)$
skip	skip
$x{:=}e$	$x{:=}e$
$C_1; C_2$	$\delta(C_1); \delta(C_2)$
if e then C_1 else C_2	$z^{\mathbf{pc}}{:=}\mathbf{join}\ [e]\ [z^{\mathbf{pc}}]; \mathbf{if}\ e\ \mathbf{then}\ \delta(C_1)\ \mathbf{else}\ \delta(C_2)$
while e do C'	$z^{\mathbf{pc}}{:=}\mathbf{join}\ [e]\ [z^{\mathbf{pc}}]; \mathbf{while}\ e\ \mathbf{do}\ (\delta(C'); z^{\mathbf{pc}}{:=}\mathbf{join}\ [e]\ [z^{\mathbf{pc}}])$

Fig. 6. Synthesis of termination-sensitive data-tracking programs $\delta(C)$

$(s, G, M') \xrightarrow{\iota(F,C)}_\lrcorner (t', D', N')$, $M \approx M'$ implies $t = t'$, $D = D'$ and $N \approx N'$. In particular, the claim in Theorem 5 remains valid if we replace $\iota(F,C)$ by $\xi(F,C)$.

The static counterpart to path tracking is an extension of the type system from Figure 1 to a system with judgements $\vdash_q \{\Gamma\} C \{\Delta\}$, where $q \in \mathcal{L}$ represents a (static) upper bound on the taints of branch conditions. We give the rules of this system in Figure 5 and note that $\vdash_q \{\Gamma\} C \{\Delta\}$ implies $\vdash \{\Gamma\} C \{\Delta\}$ and also $\vdash_p \{\Gamma\} C \{\Delta\}$ for any $p \sqsupseteq q$. A similar type system is given by Hunt and Sands [17], but not linked to dynamic taint tracking as we do in Theorem 7 below.

The property guaranteed by the static system is *equitermination* between executions starting in initial states that are Γ-indistinguishable below q:

Lemma 7. *Let* $\vdash_q \{\Gamma\} C \{\Delta\}$ *and* $s =_{\sqsubseteq q}^{|\Gamma|} s'$. *Then* $\exists t.\ s \xrightarrow{C} t$ *iff* $\exists t'.\ s' \xrightarrow{C} t'$.

Note that equitermination is symmetric and taint ignorant, i.e. applies to pairs of native executions (but can be extended to tainted executions by the erasure lemma).

Path tracking refines the static termination analysis, extending Lemma 6:

Theorem 7. *For* $\sqcup_{i \in F} M(z^i) \sqsubseteq \Gamma(\mathbf{pc})$ *let* $\vdash_q \{\Gamma\} C \{\Delta\}$ *and* $(s, G, M) \xrightarrow{\xi(F,C)}_\lrcorner (t, D, N)$. *If* $G \triangle M \sqsubseteq |\Gamma|$ *and* $M(z^{\mathbf{pc}}) \sqsubseteq q$ *then* $D \triangle N \sqsubseteq |\Delta|$ *and* $N(z^{\mathbf{pc}}) \sqsubseteq q$.

Interestingly, path tracking can also be carried out in the absence of control flow taints, i.e for pure data flow tracking. To this end, define the synthesis $\delta(C)$ by erasing from

$\xi(F, C)$ all **join** instructions (including those in **Join**) that define taint registers other than $z^{\mathbf{pc}}$, and modify instructions $z^{\mathbf{pc}}:=\mathbf{join}\ [e]\ \alpha$ to $z^{\mathbf{pc}}:=\mathbf{join}\ [e]\ [z^{\mathbf{pc}}]$ (see details in Fig. 6). The resulting programs ignore all control taint registers other than $z^{\mathbf{pc}}$, but behave exactly like $\xi(F, C)$ on data taints and the data plane: for $(s, G, M) \xrightarrow{\delta(C)}_{\mathsf{J}} (t, D, N)$, we have $M \approx N$, and $(t, D) = (t', D')$ whenever $(s, G, M') \xrightarrow{\xi(F,C)}_{\mathsf{J}} (t', D', N')$. Writing $\lfloor p \rfloor$ for the control taint component that sends $z^{\mathbf{pc}}$ to p and all other z to $\bot$, we also have that $\delta(C)$ stays below $\xi(F, C)$:

Theorem 8. *Let* $(s, G, \lfloor p \rfloor) \xrightarrow{\delta(C)}_{\mathsf{J}} (t, D, N)$ *and* $(s, G, M') \xrightarrow{\xi(F,C)}_{\mathsf{J}} (t', D', N')$. *Then,* $N = \lfloor q \rfloor$ *for some* $q \sqsupseteq p$, *with* $N \sqsubseteq N'$ *whenever* $p \sqsubseteq M'(z^{\mathbf{pc}})$. *In particular,* $u =_{\sqsubseteq \kappa}^D u'$ *coincides with* $u =_{\sqsubseteq \kappa}^{D \triangle N} u'$ *and implies* $u =_{\sqsubseteq \kappa}^{D' \triangle N'} u'$, *for all* u, u', *and* κ.

Even for arbitrary M, $\delta(C)$ enjoys termination and indistinguishability:

Theorem 9. *Let* $(s, G, M) \xrightarrow{\delta(C)}_{\mathsf{J}} (t, D, N)$ *and* $s =_{\sqsubseteq N(z^{\mathbf{pc}})}^G s'$. *Then, for any* G' *and* M', *there are* t', D', *and* N' *such that* $(s', G', M') \xrightarrow{\delta(C)}_{\mathsf{J}} (t', D', N')$. *Furthermore,* $tx = t'x$ *holds for any* x *with* $s =_{\sqsubseteq Dx}^G s'$, *and* $Dx = D'x$ *holds additionally whenever all* y *with* $Gy \sqsubseteq Dx$ *satisfy* $Gy = G'y$.

Finally, we transfer Theorem 9's conclusion to native executions and express security as an implication over multilevel indistinguishabilities using Lemma 3.

Corollary 2. *Let* $(s, G, M) \xrightarrow{\delta(C)}_{\mathsf{J}} (t, D, N)$ *and* $s =_{\sqsubseteq N(z^{\mathbf{pc}})}^G s'$. *Then,* $s' \xrightarrow{C} t'$ *for some* t', *and for all* κ, $s =_{\sqsubseteq \kappa}^G s'$ *implies* $t =_{\sqsubseteq \kappa}^D t'$.

To our knowledge, this represents the first extensional interpretation of data tracking.

6 Discussion

We presented an analysis of hybrid information flow by proving selected instrumentation schemes sound with respect to RIFLE-inspired interpretations of taint tracking.

Building upon Moore & Chong's analysis [24], we envision that our analysis can be extended to memory operations if side effects are tracked at the level of memory abstractions, for example by introducing one taint register (and associated compensation code) per region. Additional future work includes the support of (infinite) computations with output, a more detailed study of path tracking, and a comparison of taint tracking with Boudol's formulation of security as safety property [11,12].

Jee et al. [18] propose *taint flow algebras* as a generic framework for transferring traditional compiler optimizations to byte-level taint tracking. Fine-grained tracking below the level of words does not appear to have been studied in the language-based security community yet, but a unifying treatment of taint- and native optimizations may potentially emerge in explicitly relational formulations [8], extending Moore & Chong's use of two-level noninterference for selective monitoring.

Nanevski et al. [25] employ dependent types and relational Hoare Type Theory to enforce information flow and access control policies, although program verification is mostly carried out manually, by interactive verification in Coq.

Finally, separating control and data taints from each other and from the data plane appears in principle compatible with multicore execution, if the respective instruction streams are mapped onto different cores: as communication is orchestrated in an acyclic fashion, efficient loop pipelining may be enabled [26].

References

1. Amtoft, T., Dodds, J., Zhang, Z., Appel, A., Beringer, L., Hatcliff, J., Ou, X., Cousino, A.: A Certificate Infrastructure for Machine-Checked Proofs of Conditional Information Flow. In: Degano, P., Guttman, J.D. (eds.) POST 2012. LNCS, vol. 7215, pp. 369–389. Springer, Heidelberg (2012)
2. Appel, A.W.: Verified software toolchain - (invited talk). In: Barthe (ed.) [6], pp. 1–17
3. Austin, T.H., Flanagan, C.: Efficient purely-dynamic information flow analysis. In: Chong, S., Naumann, D. (eds.) PLAS 2009: Proceedings of the 4th ACM SIGPLAN Workshop on Programming Languages and Analysis for Security, pp. 113–124. ACM (2009)
4. Austin, T.H., Flanagan, C.: Permissive dynamic information flow analysis. In: Banerjee, A., Garg, D. (eds.) PLAS 2010: Proceedings of the 5th ACM SIGPLAN Workshop on Programming Languages and Analysis for Security, pp. 3:1–3:12. ACM (2010)
5. Austin, T.H., Flanagan, C., Abadi, M.: A functional view of imperative information flow. Technical Report UCSC-SOE-12-15, Department of Computer Science, University of California at Santa Cruz (2012)
6. Barthe, G. (ed.): ESOP 2011. LNCS, vol. 6602. Springer, Heidelberg (2011)
7. Barthe, G., Pichardie, D., Rezk, T.: A Certified Lightweight Non-interference Java Bytecode Verifier. In: De Nicola, R. (ed.) ESOP 2007. LNCS, vol. 4421, pp. 125–140. Springer, Heidelberg (2007)
8. Benton, N.: Simple relational correctness proofs for static analyses and program transformations. In: Jones, N.D., Leroy, X. (eds.) Proceedings of the 31st ACM Symposium on Principles of Programming Languages, POPL 2004, pp. 14–25. ACM (2004)
9. Beringer, L.: End-to-end multilevel hybrid information flow control - Coq development (2012), http://www.cs.princeton.edu/~eberinge/HybridIFC.tar.gz
10. Beringer, L., Hofmann, M.: Secure information flow and program logics. In: Proceedings of the 20th IEEE Computer Security Foundations Symposium, CSF 2007, pp. 233–248. IEEE Computer Society (2007)
11. Boudol, G.: On Typing Information Flow. In: Van Hung, D., Wirsing, M. (eds.) ICTAC 2005. LNCS, vol. 3722, pp. 366–380. Springer, Heidelberg (2005)
12. Boudol, G.: Secure Information Flow as a Safety Property. In: Degano, P., Guttman, J., Martinelli, F. (eds.) FAST 2008. LNCS, vol. 5491, pp. 20–34. Springer, Heidelberg (2009)
13. Chudnov, A., Naumann, D.A.: Information flow monitor inlining. In: CSF 2010 [15], pp. 200–214 (2010)
14. Clause, J.A., Li, W., Orso, A.: Dytan: a generic dynamic taint analysis framework. In: Rosenblum, D.S., Elbaum, S.G. (eds.) Proceedings of the ACM/SIGSOFT International Symposium on Software Testing and Analysis, ISSTA 2007, pp. 196–206. ACM (2007)
15. Proceedings of the 23rd IEEE Computer Security Foundations Symposium, CSF 2010. IEEE Computer Society (2010)
16. Hunt, S., Sands, D.: On flow-sensitive security types. In: Morrisett, J.G., Jones, S.L.P. (eds.) Proceedings of the 33rd ACM Symposium on Principles of Programming Languages, POPL 2006, pp. 79–90. ACM (2006)
17. Hunt, S., Sands, D.: From exponential to polynomial-time security typing via principal types. In: Barthe (ed.) [6], pp. 297–316

18. Jee, K., Portokalidis, G., Kemerlis, V.P., Ghosh, S., August, D.I., Keromytis, A.D.: A general approach for efficiently accelerating software-based dynamic data flow tracking on commodity hardware. In: Proceedings of the 19th Network and Distributed System Security Symposium, NDSS 2012. The Internet Society, ISOC (2012)

19. Kang, M.G., McCamant, S., Poosankam, P., Song, D.: DTA++: Dynamic taint analysis with targeted control-flow propagation. In: Proceedings of the 18th Network and Distributed System Security Symposium, NDSS 2011. The Internet Society, ISOC (2011)

20. Le Guernic, G.: Precise Dynamic Verification of Confidentiality. In: Beckert, B., Klein, G. (eds.) Proceedings of the 5th International Verification Workshop. CEUR Workshop Proceedings, vol. 372, pp. 82–96. CEUR-WS.org (2008)

21. Le Guernic, G., Jensen, T.: Monitoring Information Flow. In: Sabelfeld, A. (ed.) Proceedings of the Workshop on Foundations of Computer Security, FCS 2005, pp. 19–30. DePaul University (June 2005) (Affiliated with LICS 2005)

22. Magazinius, J., Russo, A., Sabelfeld, A.: On-the-fly Inlining of Dynamic Security Monitors. In: Rannenberg, K., Varadharajan, V., Weber, C. (eds.) SEC 2010. IFIP AICT, vol. 330, pp. 173–186. Springer, Heidelberg (2010)

23. Masri, W., Podgurski, A., Leon, D.: Detecting and debugging insecure information flows. In: Proceedings of the 15th International Symposium on Software Reliability Engineering, ISSRE 2004, pp. 198–209. IEEE Computer Society (2004)

24. Moore, S., Chong, S.: Static analysis for efficient hybrid information-flow control. In: Proceedings of the 24th IEEE Computer Security Foundations Symposium, CSF 2011, pp. 146–160. IEEE Computer Society (2011)

25. Nanevski, A., Banerjee, A., Garg, D.: Verification of information flow and access control policies with dependent types. In: 32nd IEEE Symposium on Security and Privacy, S&P 2011, pp. 165–179. IEEE Computer Society (2011)

26. Rangan, R., Vachharajani, N., Vachharajani, M., August, D.I.: Decoupled software pipelining with the synchronization array. In: Proceedings of the 13th International Conference on Parallel Architectures and Compilation Techniques, PACT 2004, pp. 177–188. IEEE Computer Society (2004)

27. Russo, A., Sabelfeld, A.: Dynamic vs. static flow-sensitive security analysis. In: CSF 2010 [15], pp. 186–199 (2010)

28. Sabelfeld, A., Russo, A.: From Dynamic to Static and Back: Riding the Roller Coaster of Information-Flow Control Research. In: Pnueli, A., Virbitskaite, I., Voronkov, A. (eds.) PSI 2009. LNCS, vol. 5947, pp. 352–365. Springer, Heidelberg (2010)

29. Vachharajani, N., Bridges, M.J., Chang, J., Rangan, R., Ottoni, G., Blome, J.A., Reis, G.A., Vachharajani, M., August, D.I.: Rifle: An architectural framework for user-centric information-flow security. In: 37th Annual International Symposium on Microarchitecture (MICRO-37), pp. 243–254. IEEE Computer Society (2004)

30. Venkatakrishnan, V.N., Xu, W., DuVarney, D.C., Sekar, R.: Provably Correct Runtime Enforcement of Non-interference Properties. In: Ning, P., Qing, S., Li, N. (eds.) ICICS 2006. LNCS, vol. 4307, pp. 332–351. Springer, Heidelberg (2006)

Succour to the Confused Deputy
Types for Capabilities

Radha Jagadeesan, Corin Pitcher, and James Riely

DePaul University

Abstract. The possession of secrets is a recurrent theme in security literature and practice. We present a refinement type system, based on indexed intuitonist S4 necessity, for an object calculus with explicit locations (corresponding to principals) to control the principals that may possess a secret. Type safety ensures that if the execution of a well-typed program leads to a configuration with an object p located at principal a, then a possesses the capability to p. We illustrate the type system with simple examples drawn from web applications, including an illustration of how Cross-Site Request Forgery (CSRF) vulnerabilities may manifest themselves as absurd refinements on object declarations during type checking.

A fuller version of the paper is available at fpl.cs.depaul.edu/jriely/papers/2012-aplas.pdf.

1 Introduction

Many systems depend upon a prescribed usage of secrets to enforce policies that incorporate secrecy, integrity, authentication, authorization, and auditing concerns. Nevertheless, it may be computationally expensive, or impossible in some adversarial models, to control the *use* of secrets directly. For this reason, it is common to control the *possession* of secrets instead of their use. However, invariants about the possession of secrets can fail due to inadequately-specified interfaces or a lack of agreement between software components. We illustrate some of the issues with two examples.

Object References. The Java security manager permits access control checks based upon permissions assigned to code [19]. This allows control over systems composed of code from different sources. The `java.io.FileOutputStream` system class utilizes access control checks in the following manner:

- The `FileOutputStream` constructor checks for the relevant file write permission.
- For performance, `FileOutputStream` methods do not have access control checks. The lack of access control checks after construction means that references to instances of `FileOutputStream` can be used to write a file by untrusted code, *if* the reference is made available to the untrusted code. For this reason, sensitive object references must be confined to trusted code.

Cross-Site Request Forgery and the Confused Deputy. Cross-Site Request Forgery (CSRF) attacks [13] are acknowledged as an instance of the Confused Deputy problem [22]. A principal is a Confused Deputy if it uses its authority to mistakenly act

R. Jhala and A. Igarashi (Eds.): APLAS 2012, LNCS 7705, pp. 66–81, 2012.

on behalf of an initiating principal. The capability-based solution [22] to the Confused Deputy problem requires the initiating principal to provide a capability to the Deputy, which the Deputy requires to complete its actions. Since capabilities authorize access to a resource without further checks, their possession must be constrained programmatically. For example, one might ask:

- If the initiating principal hands a capability to the Deputy, to whom can the Deputy pass the capability?
- Is the Deputy permitted to add its own capabilities to any request from the initiating principal?

In the case of a web browser, acting as a Deputy for both user and JavaScript behavior on web pages, it is permitted to add cookies to outgoing HTTP requests based on the URLs determined from the web pages. Several browser extensions provide a more restrictive policy on forwarding cookies for cross-site requests to prevent misunderstandings in web applications vulnerable to CSRF attacks.

In this paper, we address control over the possession of secrets via the use of logical specifications embedded in the types of a distributed programming language. Static analysis is used to verify that programs comply with possession policies, yielding an upper bound on the principals that may possess a secret.

Approach. The main contribution of this paper is the application of a *refinement type system for a distributed object-oriented language*. The type system controls possession of object references, representing secrets, via specifications in a principal-indexed variant of intuitionist S4.

We specify possession of secrets using intuitionist S4 logic [6,28]. Instead of a single modality, we consider modalities indexed by principals. An indexed modality of the form $\square_a \Phi$ represents a predicate Φ that is permissible for principal a [17,10]. We use a "may possess" predicate $mp(s)$ representing possession of a secret s. Thus $\square_a mp(s)$ means that principal a is permitted to possess secret s.

It is key to our approach that indexed modalities allow different principals to have different possession policies. In particular, $\square_a mp(s)$ and $\square_b mp(s)$ are independent statements about whether the different principals a and b may possess s. The underlying logic then provides relationships between uses of modalities:

- Indexed modalities commute, i.e., $(\square_a \square_b \Phi) \Rightarrow (\square_b \square_a \Phi)$. This permits a sequence of indexed modalities to be treated as a multiset.
- The counit $(\square_a \Phi) \Rightarrow \Phi$ allows a modality to be eliminated. The converse does not hold in general. Consequently, a right for principal a can be forgotten during logical deduction, but cannot be manufactured.
- From $\square_a(\Phi_1 \Rightarrow \Phi_2)$ and $\square_a \Phi_1$, we can deduce $\square_a \Phi_2$; thus, the possessions of a principal are closed under deduction. From comultiplication, $(\square_a \Phi) \Rightarrow (\square_a \square_a \Phi)$, we deduce that the deductions in the scope of a principal a includes the knowledge of a's posessions.
- If b is less secure than a and $\square_b \Phi$ then we can deduce $\square_a \Phi$; so, by this principle of Principal naturality, more secure principals have access to more secrets.

These relationships yield an indexed intuitionist S4 necessity modality, representing layers of permission for principals, over the underlying logic. This distinction in the logic between permissions and who has those permissions, represented by principal-indexed modalities, greatly reduces the need to quantify over principals during reasoning. For example, if a policy states that s2 may be possessed if s1 may be possessed, written $mp(s1) \Rightarrow mp(s2)$, then the indexed intuitionist S4 necessity modality structure allows this implication to be lifted to any principal a as $(\Box_a mp(s1)) \Rightarrow (\Box_a mp(s2))$.

Noninterference theorems [25] justify the use of indexed intuitionist S4 necessity modalities in this modeling. In that paper, we show that noninterference captures the idea that there is no information flow between differently indexed modalities. Let α be a modality free formula. The intuitive idea behind non interference is that if $\Box_a \alpha$ is derivable from some deductively closed set of hypothesis, then it is derivable from a subset of those hypothesis that are in the scope of the modality indexed by a, i.e. the formulas of the form $\Box_a \cdot$. In particular, noninterference implies the unprovability of the following formulas:

– $\Box_a mp(s1) \Rightarrow \Box_b mp(s1)$
– $(\Box_a(mp(s1) \Rightarrow mp(s2)) \wedge \Box_b mp(s1)) \Rightarrow \Box_a mp(s2)$

The unprovability of $\Box_a mp(s1) \Rightarrow \Box_b mp(s1)$ shows that the logical reasoning does not transfer capabilities unrestrictedly between principals. The unprovability of the second formula $(\Box_a(mp(s1) \Rightarrow mp(s2)) \wedge \Box_b mp(s1)) \Rightarrow \Box_a mp(s2)$ ensures that the acquisition of a new capability (s1) by another principal (b) does not create new capabilities for principal a by purely logical reasoning. Thus, non-interference facilitates distribution and decentralized enforcement of policies in the following sense. The reference monitor at a location uses logical reasoning to deduce whether a principal has sufficient capabilities to access the resource available at the location. Noninterference ensures that this reasoning is not dependent on other principals; so, the reference monitor at a location can function without knowledge of the principals at other locations.

We present three analyses to establish the utility of our approach:

– Sealed objects (Section 2) that demonstrate modeling of symmetric cryptography [2].
– An object encoding (Section 5) of Hardy's Confused Deputy [22].
– A web browser and server model to explore browser security policies and Cross-Site Request Forgery prevention solutions. For space reasons, this example is in the full version of this paper at fpl.cs.depaul.edu/jriely/papers/2012-aplas.pdf.

Related Work

Capability-Based Systems. Capabilities have been used to realize security policies in a variety of systems, e.g., [23,29,5] to name but a few. Distributed object languages such as E [12] illustrate the "capabilities-as-object references" paradigm where both subjects and resources are represented uniformly as objects, and classical object-oriented mechanisms are used to structure the exchange and invocation of capabilities. This viewpoint underlies Caja, a safe subset of Javascript. Caja eschews direct references to DOM objects, instead providing references to wrappers that restrict the capabilities provided on DOM objects. [26] formalize a notion of capability-safety, show that the subset Cajita satisfies this property and derive that Cajita programs have inter-component isolation.

Type Systems for Secrecy, Confinement, and Access Control. In object-oriented languages, ownership and confinement types (see [11] for a survey of ownership type system) aim to delimit the portions of the object reference graph that can have references to the objects under consideration. In this paper, we generalize from confinement types to multi-party secrecy types using refinement types built on intuitionist S4 to express dependencies.

Abadi [4] describes a type system for controlling secret keys in the spi calculus, using a binary division of code as either fully trusted or untrusted. This paper explores an idea stated there: "distinguish various principals within the system, and enable us to discuss which of these principals have a given piece of data".

Language-based approaches to access control have long been studied in the setting of process calculi, though these approaches are not based explicitly in logic; two early references are [27,24]. In [15], Fournet, Gordon and Maffeis validate authorization policies statically using a specification language with "expect" assertions in a Datalog-style language. The says family of principal-indexed modalities is used in logics for reasoning about authorization statements made by different principals [18,1]. The says modality has a monadic structure, as exemplified by the unit law ($\Phi \Rightarrow a$ says Φ). In our prior work [9] we develop a type system based on authorization logic to capture provenance in a distributed object calculus. [14] explores the impact of compromised principals on authorization policies in a distributed setting.

In this paper, we carry out a similar program, albeit in the logical setting of intutionist S4, by reusing the infrastructure of *refinement types* [16] developed in the literature: policies (and therefore types) may quantify over object references of a given class. Object references (and variables) appear in logical formulae in equality predicates and in the "may-possess" predicate mp(.) described previously. Our semantics and notion of safety are from [9] and derive, ultimately, from [20] and [21].

2   Sealed Objects

In this section, we introduce the computational model and logic, by way of an example. The details of the logic can be found in a companion paper [25]; here we summarize the properties of the logic required to understand the example.

Computation is based on threads that communicate via a shared heap. Threads are "located" at the principal for which the thread is running; similarly objects are "located" at the principal that created the object. We use the terms "principal" and "location" interchangeably. For an object p, the location is available to the programmer via the pseudo-field p.loc.

Neither threads nor objects can change location; however, object references can be communicated between threads using shared objects. A method invocation on an object leads to code execution at the location of the callee object. Thus, when the caller and callee objects are located at different locations, method invocation leads to a change of location context.

We conflate opponents, representing them all via $\bot$. Threads acting on behalf of opponents can only instantiate classes with trivial invariants, discussed below. Threads acting on behalf of non-opponents must obey a global policy. All threads must be well typed according to typical object-oriented programming rules, e.g., as in Java. Additionally, our type system controls communication of object references by non-opponent threads.

Principals are ordered by a partial order with least principal being the Opponent $\bot$. Principal naturality allows that whenever $\Box_\bot \Phi$ is deducible, then so is $\Box_a \Phi$, for any a. In particular, this means that any of the Opponent capabilities are available to all principals. Thus, our type system does not impose any restrictions more than those of usual object oriented programming on Opponent programs.

A program is *safe* if every object reference that is available to a principal at runtime is permitted by the global specification of permitted capabilities. Our type system ensures that safe well-typed programs remain safe under evaluation in the face of arbitrary opponent processes.

Consider `javax.crypto.SealedObject`. It permits a serializable object to be encrypted with a secret key and a symmetric-key cipher. The constructor is responsible for serialization and encryption. The resulting `SealedObject` contains only ciphertext. The original object can be recovered by passing the same secret key to `getObject`. We model `SealedObject` as:

```
class SealedObject {
  private final SecretKey key;
  private final Object contents;
  public SealedObject (SecretKey key, Object contents) {
    this.key = key; this.contents = contents;
  }
  public Object getObject (Section key) {
    if (key == this.key) return this.contents;
    else return null;
  }
}[ □⊥(mp(this.key) ⇒ mp(this.contents)) ]
```

By controlling possession of the `key`, one controls access to the `contents`. This code uses private fields guarded by object equality rather than encryption. This is sufficient since the type system enforces that the caller of `getObject` must possess `key`.

Specifications in our system are divided between a *global policy* and a set of *class invariants*. Intuitively, the combinatation of these policies indicates upper bounds on the capabilities that can be possessed by a principal. Our safety theorem shows that at any stage in the evolution of a system, even in the presence of opponents, any principal only possesses references that are provided for in the policy.

The global policy describes the distribution of initial secrets, and also any potential relationships between classes. It is informative to consider the following extremal global policies. Suppose that all class invariants are trivial (i.e., `tt`).

- The extremely permissive global policy $\forall \eta.\ \Box_\bot mp(\eta)$ does not forbid any transmission of objects. Thus, typing under this global policy is essentially the same as standard object-oriented typing.
- The extremely restrictive global policy `tt` in the case where there are only two principals — Opponent ($\bot$) and Secret ($\top$) — forbids all transmission of objects from $\top$ to $\bot$. Thus, typing under this global policy is essentially the same as standard information flow.

The class invariant is intended to describe the private internals of a single class. The mutable state in our objects is only in the form of private instance variables. The class invariant is written at the end of each class, in square brackets. Because we are in a concurrent setting, we make the simplifying assumption that only final fields may be mentioned in the class invariant and that constructors may do nothing but assign fields — we also disallow reassignment of method parameters and local variables. Thus, the class invariant holds for every object at the point its constructor terminates.

References to SealedObjects can be safely sent anywhere because they do not leak their contents arbitrarily. The fact that they are allowed anywhere is exemplified by the global policy $(\forall o : \texttt{SealedObject}. \; \Box_\bot \texttt{mp}(o))$ — type-sorted quantification is shorthand for quantification using a "type" predicate on objects. This policy allows SealedObjects to be given to opponents; however, they can only retrieve the contents if they have the matching key. More restrictive policies are also possible.

The class invariant of SealedObject indicates that any principal that may possess this.key may also possess this.contents. Opponents cannot create secrets, and therefore are restricted to creating instances of "global" classes with invariants (i.e. "true") that are trivially satisfied. The invariant of SealedObject is nontrivial, and therefore opponents may not create instances of the class.

The invariant must be statically justifiable by any code that creates an instance of the class. For example, consider the code new SealedObject (key, acct), where key is an instance of SecretKey and acct is an instance of a BankAccount class. We must establish that every principal that may possess key may also possess acct, written $\Box_\bot(\texttt{mp}(\texttt{key}) \Rightarrow \texttt{mp}(\texttt{acct}))$. This might be accomplished using a global policy that allows acct to be possessed anywhere, written $\Box_\bot(\texttt{mp}(\texttt{acct}))$. Stricter policies could be specified pairwise, including $\Box_\bot(\texttt{mp}(\texttt{key}) \Rightarrow \texttt{mp}(\texttt{acct}))$ as a fact. More flexible arrangements are also possible, for example, using the invariant of the factory class that creates new keys. In any case, the implication must be deduced from the available policy in order to instantiate SealedObject. In all non-trivial cases, the initial ability to create SealedObjects is specified as part of the global policy; indeed, the non-interference theorems ensure that there is no possible creation of SealedObjects otherwise.

In order to justify safety of the getObject method, we first observe that the caller to getObject must possess the key, i.e., $\Box_{\text{caller}}(\texttt{mp}(\texttt{key}))$. From the SealedObject class invariant, we know that:

$$\Box_\bot(\texttt{mp}(\texttt{this.key}) \Rightarrow \texttt{mp}(\texttt{this.contents}))$$

From which we can deduce that (note the principal on $\Box$):

$$\Box_{\text{caller}}(\texttt{mp}(\texttt{this.key}) \Rightarrow \texttt{mp}(\texttt{this.contents}))$$

After the reference equality test (key==this.key), the callee knows key=this.key. Moreover, equality can be lifted to comodalities, and we have $\Box_{\text{caller}}(\texttt{key} = \texttt{this.key})$. From $\Box_{\text{caller}}(\texttt{mp}(\texttt{key}))$ and $\Box_{\text{caller}}(\texttt{key} = \texttt{this.key})$, we deduce $\Box_{\text{caller}}(\texttt{mp}(\texttt{this.key}))$. In conjunction with the implication above, we find that $\Box_{\text{caller}}(\texttt{mp}(\texttt{this.contents}))$. This justifies return of this.contents to the caller. In the case where the equality test fails, we use the property that null may be possessed anywhere, written $\Box_\bot(\texttt{mp}(\texttt{null}))$.

If the SealedObject class had public fields, then a higher threshold must be met to instantiate the class. In this case, one would also need to establish that any principal that may possess the object may also possess the values placed into the public fields.

It is worth noting that other symmetric cryptography schemes can be encoded as simple variants of SealedObject. For example, using nested conditionals, one can encode an object requiring n keys to encrypt and $k \leq n$ keys to decrypt.

3 Language

To formalize the preceding discussion, we first describe a distributed class-based language with mutable objects [9]. The operational semantics borrows heavily from [20], adding distribution [7,8] and classes. We consider typing in Section 4.

Syntax. Names for classes (c, d), methods (ℓ), fields (f, g), variables (x, y, z), objects (p, q) and principals (a, b) are drawn from separate namespaces, as usual. Predicate variables (α, β) and predicate constructors (γ) occur in static annotations used during type-checking.

The reserved words of the language include: the variable name "this"; the principal "caller"; the class name Object; the predicate constructors "tt", "ff", "⇒", "∧", "∨", "¬" and "□". We write binary constructors infix.

The language is explicitly typed. Object types $(c<\vec{\phi}>)$ include the actual predicate parameters $\vec{\phi}$, which we treat formally as *extended values*. Value types include objects (C), principals (Prin) and Unit. Extended value types include predicate types (P), which are resolved during typechecking. The process type (Proc) has no values.

One may write classes and methods that are generic in the predicate variables, achieving ML-style polymorphism with respect to effects. Class declarations thus include the formal predicate parameters $\vec{\alpha}$, which may occur in the effect Φ (see next table) associated with instances of the class. In addition to effects, class declarations include field and method declarations, but omit implicit constructor declarations. Fields include mutability annotations that are used in the statics. The syntax is as follows[1].

Types, Annotations, Class and Method Declarations

$C,D ::= c<\vec{\phi}>$	Object Types
$T,S ::= C \mid \text{Prin} \mid \text{Unit}$	Value Types
$P,Q ::= \text{Pred}(\vec{\mathcal{T}})$	Predicate Types
$\mathcal{T},\mathcal{S} ::= T \mid P \mid \text{Proc}$	Types
$\mu ::= \text{private final} \mid \text{private mutable} \mid \text{public final}$	
$\mathcal{D} ::= \text{class } c<\vec{\alpha}:\vec{P}>\triangleleft D\{\vec{\mu}\ \vec{T}\ \vec{f};\ \vec{\mathcal{M}}\}[\Phi]$	
$\mathcal{M} ::= <\vec{\beta}:\vec{Q}>S\ \ell(\vec{T}\ \vec{x})\{M\}$	

---

[1] When writing definitions using classes and methods, we sometimes omit irrelevant bits of syntax, e.g., we leave out the parameters to classes when empty, such as writing Object rather than Object<∅>. We identify syntax up to renaming of bound names, and write $M\{\!\{^V\!/x\}\!\}$ for substitution of V for x in M (and similarly for other categories). We often omit type information. We use standard syntactic sugar in place of explicit sequencing. For example, we may write "$y.f.g$" to abbreviate "let $x = y.f; x.g$".

Values, Terms, Evaluation Contexts

$$V, W, U, A, B, \phi, \psi ::= x \mid p \mid a \mid \text{unit} \mid \alpha \mid \gamma \mid \phi(\vec{V})$$
$$M, N, L, \Phi, \Psi ::= V \mid V.f \mid V.\text{loc}$$
$$\quad \text{if } V = W \text{ then } M \text{ else } N \mid \text{let } x = N; M \mid N \parallel M$$
$$\quad V.f := W \mid \text{let } x = \text{new } c{<}\vec{\phi}{>}(\vec{V}); M \mid \text{let } x = V.\ell{<}\vec{\phi}{>}(\vec{W}); M$$
$$\quad p : C\{\vec{f} = \vec{V}\} \mid (\nu p : C) M \mid a[M]_c^b$$
$$\mathbb{E} ::= [-] \mid a[\mathbb{E}]_c^b \mid \text{let } x = \mathbb{E}; M \mid \mathbb{E} \parallel N \mid M \parallel \mathbb{E} \mid (\nu p)\,\mathbb{E}$$

We use the metavariables ϕ, ψ, Φ and Ψ to represent values and terms of predicate type, and the other metavariables to represent runtime values and terms, with A and B reserved for values of principal type. Predicates are static annotations used in type-checking; they play no role in the dynamics. An *expectation* "expect Φ" as in [15] can be coded as "new Proof<Φ>()", where class Proof is defined "class Proof<α : Pred>{}[α]".

The last three constructs in the definition of terms — $p : C\{\vec{f} = \vec{V}\}$, $(\nu p : C)\,M$, and $a[M]_c^b$ — are *dynamic constructs*. These constructs are not allowed in method declarations or initial code.

With the exception of $V.\text{loc}$, $N \parallel M$, and the terms on the last line of the definition, the constructs of the language are standard for class-based languages with generics.

The special "field" loc returns the location of an object. Concurrent composition ($\parallel$) is asymmetric. In $N \parallel M$, the returned value comes from M; the term N is available only for side effects. The terms on the last line are are not allowed to appear in declarations, as they model the runtime heap and call stack. These include heap elements $p : C\{\cdots\}$ (indicating that p is located at a with actual class C and fields $\vec{f} = \vec{V}$), name restriction (νp) (indicating that p is a fresh name) and frames $a[M]_c^b$ (indicating that M is running under authority of principle a and class c, with result available to b). We write irreducible frames simply as $a[M]$.

Evaluation is defined using a structural congruence on terms. Let $\equiv$ be the least congruence on terms that satisfies the following axioms. The rules for concurrent composition are from [20]. They capture properties of concurrent composition, including semi-associativity and the interaction with let. The rules for distribution are inspired by [8]. The interpretation of a value is independent of the location at which it occurs and the computation of a frame does not depend upon the location from which the frame was invoked (eg. $a[b[M]_d^{b'}]_c^{a'} \equiv b[M]_d^{b'}$) and axiomatize the interaction of let with distribution (eg. $a[\text{let } x = N; M]_c^{a'} \equiv \text{let } x = a[N]_c^{a'}; a[M]_c^{a'}$).

Structural Congruence $(M \equiv M')$ (where $p \notin fn(M)$)

$$(M \parallel N) \parallel L \equiv M \parallel (N \parallel L)$$
$$(M \parallel N) \parallel L \equiv (N \parallel M) \parallel L$$
$$((\nu p)\,N) \parallel M \equiv (\nu p)(N \parallel M)$$
$$M \parallel ((\nu p)\,N) \equiv (\nu p)(M \parallel N)$$
$$\text{let } x = (L \parallel N); M \equiv L \parallel (\text{let } x = N; M)$$
$$\text{let } x = ((\nu p)\,N); M \equiv (\nu p)(\text{let } x = N; M)$$

$$a[\text{let } x = b[V]_d^a; M]_c^{a'} \equiv a[\text{let } x = V; M]_c^{a'}$$
$$a[b[M]_d^{b'}]_c^{a'} \equiv b[M]_d^{b'}$$
$$a[N \parallel M]_c^{a'} \equiv a[N]_c^{a'} \parallel a[M]_c^{a'}$$
$$a[(\nu p)\,N]_c^{a'} \equiv (\nu p)\,a[N]_c^{a'}$$
$$a[\text{let } x = N; M]_c^{a'} \equiv \text{let } x = a[N]_c^{a'}; a[M]_c^{a'}$$

The evaluation relation is defined with respect to an arbitrary fixed class table. The class table is referenced indirectly in the semantics through the lookup functions *fields* and *body*. We refer the reader to the full paper for the routine definitions of these functions.

Term Evaluation $(M \rightarrow M')$

---

let $y = \text{new } C(\vec{V}); L \rightarrow (\nu p:C)(p:C\{\vec{f}=\vec{V}\} \parallel L\{^p/y\})$
  if $\text{fields}(C) = \vec{f}$ and $|\vec{f}| = |\vec{V}|$
$b[p:C\{\cdots\}] \parallel a[\text{let } y = p.\ell(\vec{W}); L]^{a'}_d \rightarrow b[p:C\{\cdots\}] \parallel a[\text{let } y = b[M']^a_c; L']^{a'}_d$
  if $\text{body}(C.\ell) = (\vec{x})\{M\}$ and $|\vec{x}| = |\vec{W}|$ and $M' = M\{^a/\text{caller}\}\{^p/\text{this}\}\{^{\vec{W}}/\vec{x}\}$ and $C = c<\cdots>$
$b[p:C\{\cdots\}] \qquad \parallel p.\text{loc} \rightarrow b[p:C\{\cdots\}] \qquad \parallel b$
$b[p:C\{f=V\cdots\}] \parallel p.f := W \rightarrow b[p:C\{f=W\cdots\}] \parallel \text{unit}$
$b[p:C\{f=V\cdots\}] \parallel p.f \quad \rightarrow b[p:C\{f=V\cdots\}] \parallel V$
if $V = V$ then M else $N \rightarrow M$
if $V = W$ then M else $N \rightarrow N$ if $V \neq W$ $\qquad \dfrac{M \equiv N \rightarrow N' \equiv M'}{M \rightarrow M'} \qquad \dfrac{M \rightarrow M'}{\mathbb{E}[M] \rightarrow \mathbb{E}[M']}$
let $x = V; M \rightarrow M\{^V/x\}$

The new construct creates an object and returns a reference to it. The result is a concurrent composition: the new object appears on the left, the return value on the right. Method invocation happens at the callee site, and thus a new frame is introduced in the consequent $b[M']^a_c$; the result of the method call will be made available to a. In M', the distinguished variables caller and this are bound to the calling principal and the object upon which the method is invoked respectively.

4   Types

The type system controls the distribution of object references via logical policies. We follow [15], as adapted to distributed OO languages with localities in [9].

By allowing predicates to include open values, we can reason about terms that include variables, such as x; however, we cannot reason about $x.f$. Thus we extend the type system to include equations between terms and values. Allowing any term is unsound, however, since our language includes mutability. Thus we identify a subset of *pure* terms which do not include mutable features. In addition, we require that evaluation of pure terms must terminate, and therefore we disallow method calls in pure terms. To shorten some definitions, we define a category of *identifiers*, η, which include bound names and principals.

$$\eta ::= x \mid p \mid a \mid \alpha$$

Environments have two types of data: type bindings for names (as usual) and logical phrases, including equalities and predicates. Define $\text{dom}(\Delta) = \{\eta \mid \eta : \mathscr{T} \in \Delta\}$.

$$\Delta ::= \emptyset \mid \Delta, \eta : \mathscr{T} \mid \Delta, \Phi \mid \Delta, V = M$$

Predicate lookup $(\text{effect}(C) = \Phi)$ is similar to method lookup. Here "$\Phi_D \wedge \Phi\{^{\vec{\phi}}/\vec{\alpha}\}$" is sugar for "let $x = \Phi_D$; let $y = \Phi\{^{\vec{\phi}}/\vec{\alpha}\}$; $x \wedge y$".

$$\dfrac{}{\text{effect}(\text{Object}) = \text{true}} \qquad \dfrac{\mathscr{D} \ni \text{class } c<\vec{\alpha}:\vec{P}>\triangleleft D\{\cdots\}[\Phi] \quad \text{effect}(D\{^{\vec{\phi}}/\vec{\alpha}\}) = \Phi_D}{\text{effect}(c<\vec{\phi}>) = \Phi_D \wedge \Phi\{^{\vec{\phi}}/\vec{\alpha}\}}$$

We also define a function $(\text{env}_a(M) = \Delta)$ to create an environment from a term.

$$env_a(\eta : C\{\vec{f} = \vec{V}\}) = \Box_a\mathtt{mp}(\eta), a = \eta.\mathtt{loc}, V_1 = \eta.f_1, \ldots, V_n = \eta.f_n$$
$$env_a(\mathtt{let}\, x = N;\, M) = env_a(N) \qquad env_a(N \,|\!|\, M) = env_a(N), env_a(M)$$
$$env_a(b\,[M]_c^{a'}) = env_b(M) \quad env_a((\nu p{:}C)\,M) = p{:}C, env_a(M) \qquad env_a(M) = \emptyset,\ otherwise$$

The type system is parameterized with respect to a semantic entailment relation $(\Delta \vDash \Psi)$. In addition to the rules arising from indexed intuitionist necessity modalities, we expect the relation to support domain specific axioms and satisfy the following properties. Let σ stand for substitutions of pure terms M for x.

1. If $\Delta \vDash \Psi$ then $\Delta\sigma \vDash \Psi\sigma$, for any substitution σ from variables to values, or from principals to principals.
2. If $\Delta, V = V, \Delta' \vDash \Psi$ then $\Delta, \Delta' \vDash \Psi$.
3. If $\Delta, x{:}T, x = M, \Box_a\mathtt{mp}(x), \Delta' \vDash \Psi$ and $\Delta, \Delta' \vDash \Box_a\mathtt{mp}(M)$ then $\Delta, \Delta' \vDash \Psi\{\!\{^M/x\}\!\}$.

In examples, we assume that whenever $\Box_a\mathtt{mp}(\eta)$ and $\eta : C$ are deducible, then so is $\Box_a\mathtt{mp}(\eta.f)$ for every public field of C.

The standard judgements required for the type system are relegated to the full paper, including subtyping $(\vdash \mathcal{T}' <: \mathcal{T})$, well-formed overriding $(\vdash <\vec{\beta} : \vec{Q}>S(\vec{T})$ overrides $D.\ell)$, well-formed types $(\Delta \vdash \mathcal{T})$, and well-formed environments $(\Delta \vdash \diamond)$. The only noteworthy aspect of these definitions is that the implication of the effects for the same base class also yields subtyping:

$$\frac{\mathcal{D} \ni \mathtt{class}\, c{<}\vec{\alpha}{>} \quad \vec{\phi} \vDash \vec{\psi} \quad |\vec{\alpha}| = |\vec{\phi}| = |\vec{\psi}|}{\vdash c{<}\vec{\phi}{>} <: c{<}\vec{\psi}{>}}$$

The judgments for declarations have the standard format. The judgment for values include a script a, indicating that the value is well typed at a specific location. The judgment for terms carries additional structure. In $\Delta \,\overset{a'}{\vdash_a}\, M : \mathcal{T}\, \rho\, d$, a should be read as the location of the term, a' as the location of the caller, $\mathcal{T}$ as the type of the resulting value, d as the class from which the code is derived, and $\rho \in \{\mathsf{Pure}, \mathsf{Impure}\}$ as a *purity annotation*.

The effect on a class must be a pure term of type Pred. The rule for typing methods uses a standard well-formed overriding definition. The typing of the method body occurs in the context of an abstract principal a that is constrained to coincide with the location of the ambient object. Similarly, the abstract principal caller is constrained to coincide with the annotation on the typing of the body of the method. In typing the method body, one can use the logical variables of the class, the method declaration and assume that the caller was permitted to possess the arguments.

Well-Formed Declarations $(\Delta \vdash \mathcal{D})\quad (\Delta \vdash \mathcal{M}\ in\ c{<}\vec{\alpha} : \vec{P}{>}{\lhd}D)$

$$\frac{\Delta, \vec{\alpha} : \vec{P} \vdash D, \vec{T} \quad \Delta, \vec{\alpha} : \vec{P}, a : \mathsf{Prin}, \mathtt{this} : c{<}\vec{\alpha}{>}, a = \mathtt{this.loc}, \Box_a\mathtt{mp}(\mathtt{this}) \,\overset{a}{\vdash_a}\, \Phi : \mathsf{Pred}\ \mathsf{Pure}\ c}{\Delta \vdash \mathtt{class}\ c{<}\vec{\alpha} : \vec{P}{>}{\lhd}D\{\vec{\mu}\ \vec{T}\ \vec{f};\ \mathcal{M}\}[\Phi]}\ \begin{array}{l}\Delta \vdash \mathcal{M}\ in\ c{<}\vec{\alpha} : \vec{P}{>}{\lhd}D \quad \mathtt{fields}(D) = \vec{\mu}_D\ \vec{T}_D\ \vec{f}_D \quad \vec{f}_D \cap \vec{f} = \emptyset \\[2pt] \hfill a \notin fn(M)\end{array}$$

$$\frac{\Delta, \vec{\alpha} : \vec{P}, \vec{\beta} : \vec{Q} \vdash S, \vec{T} \quad \vdash S' <: S \quad \vdash <\vec{\beta}{>}S(\vec{T})\ overrides\ D.\ell}{\begin{array}{c}\Delta, \vec{\alpha} : \vec{P}, \vec{\beta} : \vec{Q}, \vec{x} : \vec{T}, a : \mathsf{Prin}, \mathtt{this} : c{<}\vec{\alpha}{>}, a = \mathtt{this.loc}, \Box_a(\mathtt{mp}(\mathtt{this}) \wedge \mathtt{mp}(\vec{x})), \\ \mathtt{caller} : \mathsf{Prin}, \Box_{\mathtt{caller}}\mathtt{mp}(\vec{x}) \,\overset{\mathtt{caller}}{\vdash_a}\, M : S'\, \rho\, c \quad a \notin fn(M)\end{array}}{\Delta \vdash <\vec{\beta} : \vec{Q}>S\ \ell(\vec{T}\ \vec{x})\,\{M\}\ in\ c{<}\vec{\alpha} : \vec{P}{>}{\lhd}D}$$

The judgment for values requires that well-formed objects satisfy their class invariants. In addition, the object value, as well as the objects held in its public fields must be permitted at the given location.

Well-Formed Values and Terms $(\Delta \vdash_{\overline{a}} V : \mathcal{T})$ $(\Delta \vdash_{\overline{a}}^{a'} M : \mathcal{T} \rho d)$ $(\rho ::= \text{Pure} \mid \text{Impure})$

$$\frac{\Delta \ni b : \text{Prin}}{\Delta \vdash_{\overline{a}} b : \text{Prin}} \quad \frac{\Delta \ni x : T \quad \Delta \vDash \Box_a \text{mp}(x)}{\Delta \vdash_{\overline{a}} x : T} \quad \frac{\Delta \ni p : C \quad \Delta \vDash \Box_a \text{mp}(p)}{\Delta \vdash_{\overline{a}} p : C} \quad \frac{}{\Delta \vdash_{\overline{a}} \text{unit} : \text{Unit}}$$

$$\frac{\Delta \ni \alpha : \text{Pred}(\vec{\mathcal{T}})}{\Delta \vdash_{\overline{a}} \alpha : \text{Pred}(\vec{\mathcal{T}})} \quad \frac{arity(\gamma) = \vec{\mathcal{T}}}{\Delta \vdash_{\overline{a}} \gamma : \text{Pred}(\vec{\mathcal{T}})} \quad \frac{\Delta \vdash_{\overline{a}} \phi : \text{Pred}(\vec{\mathcal{T}}) \quad \Delta \vdash_{\overline{a}} \vec{V} : \vec{\mathcal{T}}}{\Delta \vdash_{\overline{a}} \phi(\vec{V}) : \text{Pred}}$$

$$\frac{\Delta \vdash \diamond \quad \Delta \vdash_{\overline{a}} p : C \quad fields(C) = \vec{\mu} \; \vec{T} \; \vec{f} \quad \Delta \vdash_{\overline{a}} \vec{V} : \vec{T}' \quad \vdash \vec{T}' <: \vec{T}}{\Delta, env_a(p : C\{\vec{f} = \vec{V}\}) \vDash effect(C)\{p/\text{this}\}}{\Delta \vdash_{\overline{a}}^{a'} p : C\{\vec{f} = \vec{V}\} : \text{Proc} \; \rho \; d}$$

$$\frac{\Delta \vdash \diamond \quad \Delta \vdash C \quad fields(C) = \vec{\mu} \; \vec{T} \; \vec{f} \quad \Delta \vdash_{\overline{a}} \vec{V} : \vec{T}' \quad \vdash \vec{T}' <: \vec{T}}{\Delta, env_a(x : C\{\vec{f} = \vec{V}\}) \vDash effect(C)\{x/\text{this}\} \quad \Delta, x : C, env_a(x : C\{\vec{f} = \vec{V}\}) \vdash_{\overline{a}}^{a'} M : \mathcal{T} \; \rho \; d}{\Delta \vdash_{\overline{a}}^{a'} \text{let} \; x = \text{new} \; C(\vec{V}); M : \mathcal{T} \; \text{Impure} \; d}$$

$$\frac{\Delta \vdash \diamond \quad \Delta \vdash_{\overline{a}} V : C \quad body(C.\ell) = <\vec{\beta} : \vec{Q}>S(\vec{T}) \quad \Delta \vdash_{\overline{a}} \vec{\phi} : \vec{Q} \quad \Delta \vdash_{\overline{a}} \vec{W} : \vec{T}' \quad \vdash \vec{T}' <: \vec{T}\{\vec{\phi}/\vec{\beta}\}}{\Delta, b : \text{Prin}, b = V.\text{loc} \vDash \Box_b \text{mp}(\vec{W}) \quad b \notin dom(\Delta) \quad \Delta, x : S\{\vec{\phi}/\vec{\beta}\}, \Box_a \text{mp}(x) \vdash_{\overline{a}}^{a'} M : \mathcal{T} \; \rho \; d}{\Delta \vdash_{\overline{a}}^{a'} \text{let} \; x = V.\ell<\vec{\phi}>(\vec{W}); M : \mathcal{T} \; \text{Impure} \; d}$$

$$\frac{\Delta \vdash \diamond \quad \Delta \vdash_{\overline{a}} V : d<\vec{\phi}> \quad fields(d<\vec{\phi}>) = \vec{\mu} \; \vec{T} \; \vec{f} \quad \mu_i = \text{private mutable} \quad \Delta \vdash_{\overline{a}} W : T' \quad \vdash T' <: T_i}{\Delta \vdash_{\overline{a}}^{a'} V.f_i := W : \text{Unit} \; \text{Impure} \; d}$$

$$\frac{\Delta \vdash \diamond \quad \Delta \vdash_{\overline{a}} V : c<\vec{\phi}> \quad fields(c<\vec{\phi}>) = \vec{\mu} \; \vec{T} \; \vec{f} \quad \text{If} \; \mu_i \ni \text{private then} \; c = d}{\text{If} \; \mu_i \ni \text{mutable then} \; \rho = \text{Impure}}{\Delta \vdash_{\overline{a}}^{a'} V.f_i : T_i \; \rho \; d}$$

$$\frac{\Delta \vdash \diamond \quad \Delta \vdash_{\overline{a}} V : T \quad \Delta \vdash_{\overline{a}} W : S \quad \Delta, V = W \vdash_{\overline{a}}^{a'} M : \mathcal{T} \; \rho \; d \quad \Delta \vdash_{\overline{a}}^{a'} N : \mathcal{T}' \; \rho \; d}{\text{Either} \; \vdash \mathcal{T}' <: \mathcal{T} = \mathcal{T}'' \; \text{or} \; \vdash \mathcal{T} <: \mathcal{T}' = \mathcal{T}''}{\Delta \vdash_{\overline{a}}^{a'} \text{if} \; V = W \; \text{then} \; M \; \text{else} \; N : \mathcal{T}'' \; \rho \; d}$$

$right(N) = N'$

$$\frac{\Delta \vdash_{\overline{a}}^{a} N : T \; \text{Impure} \; d}{\Delta, env_a(N), x : T, \Box_a \text{mp}(x) \vdash_{\overline{a}}^{a'} M : \mathcal{T} \; \rho \; d}{\Delta \vdash_{\overline{a}}^{a'} \text{let} \; x = N; M : \mathcal{T} \; \text{Impure} \; d}$$

$$\frac{\Delta \vdash_{\overline{a}}^{a} N : T \; \rho \; d \quad \Delta, env_a(N) \vdash_{\overline{a}}^{a} N' : T \; \text{Pure} \; d}{\Delta, env_a(N), x : T, x = N', \Box_a \text{mp}(x) \vdash_{\overline{a}}^{a'} M : \mathcal{T} \; \rho \; d}{\Delta \vdash_{\overline{a}}^{a'} \text{let} \; x = N; M : \mathcal{T} \; \rho \; d}$$

$$\frac{\Delta, env_a(M) \vdash_{\overline{a}}^{a''} N : \mathcal{T}' \; \rho \; d \quad \Delta, env_a(N) \vdash_{\overline{a}}^{a'} M : \mathcal{T} \; \rho \; d}{\Delta \vdash_{\overline{a}}^{a'} N \Vert M : \mathcal{T} \; \rho \; d} \quad \frac{\Delta, p : C \vdash_{\overline{a}}^{a'} M : \mathcal{T} \; \rho \; d}{\Delta \vdash_{\overline{a}}^{a'} (\nu p : C) M : \mathcal{T} \; \rho \; d}$$

$$\frac{\Delta \vdash \diamond \quad \Delta \vdash_{\overline{a}} V : \mathcal{T}}{\Delta \vdash_{\overline{a}}^{a'} V : \mathcal{T} \; \rho \; d} \quad \frac{\Delta \vdash \diamond \quad \Delta \vdash_{\overline{a}} V : C}{\Delta \vdash_{\overline{a}}^{a'} V.\text{loc} : \text{Prin} \; \rho \; d} \quad \frac{\Delta \vdash_{\overline{a}} b : \text{Prin} \quad \Delta \vdash_{\overline{b}}^{b'} M : \mathcal{T} \; \rho \; c}{\Delta \vdash_{\overline{a}}^{a'} b[M]_c^{b'} : \mathcal{T} \; \rho \; d}$$

The typing rules for terms are designed to establish several invariants, which we now discuss.

Well Located. The rules for terms use the value judgment to ensure that value occurrences are available at a given location. The rule for located terms switches principals as expected.

Purity Annotations. Field updates and constructor calls are impure because they mutate the heap. Field accesss to mutable fields are impure because they rely on mutable state. Method invocations are impure because they might not terminate. In all other cases, the purity annotation is constructed inductively. For example, a let is pure only if both terms involved are pure. Similarly for concurrent composition and conditionals.

Equations. The rule for pure let terms uses the function *right*. Intuitively, for any term N, $right(N)$ returns the rightmost subterm of N after it has been rewritten to a normal form. Routine details are omitted. Conditionals and let expression on pure terms introduce equations to the environment. Equations are also generated by the rules for heap objects ($\eta : C\{\cdots\}$) and new.

Caller Annotations. The caller annotation is carried inductively through all rules but two. In the rule for the concurrent composition, only the right term is constrained; the value of the left term is ignored. The purpose of the caller annotation is revealed by the rule for values which appear as terms — these are the return values. The rule ensures that the caller principal is permitted to have a reference to the value.

Checking Effects and the $\mathrm{mp}(\cdot)$ *Predicate.* The rule for new illustrates the methodology. (The rule for heap objects enforces similar proof obligations.) In this rule, the hypothesis for typing fields is standard. The lookup of the effect obligation via *effect*(C) yields a conjunction of the effects for this class and all its superclasses. The proof obligations ensure that the created object conforms to the class predicate, and that the reference and its public fields are permitted to be at the principal at which the object is located. The facts used to discharge this proof obligation are derived from the environment via Δ which accumulates the benefits derivable from the objects declared in the environment and the equations accumulated in the environment via lets and conditionals. The parameters to the constructor have to be available at the current location a.

In field update and lookup, the class annotation on the typing judgment is ensured to be the class of the object if the field is private.

In the rule for "generic" methods, we substitute concrete formulas for the logical variables being carried in the method definition. Since methods are executed at the location of the callee, we check to ensure that the location of the callee object possesses the right to hold references to the objects being passed in as actual parameters.

Conjoining Specifications. The rule for concurrent composition reflects the ideas from conjoining specifications of concurrent systems [3] — each component can assume the information exposed by the other component.

Results. An *initial program* is one that contains no dynamic constructs.

An *opponent class* is one whose effect is trivial, i.e., $\mathtt{tt}$. An *opponent program* is one that can be typed only allowing the constructor rule for opponent classes. In typing opponents, we allow the assumption $\forall \eta.\ \square_\perp \mathrm{mp}(\eta)$. Thus opponents are typed using a restricted class table, but under a permissive policy. This permissive policy is essentially the same as standard object-oriented typing.

An opponent can instantiate opponent classes. By Principal Naturality, the opponent can unconstrainedly pass arguments or return results in method invocations. Thus, the opponent typability requirement in the following safety result means only that the opponent program is typable in the sense of classic object-oriented programming.

Recall that a frame is a term of the form $a\,[M]_c^b$.

Definition 1. A term M is *safe for* Δ if whenever $M \to^* N$, $N \equiv \mathbb{E}[a\,[N']_c^b]$, N' contains no frames and $p \in fn(N)$ then $\Delta, env_\perp(N) \vDash \square_a \mathrm{mp}(p)$. $\qquad\qquad\square$

```
class User {
  private final Compiler compiler;
  private FileOutputStream fDebug;
  void action () {
    ...
    this.compiler.compile (this.fDebug, ...); // Invoke with current fDebug.
  }
  void setDebug (FileOutputStream fDebug) {
    this.fDebug = fDebug;
  }
}[ ∀o : FileOutputStream.□_this.loc mp(o) ⇒ □_this.compiler.loc mp(o) ]

class Compiler {
  private final FileOutputStream fStats;
  public void compile (FileOutputStream fDebug, String source) {
    ...
    this.fStats.write (...); // Write statistics to fStats.
    fDebug.write (...); // Write debugging output to fDebug.
  }
}
```

Fig. 1. User and Compiler Code

Proposition 2. Suppose that $\Delta \vdash_{\overline{1}} M$ and $\Delta, env_{\perp}(M), (\forall \eta. \ \Box_{\perp} mp(\eta)) \vdash_{\overline{1}} N$ for an initial opponent program N. Then N $\parallel$ M is safe for Δ. $\qquad\square$

The safety result ensures that well-typed trustworthy programs are safe when combined with arbitrary (typed but untrustworthy) opponents.

5   The Confused Deputy

In this section, we examine how to typecheck code that addresses the Confused Deputy problem using object references as capabilities.

Hardy [22] discusses a system with a compiler invoked by a user. The compiler writes two files, in addition to any generated code. The first is a statistics file. The name of the statistics file is hardcoded into the compiler, and the compiler is explicitly granted permission to write to that file. The second is a debugging file, chosen by the user. In order to write to the user's choice of debugging file, the compiler must be granted a broad permission. Hardy describes an occasion when a user selected a sensitive file—subsequently overwritten by the compiler—and dubs the compiler a Confused Deputy.

Hardy's solution requires the user to obtain a capability to write to the debugging file, and to send that capability to the compiler. The compiler can use the user's capability to write to the debugging file.

Modeling. We model Hardy's solution using the code in Figure 1. Following the object references as capabilities paradigm, the capabilities to write to files are represented by a FileOutputStream class (as in Java).

The User class invokes a compiler, passing the FileOutputStream contents of the fDebug field. The User class allows its fDebug field to be updated via a method setDebug—we examine the typing consequences below.

The Compiler class must be initialized with a final FileOutputStream field fStats at construction. When it compiles, it uses its own fStats field and the fDebug method parameter supplied by the caller to write to the statistics and debugging files.

Controlling Capabilities. The capability solution improves upon the Confused Deputy situation, with respect to the principle of least privilege, because the compiler lacks the broad permission to write to many files in the object/capability solution. Hardy observes that achieving a comparable system with a traditional access control policy for the compiler is challenging, e.g., because the compiler may be invoked by different users with access to different files.

However, the capability solution is not entirely satisfactory. As discussed in the introduction, an untrustworthy compiler might forward capabilities that it receives to objects at different locations (principals).

Type Assignment. We now consider how to typecheck the code of Figure 1 in a way that allows the Compiler to receive the fDebug object reference but not forward it to another location. We omit discussion of the source code given to the compiler, and any executable output, for reasons of space.

The typing of the compiler's use of FileOutputStream references is straightforward. The compiler receives permission to possess the field fStats implicitly. More generally, our type system implicitly allows every object to access its own fields. On the other hand, code that constructs a Compiler instance is responsible for ensuring that the chosen location of the compiler is able to possess fStats. That is, if a newly created Compiler instance is referenced via c, then the proof obligation is $\Box_{c.loc}mp(c.fStats)$. Similarly, our type system implicitly grants the compiler permission to possess the method parameter fDebug, and the obligation lies with the caller to ensure that the location of the callee may possess fDebug.

Typechecking the body of the compile method does not introduce proof obligations involving fStats or fDebug, because those values are passed as this, and the type system automatically validates $(\forall o.\Box_{o.loc}mp(o))$. That is, a location may possess a reference to any object stored at that location.

The user has a more interesting policy, because it has to permit forwarding of fDebug to the compiler. The form of the policy hinges upon the mutability of the fDebug field. For example, if fDebug was a final field, it could be referred to in the class invariant, e.g., with form:

$$\Box_{this.compiler.loc}\Box_{this.loc}mp(this.fDebug)$$

which entails:

$$(\Box_{this.loc}mp(this.fDebug)) \wedge (\Box_{this.compiler.loc}mp(this.fDebug))$$

To demonstrate a more flexible alternative, we chose to make fDebug non-final (mutable) in the code of Figure 1. Since we can no longer refer to the field in a class invariant, we instead state that all FileOutputStream references that may be possessed at the location of User may also be possessed at the location of the corresponding compiler. This class invariant is written:

$$\forall o : \texttt{FileOutputStream}. \square_{\texttt{this.loc}} mp(o) \Rightarrow \square_{\texttt{this.compiler.loc}} mp(o)$$

With this class invariant, typechecking justifies forwarding of this.fDebug to this.compiler using implication together with the facts that: (1) this.loc may possess this.fDebug (the location of an object implicitly possesses its fields); and (2) this.fDebug is declared to be an instance of FileOutputStream.

Finally, code that constructs an instance of User has an obligation to show that the associated Compiler instance is usable with any FileOutputStream object reference that the User receives.

6   Conclusion

The control of the possession and transmission of secrets is a recurrent theme in security literature and practice. The policies on possession in this paper describe an upper bound on the principals who can possess a secret. We describe a static analysis to ensure programs in a distributed object-oriented language comply with such policies. Our static analysis takes the form of a refinement type system, based on indexed necessity modalities from intuitionist S4, for an object calculus with locations. The safety result ensures that in the configurations that arise from the execution of well-typed programs, objects are only accessible to principals who are permitted to do so by the system policy, even in the presence of attackers who try to subvert the policies by inserting malicious objects and code into the system. Our results suggest that type systems are a practical tool to debug secrecy errors in the design of user-defined APIs in distributed systems.

Acknowledgements. We thank the referees of a previous version of this paper for useful comments. This research was supported by NSF CCF-0915704.

References

1. Abadi, M.: Access control in a core calculus of dependency. ENTCS 172, 5–31 (2007)
2. Abadi, M., Gordon, A.D.: A calculus for cryptographic protocols: The spi calculus. Information and Computation 148, 36–47 (1999)
3. Abadi, M., Lamport, L.: Conjoining specifications. ACM Trans. Program. Lang. Syst. 17(3), 507–535 (1995)
4. Abadi, M.: Secrecy by typing in security protocols. Journal of the ACM 46, 611–638 (1998)
5. Anderson, M., Pose, R.D., Wallace, C.S.: A password-capability system. Comput. J. 29(1), 1–8 (1986)
6. Bierman, G.M., de Paiva, V.C.V.: On an intuitionistic modal logic. Studia Logica 65 (2001)
7. Cardelli, L.: A language with distributed scope. In: POPL, pp. 286–297 (1995)
8. Castellani, I.: Process algebras with localities. In: Handbook of Process Algebra, ch. 15, pp. 945–1045 (2001)
9. Cirillo, A., Jagadeesan, R., Pitcher, C., Riely, J.: TAPIDO: Trust and Authorization Via Provenance and Integrity in Distributed Objects (Extended Abstract). In: Drossopoulou, S. (ed.) ESOP 2008. LNCS, vol. 4960, pp. 208–223. Springer, Heidelberg (2008)

10. DeYoung, H., Pfenning, F.: Reasoning about the consequences of authorization policies in a linear epistemic logic. Tech. Rep. 1213, CMU (2009)
11. Drossopoulou, S.: Ten years of ownership types or the benefits of putting objects into boxes, invited talk at BCS (2008), Talk available at http://www.doc.ic.ac.uk/~scd/BCS.pdf
12. E: Open source distributed capabilities, http://www.erights.org
13. Feil, R., Nyffenegger, L.: Evolution of cross site request forgery attacks. Journal in Computer Virology 4(1), 61–71 (2007)
14. Fournet, C., Gordon, A.D., Maffeis, S.: A type discipline for authorization in distributed systems. In: CSF (2007)
15. Fournet, C., Gordon, A.D., Maffeis, S.: A type discipline for authorization policies. ACM Trans. Program. Lang. Syst. 29(5) (2007)
16. Freeman, T., Pfenning, F.: Refinement types for ML. In: PLDI 1991, pp. 268–277. ACM, New York (1991)
17. Garg, D., Bauer, L., Bowers, K.D., Pfenning, F., Reiter, M.K.: A Linear Logic of Authorization and Knowledge. In: Gollmann, D., Meier, J., Sabelfeld, A. (eds.) ESORICS 2006. LNCS, vol. 4189, pp. 297–312. Springer, Heidelberg (2006)
18. Garg, D., Pfenning, F.: Non-interference in constructive authorization logic. In: CSFW, pp. 283–296 (2006)
19. Gong, L., Mueller, M., Prafullch, H.: Going beyond the sandbox: An overview of the new security architecture in the Java Development Kit 1.2. In: USENIX Symposium on Internet Technologies and Systems, pp. 103–112 (1997)
20. Gordon, A.D., Hankin, P.D.: A concurrent object calculus: Reduction and typing. In: Proceedings HLCL 1998 (1998)
21. Gordon, A.D., Jeffrey, A.: Authenticity by typing for security protocols. Journal of Computer Security 11(4), 451–520 (2003)
22. Hardy, N.: The confused deputy: (or why capabilities might have been invented). SIGOPS Oper. Syst. Rev. 22, 36–38 (1988)
23. Hardy, N.: KeyKOS architecture. SIGOPS Oper. Syst. Rev. 19, 8–25 (1985)
24. Hennessy, M., Riely, J.: Resource access control in systems of mobile agents. Information and Computation 173, 2002 (1998)
25. Jagadeesan, R., Pitcher, C., Riely, J.: Non interference for intuitionist necessity. Tech. Rep. 12-003, School of Computing, DePaul University (2012)
26. Maffeis, S., Mitchell, J.C., Taly, A.: Object capabilities and isolation of untrusted web applications. In: IEEE Symposium on Security and Privacy, pp. 125–140 (2010)
27. Nicola, R.D., Ferrari, G., Pugliese, R.: Klaim: a kernel language for agents interaction and mobility. IEEE Transactions on Software Engineering 24, 315–330 (1997)
28. Pfenning, F., Wong, H.C.: On a modal λ-calculus for S4. In: Proceedings of MFOS, New Orleans, Louisiana. ENTCS, vol. 1. Elsevier (March 1995)
29. Shapiro, J.S., Smith, J.M., Farber, D.J.: EROS: a fast capability system. SIGOPS Oper. Syst. Rev. 33, 170–185 (1999)

Types and Access Controls for Cross-Domain Security in Flash

Aseem Rastogi[1,*], Avik Chaudhuri[2], and Rob Johnson[3]

[1] University of Maryland, College Park and Adobe Systems Inc.
aseem@cs.umd.edu
[2] Adobe Systems Inc.
avik.chaudhuri@adobe.com
[3] Stony Brook University
rob@cs.stonybrook.edu

Abstract. The ubiquitous Flash platform enables programmers to build sophisticated web application "mash-ups" that combine Flash executables loaded from multiple trust domains with complex, asymmetric trust relationships. Flash provides APIs and run-time checks to help programmers declare and enforce trust relationships between different domains, but there is currently no formal security model for Flash.

This paper presents the first formal security model for the Flash platform. Our formal model instantly reveals that the run-time checks performed by the Flash runtime are not sufficient to enforce data integrity – we present simple example programs that are vulnerable to attacks. We then develop a static type system for Flash programs that lets programmers specify fine-grained trust relationships, and we show that, combined with the run-time checks already performed by the Flash runtime, well-typed programs cannot violate data integrity at run-time.

Keywords: Flash Security, Security Model, Dynamic Access Control, Type System.

1 Introduction

Adobe Flash is a widely-used multimedia platform for building interactive Internet applications. Flash is frequently used for video and audio applications, advertisements, and games, making it nearly ubiquitous on the web. Flash applications can load additional Flash applications from the same or other web domains, allowing developers to create mashups that combine functionality provided by several different domains.

Flash implements the "same origin policy" that is also used in JavaScript, but Flash applications can explicitly grant access to some trusted domains, enabling scripts running in the context of one domain to access data and functions of scripts loaded in another domain. This enables Flash components from different domains to communicate with each other in a controlled manner.

---

* Work performed while the author was at Stony Brook University.

R. Jhala and A. Igarashi (Eds.): APLAS 2012, LNCS 7705, pp. 82–97, 2012.
© Springer-Verlag Berlin Heidelberg 2012

However, there is currently no formal specification of the Flash security model. Without a formal specification, the guarantees of the model are unclear. Programmers cannot reason about the security of their applications – e.g. they cannot easily verify that a security-critical function in their application cannot be called with an argument coming from an untrusted application.

To that end, we make the following contributions in this paper:

- We present a formal specification of the Flash security model. The specification includes carefully modeled semantics for the dynamic access control checks and the APIs for dynamically loading other Flash applications.
- We show that the run-time checks performed by the Flash runtime are not by themselves sufficient to guarantee data integrity for Flash applications. We formalize the data integrity property and give simple examples that violate the property under the current semantics.
- We present a security extension to the Flash static type system that enables programmers to express and enforce data integrity invariants. We give a soundness theorem of our type system and prove that the runtime access control checks are sufficient to maintain the data integrity invariants of the well-typed Flash applications.
- We strengthen our threat model by allowing an attacker to by-pass the static security checks and show how our type system, in conjunction with the run-time checks, still guarantees that data integrity is maintained for a well-typed victim application executing in the same environment as the attacker's application.

We mainly focus on the data integrity property in Flash applications. This helps us prevent Cross Site Scripting attacks (and other injection attacks [1]) which are instances of data integrity violations (Section 3), and more importantly, one of the most common types of real world attacks on Flash applications [2].

Our type system is based on the crucial observation that in the Flash security model, if an application is compromised, only itself and other applications from the domains it trusts, are to be blamed. Hence, it is possible to impose a static discipline on the trusted programs, that combined with the existing run-time checks, can prevent data integrity violations.

The type system adds labels $\mathcal{D}$ to the types in the language, where each label is a set of some domains. The interpretation of the labels is that, a type with label $\mathcal{D}$ must admit only those values that *come from* one of the domains in $\mathcal{D}$. We present a static consistency relation over types, that enforces the following safety property for all the flows in the program: if a term with label $\mathcal{D}_1$ flows to a context that expects a term with label $\mathcal{D}_2$, then $\mathcal{D}_1 \subseteq \mathcal{D}_2$ must hold.

Interestingly, we can afford to allow the attacker to by-pass the safety checks mentioned above. We prove that as long as the victim makes the *worst* assumptions about the attacker's code – a value coming from the attacker's code could have originated anywhere – while type checking its own code, the data integrity property is maintained at run-time.

We present an overview of the Flash security model in Section 2. We give our threat model and some example data integrity violation attacks in Section 3. We use these examples throughout the paper to exemplify the runtime semantics (Section 4) and the type system (Section 5). We state the soundness theorem of our type system in Section 5.1. We discuss related work in Section 6 and finally conclude in Section 7.

2   Overview

Adobe Flash platform [3] is a complete application development stack. The programmer writes code in the ActionScript language and compiles it to a bytecode representation, called the swf. The swfs are typically deployed over HTTP and are included by their URL inside the HTML pages. When the HTML pages are rendered by the web browser, the Flash Player plugin in the browser loads the swfs from their URL and executes them.

Flash platform enables programmers to design and develop rich functionality applications. In particular, the platform provides APIs to load and execute other swfs, and possibly access their data and functions. A detailed account of the API can be found in [1].

Domain Based Sandboxing. The Flash Player partitions the execution environment into multiple security contexts that are defined by the source domains of the comprising swfs. For every source domain in the environment, there exists a security context, in which all the swfs loaded from that source domain execute.

The Flash Player always allows a swf to access data and functions of any other swf in the same security context. This is called the *same origin policy*, wherein the swfs loaded from the same domain can freely script into each other. However, by default, any attempt by a swf in one security context to access data and functions of a swf in another security context, generates a runtime security error.

Extension to the Same Origin Policy. To handle the situations where cross-domain scripting is sometimes desirable, the Flash platform allows for an extension to the same origin policy. A swf may express trust on some domain(s) (other than its own source domain). The implication is that, any swf from the trusted domain(s) is allowed to freely script into the trusting swf.

However, it only opens up a one way communication channel, from the trusted domain swfs to the trusting swf. For the communication in the other direction, the receiving swf has to explicitly express trust itself.

Content Loading and Import Loading. When a swf loads another swf, the loaded swf executes in the security context defined by its own source domain. This regular loading mechanism is called *Content Loading*. The Flash platform provides another loading mechanism, known as *Import Loading*, in which the loaded swf is executed in the same security context as that of the loader swf. Thus, the effect is as if the loaded swf comes from the same domain as the loader swf.

However, the source domain of the loaded swf has to allow the loader domain to import load – by placing on its webserver a crossdomain policy file having an entry for the loader domain. Before import loading, the Flash Player checks that the webserver of the loaded swf has a crossdomain policy file and that this file contains an entry for the loader domain. On the other hand, the loader must also be careful before import loading a swf from another domain, since import loading grants the loaded swf all the privileges of the loader domain.

3 Threat Model and Examples

Threat Model. We assume that the attacker owns some web domains, which are not trusted by the victim. Furthermore, it creates some swfs using the Flash platform tools and hosts them on its web domains. Thus, the attacker's swfs are capable of doing all that is allowed by the language. Moreover, we allow the attacker's programs to by-pass the static security checks of our type system. Since the victim's swfs and the attacker's swfs can load one another, the Flash runtime environment could contain the victim's swfs and the attacker's swfs together. Our goal is to maintain the data integrity property at run-time. We formalize the data integrity property in the next section.

Examples. We now give some examples of possible data integrity violations in the Flash programs. We use these examples throughout the rest of the paper to show whether and how they are prevented by the runtime semantics and our type system.

For the purpose of the examples, the functions are written as $fun(x) \{ .. \}$, where x is the function parameter. The object literals are written as $\{f_1 = t_1, f_2 = t_2, ...\}$, where f_1, f_2, ... are the property names and t_1, t_2, ... are the terms. The object properties are evaluated left to right. The function $load(i)$ loads a swf i. We denote the attacker's swf and domain by a and d respectively, and the victim's swf and domain by v and d' respectively. A swf is modeled like an object literal and written as $[\![f_1 = t_1, f_2 = t_2, ...]\!]$.

As mentioned above, we assume that the victim does not trust the attacker. However, the attacker trusts the victim since it's in the attacker's interest to allow the victim to interact with it as much as possible to create the opportunities for exploiting the victim's swf (as we see in the Example 2 below).

Example 1. Attacker's swf directly scripts into the victim's swf:

```
v = [[s_fn = fun(x) { /* transfer $100 to account x */; return 0 }]]
a = [[v_swf = load(v), f = v_swf.s_fn(a_acc)]]
```

The attacker's swf loads the victim's swf and directly calls the sensitive function in that swf with an arbitrary argument. This attack is known as the Cross Domain Scripting attack [1], and is prevented by the run-time checks in the Flash Player.

Example 2. Victim's swf passes a sensitive function to the attacker's swf

```
v = ⟦s_fn = /* as before */, a_swf = load(a), f = a_swf.f'(s_fn)⟧
a = ⟦f' = fun(g) { g(a_acc) }⟧
```

The victim's swf loads the attacker's swf and ends up passing a sensitive function to the attacker. The attacker can then call that sensitive function with an arbitrary argument. This example is a more general form of the Cross Domain Scripting attack, but is not pointed out in the existing documentation on Flash security [1]. Not surprisingly, this attack is not prevented by the Flash Player. However, our type system catches this violation in the victim's code at compile time.

Example 3. Victim's swf passes a non-sensitive function to the attacker's swf

```
v = ⟦ns_fn = fun(x) {return x + 1}, a_swf =.., f = a_swf.f'(ns_fn)⟧
a = ⟦f' = fun(g) { g(a_acc) }⟧
```

As before, the victim's swf loads the attacker's swf but this time, passes a non-sensitive function to the attacker. Since it's not a violation of data integrity, this code is successfully type checked in our type system (and runs successfully too).

Example 4. Cross Site Scripting

Finally, the Cross Site Scripting attacks [1], which are one of the most common types of real world attacks on the Flash applications, are also instances of data integrity violations. In such attacks, the victim uses the untrusted run-time inputs, called FlashVars, as arguments to the function that navigates to a URL. The attacker can then provide malicious JavaScript code in the FlashVars, and that code ends up executing with the end-user privileges. Our type system can flag Cross Site Scripting vulnerabilities in the victim's swfs at compile time.

4   Evaluation Semantics

In this section we formalize the Flash security model.

Language Syntax. The language syntax is shown in Figure 1. The set of web domains is denoted by $\mathbb{D}$. We assume that every swf has a unique identifier coming from a set $\mathbb{I}$. The identifiers are used as arguments to the loading functions.

The basic types consists of the base type ($\bot$), the function type ($\sigma_1 \rightarrow \sigma_2$), the object type ($\{x_i^{\kappa_i} : \sigma_i\}^{i \in [m]}$), and the type for the top level swf term ($[x_i^{\kappa_i} : \sigma_i]^{i \in [m]}$). We model the top level swf terms like the objects. The properties in the object and the swf type have read-write capability κ, which is a subset of $\{r, w\}$. In particular, a property can be read (resp. written) if it has read (resp. write) capability r (resp. w). Types in the language are the basic types augmented with the integrity labels, $\mathcal{D}$. Each label is a set of some domains coming from $\mathbb{D}$. The interpretation of the labels is that a type with label $\mathcal{D}$ should admit only those values at run-time that *come from* one of the domains in $\mathcal{D}$.

Domain	d	$\in$	$\mathbb{D}$
Identifier	a, b, c	$\in$	$\mathbb{I}$
Capability	κ	$\subseteq$	$\{r, w\}$
Label	$\mathcal{D}$	$\subseteq$	$\mathbb{D}$
Basic Type	τ	::=	$\perp \mid \sigma_1 \to \sigma_2 \mid \{x_i^{\kappa_i} : \sigma_i\}^{i \in [m]} \mid [\![x_i^{\kappa_i} : \sigma_i]\!]^{i \in [m]}$
Type	σ	::=	$\tau_\mathcal{D}$
Term	t	::=	$\mathsf{null} \mid \mathsf{fun}\ (x : \sigma)\ t : \sigma' \mid t(t')$
			$\mid \{x_i^{\kappa_i} : \sigma_i = t_i\}^{i \in [m]} \mid t.x \mid t.x = t'$
			$\mid [\![x_i^{\kappa_i} : \sigma_i = t_i]\!]^{i \in [m]} \mid x \mid x = t$
			$\mid \mathsf{if}\ t\ \mathsf{then}\ t'\ \mathsf{else}\ t'' \mid \mathsf{ld}(a) \mid \mathsf{i\_ld}(a)$

Fig. 1. Language Syntax

Although ActionScript is a gradually typed language [4], we do not model the dynamic type here. In our previous work [5], we have designed a type inference algorithm that can be used to evolve a gradually typed program to a statically typed program. In the current setting, we assume that the programmer has already removed all the dynamic types from his code and start from a statically typed language, focusing mainly on the security aspects of the platform.

The terms in the language include (read from left to right and top to bottom in Figure 1): the base value, function definitions, function applications, object literals, property reads and writes (from both objects and top level swfs), top level swf, variables reads and writes, and null checks. There are two special variables in the language x_{parent} and x_{self}. x_{parent} is used to access the swf that loads the current swf and x_{self} is used to access the current swf. For the first swf loaded in the runtime, x_{parent} and x_{self} evaluate to the same value.

Finally, the terms $\mathsf{ld}(a)$ and $\mathsf{i\_ld}(a)$ represent the content loading and import loading, respectively, of the swf a. We note that the term $[\![x_i^{\kappa_i} : \sigma_i = t_i]\!]^{i \in [m]}$ cannot be a subterm of any swf. A swf does not contain the code for another swf, it just loads or import loads another swf at run-time.

Evaluation Semantics. The evaluation judgments are shown in Figure 2 and Figure 3. The syntax of the values is as follows:

$$\text{Value } v ::= \mathsf{null}^d \mid \ell^d \mid \mathcal{L}_d \mid \lambda_{S,d} x^\sigma.\ t^{\sigma'} \mid \mathsf{abort}$$

The d annotation in the values represents the run-time domain of the swf where the corresponding value originates. The value null^d represents the value of the base type, ℓ^d denotes a location, and $\mathcal{L}_d$ denotes the top level swf location for a swf executing in domain d.

S represents a stack: a sequence of locations. The value $\lambda_{S,d} x^\sigma.\ t^{\sigma'}$ denotes a function definition with the closure S. The type annotations σ and σ' are the static type annotations on the function parameter and the return type.

The d annotations in null^d, ℓ^d, and the σ and σ' annotations in $\lambda_{S,d} x^\sigma.\ t^{\sigma'}$ (all the superscripts in the values), are not carried and used by the actual Flash

Evaluation judgment $S \vdash_\rho^d (H, t) \Downarrow (H', v)$

(E-Null)

$$S \vdash_\rho^d (H, \mathsf{null}) \Downarrow (H, \mathsf{null}^d)$$

(E-VarR)

$$\frac{H[x]_S = v}{S \vdash_\rho^d (H, x) \Downarrow (H, v)}$$

(E-VarW)

$$\frac{S \vdash_\rho^d (H, t) \Downarrow (H', v) \qquad H'[x \mapsto v]_S = H''}{S \vdash_\rho^d (H, x = t) \Downarrow (H'', v)}$$

(E-Fun)

$$S \vdash_\rho^d (H, \mathsf{fun}\ (x : \sigma)\ t : \sigma') \Downarrow (H, \lambda_{S,d} x^\sigma.\ t^{\sigma'})$$

(E-Obj)

$$\frac{\begin{array}{c} \ell^d \text{ is fresh} \\ H_1 = H[\ell^d \mapsto [x_1^{\kappa_1,\sigma_1} \mapsto \mathsf{null}, \ldots, x_m^{\kappa_m,\sigma_m} \mapsto \mathsf{null}]] \\ \forall i \in [m].\quad S :: \ell^d \vdash_\rho^d (H_i, t_i) \Downarrow (H'_i, v_i) \quad H'_i[x_i \mapsto v_i]_{S::\ell^d} = H_{i+1} \end{array}}{S \vdash_\rho^d (H, \{x_i^{\kappa_i} : \sigma_i = t_i\}^{i \in [m]}) \Downarrow (H_{m+1}, \ell^d)}$$

(E-PropR)

$$\frac{S \vdash_\rho^d (H, t) \Downarrow (H', \ell^{d'}) \qquad v_j = H'(\ell^{d'})(x_j^{\kappa_j,\sigma_j})}{S \vdash_\rho^d (H, t.x_j) \Downarrow (H', v_j)}$$

(E-PropW)

$$\frac{\begin{array}{c} S \vdash_\rho^d (H, t) \Downarrow (H', \ell^{d'}) \\ S \vdash_\rho^d (H', t_j) \Downarrow (H_j, v_j) \qquad H'' = H_j[\ell^{d'} \mapsto H_j(\ell^{d'})[x_j^{\kappa_j,\sigma_j} \mapsto v_j]] \end{array}}{S \vdash_\rho^d (H, t.x_j = t_j) \Downarrow (H'', v_j)}$$

(E-App)

$$\frac{\begin{array}{c} S \vdash_\rho^d (H, t) \Downarrow (H', (\lambda_{S',d'} x^\sigma.\ t_2^{\sigma_2})) \qquad S \vdash_\rho^d (H', t_1) \Downarrow (H_1, v_1) \\ \ell^{d'} \text{ is fresh} \quad H'' = H_1[\ell^{d'} \mapsto [x^{\{r,w\},\sigma} \mapsto v_1]] \\ S' :: \ell^{d'} \vdash_\rho^{d'} (H'', t_2) \Downarrow (H_2, v_2) \end{array}}{S \vdash_\rho^d (H, t\ (t_1)) \Downarrow (H_2, v_2)}$$

(E-If)

$$\frac{\begin{array}{c} S \vdash_\rho^d (H, t) \Downarrow (H', v) \\ v \neq \mathsf{null} \Rightarrow i = 1 \qquad v = \mathsf{null} \Rightarrow i = 2 \qquad S \vdash_\rho^d (H', t_i) \Downarrow (H'', v') \end{array}}{S \vdash_\rho^d (H, \mathsf{if}\ t\ \mathsf{then}\ t_1\ \mathsf{else}\ t_2) \Downarrow (H'', v')}$$

Fig. 2. Evaluation Judgments

Evaluation judgment $S \vdash^d_\rho (H, t) \Downarrow (H', v)$

(E-SwfR)

$$\frac{S \vdash^d_\rho (H, t) \Downarrow (H', \mathcal{L}_{d'}) \qquad d \in \rho(d') \qquad v_j = H'(\mathcal{L}_{d'})(x_j^{\kappa_j, \sigma_j})}{S \vdash^d_\rho (H, t.x_j) \Downarrow (H', v_j)}$$

(E-SwfW)

$$\frac{d \in \rho(d') \qquad S \vdash^d_\rho (H, t) \Downarrow (H', \mathcal{L}_{d'}) \qquad S \vdash^d_\rho (H', t_j) \Downarrow (H_j, v_j) \qquad H'' = H_j[\mathcal{L}_{d'} \mapsto H_j(\mathcal{L}_{d'})[x_j^{\kappa_j, \sigma_j} \mapsto v_j]]}{S \vdash^d_\rho (H, t.x_j = t_j) \Downarrow (H'', v_j)}$$

(E-Swf)

$$\frac{\mathcal{L}_{d'} = H[x_{\mathsf{self}}]_S \qquad \mathcal{L}_d \text{ is fresh}}{\begin{array}{c} H_1 = H[\mathcal{L}_d \mapsto [x_{\mathsf{parent}} \mapsto \mathcal{L}_{d'}, x_{\mathsf{self}} \mapsto \mathcal{L}_d, x_1^{\kappa_1, \sigma_1} \mapsto \mathsf{null}, \dots, x_m^{\kappa_m, \sigma_m} \mapsto \mathsf{null}]] \\ \forall i \in [m]. \quad \mathcal{L}_d \vdash^d_\rho (H_i, t_i) \Downarrow (H'_i, v_i) \qquad H'_i[x_i \mapsto v_i]_{\mathcal{L}_d} = H_{i+1} \end{array}}{S \vdash^d_\rho (H, [\![x_i^{\kappa_i} : \sigma_i = t_i]\!]^{i \in [m]}) \Downarrow (H_{m+1}, \mathcal{L}_d)}$$

(E-Load)

$$\frac{d' \text{ is domain of } a}{\delta_{\mathsf{ld}}(a) = [\![x_i^{\kappa_i} : \sigma_i = t_i]\!]^{i \in [m]} \qquad S \vdash^{d'}_\rho (H, [\![x_i^{\kappa_i} : \sigma_i = t_i]\!]^{i \in [m]}) \Downarrow (H', \mathcal{L}_{d'})}{S \vdash^d_\rho (H, \mathsf{ld}(a)) \Downarrow (H', \mathcal{L}_{d'})}$$

(E-ImportLoad)

verify that there is an entry for d in the crossdomain policy file on a's webserver

$$\frac{\delta_{\mathsf{ld}}(a) = [\![x_i^{\kappa_i} : \sigma_i = t_i]\!]^{i \in [m]} \qquad S \vdash^d_\rho (H, [\![x_i^{\kappa_i} : \sigma_i = t_i]\!]^{i \in [m]}) \Downarrow (H', \mathcal{L}_d)}{S \vdash^d_\rho (H, \mathsf{i\_ld}(a)) \Downarrow (H', \mathcal{L}_d)}$$

Fig. 3. Evaluation Judgments - SWF Loading and Cross-Scripting

runtime semantics. We keep them around for formalization purposes. The rules in Figure 2 and Figure 3 do not depend on these.

The special value abort denotes a failed run-time access control check, terminating the Flash Player execution.

A record is a map from variables to values. As with the superscripts in the values, we carry around the capability κ and the static type annotation σ, with the variables. A heap H is a map from locations to records.

When a swf tries to query or update the heap, under a stack S, the following rules apply:

$$H[x \mapsto v]_{S::\ell^d} = \begin{cases} H[\ell^d \mapsto H(\ell^d)[x^{\kappa, \sigma} \mapsto v]] & \text{if } x^{\kappa, \sigma} \in \mathrm{dom}(H(\ell^d)) \\ H[x \mapsto v]_S & \text{otherwise} \end{cases}$$

$$H[x]_{S::\ell^d} = \begin{cases} H(\ell^d)(x^{\kappa, \sigma}) & \text{if } x^{\kappa, \sigma} \in \mathrm{dom}(H(\ell^d)) \\ H[x]_S & \text{otherwise} \end{cases}$$

We say $H[x]_S$ resolves to $x^{\kappa, \sigma}$ whenever the query operation above finds a $x^{\kappa, \sigma}$ in the scope.

We model trust assumptions by $\rho : \mathbb{D} \to 2^{\mathbb{D}}$, where $\rho(d)$ is the set of domains that d trusts. In the actual Flash API, ρ is a function of swf identifiers $\mathbb{I}$ rather than $\mathbb{D}$. However, since same domain swfs can freely script into each other, it is advisable to host swfs with different trust assumptions on different domains [1]. Also, the actual Flash API builds up the trust relationship dynamically. We, on the other hand, assume ρ to be fixed. We believe this is a reasonable assumption for security critical swfs.

The evaluation judgments are of the form $S \vdash_\rho^d (H, t) \Downarrow (H', v)$, where d is the domain under which t is evaluating.

The rules (E-VARR) and (E-VARW) use the heap query and update operations defined above. The rule (E-FUN) records the stack S and the current domain d with the function value. A function, upon application, evaluates in the context of the domain where it originates. In the rule (E-APP), the function body evaluation takes place in the context of d', even if the application term t (t') is executing in d. Thus, irrespective of whether d' trusts d or not, if a swf from domain d can get access to a function defined in d', it can execute the function on arbitrary arguments with the privileges of d'.

The rule (E-OBJ) evaluates each property in the object. In the rules (E-PROPR), and (E-PROPW), there are no access checks (just like (E-APP)). As long as a swf from domain d can get access to a location $\ell^{d'}$, it can read or write to it freely, irrespective of whether d' trusts d or not.

The rules for the swf loading and the top level swf accesses are given in Figure 3. When a swf from domain d tries to script directly into another swf from d' through the top level location $\mathcal{L}_{d'}$, the semantics of (E-SWFR) and (E-SWFW) verify that d' must trust d, i.e. $d \in \rho(d')$. If these checks do not succeed, the execution terminates and results in the value abort (we do not show the rules for abort for space limitation).

The rule (E-SWF) evaluates the top level swf term. It also sets up the variable x_{parent} for the new swf as the value of x_{self} in current stack, which is the top level swf location of the loading swf. For the rule (E-LOAD), $\delta_{\mathsf{ld}}(a)$ denotes the runtime operation of loading the swf a over the network. The loading operation results in a term of the form $\llbracket x_i^{\kappa_i} : \sigma_i = t_i \rrbracket^{i \in [m]}$. The term is then evaluated under a's own domain.

For import loading, as mentioned in Section 2, the Flash Player verifies that crossdomain policy file on a's webserver contains an entry for d. The swf a is then evaluated in the context of d.

We now revisit the examples introduced earlier to see their behavior under the runtime semantics.

Example 1. During the execution of the attacker's swf a, the victim's swf v is loaded and evaluated using the (E-LOAD) rule. The rule results in a location $\mathcal{L}_{d'}$ s.t. in the heap, the variable s_fn in $H(\mathcal{L}_{d'})$ is mapped to the sensitive function. The variable v_swf, during the evaluation of the property f in the attacker's swf, evaluates to $\mathcal{L}_{d'}$. But the read of s_fn fails in the rule (E-SWFR), because d $\notin \rho$(d'), as the victim does not trust the attacker. This way, the attack is prevented by the runtime semantics.

Example 2. In the victim's swf v, the property a_swf evaluates to a location $\mathcal{L}_d$. During the evaluation of f in the victim's swf, the access of f' in the attacker's swf succeeds, since d' $\in \rho$(d). Thus, the code in attacker's swf, g(a_acc), executes in the attacker's context, as per the rule (E-APP). The variable g evaluates to the victim's sensitive function which then executes in the victim's context with the attacker provided argument a_acc. Thus, the runtime semantics fails to prevent this attack.

Example 3. As with Example 2, the victim's (and the attacker's) swf executes successfully in this case too.

Cross Site Scripting. Since the semantics does not reason about data integrity, it fails to prevent the Cross Site Scripting attacks also.

4.1   Formal Definition of Data Integrity

We first define an origin function on the values as follows:

Definition 1 (Value Origin). *The* origin *function for the values is defined as:* $\text{origin}(\text{null}^d) = d$, $\text{origin}(\ell^d) = d$, $\text{origin}(\mathcal{L}_d) = d$, $\text{origin}(\lambda_{S,d}x^\sigma. t^{\sigma'}) = d$

We define a location as trusted if for all the variables in the location, the contained value has an origin consistent with the static type of the variable.

Definition 2 (Trusted Location and Trusted Heap). *A location ℓ^d in heap H is trusted if $\forall x^{\kappa,\sigma} \in dom(H(\ell^d))$, whenever $H(\ell^d)(x^{\kappa,\sigma}) = v$, we have* $\text{origin}(v) \in \mathcal{D}$ *s.t.* $\sigma = \tau_\mathcal{D}$ *for some τ. A heap H is trusted, written as $H\checkmark$, if $\forall \ell^d \in dom(H)$, ℓ^d is trusted.*

The data integrity property is now defined as:

Definition 3 (Data Integrity for a Code Execution). *Let $S \vdash_\rho^d (H,t) \Downarrow (H',v)$ be an execution. Suppose $H\checkmark$. Then, either $v = $ abort or $H'\checkmark$.*

In Example 2 above, since s_fn is expected to be called with a trusted argument, its parameter type has the integrity label {d'}. However, at run time, the value a_acc which has label {d}, since it originates in the attacker's swf, is able to flow into the s_fun parameter. Thus, the data integrity property is violated.

5   Type System

In this section we present a type system that, in conjunction with the Flash run-time checks, enforces the data integrity property.

We first define a static consistency relation, $\preceq$, over the basic types τ, and the types σ. As with the usual subtyping relation, the interpretation of $\sigma_1 \preceq \sigma_2$ is that it is safe for a term of type σ_1 to flow to a context that expects a term of type σ_2. The static consistency relation verifies that the types obey the *comes from* invariants at each level, by checking that the sub-parts in the types also satisfy the relation.

The judgments for $\preceq$ are shown in Figure 4. The rule (S-TYPE) checks that $\tau_1 \preceq \tau_2$ and $\mathcal{D}_1 \subseteq \mathcal{D}_2$. The label check ensures that if the context expects a value originating in one of the domains from $\mathcal{D}_2$, then σ_1 should satisfy this invariant. The rules (S-FUN) and (S-OBJ) are standard, and (S-OBJ) also admits the usual record subtyping. As a minor technical convenience, we do not allow record depth subtyping in the rule (S-SWF).

Type Checking. The typing judgments are shown in Figure 4. These judgments are of the form $\Gamma \vdash_{\rho}^{d} t :: \sigma$, where d is the expected run-time domain of the swf. The type environment Γ has two components: (Γ_s, Γ_v). Γ_s contains the type assumptions about the parent swf that would load the current swf at run-time, and about the swfs that the current swf might load itself. Γ_v contains the standard type bindings for the free variables in t.

The rule (C-NULL) assigns the type $\perp_{\{d\}}$ to the value null, which denotes that this base value *comes from* the domain d. Similarly the rules (C-FUN) and (C-OBJ) assign the integrity label $\{d\}$ to the final type. The rules (C-PARENT), (C-LOAD), and (C-IMPORTLOAD) look up the top level swf type from Γ_s. (C-IMPORTLOAD) also ensures the swf a comes from a trusted domain.

The rules for objects and functions are standard and use the static consistency relation, $\preceq$, in place of the subtyping relation. The rules (E-SWFR) and (E-SWFW) additionally verify that the swf access is allowed per the trust assumptions, i.e. $d \in \rho(d')$, where d is the current domain and d' is the domain of the swf being accessed. The rule (C-SWF) type checks the top level swf term.

The rules (C-SWFR') and (C-SWFW') are interesting. As a first step towards strengthening the attacker capabilities, we allow the attacker to evade the trust assumptions, ρ, when type checking its own code. If the attacker's code tries to script into a swf, which does not trust the attacker's domain, we do not raise a type error. Since the Flash Player runtime already has dynamic access control checks, we can allow for these relaxed static rules. We define a lowering operation on the types that changes all the labels in a type to $\mathbb{D}$, unless it's a top level swf type.

Definition 4 (Lowering Type). *The lowering operation, $\sigma \downarrow$, is defined as:*

$$- \perp_{\mathcal{D}} \downarrow \; = \perp_{\mathbb{D}}, \; (\sigma_1 \rightarrow \sigma_2)_{\mathcal{D}} \downarrow \; = (\sigma_1 \downarrow \rightarrow \sigma_2 \downarrow)_{\mathbb{D}}$$
$$- \{x_i^{\kappa_i} : \sigma_i\}_{\mathcal{D}}^{i \in [m]} \downarrow \; = \{x_i^{\kappa_i} : \sigma_i \downarrow\}_{\mathbb{D}}^{i \in [m]}, \; [\![x_i^{\kappa_i} : \sigma_i]\!]_{\{d\}}^{i \in [m]} \downarrow \; = [\![x_i^{\kappa_i} : \sigma_i]\!]_{\{d\}}^{i \in [m]}$$

We use this lowering operation in the rules (C-SWFR') and (C-SWFW') to assign the final type as $\sigma_j \downarrow$, where x_j is the property that the attacker's code accesses. This choice gives the attacker maximum flexibility in type checking its code.

Note that a top level swf type remains unchanged across lowering. It can be easily seen that this does not reduce the attacker's capability.

Static Consistency $\tau_1 \preceq \tau_2 \qquad \sigma_1 \preceq \sigma_2$

(S-TYPE)
$$\frac{\sigma_1 = (\tau_1)_{\mathcal{D}_1} \quad \sigma_2 = (\tau_2)_{\mathcal{D}_2} \quad \tau_1 \preceq \tau_2 \quad \mathcal{D}_1 \subseteq \mathcal{D}_2}{\sigma_1 \preceq \sigma_2}$$

(S-BASE)
$$\bot \preceq \bot$$

(S-SWF)
$$\frac{n \leq m}{[\![x_i^{\kappa_i} : \sigma_i]\!]_{\{d\}}^{i \in [m]} \preceq [\![x_i^{\kappa_i} : \sigma_i]\!]_{\{d\}}^{i \in [n]}}$$

(S-FUN)
$$\frac{\sigma_3 \preceq \sigma_1 \quad \sigma_2 \preceq \sigma_4}{\sigma_1 \to \sigma_2 \preceq \sigma_3 \to \sigma_4}$$

(S-OBJ)
$$\frac{n \leq m \quad \forall i \in [n]. \quad \kappa_i' \subseteq \kappa_i \quad \sigma_i \preceq \sigma_i' \text{ when } r \in \kappa_i' \quad \sigma_i' \preceq \sigma_i \text{ when } w \in \kappa_i'}{\{x_i^{\kappa_i} : \sigma_i\}^{i \in [m]} \preceq \{x_i^{\kappa_i'} : \sigma_i'\}^{i \in [n]}}$$

Typing Judgment $\Gamma \vdash_\rho^d t :: \sigma$

(C-NULL)
$$\Gamma \vdash_\rho^d \text{null} :: \bot_{\{d\}}$$

(C-PARENT)
$$\Gamma \vdash_\rho^d x_{\text{parent}} :: \Gamma_s(x_{\text{parent}})$$

(C-VARR)
$$\Gamma \vdash_\rho^d x :: \Gamma_v(x)$$

(C-LOAD)
$$\Gamma \vdash_\rho^d \text{ld}(a) :: \Gamma_s(a)$$

(C-VARW)
$$\frac{\Gamma_v(x) = \sigma \quad \Gamma \vdash_\rho^d t :: \sigma' \quad \sigma' \preceq \sigma}{\Gamma \vdash_\rho^d x = t :: \sigma}$$

(C-FUN)
$$\frac{\Gamma[x \mapsto \sigma_1] \vdash_\rho^d t_2 :: \sigma_2' \quad \sigma_2' \preceq \sigma_2}{\Gamma \vdash_\rho^d \text{fun } (x{:}\sigma_1) \; t_2 {:} \sigma_2 :: (\sigma_1 \to \sigma_2)_{\{d\}}}$$

(C-IMPORTLOAD)
$$\frac{d' \text{ is } a\text{'s domain} \quad d' \in \rho(d)}{\Gamma \vdash_\rho^d \text{i\_ld}(a) :: \Gamma_s(a)}$$

(C-OBJ)
$$\frac{\Gamma' = \Gamma[x_1 \mapsto \sigma_1, \ldots, x_m \mapsto \sigma_m] \quad \forall i \in [m]. \quad \Gamma' \vdash_\rho^d t_i :: \sigma_i' \quad \sigma_i' \preceq \sigma_i}{\Gamma \vdash_\rho^d \{x_i^{\kappa_i} : \sigma_i = t_i\}^{i \in [m]} :: \{x_i^{\kappa_i} : \sigma_i\}_{\{d\}}^{i \in [m]}}$$

(C-PROPR)
$$\frac{\Gamma \vdash_\rho^d t :: \{x_i^{\kappa_i} : \sigma_i\}_{\mathcal{D}}^{i \in [m]} \quad j \in [m] \quad r \in \kappa_j}{\Gamma \vdash_\rho^d t.x_j :: \sigma_j}$$

(C-PROPW)
$$\frac{\Gamma \vdash_\rho^d t :: \{x_i^{\kappa_i} : \sigma_i\}_{\mathcal{D}}^{i \in [m]} \quad j \in [m] \quad w \in \kappa_j \quad \Gamma \vdash_\rho^d t_j :: \sigma_j' \quad \sigma_j' \preceq \sigma_j}{\Gamma \vdash_\rho^d t.x_j = t_j :: \sigma_j}$$

(C-APP)
$$\frac{\Gamma \vdash_\rho^d t :: (\sigma_1 \to \sigma_2)_{\mathcal{D}} \quad \Gamma \vdash_\rho^d t_1 :: \sigma_1' \quad \sigma_1' \preceq \sigma_1}{\Gamma \vdash_\rho^d t \, (t_1) :: \sigma_2}$$

(C-IF)
$$\frac{\Gamma \vdash_\rho^d t :: \sigma \quad \Gamma \vdash_\rho^d t_1 :: (\tau)_{\mathcal{D}_1} \quad \Gamma \vdash_\rho^d t_2 :: (\tau)_{\mathcal{D}_2}}{\Gamma \vdash_\rho^d \text{if } t \text{ then } t_1 \text{ else } t_2 :: (\tau)_{\mathcal{D}_1 \cup \mathcal{D}_2}}$$

(C-SWFR)
$$\frac{\Gamma \vdash_\rho^d t :: [\![x_i^{\kappa_i} : \sigma_i]\!]_{\{d'\}}^{i \in [m]} \quad d \in \rho(d') \quad j \in [m] \quad r \in \kappa_j}{\Gamma \vdash_\rho^d t.x_j :: \sigma_j}$$

(C-SWFW)
$$\frac{\Gamma \vdash_\rho^d t :: [\![x_i^{\kappa_i} : \sigma_i]\!]_{\{d'\}}^{i \in [m]} \quad d \in \rho(d') \quad j \in [m] \quad w \in \kappa_j \quad \Gamma \vdash_\rho^d t_j :: \sigma_j' \quad \sigma_j' \preceq \sigma_j}{\Gamma \vdash_\rho^d t.x_j = t_j :: \sigma_j}$$

(C-SWFR')
$$\frac{\Gamma \vdash_\rho^d t :: [\![x_i^{\kappa_i} : \sigma_i]\!]_{\{d'\}}^{i \in [m]} \quad d \notin \rho(d') \quad j \in [m] \quad r \in \kappa_j}{\Gamma \vdash_\rho^d t.x_j :: \sigma_j \downarrow}$$

(C-SWFW')
$$\frac{\Gamma \vdash_\rho^d t :: [\![x_i^{\kappa_i} : \sigma_i]\!]_{\{d'\}}^{i \in [m]} \quad d \notin \rho(d') \quad j \in [m] \quad w \in \kappa_j \quad \Gamma \vdash_\rho^d t_j :: \sigma_j' \quad \sigma_j' \preceq \sigma_j \downarrow}{\Gamma \vdash_\rho^d t.x_j = t_j :: \sigma_j \downarrow}$$

(C-SWF)
$$\frac{\Gamma' = \Gamma[x_1 \mapsto \sigma_1, \ldots, x_m \mapsto \sigma_m] \quad \forall i \in [m]. \quad \Gamma' \vdash_\rho^d t_i :: \sigma_i' \quad \sigma_i' \preceq \sigma_i}{\Gamma \vdash_\rho^d [\![x_i^{\kappa_i} : \sigma_i = t_i]\!]^{i \in [m]} :: [\![x_i^{\kappa_i} : \sigma_i]\!]_{\{d\}}^{i \in [m]}}$$

Fig. 4. Type Checking Rules

Value Typing $\vdash_H v :: \sigma$

(V-Null)	(V-Loc) $x_i^{\kappa_i,\sigma_i} \in \text{dom}(H(\ell^d))$	(V-Fun) $\sigma_1 = (\sigma \rightarrow \sigma')_{\{d\}}$	(V-SwfLoc) $x_i^{\kappa_i,\sigma_i} \in \text{dom}(H(\mathcal{L}_d))$
$\vdash_H \text{null}^d :: \bot_{\{d\}}$	$\vdash_H \ell^d :: \{x_i^{\kappa_i} : \sigma_i\}^i_{\{d\}}$	$\vdash_H \lambda_{S,d}x^\sigma.\ t^{\sigma'} :: \sigma_1$	$\vdash_H \mathcal{L}_d :: [\![x_i^{\kappa_i} : \sigma_i]\!]^i_{\{d\}}$

Fig. 5. Value Typing

5.1   Soundness

We now describe the soundness properties of our type system. We first define the typing for values, written as $\vdash_H v :: \sigma$. The judgments for this relation are shown in Figure 5. We also define consistency of the type environment with the runtime environment as follows:

Definition 5 (Consistency of Type Environment with Loading Function). Γ_s *is said to be consistent with the swf loading function* δ_{ld}, $\Gamma_s \sim \delta_{\text{ld}}$, *if whenever* $\delta_{\text{ld}}(a) = [\![x_i^{\kappa_i} : \sigma_i = t_i]\!]^{i\in[m]}$ *and a is loaded under domain d, then* $(\Gamma_s, \phi) \vdash_\rho^d [\![x_i^{\kappa_i} : \sigma_i = t_i]\!]^{i\in[m]} :: [\![x_i^{\kappa_i} : \sigma_i]\!]^{i\in[m]}_{\{d\}}$ *and* $[\![x_i^{\kappa_i} : \sigma_i]\!]^{i\in[m]}_{\{d\}} \preceq \Gamma_s(a)$.

Definition 6 (Consistency of Type Environment with Stack and Heap). $\Gamma \sim_{\rho,H} S$ *if whenever* $\Gamma_v(x) = \sigma$ *and* $H[x]_S$ *resolves to* $x^{\kappa,\sigma'}$, *we have* $\sigma' \preceq \sigma$. *Also, if* $H[x_{\text{parent}}]_S = \mathcal{L}_d$, $\vdash_H \mathcal{L}_d :: \sigma''$, *then* $\sigma'' \preceq \Gamma_s(x_{\text{parent}})$.

Our type system supports a stronger notion of trusted locations that subsumes Definition 2.

Definition 7 (Stronger Definition of Trusted Location). *In a heap H, a location* ℓ^d *is trusted if* $\forall x^{\kappa,\sigma} \in \text{dom}(H(\ell^d))$, *if* $v = H(\ell^d)(x^{\kappa,\sigma})$ *then* $\vdash_H v :: \sigma'$ *s.t.* $\sigma' \preceq \sigma$.

The definitions of trusted heap and data integrity under code execution remain same except for the use of the new definition of trusted locations.

Our main soundness theorem says that for an execution of a well-typed term, starting from a trusted heap, either the execution results in an error or in a new heap that is also trusted. Moreover, the type of the value is statically consistent with the type of the term.

Theorem 1 (Soundness of Type System). *If* $\Gamma \vdash_\rho^d t :: \sigma$, $S \vdash_\rho^d (H,t) \Downarrow (H',v)$, $\Gamma_s \sim \delta_{\text{ld}}$, $\Gamma \sim_{\rho,H} S$, *and* $H\sqrt{}$, *then either* $v = \text{abort}$ *or* $\vdash_{H'} v :: \sigma'$ *s.t.* $\sigma' \preceq \sigma$ *and* $H'\sqrt{}$.

A More Powerful Attacker. The interesting property of our type system is that it allows an attacker to by-pass the integrity labels type checking completely. We place only two restrictions on the attacker's code: (a) it must be *structurally* *well-typed*, and (b) it must use the other top level swf types correctly. The restriction (b) does not limit the attacker's capability since it can always type check the other swfs' properties accesses via (C-SwfR') and (C-SwfW').

When type checking its own swf, the victim must make the worst possible assumptions about the type labels in such an attacker's code. In particular, it must assume that all the values that come from such an attacker's swf could have originated anywhere, and therefore it must use the integrity label $\mathbb{D}$ in the type assumptions about the attacker's code. However, it need not change the labels inside the top level swf types used in the attacker's swf. We define $\Gamma_s \downarrow$ as:
$\Gamma_s \downarrow (a) = \Gamma_s(a)$ if a is a victim's swf, or $[\![x_i^{\kappa_i} : \sigma_i \downarrow]\!]_{\{d\}}^{i \in [m]}$ if a is an attacker's swf
s.t. $\Gamma_s(a) = [\![x_i^{\kappa_i} : \sigma_i]\!]_{\{d\}}^{i \in [m]}$. The victim should use $\Gamma_s \downarrow$ to type check its code.

However, the type soundness theorem requires the Γ_s to be consistent with the loading function. We prove that if an attacker's swf follows the above restrictions (a) and (b) *only*, then it can be labeled to be well-typed under $\Gamma_s \downarrow$.

Let us define a typing judgment $\Gamma \vdash_\rho^{\prime d} t :: \sigma$ which is same as Figure 4, except that the rule (S-Type) does not perform the $\mathcal{D}_1 \subseteq \mathcal{D}_2$ check. Note that, however, the rule (S-Swf) still forces the attacker to use the top level swf types consistently. We define $t \downarrow$ and $\Gamma_v \downarrow$ as the obvious extensions of $\sigma \downarrow$. Then:

Theorem 2 (Attacker SWF Typing). *Let $t = [\![x_i^{\kappa_i} : \sigma_i = t_i]\!]^{i \in [m]}$ be an attacker swf code s.t. $(\Gamma_s \downarrow, \phi) \vdash_\rho^{\prime d} t :: [\![x_i^{\kappa_i} : \sigma_i]\!]_{\{d\}}^{i \in [m]}$. Then, $(\Gamma_s \downarrow, \phi) \vdash_\rho^d [\![x_i^{\kappa_i} : \sigma_i \downarrow = t_i \downarrow]\!]^{i \in [m]} :: [\![x_i^{\kappa_i} : \sigma_i \downarrow]\!]_{\{d\}}^{i \in [m]}$.*

This theorem is a direct corollary of the following lemma:

Lemma 1 (Attacker Term Typing). *Let t be a subterm in the attacker's code s.t. $(\Gamma_s \downarrow, \Gamma_v) \vdash_\rho^{\prime d} t :: \sigma$. Then, $(\Gamma_s \downarrow, \Gamma_v \downarrow) \vdash_\rho^d t \downarrow :: \sigma'$ s.t. $\sigma' \preceq \sigma \downarrow$.*

So now, $\Gamma_s \downarrow$ is consistent with δ_{ld} for the victim's swfs as well as for any attacker's swf that is structurally well-typed but is not subjected to the static integrity labels checking. Hence $\Gamma_s \downarrow \sim \delta_{\mathsf{ld}}$. The type soundness theorem now ensures that the data integrity property is maintained at run time for the swfs typed under $\Gamma_s \downarrow$. Thus, the victim can enforce data integrity all by itself.

We now see how the type system works for our running examples.

Example 2. When type checking its code, the victim would use the following type for the attacker's swf:

$\Gamma(\mathtt{a}) = \{\mathtt{f'} : ((\mathtt{int}_\mathbb{D} \rightarrow \mathtt{int}_\mathbb{D})_\mathbb{D} \rightarrow \mathtt{int}_\mathbb{D})_\mathbb{D}\}_{\{d\}}$

The sensitive function has the type:

$\mathtt{s\_fn} : (\mathtt{int}_{\{d'\}} \rightarrow \mathtt{int}_{\{d'\}})_{\{d'\}}$

As expected, the victim's code fails to type check under these assumptions. For the function call $\mathtt{a\_swf.f'(s\_fn)}$, the type checker checks that the type of $\mathtt{s\_fn}$ is statically consistent with the argument type of $\mathtt{a\_swf.f'}$, which fails as shown in the following derivation:

$$\frac{\text{int} \preceq \text{int} \quad \boxed{\mathbb{D} \subseteq \{d'\}}}{\frac{\text{int}_{\mathbb{D}} \preceq \text{int}_{\{d'\}} \qquad \text{int}_{\{d'\}} \preceq \text{int}_{\mathbb{D}}}{\frac{\text{int}_{\{d'\}} \to \text{int}_{\{d'\}} \preceq \text{int}_{\mathbb{D}} \to \text{int}_{\mathbb{D}} \qquad \{d'\} \subseteq \mathbb{D}}{(\text{int}_{\{d'\}} \to \text{int}_{\{d'\}})_{\{d'\}} \preceq (\text{int}_{\mathbb{D}} \to \text{int}_{\mathbb{D}})_{\mathbb{D}}}}}$$

Since $\mathbb{D} \not\subseteq \{d'\}$, the typing derivation fails, and thus, the data integrity violation is prevented at compile time at the victim's end.

Example 3. In this case the non-sensitive function has the type:

   ns_fn : $(\text{int}_{\mathbb{D}} \to \text{int}_{\mathbb{D}})_{\{d'\}}$

and we can now see that the victim's code will successfully typecheck.

Cross Site Scripting. Our type system can also prevent Cross Site Scripting attacks. FlashVars can be annotated with the integrity label $\mathbb{D}$ and the parameter of the URL navigation function can be assigned the label $\{d'\}$, where d' is the victim's domain. Once this is done, the type checker ensures that the FlashVars cannot be passed as arguments to the URL navigation function.

6   Related Work

Flash Security Model. Unlike JavaScript's binary trust model, where it's either no trust or full trust between the principals, Flash allows controlled communication among otherwise isolated clients. The existing model when combined with our type system, provides stronger data integrity guarantees to the programmers. Thus, it could be worthwhile to explore Flash as the platform for client mashups investigated in [6].

Flash Security Analysis. DeVries et. al. [7] developed an inline reference monitoring system for enforcing security policies in malicious ActionScript code. They first inject runtime security guards in untrusted swf bytecode and then verify that it obeys the desired security policies.

   However, they do not present a formal study of the Flash security model, as we do here. Moreover, their problem statement is fundamentally different from ours. They seek to sanitize untrusted swfs according to certain security policies whereas the goal of our type system is to help the victim ensure that its code maintains data integrity invariants, even in the presence of untrusted swfs.

   Jang et. al. [8] study the server based aspect of Flash security – the crossdomain policy files. They present an empirical study of crossdomain policy files for Alexa top 50,000 websites. In this paper, we have mainly focused on the client side aspect of Flash security.

Security Type Systems. A characteristic feature of our system is the combination of static and dynamic checks to enforce data integrity. In that sense, our system is similar to hybrid type checking [9]. Chaudhuri et. al. [10] present a similar type system, that in conjunction with the dynamic checks, enforces data integrity in Windows Vista.

Our type system maintains *comes from* invariants, where the static type of a term is an over-approximation of the origin of the run-time value that the term evaluates to. There is a long history of security type systems that guarantee various properties for well-typed programs ([11–13]). Sabelfeld et. al. [14] present a detailed survey of language based information flow security.

7 Conclusion

In this paper, we have presented the first formal model of the security features in the Flash platform. We find that in its current form, the model is vulnerable to attacks violating data integrity property in victim's programs when they execute alongside untrusted programs. We presented a static type system, that in conjunction with existing runtime checks, prevents such attacks. We stated the soundness theorem of our type system and proved that a well-typed program maintains its data integrity invariants, even when co-executing with untrusted programs.

References

1. Adobe: Creating more secure SWF web applications,
   http://www.adobe.com/devnet/flashplayer/articles/secure_swf_apps.html
2. OWASP: Example Vulnerabilities, https://www.owasp.org/index.php/Category:
   OWASP_Flash_Security_Project#Example_Vulnerabilities
3. Adobe: Adobe Flash Platform, http://www.adobe.com/flashplatform/
4. Siek, J.G., Taha, W.: Gradual Typing for Functional Languages. In: Scheme and Functional Programming Workshop (2006)
5. Rastogi, A., Chaudhuri, A., Hosmer, B.: The ins and outs of gradual type inference. In: POPL. ACM (2012)
6. Howell, J., Jackson, C., Wang, H.J., Fan, X.: Mashupos: operating system abstractions for client mashups. In: HotOS. USENIX Association (2007)
7. DeVries, B.W., Gupta, G., Hamlen, K.W., Moore, S., Sridhar, M.: Actionscript bytecode verification with co-logic programming. In: PLAS. ACM (2009)
8. Jang, D., Venkataraman, A., Sawka, G.M., Shacham, H.: Analyzing the cross-domain policies of flash applications. In: W2SP (2011)
9. Flanagan, C.: Hybrid Type Checking. In: POPL, pp. 245–256. ACM (2006)
10. Chaudhuri, A., Naldurg, P., Rajamani, S.K.: A type system for data-flow integrity on windows vista. In: PLAS. ACM (2008)
11. Heintze, N., Riecke, J.G.: The slam calculus: programming with secrecy and integrity. In: POPL. ACM (1998)
12. Myers, A.C.: Jflow: practical mostly-static information flow control. In: POPL. ACM (1999)
13. Banerjee, A., Naumann, D.A.: Secure information flow and pointer confinement in a java-like language. In: CSF. IEEE Computer Society (2002)
14. Sabelfeld, A., Myers, A.C.: Language-based information-flow security. IEEE Journal on Selected Areas in Communications (2003)

Linear Approximation of Continuous Systems with Trapezoid Step Functions

Giulia Costantini[1], Pietro Ferrara[2], and Agostino Cortesi[1]

[1] University Ca' Foscari of Venice, Italy
{costantini,cortesi}@dsi.unive.it
[2] ETH Zurich, Switzerland
pietro.ferrara@inf.ethz.ch

Abstract. We introduce a novel abstract domain for the safe approximation of continuous functions in the context of abstract interpretation-based static analysis. The key-idea is to represent $\mathcal{C}_+^2$ functions by a finite sequence of trapezoids. In this way, we get a strictly more precise approximation of the actual values with respect to existing approaches in the literature. Experimental results underline the effectiveness of the approach in terms of both precision and efficiency.

1 Introduction

Embedded software is composed by discrete (that is, the program) and continuous (that is, the physical environment) components. The program receives inputs from the physical environment through sensors that are usually modelled by volatile variables. The reliability of these systems is crucial: a single bug can produce catastrophic effects, and this is a relevant challenge for formal verification methods. On the one hand, there is a large literature on the static analysis of discrete programs. On the other hand, these approaches do not perform well when they are applied to continuous environments. For instance, in the context of the abstract interpretation framework [11,12], the Interval domain [11] abstracts continuous systems with the minimal and maximal values a sensor can return at any time. To refine this approach, Bouissou and Martel [5] proposed the Interval Valued Step Functions (IVSF) domain, for approximating the behavior of a function in a given interval of time (i.e, a step) with the minimal and maximal values the function could achieve during that period of time.

In this paper, we go one step further by introducing the Trapezoid Step Functions (TSF) domain. TSF abstracts the values of a function in a given slot of time with two linear functions, tracking linear relationships between the time and the output value. The two linear functions, together with the two vertical lines that delimit the time slot, form a trapezoid. We approximate the function with a finite number of trapezoids, one for each step.

Consider, for instance, Figure 1. It compares the 4-steps abstraction of $f = \sin(x)$ by TSF (on the left) and by IVSF (on the right) in the interval $[0, 2\pi]$. On the one hand, these plots make clear that TSF better approximates the

R. Jhala and A. Igarashi (Eds.): APLAS 2012, LNCS 7705, pp. 98–114, 2012.

shape of the function. On the other hand, IVSF gives more precise bounds on the maximum and minimum values assumed by the function. Therefore, TSF could be used in combination with IVSF to improve the precision of the overall analysis, and in particular to precisely bound the minimal and maximal values of the function. For instance, we could combine TSF and IVSF in a Cartesian product [11]. In the example of Figure 1, this combination discovers that, when $x = \frac{\pi}{2}$, the abstracted function has exactly value 1, since (i) TSF tracks that its minimal value is 1, and (ii) IVSF tracks that its maximal value is 1.

The main contributions of this paper are (i) the formal definition of TSF and its lattice operators, (ii) the introduction of a sound abstraction function that, given a continuous and derivable function, builds up its abstraction in TSF, and (iii) the discussion of some experimental results and the comparison with the ones obtained by IVSF.

The paper is structured as follows. The rest of this Section introduces a motivating example and recalls some basic concepts of abstract interpretation. Sections 2 and 3 formalize the domain and the abstraction function. In Section 4 we present some experimental results when applying TSF to the abstraction of different functions, and show how our results compare with IVSF. Section 5 discusses the related work and Section 6 concludes.

1.1   Motivating Example

Our motivating example regards a special case of hybrid system, where we have a discrete system (an embedded program) which takes a continuous environment as input.

Consider the program in Figure 2. This is the code of an integrator, a quite common component of embedded programs. It has been inspired by [15], and it is the example used in [5] in order to show the main features of IVSF. This code integrates a function (whose values are provided through the volatile variable x) using the rectangle method on a sampling step h. We assume that the function we integrate is $\sin(2\pi t)$, and that the input data are given by a sensor

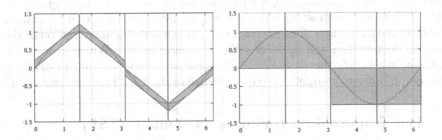

Fig. 1. TSF (left) and IVSF (right) abstractions of $\sin(x)$, with 4 steps, on the domain $[0, 2\pi]$

```
1 volatile  float  x;
2 static  float  intgrx=0.0, h=1.0/8;
3 void main() {
4         while( true ) { // assume frequency = 8 KHz
5                 float  xi=x;
6                 intgrx+=xi*h;
7         }
8 }
```

Fig. 2. Simple integrator

(hence the `volatile` variable x) at a frequency of 8KHz. This scenario is particularly interesting for the analysis of numerical precision, since the sensor will produce the sequence of values $[0, \frac{\sqrt{2}}{2}, 1, \frac{\sqrt{2}}{2}, 0, -\frac{\sqrt{2}}{2}, -1, -\frac{\sqrt{2}}{2}]$ on x. Therefore, in a perfect arithmetic computation the summation of these values multiplied by h will be equal to zero after $8 \times i$ iterations $\forall i \in \mathbb{N}$. Nevertheless, in a real system this summation would produce some approximate values because of floating point approximation. This code is particularly interesting to test the precision of abstract domains since it propagates the approximation error of our abstract domain at each iteration of the `while` loop, and therefore it is a good candidate to test the precision of TSF.

1.2   Abstract Interpretation

Abstract interpretation is a framework to define and prove the soundness of approximations. The concrete domain formalizes the information we want to approximate, while the abstract domain specifies which approximated information we track. Usually, concrete states are composed by sets of elements (e.g., all the possible computational states), that are approximated by a unique element (also referred to as an *abstract state*) in the abstract domain. Formally, the concrete domain $\wp(D)$ forms a complete lattice $\langle \wp(D), \subseteq, \emptyset, D, \cup, \cap \rangle$. Similarly, the abstract domain $\overline{A}$ has to form a complete lattice $\langle \overline{A}, \leq_{\overline{A}}, \perp_{\overline{A}}, \top_{\overline{A}}, \sqcup_{\overline{A}}, \sqcap_{\overline{A}} \rangle$ as well. The concrete and abstract domains are related by a concretization $\gamma_{\overline{A}}$ and an abstraction $\alpha_{\overline{A}}$ functions. The abstract domain is a sound approximation of the concrete domain if $\gamma_{\overline{A}}$ and $\alpha_{\overline{A}}$ form a Galois connection [11]. When abstract domains do not satisfy the ascending chain condition, a widening operator $\nabla_{\overline{A}}$ is required in order to guarantee the convergence of the fixed point computation.

2   The Trapezoid Step Functions Domain (TSF)

In this Section, we first present the concrete domain. Then, we introduce TSF, with the partial order and the least upper bound operator, to show its lattice structure. Finally, we introduce a widening operator that is crucial to ensure the convergence of the analysis on this domain. In this way, we provide a complete definition of an abstract domain that can be used not only to abstract single functions (as we did in the experimental results), but also to abstract set of functions (e.g., to take into account some rounding approximations).

2.1 Concrete Domain

The concrete domain is defined as the powerset of continuous functions in $\mathbb{R}^+ \to \mathbb{R}$ which have two continuous derivatives (i.e., the set $\mathcal{C}_+^2$). We focus our attention to a scenario in which the input variable represents the time, so the functions domain is $\mathbb{R}^+$ instead of $\mathbb{R}$.

2.2 Abstract Domain Elements

Let us first formalize the key-idea behind our domain. Given a function f and a set of ordered indices $\{t_i\}_{0 \leq i \leq N}$, we approximate the values of f in a step $[t_i, t_{i+1}]$ by a trapezoid whose (i) two parallel sides are vertical, in correspondence of t_i and t_{i+1}, and (ii) the two other sides are in the form $f^-(t) = m^- t + q^-$ and $f^+(t) = m^+ t + q^+$ and approximate lower and upper values of f inside $[t_i, t_{i+1}]$. Figure 3 depicts a trapezoid defined on the step $[0, 3]$ and having $f^-(t) = 0.33t + 1$ and $f^+(t) = -0.17t + 3.5$ as, respectively, lower and upper sides.

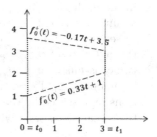

Fig. 3. Example of a trapezoid defined on $[0, 3]$

Formally, given a step $[t_i, t_{i+1}]$, a single trapezoid is defined by two linear functions, and each of these two functions is defined by two real numbers (representing the slope and the intercept). Therefore, the pair of sides of each trapezoid is defined by a tuple $\mathbf{v} = (m^-, q^-, m^+, q^+)$, where $m^-, q^-, m^+, q^+ \in \mathbb{R}$ represent the two lines $f^-(t) = m^- t + q^-$ and $f^+(t) = m^+ t + q^+$. We denote by f^- and f^+ the lower and the upper side, respectively. TSF can be seen as a generalization of IVSF, whose lower and upper sides are parallel and horizontal, i.e., with $m^- = m^+ = 0$.

Following the standard notation [5], given a set V of values, we represent a step function from time to V as a conjunction of constraints of the form "$t_i : \mathbf{v_i}$" such that $t_i \in \mathbb{R}^+ \wedge \mathbf{v_i} \in V$. This means that the step function switches to $\mathbf{v_i}$ at time t_i. The sequence of constraints can be finite or infinite but we only consider finite ones, otherwise the abstract operations of our domain would not be computable. A finite sequence of constraints $f = t_0 : \mathbf{v_0} \wedge t_1 : \mathbf{v_1} \wedge \cdots \wedge t_N : \mathbf{v_N}$ represents the step function f such that $\forall t \in \mathbb{R}^+ : f(t) = \mathbf{v_i}$ with $i = \max(\{j \in [0, N] : t_j \leq t\})$. We use the compact notation $f = \bigwedge_{0 \leq i \leq N} t_i : \mathbf{v_i}$, with $N \in \mathbb{N} \wedge t_i \in \mathbb{R}^+ \wedge \mathbf{v_i} \in V \,\forall i$. V is the set of tuples $\{(m^-, q^-, m^+, q^+) : m^-, q^-, m^+, q^+ \in \mathbb{R}\}$. We will alternatively denote the value in a step as $\mathbf{v_i} = (m_i^-, q_i^-, m_i^+, q_i^+)$ or $\mathbf{v_i} = (f_i^-, f_i^+)$ where $f_i^-(t) = m_i^- t + q_i^-$ and $f_i^+(t) = m_i^+ t + q_i^+$.

Normal Form and Equivalence Relation: This notation is not unique. For example, the conjunctions $(0 : [0,0,1,1])$ ∧ $(4 : [0,0,1,1])$ and $(0 : [0,0,1,1])$ ∧ $(7 : [0,0,1,1])$ define the same step function which, for every input $t \in [0,+\infty)$, returns as output value the interval $[0, t+1]$. For this reason, we use the same notion of normal form defined in [5]: the switching times t_i of a conjunction are sorted and different; moreover two consecutive constraints cannot have equal values (each $\mathbf{v_i}$ must be different from $\mathbf{v_{i+1}}$). With these conditions, the representation is unique. We will denote by *Norm* the normalization procedure. In our previous example, we would obtain a representation with a single constraint $0 : [0,0,1,1]$. The normalization process induces an equivalence relation $(f \equiv g \Leftrightarrow Norm(f) = Norm(g))$.

Constraints: We impose two constraints on abstract elements:

1. inside each step $[t_i, t_{i+1}]$, the two lines f_i^- and f_i^+ do not intersect. This assumption is not restrictive: we can always split the invalid step with intersecting sides into two smaller and valid steps with non-intersecting sides through the *refine* operator that will be defined in Section 2.5;
2. two consecutive steps $[t_i, t_{i+1}]$ and $[t_{i+1}, t_{i+2}]$ must have at least one point in common at t_{i+1}. This constraint is needed because otherwise the concrete functions represented by the abstract element would not be continuous. Observe that an abstract state which violates this constraint is equivalent to bottom.

Formally, these constraints can be stated as follows:

$$\forall i \in [0, N] : f_i^-(t_i) \leq f_i^+(t_i) \land f_i^-(t_{i+1}) \leq f_i^+(t_{i+1}) \tag{1}$$

$$\forall i \in [0, N-1] : [f_i^-(t_{i+1}), f_i^+(t_{i+1})] \cap [f_{i+1}^-(t_{i+1}), f_{i+1}^+(t_{i+1})] \neq \emptyset \tag{2}$$

Note that we do not require that the intervals of two consecutive steps are exactly the same at the border between them (i.e., neither the upper nor the lower sides have to link exactly the upper or the lower sides of the following step). We want our approach to be generic and for this reason we give as much freedom as we can to the abstract element definition.

The elements of our abstract domain, denoted by $D^\sharp$, are normalized finite conjunctions of constraints $f = \bigwedge_{0 \leq i \leq N} t_i : \mathbf{v_i}$ (with $N \in \mathbb{N} \land t_i \in \mathbb{R}^+ \land \mathbf{v_i} \in V \; \forall i$) which satisfy the equations (1) and (2).

2.3   Concretization Function

The abstract step function $f = \bigwedge_{0 \leq i \leq N} \{t_i : \mathbf{v_i}\}$, where $\mathbf{v_i} = (f_i^-, f_i^+) = (m_i^-, q_i^-, m_i^+, q_i^+)$, represents the set of continuous, differentiable functions that are bounded by the lines $f_i^-(t) = m_i^- t + q_i^-$ and $f_i^+(t) = m_i^+ t + q_i^+$ for any time $t \in [t_i, t_{i+1}]$. The concretization function γ is thus defined by:

$$\gamma(\bigwedge_{0 \leq i \leq N} \{t_i : \mathbf{v_i}\}) = \{g \in \mathcal{C}_+^2 | \forall i \in [0, N], \forall t \in [t_i, t_{i+1}], g(t) \in [f_i^-(t), f_i^+(t)]\}$$

where t_{N+1} is either $+\infty$ if $dom(f) = \mathbb{R}^+$, or k if $dom(f) = [0, k]$, with k constant.

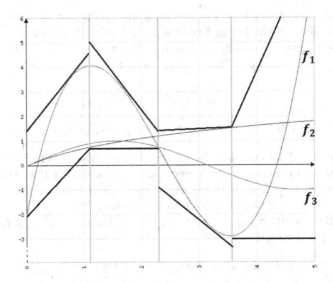

Fig. 4. Concretization function

Figure 4 depicts an example of an abstract state defined on the domain $[0, 5]$ with 4 steps (note that here $t_{N+1} = 5$). In the Figure we can see three possible concrete functions ($f_1 = x^3 - 7x^2 + 12x - 2$, $f_2 = ln(x + 1)$ and $f_3 = sin(x)$) that are all approximated by such abstract state.

2.4 Partial Order

The partial order $\subseteq^\sharp$ on two functions $f, g \in D^\sharp$ is defined point-wisely, that is, for all possible inputs t we check that the set of values assumed by f in that point is a subset of the set of values assumed by g at the same point. Formally, $f \subseteq^\sharp g \Leftrightarrow \forall t \in \mathbb{R}_+ : f(t) \subseteq g(t)$, where $f(t) = \{v : f_i^-(t) \leq v \leq f_i^+(t) \wedge t \in [t_i, t_{i+1}]\}$ and the same holds for $g(t)$.

To define the partial order on step functions, we first define a partial order on single steps. Let $\mathbf{v_i} = (f_i^-, f_i^+)$ and $\mathbf{w_j} = (g_j^-, g_j^+)$ be the values of two steps on the same domain $[a, b]$. Then:

$$\mathbf{v_i} \sqsubseteq_{[a,b]} \mathbf{w_j} \Leftrightarrow \forall t \in [a, b] : f_i^-(t) \geq g_j^-(t) \wedge f_i^+(t) \leq g_j^+(t)$$
$$\Leftrightarrow \forall t \in [a, b] : [f_i^-(t), f_i^+(t)] \subseteq [g_j^-(t), g_j^+(t)]$$
$$\Leftrightarrow [f_i^-(a), f_i^+(a)] \subseteq [g_j^-(a), g_j^+(a)] \wedge [f_i^-(b), f_i^+(b)] \subseteq [g_j^-(b), g_j^+(b)]$$

In other words, $\mathbf{v_i}$ is smaller than $\mathbf{w_j}$ if the area of the trapezoid identified by $\mathbf{v_i}$ (in the domain $[a, b]$) is contained in the area of the trapezoid identified by $\mathbf{w_j}$ (in $[a, b]$ as well). We have to compare only the upper and lower sides of the trapezoids. To do this, we check that $f_i^- \geq g_j^- \wedge f_i^+ \leq g_j^+$ for all inputs $t \in [a, b]$.

Since the sides are defined by straight lines, it is sufficient to check only the values of such lines at the left and right extremes of the trapezoid.

Now we can give a computable condition for testing whether $f \subseteq^\sharp g$. Let $f = \bigwedge_{0 \leq i \leq N}\{t_i : \mathbf{v_i}\}$ and $g = \bigwedge_{0 \leq j \leq M}\{u_j : \mathbf{w_j}\}$, then:

$$f \subseteq^\sharp g$$
$$\Updownarrow \qquad\qquad\qquad (3)$$
$$\forall(i,j) \in [0,N] \times [0,M] : [a,b] = [t_i, t_{i+1}] \cap [u_j, u_{j+1}] \neq \emptyset \Rightarrow \mathbf{v_i} \sqsubseteq_{[a,b]} \mathbf{w_j}$$

Observe that in (3) we compare the values of pairs of steps which have a part of their domain in common. If each step value of f is smaller than the value of every intersected step of g (with respect to their intersection on the domain), then $f \subseteq^\sharp g$. To check if two steps have an intersection ($[t_i, t_{i+1}] \cap [u_j, u_{j+1}] \neq \emptyset$), we can use the condition ($u_j \leq t_{i+1} \wedge u_{j+1} \geq t_i$). Moreover, if $u_j \leq t_i$ we have $[a,b] = [t_i, u_{j+1}]$ else $[a,b] = [u_j, t_{i+1}]$.

Lemma 1. *If $f, g \in D^\sharp$ are normalized, then $f \subseteq^\sharp g \Leftrightarrow \forall t \in \mathbb{R}_+, f(t) \subseteq g(t)$.*

The top element of the domain is defined by $T^\sharp = 0 : [0, -\infty, 0, \infty]$ (that is, the step function with only one step with value $\mathbb{R}$), while $\bot^\sharp$ is a special element such that $\gamma(\bot^\sharp) = \emptyset \wedge \forall f \in D^\sharp, \bot^\sharp \subseteq^\sharp f$. $D^\sharp \cup \{\bot^\sharp\}$ is a lattice.

2.5   *Refine* Operator

We define a *refine* operator, which, given an abstract state of TSF and a set of indices, adds these indices to the step list of the state, thus augmenting its number of steps. This operation has no impact on the concretization of the abstract state, since the values $\mathbf{v_i}$ are not modified. This operator will be useful to make two abstract states directly comparable, by making them defined on the same set of steps.

Consider an abstract state $f = \bigwedge_{0 \leq i \leq N}\{t_i : \mathbf{v_i}\}$ where $T = \{t_i : 0 \leq i \leq N\}$ and a set of indices $U = \{u_j : 0 \leq j \leq M\}$. Let $S = \{s_k : s_k \in (T \cup U) \wedge s_k < s_{k+1} \forall k \in [0, P]\}$ be the set of all the indices contained in T and U, ordered and without repetitions (therefore $P = N + M - |T \cap U|$). The *refine* operator on this state is defined by $Refine(f, U) = \bigwedge_{0 \leq k \leq P}\{s_k : \widehat{\mathbf{v_k}}\}$ where $\widehat{\mathbf{v_k}} = \mathbf{v}_{\max\{i : t_i \leq s_k\}}$.

2.6   *Compact* Operator

The opposite operator with respect to *refine* is *compact*. This operator reduces the number of steps contained in an abstract state, and it will be useful in order to keep such number below a given threshold. The *compact* function works by merging a pair of steps, and repeating this procedure until a given threshold is reached. While *refine* leaves the precision of an abstract state unchanged, the *compact* operator induces some loss of precision.

Let $f = \bigwedge_{0 \leq i \leq N}\{t_i : \mathbf{v_i}\}$ be an abstract state, composed by $N + 1$ steps, and let M be a given threshold, with $M < (N + 1)$. The algorithm: (i) chooses the step with the minimum width ($w_i = t_{i+1} - t_i$), (ii) merges it with the successive one, and (iii) repeats (i) and (ii) iteratively until the threshold M is reached. We arbitrarily choose the step to be merged as the one with smallest width, but alternative solutions are possible and can be supported by our approach as well.

Let A_i and B_i be the two extremes (the left and right one, respectively) of f_i^+ in $[t_i, t_{i+1}]$, and let A_{i+1} and B_{i+1} be the two extremes of f_{i+1}^+ in $[t_{i+1}, t_{i+2}]$. Then, the upper side f'^+ of the merged step will have the slope of the side linking A_i and B_{i+1}. If the point $P = \max(B_i, A_{i+1})$ is greater than such side, the intercept will be such that the side covers exactly P, otherwise we keep the original intercept of the side linking A_i and B_{i+1}. Figure 5 depicts this situation. The same applies symmetrically for the lower side. A slightly different process is required if the selected step is next to the last one (that is, $i = N - 1$), since in such case we cannot rely on t_{i+2}. For the upper side, we consider f_N^+ and we simply increase its intercept if one of the extremes of f_{N-1}^+ in $[t_{N-1}, t_N]$ is higher than such side. The same procedure applies for the lower side.

Note that this is not the only possible way to merge two steps. For example, in Figure 5, it could have been chosen the line passing through P and parallel to f_{i+1}^+ or others as well, but our method is the one which we found (empirically) to work best in most cases (i.e., it does not introduce too much approximation).

In addition, we can specify a list of steps which we do not want to remove from the state. Let T be the set of steps of the abstract state f, and let $X \subseteq T$ be the set of steps of f that have to be preserved. Then, $g = Compact_X(f, M)$ is an abstract state obtained by compacting f to M steps, while discarding only steps coming from $T \setminus X$.

Lemma 2. *Let $f \in D^\sharp$ and $M \in \mathbb{N}^+$. If $g = Compact(f, M)$, then $f \sqsubseteq^\sharp g$.*

2.7   Least Upper Bound

Given two elements x and y of the abstract domain, the least upper bound operator $\sqcup^\sharp$ defines the least element z that overapproximates both x and y. In TSF, this means that we have to create a sequence of trapezoids that are as narrow as possible and that, at the same time, contain the two given sequences of trapezoids.

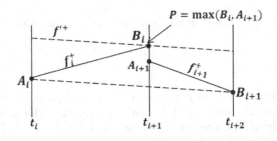

Fig. 5. Merging of two steps within the *compact* operation

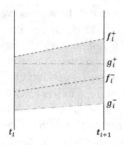 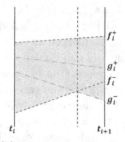 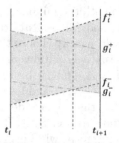

(a) No intersections, the step remains unsplit. The grey area represents the resulting trapezoid

(b) One intersection between f_i^- and g_i^-, resulting in two sub-steps and, thus, two trapezoids (colored in grey)

(c) Two intersections, one between f_i^-, g_i^- and one between f_i^+, g_i^+, resulting in three sub-steps and, thus, three trapezoids (colored in grey)

Fig. 6. Examples of the LUB computation

Let $f' = \bigwedge_{0 \le k \le N} \{x_k : \mathbf{v_k}\}$ and $g' = \bigwedge_{0 \le j \le M} \{u_j : \mathbf{w_j}\}$ be two abstract states. In order to define the least upper bound of f' and g', we use the following algorithm. First, we refine f' and g' on the same set of steps, obtaining $f = Refine(f', U)$ and $g = Refine(g', X)$, where X and U are the steps sets of f' and g', respectively. Then, for each step t_i of f and g, we look at the two trapezoids and check if there are intersections either between the two lower sides (f_i^-, g_i^-) or between the two upper sides (f_i^+, g_i^+). We split the step with respect to such intersections. In each of these new steps, we are sure that nor the upper sides nor the lower sides of f, g intersect each other. So, the resulting trapezoid for each new step is made by the greatest of the two upper sides and the lowest of the two lower sides. See Figure 6 for some representative examples.

Lemma 3. $\sqcup^\sharp$ *is the least upper bound operator.*

Lemma 4. *Let f and g be two TSF elements that satisfy the validity conditions stated in Section 2.2. Then, $f \sqcup^\sharp g$ satisfies the same conditions too.*

Similarly, we can also define the greatest lower bound operator.

2.8 Widening

The widening operator $\nabla_{D^\sharp}$ is parameterized on (i) k_S, the maximum number of steps allowed in an abstract state, (ii) k_M and k_Q, the maximum values allowed for the slope and intercept of trapezoid sides, respectively, (iii) k_I and k_L, the increment constants for the slope and intercept, respectively. All these parameters have to be ≥ 0. $\nabla_{D^\sharp}$ is then defined as follows.

$$f\nabla_{D^\sharp}g = \begin{cases} \top^\sharp & \text{if } |U| > k_S \\ f & \text{if } g \subseteq^\sharp f \\ Norm(Compact_U(h_{MQ}, k_S)) & \text{otherwise} \end{cases}$$

where U is the set of steps of the abstract state f.

We distinguish three cases: a) $|U| > k_S$; b) $g \subseteq^\sharp f$; c) otherwise. In case a), f exceeds the maximum number of steps allowed in an abstract state, k_S, and we return $\top^\sharp$. In case b), we do not have an ascending chain and we simply return f, which is already normalized, being an element of $D^\sharp$. In case c), we return the normalized and compacted version of h_{MQ}, keeping all the steps U of f. In this way, we are sure that U will be a subset of the steps set of $f\nabla_{D^\sharp}g$ and this is important for proving the convergence of $\nabla_{D^\sharp}$. The abstract state h_{MQ} is built as follows. Let g be defined on the indices set V. Let $f' = Refine(f, V)$ be the refined version of f with the addition of the indices of g and let $g' = Refine(g, U)$ be the refined version of g with the addition of the indices of f. Then f' and g' are defined on the same set of steps $T = U \cup V$. Calling t_i the elements of T, we have: $f' = \bigwedge_{0 \leq i \leq N}\{t_i : \mathbf{v_i} = (f_i^-, f_i^+)\}$ and $g' = \bigwedge_{0 \leq i \leq N}\{t_i : \mathbf{w_i} = (g_i^-, g_i^+)\}$. We define $h_{MQ} = \bigwedge_{0 \leq i \leq N}\{t_i : \mathbf{z_i} = (h_i^-, h_i^+)\}$ where (h_i^-, h_i^+) are as follows:

$$h_i^-(t) = \begin{cases} g_i^-(t) & \text{if } f_i^- = g_i^- \\ -\infty & \text{if } (m_{g_i^-} \leq -k_M) \vee (q_{g_i^-} \leq -k_Q) \\ & \quad \vee (m_{f_i^-} \leq -k_M) \vee (q_{f_i^-} \leq -k_Q) \\ (g_i^-)^\bullet(t) & \text{otherwise} \end{cases}$$

$$h_i^+(t) = \begin{cases} g_i^+(t) & \text{if } f_i^+ = g_i^+ \\ +\infty & \text{if } (m_{g_i^+} \geq k_M) \vee (q_{g_i^+} \geq k_Q) \vee (m_{f_i^+} \geq k_M) \vee (q_{f_i^+} \geq k_Q) \\ (g_i^+)^\circ(t) & \text{otherwise} \end{cases}$$

and

$$(g_i^-)^\bullet(t) = (m_{MIN_i^-} - k_I) \times t + (q_{MIN_i^-} - k_L)$$
$$(g_i^+)^\circ(t) = (m_{MAX_i^+} + k_I) \times t + (q_{MAX_i^+} + k_L)$$
$$m_{MIN_i^-} = \min(m_{f_i^-}, m_{g_i^-}), \quad q_{MIN_i^-} = \min(q_{f_i^-}, q_{g_i^-})$$
$$m_{MAX_i^+} = \max(m_{f_i^+}, m_{g_i^+}), \quad q_{MAX_i^+} = \max(q_{f_i^+}, q_{g_i^+})$$

The computation is symmetric for the lower and the upper side, so let us focus on $h_i^+(t)$. For each step t_i of f' and g' we consider three distinct cases: 1) $f_i^+ = g_i^+$, 2) $(m_{g_i^+} \geq k_M) \vee (q_{g_i^+} \geq k_Q) \vee (m_{f_i^+} \geq k_M) \vee (q_{f_i^+} \geq k_Q)$, 3) otherwise. In case 1) the side is the same in f' and g', so we keep it unchanged. In case 2) the slope (or the intercept) of the side of one abstract state (g' or f') exceeds the threshold k_M (or k_Q), so we move the side to $+\infty$. Otherwise (in case 3), we keep the maximum slope and intercept between their values in f_i^+ and g_i^+ and then we increase them both by a predefined constant quantity (k_I for the slope, k_L for the intercept). This last case is needed to ensure the convergence of the operator. For the soundness of this operator we refer to the definition in [10].

3   Abstraction of a Continuous Function

In this Section we show how to compute the approximation of $\mathcal{C}_+^2$ functions, both in IVSF and in TSF. We consider both domains, as in [5] the abstraction function was not defined, since the authors relied on a particular type of ODE solver [4]. For TSF, we also consider two different approaches: when the step width is constant and fixed, and when we automatically determine the steps distribution. For IVSF, we consider only the case where the step list is fixed. Note that we abstract only one concrete function; this approach can be generalized to the abstraction of a discrete (or countable) set of concrete functions C by computing the abstraction of each function in the set and then returning the least upper bound of all the resulting abstract states.

In the following subsections, we will denote by (i) $f \in \mathcal{C}_+^2$ the continuous function we want to abstract, (ii) f' and f'' its first and second derivatives, respectively, (iii) F'_0 the set containing the points of the domain where $f'(t) = 0$ (stationary points), that is $F'_0 = \{t : f'(t) = 0\}$ (iv) F''_0 the same for f'' (inflection points), (v) $F'^{[a,b]}_0 = \{f(t) : t \in ([a,b] \cap F'_0)\}$, that is, $F'^{[a,b]}_0$ is the set containing the stationary points of f restricted to the domain interval $[a,b]$, (vi) $F''^{[a,b]}_0$ the same as $F'^{[a,b]}_0$ but for the inflection points.

Note that the IVSF abstraction function needs to know only the first derivative of f (other than, obviously, f itself), while TSF requires also the second derivative.

3.1   IVSF Abstraction Function, Fixed Step Width

Given a step width w, suppose that $[a,b]$ is a generic interval ($b - a = w \wedge a = k \times w \wedge b = (k+1) \times w \wedge k, w \geq 0$). $M = \max(\{f(a), f(b)\} \cup F'^{[a,b]}_0)$ is the maximum point of the function in the interval $[a,b]$, extremes included, and $m = \min(\{f(a), f(b)\} \cup F'^{[a,b]}_0)$ is the minimum point of the function in the interval $[a,b]$, extremes included. The best abstraction in IVSF of this step is the interval $[m, M]$. To build the abstraction of the function f, we repeat this procedure for each step of the abstract state.

3.2   TSF Basic Abstraction Function, Arbitrary Step Width

In TSF we can get a better representation by choosing a step distribution using (i) the inflection points F''_0, and (ii) the stationary points F'_0. Assume that $[a,b]$ is a generic interval obtained using this schema. Then, the two sides which compose the value of such step are as follows (see Figure 7):

1. the side l_1 linking the points $P = (a, f(a))$ and $Q = (b, f(b))$;
2. the side l_2 which has the same slope as l_1 and is tangent to f inside $[a,b]$. Since we already know the slope of this side, we just need to compute its intercept. The procedure to do this is the following one:

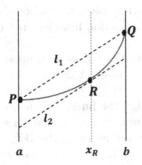

Fig. 7. The abstraction on the step $[a, b]$

(a) find the point $x_R \in [a, b]$ where the first derivative of f is equal to the slope of l_1: $f'(x_R) = m_{l_1}$. This point can be computed by bisection in $[a, b]$.

(b) let $R = (x_R, f(x_R))$. Then, l_2 is the side that goes through the point R and with slope equal to m_{l_1}, i.e., the slope of l_1.

Note that the resulting sides l_1 and l_2 are parallel, as they have the same slope. Moreover, l_2 is a tangent of the function f.

3.3   TSF Basic Abstraction Function, Fixed Step Width

Of course, also in the case of TSF we can define the abstraction on a fixed step width. Suppose that $[a, b]$ is a generic interval determined by the fixed width w. First of all, we split the interval in sub-intervals, following the schema introduced in Section 3.2. Then, for each sub-interval, we compute the upper and lower sides as specified in Section 3.2. Finally, we have to merge together these sub-intervals through the *compact* operator defined in Section 2.6. Notice that we lose some precision with this method, but we could achieve better results by adopting a more complex schema.

3.4   Dealing with Floating Point Precision Issues

Unfortunately, the abstraction technique presented in Section 3.2 is theoretically sound but it is not computable on a finite precision machine, due to the well-known problems concerning floating point representation. The abstraction function depends on various values: the points x at which $f'(x) = 0$, the points x at which $f''(x) = 0$, the point $x_r \in [a, b]$ such that $f'(x_R) = m_{l_1}$. Even knowing exactly all the points in F'_0 and F''_0 by mathematical analysis, we could not be able to precisely represent them in a machine (e.g., $\sqrt{2}$). Therefore, we can only compute an approximation of such points and not their exact value. In this Section, we introduce some restrictions on the functions we can manipulate and a refinement of the basic abstraction function. In this way, we enforce the soundness of the resulting abstraction function, not only theoretically but in a practical setting as well.

We assume that f respects the following property. If x_0 is a stationary or inflection point, then, for each interval $[\overline{x}, \overline{x} + \epsilon]$ such that $x_0 \in [\overline{x}, \overline{x} + \epsilon]$, we have: $\forall x \in [\overline{x}, \overline{x} + \epsilon] : f(x) \in [f(\overline{x}) - \tau, f(\overline{x}) + \tau]$ where τ, ϵ are parameters of the analysis. Intuitively, we ask that the function values change at most of τ around stationary and inflection points. Note that the value of ϵ can be set based on the standard in use on the machine (e.g., the IEEE 754 standard for floating points), while τ has to be set by the user: the smaller the value, the more precise the abstraction.

As in Section 3.2, we split the domain in steps with respect to the stationary and inflection points. If we cannot pinpoint those points exactly, we introduce an additional step of width ϵ in correspondence of them. The exact location of the step ($[t_i, t_{i+1}] = [\overline{x}, \overline{x} + \epsilon]$) depends on the numerical representation of the machine and it obviously must contain the exact value of the considered stationary or inflection point. The value of such additional step is $\mathbf{v_i} = (0, f(\overline{x}) - \tau, 0, f(\overline{x}) + \tau)$. For the condition imposed above, we are sure that this trapezoid (which is a rectangle, since the two sides are horizontal) soundly contains the abstracted function in the considered step.

For the steps which do not contain stationary/inflection points, the computational schema of Section 3.2 is refined as follows. The side l_1 (the one which links the extremes of f in the step) is moved up (or down, depending on the concavity of f in the step) of ϵ. This compensates for potential errors in the evaluation of the function values at the extremes. The other side l_2 goes through the point $x_R{'}$ such that $f'(x_R{'})$ is the closest value to m_{l_1} that we can reach (given the precision of the machine). The slope of l_2 is $f'(x_R{'})$ so that l_2 is tangent to the function. Since we know that the function is concave (or convex) in the sub-interval considered, we are sure that a tangent of it leaves the function always above (or below), resulting in a safe approximation.

4   Experimental Results

We present some experimental results about the use of TSF, and we compare them with the ones obtained by IVSF. First of all, we explore how the precision varies with the number of steps of the representation when analyzing some representative functions. Then, we consider a standard example of embedded software (introduced in Section 1.1) as a test-bench.

4.1   Varying the Number of Steps

Let us first compare the precision of TSF and IVSF. We apply the abstraction function to a set of representative functions (namely, $\sin(x)$, x^3, e^x, and

Table 1. Precision of TSF and IVSF varying the number of steps

#s	sin(x)			x^3			e^x			ln(x + 1)		
	TSF	IVSF	Ratio	TSF	IVSF	Ratio	TSF	IVSF	Ratio	TSF	IVSF	Ratio
4	4.14	15.10	27.4%	235.04	2500.00	9.4%	15894.07	55063.66	28.9%	0.63	5.99	10.5%
8	1.15	7.99	14.4%	58.64	1250.00	4.7%	4211.62	27531.83	15.3%	0.17	3.00	5.7%
16	0.30	4.01	7.6%	14.65	625.00	2.3%	1069.68	13765.92	7.8%	0.04	1.50	2.9%
32	0.08	2.04	3.7%	3.66	312.50	1.2%	268.50	6882.96	3.9%	0.01	0.75	1.5%
64	0.02	1.02	1.8%	0.92	156.25	0.6%	67.19	3441.48	2.0%	2.77E-03	0.37	0.7%
128	4.70E-03	0.51	0.9%	0.23	78.13	0.3%	16.80	1720.74	1.0%	6.93E-04	0.19	0.4%

$\ln(x + 1)^1$) in the interval $[0, 10]$ varying the number of steps. We measure the precision of a representation by computing the area covered by the abstract states in the Cartesian plan: the bigger the area, the rougher the abstraction. We implemented the computation of TSF in Java and we ran it on an Intel Core 2 Quad CPU 2.83 GHz with 4 GB of RAM, running Windows 7, and the Java SE Runtime Environment 1.6.0_16-b01. The execution is always extremely fast: in the worst case (function e^x), TSF requires 40 msec to compute the approximation and the area of the function for *all* the different numbers of steps. This result is not particularly surprising since the computation mainly performs arithmetic operators for whom modern processors are quite efficient. Since the execution times are very short, we could not notice any significant difference between TSF and IVSF even if we would expect that IVSF is faster. In addition, we did not notice any relevant memory consumption by the computation since it does not need to allocate memory. Table 1 reports the results of this computation. The first column reports the number of steps. Then, for each analyzed function, we report the area of the TSF and IVSF abstractions, and the ratio between the two areas. For instance, if the ratio is 50%, it means that the TSF area is half the IVSF one (i.e., twice more precise). In all cases, TSF is more precise than IVSF. In the worst case, TSF is almost 3.5 times more precise (ratio $\approx 28.9\%$). In the best case, it is approximately 330 times more precise (ratio $\approx 0.3\%$). IVSF uses rectangles to approximate portions of the curve, so its precision is greater when the curve is "flat" (i.e., similar to a horizontal line), while it is lower when the slope of the curve is high. So the amount of precision depends more on the kind of function than on the steps width. The precision of TSF, instead, does not depend on the curve slope, since the trapezoids are able to well approximate various kinds of slope. The precision of TSF depends only on how much the curve differs from a straight line *within a single step*. If in a single step the curve is similar to a straight line, then the error is near to zero; if in a single step the curve is very concave or convex, then there is a lack of precision. When increasing the number of steps in a given domain, each step has a smaller width: for this reason, the bigger the number of steps, the more the function resembles to a straight line in each single step (instead that a convex or concave curve) and the more the TSF precision increases.

---

[1] Note that, since $\ln(x)$ is not continuous in $x = 0$, we apply it to $x + 1$ in order to have a continuous function in $[0, 10]$.

Table 2. Values computed by TSF and IVSF on `intgrx`

Num. steps	TSF	IVSF	Ratio (%)
4	[-1.0263, 1.7367]	[-4.8750, 4.8750]	28
8	[-0.2772, 0.3778]	[-0.4760, 0.4760]	69
16	[-0.0740, 0.0870]	[-0.1237, 0.1237]	65
32	[-0.0188, 0.0204]	[-0.0312, 0.0312]	63
64	[-0.0047, 0.0049]	[-0.0078, 0.0078]	62
128	[-0.0012, 0.0012]	[-0.0020, 0.0020]	61

4.2   An Integrator

Consider the motivating example presented in Section 1.1. Table 2 reports the intervals of the values of `intgrx` computed by TSF and IVSF after 104 iterations of the `while` loop. The smaller the interval, the more precise the analysis. The last column reports the ratio between the widths of the two intervals. TSF obtains more precise results in all the cases. Note that augmenting the numbers of steps in the abstraction improves the precision of both domains, and the error ratio of TSF vs. IVSF stabilizes around 60% even if it is slightly better when augmenting the number of steps.

4.3   Combination of TSF with IVSF

We have seen that the TSF domain is able to approximate more closely the shape of the abstracted function than IVSF. Moreover, we noticed that our abstraction gets more and more precise (with respect to IVSF) every time we increase the number of steps in the representation. On the other hand, IVSF has the advantage to preserve the minimum and maximum values assumed by the function, while, unfortunately, TSF does not preserve such information, since the trapezoids vertices might exceed these values. Then, it could be useful in some applications, especially the ones where the stationary points of the function are relevant (e.g., $sin(x)$), to consider the product of these two domains, by using the Cartesian or the reduced product of the two [11]. For instance, in the analysis of the integrator code presented in Section 1.1 we can *precisely* abstract the values of $sin(x)$ when it is at its maximum (or minimum) by taking the intersection of the values approximated by TSF (that computes that the values are greater or equal to 1 in the maximum, and less or equal than -1 in the minimum) and IVSF (that computes that the values are less or equal to 1 in the maximum, and greater or equal than -1 in the minimum).

5   Related Work

To the best of our knowledge, IVSF is the first formalism that allows the integration of the continuous environment in an abstract interpretation of embedded software. The static analyzer HybridFluctuat, based on IVSF, has been implemented [3] in order to consider the interactions between the program and the physical environments on which it acts. In Section 4 we compared extensively the precision of our approach with respect to IVSF.

A useful domain theoretical characterization of continuous function can be found in [13], but this work only describes the continuous functions at the concrete level, and there is nothing involving the abstract interpretation theory.

Feret [14] introduced domain-specific abstract domains for digital filters, in the context of ASTREE [2], but did not provide a generic treatment of continuous functions and their abstraction.

As for hybrid systems, previous work in the context of abstract interpretation is mainly related to the analysis of hybrid automata [16,18].

Regarding continuity analysis of programs, Hamlet [17] was the first one to argue for a testing methodology for Lipschitz-continuity of software. Chaudhuri et al. recently proposed a qualitative program analysis to automatically determine if a program implements a continuous function [6]. Their practical motivation is the verification of robustness properties of programs whose inputs are uncertain. This work was further extended [7] to quantify the robustness of a program. Our treatment of continuous functions should be applicable to this particular setting (continuity of programs) as well.

A Trapezoid Step Function is a sequence of trapezoids, one for each step. But a TSF element can be seen as a pair of piecewise linear (PWL) functions as well, where one PWL function bounds the approximated continuous functions from above and the other one bounds them from below. There exists an extensive literature about PWL functions, since they played an important role in approximation, regression and classification. One of the biggest problems concerns their explicit representation in a closed form [9,20]. Another important issue is to find a PWL approximation of a certain function in order to minimize or bound the overall area (or the distance in each point) between the original function and the approximation [8,19,21]. Our approach, rather than bounding the error of the representation of a function, provides a *sound* approximation of it.

6   Conclusion and Future Work

Given the encouraging experimental results, we are planning to apply TSF to other case studies. First of all, we want to apply TSF to the approximation of the solutions of Ordinary Differential Equations (as done by IVSF). Then, we aim at exploring the use of TSF to approximate the values produced by a program, e.g., a simulator of the results given by sensors in embedded systems. In addition, we plan to develop some semantic operators over TSF necessary for cost analysis [1]. Also, it could be interesting to do a formal complexity analysis on the domain operations.

Acknowledgments. Work partially supported by RAS project "TESLA - Tecniche di enforcement per la sicurezza dei linguaggi e delle applicazioni".

References

1. Albert, E., Arenas, P., Genaim, S., Puebla, G., Zanardini, D.: Cost Analysis of Java Bytecode. In: De Nicola, R. (ed.) ESOP 2007. LNCS, vol. 4421, pp. 157–172. Springer, Heidelberg (2007)
2. Blanchet, B., Cousot, P., Cousot, R., Feret, J., Mauborgne, L., Miné, A., Monniaux, D., Rival, X.: A static analyzer for large safety-critical software. In: Proceedings of PLDI 2003. ACM (2003)
3. Bouissou, O., Goubault, E., Putot, S., Tekkal, K., Vedrine, F.: HybridFluctuat: A Static Analyzer of Numerical Programs within a Continuous Environment. In: Bouajjani, A., Maler, O. (eds.) CAV 2009. LNCS, vol. 5643, pp. 620–626. Springer, Heidelberg (2009)
4. Bouissou, O., Martel, M.: GRKLib: a guaranteed runge-kutta library. In: Proceedings of SCAN 2007. IEEE Press (2007)
5. Bouissou, O., Martel, M.: Abstract Interpretation of the Physical Inputs of Embedded Programs. In: Logozzo, F., Peled, D.A., Zuck, L.D. (eds.) VMCAI 2008. LNCS, vol. 4905, pp. 37–51. Springer, Heidelberg (2008)
6. Chaudhuri, S., Gulwani, S., Lublinerman, R.: Continuity analysis of programs. In: Proceedings of POPL 2010. ACM (2010)
7. Chaudhuri, S., Gulwani, S., Lublinerman, R., NavidPour, S.: Proving programs robust. In: Proceedings of FSE 2011. ACM (2011)
8. Chou, F., Wang, C.M., Cheng, G.D.: Optimal bounding of curves by continuous piecewise linear functions. Engineering Optimization 21(4), 307–317 (1993)
9. Chua, L., Kang, S.M.: Section-wise piecewise-linear functions: Canonical representation, properties, and applications. Proceedings of the IEEE 65(6), 915–929 (1977)
10. Cortesi, A.: Widening operators for abstract interpretation. In: Proceedings of SEFM 2008. IEEE Press (2008)
11. Cousot, P., Cousot, R.: Abstract interpretation: a unified lattice model for static analysis of programs by construction or approximation of fixpoints. In: Proceedings of POPL 1977. ACM (1977)
12. Cousot, P., Cousot, R.: Systematic design of program analysis frameworks. In: Proceedings of POPL 1979. ACM (1979)
13. Edalat, A., Lieutier, A.: Domain theory and differential calculus (functions of one variable). Mathematical Structures in Comp. Sci. 14(6) (2004)
14. Feret, J.: Static Analysis of Digital Filters. In: Schmidt, D. (ed.) ESOP 2004. LNCS, vol. 2986, pp. 33–48. Springer, Heidelberg (2004)
15. Goubault, E., Martel, M., Putot, S.: Some future challenges in the validation of control systems. In: Proceedings of ERTS 2006 (2006)
16. Halbwachs, N., Proy, Y.-E., Raymond, P.: Verification of Linear Hybrid Systems by Means of Convex Approximations. In: LeCharlier, B. (ed.) SAS 1994. LNCS, vol. 864, pp. 223–237. Springer, Heidelberg (1994)
17. Hamlet, D.: Continuity in software systems. In: Proceedings of ISSTA 2002. ACM (2002)
18. Henzinger, T.A., Ho, P.-H.: A Note on Abstract Interpretation Strategies for Hybrid Automata. In: Antsaklis, P.J., Kohn, W., Nerode, A., Sastry, S.S. (eds.) HS 1994. LNCS, vol. 999, pp. 252–264. Springer, Heidelberg (1995)
19. Imai, H., Iri, M.: An optimal algorithm for approximating a piecewise linear function. Journal of Information Processing 9(3), 159–162 (1987)
20. Kahlert, C., Chua, L.: A generalized canonical piecewise-linear representation. IEEE Transactions on Circuits and Systems 37(3), 373–383 (1990)
21. Tomek, I.: Two algorithms for piecewise-linear continuous approximation of functions of one variable. IEEE Trans. Comput. 23(4), 445–448 (1974)

Signedness-Agnostic Program Analysis: Precise Integer Bounds for Low-Level Code

Jorge A. Navas, Peter Schachte, Harald Søndergaard, and Peter J. Stuckey

Department of Computing and Information Systems,
The University of Melbourne, Victoria 3010, Australia

Abstract. Many compilers target common back-ends, thereby avoiding the need to implement the same analyses for many different source languages. This has led to interest in static analysis of LLVM code. In LLVM (and similar languages) most signedness information associated with variables has been compiled away. Current analyses of LLVM code tend to assume that either all values are signed or all are unsigned (except where the code specifies the signedness). We show how program analysis can simultaneously consider each bit-string to be both signed and unsigned, thus improving precision, and we implement the idea for the specific case of integer bounds analysis. Experimental evaluation shows that this provides higher precision at little extra cost. Our approach turns out to be beneficial even when all signedness information is available, such as when analysing C or Java code.

1 Introduction

The "Low Level Virtual Machine" LLVM is rapidly gaining popularity as a target for compilers for a range of programming languages. As a result, the literature on static analysis of LLVM code is growing (for example, see [2,7,9,11,12]). LLVM IR (Intermediate Representation) carefully specifies the bit-width of all integer values, but in most cases does not specify whether values are signed or unsigned. This is because, for most operations, two's complement arithmetic (treating the inputs as signed numbers) produces the same bit-vectors as unsigned arithmetic. Only for operations that must behave differently for signed and unsigned numbers, such as comparison operations, does LLVM code indicate whether operands are signed or unsigned. In general it is not possible to determine which LLVM variables are signed and which are unsigned.

Surprisingly, current analyses of LLVM code tend to either assume unlimited precision of integers, or else not to take the necessarily signedness-agnostic nature of LLVM analysis into account. An exception is Dietz *et al.* [1] who are very aware of the problems that come from the agnosticism but resolve, as a consequence, to move analysis to the front end of their compiler (Clang). They explain that this design decision has been made after LLVM IR analysis *"proved to be unreliable and unnecessarily complicated, due to requiring a substantial amount of C-level information in the IR ... for any IR operation the transformation needs to know the types involved (including the size and signedness) ... "* [1].

R. Jhala and A. Igarashi (Eds.): APLAS 2012, LNCS 7705, pp. 115–130, 2012.
© Springer-Verlag Berlin Heidelberg 2012

In this paper we show how precise static analysis *can* be performed on the LLVM IR, even when signedness information would seem essential to the analysis. As a consequence we can make the most of LLVM's unifying role and avoid any need to separately implement the same analyses for different source languages. Key to our solution is a way of allowing abstract operations (in the sense of abstract interpretation) to superpose the signed and unsigned cases.

At first it may seem surprising that there is any issue at all. On a fixed-width machine utilising two's complement, the algorithm for addition is the same whether the operands are signed or unsigned. The same holds for multiplication. Why should program analysis then have reason to distinguish the signed and unsigned cases? The answer is that most numeric-type abstract domains rely on an integer ordering $\leq$. Such an ordering is not available when we do not know whether a bit-vector such as $101\cdots100$ should be read as a negative or a positive integer. For example, in performing interval analysis, the rule for $[a,b] \times [c,d]$ varies with the signs of the integers that are being approximated. Any of $[bd,ac]$, $[ad,bc]$, $[bc,ad]$ and $[ac,bd]$ could be the right answer [5]. Note that we cannot conservatively appeal to the *minimum* and *maximum* of the set $\{ac,ad,bc,bd\}$, as these are ill-defined in the absence of signedness information.

We could treat all variables as signed, but this will dramatically lose precision in some cases. In the case of *unsigned* 4-bit variables[1] $x = 0110$ and y known to lie in the interval $[0001,0011]$ clearly $x+y$ must lie in the interval $[0111,1001]$, and if the variables are treated as unsigned, this is what is determined. However, if the variables are treated as signed, the addition will be deemed to "wrap around", giving $1000 = -8$ as the smallest possible sum, and $0111 = 7$ as the largest. Thus no useful information will be derived. A similar situation can arise if x and y are signed and we treat them as unsigned, such as when $x = 1110$ and y lies in the interval $[0001,0011]$.

Surprisingly, the wrong signedness assumption can also lead to *stronger* results than the right assumption. Reflecting on these examples, whether it is better to treat a value as signed or unsigned is determined solely by the patterns of bits in each value, not by whether the value is intended to be interpreted as signed or unsigned. When a computation can wrap around if the operands are treated as signed, it is better to treat them as unsigned, and vice versa. As long as the set of bit-vectors specified by an interval is correct, it does not matter whether we consider the bounds to be signed or unsigned.

This suggests that it is better to treat the bounds of an interval as a superposition of signed and unsigned values, accommodating both signed and unsigned wrap-around. That is, we treat each bound as merely a bit pattern, considering its signedness only when necessary for the operation involved (such as comparison). Instead of representing bounds over fixed bit-width integer types as a range of values on the number line, we handle them as a range of values on a number circle (see Figure 1), or, in the n-dimensional case, as a (closed convex) region of an n-dimensional torus. The unsigned numbers begin with 0 near the "South Pole", proceeding clockwise to the maximum value back near the South Pole.

---

[1] We use 4-bit examples and binary notation to make examples more manageable.

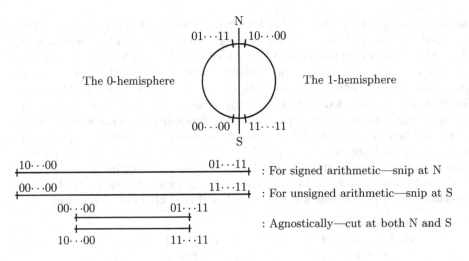

Fig. 1. Three different ways to cut the number circle open

The signed numbers begin with the smallest number near the "North Pole", moving clockwise through 0 to the largest signed number near the North Pole.

"Wrapped" intervals are permitted to cross either pole, or both. Letting an interval start and end anywhere allows for a limited type of disjunctive interval information. For example, an interval $x \in [0111, 1001]$ means $7 \leqslant x \leqslant 9$ if x is treated as unsigned, and $x = 7 \vee -8 \leqslant x \leqslant -7$ if it is treated as signed. This small broadening of the ordinary interval domain allows precise analysis of code where signedness information is unavailable. Equally importantly, it can provide more precise analysis results even where all signedness information *is* provided. We observe that this revised interval domain can pay off in the analysis of real-world programs, without incurring a significant additional cost.

It is important to note that the use of wrapped intervals, combined with signedness-agnosticism, can be worthwhile *even in the presence of signedness information*. Consider $[1000, 1010] \times [1111, 1111]$ in 4-bit arithmetic. Signed analysis gives $[-8, -6] \times [-1, -1] = [6, 8] = [0110, 1000]$, while unsigned analysis gives $[8, 10] \times [15, 15] = [120, 150]$. Here the range exceeds 2^4, so any 4-bit string is deemed possible. So even if the intervals represent *unsigned integers*, the *signed* analysis result is more accurate. Conversely, look at $[1000, 1011] \times [0000, 0001]$. Here signed analysis gives $[-8, -5] \times [0, 1] = [-8, 0]$, which we may write as $[1000, 0000]$ if we allow the interval to wrap. In this case unsigned analysis is the less accurate, as we have $[8, 11] \times [0, 1] = [0, 11]$ that is, we get $[0000, 1011]$. Each analysis provides a correct approximation to the set of five possible values, but the unsigned analysis finds 12 possible elements, whereas the signed analysis is tighter, yielding 9 possible values.

Wrapped interval arithmetic better reflects algebraic properties of the under-lying arithmetic operations than intervals without wrapping, even if signedness information is available. Consider for example the computation $x + y - z$. If we know x, y, and z are all signed 4-bit integers in the interval $[0011, 0101]$, then we determine $y - z \in [1110, 0010]$, whether using wrapped intervals or not. But wrapped intervals will also capture that $x + y \in [0110, 1010]$, while an unwrapped fixed-width interval analysis would find the sum could be as large as the largest possible integer and as small as the smallest. Therefore, wrapped intervals derive the correct bounds $[0001, 0111]$ for both $(x + y) - z$ and $x + (y - z)$. Ordinary intervals, on the other hand, can only derive these bounds for $x + (y - z)$, finding no useful information for $(x + y) - z$, although wrapping is not necessary to represent the final result. This ability to allow intermediate results to wrap around is a powerful advantage of wrapped intervals, even in cases where signedness information is available and final results do not require wrapping.

Consider the function below and assume it is entered with initial bounds information $x \in [0, 100]$ and $y \in [-10, -10]$, and that chars are 8 bits wide.

```
char modulo(char x, char y) {
    while (x >= y) {          // line 1
        x = x - y;            // line 2
    }                         // line 3
    return x;                 // line 4
}
```

Traditional interval analysis [5] would ignore the fixed-width nature of variables, in this case leading to the incorrect conclusion that line 4 is unreachable. A (traditional) *width aware* interval analysis can do better. During analysis it finds that, just before line 2, $x \in [0, 120]$. Performing line 2's abstract subtraction operation, it observes the wrap-around, and finds that $x \in [-128, 127]$ at line 3, and that $x \in [-128, -11]$ at line 4, and as the result of the function call.

While this result is correct, it is also disappointingly weak. Inspection of the code tells us that the result of such a call must always be smaller than -118, since at each iteration, x increases by 10, and if $x \in [-118, -11]$ at line 4, then on the previous iteration $x \in [-128, -11]$, so the loop would have terminated. Thus we would have hoped for the analysis result $x \in [-128, -119]$. The traditional bounds analysis misses this result because it considers "wrap around" to be a leap to the opposite end of the number line, rather than the incremental step that it is. Using our proposed domain gives the precision we hoped for. Finding again that $x \in [0, 120]$ at line 2, we derive the bounds $x \in [10, 127] \lor x \in [-128, -126]$ at line 3. On the next iteration we have $x \in [0, 127] \lor x \in [-128, -126]$ at line 1, $x \in [0, 127]$ at line 2, and $x \in [10, 127] \lor x \in [-128, -119]$ at line 3. This yields $x \in [-128, -119]$ at line 4, and one more iteration proves this to be a fixed point.

In this paper we present a novel approach to signedness-agnostic analysis of programs that manipulate fixed-width integers. The key idea is that correctness and precision of analysis can be obtained by letting abstract operations deal with states that are superpositions of signed/unsigned states. This is done without incurring great running time cost. For a concrete example of the principle, we define an abstract domain of "wrapped" intervals and associated operations and algorithms. This domain has features that appear to have been overlooked in other work. We report on the analysis cost and benefits, compared to ordinary non-wrapped intervals, as measured on a large set of benchmarks.

2   Related Work

Applications of bounds analysis include array bounds checking, overflow analysis, and bit-width frugal register allocation. However, as we have pointed out, in the context of C and similar languages using fixed-width integer types, correct bounds analysis needs to be aware of the limitations on integer precision. Simon and King [8] show how to make polyhedral analysis wrapping-aware without incurring a high additional cost. Regehr and Duongsaa [6] perform bounds analysis in a wrapping-aware manner, dealing also with bit-wise operations, but as their analysis uses conventional intervals, it is not able to maintain the precision offered by wrapped intervals.

Sen and Srikant [7] utilise *strided* wrapped intervals, which they call *Circular Linear Progressions*, for the purpose of analysis of binaries. Their abstract domain is more expressive than what we use, allowing limited relational information. They give detailed abstract operations and refer to their abstract domain as a lattice. Setting the stride in their strided intervals to 1 results in precisely the concept of wrapped intervals that we use in this paper. Hence, as will become clear, their claim that the domain of (wrapped) strided intervals has lattice structure is not correct. More importantly, closer reading of their paper makes it clear that Sen and Srikant assume signed representation. The analysis they propose is not signedness-agnostic in our sense.

Gotlieb, Leconte and Marre [3] also study wrapped, or *"clockwise"*, intervals. Their aim is to provide constraint solvers for modular arithmetic for the purpose of software verification. They show how to implement abstract addition and subtraction and also how multiplication by a constant can be handled efficiently. Again, a claim that clockwise intervals form a lattice cannot be right. Gotlieb, Leconte and Marre assume unsigned representation, that is, the treatment is not signedness-agnostic.

Signedness information is critical in the determination of the potential for under- or over-flow. In that context, the higher precision of bounds analysis that we offer is a useful additional contribution because, as shown by Dietz *et al.* [1], overflow is surprisingly common in real-world C/C++ code. They suggest, based on scrutiny of many programs, that much use of overflow is intentional and safe (though not portable), but also that the majority is probably accidental.

3   Wrapped Intervals

To accurately capture the behaviour of fixed bit-width arithmetic, we must limit the concrete domain to the values representable by the types used in the program, and correct the implementation of the abstract operations to reflect the actual behaviour of the concrete operations [8]. As we have seen, a commitment to ordinary ordered intervals $[x, y]$ (either signed or unsigned), when wrap-around is possible, can lead to severe loss of precision. Wrapped intervals not only avoid much loss of precision in the case of such wrap-around, but also provide a natural setting for signedness-agnostic analysis.

We shall use the usual arithmetic operators with their usual meaning. Operators subscripted by a number suggest modular arithmetic; more precisely, $a +_n b = a + b \bmod 2^n$ (similarly for other operations). We use $\mathcal{B}$ for the set of all *bit-vectors* of size w. We will use sequence notation to construct bit-vectors: b^k, where $b \in \{0, 1\}$, represents k copies of bit b in a row, and $s_1 s_2$ represents the concatenation of bit-vectors s_1 and s_2. For example, $01^4 0^3$ represents 01111000.

We use $\leqslant$ for the usual lexicographic ordering of $\mathcal{B}$. For example, $0011 \leqslant 1001$. In the context of wrapped intervals, a relative ordering is more useful than an absolute one. We define

$$b \leqslant_a c \text{ iff } b -_w a \leqslant c -_w a$$

Intuitively, this says that starting from point a on the number circle and travelling clockwise, b is encountered no later than c. It also means that if the number circle were rotated to put a at the South Pole (the zero point), then b would be lexicographically no larger than c. Naturally, $\leqslant_0$ coincides with $\leqslant$, and reflects the normal behaviour of $\texttt{<=}$ on unsigned w-bit integers. Similarly, $\leqslant_{2^{w-1}}$ reflects the normal behaviour of $\texttt{<=}$ on *signed* w-bit integers. When restricted to a single hemisphere (Figure 1), these orderings coincide, but $\leqslant_0$ and $\leqslant_{2^{w-1}}$ do not agree across hemispheres.

We view LLVM as a bit-vector machine—this is the key to precise analysis in the absence of signedness information, and it is what LLVM truly is. However, for convenience, when operations on bit-vectors will be independent of the interpretation, we may now and then use integers (by default unsigned) to represent bit-vectors. This is just a matter of convenience: by slight extension it allows us to use congruence relations and other modular-arithmetic concepts to express bit-vector relations that are otherwise cumbersome to express. The following definition is a good example.

Definition 1. A *wrapped interval*, or *w-interval*, is either an empty interval, denoted $\bot$, a full interval, denoted $\top$, or a delimited interval $(\!|x, y|\!)$, where x, y are w-width bit-vectors and $x \neq y +_w 1$.[2]

Let $\mathcal{W}_w$ be the set of w-intervals over width w bit-vectors. The meaning of a w-interval is given by the function $\gamma : \mathcal{W}_w \to \mathcal{P}(\mathcal{B})$:

$$
\begin{aligned}
\gamma(\bot) &= \varnothing \\
\gamma(\!|x, y|\!) &= \begin{cases} \{x, \ldots, y\} & \text{if } x \leqslant y \\ \{0^w, \ldots, y\} \cup \{x, \ldots, 1^w\} & \text{otherwise} \end{cases} \\
\gamma(\top) &= \mathcal{B}
\end{aligned}
$$

For example, $\gamma(\!|1111, 1001|\!) = \{1111, 0000, 0001, 0010, 0011, 0100, 0101, 0110, 0111, 1000, 1001\}$ represents the signed integers $[-1, 7] \cup \{-8, -7\}$ or the unsigned integers $[0, 9] \cup \{15\}$. The cardinality of a w-interval is therefore:

---

[2] The condition, which is independent of signed/unsigned interpretation, avoids duplicate names (such as $(\!|0011, 0010|\!)$ and $(\!|1100, 1011|\!)$) for the full interval.

$$\#(\bot) \;\; = 0$$
$$\#(\!|x,y|\!) = (y -_w x +_w 1)$$
$$\#(\top) \;\; = 2^w$$

In an abuse of notation, we define $e \in u$ iff $e \in \gamma(u)$. Note that $\mathcal{W}_w$ is complemented. We define the complement of a w-interval:

$$\overline{\bot} \;\;\; = \top$$
$$\overline{\top} \;\;\; = \bot$$
$$\overline{(\!|x,y|\!)} = (\!|y +_w 1, x -_w 1|\!)$$

3.1 Ordering Wrapped Intervals

We order $\mathcal{W}_w$ by inclusion: $t_1 \sqsubseteq t_2$ iff $\gamma(t_1) \subseteq \gamma(t_2)$. It is easy to see that $\sqsubseteq$ is a partial ordering on $\mathcal{W}_w$; the set is a finite partial order with least element $\bot$ and greatest element $\top$. While $(\mathcal{W}_w, \sqsubseteq)$ is partially ordered, it is *not* a lattice. For example, consider the w-intervals $(\!|0100, 1000|\!)$ and $(\!|1100, 0000|\!)$. Two minimal upper bounds are the incomparable $(\!|0100, 0000|\!)$ and $(\!|1100, 1000|\!)$, two sets of the same cardinality. So a join operation is not available. By duality, neither is a meet operation.

In fact there is no Galois connection (α, γ). For example, $\gamma(\!|1000, 0000|\!) \cap \gamma(\!|0000, 1000|\!) = \{0000, 1000\}$, a set which does not correspond to a w-interval. Furthermore, the two w-intervals $(\!|1000, 0000|\!)$ and $(\!|0000, 1000|\!)$ describe the set $\{0000, 1000\}$ equally well.

The obvious solution is a *biased* pseudo-join operation $\tilde{\sqcup}$ which selects, from the set of possible resulting w-intervals, the one with smallest cardinality, and in case of a tie, the one that contains the lexicographically smallest left bound. First we define membership testing and inclusion. Membership testing is defined:

$$e \in u \;=\; \begin{cases} true & \text{if } u = \top \\ false & \text{if } u = \bot \\ e \leqslant_x y & \text{if } u = (\!|x,y|\!) \end{cases}$$

In guarded definitions like this, the clause that applies is the first (from the top) whose guard is satisfied; that is, an 'if' clause should be read as 'else if'.

Inclusion is defined in terms of membership: either the intervals are identical or else both endpoints of s are in t and at least one endpoint of t is outside s.

$$s \sqsubseteq t \;=\; \begin{cases} true & \text{if } s = \bot \lor t = \top \\ false & \text{if } s = \top \lor t = \bot \\ a \in t \land b \in t \land (c \notin s \lor d \notin s) & \text{if } s = (\!|a,b|\!), t = (\!|c,d|\!) \end{cases}$$

Consider the cases of possible overlap between two w-intervals shown in Figure 2. Only case (a) depicts containment, but case (b) shows a situation where each w-interval has its bounds contained in the other. This explains why the third case in the definition of $\sqsubseteq$ requires that $c \notin s$ or $d \notin s$.

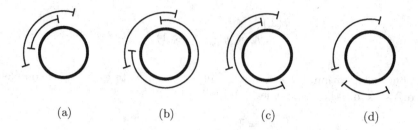

Fig. 2. Four cases of relative position of two w-intervals

Then, a biased pseudo-join operation $\tilde{\sqcup}$ is finally defined:

$$s \mathbin{\tilde{\sqcup}} t = \begin{cases} t & \text{if } s \sqsubseteq t \\ s & \text{if } t \sqsubseteq s \\ \top & \text{if } s = (\!(a,b)\!) \wedge t = (\!(c,d)\!) \wedge a \in t \wedge b \in t \wedge c \in s \wedge d \in s \\ (\!(a,d)\!) & \text{if } s = (\!(a,b)\!) \wedge t = (\!(c,d)\!) \wedge b \in t \wedge c \in s \\ (\!(c,b)\!) & \text{if } s = (\!(a,b)\!) \wedge t = (\!(c,d)\!) \wedge d \in s \wedge a \in t \\ (\!(a,d)\!) & \text{if } s = (\!(a,b)\!) \wedge t = (\!(c,d)\!) \wedge \\ & (\#(\!(b,c)\!) < \#(\!(d,a)\!) \vee (\#(\!(b,c)\!) = \#(\!(d,a)\!) \wedge a \leqslant c)) \\ (\!(c,b)\!) & \text{otherwise} \end{cases}$$

In this definition, the first two cases handle $\top$ and $\bot$, as well as Figure 2 (a); the third case handles Figure 2 (b); the fourth and fifth cases handle Figure 2 (c); and the final two cases handle Figure 2 (d). We can utilise the fact that $\mathcal{W}_w$ is complemented to define a pseudo-meet operation:

$$s \mathbin{\tilde{\sqcap}} t \;=\; \overline{\overline{s} \mathbin{\tilde{\sqcup}} \overline{t}}$$

Unfortunately the biased pseudo-join has certain shortcomings, inherited by the pseudo-meet. First, $\tilde{\sqcup}$ and $\tilde{\sqcap}$ are not associative. In fact, $(x \mathbin{\tilde{\sqcup}} y) \mathbin{\tilde{\sqcup}} z$ and $x \mathbin{\tilde{\sqcup}} (y \mathbin{\tilde{\sqcup}} z)$ may have different cardinality. This happens, for example, with $x = (\!(0010, 0110)\!)$, $y = (\!(1000, 1010)\!)$, and $z = (\!(1110, 0000)\!)$, since $(x \mathbin{\tilde{\sqcup}} y) \mathbin{\tilde{\sqcup}} z = (\!(1110, 1010)\!)$ has smaller cardinality than $x \mathbin{\tilde{\sqcup}} (y \mathbin{\tilde{\sqcup}} z) = (\!(0010, 0000)\!)$. Second, $\tilde{\sqcup}$ and $\tilde{\sqcap}$ are not monotone. For example, we have $(\!(1111, 0000)\!) \sqsubseteq (\!(1110, 0000)\!)$ and $(\!(0110, 1000)\!) \mathbin{\tilde{\sqcup}} (\!(1111, 0000)\!) = (\!(1111, 1000)\!)$. But owing to the lexicographic bias, $(\!(0110, 1000)\!) \mathbin{\tilde{\sqcup}} (\!(1110, 0000)\!) = (\!(0110, 0000)\!)$. As we do not have $(\!(1111, 1000)\!) \sqsubseteq (\!(0110, 0000)\!)$, $\tilde{\sqcup}$ is not monotone. We discuss the ramifications of this in Section 4, together with a work-around.

The lack of associativity means a generalised $\tilde{\bigsqcup}$ is not well-defined. Nevertheless, the requirement for $\bigsqcup$ is clear: Given a set S of w-intervals, we want $\bigsqcup$ to yield a w-interval t of minimal cardinality so that each interval in S is contained in t. Figure 3 gives an algorithm for computing t. Intuitively, the algorithm returns the complement of the largest un-covered gap among intervals from S. It identifies this gap by passing through S once, picking intervals lexicographically by their left bounds. However, care must be taken to ensure that any *apparent* gaps, which are in fact covered by w-intervals that cross the South Pole and

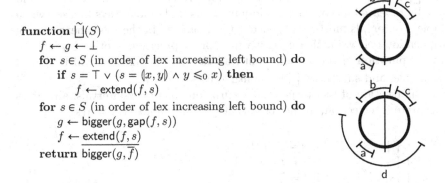

```
function ⊔̃(S)
    f ← g ← ⊥
    for s ∈ S (in order of lex increasing left bound) do
        if s = ⊤ ∨ (s = ⦇x, y⦈ ∧ y ⩽₀ x) then
            f ← extend(f, s)
    for s ∈ S (in order of lex increasing left bound) do
        g ← bigger(g, gap(f, s))
        f ← extend(f, s)
    return bigger(g, f̄)
```

Fig. 3. Finding the (pseudo) least upper bound of a set of w-intervals

may only be found later in the iteration, are not mistaken for *actual* gaps. We define the gap between two w-intervals as empty if they overlap, or otherwise the clockwise distance from the end of the first to the start of the second.

$$\mathsf{gap}(s, t) \;=\; \begin{cases} \overline{⦇c, b⦈} & \text{if } s = ⦇a, b⦈ \wedge t = ⦇c, d⦈ \wedge b \notin t \wedge c \notin s \\ \bot & \text{otherwise} \end{cases}$$

We also define an operation extend(s, t) to yield the w-interval from the start of s to the end of t, ensuring it includes all of s and t. This operation is identical to $⊔̃$, except that the last cases are omitted, and the condition on the penultimate case is relaxed to apply regardless of cardinalities. Finally, we define bigger(s, t) to be t if $\#t > \#s$, and s otherwise. The two loops in Figure 3 traverse the set of w-intervals in order of lexicographically increasing left bound; it does not matter where $⊤$ and $⊥$ appear in this sequence. The first loop assigns to f the least upper bound of all w-intervals that cross the South Pole. The invariant for the second loop is that g is the largest uncovered gap in f; thus the loop can be terminated as soon as $f = ⊤$. When the loop terminates, all w-intervals have been incorporated in f, so $f̄$ is an uncovered gap, and g is the largest uncovered gap in f. Thus the result is the complement of the bigger of g and $f̄$.

Consider Figure 3 (upper right) as an example. Here no intervals cross the South Pole, so at the start of the second loop, $f = g = ⊥$, and at the end of the loop, g is the gap between a and b, and f is the interval clockwise from the start of a to the end of c. Since the complement of f is larger than g, the result in this case is f: the interval from the start of a to the end of c.

For the lower right example of Figure 3, interval d does cross the South Pole, so at the start of the second loop, $f = $ d and $g = ⊥$. Now in the second loop, f extends clockwise to encompass b and c, and finally also d, at which point f becomes $⊤$. But because the loop starts with $f = $ d, g never holds the gap between a and b; finally it holds the gap between the end of c and the start of d. Now the complement of f is smaller than g so the final result is the complement of g, that is, the interval from the start (right end) of d to the end of c.

The $\widetilde{\bigsqcup}$ operation is useful because it may preserve information that would be lost by repeated use of the pseudo-join. Thus it should always be used when multiple w-intervals must be joined together, such as in the implementation of multiplication below. Furthermore, it will improve precision in other contexts to delay computation of pseudo-joins until all the w-intervals that will be joined are available, and substitute $\bigsqcup$ for multiple uses of $\widetilde{\sqcup}$.

The intersection of two w-intervals returns one or two w-intervals, and gives the accurate intersection, in the sense that $\bigcup \{\gamma(u) \mid u \in s \cap t\} = \gamma(s) \cap \gamma(t)$.

$$
s \cap t = \begin{cases}
\{\,\} & \text{if } s = \bot \text{ or } t = \bot \\
\{t\} & \text{if } s = t \vee s = \top \\
\{s\} & \text{if } t = \top \\
\{(\!(a,d)\!), (\!(b,c)\!)\} & \text{if } s = (\!(a,b)\!) \wedge t = (\!(c,d)\!) \wedge a \in t \wedge b \in t \wedge c \in s \wedge d \in s \\
\{s\} & \text{if } s = (\!(a,b)\!) \wedge t = (\!(c,d)\!) \wedge a \in t \wedge b \in t \\
\{t\} & \text{if } s = (\!(a,b)\!) \wedge t = (\!(c,d)\!) \wedge c \in s \wedge d \in s \\
\{(\!(a,d)\!)\} & \text{if } s = (\!(a,b)\!) \wedge t = (\!(c,d)\!) \wedge a \in t \wedge d \in s \wedge b \notin t \wedge c \notin s \\
\{(\!(b,c)\!)\} & \text{if } s = (\!(a,b)\!) \wedge t = (\!(c,d)\!) \wedge b \in t \wedge c \in s \wedge a \notin t \wedge d \notin s \\
\{\,\} & \text{otherwise}
\end{cases}
$$

3.2 Analysing Expressions

On w-intervals, addition is defined as follows:

$$
s + t = \begin{cases}
\bot & \text{if } s = \bot \text{ or } t = \bot \\
(\!(a +_w c, b +_w d)\!) & \text{if } s = (\!(a,b)\!),\, t = (\!(c,d)\!), \text{ and } \# s + \# t \leq 2^w \\
\top & \text{otherwise}
\end{cases}
$$

Here, to detect a possible overflow when adding the two cardinalities, standard addition is used. Note that $+_w$ is signedness-agnostic: treating it as signed or unsigned makes no difference. The rule for subtraction $(s - t)$ is similar—just replace the delimited interval on the left by $(\!(a -_w d, b -_w c)\!)$. The definition of abstract unary minus then follows easily, by noting that $-s = 0 - s$.

Multiplication on w-intervals is more cumbersome, even when we settle for a less-than-optimal solution. The reason is that even though unsigned and signed multiplication are the same operation on bit-vectors, signed and unsigned interval multiplication retain *different* information. The solution requires separating each interval at the North and South poles, so the segments agree on ordering for both signed and unsigned interpretations, and then performing both signed and unsigned multiplication on the fragments.

It is convenient to have names for the smallest w-intervals that straddle the poles. Let $\mathsf{np} = (\!(01^{w-1}, 10^{w-1})\!)$ and $\mathsf{sp} = (\!(1^w, 0^w)\!)$. Define the North Pole split of a delimited w-interval as follows:

$$
\mathsf{nsplit}(s) = \begin{cases}
\varnothing & \text{if } s = \bot \\
\{(\!(a,b)\!)\} & \text{if } s = (\!(a,b)\!) \text{ and } \mathsf{np} \not\sqsubseteq (\!(a,b)\!) \\
\{(\!(a, 01^{w-1})\!), (\!(10^{w-1}, b)\!)\} & \text{if } s = (\!(a,b)\!) \text{ and } \mathsf{np} \sqsubseteq (\!(a,b)\!) \\
\{(\!(0^w, 01^{w-1})\!), (\!(10^{w-1}, 1^w)\!)\} & \text{if } s = \top
\end{cases}
$$

and define the South Pole split ssplit similarly (in particular, the last case is identical). Then let the sphere cut be

$$\mathsf{cut}((\!|x,y|\!)) = \bigcup\{\mathsf{ssplit}(u) \mid u \in \mathsf{nsplit}((\!|x,y|\!))\}$$

For example, $\mathsf{cut}((\!|1111,1001|\!)) = \{(\!|1111,1111|\!), (\!|0000,0111|\!), (\!|1000,1001|\!)\}$.

Unsigned and signed multiplication of two delimited w-intervals $(\!|a,b|\!)$ and $(\!|c,d|\!)$ that do not straddle poles is straightforward:

$$(\!|a,b|\!) \times_u (\!|c,d|\!) = \begin{cases} (\!|a \times_w c, b \times_w d|\!) & \text{if } b \times d - a \times c < 2^w \\ \top & \text{otherwise} \end{cases}$$

And, letting msb be the function that extracts the most significant bit:

$$(\!|a,b|\!) \times_s (\!|c,d|\!) = \begin{cases} (\!|a \times_w c, b \times_w d|\!) & \text{if } \mathsf{msb}(a) = \mathsf{msb}(b) = \mathsf{msb}(c) = \mathsf{msb}(d) \\ & \quad \wedge\, b \times d - a \times c < 2^w \\ (\!|a \times_w d, b \times_w c|\!) & \text{if } \mathsf{msb}(a) = \mathsf{msb}(b) = 1 \wedge \mathsf{msb}(c) = \mathsf{msb}(d) = 0 \\ & \quad \wedge\, b \times c - a \times d < 2^w \\ (\!|b \times_w c, a \times_w d|\!) & \text{if } \mathsf{msb}(a) = \mathsf{msb}(b) = 0 \wedge \mathsf{msb}(c) = \mathsf{msb}(d) = 1 \\ & \quad \wedge\, a \times d - b \times c < 2^w \\ \top & \text{otherwise} \end{cases}$$

Now, signed and unsigned bit-vector multiplication agree for segments that do not straddle a pole. This is an important observation which gives us a handle on precise multiplication across arbitrary delimited w-intervals:

$$(\!|a,b|\!) \times_{us} (\!|c,d|\!) = ((\!|a,b|\!) \times_u (\!|c,d|\!)) \cap ((\!|a,b|\!) \times_s (\!|c,d|\!))$$

The use of intersection in this definition is the source of the added precision. Each of $\times_u$ and $\times_s$ gives a correct over-approximation of multiplication, and hence the intersection is also a correct over-approximation.

This now allows us to do general signedness-agnostic multiplication by joining the segments obtained from each piecewise hemisphere multiplication:

$$s \times t = \widetilde{\bigsqcup} \{m \mid u \in \mathsf{cut}(s), v \in \mathsf{cut}(t), m \in u \times_{us} v\}$$

Consider the multiplication $(\!|1111,1001|\!) \times (\!|0000,0001|\!)$. The two intervals are shown in the diagram here. The cut of the first w-interval is $\{(\!|1111,1111|\!), (\!|0000,0111|\!), (\!|1000,1001|\!)\}$, the cut of the second is $\{(\!|0000,0001|\!)\}$. The three separate segment multiplications give:

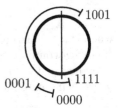

1. $(\!|1111,1111|\!) \times_u (\!|0000,0001|\!) = \top$,
   $(\!|1111,1111|\!) \times_s (\!|0000,0001|\!) = (\!|1111,0000|\!)$,
   hence $(\!|1111,1111|\!) \times_{us} (\!|0000,0001|\!) = \{(\!|1111,0000|\!)\}$.
2. $(\!|0000,0111|\!) \times_u (\!|0000,0001|\!) = (\!|0000,0111|\!)$
   $(\!|0000,0111|\!) \times_s (\!|0000,0001|\!) = (\!|0000,0111|\!)$
   hence $(\!|0000,0111|\!) \times_{us} (\!|0000,0001|\!) = \{(\!|0000,0111|\!)\}$.

3. $(1000, 1001) \times_u (0000, 0001) = (0000, 1001)$,
$\quad (1000, 1001) \times_s (0000, 0001) = (1000, 0000)$,
$\quad$ hence $(1000, 1001) \times_{us} (0000, 0001) = (0000, 1001) \cap (1000, 0000)$
$\quad = \{(1000, 1001), (0000, 0000)\}$.

Applying $\widetilde{\bigsqcup}$, we get the maximally accurate result $(1111, 1001)$. Note the crucial role played by $\times_{us}$ in obtaining this precision. For example, in the first case above, where we have no information about the result of unsigned multiplication ($(1111, 1111) \times_u (0000, 0001) = \top$), we effectively assume that multiplication is signed, obtaining a much tighter result. The role of $\times_{us}$ is to *do signed and unsigned multiplication simultaneously*. This is very different from the obvious case analysis that considers the unsigned and signed cases separately: For the example, either yields $\top$.

What is important about our approach is that the signed/unsigned case analysis happens as late as possible, at the "micro-level". This is what we have in mind when we say that the abstract operations deal with superposed signed/unsigned states. The superposition idea is general and works for other operations. However, it does not always add precision—for many abstract operations we can obtain equivalent but simpler definitions.

Unsigned and signed division are different operations, since the definition depends on the ordering of bit-vectors. Hence we need two abstract operations. Here, since the interpretation of the bit-vectors is given, the definition is straightforward but lengthy and slightly more complicated, owing to the need to carve out the sub-interval $(0^w, 0^w)$. The modulus operation is similar to division.

For the logical operations, it is tempting to simply consider the combinations of interval endpoints, at least when no interval straddles two hemispheres. But that does not work. For example, the endpoints of $(1010, 1100)$ are not sufficient to determine the endpoints of $(1010, 1100) \mid (0110, 0110)$. Namely, $1010 \mid 0110 = 1100 \mid 0110 = 1110$, but $1011 \mid 0110 = 1111$. Instead we use the unsigned versions of algorithms provided by Warren [10] (pages 58–62), but adapted to w-intervals using a South Pole split. We present the method for bitwise-or $\mid$; those for bitwise-and and bitwise-xor are similar.

$$s \mid t = \widetilde{\bigsqcup} \; \{u \mid_w v \mid u \in \mathsf{ssplit}(s), v \in \mathsf{ssplit}(t)\}$$

where $\mid_w$ is Warren's unsigned bitwise or operation for intervals [10], an operation with complexity $O(w)$.

Signed and zero extension are defined as follows. We assume words of width w are being extended to width $w + k$, with $k > 0$.

$$\mathsf{sext}(s, k) = \widetilde{\bigsqcup} \; \{((\mathsf{msb}(a))^k a, (\mathsf{msb}(b))^k b) \mid (a, b) \in \mathsf{nsplit}(s)\}$$
$$\mathsf{zext}(s, k) = \widetilde{\bigsqcup} \; \{(0^k a, 0^k b) \mid (a, b) \in \mathsf{ssplit}(s)\}$$

Truncation to $k < w$ bits (integer downcasting) keeps the lower k bits of a bit-vector of length w. Accordingly, $\mathsf{trunc}(s, k)$ is a w width w-interval s truncated to a k width w-interval. Truncation is defined as:

$$
\mathsf{trunc}(s, k) = \begin{cases}
\bot & \text{if } s = \bot \\
(\!|\mathsf{trunc}(a, k), \mathsf{trunc}(b, k)|\!) & \text{if } s = (\!|a, b|\!) \wedge a\!>\!>_a k = b\!>\!>_a k \\
& \wedge\ \mathsf{trunc}(a, k) \leqslant \mathsf{trunc}(b, k) \\
(\!|\mathsf{trunc}(a, k), \mathsf{trunc}(b, k)|\!) & \text{if } s = (\!|a, b|\!) \wedge (a\!>\!>_a k) + 1 \equiv_{2^w} b\!>\!>_a k \\
& \wedge\ \mathsf{trunc}(a, k) \nleqslant \mathsf{trunc}(b, k) \\
\top & \text{otherwise}
\end{cases}
$$

where $>\!>_a$ is arithmetic right shift. Once truncation is defined, we can easily define left shift:

$$
s << k = \begin{cases}
\bot & \text{if } s = \bot \\
(\!|a\!<\!<k, b\!<\!<k|\!) & \text{if } \mathsf{trunc}(s, w - k) = (\!|a, b|\!) \\
(\!|0^w, 1^{w-k}0^k|\!) & \text{otherwise}
\end{cases}
$$

Logical right shifting ($>\!>_l$) requires testing if the South Pole is covered:

$$
s >>_l k = \begin{cases}
\bot & \text{if } s = \bot \\
(\!|0^w, 0^k 1^{w-k}|\!) & \text{if } \mathsf{sp} \sqsubseteq s \\
(\!|a\!>\!>_l k, b\!>\!>_l k|\!) & \text{if } s = (\!|a, b|\!)
\end{cases}
$$

and arithmetic right shifting ($>\!>_a$) requires testing if the North Pole is covered:

$$
s >>_a k = \begin{cases}
\bot & \text{if } s = \bot \\
(\!|1^k 0^{w-k}, 0^k 1^{w-k}|\!) & \text{if } \mathsf{np} \sqsubseteq s \\
(\!|a\!>\!>_a k, b\!>\!>_a k|\!) & \text{if } s = (\!|a, b|\!)
\end{cases}
$$

Shifting with variable shift, for example, $s << t$, can be defined by calculating the (fixed) shift for each $k \in (\!|0, w-1|\!)$ which is an element of t, and pseudo-joining the resulting w-intervals.

3.3   Dealing with Control Flow

In LLVM, comparison operations are explicitly signed or unsigned. Taking the 'then' branch of a conditional with condition $s \leqslant_0 t$ can be thought of as prefixing the branch with 'assume $s \leqslant_0 t$', and this assume statement can narrow the bounds for s and t. We update the information for s as follows:

$$
s = \begin{cases}
\bot & \text{if } t = \bot \\
s & \text{if } 1^w \in t \\
s \mathbin{\tilde{\sqcap}} (\!|0^w, b|\!) & \text{if } t = (\!|a, b|\!)
\end{cases}
$$

Signed comparison ($\leqslant_{2^{w-1}}$) is similar, but replaces 1^w by 01^{w-1} and $(\!|0^w, b|\!)$ by $(\!|10^{w-1}, b|\!)$. Updating the second argument t in a context $s \leqslant_{2^{w-1}} t$ is defined analogously. Finally, φ-nodes in the LLVM control-flow graph are handled as usual, in our case using $\tilde{\sqcup}$.

4   Non-termination and Widening

As shown in Section 3, $\tilde{\sqcup}$ lacks desirable algebraic properties and fails to be monotone. Although $\mathcal{W}_w$ is finite, the fact that $\tilde{\sqcup}$ is not monotone raises a major problem: a *least fixed point* may not exist because multiple fixed points could be equally precise, and even worse, the analysis may not terminate. Fortunately, in practice, there is an easy solution to this problem. While $\mathcal{W}_w$ is finite, it does contain chains of length $O(2^w)$. Hence, for efficient analysis, fixed point acceleration is needed in any case. Judicious use of widening ensures termination of our analysis, side-stepping the non-monotonicity problem. We define an upper bound operator ∇, based on the idea of widening by (roughly) doubling the size of a w-interval. First, $s\nabla\bot = \bot\nabla s = s$, and $s\nabla\top = \top\nabla s = \top$. Additionally,

$$(\!|u,v|\!)\nabla(\!|x,y|\!) = \begin{cases} (\!|u,v|\!) & \text{if } (\!|x,y|\!) \sqsubseteq (\!|u,v|\!) \\ \top & \text{if } \#(\!|u,v|\!) \geqslant 2^{w-1} \\ (\!|u,y|\!) \,\tilde{\sqcup}\, (\!|u,2v -_w u +_w 1|\!) & \text{if } (\!|u,v|\!) \,\tilde{\sqcup}\, (\!|x,y|\!) = (\!|u,y|\!) \\ (\!|x,v|\!) \,\tilde{\sqcup}\, (\!|2u -_w v -_w 1, v|\!) & \text{if } (\!|u,v|\!) \,\tilde{\sqcup}\, (\!|x,y|\!) = (\!|x,v|\!) \\ (\!|x,y|\!) \,\tilde{\sqcup}\, (\!|x, x +_w 2v -_w 2u +_w 1|\!) & \text{if } u,v \in (\!|x,y|\!) \\ \top & \text{otherwise} \end{cases}$$

Then ∇ is an upper bound operator [5] and we have the property

$$s\nabla t = s \;\lor\; s\nabla t = \top \;\lor\; \# s\nabla t \geqslant 2 \# s$$

Given $f : \mathcal{W}_w \to \mathcal{W}_w$, we define the accelerated sequence $\{f_\nabla^n\}_n$ as follows:

$$f_\nabla^n = \begin{cases} \bot & \text{if } n = 0 \\ f_\nabla^{n-1} & \text{if } n > 0 \land f(f_\nabla^{n-1}) \sqsubseteq f_\nabla^{n-1} \\ f_\nabla^{n-1} \nabla f(f_\nabla^{n-1}) & \text{otherwise} \end{cases}$$

Since $\{f_\nabla^n\}_n$ is increasing (whether f is monotone or not) and $\mathcal{W}_w$ has finite height, the accelerated sequence eventually stabilises. In our implementation we perform a widening step after every fifth iterative step.

5   Experimental Evaluation

We implemented wrapped interval analysis for LLVM 3.0 and ran experiments on an Intel Core with a 2.70Gz clock and 7.8Gb of memory. For comparison we also implemented an unwrapped fixed-width interval analysis using the same fixed point algorithm. Since we analyse LLVM IR, signedness information is in general not available. Therefore, to compare the precision of "unwrapped" and "wrapped" analysis, we ran the unwrapped analysis assuming all integers are signed, similarly to [9]. We used the Spec CPU 2000 benchmark suite widely used by LLVM testers. The code for the analyses and the fixed point engine is publicly available at http://code.google.com/p/wrapped-intervals/.

Fig. 4 shows evaluation results. Columns T_U and T_W show analysis times (average of 5 runs) for the unwrapped and wrapped interval analysis, respectively. Column I shows the total number of integer intervals considered by the

Program	T_U	T_W	I	P_U	P_W	G_W
164.gzip	0.30s	0.35s	1511	152	264	115
175.vpr	1.02s	1.83s	4143	316	339	26
176.gcc	12.73s	15.27s	16711	2840	5251	2489
186.crafty	2.36s	3.20s	17679	1761	3825	2235
197.parser	1.40s	2.46s	4736	283	411	140
255.vortex	4.88s	6.40s	22813	812	1005	207
256.bzip2	0.45s	0.83s	2529	247	433	209
300.twolf	1.08s	1.20s	730	16	20	4

Fig. 4. Comparison between unwrapped and wrapped interval analyses

analyses, Column P_U shows the number of cases where the unwrapped analysis infers a proper (delimited) interval, and P_W does the same for wrapped intervals. Finally, column G_W shows the number of variables for which the wrapped analysis gave a more precise result (it is never less precise). In some cases, both analyses produce delimited intervals, but the wrapped interval is more precise. For instance, for 164.gzip, there are 3 such cases. This explains why, in most cases, $G_W > P_W - P_U$.

We note that both analyses are fast, and the added cost of wrapped analysis is reasonable. Regarding precision, the numbers of proper intervals (P_U and P_W) are remarkably low compared with the total number of tracked intervals (I). There three main reasons for this. First, our analysis is intra-procedural. Second, it does not track global variables or pointers. Third, numerous instructions that cast non-trackable types (*e.g.*, ptrtoint, fptosi) are not supported. In spite of these limitations, the numbers in column G_W show that wrapped interval analysis does infer significantly better bounds.

6   Conclusion

Analysis of programs written in LLVM IR and similar low-level languages is hampered by the fact that, for many variables, signedness information has been stripped away. While it is possible to analyse programs correctly under the assumption that such variables are unsigned (or signed, depending on taste), such an assumption leads to a serious loss of precision.

It is better for analysis to be signedness-agnostic. We have shown that, if implemented carefully, signedness-agnosticism amounts to more than simply "having a bet each way". Our key observation is that one can achieve higher accuracy of analysis by making each individual abstract operation signedness-agnostic, whenever its concrete counterpart is. This applies to important operations like addition, subtraction and multiplication.

Signedness-agnostic *bounds analysis* naturally leads to wrapped intervals, as signed and unsigned representation correspond to two different ways of ordering bit-vectors. In this paper we have detailed the first signedness-agnostic bounds analysis, based on wrapped intervals. This analysis is efficient and accurate, and is beneficial even for programs with full signedness information. Future work involves removing the limitations of our implementation discussed above. More importantly, there is a need to better assess the practical benefits of our analysis, for example, in the context of software verification. Another line of research is to generalise the analysis to relational domains, such as those based on difference logic (constraints $x - y \leqslant k$) or octagons [4].

Acknowledgments. This work was supported through ARC grant DP110102579. We thank Fernando Pereira, Victor Campos, Douglas do Couto, and Igor Rafael for fruitful discussions and for making their LLVM SSI construction pass available.

References

1. Dietz, W., Li, P., Regehr, J., Adve, V.: Understanding integer overflow in C/C++. In: Proc. 34th Int. Conf. Software Eng., pp. 760–770. IEEE (2012)
2. Falke, S., Kapur, D., Sinz, C.: Termination Analysis of Imperative Programs Using Bitvector Arithmetic. In: Joshi, R., Müller, P., Podelski, A. (eds.) VSTTE 2012. LNCS, vol. 7152, pp. 261–277. Springer, Heidelberg (2012)
3. Gotlieb, A., Leconte, M., Marre, B.: Constraint solving on modular integers. In: Proc. Ninth Int. Workshop Constraint Modelling and Reformulation (2010)
4. Miné, A.: The octagon abstract domain. Higher-Order and Symbolic Computation 19(1), 31–100 (2006)
5. Nielson, F., Riis Nielson, H., Hankin, C.: Principles of Program Analysis. Springer (1999)
6. Regehr, J., Duongsaa, U.: Deriving abstract transfer functions for analyzing embedded software. In: LCTES 2006: Proc. Conf. Language, Compilers, and Tool Support for Embedded Systems, pp. 34–43. ACM Press (2006)
7. Sen, R., Srikant, Y.N.: Executable analysis using abstract interpretation with circular linear progressions. In: Proc. Fifth IEEE/ACM Int. Conf. Formal Methods and Models for Codesign, pp. 39–48. IEEE (2007)
8. Simon, A., King, A.: Taming the Wrapping of Integer Arithmetic. In: Riis Nielson, H., Filé, G. (eds.) SAS 2007. LNCS, vol. 4634, pp. 121–136. Springer, Heidelberg (2007)
9. do Couto Teixera, D., Pereira, F.M.Q.: The design and implementation of a non-iterative range analysis algorithms on a production compiler. In: Proc. 2011 Brasilian Symp. Programming Languages (2011)
10. Warren Jr., H.S.: Hacker's Delight. Addison Wesley (2003)
11. Zhang, C., Wang, T., Wei, T., Chen, Y., Zou, W.: IntPatch: Automatically Fix Integer-Overflow-to-Buffer-Overflow Vulnerability at Compile-Time. In: Gritzalis, D., Preneel, B., Theoharidou, M. (eds.) ESORICS 2010. LNCS, vol. 6345, pp. 71–86. Springer, Heidelberg (2010)
12. Zhang, C., Zou, W., Wang, T., Chen, Y., Wei, T.: Using type analysis in compiler to mitigate integer-overflow-to-buffer-overflow threat. Journal of Computer Security 19(6), 1083–1107 (2011)

Hierarchical Shape Abstraction
of Dynamic Structures in Static Blocks[*]

Pascal Sotin and Xavier Rival

INRIA Paris–Rocquencourt / CNRS / École Normale Supérieure, Paris, France

Abstract. We propose a hierarchical shape abstract domain, so as to
infer structural invariants of dynamic structures such as lists living *inside* static structures, such as arrays. This programming pattern is often
used in safety critical embedded software as an alternative to dynamic
memory allocation. Our abstract domain precisely describes such hierar-
chies of structures. It combines several instances of simple shape abstract
domains, dedicated to the representation of elementary shape properties,
and also embeds a numerical abstract domain. This modular construction greatly simplifies the design and the implementation of the abstract
domain. We provide an implementation, and show the effectiveness of
our approach on a problem taken from a real code.

1 Introduction

Safety critical embedded systems as found in avionics should meet safety requirements fixed by regulation standards [12]. In particular, software providers
should supply evidence that the real time applications will not fail due to resource exhaustion. In practice, this constraint forbids the use of dynamic memory
allocation in highly critical software. Though, this does not mean that dynamic
data-structures (that is linked structures where pointers may be modified at any
time in the execution of the program) cannot be used: indeed, structure elements may be allocated statically (in arrays or in other static sections) and links
across elements may be re-computed at any time. Such statically allocated dynamic structures are found in many programs such as the USB driver considered
in [22] or the multi-threaded avionic software considered in [21].

In the last decade, dramatic progresses have been accomplished in the verification of absence of runtime errors in safety critical programs [3,2], yet statically
allocated dynamic structures are still very challenging for static analysis tools.
Static analyzers such as ASTRÉE [3,2] do offer some support for the summarization of large memory regions, but will not capture inductive properties of linked
data structures such as lists. Inferring that such a structure is a well formed list
may require maintaining large disjunctions of cases depending on the elements
order. Failure to do so would lead to false alarms, as proving the absence of runtime errors may require proving that the dynamic structures are well formed.

---

[*] The research leading to these results has received funding from the European Research Council under the FP7 grant agreement 278673, Project MemCAD.

R. Jhala and A. Igarashi (Eds.): APLAS 2012, LNCS 7705, pp. 131–147, 2012.

On the other hand, shape analysis techniques are very smart at summarizing unbounded linked structures [24,11,1] but typically do not track the fact that some pieces of data are stored in a fixed, static block, which may be accessed to as an array. Furthermore, existing shape analyses cannot be interfaced with a powerful numerical domain such as the one used in [2].

In this paper, we exploit the ability of the shape analysis framework proposed in [5,17] to attach numeric predicates to shape graph "nodes" that represent concrete values of arbitrary size (addresses or contents of physical memory cells) in order to tie a complex property to a memory region, in a fully modular way from the static analysis design point of view. In particular, the contents of a static region (as a sequence of bytes) is represented by a symbolic variable, which may be characterized in a value abstract domain; we can then choose to consider this sequence of bytes as a "store inside the store", and let another instance of our shape abstract domain take care of its abstraction. In this setup, the analysis uses two instances of the shape abstract domain: one is used to abstract the memory states, whereas the other is used in order to abstract the contents of the static region. The main advantage of this technique is the modularity of the abstraction, as it alleviates the need for a complex monolithic abstract domain expressing all data-structure invariants. It also allows to reuse the abstract domain of [5] as is, and can be combined with a powerful numerical abstract domain. Our main contributions are (1) the design of a framework for the abstraction of hierarchical memory states, where some memory regions are viewed as *sub-memories*, (2) the integration of an array abstraction in a shape abstract domain, to automatically infer sub-memory boundaries and (3) the implementation of the hierarchical abstraction in the MEMCAD static analyzer, which implements the framework of [5] using the APRON [16] numerical domain library, and the verification of a simplified excerpt from the avionic code discussed in [21] (leaving out features out of the scope of the issue considered in this paper).

2   Running Example

Fig. 1 describes the function considered in our running example, a simplified excerpt of the safety critical application considered in [21]. The data-type (Fig. 1a) is a form of singly linked list (which represents message queues), yet all elements manipulated in the program live in a global array free_pool[100]. A fragment of a concrete state is shown in Fig. 1b. At any point in the execution some of the array elements are active and are members of an existing list structure (the gray elements in the figure) whereas the others are "invalid". We call such an array a *free-pool*. Furthermore, other structural invariants are maintained throughout the program: the list is ordered by increasing priorities and its first and last cells are respectively pointed to by hd and tl. The code inserts a set of elements in the list stored in the free-pool. For each element, it searches the position and performs the insertion. Several cases were omitted for the sake of concision, and we only focus on the case of an insertion within the list, after a traversal to determine the right position. The goal of the analysis discussed in

```
1 typedef struct Cell {
    struct Cell *next;
3   int prio;
    /* other fields */
5 } Cell;
  Cell free_pool[100];
```

(a) Data-type and free-pool.

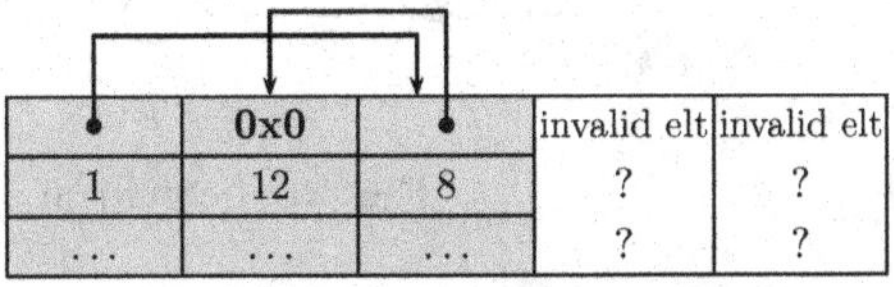

(b) A concrete structure.

```
void main() {
2   int free_idx;
    Cell *hd, *tl;
4   hd = null;
    tl = null;
6   for(free_idx = 0; free_idx < 100; free_idx++) {
      int priority; /* = computation(); */
8     if (hd == null) { /* insert first cell */ }
      else if (priority < hd->prio) { /* insert as head */ }
10    else if (priority >= tl->prio) { /* insert as queue */ }
      else {
12      Cell *cur = hd;
        while(priority >= cur->next->prio) { cur = cur->next; }
14      assert(cur != tl); // position found
        free_pool[free_idx].next = cur->next;
16      free_pool[free_idx].prio = priority;
        cur->next = &free_pool[free_idx]; } } }
```

(c) Insertion routine.

Fig. 1. A dynamic structure in a static area

the paper is to establish both the preservation of the list structural invariant, and memory safety. In particular, the inner loop should cause no null pointer dereference (although the loop condition does not explicitly check that cur is not null). Moreover, it should verify the assertion at line 14, i.e., that the insertion is not made at the tail of the list in that branch.

Existing memory abstractions. Fig. 1b shows a (simplified) concrete state encountered at the head of the main loop in our example program. At the end of the execution, the list has length 100 and occupies the whole array. Due to the size of the structure, an efficient analysis requires it be *summarized*. The abstraction of [17] allows to summarize the whole list into a predicate which expresses that hd points to a list. However, that abstraction fails to capture the fact the list is allocated inside an array, and does not allow to analyze accesses using array selectors. In the other hand, preserving a fully precise abstraction of the array would not allow the summarization of the list and would require a large case analysis over the list elements ordering, which would be prohibitively expensive.

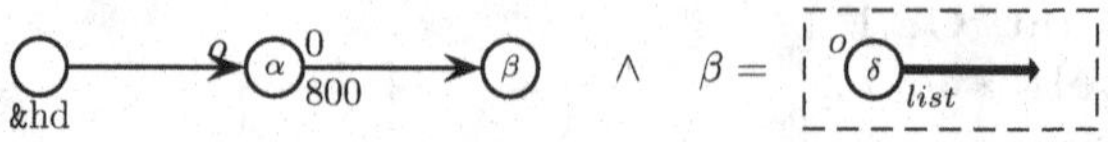

Fig. 2. Hiearchical abstraction

Hierarchical abstraction. The limitation of all the abstractions examined so far is that they fail to capture *both* the list structure and the fact that it lives inside a contiguous memory region. A solution is to perform a two steps abstraction:

1. The whole array occupies an 800 bytes long contiguous region, which can be abstracted by a single points-to predicate $\alpha \mapsto \beta$ where symbolic variables α and β respectively represent the address of the array and its *whole* contents viewed as a sequence of bytes, as shown in the left part of Fig. 2, whereas variable hd points into the array at some offset o (i.e. from base address α).

2. Symbolic variable β which denotes the array contents can be constrained by any abstraction over the sequence of bytes it represents. The trick is then to view it as a memory state in itself (which we later refer to as the *sub-memory*), and apply a classical shape abstraction to it, which expresses that it stores a well-formed singly linked list structure, the first element of which is at offset o, as shown in the right part of Fig. 2. This abstraction relies on the user-defined **list** inductive predicate below:

$$\alpha \cdot \mathbf{list} := (\mathbf{emp} \wedge \alpha = 0) \vee (\alpha \cdot \mathrm{next} \mapsto \beta_0 * \alpha \cdot \mathrm{prio} \mapsto \beta_1 * \beta_0 \cdot \mathbf{list}).$$

In this view, the analysis should use *two levels* of memory abstractions: one to describe the main memory, and another one to describe the contents of a contiguous region of the memory, viewed as a sub-memory. In that sense, our abstraction is *hierarchical*. Furthermore, we are going to show that both abstractions may share a single implementation, where the memory abstraction consists of a general and parametric shape analysis abstract domain. This approach handles arbitrary nesting of dynamic and static structures (e.g., lists of arrays containing lists...). We formalize this abstraction in Sect. 3.3.

Static analysis in the hierarchical abstract domain. Our static analysis should establish properties of array initialization and list construction routines as well as common list operations (traversal, insertion...). Overall, the analysis algorithms in the hierarchical shape abstract domain are standard shape analysis algorithms including unfolding of inductive definitions and widening over shape graphs [5]. However, a number of specific issues need be solved, such as:

  − reasoning about array regions (and about the border between the free zone and the active list) effectively requires integrating array analysis techniques such as those proposed in [8] into a shape abstract domain;
  − designing clear interfaces between domains, so as to make the analysis fully modular, letting the main memory abstraction devolve the analysis of operations to the sub-memory abstraction when possible.

Those issues will be considered carefully in Sect. 4.

3   A Hierarchical Shape Abstract Domain

We formalize our abstract domain in this section, and recall elements of the abstract domain introduced in [6,5] it is based on.

3.1   A Shape Graph Abstract Domain

Concrete model. Intuitively, a *concrete store* can be viewed as a partial function σ from addresses ($a \in \mathbb{A}$) into values ($\mathbb{V}$, where $\mathbb{A} \subseteq \mathbb{V}$). In fact, the structure of memory states is more complex as values of various sizes may be read, so a store is actually characterized by its domain $\mathbf{dom}(\sigma) \in \mathcal{P}(\mathbb{A})$, and the read operation, which maps pair of addresses $a < a' \in \mathbb{A}$ to the value $\mathbf{read}(\sigma, a, a') \in \mathbb{V}$ that can be read in σ between a and a', when $[a, a'[\sqsubseteq \mathbf{dom}(\sigma)$. A concrete value $v \in \mathbb{V}$ thus consists of a sequence of bytes.

Abstraction based on shape graphs. In the abstract level, *symbolic variables* (noted as Greek letters $\alpha, \beta, \ldots \in \mathbb{V}^\sharp$) represent concrete values. These symbolic variables may appear in constraints on the stores structure, on their contents, and possibly simultaneously on both. A *shape graph* $G \in \mathbb{D}_G^\sharp$ describes the structure of concrete stores, as a *separating conjunction* of predicates, called *edges*, which express e.g., that some symbolic variable α is the address of a memory cell containing a value abstracted by another symbolic variable β: this constraint is described by a *points-to* edge of the form $\alpha \mapsto \beta$ (the more general format of points-to edges is shown below). Therefore, concretization $\gamma_G(G)$ of shape graph $G \in \mathbb{D}_G^\sharp$ is defined indirectely. Instead of returning a set of stores, it returns a set of pairs (σ, ν) where $\nu \in \mathbb{Val} = \mathbb{V}^\sharp \to \mathbb{V}$ is a *valuation*, mapping each symbolic variable to the concrete value it abstracts, i.e., performing a physical mapping of the shape graph.

Shape graphs and concretization. The abstract domain is parameterized by the data of a finite set $\mathbb{I}$ of inductive definitions, such as the **list** definition shown in Sect. 2. The complete grammar of shape graphs is defined below:

$$
\begin{aligned}
G &::= e_0 * e_1 * \ldots * e_k & \text{separating conjunction} \\
e &::= \alpha_{[o_0, o_1[} \mapsto \beta + o_2 & \text{points-to edge } (\alpha, \beta \in \mathbb{V}^\sharp) \\
&\mid \alpha \cdot \iota & \text{inductive edge} \\
&\mid \alpha \cdot \iota \mathrel{*\!\!=} \beta \cdot \iota & \text{segment edge}
\end{aligned}
$$

Points-to edge $\alpha_{[o_0, o_1[} \mapsto \beta + o_2$, where o_0, o_1, o_2 are linear expressions over symbolic variables, describes a contiguous region between the addresses represented by $\alpha + o_0$ and $\alpha + o_1$ and storing the value represented by $\beta + o_2$ (thus its size corresponds to $o_1 - o_0$). Edge $\alpha \cdot \iota$ abstracts complete structures described by inductive definition ι, at address α. Segment $\alpha \cdot \iota \mathrel{*\!\!=} \beta \cdot \iota$ abstracts *incomplete* structures, that is a structures starting at address α with a *hole* at address β, i.e. a missing sub-structure at address β. The semantics of inductive and segment edges is defined by syntactic unfolding of their definitions, using rewrite relation $\leadsto_{\text{unfold}}$. For instance, the unfolding rules of inductive definition **list** are:

$$
\begin{aligned}
\alpha \cdot \textbf{list} &\quad\leadsto_{\text{unfold}} (\textbf{emp} \wedge \alpha = 0) \\
\alpha \cdot \textbf{list} &\quad\leadsto_{\text{unfold}} (\alpha \cdot \text{next} \mapsto \beta_0 * \alpha \cdot \text{prio} \mapsto \beta_1 * \beta_0 \cdot \textbf{list}) . \\
\alpha \cdot \textbf{list} \mathrel{*\!\!=} \delta \cdot \textbf{list} &\quad\leadsto_{\text{unfold}} (\textbf{emp} \wedge \alpha = \delta) \\
\alpha \cdot \textbf{list} \mathrel{*\!\!=} \delta \cdot \textbf{list} &\quad\leadsto_{\text{unfold}} (\alpha \cdot \text{next} \mapsto \beta_0 * \alpha \cdot \text{prio} \mapsto \beta_1 * \beta_0 \cdot \textbf{list} \mathrel{*\!\!=} \delta \cdot \textbf{list}.) .
\end{aligned}
$$

Concretization. We can now formalize the concretization $\gamma_G : \mathbb{D}_G^\sharp \to \mathcal{P}(\mathbb{M} \times \mathbb{Val})$ of edges and of shape graphs. First, let us consider an edge e, and define its concretization $\gamma_G(e)$.

- If e is $\alpha_{[o_0,o_1[} \mapsto \beta + o_2$, then $(\sigma, \nu) \in \gamma_G(e)$ if and only if:

$$
\begin{cases}
\textbf{dom}(\sigma) = [\nu_{\mathcal{L}}(\alpha + o_0), \nu_{\mathcal{L}}(\alpha + o_1)[\\
\textbf{read}(\sigma, \nu_{\mathcal{L}}(\alpha + o_0), \nu_{\mathcal{L}}(\alpha + o_1)) = \nu_{\mathcal{L}}(\beta + o_2)
\end{cases}
$$

  where $\nu_{\mathcal{L}}$ denotes the extension of ν to linear expressions over symbolic variables (for instance, $\nu_{\mathcal{L}}(8 + \alpha + 2\beta) = 8 + \nu(\alpha) + 2\nu(\beta)$). This indeed captures the property that this points-to edge covers the range of addresses corresponding to symbolic range $[\alpha + o_0, \alpha + o_1[$ and contains symbolic value $\beta + o_2$.
- If e is either an inductive edge $\alpha \cdot \iota$ or a segment edge $\alpha \cdot \iota \mathrel{*\!\!=} \beta \cdot \iota$, then its concretization is defined by unfolding; thus $(\sigma, \nu) \in \gamma_G(e)$ if and only if:

$$
\exists G, e \leadsto_{\text{unfold}} G \wedge (\sigma, \nu) \in \gamma_G(G).
$$

Concretization γ_G calculates the separating conjunction of the concretizations of the edges of shape graphs:

$$
\gamma_G(e_0 * e_1 * \ldots * e_k) = \{(\sigma_0 \circledast \sigma_1 \circledast \ldots \circledast \sigma_k, \nu) \mid \forall i, (\sigma_i, \nu) \in \gamma_G(e_i)\}.
$$

where $\circledast$ is the fusion of functions with disjoint domains ($\sigma_0 \circledast \sigma_1$ is defined if and only if $\textbf{dom}(\sigma_0) \cap \textbf{dom}(\sigma_1) = \emptyset$ and then $\textbf{read}(\sigma_0 \circledast \sigma_1, a, a') = \textbf{read}(\sigma_i, a, a')$ if $[a, a'[\subseteq \textbf{dom}(\sigma_i))$. In general, due to inductive and segment edges, the concretization of a shape graph has to be defined as a least-fixpoint.

Examples. In practice, a contiguous concrete memory region (or *block*) may be described by one or more points-to edges from one single node, that denote fragments of that memory region. We call such a set of points-to edges starting from a same source node α a *segmentation* of the block. As a very simple example, Fig. 3 shows two possible segmentations (with two edges in Fig. 3b or with one edge in Fig. 3c) to abstract a concrete array of two unsigned 2-bytes integers shown in Fig. 3a. As a convention, we insert segmentation offsets between points-to edges (offsets 0, 2 and 4 in Fig. 3b) and destination offsets at the end of points-to edges (offsets +0 in Fig. 3b): Fig. 3b represents shape graph $\alpha_{[0,2[} \mapsto \beta_0 + 0 * \alpha_{[2,4[} \mapsto \beta_1 + 0$. Segmentations with linear expressions over symbolic variables as offsets rely on the same principle and will appear in Sect. 4.

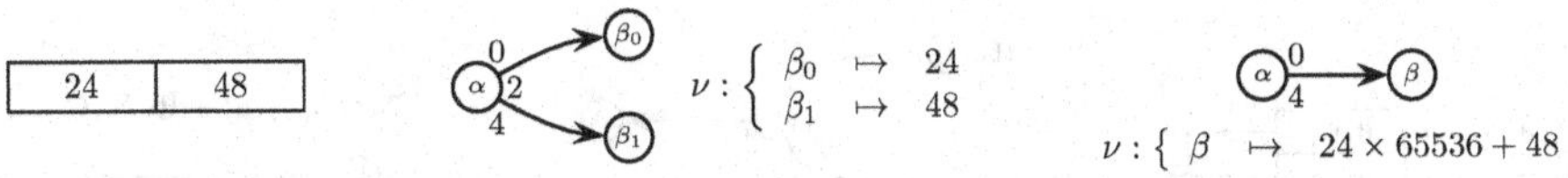

(a) Concrete array.   (b) Pair of edges.   (c) Single edge.

Fig. 3. Segmentations representing an array of two unsigned short integers

3.2 Combination with a Value Domain

The advantage of the notion of shape graphs presented in Sect. 3.1 is that they allow a nice decomposition of the abstract domain: in particular, other forms of properties (such as arithmetic constraints) over symbolic variables can be described in a separate value abstract domain $\mathbb{D}_V^\sharp$, with concretization $\gamma_V :$ $\mathbb{D}_V^\sharp \to \mathcal{P}(\mathbb{V}\text{al})$. An abstract memory state is a pair $(G, V) \in \mathbb{D}_G^\sharp \times \mathbb{D}_V^\sharp$, and concretizes into $\{\sigma \mid \exists \nu \in \gamma_V(V), \ (\sigma, \nu) \in \gamma_G(G)\}$.

In most cases, $\mathbb{D}_V^\sharp$ can be chosen among numerical abstractions. For instance, in the case of Fig. 3b, the octagon abstract domain [20] allows to express relation $\beta_0 < \beta_1$ which is satisfied in valuation ν used to concretize that shape graph into the concrete store of Fig. 3a. However, non purely numerical abstractions may be used as well. For instance, in the case of the shape graph of Fig. 3c, symbolic variable β denotes an array of unsigned 2-bytes integers, and array specific abstractions may be used to abstract β; for instance, that array is sorted, so we could choose $\mathbb{D}_V^\sharp$ in order to express array sortedness.

Moreover, a concrete state M also encloses an environment $E \in \mathbb{E} = \mathbb{X} \mapsto \mathbb{A}$ mapping program variables into addresses, thus is a pair $M = (E, \sigma)$. Likewise, an abstract state $M^\sharp \in \mathbb{S}^\sharp$ also includes an abstract environment $E^\sharp \in \mathbb{E}^\sharp = \mathbb{X} \mapsto \mathbb{V}^\sharp$, and the concretization simply asserts the compatibility of the concrete environment with the abstract environment up to the valuation. We write $\mathbb{S}$ for $\mathbb{E} \times \mathbb{M}$ and $\mathbb{S}^\sharp$ for $\mathbb{E}^\sharp \times \mathbb{D}_G^\sharp \times \mathbb{D}_V^\sharp$. The concretization writes down as follows:

$$(E, \sigma) \in \gamma_S(E^\sharp, G, V) \iff \exists \nu \in \gamma_V(V), \ E = \nu \circ E^\sharp \wedge (\sigma, \nu) \in \gamma_G(G).$$

3.3 Hierarchical Abstraction

At this stage, we are ready to formalize the final step of our hierarchical abstraction: indeed, we noticed in Sect. 3.2 that symbolic variables denote values (as sequences of bytes), that can be constrained both in the shape graph and in some *underlying* value abstraction; thus, we simply need to let our shape abstraction be a possible instance of the value abstraction.

In order to ensure correct mapping with the main memory, the sub-memory abstraction should carry not only a shape graph, but also a *local environment* describing how sub-memory cells are accessed. Therefore, the general form of a *sub-memory value abstract domain* predicate is:

$$\mathfrak{Mem}\langle \beta, \alpha + o_0, \alpha + o_1, E_s, G_s \rangle$$

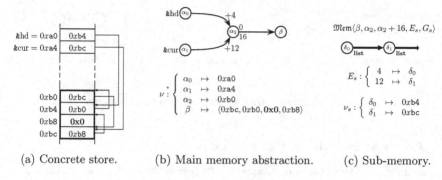

(a) Concrete store.   (b) Main memory abstraction.   (c) Sub-memory.

Fig. 4. Hierarchical abstraction

where:

- $\beta \in \mathbb{V}^{\sharp}$ denotes the sub-memory contents;
- $[\alpha + o_0, \alpha + o_1[$ denotes the range of addresses covered by the sub-memory (where $\alpha \in \mathbb{V}^{\sharp}$ is the base address of the block the sub-memory belongs to);
- $G_s \in \mathbb{D}_G^{\sharp}$ is a shape graph describing the sub-memory;
- $E_s : \mathbb{V}_{\mathcal{L}}^{\sharp} \to \mathbb{V}^{\sharp}$ is a partial map from symbolic offsets (linear combination of symbolic variables) relative to α into nodes of sub-shape graph G_s.

In practice, a store may contain several sub-memories, thus an abstract value of $\mathbb{D}_V^{\sharp}$ consists of a finite set of sub-memory predicates together with a regular abstract element of some other numerical domain to express arithmetic constraints among symbolic variables. We write $\mathbb{D}_{V[\mathbf{sub}]}^{\sharp}$ (resp., $\gamma_{V[\mathbf{sub}]}$) for the sub-memory abstract domain (resp., concretization). Concretization function $\gamma_{V[\mathbf{sub}]} : \mathbb{D}_{V[\mathbf{sub}]}^{\sharp} \to \mathcal{P}(\mathbb{V}\mathfrak{al})$ is formally defined as follows:

$$
\nu \in \gamma_{V[\mathbf{sub}]}(\mathfrak{Mem}\langle \beta, \alpha + o_0, \alpha + o_1, E_s, G_s \rangle)
$$
$$
\iff \quad \exists (\sigma_s, \nu_s) \in \gamma_G(G_s), \quad
\begin{cases}
\mathbf{dom}(\sigma_s) = [\nu_{\mathcal{L}}(\alpha + o_0), \nu_{\mathcal{L}}(\alpha + o_1)[\\
\nu(\beta) = \mathbf{read}(\sigma_s, \nu_{\mathcal{L}}(\alpha + o_0), \nu_{\mathcal{L}}(\alpha + o_1)) \\
\forall l \in \mathbb{V}_{\mathcal{L}}^{\sharp}, \; E_s(l) = \delta \implies \nu_{\mathcal{L}}(\alpha + l) = \nu_s(\delta)
\end{cases}
$$

As an example, we consider in Fig. 4 the case of an array, used as a sub-memory which contains a list occupying the whole array (for the sake of simplicity, we assume list elements only have a next field). Fig 4a shows a concrete state, where the array has length 4, and all cells are part of a list. All physical addresses are shown and thin edges help visualize pointers. Fig. 4b shows the shape graph which abstracts the main memory together with the valuation used to concretize it into the store of Fig. 4a. Note that symbolic variable β is mapped into the concatenation of four 4-bytes values (we assume a 32 bits architecture), hence a value of length 16 bytes. The associated sub-memory predicate is displayed in Fig. 4c, with its shape graph, its environment and the valuation ν_s used to concretize it appropriately. As G_s summarizes the list into a segment predicate and an inductive predicate, some physical addresses ($0x$b0 and $0x$b8) do not even appear in ν_s.

In practice, the abstract states manipulated in order to analyze programs such as the code shown in Fig. 1c are more complex, yet the principle is the same as in the example of Fig. 4:

- list elements have additional fields, so that the size of one structure element is 8 bytes or more, and the strides of the pointers in the free-pool region are multiple of that size s;
- the overall size of the free-pool may be much larger, and could actually be kept abstract (i.e., the analysis would only know it is an unsigned number, that would be a multiple of s);
- the sub-memory may not occupy the whole free-pool space (as is the case in the concrete store shown in Fig. 1b), so the free-pool corresponds to a segmentation with several outgoing edges;
- the offsets in the main shape graph and in the sub-environment are non constant linear expressions over symbolic variables.

4 Static Analysis Algorithms in the Hierarchical Abstract Domain

We now describe the static analysis algorithms, which allow to infer precise invariants over both the main memory and the sub-memory for programs such as the insertion routine in Fig. 1c.

4.1 Structure of the Analysis

For the most part, the analysis consists of a standard shape analysis following the principles of [6,5], which can be formalized as a forward abstract interpretation [7]. The concrete semantics $[\![P]\!]$ of program P collects the set of states (ℓ, M) which are reachable from the entry point of P, after any sequence of execution steps: $(\ell, M) \in [\![P]\!]$ if and only if $(\ell_0, M_0) \rightarrow (\ell_1, M_1) \rightarrow \ldots \rightarrow (\ell_n, M_n) \rightarrow (\ell, M)$, where ℓ_0 is the entry point of P and $\rightarrow$ denotes the transition relation of P. The analysis computes invariants I_ℓ for all control states ℓ, which consist of finite disjunctions of abstract states. The analysis is sound in the following sense:

Theorem 1 (Soundness). *For all* $(\ell, M) \in [\![P]\!]$, *there exists* $M^\sharp \in I_\ell$ *such that* $M \in \gamma_S(M^\sharp)$.

To achieve this, we use sound transfer functions to compute abstract post-conditions and sound abstract join and widening operators to over-approximate the effect of control flow joins. The abstract join operator is especially interesting in the sense that it may introduce or merge existing sub-memory predicates, which is why we consider it first (Sect. 4.2). Furthermore, another novelty is the need for all abstraction layers (main memory, sub-memory and other value abstract domains) to exchange information, as one analysis step typically requires some steps of computation be done in all layers (Sect. 4.3).

4.2   Abstract Join and Management of Sub-Memory Predicates

In the beginning of the analysis, the contents of the memory is unknown, so no information is available in $\mathbb{D}^{\sharp}_{V[\mathbf{sub}]}$ (the empty set of sub-memory predicates denotes the absence of sub-memory information). As the analysis progresses, sub-memory predicates may be introduced or be combined into new sub-memory predicates. Those operations are performed at control flow join points, by the shape abstract join (which serves both as an abstract union and as a widening).

The abstract join operator takes two inputs $M^{\sharp}_l = (E^{\sharp}_l, G_l, V_l)$, $M^{\sharp}_r = (E^{\sharp}_r, G_r, V_r)$, and computes an over-approximation $M^{\sharp}_o = (E^{\sharp}_o, G_o, V_o)$. To achieve such a result, the shape graph join computes matching partitions of the edges of G_l and G_r and approximates such corresponding sets of edges with edges into G_o. These partitions are described by functions $\Psi_l, \Psi_r : \mathbb{V}^{\sharp} \to \mathbb{V}^{\sharp}$, where Ψ_l (resp., Ψ_r) maps nodes of G_o into the nodes of G_l (resp., G_r) that they over-approximate. In the following, we let $\Psi(G)$ (resp., $\Psi(o)$) denote the renaming of all symbolic variables in graph G (resp., in offset o) by applying function Ψ. Then, the computation of G_o takes the form of a sequence of rewriting steps over graph tuples:

$$(G_l, G_r, \mathbf{emp}) = (G^0_l, G^0_r, G^0_o) \overset{\sqcup}{\leadsto} (G^1_l, G^1_r, G^1_o) \overset{\sqcup}{\leadsto} \dots$$
$$\dots \overset{\sqcup}{\leadsto} (G^{k-1}_l, G^{k-1}_r, G^{k-1}_o) \overset{\sqcup}{\leadsto} (G^k_l, G^k_r, G^k_o) = (\mathbf{emp}, \mathbf{emp}, G_o)$$

where each step i is sound in the sense that

$$\forall s \in \{l, r\}, \; \gamma_{\mathbb{S}}(E^{\sharp}_s, G^i_s * \Psi_s(G^i_o), V_s) \subseteq \gamma_{\mathbb{S}}(E^{\sharp}_s, G^{i+1}_s * \Psi_s(G^{i+1}_o), V_s)$$

Each step corresponds to a rule, as defined in [5], such as, for instance:
- Rule **(r-pt)** over-approximates a pair of points-to edges with a new one:

$$\left(\begin{array}{c} \Psi_l(\alpha)_{[\Psi_l(o), \Psi_l(o')[} \mapsto \Psi_l(\beta), \\ \Psi_r(\alpha)_{[\Psi_r(o), \Psi_r(o')[} \mapsto \Psi_r(\beta), \\ \mathbf{emp} \end{array} \right) \overset{\sqcup}{\leadsto} \left(\begin{array}{c} \mathbf{emp}, \\ \mathbf{emp}, \\ \alpha_{[o, o'[} \mapsto \beta \end{array} \right).$$

- Rule **(r-emp-seg)** matches an empty region in G_l with a region of G_r that can be proved a particular case of a segment; one case of **(r-emp-seg)** is:

$$\left(\begin{array}{c} \mathbf{emp}, \\ \Psi_r(\alpha)_{[\Psi_r(o), \Psi_r(o')[} \mapsto \Psi_r(\beta), \\ \mathbf{emp} \end{array} \right) \overset{\sqcup}{\leadsto} \left(\begin{array}{c} \mathbf{emp}, \\ \mathbf{emp}, \\ \alpha \cdot \mathbf{list} \mathbin{*\!=} \beta \cdot \mathbf{list} \end{array} \right) \text{ if } \Psi_l(\alpha) = \Psi_l(\beta).$$

All rules are shown in [5]. The soundness of each step guarantees the soundness of the result, given value the abstract element $V_o = (\Psi_l)^{-1}(V_l) \triangledown_V (\Psi_r)^{-1}(V_r)$, where $\triangledown_V$ is a widening operator in $\mathbb{D}^{\sharp}_V$ (symbolic variables of inputs need be renamed using Ψ_l, Ψ_r to make value abstractions consistent), and environment $E^{\sharp}_o = (\Psi_l)^{-1} \circ E^{\sharp}_l$. In our setup, with points-to edges of non statically known size (Sect. 3.1) and with sub-memory predicates (Sect. 3.3), additional join rewriting rules need be considered, resulting in the *introduction* and in the *fusion* of sub-memory predicates, as part of $\triangledown_V$.

Theorem 2 (Soundness). *For all* $s \in \{l, r\}$, $\gamma_{\mathbb{S}}(E^{\sharp}_s, G_s, V_s) \subseteq \gamma_{\mathbb{S}}(E^{\sharp}_o, G_o, V_o)$.

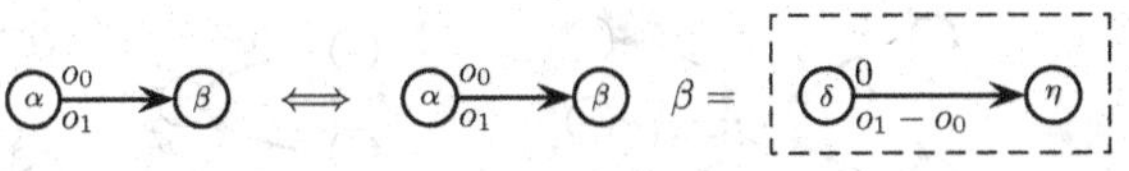

(a) Introduction of a sub-memory predicate.

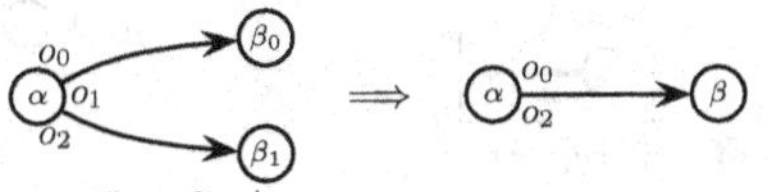

$\mathfrak{Mem}\langle \beta_0, \alpha + o_0, \alpha + o_1, E_{s,0}, G_{s,0}\rangle$
$\mathfrak{Mem}\langle \beta_1, \alpha + o_1, \alpha + o_2, E_{s,1}, G_{s,1}\rangle$

$\mathfrak{Mem}\langle \beta, \alpha + o_0, \alpha + o_2, E_{s,0} \uplus E_{s,1}, G_{s,0} * G_{s,1}\rangle$

(b) Fusion of sub-memory predicates.

Fig. 5. Management of sub-memory predicates

Join over contiguous points-to edges. Unlike the abstract domain of [5], the abstraction shown in Sect. 3 copes with arrays, thus new rewriting rules need be added for the case where matching nodes $\Psi_l(\alpha), \Psi_r(\alpha)$ are the origin of different numbers of points-to edges in both arguments. Thus, the extended algorithm adds a general rule **(r-fusion)** to re-partition such segmentations from a same node, as in array analyses such as [8]. When the left segmentation has one edge and the right segmentation has two, **(r-fusion)** writes down as follows:

$$\begin{pmatrix} \Psi_l(\alpha)_{[\Psi_l(o), \Psi_l(o'')[} \mapsto \Psi_l(\beta), \\ \Psi_r(\alpha)_{[\Psi_r(o), \Psi_r(o')[} \mapsto \beta_0 * \Psi_r(\alpha)_{[\Psi_r(o'), \Psi_r(o'')[} \mapsto \beta_1, \\ \mathbf{emp} \end{pmatrix} \overset{\sqcup}{\rightsquigarrow} \begin{pmatrix} \mathbf{emp}, \\ \mathbf{emp}, \\ \alpha_{[o, o''[} \mapsto \beta \end{pmatrix}$$

where Ψ_r maps β into the *sequence* $\langle \beta_0, \beta_1 \rangle$, i.e. expresses that symbolic variable β should over-approximate values corresponding to the concatenation of the values represented by β_0 and β_1 in G_r. General **(r-fusion)** subsumes **(r-pt)**.

Introduction and fusion of a sub-memory predicate. Whenever a shape graph contains a points-to edge, a sub-memory predicate can be introduced, as shown in Fig. 5a. When applying rule **(r-fusion)**, such sub-memory predicates can be introduced in both join inputs, so as to capture the meaning of points-to edges in both inputs. However, this process generates two sub-memory predicates in the right hand side (and one in the left hand side), thus those sub-memory predicates need be combined together. This operation can be performed as shown in Fig. 5b.

Example of an abstract join. Fig. 6 shows a join similar to those found in the analysis of the code of Fig. 1c. For the sake of clarity, we show only a relevant fragment of the abstract states, and we express the relation between β_1^1 and α^1 in the value abstraction (in the analysis, it is actually represented as a looping points-to edge $\alpha^1_{[o'_1, o'_1+4[} \mapsto \alpha^1 + o''_1$). The abstract state shown in Fig. 6a describes a list stored in a sub-memory and pointed to by cur. Fig. 6b describes the situation after allocating an additional element in the free-pool, pointed to by cur. Join (Fig. 6c) applies rule **(r-fusion)** to the first two edges, introduces

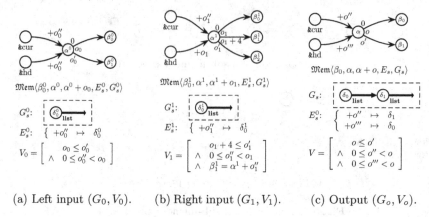

(a) Left input (G_0, V_0).   (b) Right input (G_1, V_1).   (c) Output (G_o, V_o).

Fig. 6. Abstract join at the second iteration

a sub-memory in G_1, merges that sub-memory with the pre-existing one, and then performs an abstract join in the sub-memory. This sub-memory join then introduces a segment, thanks to rule **(r-emp-seg)**.

Soundness of the abstract join and termination of the widening can be proved as in [5]. The implementation is also similar (in particular, the algorithm actually infers partitions Ψ_l, Ψ_r as part of the sequence of rewriting steps leading to G_o).

4.3   Abstract Transfer Functions

Abstract transfer functions compute over-approximated abstract post-conditions for each elementary concrete operations. When analyzing a statement (such as an allocation, an assignment, a test...) between control states ℓ and ℓ', the analyzer should evaluate a transfer function $\mathfrak{transfer}^\sharp_{\ell,\ell'}$. This transfer function should satisfy the soundness condition below:

$$M \in \gamma_S(M^\sharp) \wedge (\ell, M) \to (\ell', M') \Longrightarrow M' \in \gamma_S(\mathfrak{transfer}^\sharp_{\ell,\ell'}(M^\sharp))$$

Analysis of an assignment. In the following, we consider the analysis of the assignment $\mathtt{lv} := \mathtt{ex}$ between ℓ and ℓ', where $\mathtt{lv}$ is an l-value and $\mathtt{ex}$ an expression (the other transfer functions are similar, thus we formalize only $\mathfrak{assign}$). In the concrete level, $[\![\mathtt{lv}]\!]$ (resp., $[\![\mathtt{ex}]\!]$) denotes the semantics of $\mathtt{lv}$ (resp., $\mathtt{ex}$); it maps a memory state into an address (resp., a numeric or pointer value). Then, the concrete transitions corresponding to that assignment are of the form $(E, \sigma) \to (E, \sigma')$, where $\sigma' = \sigma[[\![\mathtt{lv}]\!](E, \sigma) \leftarrow [\![\mathtt{ex}]\!](E, \sigma)]$. In the abstract level, $[\![\mathtt{lv}]\!]^\sharp$ (resp., $[\![\mathtt{ex}]\!]^\sharp$) returns a node with offset $\alpha + o$ denoting the address of the cell to modify (resp., a node with offset $\beta' + o'$ denoting the value to assign). When the abstract pre-condition shape graph G contains a points-to edge $\alpha + o \mapsto \beta$, $\mathfrak{assign}$ should simply replace this edge with points-to edge $\alpha + o \mapsto \beta' + o'$. However, some transformations may need be done on G before this trivial $\mathfrak{assign}$ can be applied:

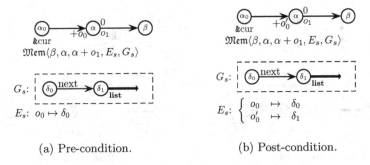

(a) Pre-condition.   (b) Post-condition.

Fig. 7. Analysis of the assignment $cur = cur{-}{>}next$

- When the evaluation of either lv or ex requires accessing fields which are not materialized, as they are summarized as part of inductive or segment edges, those should be unfolded first [5].
- When ex is a non trivial numeric expression, it should be analyzed in the value domain. Let us consider the case where ex is $4*x+8$. That expression should be transformed by replacing all l-values with nodes corresponding to their addresses, which gives an expression of the form $4 \cdot \delta + 8$. A fresh node β' should be added to G. The assignment $\beta' \leftarrow 4 \cdot \delta + 8$ should be analyzed in the value domain, using sound abstract transfer function $\mathsf{assign}_{\mathsf{V}^\sharp}$. Then, the assign proceeds as above, by switching a points-to edge.

In the following, we extend this operator to the hierarchical abstract domain. We assume abstract pre-condition $(E^\sharp, G, V)$ contains at least one sub-memory $\mathfrak{Mem}\langle \beta, \alpha + o_0, \alpha + o_1, E_s, G_s \rangle$, and describe the analysis assignment $lv := ex$. As cases where the assignment only affects the main memory are unchanged, we consider only the cases where it involves a read or a write into the sub-memory, and show what changes need be done to the classic assign operator.

Read in a sub-memory. Let us consider statement $cur = cur{-}{>}next$, with the abstract pre-condition shown in Fig. 7a. Then, l-value cur evaluates into α_0, which is the origin of points-to edge $\alpha_0 \mapsto \alpha + o_0$. The evaluation of r-value $cur{-}{>}next$ is more complex, as cur points into the sub-memory, at offset o_0. However, the environment maps o_0 into sub-memory node δ_0, which has a next field, pointing to δ_1. Thus, in the sub-memory, the r-value evaluates to δ_1. The effect of the assignment is thus captured by an update to the main memory edge destination offset (o'_0 instead of o_0) and an update to the sub-environment to reflect this new mapping (Fig. 7b). To summarize, sub-memory pointer reads can be handled like normal pointer reads, where the base address is represented by the sub-memory based node.

When the read operation returns a node that does not appear in the sub-memory environment (and thus, cannot be seen from the outside), an equality constraint between that node and an external fresh node should be generated in $V^\sharp$, so as to capture the effect of the assignment.

Write in a sub-memory. We now consider the case of an assignment to a structure field *inside* a sub-memory. In Fig. 8, we show an abstract pre-condition

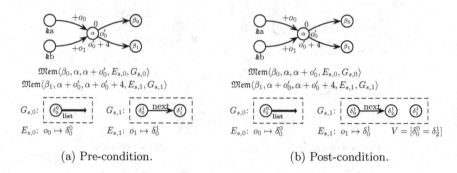

(a) Pre-condition.   (b) Post-condition.

Fig. 8. Analysis of the assignment b−>next = a

and an abstract post-condition computed from it, in the case of assignment b−>next = a where a and b are two pointers into a free-pool. This abstract state arises after introduction of two sub-memories, and before their fusion by a join operator (Sect. 4.2). The effect of the assignment is local to the sub-memory where b points to:

- a new node δ_2^1 is created with the equality constraint that it is equal to δ_0^0;
- sub-memory points-to edge $\delta_0^1 \cdot \text{next} \mapsto \delta_1^1$ is replaced with $\delta_0^1 \cdot \text{next} \mapsto \delta_2^1$.

The second operation is actually performed as part of the evaluation of $\text{assign}_{\mathbb{V}^\sharp}$ over the sub-memory which content is bound to β_1. Past this step, the invariant attached to that sub-memory includes pointers *leaving* the sub-memory itself (to the other sub-memory). Similar situations arise in the program of Fig. 1c, when updates are done inside the free-pool. Moreover, when the sub-memory cell that need be assigned is part of a folded inductive predicate, classical inductive predicate unfolding techniques [5] apply.

Soundness. Operator assign is sound:

Theorem 3 (Soundness). *Let $M = (E, \sigma) \in \gamma_S(M^\sharp)$. If we let $a = [\![lv]\!](M)$ and $v = [\![ex]\!](M)$, then $(E, \sigma[a \leftarrow v]) \in \gamma_S(\text{assign}(lv, ex, M^\sharp))$.*

5   Prototype and Implementation

We integrated the hierarchical abstraction into the MEMCAD analyzer (*Memory Compositional Abstract Domain*, http://www.di.ens.fr/~rival/memcad.html). It was implemented as a functor, which lifts a shape abstract domain into a value abstract domain, which can in turn be fed into the shape abstract domain functor. Numerical abstract invariants ($\mathbb{D}_V^\sharp$) are represented in a numerical domain complying with the Apron [16] interface. The experiments below use convex polyedra [9]. The results obtained when running it on a series of routines that build and manipulate a sub-structure in a free-pool are shown in the table below (in the third column), and are compared with times to analyze similar routines using regular memory allocation system call **malloc** (second column), which do not require the hierarchical abstraction. Run-times are given in seconds, as observed with an Intel Core i3 CPU laptop running at 2.10 GHz, with 4 Gb of RAM. The analysis is fully automatic and inputs only a generic list inductive definition (Sect. 2) and the unannotated source code. The set of codes considered in the table below includes `running`, our main example (Fig. 1c), as well as other basic operations on the dynamic structure (head and tail insertion, flipping of cells, drop of a cell). Those comprise all typical features of a the user defined allocator based on a static free-pool as found in `running`. While the industrial code of [21] never "deallocates" cells (instead, it sometimes reset the free-pool, before building a new structure in it), we included a `drop` example, where a cell is selected and removed from the linked list, yet cannot be reused; such cells are abstracted from the sub-memory contents (those cells are abstracted into a ... ∗ **true** predicate [23] i.e., a heap region nothing is known about).

Program	Allocation method		Description
	malloc	free-pool array	
`running`	0.195	0.520	The running example
`head`	0.019	0.034	List, head-insertion
`tail`	0.027	0.050	List, tail-insertion
`traversal`	0.056	0.107	List, tail-insertion then traversal
`flip`	0.139	0.323	List, flipping two cells after selection
`drop`	0.104	0.289	List, dropping a cell after selection
`integers`	NA	0.016	Initialization of an array to zeros

In all those examples, MEMCAD infers a precise abstract description of all dynamic structures in the free-pool or in the main memory, and proves memory safety. We observe a 2X to 3X slowdown in the analyses of codes using a free-pool. The difference is justified by the extra burden of maintaining the sub-memory predicates together with the array segmentation and side numerical predicates over offsets. While noticeable, this slowdown is very reasonable, as the properties which are inferred are strong and memory safety is proved. Last, we remarked that the current implementation of the MEMCAD analyzer does not feature a very efficient management of symbolic disjunctions of abstract states; addressing that separate issue would improve timings significantly.

6   Related Works and Conclusion

Our hierarchical abstract domain allows to design memory abstractions in a modular way, which relates to the layout of data-structures used in programs. This modularity makes the analysis design simpler while preserving its characteristics (precision and performance). Our abstract domain is parametric in the data of an underlying value abstraction (so that more complex abstract domains could be used in order to deal with values), and in the data of a set of structure inductive definitions (our test case uses only lists, but the analysis would be very similar if doubly-linked lists or trees were built inside the free-pool instead of singly linked lists). Furthermore, our proposal integrates much of the power of array analyses such as [13,15,8] into a shape analysis framework [6,5]. This was made possible by the structure of the abstraction proposed in [5], which allows a nice combination with a value abstraction. While that value abstraction was initially set to be a numerical abstraction, our hierarchical abstract domain shows that much more complex structures can be devolved to an underlying domain. This allows a very modular design for the static analyses. We notice that the notion of array partition of [8] plays a similar role as the partition used in abstract join [5] of shape graphs. Like [8], our analysis does not require a pre-analysis to discover array partitions, following the principles of the shape join of [5]. Composite structures are a common issue in the shape analysis field [19,11,10]. An important contribution of our proposal is to decompose the abstract domain into smaller domains, which are easier to implement and to reason about.

Gulwani et al. [14] enhance shape abstract domains with numerical information so as to reason about the size of arrays stored in linked list elements. Their analysis does not allow to reason about the structure contents whereas our approach allows to delegate such a description to a generic value domain (which may store shape information, when the arrays store complex structures). In [4], Calcagno et al. address the safety of general memory allocators, like the C **malloc**, using an ad-hoc abstract domain based on separation logic, which embeds both shape and numerical information. Their work addresses a separate set of cases than ours, as their approach could not deal with our user-defined pseudo-allocator whereas MEMCAD does not handle their examples at this point. As this analysis considers the allocator separately from the code, it can abstract away the contents of memory block. The analysis of [18] targets overlaid dynamic structures, which is also a completely separate issue than that of our application specific memory allocator, and relies on very different techniques.

The most important future work is the integration of our shape abstraction into an analyzer such as ASTRÉE [3], which would effectively improve the analysis of embedded applications such as those considered in [22,21]. This represents a considerable amount of work as no standard interface has been set up so far for memory abstractions, unlike numerical abstractions. We believe our work actually achieves a step in that direction, as the design of the hierarchical abstraction imposed a careful assessment of abstract domain component interfaces. Other future works include the support of non-contiguous segmentations, which would allow the analysis of a wide family of memory allocators. Last, our framework supports the composition of more than two levels of hierarchical abstractions, e.g., to analyze lists of elements containing arrays, that are stored inside large static zones, thus we could consider such examples.

Acknowledgments. We thank the members of the MEMCAD group for discussions and the reviewers for suggestions that helped improving this paper.

References

1. Berdine, J., Calcagno, C., Cook, B., Distefano, D., O'Hearn, P.W., Wies, T., Yang, H.: Shape Analysis for Composite Data Structures. In: Damm, W., Hermanns, H. (eds.) CAV 2007. LNCS, vol. 4590, pp. 178–192. Springer, Heidelberg (2007)

2. Bertrane, J., Cousot, P., Cousot, R., Feret, J., Mauborgne, L., Miné, A., Rival, X.: Static analysis and verification of aerospace software by abstract interpretation. In: AIAA Infotech@Aerospace, I@A 2010 (2010)
3. Blanchet, B., Cousot, P., Cousot, R., Feret, J., Mauborgne, L., Miné, A., Monniaux, D., Rival, X.: A static analyzer for large safety-critical software. In: PLDI (2003)
4. Calcagno, C., Distefano, D., O'Hearn, P.W., Yang, H.: Beyond Reachability: Shape Abstraction in the Presence of Pointer Arithmetic. In: Yi, K. (ed.) SAS 2006. LNCS, vol. 4134, pp. 182–203. Springer, Heidelberg (2006)
5. Chang, E., Rival, X.: Relational inductive shape analysis. In: POPL (2008)
6. Chang, B.-Y.E., Rival, X., Necula, G.C.: Shape Analysis with Structural Invariant Checkers. In: Riis Nielson, H., Filé, G. (eds.) SAS 2007. LNCS, vol. 4634, pp. 384–401. Springer, Heidelberg (2007)
7. Cousot, P., Cousot, R.: Abstract interpretation: A unified lattice model for static analysis of programs by construction or approximation of fixpoints. In: POPL (1977)
8. Cousot, P., Cousot, R., Logozzo, F.: A parametric segmentation functor for fully automatic and scalable array content analysis. In: POPL (2011)
9. Cousot, P., Halbwachs, N.: Automatic discovery of linear restraints among variables of a program. In: POPL (1978)
10. Dillig, I., Dillig, T., Aiken, A.: Precise reasoning for programs using containers. In: POPL (2011)
11. Distefano, D., O'Hearn, P.W., Yang, H.: A Local Shape Analysis Based on Separation Logic. In: Hermanns, H. (ed.) TACAS 2006. LNCS, vol. 3920, pp. 287–302. Springer, Heidelberg (2006)
12. DO-178C: Software considerations in airborne systems and equipment certification. Technical report, Radio Technical Commission on Aviation (2011)
13. Gopan, D., Reps, T.W., Sagiv, S.: A framework for numeric analysis of array operations. In: POPL (2005)
14. Gulwani, S., Lev-Ami, T., Sagiv, M.: A combination framework for tracking partition sizes. In: POPL (2009)
15. Halbwachs, N., Péron, M.: Discovering properties about arrays in simple programs. In: PLDI (2008)
16. Jeannet, B., Miné, A.: Apron: A Library of Numerical Abstract Domains for Static Analysis. In: Bouajjani, A., Maler, O. (eds.) CAV 2009. LNCS, vol. 5643, pp. 661–667. Springer, Heidelberg (2009)
17. Laviron, V., Chang, B.-Y.E., Rival, X.: Separating Shape Graphs. In: Gordon, A.D. (ed.) ESOP 2010. LNCS, vol. 6012, pp. 387–406. Springer, Heidelberg (2010)
18. Lee, O., Yang, H., Petersen, R.: Program Analysis for Overlaid Data Structures. In: Gopalakrishnan, G., Qadeer, S. (eds.) CAV 2011. LNCS, vol. 6806, pp. 592–608. Springer, Heidelberg (2011)
19. Marron, M., Stefanovic, D., Hermenegildo, M.V., Kapur, D.: Heap analysis in the presence of collection libraries. In: PASTE (2007)
20. Miné, A.: The octagon abstract domain. HOSC 19(1) (2006)
21. Miné, A.: Static Analysis of Run-Time Errors in Embedded Critical Parallel C Programs. In: Barthe, G. (ed.) ESOP 2011. LNCS, vol. 6602, pp. 398–418. Springer, Heidelberg (2011)
22. Monniaux, D.: Verification of device drivers and intelligent controllers: a case study. In: EMSOFT (2007)
23. Reynolds, J.: Separation logic: A logic for shared mutable data structures. In: LICS (2002)
24. Sagiv, S., Reps, T.W., Wilhelm, R.: Parametric shape analysis via 3-valued logic. In: POPL (1999)

Vinter: A Vampire-Based Tool for Interpolation*

Kryštof Hoder[1], Andreas Holzer[2], Laura Kovács[2], and Andrei Voronkov[1]

[1] University of Manchester
[2] TU Vienna

Abstract. This paper describes the Vinter tool for extracting interpolants from proofs and minimising such interpolants using various measures. Vinter takes an input problem written in either SMT-LIB or TPTP syntax, generates so called local proofs and then uses a technique of *playing in the grey areas of proofs* to find interpolants minimal with respect to various measures. Proofs are found using either Z3 or Vampire, solving pseudo-boolean optimisation is delegated to Yices, while localising proofs and generating minimal interpolants is done by Vampire. We describe the use of Vinter and give experimental results on problems from bounded model checking.

1 Introduction

Craig's interpolation [3] has become a useful technique for various tasks in software verification, such as bounded model checking [10], predicate abstraction [8], and loop invariant generation [11]. It provides a systematic way to generate predicates over program states, which are precise enough to prove particular program properties.

Let us introduce some notation and define interpolation through colors. All formulas in this paper are first-order. We will use the standard notion of an *inference*, written as $\frac{A_1 \dots A_n}{A}$, where $A_1, \dots, A_n$ denote the premises and A the conclusion of the inference. By a *derivation* or a *proof* we mean a tree built using inferences, see [9] for details. We assume that for every inference its conclusion is a logical consequence (in first-order predicate logic or in some theory) of its premises. If a formula A is derivable from a set of formulas S, we will write $S \vdash A$ and omit S if it is empty.

We will use three colors: blue, red and grey. Each symbol is colored in exactly one of these colors. By a symbol we mean a function or a predicate symbol; logical variables are not symbols. We say that a formula is *red* if it has at least one red symbol and contains only red and grey symbols. Similarly, a *blue* formula has at least one blue symbol and contains only blue and grey symbols. A formula is *grey* if all symbols in this formula are grey. Let R be a red formula, B a blue formula and $\vdash R \rightarrow B$. We call an *interpolant* of R and B any grey formula I such that (i) $\vdash R \rightarrow I$ and (ii) $\vdash I \rightarrow B$. That is, an interpolant I is in intermediate in power between R and B, and uses only grey symbols. Likewise, if $\{R, B\}$ is unsatisfiable, then a *reverse interpolant* of R and B is any grey formula I such that (i) $\vdash R \rightarrow I$ and (ii) $\{I, B\}$ is

---

* We acknowledge funding from the University of Manchester and an EPSRC grant (Hoder and Voronkov), the FWF Hertha Firnberg Research grant T425-N23, the FWF National Research Network RiSE S11410-N23 and S11403-N23, the WWTF PROSEED grant ICT C-050 and the CeTAT project (Holzer and Kovács).

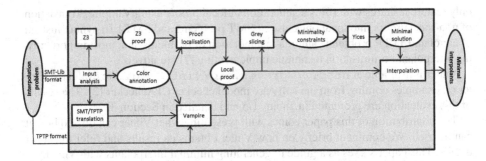

Fig. 1. Architecture of Vinter

unsatisfiable. Interpolation-based verification methods make use of reverse interpolants, where R typically encodes a bounded program trace and B describes a property which is violated at the end of the trace.

If $\{R, B\}$ is unsatisfiable and we have a derivation Π of $\bot$ from $\{R, B\}$, where $\bot$ denotes a (grey) formula which is always false, we are interested in extracting a reverse interpolant from Π. There are algorithms [10,9] for extracting a reverse interpolant from derivations satisfying a locality condition: a derivation is called *local* if no inference in this derivation contains both a red and a blue symbol. A derivation that is not local is called non-local.

In [7] we observe that changes in the grey parts of local proofs, that is, parts consisting of only grey formulas, can make significant changes in the interpolants extracted from proofs. Based on this observation, we defined the notion of *grey slicing* transformations of proofs and showed that all such transformations can be captured by a propositional formula in the following sense. Given a proof Π we can find a propositional formula p such that p is true on a proof Π' if and only if Π' is a local proof obtained from Π by grey slicing. This propositional formula, together with some size measures of formulas, can be used for building small interpolants by running a pseudo-boolean optimisation tool. Small interpolants are believed to be good for end-applications since they are easier to use in proofs and are more likely to generalise than larger ones.

While the method of [7] is general and can be used for generating small interpolants, the power of the method was not well understood. One of the reason was lack of realistic examples coming from state-of-the-art model checkers. Another major obstacle to the evaluation of [7] on realistic examples was lack of a standalone tool that would take as input an interpolation problem generated by a model checker and output minimal interpolants in a fully automatic way.

We address these problem by implementing the Vinter tool that implements the interpolant minimisation technique together with the technique of localising non-local proofs (Section 2). Vinter takes an input problem written in either SMT-LIB [1] or TPTP syntax [14], generates local proofs and then finds interpolants minimal with respect to various measures. Proofs are found using either Z3 [4] or Vampire [13], solving pseudo-boolean optimisation is delegated to Yices [5], while localising proofs and generating minimal interpolants is done by Vampire.

In our previous paper [6] we already described an implementation of interpolation in Vampire. Vinter is a new tool whose aim is to generate a *minimal* interpolant. The only feature it shares with [6] is a generation of local proofs using Vampire. Translation of non-local proofs into local ones, use of SMT problems and SMT-LIB syntax instead of annotated TPTP problems, automatic annotation of problems and, most importantly, the interpolant minimisation technique implementing [7] are novel.

Vinter is available at http://vprover.org/vinter.cgi. We evaluated Vinter on examples coming from the software model checker CPAchecker [2]. The results of this evaluation are presented in Tables 1-5 and detailed in Section 3.

The contribution of this paper comes with presenting what Vinter can do and how it can be used. We comment briefly on how Vinter obtains its results and refer to [7] for details. This paper serves as a guide to generating minimal interpolants with Vinter.

2   Tool Description

Figure 1 shows the architecture of Vinter. Vinter is run on an input problem, called the interpolation problem, and accepts two options denoting the input syntax (SMT-LIB or TPTP) and the theorem prover (Vampire or Z3) used for proving.

Given an input formula, Vinter makes the following steps: (i) creation of an interpolation problem (formulas annotated with coloring information); (ii) generation of a local proof; (iii) grey slicing analysis resulting in a pseudo-boolean constraint; (iv) solving the constraint; (v) generation of a minimal interpolant. In this section we explain all these steps in some detail.

Annotated Formulas and Interpolation Problems. To specify an interpolation problem, one needs to specify two formulas R and B, together with the coloring information. However, both the SMT-LIB and TPTP syntax describe only first-order problems. To specify interpolation problems, we extended the TPTP syntax as described in [6]. For example, one can use the following annotations to specify colors:

vampire(symbol,function,symbol_name,symbol_arity,symbol_color).

However, these *color annotations* can only be understood by Vampire, and are used by Vampire to produce local proof.

For the SMT-LIB syntax we chose a different convention to specify colors. This convention was chosen by analysing bounded model checking problems in SMT-LIB. Such problems describe several unfoldings of computations going through several program states $0, 1, \ldots$. One common way of describing such problems in the SMT community is to turn state variables into functions of one argument (the state). For example, the term $f(1)$ denotes the value of state variable f at state 1.

To extract an interpolation problem from an SMT problem we "reverse engineer" SMT problems in the following way. If the SMT problem contains a unary function f which is only applied to integer constants, we consider it a state variable and replace any term of the form $f(i)$ by a constant f_i. After that we take a "middle state" m (the average integer value of all states) and consider all terms f_k for $k < m$ red and terms f_k for $k > m$ blue. The term f_m is considered grey. This corresponds to the standard use of interpolation in bounded model checking. Further, we consider the conjunction of all formulas containing red symbols as R and the conjunction of all formulas containing blue symbols as B.

Finally, if Vinter is run with Vampire, the interpolation problem written in the SMT-LIB syntax is translated into a TPTP problem with color annotations.

$$\frac{\dfrac{R_1 \quad G_1}{G_2 \qquad G_3 \quad B_1}}{\dfrac{G_4 \qquad G_5}{\bot}}$$

Fig. 2. Local proof Π_1

$$\frac{\dfrac{R_1 \quad G_1 \quad G_3 \quad B_1}{G_4 \qquad G_5}}{\bot}$$

Fig. 3. Local proof Π_2 obtained by slicing off G_2 in Figure 2

Generation of a Local Proof. This step depends on which theorem prover we use. We need a proof-producing theorem prover and ideally a prover producing local proofs. So far, there is not much choice on the market. Z3 seems to be the most efficient SMT solver that produces proofs which are usually non-local. Many first-order theorem provers produce proofs but only Vampire can produce local proofs [6].

If Vinter is run using Vampire, we pass the interpolation problem to Vampire and use the option that makes it search only for local refutations. That is, if Vampire produces a proof, the proof is local.

If Vinter is run using Z3, in general we can only obtain non-local proofs. Then we use the technique of [7] to transform them into local proofs. This technique existentially quantifies away uninterpreted colored constants to make a non-local proof into a local one. In this paper however we do a bit more than [7]: instead of quantifying away only red symbols, we also existentially quantify away blue symbols. Tables 1-3 show the effect of quantifying away different colors.

Transforming non-local Z3 proofs into local ones by quantifying away colored symbols is also used in [12]. The method described in [12] also implements additional steps, such as eliminating quantifier instantiations and using a secondary interpolating prover for proof subtrees that cannot be localised. While the approach of [12] is more general than ours when it comes to localise Z3 proofs, it is quite specific to the set of proof rules used by Z3. Let us therefore note that our proof localisation can be applied to arbitrary SMT proofs. Moreover, Vinter is not restricted to SMT proofs only. To the best of our knowledge, Vinter is the first tool that generates interpolants both from SMT proofs and first-order resolution proofs, and minimises interpolants wrt various measures.

Grey Slicing. After obtaining a local proof Π, either by Vampire or by localising a Z3 proof, Vinter implements the main idea of the interpolant minimisation method: it encodes all *grey slicing transformations* of this local proof by a propositional formula P. Grey slicing is described in [7]. It is based on the idea that some grey formulas can be removed from a local proof without destroying locality and their removal can change the interpolant extracted from the proof.

Example 1. Let us illustrate how grey slicing changes the interpolants extracted from a local proof. Consider the local proof Π_1 given in Figure 2. Using the method of [9], the reverse interpolant extracted from Π_1 is $\neg G_2$.

By slicing off the grey formula G_2, that is by performing grey slicing with G_2 in Π_1, we obtain the local proof Π_2 given in Figure 3. The reverse interpolant extracted from Π_2 is $\neg G_4$. Note that both $\neg G_2$ and $\neg G_4$ can be used as a reverse interpolant extracted from Π.

Table 1. Vinter results using Vampire, respectively Z3

	♯ benchmarks	♯ local proofs
Vampire	4217	1903
Z3	4217	3593
red		3501
blue		3517

The propositional formula P encoding all grey slicing transformations of a local proof Π is built by Vinter such that every satisfying assignment to P represents a local proof obtained from Π by grey slicing. Moreover, for every grey formula G in Π the formula P contains a variable p_G that is true if and only if G occurs in the interpolant. When constructing the formula P we use the property that Π is local. That is, a grey formula G in Π is either a leaf of Π or the conclusion of an inference satisfying exactly one of the following conditions: (i) the inference has only grey premises; (ii) the inference has at least one red premise and its all other premises are red or grey; (iii) the inference has at least one blue premise and its all other premises are blue or grey. Depending on the inference introducing G in Π, we generate formulas over p_G expressing under which conditions G is used in the interpolant constructed from Π. We then take P as the conjunction of all formulas over p_G.

The derived formula P allows us to optimise the extracted interpolant using various measures, such as the total number of different symbols in the interpolant, the total number of different atoms, or the total number of quantifiers in such atoms. The minimisation problem can be described as a pseudo-boolean constraint using P and a linear expression built from variables p_G. For example, if we are interested in generating an interpolant that uses a minimal number of quantifiers, we construct the linear expression $\sum_G \text{quant}(G) \cdot p_G$ and derive the pseudo-boolean constraint $min_G(\sum_G \text{quant}(G) \cdot p_G \wedge P)$, where $\text{quant}(G)$ denotes the number of quantifiers in G. A solution to this constraint yields an interpolant that is minimal in the number of quantifiers.

The grey slicing and the pseudo-boolean constraint construction steps of Vinter are implemented in Vampire.

Solving the Constraint. We pass the resulting pseudo-boolean constraint to Yices [5] and generate a satisfying assignment that it is minimal wrt a given measure. In order to compute the minimal solution of the pseudo-boolean constraint, we use a divide-and-conquer approach to constrain the minimal value of the solution. That is, we make iterative calls to Yices until the upper and lower bounds on the solution become tight. For solving pseudo-boolean constraints we chose Yices since Yices runs under all recent versions of Windows, Linux and MacOS. One could expect that using pseudo-boolean constraint solvers instead of Yices and generating suboptimal solutions will give a considerable improvement in the pseudo-boolean constraint solving part of Vinter. We leave this task for future work.

Generation of a Minimal Interpolant. If Yices finds a minimal solution, we reconstruct a local derivation corresponding to this solution and use the algorithm of [9] to extract an interpolant from it. This part of Vinter is also implemented in Vampire.

3   Experimental Results

Generating interpolation problems, localising proofs, grey slicing and minimising interpolants are written in C++, using all together 4209 lines of C++ code. In addition, Vinter contains about 200 lines of shellscript code for merging its various parts and realising the architecture of Figure 1. All experiments described in this section were obtained on a 64-bit 2.33 GHz quad core Dell machine with 12 GB RAM.

Benchmarks. In [7] we reported on initial results on generating minimal interpolants, by using examples from the TPTP and the SMT-LIB libraries. Experiments on more realistic verification benchmarks, that is on examples coming from concrete verification tools were left for future study.

In this paper, we address this task and evaluate Vinter on 4217 examples generated by the software model checker CPAchecker [2]. Some of these examples are also used in the *software verification competition* – see http://sv-comp.sosy-lab.org/benchmarks.php. To be precise, we took the following three benchmark suites: *ControlFlowInteger* examples that express properties about the control-flow structure and the integer variables of programs; *SystemC* examples about concurrent programs; and *Nested* loop examples. From each of these 4217 examples we generated interpolation problems for Vinter, as follows. We used CPAchecker to determine the reachability of error locations in the benchmark files. Each time an error location was encountered, the unsatisfiable formula encoding the infeasibility of the error-prone program path was output in the SMT-LIB format. These SMT-LIB examples were further used as inputs to Vinter. All SMT-LIB examples we used CPAchecker involved linear arithmetic and uninterpreted functions.

Generating Local Proofs. The interpolation problems coming from CPAchecker are using few quantifiers, but have a deeply nested linear arithmetic structure. Such problems can be efficiently proved by SMT solvers, such as Z3. On the contrary, first-order theorem provers, such as Vampire, are good in dealing with quantifiers but have difficulties with theory reasoning. Theory reasoning in Vampire is supported by using sound but incomplete theory axiomatisations. On the other hand, when we run Vinter with Vampire, whenever Vampire produces a proof, the proof is local. This is not the case with Z3, essentially proofs produced by Z3 are non-local and thus need to be localised for interpolant generation. Depending which theorem prover Vinter is using, generating minimal interpolants is challenging due to theory reasoning and/or proof localisation.

Table 1 gives an overview of Vinter's results on the CPAChecker benchmarks. The first column of Table 1 specifies the prover used for finding proofs, the second column the number of interpolation problems, and the third column the number of examples for which a local proof was found. When Vinter was run with Z3, Table 1 also list the number of localised proofs by quantifiying away the red, respectively the blue constants.

When we ran Vinter with Z3, all 4217 CPAchecker examples were proved by Z3 in essentially no time. However, when considering color annotations over the proof symbols, the proof localisation step of Vinter generated local proofs for 3593 examples out of the 4217 examples. Some of these proofs could only be localised by quantifying away the blue (respectively, the red) constants. More precisely, by analysing our results, we observed that 3501 Z3 proofs were localised by quantifying away the red constants, and 3517 Z3 proofs were localised when we quantified away the blue constants.

Table 2. Minimal interpolants extracted from localised Z3 proofs, after quantifying away red symbols

benchmark	measure	no	>1	>2	>3	>5
all	weight	3219	282	54	24	4
all	atoms	3417	84	25	5	
all	quant	3501				
ssh	weight	99	62	18		
ssh	atoms	160	1			
ssh	quant	161				
systemc	weight	806	199	22	17	2
systemc	atoms	936	69	18	3	
systemc	quant	1005				
nested	weight	2314	21	14	7	2
nested	atoms	2321	14	7	2	
nested	quant	2335				

Table 3. Minimal interpolants extracted from localised Z3 proofs, after quantifying away blue symbols

benchmark	measure	no	>1	>2	>3	>5
all	weight	2096	1367	30	20	4
all	atoms	3434	54	24	5	
all	quant	2392	10	1115		
ssh	weight	74	72	18		
ssh	atoms	162	2			
ssh	quant	159		5		
systemc	weight	804	192	5	15	2
systemc	atoms	951	45	19	3	
systemc	quant	995	10	13		
nested	weight	1218	1103	7	5	2
nested	atoms	2321	7	5	2	
nested	quant	1238		1097		

Our experiments give thus practical evidence that our extension to [7] for quantifying away either red or blue symbols effects interpolant minimisation. Combining red *and* blue symbol quantification in the *same* non-local proof is an interesting task to investigate.

When evaluating Vinter using Vampire on the 4217 CPAchecker examples, we ran Vampire with a 60 seconds time limit. The CPAchecker examples expressed in the SMT-LIB syntax were translated by Vinter into an annotated Vampire input. Using the coloring annotations over the input symbols, Vampire produced local proofs for 1903 benchmarks out of the 4217 examples. For the remaining 2314 examples, Vampire failed to generate a proof. One reason why Vampire failed to produce a proof was that these examples have a deeply nested linear arithmetic structure. In addition, we also observed that the coloring annotations may lead to performance degradation in Vampire's reasoning processes. We believe that improving the theory reasoning and the local proof generation engines of Vampire would yield better performances of Vinter.

Generating Minimal Interpolants. Vinter implements the following three measures to minimise interpolants: (i) the number of symbols (*weight* measure), (ii) the number of atoms (*atom* measure), and (iii) the number of quantifiers (*quant* measure) in the interpolant. For solving the pseudo-boolean optimization problems describing minimality constraints over interpolant formulas, we ran Yices with a timeout of 126 seconds.

Tables 2 and 3 summarise our results on minimising interpolants extracted from Z3 proofs, whereas Table 4 reports on our experiments for generating minimal interpolants from Vampire proofs. The first column of these tables lists the set of CPAchecker examples: *all* refers to all benchmarks for which minimal interpolants were generated, whereas *ssh*, *systemc* and *nested* denote examples out of all these benchmarks which come from the *ControlFlowInteger*, *SystemC*, and *Nested* benchmark suites. For each benchmark set, the second column shows the measure used for minimising interpolants. Similarly, for each benchmark set, columns starting with column three present the number of those examples for which the measure decreased and by the factor given in the headers of the columns. For example > 2 means that the measure increased by a factor greater than 2. Note that the best improvement was obtained by running Vampire, and especially on the *nested* benchmarks. This means that having initial proofs of good quality is crucial for the success of the method.

Table 4. Minimal interpolants extracted from Vampire proofs

benchmark	measure	no	> 1	> 2	> 3	> 5	> 10	> 20	> 50
all	weight	1266	637	217	152	81	22	8	2
	atoms	1702	201	111	18	2			
	quant	1833	70	47	8				
ssh-simpl	weight	85	8	4	4	3	1		
	atoms	84	1	1					
	quant	85							
systemc	weight	592	53	29	16	11	8		
	atoms	616	16	13					
	quant	645							
nested	weight	597	576	184	132	67	13	8	2
	atoms	1002	171	97	18	2			
	quant	1103	70	47	8				

Table 5. Weight of interpolants before and after minimisation, using Vampire proofs

benchmark		0	≥ 1	≥ 3	≥ 5	≥ 10	≥ 20	≥ 50	≥ 100
all	before	524	1379	1303	770	348	121	37	6
	after	524	1379	1248	396	226	46	5	
ssh-simpl	before	8	77	75	13	3	1	1	
	after	8	77	71	6	2	1	1	
systemc	before	360	285	227	152	41	9	3	
	after	360	285	219	124	17	2		
nested	before	156	1017	1001	605	304	111	33	6
	after	156	1017	958	266	207	43	4	

Table 5 illustrates the sizes of interpolants before and after weight minimisation. For example, one can see that on all examples, 37 interpolants had the weight ≥ 50 before minimisation and only 5 of them had a weight ≥ 50 after the minimisation. Note that the largest interpolants (with 100–500 symbols) were all minimised.

By analysing our results, we also encountered problems on which Vampire produced local proofs, and hence interpolants, but the Z3 proof could not be localised and thus interpolants could not computed.

Summarising, we believe that the experimental results of Tables 2-5 indicate that Vinter can be successfully used for generating *small* interpolants and that the effect of minimisation is better when the initial proofs are local. For example, Vinter could sometimes decrease the weight of interpolants by a factor of more than 100. We believe that Vinter can help software verification tools deal with significantly smaller interpolants.

4 Conclusions

We describe the Vinter tool for localising proofs, extracting interpolants from local proofs and minimising interpolants using various measures. We present the use of Vinter and evaluate Vinter on a collection of bounded model checking examples. Future work includes integrating Vinter with end-applications and generating interpolation-friendly proofs.

References

1. Barrett, C., Stump, A., Tinelli, C.: The Satisfiability Modulo Theories Library (SMT-LIB) (2010), www.SMT-LIB.org

2. Beyer, D., Keremoglu, M.E.: CPACHECKER: A Tool for Configurable Software Verification. In: Gopalakrishnan, G., Qadeer, S. (eds.) CAV 2011. LNCS, vol. 6806, pp. 184–190. Springer, Heidelberg (2011)
3. Craig, W.: Three uses of the Herbrand-Gentzen Theorem in Relating Model Theory and Proof Theory. Journal of Symbolic Logic 22(3), 269–285 (1957)
4. de Moura, L., Bjørner, N.: Z3: An Efficient SMT Solver. In: Ramakrishnan, C.R., Rehof, J. (eds.) TACAS 2008. LNCS, vol. 4963, pp. 337–340. Springer, Heidelberg (2008)
5. Dutertre, B., de Moura, L.: A Fast Linear-Arithmetic Solver for DPLL(T). In: Ball, T., Jones, R.B. (eds.) CAV 2006. LNCS, vol. 4144, pp. 81–94. Springer, Heidelberg (2006)
6. Hoder, K., Kovács, L., Voronkov, A.: Interpolation and Symbol Elimination in Vampire. In: Giesl, J., Hähnle, R. (eds.) IJCAR 2010. LNCS, vol. 6173, pp. 188–195. Springer, Heidelberg (2010)
7. Hoder, K., Kovacs, L., Voronkov, A.: Playing in the Grey Area of Proofs. In: Proc. of POPL, pp. 259–272 (2012)
8. Jhala, R., McMillan, K.L.: A Practical and Complete Approach to Predicate Refinement. In: Hermanns, H. (ed.) TACAS 2006. LNCS, vol. 3920, pp. 459–473. Springer, Heidelberg (2006)
9. Kovács, L., Voronkov, A.: Interpolation and Symbol Elimination. In: Schmidt, R.A. (ed.) CADE 2009. LNCS, vol. 5663, pp. 199–213. Springer, Heidelberg (2009)
10. McMillan, K.L.: An Interpolating Theorem Prover. Theor. Comput. Sci. 345(1), 101–121 (2005)
11. McMillan, K.L.: Quantified Invariant Generation Using an Interpolating Saturation Prover. In: Ramakrishnan, C.R., Rehof, J. (eds.) TACAS 2008. LNCS, vol. 4963, pp. 413–427. Springer, Heidelberg (2008)
12. McMillan, K.L.: Interpolants from Z3 Proofs. In: Proc. of FMCAD, pp. 19–27 (2011)
13. Riazanov, A., Voronkov, A.: The Design and Implementation of Vampire. AI Communications 15(2-3), 91–110 (2002)
14. Sutcliffe, G.: The TPTP Problem Library and Associated Infrastructure. J. Autom. Reasoning 43(4), 337–362 (2009)

Side-Effecting Constraint Systems:
A Swiss Army Knife for Program Analysis

Kalmer Apinis, Helmut Seidl, and Vesal Vojdani

Lehrstuhl für Informatik II, Technische Universität München
Boltzmannstraße 3, D-85748 Garching b. München, Germany
{apinis,seidl,vojdanig}@in.tum.de

Abstract. Side-effecting constraint systems were originally introduced for the analysis of multi-threaded code [22]. In this paper, we show how this formalism provides a unified framework for realizing efficient interprocedural analyses where the amount of context-sensitivity can be tweaked and where the context-sensitive analyses of local properties can be combined with *flow-insensitive* analyses of global properties, e.g., about the heap. Side-effecting constraint systems thus form the ideal basis for building general-purpose infrastructures for static analysis. One such infrastructure is the analyzer generator GOBLINT, which we used to practically evaluate this approach on real-world examples.

1   Introduction

Due to the complicated semantics of modern programming languages, analyzers inferring non-trivial program invariants require auxiliary analyses for many different properties. When checking multi-threaded C for absence of data-races, for example, one needs auxiliary analyses for disambiguating function pointers, may- and must-alias analysis for ordinary pointers, and if control-flow is to be tracked with higher precision, some form of value analysis is additionally required [29].

One choice, when combining various kinds of analyses, is to proceed in stages where later stages have access to the invariants previously computed. The advantage of the staged approach is that each stage has to deal with a small set of different concepts only and thus can be kept rather simple. The disadvantage, though, is that an unnecessary loss of precision may be incurred, since information only flows in one direction across stages.

Thus, when precision is crucial, an integrated approach is preferred. This is the case in sound static analyzers, such as ASTRÉE [6] or GOBLINT [23]. In these frameworks, the different analyses are joined into one global analysis which determines all required invariants in one go, so that the distinct analyses reciprocally benefit from one another. Additionally, GOBLINT allows the user to configure, for each analysis, whether it should run context-, path-sensitively, or not at all: the different analyses communicate through a query-system such that multiple analyses can complement each other in answering, e.g., aliasing queries. Such flexible integration is only possible, however, when the *algorithmics* of the different analyses harmonize. The goal, therefore, is to abandon dedicated analysis

R. Jhala and A. Igarashi (Eds.): APLAS 2012, LNCS 7705, pp. 157–172, 2012.
© Springer-Verlag Berlin Heidelberg 2012

algorithms and instead provide one specification formalism together with a single solver engine to compute the invariants. Proofs of soundness are then vastly simplified as the verification task is separated into proving the constraint system correct and independently proving the correctness of a generic fixpoint engine, along the lines of [13].

We suggest that *side-effecting* constraint systems, introduced in [22] for the analysis of multi-threaded code, is the ideal tool to achieve the desired harmonization. Intuitively, in each constraint of a side-effecting constraint system, the right-hand side does not only specify a sequence of reading accesses to some constraint variables, whose values are queried and used to provide a contribution to the variable on the left-hand side, but may additionally disperse write contributions to further constraint variables in-between. The key contribution of this paper is to show that many analysis problems, whose solving seem to require different algorithms, can all be expressed using this single formalism. In particular, we show that this idea provides a uniform solution to the following interprocedural analysis problems:

1. tabulation of procedure summaries for parts of the calling context only, also in the presence of dynamic procedure calls;
2. integrated analysis which accumulates certain data flow information flow-insensitively, while at the same time tracking other data, such as (an abstraction of) the local state, flow- as well as context-sensitively.

These problems can be expressed by ordinary constraint systems which thus may serve as a formal specification of the analysis problem. For non-trivial analyses, including constant propagation, these constraint systems are infinite. *Local* fix-point solvers, which only solve those variables that are required for the analysis, can be used to solve infinite systems. However, these constraints are not only infinite, but some variables of the constraint system may formally depend on infinitely many other variables. Therefore, they do not lend themselves to implementations by means of generic local solvers.

We show instead that these constraint systems can be reformulated by introducing side-effecting constraints. The side-effects are triggered during constraint solving and may depend on the values of other variables. Side-effecting constraints thus cannot generally be replaced by an equivalent constraint system with finite variable dependencies by factoring out side-effects as individual constraints. The reformulated constraint systems, however, can be solved efficiently by means of generic local solvers adapted to side-effecting constraints. A local solver will try to solve only variables that are required for the analysis. These adapted generic local solvers together with side-effecting constraint systems may thus serve as a Swiss army knife for efficient integrated whole-program analysis. All proofs in this paper have been omitted — but can be found in the technical report [2].

Related Work. The seminal paper by Kildall [15] can already be interpreted as an attempt to provide a unifying framework for various program analysis techniques at his time. It did not incorporate, however, direct support for more advanced language features such as procedures or threads. The approach of abstract interpretation by Cousot and Cousot [4] not only provides the foundations for reasoning about the correctness, but also serves as the basis for a variety of program analyses which algorithmically translate into solving appropriate constraint systems [7] or directly interpreting the input program abstractly [6]. As one instance, also a framework for analyzing programs with procedures has been provided [5].

Various further approaches to interprocedural analysis are reviewed by Sharir and Pnueli [25] — one based on call-strings while the other, similar to [5], relies on (partially) computing abstract procedure summaries. Following Sharir and Pnueli, later, restricted frameworks for interprocedural analyses have been provided [20] which, however, only work for specific simple domains and therefore may not serve as general program analysis frameworks.

Partial contexts are important for scalability since it enables more compositional approaches. It is particularly useful for heap analysis, though the analysis designer must provide a way to isolate the procedure-relevant portion of the heap and retrofit the partial effect of a procedure into the wider context at a call site [3, 21]. For object-oriented languages, *object-sensitivity*, which distinguishes call-contexts using only the receiver object at a method invocation site, rather than the entire points-to information, is sufficiently precise [18].

Generic frameworks for program analysis and code optimization [16, 19, 27, 30] follow the multi-stage analysis paradigm and do not provide a unified solving algorithm that allows one to combine mutually dependent flow-sensitive and flow-independent analyses. However, specific pointer-analyses have been proposed which flow-sensitively track a subset of relevant pointers. The *client-driven* pointer analysis by Guyer and Lin [12] monitors the performance of an initial flow-insensitive analysis to decide which pointers to track flow-sensitively. Lhoták and Chung [17], wishing to perform strong updates, track pointers with singleton points-to sets flow-sensitively, while relying on fast flow-insensitive approaches for points-to sets where precision is already lost.

Organization of the paper. Section 2 is meant as a gentle introduction to constraint systems for specifying program analyses. Basic notions are introduced for the case of intra-procedural analyses. Section 3 extends the specification formalism of constraint systems so that it also covers interprocedural analysis in the sense of [5] and indicates how these systems can be extended to make reachability information explicit. Section 4 extends these constraint systems to allow for fine-tuning the amount of context by which procedure calls are distinguished. The resulting constraint systems may be neither monotonic, nor finite. Even worse, some variables of the constraint system may formally depend on infinitely many other variables. Section 5 provides further extensions to the constraint system which supports a flow-insensitive treatment of global information. Section 6 indicates how side-effects, added to the specification formalism of constraints, allow for smooth reformulations of the constraint systems from Sections 4 and 5. The new constraint systems, however, have the advantage that for every abstract lattice, the variables only depend on *finitely* many other variables — thus allowing to apply generic local fixpoint algorithms as universal solver engines. Sections 7 and 8 provide further evidence of the usefulness of the framework by indicating how dynamic procedure calls as well as the alternative approach to interprocedural analysis of Sharir/Pnueli [25] can also be specified. Section 9 demonstrates that this approach is not only expressive but also results in competitive realizations of analyzers.

2 Intra-procedural Constraint Systems

We consider programs which consist of a finite set Proc of procedures. Each procedure g is given by a distinct control flow graph (N_g, E_g), where N_g is the set of program points of g and $E_g \subseteq N_g \times L \times N_g$ the set of edges with labels from a set L. An edge label $s \in L$ represents either elementary statements or conditional guards of the source language. Additionally, we have call edges with labels $f()$. The call edge syntax does not allow explicit arguments to functions; passing of arguments or returning results may be simulated, e.g., by means of global variables. Each procedure g has one start node s_g and one return node r_g, and we ensure that every program point $v \in N_g$, even when semantically unreachable, can be formally (i.e., ignoring the semantics of edge labels) reached from s_g, and likewise, r_g can be formally reached from v.

The goal of the analysis of such a program is to infer program invariants. Following the approach of abstract interpretation, program invariants are represented by elements from a complete lattice $(\mathbb{D}, \sqsubseteq)$, where $\mathbb{D}$ is the set of program invariants, and $\sqsubseteq$ the implication ordering between invariants. Let us for the moment consider a program with just one procedure main and without procedure calls. Analyzing such programs is referred to as *intra-procedural* analysis. Assume that we are interested in inferring one invariant for each program point of the analyzed program. Such an analysis is referred to as *flow-sensitive*. Flow-sensitive intra-procedural invariants can conveniently be expressed as solutions of a *constraint system*.

Let V denote a set of constraint variables or unknowns. For intra-procedural analysis, the set of unknowns are simply program points $V = N_{\mathsf{main}}$. Any pair (x, f) where $x \in V$ and f is a function $(V \to \mathbb{D}) \to \mathbb{D}$ is called a constraint, were the right-hand side f is meant to provide a contribution to the value of x depending on some other values of constraint variables. The variable x is called the left-hand side of the constraint, whereas we refer to f as the right-hand side. A set of constraints form a *constraint system*. A variable assignment $\sigma \in V \to \mathbb{D}$ is a *solution* of the constraint system $\mathcal{C}$ if for all $(x, f) \in \mathcal{C}$, we have $\sigma\, x \sqsupseteq f\, \sigma$. Every constraint system has one trivial solution, namely, a function which maps all variables to the top element $\top \in \mathbb{D}$. In practice, though, we aim at computing *least*, or at least *non-trivial*, solutions of constraint systems.

Assume that $d_0 \in \mathbb{D}$ describes the program state before starting procedure main and that for each statement or guard s occurring at an edge, we are given the abstract semantics $[\![s]\!]^\sharp \in \mathbb{D} \to \mathbb{D}$, which describes how the abstract state after the execution of s is obtained from the abstract state before the execution.

As usual in program analysis, these functions are assumed to be monotonic. Also, we assume the functions $[\![s]\!]^\sharp$ to be *strict*, i.e., preserve the value $\bot$. In the following, the value $\bot \in \mathbb{D}$ always represents the empty set of concrete program states, i.e., can only be assumed at a program point which is *unreachable*. Then, an initial abstract state $\bot \neq d_0 \in \mathbb{D}$ for the start point s_{main} together with the edges of the control flow graph give rise to the following system of constraints:

$$[s_{\mathsf{main}}] \sqsupseteq d_0$$
$$[v] \sqsupseteq [\![s]\!]^\sharp \,(\mathsf{get}\,[u]) \qquad \forall (u, s, v) \in E_{\mathsf{main}} \tag{0}$$

For better readability, each constraint $(x, \mathbf{fun}\ \mathsf{get} \to e)$ is denoted as "$x \sqsupseteq e$"; that is, get will always be the name of the first parameter of functions representing right-hand sides.

Since all abstract functions $[\![s]\!]^\sharp$ are assumed to be monotonic, constraint system (0) has a unique least solution. Moreover, the whole constraint system uses finitely many unknowns only, where the evaluation of the right-hand side of each constraint may also access finitely many unknowns. In case that the domain $\mathbb{D}$ does not contain infinite strictly ascending chains, a solution of (0) can be computed, e.g., with Round-Robin iteration or some variant of worklist solver [14, 15, 28].

3   Analyzing Procedures

Sharir and Pnueli [25] describe two approaches to interprocedural program analysis. The *functional* approach tries to summarize the abstract effect of a procedure into a summary function. Many practical inter-procedural analyses, though, are based on complete lattices $\mathbb{D}$ where no effective representations for procedure summaries are known. This is already the case for inter-procedural full constant propagation. For such cases, Sharir and Pnueli propose an approach which conceptually represents procedure summaries by their value tables of which only those entries are computed which may affect the analysis result. Formulated as a constraint system, following Cousot and Cousot [5], the constraint variables for this approach are pairs $V = N \times \mathbb{D}$ where the second component records the *calling-context* of the current instance of the procedure. The value for the unknown $[v, d]$, where v belongs to a function g, thus represents the abstract value attained at program point v when g is called in context d. For the moment, we just consider *static* procedure calls, i.e., call edges of the form $(u, g(), v)$ where the parameterless procedure g is called. We obtain the following constraint system for the variables $[v, d]$:

$$[s_g, d] \sqsupseteq d \qquad\qquad\qquad\qquad\qquad \forall g \in \mathsf{Proc}$$
$$[v, d] \sqsupseteq [\![s]\!]^\sharp \,(\mathsf{get}\,[u, d]) \qquad\qquad \forall (u, s, v) \in E$$
$$[v, d] \sqsupseteq \mathsf{comb}_e^\sharp \,(\mathsf{get}\,[u, d])\,(\mathsf{get}\,[r_g, \mathsf{enter}_e^\sharp \,(\mathsf{get}\,[u, d])]) \tag{1}$$
$$\forall e = (u, g(), v) \in E$$

Here the functions $\mathsf{enter}_e^\sharp \in \mathbb{D} \to \mathbb{D}$ and $\mathsf{comb}_e^\sharp \in \mathbb{D} \to \mathbb{D} \to \mathbb{D}$ describe the abstract semantics of procedure calls. Just as for the abstract semantics of statements, we demand these functions to be monotonic and strict in each of their arguments. For an abstract state d, the application $\mathsf{enter}_e^\sharp\, d$ returns the abstract state in which g is called. The function $\mathsf{comb}_e^\sharp$ on the other hand, describes how the abstract value d_1 before the call must be combined with the abstract value d_2 returned by the call to obtain the abstract value after the call. The constraint for calling a procedure g at program point u, where d is the context of the caller, computes $d_1 = \mathsf{get}\,[u,d]$ and the context $d' = \mathsf{enter}_e^\sharp\, d_1$ of the called procedure g, and combines d_1 with the return state of the call $d_2 = \mathsf{get}\,[r_g, d']$.

Even if all abstract functions $[\![s]\!]^\sharp$ and all $\mathsf{enter}_e^\sharp$ and $\mathsf{comb}_e^\sharp$ are monotonic, the right-hand sides of the constraint system (1) are not necessarily monotonic themselves. The second argument to combine is of the form $\mathsf{get}\,[x, \mathsf{get}\,[y,d]]$, and there is no guarantee that $\sigma_1\,[x, a_1] \sqsubseteq \sigma_2\,[x, a_2]$ just because $a_1 \sqsubseteq a_2$ and $\sigma_1 \sqsubseteq \sigma_2$. The expressions is, however, monotonic for variable assignments of which at least one is a *monotonic assignment*. In our setting, a variable assignment σ is monotonic, if for all program points v, we have $\sigma\,[v, a_1] \sqsubseteq \sigma\,[v, a_2]$ whenever $a_1 \sqsubseteq a_2$. This monotonicity is sufficient to enforce that constraint system (1) has a unique least solution which is monotonic [10]. The least solution describes in some sense the procedure summaries, i.e., the abstract effect of every function g for every context $a \in \mathbb{D}$ – no matter whether the procedure g is called for a or not. E.g. $[s_g, \top]$ equals $\top$ by the first constraint in (1), regardless if $\mathsf{enter}^\sharp$ for an edge calling g will ever return $\top$.

Computing the least solution using an ordinary worklist algorithm, however, is not generally possible. Adding contexts to variables makes the set of variables infinite, given that $\mathbb{D}$ is infinite. And even if $\mathbb{D}$ is finite, the number of unknowns depends on the number of elements in $\mathbb{D}$, which might be large. Often procedures are only called in few distinct abstract calling-contexts. In this case, *local fixpoint iteration* may succeed by starting from a set X of interesting variables, such as $X = \{[r_{\mathsf{main}}, d_0]\}$, and return a *partial* solution which contains the return values of the procedure summary for the required abstract calling-contexts only. Assume that local fixpoint computation terminates with a *partial* solution $\eta \in X' \to \mathbb{D}$ where $X \subseteq X'$. Then it follows that the entry point s_g of a procedure g can only be reached with abstract values from $a \in \mathbb{D}$ with $[s_g, a] \in X'$. Accordingly, a program point v can only be reached by abstract values bounded by $\bigsqcup\{\eta\,[v, a] \mid [v, a] \in X'\}$, as observed in [9, 10].

Thus, the least solution of constraint system (1) does not contain reachability information, and it is only by local fixpoint iteration that a set of possibly occurring contexts is identified. Instead of referring to the operational behavior of solvers, we prefer to express reachability directly by means of the constraint system. In order to do so, we modify (1) by replacing the constraints $[s_g, a] \sqsupseteq a$ with

$$[s_{\mathsf{main}}, d_0] \sqsupseteq d_0$$
$$[s_f, a] \sqsupseteq \bigsqcup\{a \mid \exists a' \in \mathbb{D}, a = \mathsf{enter}_e^\sharp\, (\mathsf{get}\,[u, a'])\,\} \qquad (1')$$
$$\forall e = (u, f(), v) \in E$$

Note that for each potential entry state $a \in \mathbb{D}$, the second constraint joins over the same value a, so the result is either $\bigsqcup \emptyset = \bot$ or a. The entry point of the called procedure f is constrained by the context a if there exists a call to f in some context a' (of the caller) that produces the entry state a (for the callee). This explicitly encodes reachability into the system. Therefore, in contrast to the constraint system (1), we require a dedicated constraint for the initial call of the main procedure. Assuming that the initial local state is d_0, the initial context is also d_0, as encoded by the first constraint.

The constraint system (1'), however, may have minimal solutions which are not monotonic. Assume, e.g., the case where the procedure main consists just of the program point s_{main}. Then the unique least solution is given by $[s_{\mathsf{main}}, b] = \bot$ for $b \neq d_0$ and $[s_{\mathsf{main}}, d_0] = d_0$ — which is not a monotonic variable assignment. For non-monotonic variable assignments, however, right-hand sides of constraints need no longer be monotonic. As any constraint system over a complete lattice, the constraint system (1') has solutions, and if the domain is finite one may compute it by an accumulating fix-point iteration, i.e., joining the new value of an known with the one from previous iteration.

If the lattice $\mathbb{D}$ is infinite, however, then the constraint system (1') not only contains infinitely many variables, but also has constraints where the evaluation of a single right-hand side may access infinitely many unknowns. This is the case for the newly introduced constraints for the entry points of procedures. In order to terminate, local solving requires that there be only finitely many right-hand sides for each variable, and that each constraint depend on finitely many variables only. Therefore, it cannot be applied to solve system (1').

4   Partial Context-Sensitivity

Local solving has difficulties when reachability is explicitly encoded in the constraint. We now consider analyses where tracking reachability explicitly is necessary not just for termination, but also for the result of the analysis. This is the case, e.g., if only *parts* of the abstract state are used to distinguish between different procedure calls. Consider a complete lattice $\mathbb{D} = \mathbb{D}_1 \times \mathbb{D}_2$ which is the Cartesian product of complete lattices $\mathbb{D}_1, \mathbb{D}_2$, and assume that calls to procedures f are disambiguated by means of the second component b of a reaching abstract state $(a, b) \in \mathbb{D}$, while the first components corresponding to the same b are merged. Conceptually, the constraints for handling function calls then take the following form:

$$[s_{\mathsf{main}}, \langle d_0 \rangle_2] \sqsupseteq d_0$$
$$[v, b] \sqsupseteq [\![s]\!]^{\sharp} \, (\mathsf{get}\,[u, b]) \qquad\qquad \forall (u, s, v) \in E$$
$$[s_g, b] \sqsupseteq \bigsqcup \{ d \mid \exists b' {\in} \mathbb{D}_2, d {=} \mathsf{enter}_e^{\sharp}\,(\mathsf{get}\,[u, b']), \langle d \rangle_2 = b \}$$
$$\qquad\qquad\qquad \forall e = (u, g(), v) \in E \quad (2)$$
$$[v, b] \sqsupseteq \mathbf{let}\ d = \mathsf{enter}_e^{\sharp}\,(\mathsf{get}\,[u, b])$$
$$\qquad \mathbf{in}\ \mathsf{comb}_e^{\sharp}\,(\mathsf{get}\,[u, b])\,(\mathsf{get}\,[r_g, \langle d \rangle_2]) \qquad \forall e = (u, g(), v) \in E$$

Here, the operator $\langle \cdot \rangle_i$ extracts the i-th component of a tuple. Technically, this constraint system is a smooth generalization of constraint system (1') — only that now program points v are not distinguished by the full context d in which the procedure of v has been called, but only the second component of d. Similarly to constraint system (1'), the constraint system (2) explicitly keeps track of reachability. In the particular case where $\mathbb{D}_2$ is the unit domain $\mathbf{1} = \{\bullet\}$, constraint system (2) generalizes a constraint system for callstring 0. In this case no contexts are distinguished, and all right-hand sides of the constraint system are monotonic. For nontrivial contexts, though, constraint system (2), just as constraint system (1'), may have minimal solutions which are not monotonic. Still, every solution of (2) provides a *sound* analysis information [2].

Assume for a moment that the complete lattice $\mathbb{D}_2$ of partial contexts is infinite. Then the same argument as in the last section for constraint system (1') can be applied to rule out local fixpoint iteration for solving the constraint system (2). But even if the number of partial contexts is finite, use of general fixpoint engines may be infeasible. According to the constraint of (2) for the starting states of procedure g with the context b, the solver has to track contributions from *all* call sites that *may* call g in context b. Also in complete absence of context-sensitivity (i.e., where $\mathbb{D}_2 = \mathbf{1}$) but in presence of dynamic procedure calls, a local solver, for instance, will explore *all* possible call sites in order to determine the abstract value for the start node of g. The same already holds true in presence of partial context-sensitivity (i.e., both $\mathbb{D}_1$ and $\mathbb{D}_2$ are different from $\mathbf{1}$). We conclude that even in these simple cases, the number of variables considered by the local solver on constraint system (2) might be excessively large.

5   Flow-Insensitive Analyses

One further challenge for general frameworks for automatic program analysis is added when certain pieces of information are meant to be accumulated *flow-insensitively*. Flow-insensitive analyses try to infer invariants which hold throughout the program execution. Such invariants are used, e.g., to reason about dynamic data-structures [1, 24, 26] or concurrently running threads [29].

Technically, flow-insensitive analyses can be constructed by introducing an extra finite set G of entities for which values are accumulated. Depending on the application, the elements of G can, e.g., be viewed as *global* variables, abstract locations of heap objects or the components of the interface through which concurrently running threads communicate. Thus, the effect of the statement s at an edge in the control flow graph may now additionally depend on the values of the globals in G as well as the predecessor state and may also return contributions to the values of some of the globals. In the following we assume that global and local information are represented by the same lattice $\mathbb{D}$ — if this is not the case, one can, for example, use the Cartesian product (with product ordering) of the domains and set the unused pair entry to $\bot$. One way to describe the effects of a statement s then is by modifying the abstract semantics $[\![s]\!]^{\sharp}$ to a function:

$$[\![s]\!]^\sharp \in \mathbb{D} \to (G \to \mathbb{D}) \to \mathbb{D} \times (G \to \mathbb{D})$$

which jointly specifies the contribution to the next program point as well as to certain elements of G. Again, we assume this function to be monotonic in its arguments and strict, at least in its first argument. This means that any call $[\![s]\!]^\sharp \perp \tau$ should return a pair $(\perp, \perp)$ where $\perp$ maps every global to $\perp$. In absence of procedures, we thus may put up the following constraint system for approximating invariants for the globals in G:

$$
\begin{aligned}
[v] &\sqsupseteq \langle [\![s]\!]^\sharp \, (\text{get } [u]) \, \text{get} \rangle_1 & \forall (u, s, v) \in E \\
[y] &\sqsupseteq \langle [\![s]\!]^\sharp \, (\text{get } [u]) \, \text{get} \rangle_2 \, y & \forall y \in G, (u, s, v) \in E
\end{aligned}
\tag{3}
$$

In absence of procedures, this constraint system can be solved with Round-Robin iteration or some kind of worklist algorithm. While it cannot easily be combined with constraint system (1), it can be combined with the constraint system (2). Assume the complete lattice $\mathbb{D}$ is of the form $\mathbb{D} = \mathbb{D}_1 \times \mathbb{D}_2$ where elements $b \in \mathbb{D}_2$ may serve as contexts. Then we modify the constraint system (2) by replacing the constraints for statements s with:

$$
\begin{aligned}
[v, b] &\sqsupseteq \langle [\![s]\!]^\sharp \, (\text{get } [u, b]) \, \text{get} \rangle_1 & \forall (u, s, v) \in E \\
[y] &\sqsupseteq \bigsqcup \{ \langle [\![s]\!]^\sharp \, (\text{get } [u, b]) \, \text{get} \rangle_2 \, y \mid b \in \mathbb{D}_2 \} & \forall y \in G, (u, s, v) \in E
\end{aligned}
\tag{4}
$$

Just as for constraint system (2), a local fixpoint algorithm for the enhanced constraint system will behave badly: in order to determine the value for some global y, the algorithm would explore *all* unknowns $[u, b]$ for which there is a control-flow edge (u, s, v) which *may* contribute to the value of y. If the number of potential contexts is infinite, we again obtain constraints where right-hand sides access infinitely many constraint variables. In the next section, though, we provide alternative formulations of constraint systems (2) and (4) which can be solved by means of partial tabulation.

6   Constraint Systems with Side-Effects

Ordinary constraints allow to specify precisely in which order variables are read while the single writing occurs at the very end, namely, to the variable at the left-hand side. Side-effecting constraints generalize this by allowing multiple writes and also to specify precisely in which order constraint variables are not only read, but also written to. In particular, which variable to read or write to next can depend on the values previously read. Even the sets of accessed variables may change. Each execution of a constraint thus yields a sequence of reads and writes which is terminated with an assignment to a left-hand side. In side-effecting constraint systems, a constraint is given by a pair (x, f) where the right-hand side f now is a function $f \in (V \to \mathbb{D}) \to (V \to \mathbb{D} \to \text{unit}) \to \mathbb{D}$. A call get y of the first argument function of f to some unknown $y \in V$ is meant to return the value of y in the current variable assignment. A call **set** $y\ d$ of the second argument function during the evaluation of f for $y \in V$, $d \in \mathbb{D}$ is meant to provide the contribution d to the value of y in the current variable assignment. A variable assignment $\sigma \in V \to \mathbb{D}$ is a *solution* to the constraint system $\mathcal{C}$ if for all constraints $(x, f) \in \mathcal{C}$ we have that $\sigma\ x \sqsupseteq f\ \sigma$ **set** where for every call **set** $y\ d$ arising from the evaluation of f we have $\sigma\ y \sqsupseteq d$. If f is given by **fun get** $\to$ **fun set** $\to e$ for an expression e, we again represent the constraint (x, f) by "$x \sqsupseteq e$".

Side-effecting constraint systems allow us to conveniently specify partially context-sensitive interprocedural analyses. Instead of defining the constraints for the starting point of some function g by means of the *inverse* of the $\mathsf{enter}_e^\sharp$ function as in constraint system (2), we attribute the contributions to the respective call sites as *side-effects*. As in Section 4, consider an analysis where the domain is the Cartesian product $\mathbb{D}_1 \times \mathbb{D}_2$ of two complete lattices $\mathbb{D}_1$ and $\mathbb{D}_2$. Assume again that calls to procedures should only be distinguished w.r.t. the second component $b \in \mathbb{D}_2$ of reaching states. The constraints for statements or guards are identical to the constraint system (2). We modify the constraints generated for every procedure call edge $(u, g(), v) \in E$ in the following way:

$$[v, b] \sqsupseteq \mathbf{let}\ d = \mathsf{enter}_e^\sharp\ (\mathsf{get}\ [u, b])$$
$$() = \mathsf{set}\ [s_g, \langle d \rangle_2]\ d \tag{5}$$
$$\mathbf{in}\ \mathsf{comb}_e^\sharp\ (\mathsf{get}\ [u, b])\ (\mathsf{get}\ [r_g, \langle d \rangle_2])$$

For an infinite complete lattice $\mathbb{D}_2$, the constraint system (5) requires infinitely many constraint variables. This is identical to constraint system (2). In contrast, however, to system (2), the number of constraint variables accessed in the right-hand side of every single constraint is finite, while there are still only finitely many right-hand sides for each unknown. Moreover, we have:

Theorem 1. *The constraint systems* (5) *and* (2) *are equivalent. This means that every solution of the constraint system* (2) *is a solution of the constraint system* (5) *and vice versa, every solution of the constraint system* (5) *is a solution of the constraint system* (2).

Since every solution of constraint system (2) is a sound abstraction of the concrete semantics, Theorem 1 implies that every solution of constraint system (5) is a sound abstraction of the concrete semantics. In contrast to constraint system (2), constraint system (5) now can be solved by means of local fixpoint iteration.

Side-effecting constraint systems also provide a way to realize flow-insensitive invariants as considered in Section 5 — even in presence of procedure calls which are analyzed by means of partial tabulation of summaries. The corresponding constraint system is obtained from the constraint system (5) by modifying the constraints for statement or guard edges $(u, s, v) \in E$ by taking the modified abstract semantics $[\![s]\!]^\sharp$ into account:

$$[v, b] \sqsupseteq \mathbf{let}\ (d, \tau) = [\![s]\!]^{\sharp}\ (\mathbf{get}\ [u, b])\ \mathbf{get}$$
$$() = \mathbf{forall}\ (y \in G\ \mathbf{with}\ \tau\, y \neq \bot)$$
$$\mathbf{set}\ y\ (\tau\, y) \tag{6}$$
$$\mathbf{in}\ d$$

The remaining constraints are as for (5). Due to this formulation, contributions to globals y are only collected for contexts b which occur during fixpoint iteration.

7   Dynamic Procedure Calls

Constraints for procedure calls can be extended to deal with *dynamic* calls, i.e., the procedure, to be called, may depend on the current program state. Let this dependence be formalized by means of a modified functionality

$$\mathsf{enter}_e^{\sharp} \in \mathbb{D} \to \mathsf{Proc} \to \mathbb{D}$$

of the abstract functions $\mathsf{enter}_e^{\sharp}$ where $\mathsf{enter}_e^{\sharp}\, d\, g = \bot$ indicates that procedure g is definitely not called at the edge e when the concrete state is described with d. Here we only consider the extension of the side-effecting constraint system for partial contexts with dynamic calls. Therefore, assume again that the complete lattice $\mathbb{D}$ of abstract states is of the form $\mathbb{D} = \mathbb{D}_1 \times \mathbb{D}_2$ where the elements in $\mathbb{D}_2$ are used to distinguish between different calls. We get the constraint system by replacing the procedure call constrains in (5) with constraints for every procedure $g \in \mathsf{Proc}$:

$$[v, b] \sqsupseteq \mathbf{let}\ d = \mathsf{enter}_e^{\sharp}\ (\mathbf{get}\ [u, b])\ g$$
$$() = \mathbf{set}\ [s_g, \langle d \rangle_2]\ d \tag{7'}$$
$$\mathbf{in}\ \mathsf{comb}_e^{\sharp}\ (\mathbf{get}\ [u, b])\ (\mathbf{get}\ [r_g, \langle d \rangle_2])$$

For efficiency reasons, we do not want to analyze procedures which are not called, i.e., for which $\mathsf{enter}_e^{\sharp}$ returns $\bot$. In order to avoid that, an extra test first checks whether $\mathsf{enter}_e^{\sharp}\, d\, g$ has returned $\bot$ or not. Only if that value is different from $\bot$, a side-effect to the start point of g is triggered and the return value of g is combined with the state before the call. This optimization results in:

$$[v, b] \sqsupseteq \mathbf{match}\ \mathsf{enter}_e^{\sharp}\ (\mathbf{get}\ [u, b])\ g\ \mathbf{with}$$
$$|\, \bot \to \bot$$
$$|\, d \to \mathbf{let}\ () = \mathbf{set}\ [s_g, \langle d \rangle_2]\ d \tag{7}$$
$$\mathbf{in}\ \mathsf{comb}_e^{\sharp}\ (\mathbf{get}\ [u, b])\ (\mathbf{get}\ [r_g, \langle d \rangle_2])$$

8   Forward Propagation

The algorithm of Sharir and Pnueli for partially tabulating procedure summaries has proven to be surprisingly efficient in practice. It can also be applied to partially tabulating partial contexts. Interestingly, its algorithmic characteristics are quite different from locally solving ordinary constraint systems. Instead of recursively descending into variable dependences starting from the return point the initial call to main, i.e. $[r_{\mathsf{main}}, d_0]$, it is based on *forward propagation*: whenever the abstract state at an unknown $[u, b]$ changes, the abstract effects corresponding to all outgoing edges (u, s, v) are executed to trigger the necessary updates for the end points v. This behavior is mandatory for the analysis of *binary* code where the control-flow graphs are not given before-hand but are successively built up while the program is decoded [11]. We show that this forward propagation can be achieved if the following variant of the side-effecting constraint system (5) is used:

$$[s_{\mathsf{main}}, \langle d_0 \rangle_2] \sqsupseteq d_0$$
$$[u, b] \sqsupseteq \mathbf{let}\ () = \mathsf{set}\ [v, b]\ ([\![s]\!]^\sharp\ (\mathsf{get}\ [u, b]))\ \mathbf{in}\ \bot \qquad \forall (u, s, v) \in E$$
$$[u, b] \sqsupseteq \mathbf{let}\ d = \mathsf{enter}_e^\sharp\ (\mathsf{get}\ [u, b])$$
$$() = \mathsf{set}\ [s_g, \langle d \rangle_2]\ d \qquad\qquad\qquad (5')$$
$$() = \mathsf{set}\ [v, b]\ (\mathsf{comb}_e^\sharp\ (\mathsf{get}\ [u, b])\ (\mathsf{get}\ [r_g, \langle d \rangle_2]))$$
$$\mathbf{in}\ \bot$$
$$\forall e = (u, g(), v) \in E$$

Theorem 2. *The constraint systems* (5) *and* (5') *are equivalent, which means that every solution to constraint system* (5) *is also a solution to constraint system* (5'), *and vice versa, every solution to constraint system* (5') *is also a solution to system* (5).

Assume that local solving is applied to the constraint system (5'), and a variable $[u, b]$ has changed its value. Since for every constraint (but the very first one) the variable of the left-hand side also occurs on the right-hand side, all constraints for $[u, b]$ will be evaluated and the change be propagated through the control-flow graph and into calls via side effects. If then a variable $[r_g, b']$ (corresponding to the return point of the procedure g) changes its value, re-evaluation will be triggered for every constraint for a corresponding call to procedure g and produce the required contributions to the end points of these calls. Thus, the *operational* behavior of a local fixpoint solver applied to this system emulates the behavior of the original algorithm of Sharir/Pnueli. The advantage, though, is that this effect is not achieved by implementing a dedicated algorithm, but solely by changing the specification of the constraints. Moreover, this formulation is flexible enough to allow for an extension which deals with side effects to globals as well.

9   Experimental Evaluation

Side-effecting constraint systems are at the heart of GOBLINT — a analyzer generator for concurrent C programs. This implementation of our Swiss army knife approach allows us to conduct experimental comparisons between configurations for the same analysis. For this paper, we considered a lockset analysis, where the goal is to guarantee absence of data races by accumulating for every global g, sets of definitely held static locks when accessing g. This analysis requires a detailed value analysis which provides points-to information for pointers as well as constant values for variables and resolves function pointers on-the-fly. Given that, the actual sets of definitely held locks are propagated and recorded at each access to a shared variable. In order to increase precision, path-sensitivity is added to relate conditional lock operations with corresponding conditional unlock operations [8].

We considered a suite of the following concurrent programs using POSIX threads:

aget A multithreaded HTTP download accelerator, version 0.4.
automount Autofs kernel-based automounter for Linux, version 5.0.2.
ctrace C tracing library sample program, version 1.2.
knot Knot web-server, stable release from SOSP CD.
pfscan Parallel file scanner, version 1.0.
smtprc Smtp relay checker is a network open mail relay checker, version 2.0.3.
ypbind Linux NIS daemon: ypbind-mt, version 1.19.1.
zfs-fuse ZFS filesystem for FUSE/Linux: release 0.4.0_beta2.

The sizes of these benchmarks vary between 1280 LoC and 24097 LoC where LoC counts the lines of post-processed and merged C code.

For these benchmarks, we compared the analysis based on Cousot-style constraint system (5) (extended with dynamic function calls and side effects) with the analysis based on constraint system (5') corresponding to Sharir/Pnueli's forward propagating algorithm. In both cases, we considered three instances where procedures are analyzed with full context, with partial context or no context, respectively. As partial context, we chose the information about the pointer variables together with the lockset information.

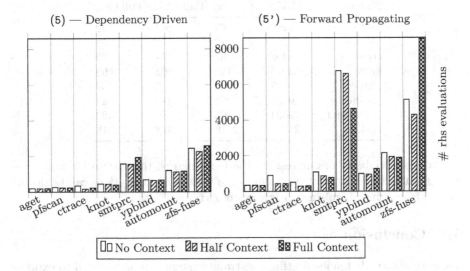

Fig. 1. Timing results

For benchmarking we used an Ubuntu 11.04 machine with an Intel Core 2 Quad Q9650 3GHz processor, of which the analyzer currently utilizes a single core, and 4.0GB DDR2(800 MHz) memory. For all benchmarks and all configurations, the analyzer performs reasonably well — the full context analysis of the 24kloc program zfs-fuse takes 3.7 seconds only. For a fair comparison between the different configurations, we counted the number of evaluations of right-hand sides. Figure 1 displays these numbers for the given list of benchmarks, sorted according to their sizes. The Table 1 shows, for each program, the number of lines where a data race could not be ruled out. As expected, the analysis without context is less precise. Less expected, we found no difference in precision between full or half context in these benchmarks. Concerning precision, no distinction is made between dependency-driven solving and forward propagation, as these approaches produce the same result for the same context configuration.

Surprisingly, an analysis without context was not the most efficient — for larger programs and forward propagation, sometimes more right-hand sides had to be evaluated. This shows that trading the number of updates against the number of constraint variables does not necessarily pay off. Secondly, the half context configuration turned out to be the most efficient (with the notable exception of benchmark smt_proc and forward propagation), while sacrificing no precision. Generally, for these benchmarks forward propagation required the evaluation of significantly more right-hand sides than the dependency-driven approach. This confirms the intuition that forward propagation is prone to analyze the code, after two branches have met, twice.

Table 1. Precision Results

Name	Size(LoC)	Lines with Warnings		
		No Ctx.	Half Ctx.	Full Ctx.
aget	1280	162	162	162
pfscan	1295	72	72	72
ctrace	1407	87	79	79
knot	2255	140	62	62
smtprc	5787	1068	636	636
ypbind	6596	251	244	244
automount	20624	505	480	480
zfs-fuse	24097	2319	2318	2318

For reproducibility of our results, the benchmarks, the system GOBLINT together with scripts to run the system in the various configurations can be downloaded from http://goblint.github.com/side_effect .

10   Conclusion

We have shown that side-effecting constraint systems are well-suited to express interprocedural program analyses with quite different characteristics such as flow insensitivity for global properties, as well as flow sensitivity for locals where procedure summaries are tabulated for varying parts of the abstract state. Encoding different well-known techniques using side-effecting constraint systems allows us to freely combine different types of program analyses into a single analysis, while preserving soundness guarantees. This combination into a single analysis is critical for precision because different analyses may mutually complement each other. It also enables us to generically apply *property simulation* [8], which we used to deal with conditional locking, by letting the user select which analyses should be seen as the relevant property and which analyses are part of the simulation.

The approach through side-effecting constraint systems has been realized in the analyzer generator GOBLINT. Any analysis that can be expressed using side-effecting constraint system can be plugged into the analysis framework. An experimental evaluation on practical programs shows that competitive run times can be obtained for larger programs and quite complicated analyses.

Surprisingly, the constraint systems arising from interprocedural analysis with tabulation of partial contexts are not monotonic. Still, we plan to extend the widening/narrowing approach of Cousot and Cousot [4], that expects monotonicity, to our setting in order to allow analyses also to build upon very expressive lattices where ascending chains of elements may not be ultimately stable.

Acknowledgements. The research leading to these results has received funding from the ARTEMIS Joint Undertaking under grant agreement n° 269335 and from the German Science Foundation (DFG). The last author is partially supported by EstSF grant n° 8421.

References

1. Andersen, L.O.: Program Analysis and Specialization for the C Programming Language. Ph.D. thesis, DIKU, University of Copenhagen (1994)
2. Apinis, K., Seidl, H., Vojdani, V.: Side-Effecting Constraint Systems: A Swiss Army Knife for Program Analysis. Tech. Rep. TUM-I1213, Technische Universität München, Institut für Informatik (2012)
3. Calcagno, C., Distefano, D., O'Hearn, P., Yang, H.: Compositional shape analysis by means of bi-abduction. In: POPL 2009, pp. 289–300. ACM Press (2009)
4. Cousot, P., Cousot, R.: Abstract Interpretation: A unified lattice model for static analysis of programs by construction or approximation of fixpoints. In: POPL 1977, pp. 238–252. ACM Press (1977)
5. Cousot, P., Cousot, R.: Static Determination of Dynamic Properties of Recursive Procedures. In: IFIP Conf. on Formal Description of Programming Concepts, pp. 237–277. North-Holland (1977)
6. Cousot, P., Cousot, R., Feret, J., Mauborgne, L., Miné, A., Monniaux, D., Rival, X.: The ASTREÉ Analyzer. In: Sagiv, M. (ed.) ESOP 2005. LNCS, vol. 3444, pp. 21–30. Springer, Heidelberg (2005)
7. Cousot, P., Halbwachs, N.: Automatic discovery of linear restraints among variables of a program. In: POPL 1978, pp. 84–96. ACM Press (1978)
8. Das, M., Lerner, S., Seigle, M.: ESP: Path-sensitive program verification in polynomial time. In: PLDI 2002, pp. 57–68. ACM Press (2002)

9. Fecht, C.: Abstrakte Interpretation logischer Programme: Theorie, Implementierung, Generierung. Ph.D. thesis, Universität des Saarlandes (1997)
10. Fecht, C., Seidl, H.: A Faster Solver for General Systems of Equations. Sci. Comput. Program. 35(2), 137–161 (1999)
11. Flexeder, A., Mihaila, B., Petter, M., Seidl, H.: Interprocedural Control Flow Reconstruction. In: Ueda, K. (ed.) APLAS 2010. LNCS, vol. 6461, pp. 188–203. Springer, Heidelberg (2010)
12. Guyer, S.Z., Lin, C.: Client-Driven Pointer Analysis. In: Cousot, R. (ed.) SAS 2003. LNCS, vol. 2694, pp. 214–236. Springer, Heidelberg (2003)
13. Hofmann, M., Karbyshev, A., Seidl, H.: Verifying a Local Generic Solver in Coq. In: Cousot, R., Martel, M. (eds.) SAS 2010. LNCS, vol. 6337, pp. 340–355. Springer, Heidelberg (2010)
14. Jørgensen, N.: Finding Fixpoints in Finite Function Spaces Using Neededness Analysis and Chaotic Iteration. In: LeCharlier, B. (ed.) SAS 1994. LNCS, vol. 864, pp. 329–345. Springer, Heidelberg (1994)
15. Kildall, G.: A unified approach to global program optimization. In: POPL 1973, pp. 194–206. ACM Press (1973)
16. Lattner, C., Adve, V.: LLVM: A compilation framework for lifelong program analysis & transformation. In: CGO 2004, pp. 75–88. IEEE Press (2004)
17. Lhoták, O., Chung, K.C.A.: Points-to analysis with efficient strong updates. In: POPL 2011, pp. 3–16. ACM Press (2011)
18. Milanova, A., Rountev, A., Ryder, B.G.: Parameterized object sensitivity for points-to analysis for Java. ACM Transactions on Software Engineering and Methodology 14, 1–41 (2005)
19. Necula, G.C., McPeak, S., Rahul, S.P., Weimer, W.: CIL: Intermediate Language and Tools for Analysis and Transformation of C Programs. In: Horspool, R.N. (ed.) CC 2002. LNCS, vol. 2304, pp. 213–228. Springer, Heidelberg (2002)
20. Reps, T., Horwitz, S., Sagiv, M.: Precise interprocedural dataflow analysis via graph reachability. In: POPL 1995, pp. 49–61. ACM Press (1995)
21. Rinetzky, N., Bauer, J., Reps, T.W., Sagiv, S., Wilhelm, R.: A semantics for procedure local heaps and its abstractions. In: POPL 2005, pp. 296–309 (2005)
22. Seidl, H., Vene, V., Müller-Olm, M.: Global invariants for analyzing multithreaded applications. Proc. of the Estonian Academy of Sciences: Phys., Math. 52(4), 413–436 (2003)
23. Seidl, H., Vojdani, V.: Region Analysis for Race Detection. In: Palsberg, J., Su, Z. (eds.) SAS 2009. LNCS, vol. 5673, pp. 171–187. Springer, Heidelberg (2009)
24. Shapiro, M., Horwitz, S.: Fast and accurate flow-insensitive points-to analysis. In: POPL 1997, pp. 1–14. ACM Press (1997)
25. Sharir, M., Pnueli, A.: Two approaches to interprocedural data flow analysis. In: Muchnick, S., Jones, N. (eds.) Program Flow Analysis: Theory and Application, pp. 189–233. Prentice-Hall (1981)
26. Steensgaard, B.: Points-to analysis in almost linear time. In: POPL 1996, pp. 32–41. ACM Press (1996)
27. Vallée-Rai, R., Co, P., Gagnon, E., Hendren, L., Lam, P., Sundaresan, V.: Soot: A Java bytecode optimization framework. In: CASCON 1999. IBM Press (1999)
28. Vergauwen, B., Wauman, J., Lewi, J.: Efficient Fixpoint Computation. In: LeCharlier, B. (ed.) SAS 1994. LNCS, vol. 864, pp. 314–328. Springer, Heidelberg (1994)
29. Vojdani, V.: Static Data Race Analysis of Heap-Manipulating C Programs. Ph.D. thesis, University of Tartu (2010)
30. Wilson, R.P., French, R.S., Wilson, C.S., Amarasinghe, S.P., Anderson, J.M., Tjiang, S.W.K., Liao, S.W., Tseng, C.W., Hall, M.W., Lam, M.S., Hennessy, J.L.: SUIF: An infrastructure for research on parallelizing and optimizing compilers. SIGPLAN Not. 29, 31–37 (1994)

Inference of Necessary Field Conditions with Abstract Interpretation

Mehdi Bouaziz[1], Francesco Logozzo[2], and Manuel Fähndrich[2]

[1] École Normale Supérieure, Paris
[2] Microsoft Research, Redmond, WA, USA

Abstract. We present a new static analysis to infer necessary field conditions for object-oriented programs. A necessary field condition is a property that should hold on the fields of a given object, for otherwise there exists a calling context leading to a failure due to bad object state. Our analysis also infers the provenance of the necessary condition, so that if a necessary field condition is violated then an explanation containing the sequence of method calls leading to a failing assertion can be produced.

When the analysis is restricted to readonly fields, i.e., fields that can only be set in the initialization phase of an object, it infers object invariants. We provide empirical evidence on the usefulness of necessary field conditions by integrating the analysis into `cccheck`, our static analyzer for .NET. Robust inference of readonly object field invariants was the #1 request from `cccheck` users.

1 Introduction

Design by Contract [24] is a programming methodology which systematically requires the programmer to provide the preconditions, postconditions, and object invariants (collectively called contracts) at design time. Contracts allow the automatic generation of documentation, amplify the testing process, and naturally enable assume/guarantee reasoning for static program verification.

Assume/guarantee reasoning is a divide and conquer methodology, where the correctness proof is split between the callee and the caller. When the body of the callee is analyzed, its precondition is assumed and the postcondition must be proved. At a call site, the precondition must be proved and the postcondition can be assumed by the caller. In object-oriented programs, an *object invariant* (sometimes incorrectly called class invariant) is a property on the object fields that holds in the *steady* states of the object, i.e., it is at the same time a precondition and a postcondition of all the methods of a class.

In a perfect (Design by Contract) world, the programmer provides contracts for all the methods and all the classes, and a static verifier would leverage them to prove the program correctness. In the real world, relatively few classes and methods have contracts, for various reasons. First, the programming language or the programming environment may not support contracts at all. Programmers may add checks on the input parameters of a method and on the object fields,

R. Jhala and A. Igarashi (Eds.): APLAS 2012, LNCS 7705, pp. 173–189, 2012.
© Springer-Verlag Berlin Heidelberg 2012

but there is no systematic way of expressing those in a way that can be exploited by a static analyzer to perform assume/guarantee reasoning. Second, even if the programming environment supports contracts, programmers may have only partially annotated their code, for instance by adding preconditions only to the externally visible (public) methods, ignoring object fields. Third, the programmer may also have avoided adding contracts which may appear evident from the code, e.g., setting a private field to a non-null value in the constructor and never changing it again. Fourth, the provided contracts may be too weak, for instance a stronger object invariant may be needed to ensure the absence of errors such as runtime failures or assertion violations.

Inference has been advocated as the holy grail to solve the problems above. Ideally, an automatic static analyzer will infer preconditions and postconditions for each method, and object invariants for each class, exploiting the existing annotations and parameter checking code to get more precise results. The inferred contracts will then be propagated and used in the assume/guarantee reasoning.

Much research has been conducted to characterize *when* the object invariant can be assumed and when it should be checked, e.g. [11]. Orthogonally, some static analyses have been developed to infer object invariants when those points are known, e.g. [23, 4]. Those analyses over-approximate the strongest object invariant which in turn over-approximates the trace-based object semantics [23].

In this paper we tackle the problem of inferring *necessary* conditions on object invariants, i.e., conditions on object fields that should hold, for otherwise, there exists an execution trace starting with an object construction and a series of method invocations that leads to an assertion failure in one of the object's methods due to bad object state. Necessary object invariants differ from "usual" programmer-written object invariants in that they typically under-approximate the object invariant. Necessary object invariants are *necessary* in the sense that if they don't hold, there exists an execution trace that is guaranteed to fail. Satisfying all necessary object invariants on the other hand does not guarantee the absence of failures, due to, e.g., method internal non-determinism.

Main Contributions. We discuss and define the problem of brittleness of class-level modular analyses (Sect. 2) – solving that problem was the #1 request of cccheck [15] users[1]. We introduce a solution to the problem based on the inference of necessary field conditions (Sect. 4). Our solution builds on the top of previous work on precondition inference [8]. We show that when readonly fields are concerned, necessary conditions are object invariants (Sect. 5). We validate our analysis on large and complex libraries (Sect. 6). We compare it with: (i) a baseline run (BR) where no properties for object fields are inferred (only method preconditions and postconditions); and (ii) an optimized implementation of the class-level modular analysis (CLMA). Experimental results show that our analysis: (i) introduces a modest slowdown (and in some cases a speedup!) over BR; (ii) is up to 2× faster than CLMA; and (iii) induces a precision improvement comparable to CLMA. To the best of our knowledge we are the first to

---

[1] cccheck is the abstract interpretation-based [7] contract static checker for CodeContracts [13]. At the moment of writing it counts more than 75,000 external downloads.

```
public class Person {
  private readonly string Name;
  private readonly JobTitle JobTitle;

  public Person(string name, JobTitle jobTitle)  {
    Contract.Requires(jobTitle != null && name != null);

    this.Name = name;
    this.JobTitle = jobTitle;
  }

  public string GetFullName()  {
    if (this.JobTitle != null)
      return string.Format("{0}␣({1})", PrettyPrint(this.Name), this.JobTitle.ToString()));
    return PrettyPrint(this.Name);
  }

  public int BaseSalary() {
    return this.JobTitle.BaseSalary;
  }

  public string PrettyPrint(string s)  {
    Contract.Requires(s != null);
    // ...
  }
}
```

Fig. 1. The running example. Without the object invariant this.Name != null $\land$ this.JobTitle != null a modular static analyzer issues two false warnings.

systematically evaluate and compare different approaches to the static inference of field conditions. In the light of the experimental results, we have chosen to deploy it as the standard analysis for object-invariant inference in cccheck.

2   Motivation

Let us consider the code in Fig. 1. A Person object contains two private fields, the name of the person and his job title. The C# readonly marker specifies that those fields can *only* be assigned inside the constructors. The method GetFullName returns the name of the person and the job title, if any. The method BaseSalary returns the base salary for the job title of the given person.

2.1   Separate Method-Level Analysis

A method-level modular analysis of Person will analyze each constructor/method in isolation. At the entry point, it will assume the precondition and the object invariant. At the exit point, it will assert the postcondition and the object invariant. In our simple example the object invariant is empty (trivially the true invariant). The analysis reports 2 possible null dereferences. In the method GetFullName, the field Name may be null, violating the precondition of PrettyPrint. In the method BaseSalary the field JobTitle may be null (in GetFullName, JobTitle is checked before being dereferenced). Those are *false* warnings as both fields are initialized to non-null values in the constructor. The readonly fields semantics guarantees that they cannot be modified anymore.

The usual solution to this problem is to ask the programmer to provide the object invariant. This is for instance the approach of tools like ESC/Java [18, 3], Krakatoa [16], Spec# [1], and the default behavior of cccheck [15]. The advantage of programmer-provided invariants is that they clearly state programmer intent and can be used as documentation. The drawback is that too many annotations may be required, quickly overwhelming the programmer. Our goal is to help the programmer by inferring (or suggesting in the IDE) object invariants.

2.2   Class-Level Modular Analysis

A class-level modular analysis [22] exploits the information that the methods are executed after the constructor to improve precision. The main insight is that an object invariant can be given a fixpoint characterization as follows:

$$I = \bigsqcup_{c \in Constrs} s[\![c]\!] \sqcup \bigsqcup_{m \in Methods} s[\![m]\!](I), \tag{1}$$

i.e., an object invariant is a property that holds after the execution of the constructors and before and after the execution of the public methods[2]. Once we fix an abstract domain A and the corresponding static analysis $\bar{s}[\![\cdot]\!]$, equation (1) can be solved with standard fixpoint techniques. A widening operator may be required to enforce the convergence of the iterations.

In our example, we let A be the non-nullness abstract domain [14]. At the first iteration, the analysis infers that JobTitle and Name are not null at the exit of the constructor: $I_0 = \langle \text{Name} \mapsto \text{NN}, \text{JobTitle} \mapsto \text{NN} \rangle$. The analysis then propagates I_0 to the entry point of the two methods: $\bar{s}[\![\text{GetFullName}]\!](I_0) = \bar{s}[\![\text{BaseSalary}]\!](I_0) = I_0$ so that I_0 is an object invariant. It is easy to see that I_0 is the *strongest* state-based invariant for Person. Using the invariant I_0, a static analyzer can prove the safety of all the field dereferences in the class.

2.3   Drawbacks of Class-Level Modular Analysis

In general a class-level modular analysis is brittle with respect to source modifications. A small change in one part of a class may cause a warning in a distant (apparently) totally unrelated part of the same class, causing major confusion for the programmer. We identify two main sources of brittleness. The first source arises from adding new members (constructors, methods) to a class. The second source arises from changes to the allowed initial method states and object initialization.

Addition of New Class Members: Suppose that a new constructor is added to the class in our example as follows:

```
public Person(string name) {
  Contract.Requires(name != null);

  this.Name = name; }
```

---

[2] Here for simplicity we omit the treatment of aliasing, of inheritance, of the projection operators, and of method calls. The interested reader can find the extension of (1) for the treatment of those features in [23].

Let us call the modified class Person′. The field JobTitle is not assigned in the constructor, and it gets the default value null. The C# compiler does not issue any warning: it is perfectly legal to *not* assign a field (even if marked as readonly) in the constructor. The class-level modular analysis now considers the two constructors, and hence two ways of initializing the object. The object state after constructor invocation is:

$$J_0^0 = \bar{s}[\![Person(string, JobTitle)]\!] = \langle Name \mapsto NN, JobTitle \mapsto NN \rangle$$
$$J_0^1 = \bar{s}[\![Person(string)]\!] = \langle Name \mapsto NN, JobTitle \mapsto T \rangle$$
$$J_0 = J_0^0 \sqcup J_0^1 = J_0^1.$$

The analysis of the methods yields:

$$J_1^0 = \bar{s}[\![GetFullName]\!](J_0) = \langle Name \mapsto NN, JobTitle \mapsto T \rangle$$
$$J_1^1 = \bar{s}[\![BaseSalary]\!](J_0) = \langle Name \mapsto NN, JobTitle \mapsto NN \rangle$$
$$J_1 = J_1^0 \sqcup J_1^1 = J_0.$$

It is easy to see that J_0 is the strongest state-based object invariant for the modified class Person′. Therefore no imprecision is introduced by the abstract domain (or in general by the widening).

The analysis verifies the field dereferences in GetFullName: the explicit check for JobTitle nullness ensures that the successive access is correct. On the other hand, the analysis now issues a warning for the dereference of JobTitle in BaseSalary. This warning is no longer a false alarm, but a symptom for a real defect in the code. However, *what* is the real origin of this problem? Who should be blamed? Was the original class correct? Or, could it be that the verification of BaseSalary in the first version of Person was just a "lucky" accident? After all, the programmer was protecting against JobTitle being null in GetFullName, but she forgot to do so in the other method. The class-level static analysis on Person was smart enough to prove that the field JobTitle was always not-null. But was it the intent of the programmer?

Ideally, if the programmer wanted JobTitle to be not-null, then we should emit the warning in the new version of the class where the field is assigned a null value (i.e., the constructor). If, on the other hand, the programmer allowed JobTitle to be null, then we should emit the warning where the field is dereferenced (i.e., BaseSalary), and we should produce an inter-procedural trace leading to the alarm.

One can argue that if Person(string) is not used in the program, no warnings would have been emitted. However it is a good design pattern to consider and analyze a class as a whole, regardless of how it is used. Moreover a class can be compiled as a library and used outside the project: the analysis cannot rely on the context.

Changing the Initial State of the Object: Suppose that in the example of Fig. 1 the precondition for Person(string, JobTitle) was omitted or deleted. Call the resulting class Person″. Then the object fields can be assigned null so that invariant (1) is T (trivially true invariant). As a consequence the analysis can no longer prove the safety of the field dereference in BaseSalary, and it emits a warning in that method. While the analyzer is correct in pointing out that dereference, because that is the point where the runtime error will occur, the *real* error may be in the constructor where the programmer has not prevented her implementation from leaving jobTitle initialized to null. Catching this kind of weakness in realistic and large classes is in general quite difficult.

Usability Impact: In general, an apparently innocent and harmless code addition like a new constructor caused a warning in a piece of code that was previously verified. Adding new constructors or new methods may cause the object invariant to be weaker, hence causing the analysis to emit alarms in many places that are apparently unrelated to the changes. Debugging those problems can be very painful for the programmer: it is hard from invariant (1) to trace back the origin of a warning. In a realistic setting, a class definition may contain dozens of methods, some of them with a complex control flow graph. Furthermore, the underlying abstract domain used by the analyzer may be very complex—in general, the reduced product of many abstract domains, e.g., alias, numerical, symbolic, arrays, etc. As a consequence, the object invariant inferred according to (1) may not be immediately evident to the programmer. Pretty-printing the inferred invariant is of little help. The programmer would have to understand why the tool inferred the object invariant, and how this invariant was used to prove the assertions in the previous version of the class. Then, she would have to inspect the newly inferred invariant, understand why it is different from the previous one, i.e., to identify the root cause of the alarm. In real code this process is time consuming, and requires the programmer to have some expertise about the internals of the analyzer, something we want to avoid.

In principle, the above noted brittleness is problematic for all inference problems, e.g., loop invariants and postconditions. However, according to our experience, loop invariants and postcondition inference is pretty stable. We guess that these inferences are more stable because they are locally inferred. Object invariant inference, on the other hand, manifests a more chaotic behavior: according to equation (1), the effects of small changes are amplified by the interleaved propagation to all the other class members, *de facto* losing locality.

2.4   Necessary Object Invariants

We propose a different, new approach to the object-invariant inference problem. We detect conditions that *should* hold on the fields of an object, for otherwise we can exhibit a trace from object construction and a series of method calls that leads to an assertion failure inside a method of the class. These conditions are *necessary* for the object's correctness. Technically, instead of performing a forward analysis as in equation (1), we perform a goal-directed backward inter-procedural propagation of potentially failing assertions. By proceeding backwards, we can infer an abstract error trace, producing a more meaningful message for the programmer. We illustrate our technique with the Person example.

In the original class `Person`, we first run a method-level separate modular analysis of the methods, assuming the object invariant to be T [3]. cccheck will report the warnings as in Sect. 2.1. Using the techniques of [8] we try to infer preconditions by pushing the assertions that cannot be proven to the method entry points. In our example, we get the two following conditions on the entry state: $\mathcal{I}(\texttt{GetFullName}) = \texttt{this.Name} \mathrel{!{=}} \texttt{null}$ and $\mathcal{I}(\texttt{BaseSalary}) = \texttt{this.JobTitle} \mathrel{!{=}} \texttt{null}$. $\mathcal{I}(\texttt{m})$ denotes a necessary precondition for the method m. The conditions are necessary for the correctness of the method: if violated, an error will definitely occur. In this example, they happen to also be sufficient: if they hold at entry, then no error will appear at runtime. However, they cannot be made *pre*-conditions as they violate the visibility rules of the language: a precondition cannot be less visible than the enclosing method [24]. The two fields are *private* to the object, but the conditions are on the entry of *public* methods. Thus, there is no way for the client to understand and satisfy these conditions at call-sites. The conditions are internal to the object, but they should hold whenever the respective method is called. In particular, they should hold just after object construction, i.e., just after the constructor is done. Our analysis pushes the necessary conditions to the exit point of constructor `Person(string, JobTitle)` as postconditions that should be established by the constructor. The analyzer can easily prove the two assertions (they follow from the constructor precondition). As the fields are marked as readonly, their value cannot be changed by methods after construction, and so $\mathcal{I}(\texttt{GetFullName}) \wedge \mathcal{I}(\texttt{BaseSalary})$ is an object invariant. Overall, no warning is raised for `Person`.

In `Person'`, the conditions $\mathcal{I}(\texttt{GetFullName})$ and $\mathcal{I}(\texttt{BaseSalary})$ are propagated backwards to both constructors. In the newly added constructor, the assertion `this.JobTitle != null` is false. cccheck emits an alarm pointing to the newly added constructor (instead of the field dereference in `BaseSalary` as in Sect. 2.2). Furthermore, cccheck produces an error *trace*: the sequence of calls $\langle \texttt{Person}'(s), \texttt{BaseSalary} \rangle$, for any s, will drive the execution into a null dereference.

In `Person''`, the conditions are propagated to the constructor. None of the conditions are satisfied by the constructor at the exit point: both `this.Name` and `this.JobTitle` can be null. The analysis further propagates those assertions to the constructor entry, as preconditions: `name != null && jobTitle != null`. It also infers a provenance trace: violating the first (resp. second) precondition will point to a failure in `GetFullName` (resp. `BaseSalary`).

3   Preliminaries

A class is a tuple $\langle \texttt{F}, \texttt{C}, \texttt{M}, \texttt{I}_{\texttt{F}} \rangle$, where F is a set of fields, C is a set of object constructors, M is a set of methods, and $\texttt{I}_{\texttt{F}}$ is an object invariant. A field $\texttt{f} \in \texttt{F}$ has a type, a visibility modifier `private` or `public`, and an optional `readonly` flag specifying if the field can be assigned only in constructors. We refer to constructors and methods as members ($\texttt{m} \in \texttt{C} \cup \texttt{M}$). Each member has a signature

---

[3] If the class contains a programmer-provided invariant, we will use it.

(return type, parameter types), a visibility modifier private or public, a body $b_f \in \mathbb{S}$, an optional precondition Pre$_f$, and an optional postcondition Post$_f$. When clear from the context, we omit the subscript for the member from the body, the precondition, and the postcondition. The optional object invariant I$_F$ is a property only on the fields in F. We assume the contracts are expressed in a side-effect free language $\mathbb{B}$. For the sake of simplicity, we focus our attention on private fields and public constructors and methods. It is difficult to state an object invariant on public fields (preconditions and postconditions are better suited for it) and private methods do not contribute to the object invariant. We do not consider inheritance in this paper.

Let Σ be a set of states and $\tau \in \mathcal{P}(\Sigma \times \Sigma)$ be the transition function. The partial-trace semantics of the body b of a member has a fixpoint characterization:

$$\tau_b^+(S) = \mathsf{lfp}\lambda T.\ S \cup \{\sigma_0 \ldots \sigma_n \sigma_{n+1} \mid \sigma_0 \ldots \sigma_n \in T \wedge \tau_b(\sigma_n, \sigma_{n+1})\}.$$

The concretization function $\gamma_\mathbb{B} \in \mathbb{B} \to \mathcal{P}(\Sigma)$ gives the semantics of a contract in terms of the set of states Σ. The initial states for the execution of a member are $S_0 = \gamma_\mathbb{B}(I_F) \cap \gamma_\mathbb{B}(\text{Pre})$. The partial-trace semantics of a member is $\tau_b^+(S_0)$. The bad states B are the ones violating some code or language assertions ($B_s \subseteq \Sigma$), or the postconditions: $B = B_s \cup \gamma_\mathbb{B}(\neg\text{Post})$. The finite bad traces are those that contain at least one bad state: $B^* = \{\sigma_0 \ldots \sigma_n \in \Sigma^* \mid \exists i \in [0, n].\sigma_i \in B\}$. The good runs of a member from $S \subseteq S_0$ are $\mathcal{G}(b, S) = \tau_b^+(S) \setminus B^*$. Dually, the bad runs of a member from $S \subseteq S_0$ are $\mathcal{B}(b, S) = \tau_b^+(S) \cap B^*$.

We assume an abstract domain $\mathcal{A}$ soundly approximating the set of states, i.e., $\langle \mathcal{P}(\Sigma), \subseteq \rangle \xleftrightarrow[\alpha]{\gamma} \langle \mathcal{A}, \sqsubseteq \rangle$ [7]. When $\bar{a} \in \mathcal{A}$ is such that $S_0 \subseteq \gamma(\bar{a})$, then the abstract semantics $\bar{s}[\![b]\!](\bar{a}) \in \mathcal{A}$ overapproximates $\alpha_\Sigma(\tau_b^+(S_0))$ — α_Σ being the abstraction collecting the states in a set of traces.

In [8] we defined the problem of necessary initial conditions inference as finding an initial condition $e \in \mathbb{B}$ such that: $\mathcal{G}(b, \gamma_\mathbb{B}(e) \cap S_0) = \mathcal{G}(b, S_0)$ and $\mathcal{B}(b, \gamma_\mathbb{B}(e) \cap S_0) \subseteq \mathcal{B}(b, S_0)$, i.e., e is a condition at the entry of b such that: (i) all good runs are preserved; and (ii) only bad runs are eliminated. Please note that the conditions for the necessary precondition inference are equivalent, because of monotonicity, to only requiring that $\mathcal{G}(b, \gamma_\mathbb{B}(e) \cap S_0) \supseteq \mathcal{G}(b, S_0)$. Also, the problem is different from the inference of the weakest (liberal) preconditions, which imposes that *all* the bad traces are eliminated. For instance, a trivial solution to our problem is $e = \text{true}$, but true is not (in general) a solution of $\lambda X.X \implies \mathsf{wlp}(b, \text{Post})$. Cousot, Cousot, and Logozzo [8] presented several static analyses $\mathcal{I}(b) \in \mathcal{A} \to \mathbb{B}$ to infer non-trivial initial necessary conditions, parameterized by the abstract domain $\mathcal{A}$. Those analyses are more or less precise. They can discover simple predicates (e.g., x != null), disjunctive conditions (e.g., $x \leq 0 \vee 0 < y$), or quantified conditions over collections (e.g., $\forall i.0 \leq \text{arr}[i]$ or $\exists i.\text{arr}[i] = 123$). The common idea behind the analyses of [8] is to find a Boolean expression e in terms of the member entry point values, such that if e is violated at the entry point, then an assertion a will later definitely fail (up to non-termination). We denote this relation as $e \leadsto a$. We do not repeat the details of these analyses here, leaving them as a building block to our analysis of necessary object field conditions. Our goal here is: (i) to show how such analyses can be lifted to infer necessary field conditions; and (ii) to prove that this inference is competitive with the forward class-level modular analysis in terms of precision and performance.

4   Inference of Necessary Conditions on Object Fields

Our goal is the inference of necessary conditions on object fields. A necessary field condition is a property that should hold on the instance fields of an object, otherwise there exists a context (sequence of public method calls) that causes the object to be in a bad state. In this section we design a new static analysis, built on the top of a generic abstract interpretation of the class members, to infer such conditions.

The verification of a member m, $\texttt{cccheck}(\texttt{m}, \textbf{out } \bar{\texttt{a}})^4$, works in two steps: (i) first analyze the member to infer program-point specific invariants, call these $\bar{\texttt{a}}$; (ii) use these inferred invariants to prove the assertions in m body. Assertions can be user-defined assertions or language assertions (e.g., pointer dereference, arithmetic overflow, division by zero . . .). The member precondition and the postconditions of the called functions are turned into assumptions (nothing to be proven). The member postcondition, the object invariant, and the preconditions of the called functions are turned into assertions (they should be proven). For methods only, the object invariant is assumed at their entry point.

If no alarm is raised, i.e., the member has been verified, there is nothing to do. Otherwise, cccheck tries to infer an initial condition. The necessary initial condition for a member m is $\mathcal{I}_0 := \mathcal{I}(\texttt{m})(\bar{\texttt{a}})$. If $\mathcal{I}_0 \equiv \texttt{true}$ we are done: there is no way to push any of the failing assertions to the entry point.

If m is a constructor, then $\mathcal{I}_0$ contains predicates on parameters, on the public fields reachable from the parameters, or on private fields of an object of the same type as the type m belongs to.

In the first two cases, $\mathcal{I}_0$ can be made a precondition of m. We denote by $\phi_P := \pi_1(\mathcal{I}_0)$ the components of $\mathcal{I}_0$ that are valid preconditions according to the language visibility rules. Note that in general, when m contains loops, ϕ_P does not guarantee its *safety*. The safety in general can be checked by re-running the verification with the new precondition: $\texttt{cccheck}(\texttt{m}[\texttt{Pre} \mapsto \texttt{Pre}_\texttt{m} \wedge \phi_P], \textbf{out } \bar{\texttt{a}})$. In some cases, safety can be guaranteed by construction, e.g., if m contains no loops. If we can prove safety, we can mask the warning (the precondition is a necessary and sufficient condition).

In the last case, when an object of the same type as the type m belongs to is passed as a parameter, we emit the warning, and point out the assumption the programmer is making on the private field of a different object, suggesting a refactoring.

If m is a method then there is a fourth case for $\mathcal{I}_0$: it may contain some condition ϕ_I on the private fields of the this object. The condition ϕ_I cannot be made a precondition of m as a precondition less visible than the enclosing member is not

---

[4] As usual in programming languages the keyword **out** denotes out parameters.

Result: A necessary condition $\mathcal{J}^*$ on object fields

```
while true do
    φ ← true
    foreach m ∈ M do
        if ¬cccheck(m, out ā) then  // Strengthen precondition and invariant
            ⟨φ_P, φ_I⟩ ← π_2(𝒥(m)(ā))
            Pre_m ← Pre_m ∧ φ_P
            φ ← φ ∧ φ_I
        end
    end
    if φ = true then
        break// no change on I_F, we are done
    else
        I_F ← I_F ∧ φ
    end
end
foreach c ∈ C do
    if ¬cccheck(c, out ā) then  // Strengthen the precondition
        Pre_c ← Pre_c ∧ π_1(𝒥(c)(ā))
    end
end
```

Algorithm 1. The necessary field conditions inference algorithm. The algorithm can be easily instrumented to trace the provenance of the ϕs appearing in $\mathcal{J}^*$ and hence to construct a failing context.

allowable by the Design-by-Contracts methodology: there is no way for the client to satisfy the precondition[5]. Nevertheless, ϕ_I is a necessary condition on the object fields, which should hold whenever the method is invoked. In particular, it is a condition that should hold just after any of the constructors c or any of the (public) methods m' are executed. Otherwise we can construct a context where the call to c or m' is immediately followed by a call to m, and we know by construction that invoking m in a state satisfying $\neg\phi_I$ will definitely cause a failure (up to termination). Therefore we can strengthen the object invariant to $I_F \mapsto I_F \wedge \phi_I$, and repeat the analysis of all the class members. We denote by $\langle\phi_p, \phi_I\rangle := \pi_2(\mathcal{J}_0)$ the pair containing the new precondition for m and the necessary condition on the object field.

For each new condition ϕ added to the object invariant we can remember its provenance (the failing assertion and the containing member). In general, we can generate a provenance chain $a_n \rightsquigarrow a_{n-1} \rightsquigarrow \ldots a_0$. Suppose that a_n is an assertion in one of the object constructors. By construction we know (up to termination) that if a_n is violated, then we can construct a sequence of public method calls (the ones containing the assertions $a_i, i \in [0, n]$) causing a_0 to fail at runtime. Therefore, we can produce more meaningful warnings to the programmer by pointing out the assertion a_n and the sequence of public method calls that will lead to an assertion failure at runtime if a_n is violated.

Algorithm 1 formalizes our explanations above. It computes a greatest fixpoint on the abstract domain $\mathbb{B} \times (C \to \mathbb{B}) \times (M \to \mathbb{B})$. The partial order is the pointwise lifting of the logical implication $\Rightarrow$. Please note that the algorithm may not

---

[5] Remember that we are only considering public methods. If the method was private, then the condition could have been made a precondition.

terminate, necessitating widening for convergence. A simple widening is to limit the number of iterations (k-widening). The algorithm can be optimized using Gauss-Seidl chaotic iterations [6], i.e., by strengthening I_F after the analysis of each method.

It is easy to modify it to track the origin of the assertions. The object condition is in conjunctive form: $\phi_I = \phi_I^0 \wedge \cdots \wedge \phi_I^n$. By construction of $\mathcal{J}$, each $\phi_I^i, i \in [0, n]$ originates from some assertion $\mathbf{a}$ that cannot be proven: $\exists \mathbf{a}. \ \phi_I^i \rightsquigarrow \mathbf{a}$. In turn, $\mathbf{a}$ may be an inferred condition with its own provenance, and so on, effectively building a provenance chain. We denote by $\mathcal{J}^*$ the conjunction of the ϕs computed by the algorithm at each step.

5   Object Invariants for Readonly Fields

The predicate $\mathcal{J}^*$ inferred by the Algorithm 1 is a necessary condition on the object fields. It states a condition that must hold on the object's fields in between calls to public methods for otherwise, there exists a series of method calls from object construction to a guaranteed assertion failure. In general, the definition of object invariants is tied to a particular methodology for when object invariants are supposed to be valid. These programming methodologies define at which program points the object invariant holds, and which aliasing containment policy is assumed and enforced. Different methodologies adopt different policies (e.g., cccheck [15], Spec# [1], jStar [10] or VeriFast [20]). The programming methodology is an orthogonal issue to the solution presented in this paper, since it is mainly concerned with guaranteeing that object invariants are *sufficient* for proving the safety of all methods. In contrast, we are inferring *necessary* conditions on fields without which failure is guaranteed. This distinction is analogous to the distinction between necessary and sufficient preconditions [8]. Thus, in this paper we do not consider any particular object invariant methodology.

Yet, it is still useful to point out one special case, where we can indeed talk about an object invariant: If we restrict ourselves to include in Algorithm 1 only **readonly** fields, then the inferred predicate is truly an object invariant, since it needs to hold at every program point after construction (independent of methodology).

A field marked as readonly can only be updated in a constructor of the class it belongs to [19]. Assignment to a readonly field is not compulsory. If a readonly field is not initialized, it gets the default value (e.g., **null** for heap objects). A readonly field is different from a *constant* field in that it is not a compile time constant.

The algorithm for the inference of object invariants for readonly fields differs from Algorithm 1 in the way the inferred necessary conditions for the methods are selected: $\langle \phi_p, \phi_I, \phi_A \rangle := \pi_3(\mathcal{J}(\mathbf{m})(\bar{\mathbf{a}}))$. The function $\pi_3 \in \mathbb{B} \rightarrow \mathbb{B}^3$ partitions the inferred conditions according to visibility rules. The precondition ϕ_P contains only variables as-visible-as the method. The readonly object invariant ϕ_I contains only readonly fields of the **this** object. Finally the input assumption ϕ_A contains conditions necessary for the method correctness, but which cannot be included in the method precondition or the readonly invariant.

It is easy to see that $\mathcal{I}^*$ computed by this modified algorithm is an invariant on object fields, no matter which methodology for object invariants is chosen. Indeed, the initial, programmer-provided condition I_F is an invariant. All the successive additions are properties on readonly fields that should hold at the end of the constructor and — by the semantics of readonly fields — cannot be further changed.

6   Experiments

We evaluate the cost and the precision of our analysis by comparing it to runs of cccheck: (i) without object invariants inference; (ii) with object invariants inference based on class-level modular analysis. We want to measure the extra cost and precision induced by our analysis. We use the main libraries of the .NET framework (mscorlib, System, System.Core) and some randomly chosen libraries as benchmarks. The libraries are available in all Windows installations.

Experimental Setting. We ran cccheck with four different settings:

- (BR)   with the object invariant inference disabled;
- (NCR) with the object invariant inference enabled for readonly fields only (Sect. 5);
- (NC1) with the object invariant inference enabled for all fields (Sect. 4), with the constraint of analyzing every method only once;
- (CLMAR) with the forward class-level modular analysis enabled for readonly fields only (Sect. 2.2).

In the (BR) experience, we ran cccheck with the default abstract domains and options. The default abstract domains include a domain for the heap analysis, one for the non-null checks, several numerical abstract domains, and an abstract domain for collections (more details in [15]). In this configuration, cccheck verifies the absence of: (i) contract violations, (ii) null dereferences, and (iii) out-of-bounds array accesses. cccheck performs intra-procedural modular analysis: it infers invariants on the member body which it uses to discharge the proof obligations. It exploits contracts to achieve inter-procedural analysis. To reduce the annotation burden, cccheck infers and propagates preconditions and postconditions. First, cccheck computes an approximation of the call-flow graph of the assembly under analysis. Then it schedules the analysis of the members in a bottom-up fashion: callees are analyzed before callers. Inferred preconditions (resp. postconditions) are propagated to the callers as additional asserts that should be proven (resp. assumes it can rely over). Finally, to improve performance, cccheck implements a caching mechanism to avoid re-analysis: if it detects that a member has not changed (in our case, no new contract has been added to the member or to its callees) it skips its analysis, and simply replays the previous result (warnings, inferred contracts).

(NCR) adds to (BR) the algorithm to infer object invariants for *readonly* fields. We include (NC1) in the experiments to get a better sense of the power of inferring necessary field conditions. It computes field conditions for *all* fields, but

Library	# Meth.	(BR) Checks	Top	Time	(NCR) Checks	Top	Time	(NC1) Checks	Top	Time	(CLMAR) Checks	Top	Time
mscorlib	22,904	113,551	13,240	31:41	113,750	13,084	27:36	115,002	11,053	32:22	116,116	13,152	26:12
Addin	552	4,170	682	4:15	4,148	605	4:07	4,295	485	4:11	4,067	571	12:55
Composition	1,340	6,228	909	0:44	6,356	791	0:46	6,302	743	0:47	8,095	885	1:57
Core	5,952	34,324	5,323	29:57	36,100	4,820	33:50	36,196	4,463	34:54	42,602	5,715	72:31
Data.Entity	15,239	88,286	12,460	23:13	87,743	11,719	24:02	91,591	15,861	27:59	88,125	11,569	43:36
Data.OracleClient	1,961	9,596	1,070	2:38	9,738	1,025	2:21	9,736	887	2:26	107,23	1,018	3:25
Data.Services	2,448	18,255	3,118	6:45	18,518	2,938	7:23	18,733	2,749	6:54	21,818	2,989	24:18
System	15,586	94,038	8,702	15:03	93,948	8,644	15:15	96,154	10,693	15:30	94,008	8,648	17:37

Fig. 2. Experiments results showing the impact of our static analysis in reducing the false warnings and its comparison with a class-level modular analysis. Time is in minutes and seconds. Columns Checks and Top are respectively the total number of proof obligations and the number of proof obligations that cannot be decided.

without iterating the propagation until a fixpoint is reached. It is essentially Algorithm 1 instantiated with the Gauss-Seidl iteration schema with a 1-widening (i.e., the widening is set to one iteration). (CLMAR) adds to (BR) object invariants inference for readonly fields using a class-level modular analysis.

Results. In Fig. 2, we report, for each library, the total number of methods, the number of proof obligations (language assertions or inferred contracts) generated during the analysis, the number of proof obligations that cannot be proven and the overall execution time. The first thing to note is the increase on checks. This is due to the field conditions being inserted as postconditions to be checked at constructor exits and method exits, as well as propagation of necessary field conditions to preconditions of constructors, and on to call-sites. In return, we assume the invariant at method entries. The increase in proof obligations is paid for by the reduction in overall warnings. In the (NCR) experience, we have at worst 45 (Data.OracleClient) and at most 741 (Data.Entity) fewer warnings. When percentages are observed, the best improvement is in the Core benchmark (2.16 %). (NC1) in general provides an even more dramatic reduction of the total number of warnings (up to 2, 187 less in mscorlib) but in two cases it adds to the baseline (e.g., 3, 401 more warnings for Data.Entity). The reason for it is that in some cases the inferred object invariant is quite complex (many disjuncts). It gets propagated as precondition for the constructor. The constructor is called in many places and either cccheck cannot prove the precondition at those call sites, or it is further propagated, sometime originating in an even more complex call-site assertions, etc. As one may expect (CLMAR) is generally more precise than (BR) – up to 891 fewer warnings on Data.Entity. Nevertheless there is no definite answer whether (CLMAR) is more precise than (NCR). When absolute numbers are compared, in 5 cases (mscorlib, Composition, Core, Data.Services, System) (NCR) emits fewer warnings than (CLMAR). On the other hand, when the ratio Top/Checks is considered, in 6 cases (mscorlib, Addin, Composition, Data.Entity, Data.OracleClient, Data.Services) (CLMAR) provides better results than (NCR). Overall, precision-wise there is no big difference between (NCR) and (CLMAR).

When performances are considered, results are somehow surprising. A more precise analysis does not always mean a slower analysis. For instance the

Library	(NCR)		(NC1)		(CLMAR)
	Inferred	Violations	Inferred	Violations	Inferred
mscorlib	41	1	823	80	61
AddIn	9	5	48	8	2
Composition	36	0	63	0	33
Core	150	0	323	6	81
Data.Entity	230	4	531	18	378
Data.OracleClient	13	0	75	8	54
Data.Services	53	1	96	11	49
System	22	0	349	55	131

Fig. 3. Experiments results showing the number of inferred conditions and the number of definite violations found

analyis of mscorlib was faster in both (NCR) and (CLMAR) than in (BR). On the other hand, in some benchmarks (CLMAR) was way slower than (NCR) and (NC1) (e.g., Addin, Core, Data.Entity, Data.Service). In those benchmarks the bottom-up propagation of inferred pre/post-conditions caused (CLMAR) to converge very slowly. For instance, a new inferred contract may trigger the re-analysis of a constructor, originating in a new object invariant, which at its turn impacts, e.g., the postconditions inferred for the methods of this type, etc. Of course, theoretically (NCR) may suffer from the same problem, but we did not experienced it in our experiments. Overall, performance-wise (NCR) seems a better choice than (CLMAR): in all but one experiment (mscorlib) it is faster, it adds a modest slowdown w.r.t. (BR), and it seems to be less prone to hit performance corner cases.

In Fig. 3 we report the number of field conditions inferred (after simplification, to remove redundant ones). For (NCR) and (NC1) we also report the number of violations, i.e., the number of necessary field conditions for which cccheck was able to automatically find an instantiation context that *definitely* leads to a failure. When comparing (NCR) and (NC1), it is worth noting that the effectiveness of invariant inference is limited by the fact that in "old" libraries (e.g., mscorlib) few fields are actually declared as readonly. The inferred conditions distribute evenly between (NCR) with (CLMAR): in 4 benchmarks (NCR) infers more conditions than (CLMAR), and vice versa. Our static analysis was able to find several instantiation contexts definitely leading to a failure in some classes. Experiment (NCR) shows that in 11 cases (overall) it is possible to cause a class to fail by breaking an invariant on readonly fields. The failing context creates the object by invoking a particular constructor and just after calling a particular method (*e.g.*, the sequence Person(string), BaseSalary in Sect. 2). In general, in experiment (NC1) the instantiation context is more complex, requiring longer invocation sequences to manifest.

Discussion. The experimental results are encouraging, but they require further study. In particular, given that programs are partially specified only, important usage conditions may be absent from the code. To the programmer, our necessary field conditions may appear too strong or the failing context may appear unfeasible. E.g., consider a class that requires an initialization method A to be called before allowing a call to B. If this initialization pattern is not specified using preconditions and postconditions on A and B, necessary field condition inference will probably find a condition for B that is only established after A, but not by the constructors. Our analysis will suggest it as an invariant to be added to the constructors, which may confuse the programmer.

In general, a necessary field condition ϕ_m can be decomposed into a precondition Pre_m and a weaker invariant I, such that $Pre_m \wedge I \Rightarrow \phi_m$. In our example above, assume a public flag `init` is used to indicate that the object is initialized. In that case, the precondition for B is `init`, and the weaker invariant I is `init` $\Rightarrow \phi_m$. We plan to investigate how to decompose necessary field conditions into the above form.

Overall Evaluation. The inference of field conditions improves the precision of the basic modular analysis (BR) – this was expected. The question is then which analysis to use, and in particular which one to provide to our users, who were asking for a readonly fields inference algorithm. When precision is considered (NC1) generally performs slightly better than (NCR) and (CLMAR), except one case where it adds thousands more warnings. Precision-wise, there is no clear winner between (NCR) and (CLMAR) – the choice seems to depend on the particular code base. When the extra cost of the analysis is considered, (NCR) performs better than (NC1) and way better than (CLMAR) in most cases. As far as usability is concerned, (NCR) and (NC1) should produce a better programmer experience since warnings are more understandable and easier to fix. We have no formal user study on that issue, only anedoctal evidence from the interaction with our customers (e.g., on the CodeContracts MSDN forum [25]). Overall, we think that (NCR) is the analysis best suited for our users, and we decided to set it as the default object invariant inference in the CodeContracts distribution.

7 Related Work

Daikon [12] pioneered the dynamic invariant inference approach. Given a suite of test cases, Daikon observes the values, and then generalizes it to likely invariants (pre, post, and object invariants). As a dynamic technique, Daikon requires a good set of test cases in order to produce useful invariants. In contrast, our approach is purely static, it works without test inputs and it is not limited by the pre-set candidate invariants. DySy [9] uses dynamic symbolic execution to infer preconditions, postconditions, and invariants. Like Daikon, the approach depends on test suites but uses symbolic path condition computations to identify candidate invariants (so it is not limited to a pre-defined set of invariants).

On the purely static side of invariant inference, Logozzo [23] introduced the forward analysis described in the introduction (equation (1)). Chang and Leino [4] instantiated [23] using the Spec# methodology [1] and stronger heap invariants. Houdini [17] is an annotation inference system based on ESC/Java. It guesses invariants and uses ESC/Java to prove them. Houdini is limited by the pre-set initial candidates for invariants.

What sets our work apart from all the above is the focus on *necessary* conditions that, when violated, lead to failures. Instead, all the above analyses compute a form of strongest invariants given a set of possible candidates or abstract domains. We are not aware of work describing the problem of analysis brittleness with respect to small or simple program changes.

Surprisingly little research focuses on the problem of detecting the origin of alarms in abstract interpretation-based analyzers. We are aware of Rival [26] who studies the source of warnings in the context of the ASTREE analyzer, and Brauer and Simon [2] who use under-approximations to present a counter-example to the programmer. Our work differs from theirs because we do not only want to report the cause for a warning but we also want to infer a contract for the program. The problem is studied more widely in model checking [5] and deductive verification, e.g., [21], where the finiteness hypotheses make the problem more tractable. Our traces leading to failure can be viewed as an approach to finding the origin and explanations of warnings.

8   Conclusion

Necessary object field conditions provide an alternative approach to finding predicates that are candidates for object invariants. These conditions are computed using a backward analysis from assertions within methods that will fail, unless the object field condition is satisfied on entry to the method. This approach produces invariant candidates that are demand-driven, as opposed to accidental implementation details that are often inferred by forward analyses, drastically eliminating the usual brittleness of object invariant inference caused by changes in the program. We evaluated our analysis in the context of the CodeContract static checker and found that it significantly reduces the number of warnings in a variety of large code bases.

References

[1] Barnett, M., Fähndrich, M., Leino, K.R.M., Müller, P., Schulte, W., Venter, H.: Specification and verification: the Spec# experience. CACM 54(6), 81–91 (2011)

[2] Brauer, J., Simon, A.: Inferring Definite Counterexamples through Under-Approximation. In: Goodloe, A.E., Person, S. (eds.) NFM 2012. LNCS, vol. 7226, pp. 54–69. Springer, Heidelberg (2012)

[3] Chalin, P., Kiniry, J.R., Leavens, G.T., Poll, E.: Beyond Assertions: Advanced Specification and Verification with JML and ESC/Java2. In: de Boer, F.S., Bonsangue, M.M., Graf, S., de Roever, W.-P. (eds.) FMCO 2005. LNCS, vol. 4111, pp. 342–363. Springer, Heidelberg (2006)

[4] Chang, B.-Y.E., Leino, K.R.M.: Inferring object invariants: Extended abstract. ENTCS 131 (2005)

[5] Clarke, E.M., Grumberg, O., Peled, D.: Model checking. MIT Press (2001)

[6] Cousot, P.: Asynchronous iterative methods for solving a fixed point system of monotone equations in a complete lattice. Res. rep. 88, Laboratoire IMAG, Université scientifique et médicale de Grenoble, France (1977)

[7] Cousot, P., Cousot, R.: Abstract interpretation: a unified lattice model for static analysis of programs by construction or approximation of fixpoints. In: POPL (1977)

[8] Cousot, P., Cousot, R., Logozzo, F.: Precondition Inference from Intermittent Assertions and Application to Contracts on Collections. In: Jhala, R., Schmidt, D. (eds.) VMCAI 2011. LNCS, vol. 6538, pp. 150–168. Springer, Heidelberg (2011)

[9] Csallner, C., Tillmann, N., Smaragdakis, Y.: DySy: dynamic symbolic execution for invariant inference. In: ICSE (2008)

[10] Distefano, D., Parkinson, M.J.: jStar: Towards practical verification for Java. In: OOPSLA (2008)

[11] Drossopoulou, S., Francalanza, A., Müller, P., Summers, A.J.: A Unified Framework for Verification Techniques for Object Invariants. In: Dell'Acqua, P. (ed.) ECOOP 2008. LNCS, vol. 5142, pp. 412–437. Springer, Heidelberg (2008)

[12] Ernst, M.D.: Dynamically Discovering Likely Program Invariants. PhD thesis, University of Washington (2000)

[13] Fähndrich, M., Barnett, M., Logozzo, F.: Code Contracts (2009)

[14] Fähndrich, M., Leino, K.R.M.: Declaring and checking non-null types in an object-oriented language. In: OOPSLA (2003)

[15] Fähndrich, M., Logozzo, F.: Static Contract Checking with Abstract Interpretation. In: Beckert, B., Marché, C. (eds.) FoVeOOS 2010. LNCS, vol. 6528, pp. 10–30. Springer, Heidelberg (2011)

[16] Filliâtre, J.-C., Marché, C.: The Why/Krakatoa/Caduceus Platform for Deductive Program Verification. In: Damm, W., Hermanns, H. (eds.) CAV 2007. LNCS, vol. 4590, pp. 173–177. Springer, Heidelberg (2007)

[17] Flanagan, C., Leino, K.R.M.: Houdini, an Annotation Assistant for ESC/Java. In: Oliveira, J.N., Zave, P. (eds.) FME 2001. LNCS, vol. 2021, pp. 500–517. Springer, Heidelberg (2001)

[18] Flanagan, C., Leino, K.R.M., Lillibridge, M., Nelson, G., Saxe, J.B., Stata, R.: Extended static checking for java. In: PLDI (2002)

[19] Hejlsberg, A., Torgersen, M., Wiltamuth, S., Golde, P.: The C# Programming Language. Addison-Wesley Professional (2010)

[20] Jacobs, B., Smans, J., Piessens, F.: A Quick Tour of the VeriFast Program Verifier. In: Ueda, K. (ed.) APLAS 2010. LNCS, vol. 6461, pp. 304–311. Springer, Heidelberg (2010)

[21] Le Goues, C., Leino, K.R.M., Moskal, M.: The Boogie Verification Debugger (Tool Paper). In: Barthe, G., Pardo, A., Schneider, G. (eds.) SEFM 2011. LNCS, vol. 7041, pp. 407–414. Springer, Heidelberg (2011)

[22] Logozzo, F.: Class-Level Modular Analysis for Object Oriented Languages. In: Cousot, R. (ed.) SAS 2003. LNCS, vol. 2694, pp. 37–54. Springer, Heidelberg (2003)

[23] Logozzo, F.: Modular static analysis of Object-oriented languages. PhD thesis, École polytechnique (2004)

[24] Meyer, B.: Eiffel: The Language. Prentice Hall (1991)

[25] MSDN. CodeContracts Forum,
http://social.msdn.microsoft.com/Forums/en-US/codecontracts/threads/

[26] Rival, X.: Understanding the Origin of Alarms in ASTRÉE. In: Hankin, C., Siveroni, I. (eds.) SAS 2005. LNCS, vol. 3672, pp. 303–319. Springer, Heidelberg (2005)

Lazy v. Yield:
Incremental, Linear Pretty-Printing

Oleg Kiselyov, Simon Peyton-Jones[1], and Amr Sabry[2]

[1] Microsoft Research, Cambridge, UK
simonpj@microsoft.com
[2] Indiana University, Bloomington, USA
sabry@cs.indiana.edu, oleg@okmij.org

Abstract. We propose a programming style for incremental stream processing based on typed *simple generators*. It promotes modularity and decoupling of producers and consumers just like lazy evaluation. Simple generators, however, expose the implicit suspension and resumption inherent in lazy evaluation as computational effects, and hence are robust in the presence of other effects. Simple generators let us accurately reason about memory consumption. To substantiate our claims we give a new solution to the notorious pretty-printing problem. Like earlier solutions, it is linear, backtracking-free and with bounded latency. It is also simpler to write and reason about, and is compatible with effects including IO, letting us read the source document from a file, and format it as we read.

1 Introduction

Lazy evaluation is regarded as one of the main reasons why functional programming matters [1]. Lazy evaluation lets us write *producers* and *consumers* separately, whereas the two are inextricably intertwined in a call-by-value language. This separation allows a modular style of programming, in which a variety of producers, consumers, and transformers can readily be "plugged together." Lazy evaluation is also an elegant implementation of a form of coroutines, suspending and resuming computations based on the demand for values, giving us memory-efficient, incremental computation 'for free' [2–4].

Extensive experience in Haskell has, however, exposed severe drawbacks of lazy evaluation, which are especially grievous for stream processing of large amounts of data. Lazy evaluation is fundamentally incompatible with computational effects, can cause fatal memory leaks, and greatly inhibits modular reasoning, especially about termination and space consumption. Seemingly innocuous and justified changes to the code or code compositions may lead to divergence, or explosion in memory consumption. We review and illustrate these drawbacks in more detail in §2.

It is therefore worth investigating alternatives to lazy evaluation, which are nearly as convenient, modular, and conducive to incremental computation, and yet are more robust under composition with computational effects. Since lazy evaluation corresponds to an *implicit* and stylized use of coroutines [5–8], it is

R. Jhala and A. Igarashi (Eds.): APLAS 2012, LNCS 7705, pp. 190–206, 2012.
© Springer-Verlag Berlin Heidelberg 2012

natural to consider an *explicit* stylized use of coroutines. Such alternatives, historically known as *generators* or *iterators*, have indeed been used to structure programs using "pipelines" of producers and consumers [9] following Jackson's principles of program design [10]. They have recently re-emerged in various modern languages such as Ruby, Python, C#, and JavaScript. Although the details differ, such languages offer an operator yield that captures a particular pattern in which a computation is suspended, allowed to communicate with another context, and then resumed.[1]

Survey [11] documents a rich variety of yield operators, whose most general variant is tantamount to full first-class delimited continuations. In this paper we study a much lighter-weight variant of yield, which we call *simple generators*. We make the following specific contributions:

- We introduce *typed simple generators* (§3), offering a library of combinators that support efficient stream producers, transducers, and consumers. Despite their simplicity (implementable on a single linear stack without copying), simple generators are capable to solve a variety of stream-processing problems that would normally require lazy evaluation, and yet compose readily with effects.
- We show that simple generators are expressive enough to efficiently implement a particularly recondite problem: that of bounded-lookahead, linear-time, incremental, pretty-printing (§4). This problem has been widely considered to require full coroutines or 'tying of the knot,' which in turn demands lazy evaluation. Our new solution, derived in §5, is distinguished by modularity and ease and precision of the analysis about latency, time, and especially space. The overall pretty-printing becomes a composition of independently developed, tested, and analyzed components. We can swap the components, for example, replacing the component that traverses an in-memory document with a generator that reads the document from a file. The new structure helped us discover and correct edge cases neglected in previous implementations.
- We give benchmarks in §5.4 to validate our analyses of space and time.
- Although we mostly use Haskell for concreteness and the ease of contrasting yield and lazy evaluation, our approach extends to other languages. Monadic style, needed to work with generators in Haskell, is a model of call-by-value languages. Since monads make effects (sometimes painfully) explicit, they give good guidance to implementing and using generators in strict languages – as we demonstrate for OCaml.

Appendix A of the full paper http://okmij.org/ftp/continuations/PPYield/yield-pp.pdf gives the derivation of optimal pretty-printing in all detail. The complete Haskell and OCaml code accompanying the paper is available online in the same directory.

---

[1] In some other languages such as Java, the interleaving of execution between producers and consumers is achieved with threads or even bytecode post-processing (weaving).

2   The Problem with Laziness

The real virtue of lazy evaluation, emphasized in Hughes's famous paper [1], is that it supports *modular programming* by allowing the *producer* and *consumer* of a data structure to be separated, and then composed in a variety of ways in "plug-and-play" fashion. Alas, lazy evaluation is also fragile:

- Coroutining via lazy evaluation is incompatible with computational effects. With effects, the evaluation order is significant and cannot be left implicit. Adding effects requires re-writing of the code, and, as in call-by-value languages, tangles data producers and consumers (see §2.1);
- Lazy evaluation allows us to implement *cyclic* data transformers as well as linear ones; this is called 'tying the knot.' A number of elegant Haskell algorithms are written that way, e.g., the famous repmin [3]. Alas, it is particularly hard to reason about the termination of such algorithms, in part because the types do not tell us anything about demand and supply of values (see §2.2).
- Reasoning about space requirements of lazy algorithms is notoriously hard, and non-modular: how much space a function may need depends on the context. One case study [12] reports that it took three weeks to write a prototype genomic data mining application in Haskell, and two months to work around laziness frequently causing heap overflows. More examples are discussed at the end of §3 and in a recent paper by the first author [13].

The rest of the section illustrates these problems and the next one demonstrates how yield answers them.

2.1   Effects

Our running example is typical file processing: to read and print a file expanding all tabs[2]. Ideally, reading file data, tab expansion itself, and writing the result should be separated, so each can be replaced. For example, the programmer may chose between two tab expansion algorithms: the naïve replacement of '\t' with 8 spaces, and the sophisticated one, adding spaces up to the next tab stop (the multiple of 8). In idiomatic, lazy Haskell we start by writing the naïve tabX0 and sophisticated algorithms tabX1 assuming that the input data are all in memory, in a String. We do not worry how data got into memory or how it is written out:

```
tabX0, tabX1 :: String → String
tabX0 []           = []
tabX0 ('\t': rest ) = replicate  8 ' '  ++ tabX0 rest
tabX0 (c: rest )    = c :  tabX0 rest

tabX1 = go 0 where
  go pos []           = []
  go pos ('\t': rest ) = let pos' = (pos +8) − pos `mod` 8 in
                           replicate  (pos' − pos) ' '  ++ go pos' rest
  go pos (c: rest )    = c : go (if  c == '\n' then 0 else pos +1) rest
```

---

[2] We do *not* assume that the file is made of lines of bounded width.

The sophisticated version keeps a bit of local state, the pos argument, for the current output position. The complete function is as follows:

```
expandFile_lazy  :: String → IO ()
expandFile_lazy  filename = do h  ← openFile filename ReadMode
                               str ← hGetContents h
                               putStr (tabX0 str)
```

It opens the file, reads its contents, calls tabX0 to transform the contents, and writes out the result. It is modular, in the sense that it would be the work of a moment to replace tabX0 with tabX1, or by some other transformation entirely.

But we obviously don't want to read in the entire contents of the file into memory, then transform it, and then write it out. We would prefer to read the file on demand, so to process arbitrarily large files in bounded memory. Haskell's hGetContents function does exactly that, returning a string containing lazy thunks that, when forced (ultimately by putStr), read the file.

This on-demand input/output is called "lazy IO." Although very convenient, it is fraught with problems, including deadlocks and leaks of space, file descriptors and other resources [13]. The problems are apparent already in our code. For example, on file reading error an exception would be raised not in hGetContents but rather at some later indeterminate point in putStr. Moreover, file reading operations interleave uncontrollably with other IO operations, which may be fatal if the input file is actually a pipe. These problems really do arise in practice; the standard response is "you should use strict I/O."[3]

Thus lazy evaluation indeed does not work with effects. If we use effects, we have to re-write our tab-expansion code, for example, as follows:

```
expandFile_strict  :: String → IO ()
expandFile_strict  filename = do
  h ← openFile filename ReadMode; loop h; hClose h
  where loop h = do done ← hIsEOF h
                    if done then return () else hGetChar h ≫= check ≫ loop h
        check '\t' = putStr (replicate  8 ' ')
        check c    = putStr [c]
```

We now distinguish EOF from other input errors. We explicitly close the file as soon as we do not need it. Alas, the tab expansion, reading, and checking for the end of data are all intertwined. Although we can abstract out processing of a character, we cannot abstract out the processing of the entire stream, or easily replace the naïve tab expansion algorithm with the smart tab expansion: we have to re-write the whole reading-writing loop to thread the output pos. We clearly see what John Hughes meant when saying that strict evaluation entangles consumers and producers and inhibits modularity.

The same considerations would apply to any effectful producer or transformer. Thus, there is a real tension between the modular programming style advocated in "Why functional programming matters" and computational effects.

---

[3] e.g. http://stackoverflow.com/questions/2981582/
haskell-lazy-i-o-and-closing-files.

2.2 Recursive Knots

Richard Bird's famous repmin function [3], shown below, has made a compelling case for lazy evaluation. The function takes a tree and returns a new tree of the same shape, with every leaf value replaced by the minimum leaf value of the original tree. The new tree is constructed on-the-fly and the original tree is traversed only *once*:

```
data Tree = Leaf Int | Node Tree Tree
repmin :: Tree → Tree
repmin t = tr where (mn, tr) = walk mn t

walk :: Int → Tree → (Int, Tree)
walk mn (Leaf n)    = (n,              Leaf mn)
walk mn (Node t1 t2) = (n1 `min` n2, Node tr1 tr2)
  where (n1,tr1) = walk mn t1
        (n2,tr2) = walk mn t2
```

The main function walk takes the value to put into leaves and a tree and returns its minimum leaf value and the transformed tree. In repmin we pass the minimum leaf value computed by walk as an argument to walk itself, "tying the knot." Crucial is putting the minimum computation mn into a Leaf without evaluating it. Once the computation is eventually evaluated, the resulting minimum value shows up in all leaves. Lazy evaluation is indispensable for repmin.

Alas, small changes easily make the program diverge. For example, suppose we only wish to replace those leaves whose value is more than twice the minimum. If we replace the Leaf n case in walk with the following:

```
walk mn (Leaf n) | n > 2 * mn = (n, Leaf mn)
                 | otherwise  = (n, Leaf n)
```

we get a divergent repmin. Now walk *does* need the value of mn before finishing the traversal, demanding the value it is yet to produce. We may try one of the following fixes:

```
walk mn (Leaf n) = (n, if n > 2 * mn then Leaf mn else Leaf n)
walk mn (Leaf n) = (n, Leaf (if n > 2 * mn then mn else n))
```

We leave it as an exercise to determine which one works. The answer is non-obvious, requiring us to do global dataflow analysis in our head, determining which terms are evaluated when. Even experienced functional programmers can make mistakes, and often confess a lack of complete certainty about whether the program is now right. However elegant, "tying the knot" is fragile. To make matters worse, just imagine needing to modify repmin to print the leaves as they are walked!

3 Yield

We now describe how yield can be used as an alternative to lazy evaluation that is robust and compatible with arbitrary effects, and yet has attractive features of lazy evaluation in untangling producers from consumers and allowing them to be developed separately. Since there are many possible variants of yield [11], as well as several Haskell libraries based on *iteratees* that are similar to ours, we begin by reviewing some background, and then present our particular design contrasting it others. Finally, we revisit the examples in the previous section using our library.

Although we will be using Haskell to introduce yield, we will rely on monadic style, which is a model of call-by-value languages. The modeling of simple generators in Haskell helps implementing them in other languages, such as OCaml.

3.1   Background

Our design of *simple generators* is inspired by CLU's iterators [14] which are themselves inspired by the generators of Alphard [15]. Generators of Alphard were meant as a compositional abstraction of iteration: "generators abstract over control as functions abstract over operations" [15]. These simple generators can be viewed as asymmetric coroutines, a producer and a consumer, that pass data in one direction only, from the producer to the consumer. Besides unidirectionality, simple generators are further restricted: they can be nested but they cannot run side-by-side (and so cannot solve problems like 'same-fringe').

More generally, generators with varying degrees of expressiveness have spread to many languages. A uniform way to understand the variations in expressiveness is to view the various designs as imposing restrictions on delimited continuations [11]. The most general design gives full first-class delimited continuations. Some other (like that of Javascript) expose the continuation as a first-class object in the form of an *external iterator* but restrict the continuation to be a *one-shot* continuation. Even more restricted designs such as Ruby's never expose the continuation and only provide *internal iterators* that can only be used in the context of a foreach-like loop. One simple generators are also restricted in that sense: they never expose the continuation and restrict the implicit continuation to be *one-shot*. The restriction enables a simple and efficient implementation of simple generators on a single linear stack without copying [14].

Haskell's Hackage has a package generator for a very simple version of Python generators. It is inefficient, relying on the full delimited continuation monad, and, mainly, does not offer stream transducers.

Like generators, iteratees [13] provide incremental, compositional input processing and a sound alternative to lazy IO. Whereas generators focus on production of values, iteratees are designed around consumption [16]. There are many implementations of iteratees in many languages: just Haskell Hackage has the libraries iteratee, enumerator, monad-coroutine, iterIO, pipes, conduit and even broad categories 'Enumerator' and 'Conduit'. Underlying all these iteratee implementations is the resumption monad, which is tantamount to first-class, multi-shot delimited continuations. Compared to simple generators, iteratees are thus more expressive but much more heavier-weight. They cannot be implemented on linear stack without copying or building auxiliary data structures. The remarkable implementation simplicity and efficiency of simple generators strongly motivates investigating and pushing the limits of their expressiveness.

```
-- Simple generators
type GenT e m                = ReaderT (e → m ()) m
type Producer m e            = GenT e m ()
type Consumer m e            = e → m ()
type Transducer m1 m2 e1 e2 = Producer m1 e1 → Producer m2 e2

yield     :: Monad m ⇒ e → Producer m e
runGenT :: Monad m ⇒ Producer m e → Consumer m e → m ()
foldG     :: Monad m ⇒ (s → e → m s) → s → Producer (StateT s m) e → m s

newtype ReaderT env m a = ReaderT { runReaderT :: env → m a }
ask       :: ReaderT env m r

newtype StateT s m a = StateT { runStateT :: s → m (a, s) }
```

Fig. 1. The interface of our Haskell yield library. For completeness, we also include the ReaderT and StateT types from the **transformers** library.

```
type 'a gen        = unit → 'a
type producer      = unit gen
type consumer      = exn → unit
type 'a transducer = 'a gen → 'a gen

val yield    : exn → unit
val iterate  : producer → consumer → unit
val foldG    : ('s → exn → 's) → 's → producer → (unit → 's)
```

Fig. 2. The interface of our OCaml library of simple generators. A yielded value is encapsulated in an exception object.

3.2   Producers, Consumers, Transducers

Our design is lightweight: other than type abbreviations, it consists of just three functions. It is summarized in the top portion of Fig. 1 and discussed in detail in the remainder of this section. For comparison, Fig. 2 shows the corresponding interface in OCaml.

The users of simple generators may regard GenT e m as an abstract monad: the type GenT e m a is that of computations that emit values of type e and eventually return a value of type a. The alias Producer emphasizes this interpretation. The concrete type of GenT e m reveals that a producer is structured as an environment (Reader) monad over an arbitrary m. The consumer is stored in an *environment* that the generator can query, or "ask." The consumer thus acts as a *loop body* that the producer invokes to process the 'emitted' element.

With yield being the only primitive producer, and GenT e m being a monad, we may write more complex producers, e.g., emitting characters read from a file:

```
fileGen  :: MonadIO m ⇒ Producer m Char
fileGen  = do h ← liftIO  $ openFile "/tmp/testf.txt" ReadMode
              loop h; liftIO  $ hClose h
    where loop h = do done ← liftIO  $ hIsEOF h
                      if  done then return ()
                            else liftIO  (hGetChar h) >>= yield ≫ loop h
```

The standard System.IO function putChar is a sample consumer. We hook the producer and putChar by simply saying fileGen `runGenT` putChar, which prints characters as they are read.

The type of yield is an instance of Consumer m a where m is GenT a m'. Therefore, we can build consumers that transform the received element emitting (producing) the result – in short, act as *stream transducers*. Since yield is a consumer that immediately emits the consumed element, runGenT gen yield is the same as gen, and \gen → runGenT gen yield is the identity transducer. Here is a version of the naïve tab expander tabX0 from §2.1 expressed as a transducer:

```
tabY0 ∷ Monad m ⇒ Transducer (GenT String m) m Char String
tabY0 gen = runGenT gen con
  where con '\t' = yield (replicate  8 ' ')
        con c    = yield [c]
```

Thus tabY0 fileGen is a producer that reads the file and tabifies it, and which can be combined with a consumer like putStr using runGenT.

We may regard Producer e m as an effectful analogue of [e], representing a sequence of elements whose production may require an effect m. Transducers are hence analogues of list transformers, and the list combinators map, fold, etc. have natural counterparts on generators. The following transducer is a map-like one:

```
mapG ∷ Monad m ⇒ (e1 → e2) → Transducer (GenT e2 m) m e1 e2
mapG f gen = runGenT gen (yield ∘ f)
```

Since transducers are Producer-to-Producer functions, they can be combined by functional composition – letting us add more stream processing stages by composing-in more transducers. For example, a producer which reads the file, upper-cases and tabifies it is composed as (tabY1 ∘ mapG toUpper) fileGen. The library's implementation in terms of an environment monad guarantees that such whole stream processing happens in constant memory.

So far, we merely rewrote expandFile_strict of §2.1 using our generator library. In contrast to §2.1, we can now replace the naïve tab expansion with a sophisticated one without re-writing the file reader. Recall that the sophisticated tab expansion has local state, the current output position. Since our library is parametrized over a monad m, we add local state by merely instantiating m to be the state monad.

```
tabY1 ∷ Monad m ⇒ Transducer (StateT Int (GenT String m)) m Char String
tabY1 gen = evalStateT (runGenT gen con) 0
  where con e1 = get ≫= (\s → lift (f s e1)) ≫= put
        f pos '\t' = let pos' = (pos +8) − pos `mod` 8 in
                       yield (replicate (pos' − pos) ' ') ≫ return pos'
        f pos c = yield [c] ≫ return (if c == '\n' then 0 else pos +1)
```

To add the sophisticated tab expansion, all we need is to replace tabY0 with tabY1 in the previous code fragments.

The examination of tabY1 points to further abstraction. The internal function f looks like tabX1 in the lazy evaluation example in §2.1, only without the argument rest. Its type fits the pattern s → e → m s of a monadic state transformer (with the local state s being Int). We capture the pattern in combinator similar to List.fold:

```
foldG  :: Monad m ⇒ (s → e → m s) → s → Producer (StateT s m) e → m s
foldG f s0 gen = execStateT (runGenT gen consumer) s0
  where consumer x = get ≫= (\s → lift $ f s x) ≫= put
```

We rewrite tabY1 using foldG as:

```
tabY1' = foldG t 0 ≫ return () where
  t pos '\t' = let pos' = (pos +8) − pos 'mod' 8 in
               yield (replicate (pos' − pos) ' ') ≫ return pos'
  t pos c = yield [c] ≫ return (if c == '\n' then 0 else pos +1)
```

(we will abbreviate foldG t s ≫ return () as foldG_ t s.)

3.3   Cycles

The function repmin seems out of scope for generators, which are intended for stream processing. The function repmin builds a tree rather than a stream. We can bring repmin into the scope for generators by serializing the resulting tree into a stream of XML-like nodes:

```
data TreeStream = BegNode | EndNode | LeafData Int
serializeX  :: Tree → [TreeStream]
```

We now show how to write serializeX ∘ repmin with generators, with the 'side effect' of being able to add arbitrary effects such as debug printing. We start by writing the generator traverse that turns a tree into a producer of TreeStream elements, and collect which collects the elements into a list:

```
traverse  :: Monad m ⇒ Tree → Producer m TreeStream
traverse (Leaf i)     = yield (LeafData i)
traverse (Node t1 t2) = do yield BegNode; traverse t1; traverse t2; yield EndNode

collect  :: Monad m ⇒ Producer (StateT [e] m) e → m [e]
collect  g = foldG (\s e → return $ e:s) [] g ≫= return ∘ reverse
```

Then collect ∘ traverse (in the Identity monad) is equivalent to serializeX. We now need to insert a version of repmin that processes the TreeStream elements, replacing LeafData elements by the minimum. This operation clearly needs a lookahead buffer of type [TreeStream]. The first encountered LeafData node switches on the look-ahead, triggering the accumulation, which continues through the end. We will see a similar buffering in §5.2:

```
repminT gen = foldG go (0,[]) gen ≫= \(m,buf) → mapM_ (flush m) (reverse buf)
  where go (m, []) BegNode      = yield BegNode ≫ return (m, [])
        go (m, []) EndNode      = yield EndNode ≫ return (m, [])
        go (m, []) (LeafData x) = return (x,[ LeafData x])
        go (m, b) (LeafData x)  = return (x 'min' m,LeafData x : b)
        go (m, b) e             = return (m, e:b)

        flush  m (LeafData _) = yield (LeafData m)
        flush  _ e            = yield e
```

The serialized repmin-ed tree is then the result of the modular composition collect ∘ repminT ∘ traverse. If we wish to add debug printing, we insert into the cascade a stream transformer that re-emits the elements while printing them.

The stream transformer repminT *obviously* has unbounded look-ahead. Although more difficult to discern, the original repmin also requires unbounded look-ahead, with the tree itself used as an implicit look-ahead 'buffer.'

4   Pretty-Printing Specification

Oppen [17] defined pretty-printing as a 'nice' formatting of a (tree-structured) document within a fixed page width. The core of his specification of nice formatting – used in all other Haskell implementations – takes documents of the following abstract form:

data Doc = Text String | Line | Doc :+: Doc | Group Doc

An abstract document is either a string (Text), a potential line break (Line), a composition of two documents side-by-side (:+:), or a *group*. A group specifies a unit whose linebreaks are interpreted consistently. If a group, with all Linebreaks within it interpreted as spaces, fits onto the remainder of the line, the group is formatted this way. Otherwise, the Linebreaks in the group (but not within embedded groups) are treated as newlines. For example, the following simple document:

doc1 = Group (Text "A" :+: (Line :+: Group (Text "B" :+: (Line :+: Text "C"))))

would be formatted as shown on the left if the width of the page is 5 or more characters, and as shown in the middle if the width of the page is 3 or 4 characters, and as shown on the right if the width of the page is 1 or 2 characters:

```
   A B C           A                A
                 B C                B
                                    C
```

As an executable specification of the problem we take the following inefficient pretty-printer (also used as a starting point by Chitil [18]):

```
type Fit        = Bool          type WidthLeft = Int
type Width      = Int           type PageWidth = Int
```

```
pretty1 :: PageWidth → Doc → String
pretty1 w d = fst $ format False w d where
 format :: Fit → WidthLeft → Doc → (String, WidthLeft)
 format f r (Text z)   = (z, r − length z)
 format True  r Line   = ("␣", r−1)
 format False r Line   = ("\n",w)
 format f r (d1 :+: d2) = (s1 ++ s2, r2)
   where (s1,r1) = format f r d1
         (s2,r2) = format f r1 d2
 format f r (Group d)  = format (f || width d ≤ r) r d
```

```
width :: Doc → Width
width (Text z)   = length z
width Line       = 1
width (d1 :+: d2) = width d1 + width d2
width (Group d)  = width d
```

The function pretty1 is invoked with the width of the page and the document to format. It immediately invokes an interpreter, format, which recursively traverses and formats the document maintaining a boolean-valued environment variable f and an integer-valued state variable r. The flag f tells if the current document is part of the group that fits on the current line. The flag affects the formatting of Line. The state r tells the remaining available space on the current line; the fit of a group is determined by comparing r with the expected length of the group. This length is calculated by the function width which traverses the document adding up the lengths of its constituent strings.

The executable specification of pretty-printing is clear but greatly inefficient: in the worst case, it takes time exponential in the size n of the input document. The width of an inner group may be repeatedly recomputed, as part of the width computation for ancestor groups as they are being formatted. Furthermore, we cannot begin to format a group until we computed its width; therefore the algorithm has an unbounded look-ahead and its latency is $O(n)$. In contrast, Oppen's original algorithm which is imperative and uses explicit coroutines, is linear in the size of the document, is independent of the page width w to which the document is formatted, and is incremental with a latency bounded by $O(w)$. Attempts to algebraically derive just as efficient Haskell implementation have so far failed [19, 20]. Most Haskell pretty-printing libraries use some form of backtracking and hence cannot have bounded latency. Standing out is Chitil's implementation [18], which matches the classical one in efficiency. It is written however in an iterative style, which amounts to performing a manual continuation-passing style transformation. Swierstra bolstered the case for laziness by showing that a linear, incremental lazy pretty-printing function exists after all [21]. It crucially relies on tying the knot, and its non-divergence is hard to see. Other analyses, in particular estimating space complexity, are difficult as well. The code is complex, with five state parameters, one of which is computed 'backwards.' In fact the solution was developed as an attribute grammar, and hand-translated into Haskell. (Swierstra et al. have since developed mechanical translations and even embedding of attribute grammars in Haskell [4, 22].)

5   Stepwise Generation of Pretty-Printer

We build an efficient pretty-printer by combining two key optimizations: (i) avoiding re-computations of group width by memoization or pre-computation and (ii) pruning, computing the width of a group only as far as needed to determine if the group fits on the line. These optimizations are present in one form or another in all optimal pretty-printing implementations. Our development is distinguished by a systematic, modular and compositional application of the optimizations. We build the pretty-printer as a cascade of separately developed, tested and *analyzed* stream transducers. We stress the ease of analysis and its composability.

Here is a general idea. To avoid re-computing group widths, we may compute the width of all groups beforehand – for example, by traversing the whole document tree and annotating each node with its width. The traversal is standard post-order, linear in the size of the tree. Alas, the annotated tree needs as much space as the original one. Since we have to traverse all children of the root node to compute its width, we really have to build the whole annotated tree first before we start formatting.

Applying the pruning optimization seems non-obvious, until we make the traversal of the document tree incremental, as a generator of a stream of traversed nodes. The width computation becomes a transducer that adds width annotations to stream elements. The annotated tree is never explicitly constructed. Pruning becomes a straightforward optimization of the group width transducer, bounding its look-ahead. We realize this plan below, step-wise. §5.1 converts the document tree to a stream of nodes, which we then annotate with the horizontal position. §5.2 modifies the annotations so they effectively become group width annotations. §5.3 optimizes the annotation algorithm using pruning. The width-annotated stream is formatted in §5.4. To save space, we focus on the key steps and relegate the details to Appendix A of the full paper.

5.1 Generating Document Stream

The first step of our plan is converting the document tree to a stream of nodes. The elements of the stream are of the following type:

data StreamB = TE String | LE | GBeg | GEnd

with constructors for Text and Line and a pair of constructors for entering and leaving a group. The function genB generates a bare stream by in-order traversing the document tree:

genB :: **Monad** m $\Rightarrow$ Doc $\rightarrow$ Producer m StreamB

Analysis. As genB reaches a text or a line node, it (like traverse in §3) immediately emits the corresponding stream element. Hence genB has unit latency. Since genB is a simple in-order traversal of the tree, the total time to generate the whole stream is linear in the size of the tree. The function needs stack space proportional to the depth d of the tree since genB is not tail-recursive.

We annotate the stream elements with the rolling width, or the horizontal position HP in a hypothetical formatting of the document in a single line:

type HP = Int
type HPB = Int
data StreamHPB = TE$_b$ HP String | LE$_b$ HP | GBeg$_b$ HPB | GEnd$_b$ HP

All stream elements except GBeg are annotated with the horizontal position at the end of formatting of that element on the hypothetical single line. In particular, GEnd is annotated with the final HP for its group. The node GBeg is however annotated with the horizontal position HPB at the beginning of the formatting of the group. In other words, each node is annotated with the sum of the widths of all preceding nodes including the current. The annotation is done by the simple state transducer trHPB, consuming StreamB and emitting StreamHPB of annotated elements. The horizontal position is the state:

trHPB :: **Monad** m $\Rightarrow$
    Transducer (StateT HP (GenT StreamHPB m)) m StreamB StreamHPB

Analysis. The transforming function merely increments the current horizontal position. It hence does constant amount of work, has unit latency and runs in constant space. The total transformation time is linear in the size of the input stream.

5.2   Determining Group Widths

The annotated stream is not directly suitable for formatting: when we encounter a group, that is, a GBeg element, we have to decide if the group fits; hence we need the width of the group, or the horizontal position of the group's end. Therefore, we transform StreamHPB into StreamHPA where GBeg will be annotated with final rather than initial HP of the group, that is, the HP of the GEnd element of the group. Clearly this requires look-ahead. Furthermore, since groups can be nested, the look-ahead buffer must be structured, so that we can track several groups in progress:

```
data StreamHPA = TE_a HP String | LE_a HP | GBeg_a HP | GEnd_a HP
type Buffer m = [Buf StreamHPA m]
```

The overall look-ahead Buffer m is a list of simple buffers Buf that each correspond to one unfinished, nested group. A Buf accumulates stream elements corresponding a tree branch, after GBeg and up to and including the matching GEnd. A simple buffer Buf should permit the following operations:

```
buf_empty  ∷ Monad m ⇒ Buf e m
(▷)        ∷ Monad m ⇒ Buf e m → e → Buf e m
(◁)        ∷ Monad m ⇒ e → Buf e m → Buf e m
buf_ccat   ∷ Monad m ⇒ Buf e m → Buf e m → Buf e m
buf_emit   ∷ Monad m ⇒ Buf e m → Producer m e
```

that is, the creation of the empty buffer, appending an element to the buffer b ▷ e and prepending an element e ◁ b in constant time, concatenation of two buffers in constant time, and emitting all elements in the buffer in linear time.

The producer of StreamHPA is also a state transducer, from the stream StreamHPB built in the previous section. The state is the look-ahead Buffer m:

```
type St m = StateT (Buffer m) (GenT StreamHPA m)
trHPA ∷ Monad m ⇒ Transducer (St m) m StreamHPB StreamHPA
trHPA = foldG_ go [] where
  go q (GBeg_b _)     = return (buf_empty:q)
  go (b:q) (GEnd_b p) = pop q (GBeg_a p ◁ (b ▷ GEnd_a p))
  go [] (TE_b p)      = yield (TE_a p) ≫ return []  -- ditto for LE
  go (b:q) (TE_b p)   = return ((b ▷ TE_a p):q)     -- ditto for LE

  pop [] b      = buf_emit b ≫ return []
  pop (b':q) b  = return ((buf_ccat b' b):q)
```

GBeg adds a new layer to the Buffer ready to accumulate elements of the new group. Text and Line elements outside of a group are emitted immediately to the output stream. Otherwise, they are accumulated in the Buf of their parent group. GEnd p supplies the final horizontal position p of the group, letting us emit GBeg p and flush the accumulated elements in Buf. Since the terminated group may be part of another, still unfinished group, we delay emitting elements of the terminated group and put them into the look-ahead buffer of the parent group. Only when the outer group is terminated we finally empty the look-ahead buffer emitting all its elements.

Analysis. Since we cannot emit any group element until we see GEnd, the latency is of the order of n, the size of the whole document (stream). The look-ahead Buffer m is the extra space, again linear in n. Total time is determined by amortization. Assume that each element of the input stream brings us the credit of 2. We spend one credit to yield the element, and to put the element into the buffer (in general, for any constant amount of work within go). Thus all elements in the buffer have one credit left, enough to pay for the linear-time operation buf_emit. Thus, the total time complexity is linear in n.

Hooking up the stream StreamHPA to a linear-time constant-space formatter (similar to the one in §5.4 below) gives the overall pretty-printer, with linear-time complexity but unbounded, $O(n)$ latency and the corresponding amount of extra space. To bound the look-ahead we apply the second optimization below, pruning.

5.3   Pruning

We have just seen that determining the width of each group is expensive since we have to scan the whole group first. However, the exact group width is not necessary: if the width is greater than the page width, we do not need to know by how much. We introduce an 'approximate horizontal position' HPP:

data HPP = Small HP | TooFar
data StreamHPP = TE_p HP String | LE_p HP | $GBeg_p$ HPP | $GEnd_p$ HP

to use instead of the exact final horizontal position HP to annotate GBeg elements with. GBeg is annotated with TooFar if the final horizontal position of the group is farther than the page width w away from the group's initial horizontal position. Computing HPP requires only bounded, by w, look-ahead. The stream transformer trHPP below is the pruned version of trHPA of the previous section.

The look-ahead BufferP, like the look-ahead Buffer of trHPA, is a sequence of simple Bufs that accumulate delayed elements following a GBeg up to and including the corresponding GEnd. We need to efficiently access the sequence from both ends however; the simple list no longer suffices. The Haskell basis library provides the data structure Seq with the needed algorithmic properties (we import Data.Sequence as S):

type BufferP m = (HPL, S.Seq (HPL, Buf StreamHPP m))
bufferP_empty = (0,S.empty)
type HPL = Int

If HP is the beginning horizontal position of the group, HPL is a w-offset position: any position after HPL is TooFar. For each accumulated group we compute HPL and make it easily accessible. Furthermore, fst BufferP provides the HPL for the outermost group, so we can easily see if the current HP is too far for that group. If so, we can emit GBeg TooFar and empty its look-ahead Buf.

The transformer trHPP of StreamHPB to StreamHPP is the 'pruned' version of trHPA:

```
type St m = StateT (BufferP m) (GenT StreamHPP m)
trHPP :: Monad m ⇒ PageWidth → Transducer (St m) m StreamHPB StreamHPP
trHPP w = foldG_ go bufferP_empty where
   ...
   check :: BufferP m → HP → GenT StreamHPP m ()
   check (p0,q) p | p ≤ p0 && S.length q ≤ w = return (p0,q)
   check (_,q) p | (_,b) :< q' ← S.viewl q  =
      buf_emit (GBeg_p TooFar ⊴ b) ≫ check' q' p
         check' q p | (p', _) :< _ ← S.viewl q = check (p',q) p
                    | otherwise               = return bufferP_empty
```

Except for check, it is essentially the same as trHPA of §5.2. The function check prunes the look-ahead: it checks to see if the current horizontal position p exceeds p0, the HPL of the outer group. If so, the outer group is wider than w, which lets us immediately emit $GBeg_p$ TooFar and the elements accumulated in the outer Buf. The not-yet-terminated inner group may also turn out too wide: we have to recursively check. The function check also prunes the look-ahead BufferP when it becomes deeper than w, which may happen in the edge case of a document:

   Group (Group (Group ... :+: Group ...) :+: Group (Group ... :+: Group ...))

whose StreamHPB includes an arbitrarily long sequence of GBeg p with the same initial group position p. The first pruning criterion will not be triggered then. In genB of App. A we have ensured that each group is at least one character-wide, with no group as a sole child. Therefore, a group that contains at least w descendant groups must be wider than w. Incidentally, this edge case has not been accounted for in [21]; the latter algorithm would need to add yet another state parameter to the formatting function.

Analysis. All S.Seq operations used in the code – adding to the left ($\lhd$) or to the right ($\rhd$) end of the queue and deconstructing the left or the right end with S.viewl or S.viewr – take constant amortized time. Therefore, the analysis of trHPP is similar to the analysis of trHPA, modulo the fact that the total size of the look-ahead BufferP is bounded by w. Therefore, latency and the extra space for the look-ahead buffer are bounded by the page width. The total processing time remains linear in the size of the input stream.

5.4   Putting It All Together and Benchmarking

The final step of pretty-printing is the formatting: transforming the pruned StreamHPP to a stream of Strings. To format stream elements LE as spaces or newlines, the formatter keeps track of an indicator if the current group and its ancestors fit on the remainder of the line. The formatter trFormat is straight-forward, with unit latency and the overall linear running time, operating in constant space. The complete pretty-printer of a document is a cascade of the width estimators and the formatter, applied to the initial stream generator:

```
pp :: Monad m ⇒ PageWidth → Doc → Producer m String
pp w = trFormat w ∘ trHPP w ∘ trHPB ∘ genB
```

Final Analysis. The total latency is the sum of latencies contributed by all transducers, which is bounded by the page width w. Since all transducers process the whole stream in time linear to the size of the stream, the total running time of the pretty-printer is linear in the source document size. We need extra space: $O(w)$ for the look-ahead BufferP in trHPP and $O(d)$ (where d is the document depth) for the initial generator genB.

To validate the analyses, we ran a benchmark meant to resemble the full binary tree prepared for pretty-printing. The benchmark, rather than writing

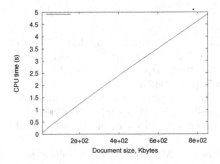 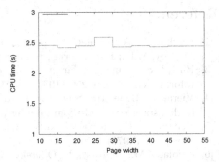

the formatted document to a file, accumulates, in the Writer monad, its total size and the number of lines. The benchmark was compiled with GHC -O2 version 7.0.4 and ran on a i386 FreeBSD 2GHz Pentium 4 system. The running times (in seconds) are the medians of five consecutive runs. The figure on the left plots the running time against the size of the formatted output, for the fixed page size $w = 50$. The figure on the right plots the running time of pretty-printing the same benchmark document (output size 414,870 bytes) against the different values of the page width w. The benchmark validates the analyzes: the running time is a linear function of the document length, independent of w.

6   Conclusions

We have described simple generators to complement or supplant lazy evaluation in stream-processing programs. Like lazy evaluation, simple generators promote modularity, stepwise development and incremental testing by decoupling stream producers, consumers and transformers. Unlike lazy evaluation, simple generators are compatible with effects including IO, and allow modular, composable reasoning about time, latency, and especially about space consumption. We have implemented simple generators as libraries in Haskell and OCaml. The Haskell monadic implementation guides implementations in other languages, making connections with the visitor pattern and dynamic binding clear. In future work, we will formalize the yield calculus and formally relate with call-by-need.

We have illustrated simple generators and demonstrated their expressive power by solving the challenging efficient pretty-printing problem. Our implementation is a new and unexpected solution: efficient pretty-printing was believed to require full delimited continuations or coroutines, which simple generators do not provide. Like the other optimal solutions, it is linear in the size of the input document and has bounded latency. Our solution however was assembled from separately developed and tested components. We have also analyzed time and space complexity component-by-component, combining the analyses at the end. Our precise analyses discovered previously overlooked edge cases.

Acknowledgments. We thank S. Doaitse Swierstra for helpful discussions. Many helpful suggestions by anonymous reviewers are gratefully acknowledged.

References

[1] Hughes, J.: Why functional programming matters. Comput. J. 32, 98–107 (1989)

[2] McIlroy, M.D.: Power series, power serious. J. Funct. Program. 9, 325–337 (1999)

[3] Bird, R.S.: Using circular programs to eliminate multiple traversals of data. Acta Informatica 21, 239–250 (1984), doi:10.1007/BF00264249

[4] Viera, M., Swierstra, S.D., Swierstra, W.: Attribute grammars fly first-class: how to do aspect oriented programming in Haskell. In: ICFP, pp. 245–256 (2009)

[5] Henderson, P., Morris Jr., J.H.: A lazy evaluator. In: POPL, pp. 95–103. ACM, New York (1976)

[6] Ariola, Z.M., Maraist, J., Odersky, M., Felleisen, M., Wadler, P.: A call-by-need lambda calculus. In: POPL, pp. 233–246. ACM, New York (1995)

[7] Garcia, R., Lumsdaine, A., Sabry, A.: Lazy evaluation and delimited control. In: POPL, pp. 153–164. ACM, New York (2009)

[8] Chang, S., Van Horn, D., Felleisen, M.: Evaluating Call-by-Need on the Control Stack. In: Page, R., Horváth, Z., Zsók, V. (eds.) TFP 2010. LNCS, vol. 6546, pp. 1–15. Springer, Heidelberg (2011)

[9] Kay, M.: You pull, I'll push: on the polarity of pipelines. In: Proc. Balisage: The Markup Conference. Balisage Series on Markup Technologies, vol. 3 (2009)

[10] Jackson, M.A.: Principles of Program Design. Academic Press, Inc., Orlando (1975)

[11] James, R.P., Sabry, A.: Yield: Mainstream deliminted continuations. In: Theory and Practice of Delimited Continuations (2011)

[12] Clare, A., King, R.D.: Data Mining the Yeast Genome in a Lazy Functional Language. In: Dahl, V. (ed.) PADL 2003. LNCS, vol. 2562, pp. 19–36. Springer, Heidelberg (2002)

[13] Kiselyov, O.: Iteratees. In: Schrijvers, T., Thiemann, P. (eds.) FLOPS 2012. LNCS, vol. 7294, pp. 166–181. Springer, Heidelberg (2012)

[14] Liskov, B.: A history of CLU. Technical Report 561, MIT LCS (1992)

[15] Shaw, M., Wulf, W.A., London, R.L.: Abstraction and verification in Alphard: defining and specifying iteration and generators. Comm. ACM 20, 553–564 (1977)

[16] Lato, J.W.: Understandings of iteratees (2012), http://johnlato.blogspot.com/2012/06/understandings-of-iteratees.html

[17] Oppen, D.C.: Prettyprinting. ACM Trans. Program. Lang. Syst. 2, 465–483 (1980)

[18] Chitil, O.: Pretty printing with lazy dequeues. ACM Trans. Program. Lang. Syst. 27, 163–184 (2005)

[19] Hughes, J.: The Design of a Pretty-Printing Library. In: Jeuring, J., Meijer, E. (eds.) AFP 1995. LNCS, vol. 925, pp. 53–96. Springer, Heidelberg (1995)

[20] Wadler, P.: A prettier printer. In: The Fun of Programming. A Symposium in Honour of Professor Richard Bird's 60th birthday, Oxford (2003)

[21] Swierstra, S.D.: Linear, online, functional pretty printing (corrected and extended version). Technical Report UU-CS-2004-025a, Utrecht University (2004)

[22] Dijkstra, A.: Stepping through Haskell. PhD thesis, Utrecht University, Department of Information and Computing Sciences (2005)

Dynamic Software Update for Message Passing Programs

Gabrielle Anderson[1] and Julian Rathke[2]

[1] University of Aberdeen, Regents Walk, Aberdeen, AB24 3FX, UK
[2] Electronics and Computer Science, University of Southampton, SO17 1BJ, UK

Abstract. Global Session Types are typically used to express communication protocols between a number of participating entities. Analyses on these types can be used to prove that message passing programs have a variety of desirable properties such as communications safety and deadlock freedom. In this paper we provide a Global Session Type analysis for queued channel message passing programs whose code may be updated during runtime (Dynamic Software Update). In particular, we prove safety and liveness properties for well-typed programs by identifying suitable restrictions on the runtime points at which dynamic updates may occur. This includes the possibility of updating several threads without requiring global thread synchronisation.

1 Introduction

Software needs to be maintained after its release; this often takes the form of applying a software patch, that is, a program to modify or update some part of the system code. The patch may be to fix bugs, to add functionality, or to simply make the system more efficient. The naive and simplest method used to update software is to halt the execution of the code, apply a patch, and then restart the program. This methodology is both intrusive and costly in terms of downtime. In order to address this, the notion of Dynamic Software Update (DSU) has been proposed [Appel(1994), Boyapati et al.(2003)]. The idea there is that programs are modified whilst they are still running. A fully realised DSU system would handle the mechanism of the update itself while ensuring the program and its state remain consistent. One challenge in such systems then is to show that correctness properties of the system being updated are maintained. In this paper we recall how one can use Session Types analyses to specify behaviours of queued message passing concurrent programs, such as can be found in Erlang and Scala, in such a way as to guarantee deadlock freedom and typeful communication. We then demonstrate that, by suitably enriching the Session Types, we can provide an analysis to preserve these guarantees of deadlock freedom and type safety even in the presence of dynamically changing code. For example, consider the following Producer/Consumer program in which the Producer thread repeatedly sends a message on some queued channel c_1 and then waits for an 'ack' on a channel c_2. The Consumer thread repeatedly receives the message on c_1 and acknowledges on c_2:

R. Jhala and A. Igarashi (Eds.): APLAS 2012, LNCS 7705, pp. 207–222, 2012.

$$t_p = \mathsf{rec}X.\mathsf{snd}(c_1, v_1).\mathsf{rcv}(c_2)(x : \textsc{Unit}).X$$
$$t_{co} = \mathsf{rec}X'.\mathsf{rcv}(c_1)(x : T_1).\mathsf{snd}(c_2, ()).X'$$

At some point we may wish to increase the asynchrony in this protocol by having the Producer send two data items before waiting for the acknowledgement. This could be achieved with a code modification as follows:

$$t'_p = \mathsf{rec}X.\mathsf{snd}(c_1, v_1).\mathsf{snd}(c_1, v_2).\mathsf{rcv}(c_2)(x : \textsc{Unit}).X$$
$$t'_{co} = \mathsf{rec}X'.\mathsf{rcv}(c_1)(x : T_1).\mathsf{rcv}(c_1)(x : T_2).\mathsf{snd}(c_2, ()).X'$$

The application of an update to transform the former in to the latter at an inopportune point in the runtime could introduce deadlock into an otherwise live program. For instance, if the update to the code were to occur in the cycle just after the Producer had sent its first message, then the Consumer would now be expecting another message before it 'ack's but the Producer won't proceed until it receives said 'ack' and so we have deadlock.

In general, we will need to identify sufficient conditions on the system and potential update to ensure that a previously live system will not create a potentially deadlocked system. We have two main approaches to doing this: firstly, we can allow an update to occur if, in the resulting system, all of the threads agree on their (possibly new) communication protocol and there are no pending messages in the channel queues. We call this approach *Global Typability*. Secondly, to avoid demanding a global consensus between threads at a point in runtime where the message queues are empty, we consider a condition in which threads may be updated independently as long as they do so in 'protocol order'. That is, threads that depend on others to proceed must be updated later than those they depend on. We call this latter approach *Local Update*.

In order to formalise these two approaches and prove their correctness we make use of a small simply typed process-calculus with support for multiple threads, queued message passing, and dynamic update. We express the behavioural properties of programs as Session Types which are extracted from programs by means of a reasonably standard type and effect system. Effects of the code and the messages in the queue at the point an update is to be applied determine the subsequent safety and liveness of the updated program. Global Typability and Local Update are expressed as predicates on these effects.

The remainder of the paper is structured as follows: we first introduce our calculus of updateable, multi-threaded, expressions and furnish it with a reduction semantics (Section 2). We then define an effect calculus using Session Types to represent the abstract communication behaviour of the message passing calculus. We also give a type system which extracts this behaviour (Section 3) and is parameterised on our two different approaches to guaranteeing safety and liveness. We then consider these two approaches to update, (Section 4.1) and (Section 4.2), by defining the appropriate predicates and proving the relevant theorems for them. We conclude the paper in Section 5 with a discussion of related and future work.

$$v ::= () \mid b \mid n \mid x \mid l$$
$$t ::= X \mid \mathsf{snd}(c, v).t \mid \mathsf{rcv}(c)(x : T).t \mid \mathsf{sel}\, c\, \mathsf{from}\, \{\widetilde{l \mapsto t}\}$$
$$\mid\; \mathsf{case}\, c\, \mathsf{of}\, \{\widetilde{l \mapsto t}\} \mid \mathsf{rec} X.t \mid f(t) \mid \mathsf{error} \qquad P ::= t \mid P \parallel P$$
$$\sigma ::= c \mapsto (v_1; v_2; \ldots; v_n) \mid \sigma, \sigma \qquad T ::= \textsc{Unit} \mid \textsc{Bool} \mid \textsc{Int}$$

Fig. 1. Grammar for the program language

2   A Calculus for Dynamic Update

We present our calculus of dynamically updateable message passing programs. This is a very simple process calculus language used primarily just to demonstrate the formalism of our update analysis. In principle one may use a more sophisticated programming language here as long as its communication behaviours are representable using the type and effect system of Section 3. The main theorems are proved via this language of effects and hence would not be disturbed by such a change. The grammar for the language is given in Figure 1. There are a few points of interest to note. We use the usual commands for sending and receiving messages on channels as well as a channel-based case statement in which one thread may send a selection l along the channel to determine which branch to take. Channel names and label names are drawn from some ambient sets of names disjoint from each other. Communication is *queued asynchronous*, in that messages are sent into a dedicated queue for each channel. We represent the runtime state of the system then as a configuration comprising a collection of channel queues σ along with a program P. We will write $[\sigma]\, P$ for these configurations and we define the reduction semantics on configurations in Figure 2. We make the assumption that recursively defined programs are identified with their unwindings (technically, a structural equivalence relation $\equiv$ is used) The main novelty in the calculus is the region annotation $f(t)$ that allows for a named delimitation of a block of code — these named blocks are used as the unit of code update. These annotations are a slight variation on the standard DSU approach that permits the bodies of functions to be changed in their entirety [Hicks and Nettles(2005), Stoyle et al.(2005)].

The reader will have observed that there is no command to perform an update within the language. This is because we model the arrival of an update as an event external to the program. Therefore, we say a *full configuration* $[\sigma]\, P, \psi$ is a pair of a configuration $[\sigma]\, P$ along with a (possibly empty) list of code updates ψ of the form:

$$\mathsf{p}_1(z_\sigma, z_P, z_{\overline{\psi}}) \mapsto \{\widetilde{f \mapsto t}\}_1 : \ldots : \mathsf{p}_n(z_\sigma, z_P, z_{\overline{\psi}}) \mapsto \{\widetilde{f \mapsto t}\}_n$$

where $\mathsf{p}_i(z_\sigma, z_P, z_{\overline{\psi}})$ are predicates over the current *full* configuration. An update can appear in the system at any point of execution. The intended semantics of these updates is that, as soon as the program reaches a runtime configuration $[\sigma]\, P, \psi$ that satisfies a predicate $\mathsf{p}_i(z_\sigma, z_P, z_{\overline{\psi}})$ then the corresponding code patches $\{\widetilde{f \mapsto t}\}_i$ associated with the predicate p_i (for least such i) are applied

$$\frac{}{[\sigma[c \mapsto q]] \, \mathsf{snd}(c,v).t \to [\sigma[c \mapsto q;v]] \, t} \qquad \frac{\vdash v : T}{[\sigma[c \mapsto v;q]] \, \mathsf{rcv}(c)(x:T).t \to [\sigma[c \mapsto q]] \, t[v/x]}$$

$$\frac{l_i \in \widetilde{l} \quad \sigma' = \sigma[c \mapsto q;l_i]}{[\sigma[c \mapsto q]] \, \mathsf{sel} \, c \, \mathsf{from} \, \{\widetilde{l \mapsto t}\} \to [\sigma'] \, t_i} \qquad \frac{l_i \in \widetilde{l}}{[\sigma[c \mapsto l_i;q]] \, \mathsf{case} \, c \, \mathsf{of} \, \{\widetilde{l \mapsto t}\} \to [\sigma[c \mapsto q]] \, t_i}$$

$$\frac{\not\vdash v : T}{[\sigma[c \mapsto v;q]] \, \mathsf{rcv}(c)(x:T).t \to [] \, \mathsf{error}} \qquad \frac{l_i \notin \widetilde{l}}{[\sigma[c \mapsto l_i;q]] \, \mathsf{case} \, c \, \mathsf{of} \, \{\widetilde{l \mapsto t}\} \to [] \, \mathsf{error}}$$

$$\frac{[\sigma] \, t \to [\sigma'] \, t'}{[\sigma] \, f(t) \to [\sigma'] \, t'} \qquad \frac{[\sigma] \, P_1 \to [\sigma'] \, P_1'}{[\sigma] \, P_1 \parallel P_2 \to [\sigma'] \, P_1' \parallel P_2} \qquad \frac{[\sigma] \, P_2 \to [\sigma'] \, P_2'}{[\sigma] \, P_1 \parallel P_2 \to [\sigma'] \, P_1 \parallel P_2'}$$

Fig. 2. Reduction Semantics $[\sigma] \, t \to [\sigma'] \, t'$

$$\frac{}{[\sigma] \, P, \psi \to [\sigma] \, P, \psi, \psi'} \, (\mathrm{U1}) \qquad \frac{\not\exists i.\mathsf{p}_i(\sigma, P, \psi) \quad [\sigma] \, P \to [\sigma'] \, P'}{[\sigma] \, P, \psi \to [\sigma'] \, P', \psi} \, (\mathrm{U2})$$

$$\frac{\text{least } i.\, \mathsf{p}_i(\sigma, P, \psi) \quad \psi' = \psi \setminus \mathsf{p}_i(z_\sigma, z_P, z_{\overline{\psi}}) \mapsto \{\widetilde{f \mapsto t}\}_i}{[\sigma] \, P, \psi \to [\sigma] \, \mathsf{upd}(P, \{\widetilde{f \mapsto t}\}_i), \psi'} \, (\mathrm{U3})$$

Fig. 3. Update Reduction Semantics $[\sigma] \, P, \psi \to [\sigma'] \, P', \psi'$

by substituting the code in each delimited block named f with new code t. We let u range over such code patches and we write $\mathsf{upd}(P, u)$ to represent the application of the patch u to P. We omit the straightforward definition of this function. The reduction relation for update between full configurations is defined in Figure 3. Rule (U1) denotes the external introduction of an update. Rule (U2) denotes a term reduction when no updates are applicable. Rule (U3) denotes the application of the oldest applicable update.

3   Type and Effect System

We use Session Types to represent the communication behaviour of programs. In order to extract the Session Types from code we make use of a standard type and effect system to determine the effect of a given message passing calculus term [Dezani-Ciancaglini and Liguoro(2010)]. A *local* Session Type, or effect, φ describes the communication behaviour of a single thread of control. The effects of parallel threads are represented simply by a parallel composition of effects Φ. The grammar for these is in Figure 4. For the most part, these effects will be recognisable to those familiar with Session Types or message-passing processes. For example, internal choice $\oplus c\{\widetilde{l \mapsto \varphi}\}$ denotes that a program may send any

$$\varphi ::= 0 \mid X \mid c!\langle T\rangle.\varphi \mid c?(T).\varphi \mid \oplus c\{\widetilde{l \mapsto \varphi}\} \mid \&c\{\widetilde{l \mapsto \varphi}\} \mid f(\varphi) \mid \mu X.\varphi \mid \text{error}$$

$$\Phi ::= \varphi \mid \Phi \parallel \Phi \qquad G ::= 0 \mid X \mid d \rightarrow d' : c\langle T \mapsto G\rangle \mid d \rightarrow d' : c\langle \widetilde{l \mapsto G}\rangle_I \mid f(G) \mid \mu X.G$$

Fig. 4. Local and Global Session Types

$$\overline{\Gamma \vdash () : \text{Unit}} \quad \overline{\Gamma \vdash b : \text{Bool}} \quad \overline{\Gamma \vdash n : \text{Int}} \quad \overline{\Gamma \vdash x : \Gamma(x)}$$

$$\frac{\varphi \wr \Gamma \vdash t \quad \Gamma \vdash v : T}{c!\langle T\rangle.\varphi \wr \Gamma \vdash \text{snd}(c,v).t} \quad \frac{\varphi \wr \Gamma, x : T \vdash t}{c?(T).\varphi \wr \Gamma \vdash \text{rcv}(c)(x : T).t}$$

$$\frac{\varphi_i \wr \Gamma \vdash t_i}{\oplus c\{\widetilde{l \mapsto \varphi}\} \wr \Gamma \vdash \text{sel } c \text{ from } \{\widetilde{l \mapsto t}\}} \quad \frac{\varphi_i \wr \Gamma \vdash t_i}{\&c\{\widetilde{l \mapsto \varphi}\} \wr \Gamma \vdash \text{case } c \text{ of } \{\widetilde{l \mapsto t}\}}$$

$$\frac{\varphi \wr \Gamma \vdash t}{f(\varphi) \wr \Gamma \vdash f(t)} \quad \frac{\varphi \wr \Gamma, X : T \vdash t}{\mu X.\varphi \wr \Gamma \vdash \mu X.t} \quad \frac{\varphi \wr \emptyset \vdash t}{\vdash t : \varphi} \quad \frac{\vdash P_i : \Phi_i}{\vdash P_1 \parallel P_2 : \Phi_1 \parallel \Phi_2}$$

Fig. 5. Type Rules

label $l_i \in \widetilde{l}$ and proceed with that label's associated effect φ_i, irrespective of its environment, and external choice $\&c\{\widetilde{l \mapsto \varphi}\}$ denotes that a program proceeds with φ_i whenever it receives a select message on label l_i on channel c. In line with our base calculus, we introduce region annotations for Session Types also.

Global Session Types describe communication protocols between multiple roles at a high level of abstraction [Bettini et al.(2008)]. Intuitively each participant role d is played out by one process in a program and given a global type we can project this to each participant role to produce a local session type. The grammar for Global Session Types is as in Figure 4. The type $d_1 \rightarrow d_2 : c\langle T \mapsto G\rangle$ denotes that participant d_1 sends a message to participant d_2 and then the protocol continues as G. The type $d_1 \rightarrow d_2 : c\langle \widetilde{l \mapsto G}\rangle_I$ denotes that participant d_1 chooses a label l_i from set $\widetilde{l}$, communicates this choice to participant d_2, and then the system continues with behaviour G_i. The notation $\langle \widetilde{l \mapsto G}\rangle_I$ denotes a vector that maps labels l_i to Global Session Type continuations G_i, where the vector is defined over indexing set I. As in [Honda et al.(2008)], we define a Global Session Type G to be well formed if and only if, for all choices $d \rightarrow d' : c\langle \widetilde{l \mapsto G}\rangle_I$ within G, and for all roles d'' which are not participating in the choice (i.e. those that are not d or d'), that the projection of each continuation G_i with respect to d'' are equal to the projections of all the other continuations G_j with respect to d''. We describe how to project Global Session Types to Local Session Types in the following section.

We use a simple typing judgement $\Gamma \vdash v : T$ to denote that a value has a given type in type environment Γ. We use a typing judgement $\varphi \wr \Gamma \vdash t$ to denote that, under variable typing assumption Γ, a term t has an effect φ. We also use a type judgement $\vdash P : \Phi$ to denote that process P has an effect Φ. The inference rules for the type and effect system are given in Figure 5.

We recall that the language of effects is essentially an asynchronous process calculus (without message-passing) and as such, has its own reduction semantics. In order to define this we consider abstract configurations to be comprised of a collection of abstract channel queues, *viz.* queues of types rather than values, Σ, and an effect Φ. We define the reduction relation $[\Sigma]\,\Phi \to [\Sigma']\,\Phi'$ between abstract configurations in an analogous way to that in Figure 2. Note that it is not possible to step into an annotated region without also reducing said region. We will use the notation $\Sigma_\emptyset$ to mean the collection of everywhere empty channel queues and the notation $\Lambda(\sigma)$ to mean the collection of queues in σ but with values replaced by their types. The update semantics is similarly defined on abstract configurations except that the function $\mathsf{upd}(\Phi, u)$ is defined in such a way that the effect of the new code, rather than the code itself, is substituted in to Φ.

4   Preserving Safety and Liveness in the Presence of Updates

In this section we consider the safety and liveness (progress) properties of our systems. It is clear that, even in the absence of update, without some immediate constraints on the communications between threads these properties do not hold. We therefore begin by identifying a condition on configurations based on Global Session Types [Bettini et al.(2008)].

Projection is defined as a relation $G \upharpoonright d = \varphi$ following [Honda et al.(2008)], that is,

$$0 \upharpoonright d = 0 \qquad\qquad X \upharpoonright d = X$$
$$(\mu X.G) \upharpoonright d = \mu X.(G \upharpoonright d) \qquad f(G) \upharpoonright d = f_d(G \upharpoonright d)$$
$$d_1 \to d_2 : c\langle T \mapsto G\rangle \upharpoonright d_1 = c!\langle T\rangle.G \upharpoonright d_1$$
$$d_1 \to d_2 : c\langle T \mapsto G\rangle \upharpoonright d_2 = c?(T).G \upharpoonright d_2$$
$$d_1 \to d_2 : c\langle T \mapsto G\rangle \upharpoonright d = G \upharpoonright d$$
$$d_1 \to d_2 : c\langle \widetilde{l \mapsto G}\rangle_I \upharpoonright d_1 = \oplus c\{l_j \mapsto \widetilde{(G_j \upharpoonright d_1)}\}_J$$
$$d_1 \to d_2 : c\langle \widetilde{l \mapsto G}\rangle_I \upharpoonright d_2 = \& c\{l_i \mapsto \widetilde{(G_i \upharpoonright d_2)}\}_I$$
$$d_1 \to d_2 : c\langle T \mapsto G\rangle_I \upharpoonright d = G \upharpoonright d$$

where we assume $d \neq d_1, d_2$ and $\emptyset \neq J \subseteq I$. As convenient notation we write $\Phi^{\upharpoonright G}$ to mean that $\Phi \equiv (G \upharpoonright d_1) \parallel \ldots \parallel (G \upharpoonright d_n)$ for a given G and for all participants $d_1, \ldots, d_n$ in G. We write $\Phi^\upharpoonright$ when the precise G is unimportant. We assume that all Global Session Types have principle channel allocation [Deni and Yoshida(2010)]; this denotes that each pair of participants d_1 and d_2 shares two unique channels, one from d_1 to d_2, and one from d_2 to d_1. The novel aspect of projection here is how to handle region annotations. The projection of annotation $f(G)$ onto a participant d makes use of a fresh region name which is the region annotated with the participant name. This permits us to ensure that the region annotation in the Global Session Type is projected to annotations with different region names in each of the participant's local Session Types. We do this in order to be able to update each thread independently.

The immediate benefit of using Global Session Types here is that any abstract configuration that is obtained by reducing any projection $[\Sigma_\emptyset] \, \Phi^\restriction$, can be proved to be error free and live [Honda et al.(2008)]. We now leverage this result to show how this can remain true in the presence of update.

4.1   Global Typability

As we outlined in the introduction, a condition to ensure safety and liveness after dynamic update might be to maintain the property that the effect of the system Φ is a projection of some global session type. This would entail checking that any updated code forms a (possibly different) projection of a global session type. The condition of being a projection, alone, is clearly inadequate to prove safety and liveness, as there may be pending messages in the channel queues. For example: $[c \mapsto 4]\,(\mathsf{snd}(c, \mathsf{true}).() \parallel \mathsf{rcv}(c)(x : \mathrm{Bool}).())$ has an effect $c!\langle\mathrm{Bool}\rangle.0 \parallel c?(\mathrm{Bool}).0$ that can be viewed as a projection of the global type $d_1 \twoheadrightarrow d_2 : c\langle\mathrm{Bool} \mapsto 0\rangle$. This program will reduce to an error, as the message at the front of the queue is of a different type to that expected by the receiver. Hence the requirement that all updated programs be projections of Global Session Types is not a sufficient property to guarantee safety and liveness. A simple remedy to this is to demand that all channel queues are empty. This then forms the basis for our Global Typability condition but before we can define this we need to make some simplifying assumptions.

We assume that during the evaluation of a system, we will see exactly one code update arrive — this update may contain code to update several threads. We will use the notation $[\sigma]\,P, (\psi)$ to mean a full configuration in which ψ is the unique update that arrives at some point during evaluation. The familiar 'optional' notation (ψ) allows for the absence of this update either due to it having not yet arrived or it having been applied already. We use a similar notation for abstract configurations. We make use of global types that are of the form $\mu X.f(G_0)$ where G_0 does not contain any instances of μ nor any region annotations and does not terminate with 0. We call these *loop global* types as they describe ongoing looping protocols and we use the notation G° to indicate that G is of this form. Define the Global Typability predicate $\mathcal{GT}(\psi)$ on code updates as

$$\mathcal{GT}(\psi) \text{ iff } (\psi = \mathsf{p}_{gt}(z_\Sigma, z_{\overline\varphi}, z_{\overline\psi}) \mapsto \{\widetilde{f_{d_i} \mapsto t_{d_i}}\} \text{ and } \exists\Phi. \vdash \prod t_{d_i} : \Phi^\restriction)$$

where $\mathsf{p}_{gt}(z_\Sigma, z_{\overline\varphi}, z_{\overline\psi})$ is the predicate $(z_\Sigma = \Sigma_\emptyset) \wedge z_{\overline\varphi}^\restriction$, and $z_{\overline\varphi}^\restriction$ denotes that $z_{\overline\varphi}$ is the projection of some Global Session Type.

If P is a well-typed program whose effect is a projection of a global session type and if the unique possible update ψ during evaluation from $[\Sigma_\emptyset]\,P$ is such that $\mathcal{GT}(\psi)$ then we claim that evaluation never reaches an error state or gets stuck. To check whether a configuration is a projection of some global type is not too onerous due to the principle channel allocation property — i.e. each channel

$$\Delta^{\restriction G} = \bigcup_{n<\omega} \Delta_n^{\restriction G} \qquad \Delta_0^{\restriction G} = \{[\Sigma_\emptyset]\, \Phi^{\restriction G}\}$$

$$\Delta_{n+1}^{\restriction G} = \{\, \delta([c \mapsto T; \Sigma], \varphi_i, \varphi_j') \mid \delta(\Sigma, \varphi_i, \varphi_j) \in \Delta_n^{\restriction G}\} \cup \Delta_n^{\restriction G}$$
$$\cup \{\, \delta(\Sigma, \varphi_i', \varphi_j') \qquad \mid \delta(\Sigma, \varphi_i, \varphi_j) \in \Delta_n^{\restriction G}\}$$

Where

$$\varphi_i' = \begin{cases} f_{d_i}(c!\langle T\rangle.\varphi_i) & \text{if } c!\langle T\rangle.\varphi_i \text{ is such that } G \restriction d_i \equiv f_i(c!\langle T\varphi_i\rangle.) \\ c!\langle T\rangle.\varphi_i & \text{otherwise} \end{cases}$$

Similarly

$$\varphi_j' = \begin{cases} f_{d_j}(c?(T).\varphi_{d_i}) & \text{if } G \restriction d_j \equiv f_{d_j}(c?(T).\varphi_j) \\ c?(T).\varphi_j & \text{otherwise} \end{cases}$$

Fig. 6. Abstract configurations heading towards the projection of G

uniquely identifies the sender and receiver participants. To formally prove safety and liveness we characterise a set of abstract configurations $\Delta^{\restriction}$ that may reduce to some $[\Sigma_\emptyset]\, \Phi^{\restriction G}$. The key observation to make here is that for projections of any looping G° then any reduction will be reducing towards G°. We then show that safety and liveness holds for all such abstract configurations. The definition of $\Delta^{\restriction}$ is given as the union of all sets $\Delta_n^{\restriction G^\circ}$ (Figure 6). Each represents configurations that may reach G° in no more than n reduction steps. Given a global type G, we use the notation $\delta(\Sigma, \varphi_i, \varphi_j)$ to represent a configuration of n participants of G with two particular participants d_i, d_j identified:

$$[\Sigma]\, \varphi_1 \parallel \cdots \parallel \varphi_i \parallel \cdots \parallel \varphi_j \parallel \cdots \parallel \varphi_n$$

By writing $\delta(\Sigma', \varphi_i', \varphi_j')$ we refer to this same configuration but with possible changes in the abstract state and identified participants' effects. There are two principle ways to extend configurations in the set $\Delta^{\restriction G}$, each of which has several cases. The first way is to add a typed message T to the front of the existing message queues, and to add a receive that expects a T to the front of the receiving process. The second way is to add a send of a given type and a receive of a given type to the front of the given sending and receiving processes. The channels used for adding a message or adding a send/receive pair must also follow principle channel allocation [Deni and Yoshida(2010)], and hence the channel used in both cases is $c = d_i d_j$, where d_i is the role of effect φ_i and d_j is the role of effect φ_j. In order to ensure that processes are well annotated we always add the relevant region annotation when the process is a projection of a global session type. Note that in Figure 6 *we omit* the cases for choice and selection. This is as they are analogous and hence are omitted for simplicity of presentation. We first show that our set of configurations reducing towards some G° is closed under reduction and that these configurations are safe and live:

Lemma 1. *If* $[\Sigma]\, \Phi \in \Delta^{\restriction G^\circ}$ *and* $[\Sigma]\, \Phi \to [\Sigma']\, \Phi'$ *then* $[\Sigma']\, \Phi' \in \Delta^{\restriction G^\circ}$

Lemma 2. *If* $[\Sigma]\, \Phi \in \Delta^{\restriction}$ *then* error $\notin \Phi$ *and* $[\Sigma]\, \Phi \to [\Sigma']\, \Phi'$ *for some* Σ', Φ'.

We also need to ensure that updating a configuration with an update ψ satisfying $\mathcal{GT}(\psi)$ results in a consistent state. Note that we only need to check this in the case in which the channel queues are empty and therefore the following suffices:

Lemma 3. *If* $\vdash P : \Phi^\uparrow$ *and* $\mathcal{GT}(\psi)$ *then* $\vdash \mathsf{upd}(P, \{\widetilde{f_{d_i} \mapsto t_{d_i}}\}) : \Phi'$ *for some* $\Phi'^\uparrow$ *where* ψ *is* $\mathsf{p}_{gt}(z_\Sigma, z_{\overline{\varphi}}, z_{\overline{\psi}}) \mapsto \{\widetilde{f_{d_i} \mapsto t_{d_i}}\}$

We show that we can infer liveness of programs from liveness of their effects.

Lemma 4. *If* $\vdash P : \Phi$ *and* $\mathcal{GT}(\psi)$ *then*

$$[\Lambda(\sigma)]\, \Phi, (\psi) \to [\Lambda(\sigma')]\, \Phi', (\psi) \text{ implies } [\sigma]\, P, (\psi) \to [\sigma']\, P', (\psi) \text{ for some } \sigma', P'$$

We now have all we need to establish the main properties of Global Typability:

Theorem 1 (Global Typability Subject Reduction). *Let* Σ *be* $\Lambda(\sigma)$, *and let* ψ *be the unique possible update during evaluation of* P *and suppose that* $\mathcal{GT}(\psi)$. *Then*

$$\vdash P : \Phi \text{ and } [\Sigma]\, \Phi \in \Delta^\uparrow \text{ and } [\sigma]\, P, (\psi) \to [\sigma']\, P', (\psi)$$

implies $\vdash P' : \Phi'$ *for some* Φ' *such that*

$$[\Sigma]\, \Phi, (\psi) \to [\Sigma']\, \Phi', (\psi) \text{ with } [\Sigma']\, \Phi' \in \Delta^\uparrow$$

Proof. By induction over $[\Sigma]\, \Phi, (\psi) \to [\Sigma']\, \Phi', (\psi)$. The interesting cases are in the reduction rules for update. The case for Rule (U1) follows immediately. The case for Rule (U2) is straightforward by Lemma 1 and the inductive hypothesis. In the case of rule (U3) we know that: $[\sigma]\, P, \psi \to [\sigma]\, P'$ where $P' = \mathsf{upd}(P, \{\widetilde{f_{d_i} \mapsto t_{d_i}}\})$. By the definition $\Delta_0^{\uparrow G}$ we know that $\Sigma = \Sigma_\emptyset$, and hence can use Lemma 3 to show that $\vdash P' : \Phi'^\uparrow$. We then have that $[\Sigma]\, \Phi'^\uparrow \in \Delta^\uparrow$.

Theorem 2 (Global Typability Safety and Liveness). *Let* ψ *be the unique possible update during evaluation of* P *such that* $\mathcal{GT}(\psi)$. *Suppose that* $\vdash P : \Phi$ *and* $[\Lambda(\sigma)]\, \Phi \in \Delta^\uparrow$. *Then, for some* σ', P',

$$\mathsf{error} \notin P, \text{ and } [\sigma]\, P, (\psi) \to [\sigma']\, P', (\psi)$$

Proof. By our type rules we clearly have that $\mathsf{error} \notin P$. By Lemma 2 we know that $[\Sigma]\, \Phi \to [\Sigma']\, \Phi'$. We can then show, using Lemma 4, that $[\sigma]\, P, (\psi) \to [\sigma']\, P', (\psi)$.

The above theorems tell us that it is safe to update programs whose current effects are projections of Global Session Types. This corresponds to a high degree of synchronisation between threads, and requires a lock on all message queues in order to check the update predicate. This approach is similar to performing a shut down and restart. We prove the safety and liveness of this approach, which has been previously assumed but not formally considered. One other disadvantage to Global Typability is that, even under fair scheduling, there is no guarantee that an update will ever be applied. This problem is particularly prominent in systems without feedback, such as a producer/consumer program without acknowledgement, as global synchronisation may never occur. In order to address updates for systems with feedback, and in order to provide an update that requires less synchronisation, we present a more relaxed approach whereby threads may be updated separately.

4.2   Local Update

A system being a projection of a global session type is only a sufficient condition to ensure safety and liveness after a dynamic update if there are no pending messages in the channel queues. As it is difficult to guarantee such a situation will occur frequently enough at runtime to ensure timely updates, we must then consider how to perform updates in the presence of pending messages. For example, consider a Producer/Consumer example that incorporates a buffer. Here the Producer repeatedly sends a message on a queued channel c_1, the Buffer repeatedly receives a value and forwards it to the Consumer, which repeatedly receives the values. Note that no participant performs an 'ack':

$$t_p = \text{rec}X.f(\text{snd}(c_1, v_1).X) \quad t_b = \text{rec}X'.f'(\text{rcv}(c_1)(x_1 : T_1).\text{snd}(c_2, x_1).X')$$
$$t_{co} = \text{rec}X''.f''(\text{rcv}(c_2)(x_1 : T_1).X'')$$

At some point we may wish to change the system so that instead of repeatedly producing and consuming values of the type T_1, that it alternates between values of type T_1 and of type T_2. This can be achieved with the new code:

$$t_p = \text{rec}X.f(\text{snd}(c_3, v_1).\text{snd}(c_3, v_2).X)$$
$$t_b = \text{rec}X'.f'(\text{rcv}(c_3)(x_1 : T_1).\text{rcv}(c_3)(x_2 : T_2).\text{snd}(c_4, x_1).\text{snd}(c_4, x_2).X')$$
$$t_{co} = \text{rec}X''.f''(\text{rcv}(c_4)(x_1 : T_1).\text{rcv}(c_4)(x_2 : T_2).X'')$$

We hence want to perform an update in such a way that all messages sent under the old protocol are consumed by the relevant process of the old program before that process migrates to the new program. The problem with Global Typability in situations without feedback is that the Producer can continue to send messages under the old program code, so that the Consumer may never finish receiving the old program's messages. In order to break this dependency we consider how to update processes separately. Specifically, we consider an approach where processes such as the Producer in the above example are updated first, so that no more messages are being produced under by the old program, and so the consuming processes (the Buffer and the Consumer) can process all the old messages, and then be updated themselves. We demonstrate this approach with an example reduction sequence. We delay the precise definition of the update, stating informally that ψ consists of three updates, one for each process, that the Producer is updated immediately, that the Buffer is updated when it has forwarded all the old messages to the Consumer, and that the Consumer is updated when it has received all the old messages. In this example the producer sends one message, and then the update is introduced on line 3. The portion of the update pertaining to the Producer is applied immediately, on line 4. The message from the old program is then received and forwarded by the buffer on lines 5-6, after which the Buffer is updated on line 7. Finally the consumer receives the message, and is updated online 9. At this point the system is back in a consistent state, and hence will continue without deadlock or error.

1	$[\sigma_\emptyset]\, t_p \parallel t_b \parallel t_c$	2	$\rightarrow [c_1 \mapsto v_1]\, t_p \parallel t_b \parallel t_c$
3	$\rightarrow [c_1 \mapsto v_1]\, t_p \parallel t_b \parallel t_c, \psi$	4	$\rightarrow [c_1 \mapsto v_1]\, t_p' \parallel t_b \parallel t_c, \psi_b, \psi_{co}$
5	$\rightarrow [\sigma_\emptyset]\, t_p' \parallel \mathsf{snd}(c_2, v_1).t_b \parallel t_c, \psi_b, \psi_{co}$	6	$\rightarrow [c_2 \mapsto v_1]\, t_p' \parallel t_b \parallel t_c, \psi_b, \psi_{co}$
7	$\rightarrow [c_2 \mapsto v_1]\, t_p' \parallel t_b' \parallel t_c, \psi_{co}$	8	$\rightarrow [\sigma_\emptyset]\, t_p' \parallel t_b' \parallel t_c, \psi_{co}$
9	$\rightarrow [\sigma_\emptyset]\, t_p' \parallel t_b' \parallel t_c'$	10	$\rightarrow \ldots$

Note that the updated processes can continue to reduce normally, after its update. In particular, once the producer and the buffer have been updated, they can communicate along the new channel c_3. In the example we omit such reductions.

An overview of Local Update is as follows. We update processes individually, starting with the process that begins each iteration of the Global Session Type, and continuing with processes in the order they are enabled in the protocol. We consider separately the processes that have been updated and the processes that have not been updated. We show that the latter are always live or updatable, and contains no errors. We then show that, after all processes have been updated, that the whole system is in the set of abstract configurations of Section 4.1, and use the results of that section to show liveness and safety.

Before we define Local Update we need to make some simplifying assumptions. We again will consider looping global types G° that are of the form $\mu X.f(G_0)$ where G_0 does not contain any instances of μ nor any region annotations. We assume that the old program is one that can evolve to the projection of a global type G_1. We assume that the new program is a projection of the global type G_2, that no channels are shared between G_1 and G_2, and that G_1 and G_2 share the same set of roles. We define a strict partial order $<_{G_1}$ over participants d of a protocol G_1 denoting the order under which the participants can begin execution of a protocol G_1. For example, for the Producer/Buffer/Consumer example we would define $d_p < d_b < d_{co}$. We omit a precise definition here but suffice to say it incorporates the per role protocol order in G_1 and the dependency between sender to receiver on a shared channel. We require that the order has a unique minimum element. This disallows protocols such as $d_1 \rightarrow d_3 : c_1\langle T_1 \mapsto d_2 \rightarrow d_3 : c_2\langle T_2 \mapsto \ldots\rangle\rangle$. We omit the subscript when the meaning is clear. We only define $<_{G_1}$ for the Global Session Type G_1 of the original program. This order does not change as a given $[\Sigma]\,\Phi$ reduces. We assume that we can partition the roles in G_1 (and hence G_2) into two disjoint sets, where $\underline{D}$ denotes the roles of processes that have not yet been updated, and $\overline{D}$ denote the roles of processes that have been updated. We write $\overline{D} < \underline{D}$ when $\forall d \in \underline{D}, d' \in \overline{D}$ we have that $d \not< d'$.

We refer to the set of channels that are received upon in an effect φ as $\mathsf{R}(\varphi)$. Define the Local Update predicate $\mathcal{LU}(\psi)$ on code updates as:

$$\mathcal{LU}(\psi) \text{ iff } (\psi = (\mathsf{p}_i(z_\Sigma, z_{\overline{\varphi}}, \widetilde{z_{\overline{\psi}}}) \mapsto (f_{d_i} \mapsto t_{d_i}))_D \text{ and } \forall d_i \in D \, . \vdash t_{d_i} : G_2 \upharpoonright d)$$

where $p_{d_i}(z_\Sigma, z_{\overline{\varphi}}, z_{\overline{\psi}})$ is $\forall c \in R(z_{\varphi_i}).z_\Sigma(c) = \emptyset \wedge \forall d_j <_{G_1} d_i.z_{\psi_j}$ is empty, ψ_j is the update for process projected from d_j, and D is the set of all roles used in G_1.

If P is a well-typed program whose effect is a projection of a global session type and if the unique update ψ during evalation from $[\Sigma_\emptyset] P$ is such that $\mathcal{LU}(\psi)$ then we claim that evaluation never reaches an error state or gets stuck.

To formally prove this we make several definitions. We relax the definition of the set of abstract configurations reducing towards G. We define the relaxed projection $\Phi_D^{\restriction G}$ to mean that $\Phi \equiv G \restriction d_1 \parallel \ldots \parallel G \restriction d_n$ for all participants $d_1, \ldots, d_n$ in a given D. Note that D need not comprise all roles in the given G.

We define the relaxed set of configurations for the non-updated roles $\underline{D}$ as $\Delta_{\underline{D}}^{\restriction G_1}$, where G_1 is the protocol of the old program (Figure 7). This definition permits the prefix of messages from processes whose role is not present in $\underline{D}$ when prefixing a receive action to a process that is present, along with prefixing send and receive actions to processes whose roles are both in $\underline{D}$. Note that we do not include the variants for assuring region well annotation, or the rules for selection, for the purposes of brevity. The full details are found in [Anderson(2012)].

We refer to the set of channels that are sent upon by an effect φ as $S(\varphi)$. We define the relaxed set of configurations for the updated roles $\overline{D}$ as $\Delta_{\overline{D}}^{\restriction G_2}$, where G_2 is the protocol of the new program (Figure 7). This set filters the non-relaxed definition $\Delta^{\restriction G_2}$ (see Figure 6) for those configurations where the effects of all the roles that are not in $\overline{D}$ are projections of the protocol G_2. That is, any roles that have not been updated should start at the beginning of their runs of G_2.

We show that relaxed sets are closed under reduction for looping types G°:

Lemma 5. *If* $[\Sigma] \Phi \in \Delta_D^{\restriction G^\circ}$ *and* $[\Sigma] \Phi \to [\Sigma'] \Phi'$ *then* $[\Sigma'] \Phi' \in \Delta_D^{\restriction G^\circ}$.

$$\text{If } [\Sigma] \Phi \in \Delta_D^{\restriction G^\circ} \text{ and } [\Sigma] \Phi \to [\Sigma'] \Phi' \text{ then } [\Sigma'] \Phi' \in \Delta_D^{\downarrow G^\circ}$$

We then show that configurations in the relaxed projection for non-updated processes are safe, and are either live, empty, or are relaxed projections of the base global type:

Lemma 6. *If* $[\Sigma] \Phi \in \Delta_D^{\restriction G}$ *then* error $\notin \Phi$ *and moreover, either* $[\Sigma] \Phi \to [\Sigma'] \Phi'$ *or* $[\Sigma] \Phi = [\Sigma_\emptyset] \Phi_D^{\restriction G}$

We need to make sure that updating a process of role d_i with an update $\mathcal{LU}(\psi)$ results in a process that conforms to the new protocol G_2.

Lemma 7. *If* $\vdash t_i : G_1 \restriction d$ *and* $\mathcal{LU}(\psi)$ *then* $\vdash \mathsf{upd}(t_i, f_{d_i} \mapsto t_{d_i}) : G_2 \restriction d_i$.

We need to show that if we extend a relaxed configuration of updated processes with a newly updated process then the new configuration will be in relaxed set, extended by the new role:

Lemma 8. *if* $[\Sigma] \Phi \in \Delta_D^{\restriction G}$ *and* $D' = D + \{d'\}$
then $[\Sigma] (\Phi \parallel G \restriction d') \in \Delta_{D'}^{\restriction G}$.

$$\Delta_{\underline{D}}^{\restriction G_1} = \bigcup_N {}_n\Delta_{\underline{D}}^{\restriction G_1} \qquad {}_0\Delta_{\underline{D}}^{\restriction G} = \{[\Sigma_0]\,\Phi_{\underline{D}}^{\restriction G}\}$$

$$
\begin{aligned}
{}_{n+1}\Delta_{\underline{D}}^{\restriction G_1} = &\quad \{\delta([c \mapsto T; \Sigma], \varphi_j') \mid \delta(\Sigma, \varphi_j) \in {}_n\Delta_{\underline{D}}^{\restriction G_1}\} \\
&\cup \{\delta(\Sigma, \varphi_i', \varphi_j') \quad\mid \delta(\Sigma, \varphi_i, \varphi_j) \in {}_n\Delta_{\underline{D}}^{\restriction G_1}\} \cup {}_n\Delta_{\underline{D}}^{\restriction G_1}
\end{aligned}
$$

$$
\Delta_{\overline{D}}^{\restriction G_2} = \{ \; [\Sigma] \textstyle\prod_{\overline{D}} \varphi_d \mid [\Sigma] \prod \varphi_{d_i} \in \Delta^{\restriction G_2} \wedge \\
\forall d_i \in \underline{D} \;.\; (\varphi_{d_i} = G_2 \restriction d_i \wedge \forall c \in \mathsf{S}(\varphi_{d_i}).\Sigma(c) = \emptyset)\}
$$

Where $\varphi_i' = c!\langle T\rangle.\varphi_i$, and $\varphi_j' = c?(T).\varphi_j$.

Fig. 7. Relaxed abstract configurations reducing to global projections

We also need to show that if we redact a relaxed configuration of non-updated processes by a newly updated process then the new configuration will be in the relaxed set, redacted by the updated role:

Lemma 9. *If $[\Sigma]\,(\Phi \parallel G \restriction d') \in \Delta_{D'}^{\restriction G}$ and $\forall c \in \mathsf{R}(G \restriction d').\Sigma(c) = \emptyset$ and $D' = D + \{d'\}$ and $\not\exists d \in D$ such that $d < d'$ then $[\Sigma]\,\Phi \in \Delta_D^{\restriction G}$.*

In Lemmas 8 and 9 we make use of disjoint union. Note that it is in the proofs of these lemmas where the ordering on roles, as stipulated in $\mathcal{LU}(\psi)$, is primarily used. Recall that the definition of the update predicates p_{d_i} includes the property that all smaller participants have already been updated.

Theorem 3 (Local Update Subject Reduction). *Let ψ be the unique possible update during evalation of P such that $\mathcal{LU}(\psi)$. Suppose the roles of G_1° (and G_2°) are are partitioned as $\overline{D} < \underline{D}$. Further suppose $[\sigma]\,P = [\sigma_1, \sigma_2]\,P_1 \parallel P_2$ for some $\sigma_1, \sigma_2, P_1, P_2$ such that $\vdash P_1 : \Phi_1$ and $\vdash P_2 : \Phi_2$ and let $\Sigma_i = \Lambda(\sigma_i)$. Then*

$$[\sigma]\,P, (\psi) \to [\sigma']\,P', (\psi') \text{ and } [\Sigma_1]\,\Phi_1 \in \Delta_{\underline{D}}^{\restriction G_1^\circ} \text{ and } [\Sigma_2]\,\Phi_2 \in \Delta_{\overline{D}}^{\restriction G_2^\circ}$$

implies $\vdash P' : \Phi_1' \parallel \Phi_2'$ for some Φ_1', Φ_2' such that

$$[\Lambda(\sigma)]\,\Phi, (\psi) \to [\Sigma_1', \Sigma_2']\,(\Phi_1' \parallel \Phi_2'), (\psi') \text{ and } [\Sigma_1']\,\Phi_1' \in \Delta_{\underline{D}'}^{\restriction G_1^\circ} \text{ and } [\Sigma_2']\,\Phi_2' \in \Delta_{\overline{D}'}^{\restriction G_2^\circ}$$

with some (different) partition of the roles $\underline{D}'$ and $\overline{D}'$ such that $\overline{D}' < \underline{D}'$.

Proof. By induction over $[\Sigma]\,\Phi, (\psi) \to [\Sigma_1', \Sigma_2']\,\Phi_1', \Phi_2', (\psi')$. Rule (U1) is immediate. Rule (U2) straightforward by Lemma 5 and induction. By rule (U3) we know that there exists a least $i.\mathsf{p}_i(z_\sigma, z_P, z_{\overline{\psi}}) = \mathsf{true}$. Hence we know that $\forall c \in \mathsf{R}(z_{\varphi_i}).z_\Sigma(c) = \emptyset \wedge \forall d_j <_{G_1} d_i.z_{\psi_j}$ is empty. By Lemma 7 we know that $\varphi_i' = G_1 \restriction d_i$ where $\varphi_i' = \mathsf{upd}(\varphi_i, f_{d_i} \mapsto t_{d_i})$. By Lemma 8 we know that $[\Sigma_2]\,(\Phi_2 \parallel \varphi_i') \in \Delta_{\overline{D}'}^{\restriction G_2^\circ}$ where $\overline{D}' = \overline{D} + \{d_i\}$. Because $\mathsf{p}_i(z_\sigma, z_P, z_{\overline{\psi}})$ holds we know that $\forall d_j <_{G_1} d_i.\psi_j$ is empty, and hence that $\not\exists d \in \underline{D}$ such that $d < d_i$. Then, by Lemma 9, we know that $[\Sigma_1]\,\Phi \in \Delta_{\underline{D}'}^{\restriction G}$, where $\underline{D} = \underline{D}' \cup \{d_i\}$.

Theorem 4 (Local Update Safety and Liveness). *Suppose that $[\sigma]\,P = [\sigma_1, \sigma_2]\,P_1 \parallel P_2$, with $\vdash P_i : \Phi_i$ such that $[\Sigma_1]\,\Phi_1 \in \Delta_{\underline{D}}^{\restriction G_1}$ and $[\Sigma_2]\,\Phi_2 \in \Delta_{\overline{D}}^{\restriction G_2}$. Then*

$$\mathsf{error} \notin P, \text{ and } [\sigma]\,P, (\psi) \to [\sigma']\,P', (\psi') \text{ for some } \sigma', P', \psi'.$$

Proof. By the proof rules, we clearly have that error $\notin P$. By Lemma 6 we know that either $[\Sigma_1]\,\Phi_1 \to [\Sigma_1']\,\Phi_1'$ or $[\Sigma_1]\,\Phi_1 = [\Sigma_\emptyset]\,\Phi_D^{\lceil G_1}$. If the former then we can reduce using (U2). If the latter then we can show that $\exists d_i \in \underline{D}$ such that $\nexists d \in \underline{D}$ such that $d < d'$. Hence we can show that $\exists i.\mathsf{p}_i(z_\sigma, z_P, z_{\overline{\psi}})$ and reduce using (U3).

The Local Update approach permits the update of individual threads of message passing programs running certain protocols. This is a significant step forward from existing work, where either global synchronisation or a significant level of indirection is required. In this approach each thread's receive queues must be empty when an update to that thread occurs, which ensures that a degree of transactional consistency is maintained so that old programs cannot communicate with new ones. Note that when an update has been partially applied the non-updated threads can continue to communicate with each other, as can the updated threads.

Local Update does require some synchronisation, namely exclusive access to the update queue, and the message queues on which the updating process receives. We believe that checking whether the update predicate holds in a given configuration is linear in the number of processes in the system (which determines the size of the update queue, and the number of channels used). The implementation of the atomicity of the check requires less synchronisation than in Global Typability. Furthermore, while a strict interpretation of the semantics requires the check to be performed at each interleaving, it could be implemented more efficiently with control messages from processes that update to those that follow them in the partial order, so that the later processes do not attempt to check their predicates before their predecessors have updated.

5   Related and Further Work

Most work on DSU concerns single threaded programs. These have focused primarily on preserving type safety, particularly with respect to changing function signatures [Stoyle et al.(2005)] [Bierman et al.(2003)]. Whilst type safety is important in updates for concurrent programs, and has been thoroughly considered [Neamtiu and Hicks(2009)], the concern of many concurrent program designers is focused elsewhere on behavioural properties such as liveness [Lea(1999)].

There are a variety of non-formal approaches to DSU for multi-threaded programs. For example, [Ajmani(2004)] discusses how to perform DSU for distributed object oriented programs, so that old and new instances of a class can interact. This is achieved, for an object with a given version of a class, by limitations on which method calls from different versions of that class can be called on the given object. The restrictions themselves change as the version of the object changes. Such approaches introduce significant overhead (there must be interface classes between every pair of versions of a given class), and do not handle liveness. This is of particular concern given the dynamic method call restrictions.

There are attempts to informally show deadlock freedom when performing DSU to multi-threaded programs. In [Hayden et al.(2011a)] update points are placed at the top of main loops for each of the threads, and it is required that no locks are held when updates are applied. This approach requires the leading thread to block and wait for all others to reach the top of their main loops. In initial experiments this has not introduced deadlock, but this property has not been proved formally. In addition, this reduces asynchrony as all threads must synchronise with the leading thread, rather than updating independently and continuing with the new protocol, as in our work. We believe that our work on Global Typability may abstract their approach, but further research is required. In [Hayden et al.(2012)] they proceed similarly, but make blocking operations interruptible, so that if an update arrives when a subservient thread is blocked it is informed and jumps to the update code at the top of the loop. They note that this approach is only applicable when the blocking operations occur at the beginning of the loop, when it is safe to jump back to the top. They explicitly do not consider how to handle blocking behaviour in the middle of loops.

One key aspect of DSU, that we have not considered in this paper, is its performance costs and overheads. The majority of the overhead concerns permitting changes to function or object signatures. In non-managed languages, such as those based on C and C++, the indirection necessary to update functions or modules introduces an overhead during steady state (non-updating) execution, often between 2-10% [Neamtiu and Hicks(2009)] [Boyapati et al.(2003)]. In managed languages such as Java, it is possible to leverage the inbuilt indirection to provide DSU with no steady-state overhead verses the managed language [Subramanian(2010)]. When whole program transformation is employed, rather than replacing functions or classes, the function indirection is not required, and DSU can be provide for non-managed languages without any steady-state overhead [Hayden et al.(2011b), Hayden et al.(2011a)].

There are several possible extensions to this work. As programming using DSU is complex for programmers to reason about, one approach to reduce it is to perform whole program transformation [Hayden et al.(2011a)]. While this technique significantly reduces the conceptual burden, it relies on programs reaching specific update points. This restriction is more consequential in multi-threaded programs when there is no guarantee that the threads will ever all be at an updatable point. We could incorporate our analysis, which uses synchronisation behaviour, into work on whole program transformation in order to provide greater confidence that updates will not be delayed indefinitely. As Session Typing techniques can be used to analyse the call graph of object oriented programs we should be able to extend our techniques to updating object oriented programs. The current state of the art for DSU of OO programs uses interrupts to detect safe update points and the garbage collector to provide object transformation [Subramanian(2010)]. We believe that we could combine our more complex safety analysis with their efficient implementation to provide an update system that, unlike Subramanian's, permits update to active methods.

References

[Ajmani(2004)] Ajmani, S.: Automatic Software Upgrades for Distributed Systems. Artificial Intelligence (Cm), 1–23 (2004)

[Anderson(2012)] Anderson, G.: Behavioural Properties and Dynamic Software Update for Concurrent Programs. Ph.D. Thesis, University of Southampton (2012)

[Appel(1994)] Appel, A.: Hot-sliding in ML. Technical report. Princeton University, Princeton, New Jersey, USA

[Bettini et al.(2008)] Bettini, L., Coppo, M., D'Antoni, L., De Luca, M., Dezani-Ciancaglini, M., Yoshida, N.: Global Progress in Dynamically Interleaved Multiparty Sessions. In: van Breugel, F., Chechik, M. (eds.) CONCUR 2008. LNCS, vol. 5201, pp. 418–433. Springer, Heidelberg (2008)

[Bierman et al.(2003)] Bierman, G., Hicks, M., Sewell, P., Stoyle, G.: Formalizing Dynamic Software Updating. In: Proceedings of the 2nd Workshop on Unanticipated Software Evolution

[Boyapati et al.(2003)] Boyapati, C., Liskov, B., Shrira, L., Moh, C.-H., Richman, S.: Lazy Modular Upgrades In Persistent Object Stores. In: Proceedings of the 18th on Object-oriented Programing, Systems, Languages, and Applications, pp. 403–417

[Deni and Yoshida(2010)] Deniélou, P.-M., Yoshida, N.: Buffered Communication Analysis in Distributed Multiparty Sessions. In: Gastin, P., Laroussinie, F. (eds.) CONCUR 2010. LNCS, vol. 6269, pp. 343–357. Springer, Heidelberg (2010)

[Dezani-Ciancaglini and Liguoro(2010)] Dezani-Ciancaglini, M., de'Liguoro, U.: Sessions and Session Types: An Overview. In: Laneve, C., Su, J. (eds.) WS-FM 2009. LNCS, vol. 6194, pp. 1–28. Springer, Heidelberg (2010)

[Hayden et al.(2011a)] Hayden, C.M., Smith, E.K., Denchev, M., Hicks, M., Foster, J.S.: Kitsune: Efficient, General-purpose Dynamic Software Updating for C

[Hayden et al.(2011b)] Hayden, C.M., Smith, E.K., Hicks, M., Foster, J.S.: State Transfer for Clear and Efficient Runtime Upgrades. In: Proceedings of the 3rd Workshop on Hot Topics in Software Upgrades

[Hayden et al.(2012)] Hayden, C.M., Saur, K., Hicks, M., Foster, J.S.: A Study of Dynamic Software Update Quiescence for Multithreaded Programs. In: Proceedings of the 4th Workshop on Hot Topics in Software Upgrades

[Hicks and Nettles(2005)] Hicks, M., Nettles, S.: Dynamic Software Updating. ACM Trans. Program. Lang. Syst. 27(6), 1049–1096 (2005) ISSN 0164-0925

[Honda et al.(2008)] Honda, K., Yoshida, N., Carbone, M.: Multiparty Asynchronous Session Types (January 2008) ISSN 0362-1340

[Lea(1999)] Lea, D.: Concurrent Programming in Java: Design Principles and Patterns, 2nd edn. Addison-Wesley Longman Publishing Co., Inc. (1999)

[Neamtiu and Hicks(2009)] Neamtiu, I., Hicks, M.: Safe and Timely Dynamic Updates to Multi-threaded Programs. In: Proceedings of the Conference on Programming Language Design and Implementation, pp. 13–24

[Stoyle et al.(2005)] Stoyle, G., Hicks, M., Bierman, G., Sewell, P., Neamtiu, I.: Mutatis Mutandis: Safe and predictable dynamic software updating. ACM Trans. Program. Lang. Syst. 29(4), 183–194

[Subramanian(2010)] Subramanian, S.: Dynamic Software Updates: A VM-Centric Approach. PhD thesis, University of Texas at Austin

A Synchronous Language with Partial Delay Specification for Real-Time Systems Programming

Rémy Wyss[1], Frédéric Boniol[1], Julien Forget[2], and Claire Pagetti[1]

[1] ONERA–Toulouse, France
[2] LIFL/USTL–Lille, France

Abstract. High-level formal programming languages require system designers to provide a very precise description of the system during early development phases, which may in some cases lead to arbitrary choices (i.e. the designer "overspecifies" the system). In this paper, we propose an extension of synchronous dataflow languages where the designer can specify that he does not care whether some communication is immediate or delayed. It is then up to the compiler to choose where to introduce delays, in a way that breaks causality cycles and satisfies latency requirements imposed on the system.

1 Introduction

Context. Implementing real-time critical systems is an increasingly complex process that calls for high-level formal programming languages. In this paper, we focus on synchronous languages [1], such as LUSTRE [6] and its commercial version SCADE [4], which have successfully been adopted for the formal specification of control systems. These languages are based on the *synchronous paradigm*, where the behaviour of a program is seen as a sequence of reactions: (1) each reaction consists in reading the current inputs, computing the current outputs and updating the internal state of the system; (2) each reaction occurs in zero *logical time* (we do not care about when computations occur during a reaction). Relying on such a language imposes very early in the development process to specify a completely deterministic system, while in some specific cases the designer might want to leave some degree of liberty in the specification. This paper details how to avoid such overspecification.

Non deterministic communication specification. Let us consider the simplified mono-periodic flight control system depicted in the Figure 1. It consists of a set of avionics functions, which acquire information on the state of the aircraft and on the pilot orders, and which objective is to control the position, speed and attitude of the vehicle thanks to its control surfaces. The right part of the figure depicts the control of the ailerons while the left part depicts the control of the elevators. Each vertex depicts a function. Edges depict data-communications between functions and are of two different kinds. Plain arrows stand for immediate communications, which induce a precedence constraint from the producer to the consumer. Dashed arrows stand for less constrained communications that do not induce precedence constraints. We illustrate this distinction below.

R. Jhala and A. Igarashi (Eds.): APLAS 2012, LNCS 7705, pp. 223–238, 2012.

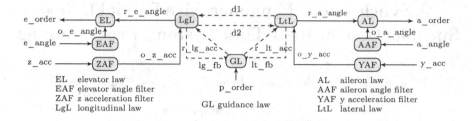

Fig. 1. A simplified flight control system

The variable `a_angle` stands for the current angle of the aileron and is acquired by the function AAF (Aileron angle filter). This function consolidates the data and sends the variable `o_a_angle` (the observed angle) to the function AL (Aileron law). AL controls the aileron and maintains the required angle `r_a_angle`. According to the observed angle and the required angle, it sends an order `a_order` that enables to reach safely the required angle. Thus, the differential equations that command the aileron surface are implemented by the data-flow $L_1 = $ `a_angle` $\to$ `o_a_angle` $\to$ `a_order`. Such a computation path, from a sensor acquisition to an actuator order is called a *functional chain*. In this case, L_1 corresponds to the discretisation of a command law and functions must be applied strictly sequentially for the computation to be correct. The elevator law behaves similarly.

The control laws of the ailerons and of the elevators communicate through the functions LtL and LgL, in order to verify that the orders sent to the different actuators (ailerons and elevators) are consistent. This consolidation is however less stringent than the command described in L_1, therefore longer latencies in the communication can be supported. As a result, communications between such functions do not impose strict precedence constraints and a function is allowed to compute using data produced by another function during the previous reaction instead of the current reaction (delayed communication). Still, the comparison and consolidation must be done on sufficiently "fresh" data. Thus, the number of delayed communications that the functional chain $L_2 = $ `z_acc` $\to$ `o_z_acc` $\to$ `d2` $\to$ `r_a_angle` $\to$ `a_order` can tolerate is bounded by a maximum latency constraint.

The last part of the system, the guidance law (GL), computes a series of accelerations to apply in order to reach a position ordered by the pilot. This is described by the chain $L_3 = $ `p_order` $\to$ `r_lt_acc` $\to$ `r_a_angle` $\to$ `a_order`. This function is temporally less constrained since the required position is reached only after several execution steps (several reactions). The function could even be implemented as a function executed less often than every logical instant. Thus, communications between GL and other functions are flexible.

This illustrates two cases where the communication specification should remain non deterministic (unspecified): (1) when loosely coupled control laws communicate, (2) when there is a global latency imposed over a functional chain; local delays between each component of the chain are not explicitly required and may remain unspecified by the designer, provided that at run time the global end-to-end latency is satisfied.

Allowing such a liberty in the way functions communicate eases the design of large systems that are typically made up of several thousand components (for instance, a flight control system is made up of about 5.000 functional nodes). In such a system, specifying the temporal semantics of all the communications (more than 20.000 in a flight control system) is not humanly reasonable. A better solution would be to let designers specify only for critical communications and to leave the rest unspecified, meaning that he "does not care" whether the communications are immediate or delayed. The second advantage of this liberty is to ease the scheduling as it allows for more parallelism, in particular when the system is implemented on a distributed platform.

Contribution. With existing synchronous languages, the designer must explicitely choose between immediate and delayed communications, even for flexible communications. In this paper we detail how to transform this manual choice into an automated choice included in the compilation process. Notice that we still allow a system to contain explicitly immediate or delayed communications (for instance to memorize the current state of the system requires a delay). The new type of flexible communications comes as an additionnal mechanism, not as a replacement for either immediate or delayed communications.

We define a synchronous language with partial delay specification that provides a higher degree of flexibility during the design phase. We introduce a new operator called "don't care" to specify communications that are allowed to be either immediate or delayed. The semantics of the language is defined formally with a Kahn's semantics in section 2. A program with "don't care" operators is partially non deterministic as it accepts several different behaviours. The language also enables to impose latency constraints expressed as bounds on the number of delays involved in functional chains.

Though the initial specification is non deterministic, we want to generate completely deterministic code in the end, as we are interested in highly critical systems. We propose to translate a program with "don't care" operators into a standard synchronous program that respects the latency requirements imposed on the functional chains and that is causal (meaning that there is no cycle without delay). We have chosen a deterministic syntactic translation (section 3), which either simply drops a "don't care" operator or replaces it by a classic delay operator (the `pre`/`fby` of Lustre/Lucid Synchrone [6,17]). We show that finding a valid translation (choosing where to keep delays) is equivalent to solving a set of pseudo-Boolean constraints and can thus be solved using existing techniques for this widely studied problem.

Related work. Real-time embedded code is often implemented as a set of threads scheduled concurrently by a scheduling policy [3]. These policies focus on ensuring the respect of temporal constraints and do not consider functional determinism as tasks are assumed to be completely independent. We might say that the system behaves as if all data-flows were tagged with a "don't care". There is however an important difference with our language: two different executions of the same system may have different functional behaviours due to timing variations (if a task executes for less than its worst-case execution time for instance). Precedence constraints can be imposed on tasks imposing direct communication and thus ensuring an order between tasks, however we lose the flexibility of the "don't care".

Architecture Description Languages such AADL (*Architecture and Analysis Design Language*) [5], MARTE (*Modeling and Analysis of Real-time and Embedded systems*) [13] or SYSML (*System Modeling Language*) [14] enable to specify detailled communication patterns between functional components. In AADL, data communications are either immediate or delayed. Immediate connections impose a precedence constraint from the producer to the consumer of the data, while delayed communications do not. End-to-end latency constraints can also be imposed on flows (a flow is a path through sub-components of a component). However, the patterns are always fully deterministic and no mechanism allows to handle "don't care" communications. The CCSL language [11] used in MARTE is closer to our work. It enables to specify clock constraints, that is to say constraints on the relation between the activation rates of the different operations of the system. This can yield several different instanciated systems that satisfy the constraints.

In [15] and [10], the authors introduce a methodology to optimise the computation time of synchronous circuits. For a given deterministic specification, the method rewrites the specification into a functionally equivalent one by modifying the equations. To this intent, a synchronous program is represented as a graph where the vertices are functional units and the edges represents the communication between two functional units. The edges are tagged with an integer which represents the number of delay registers required for the communication. The idea of the methodology, called retiming, is to apply graph transformations which insert and remove delays.

In [12], the authors define a non deterministic language based on Input/Output Boolean Automata. The semantics of a non deterministic program is defined as the set of deterministic programs which behaviour is included in the non deterministic ones. This language has a higher expressive power than our data-flow language. The authors then define the product of non deterministic specifications. To convert a non deterministic specification into a deterministic one, the designer needs to define an "oracle" and synchronise the program with this oracle. How to define an oracle is out of the scope of the paper.

2   A Synchronous Language with Partial Delay Specification

In this section, we extend synchronous data-flow languages with the ability to have partial delay specifications using a new *"don't care"* operator.

2.1   Syntax

We define the syntax of a very simple first-order synchronous data-flow language. The language is meant as a proof-of-concept and those concepts should later be included in a larger, more realistic language. The grammar is the following:

$$syst \quad ::= n\_list;$$
$$\textbf{node } N(io) \textbf{ returns } (io) \left[\textbf{ var } io; req\_list; \right] \textbf{ let } eqs \textbf{ tel}$$
$$n\_list ::= \quad imported \; node \; N(io) \; returns \; (io)$$
$$\mid \; imported \; node \; N(io) \; returns \; (io); n\_list$$
$$io \quad ::= id \mid io, id$$
$$eqs \quad ::= eq \mid eqs \; eq$$
$$eq \quad ::= io = exp;$$
$$exp \quad ::= id \mid cst \mid dop(id, \ldots, id) \mid cst \textbf{ fby } id \mid cst \textbf{ dc } id$$

A program (*syst*) is made up of a list of imported nodes (*n_list*) and a unique main node which assembles the set of imported nodes. Imported nodes are black boxes (programmed with other existing languages) that have no side effects on the rest of the program. The program takes a set of inputs, produces a set of outputs and can use local variables. All of these are described by *io*. It is possible to specify a set of requirements (*req_list*). This will be explained in section 2.3. The assembly of imported nodes is described as a set of equations (*eqs*). An equation computes a list of local or output flows using a flow expression (*expr*). A flow expression can be a flow variable (*id*), a constant (*cst*), the application of an imported node (*dop*) on flows, the application of the fby operator (the delay operator of LUCID SYNCHRONE [17]) on a flow. This *"followed by"* operator introduces a delay of one reaction between its input and its output flow (parameter cst is the initialization value for the first reaction, as it has no previous value). Finally an expression can be the application of the new *"partial delay"* operator dc (called "don't care") on a flow. The equation $x = cst$ dc x' can correspond to either $x = x'$ or $x = cst$ fby x' and thus introduces some non determinism. In the first case, the communication between x' and x is immediate and in the second it is delayed. Again, the operator dc can only be applied to identifiers and not to expressions in order to simplify our presentation. Notice that programs contain no hierarchy (no nodes decomposed into other non-imported nodes). Modular compilation/analysis is out of the scope of this paper.

Example 1. Let us illustrate our syntax with the textual version of the flight control system of Figure 1.

```
imported node AL(i1, i2) returns (o);
imported node EL(i1, i2) returns (o);
imported node GL(i1, i2, i3) returns (o1, o2);
...
node FCS(a_angle, y_acc, e_angle, z_acc, p_order)
returns (a_order, e_order)
   var o_e_angle, o_a_angle, r_a_angle, o_y_acc, r_e_angle, o_z_acc,
       lg_fb, r_lg_acc, d1, d2, r_lt_acc, lt_fb,   dc1, dc2, dc3, dc4, dc5, dc6;
let
   o_a_angle = AAF(a_angle);            o_y_acc = YAF(y_acc);
   o_z_acc = ZAF(z_acc);                o_e_angle = EAF(e_angle);
   o_z_acc = ZAF(z_acc);                o_e_angle = EAF(e_angle);
   (lg_fb, d2, r_e_angle) = LgL(dc1, o_z_acc, dc4);
   (r_a_angle, lt_fb, d1) = LtL(dc2, o_y_acc, dc6);
   (r_lt_acc, r_lg_acc) = GL(dc3, dc5, p_order);
   a_order = AL(o_a_angle,r_a_angle);
   e_order = EL(r_e_angle, o_e_angle);
```

```
   dc1 = 0 dc d1;                    dc2 = 0 dc d2;
   dc3 = 1 dc lt_fb;                 dc4 = 0 dc r_lg_acc;
   dc5 = 1 dc lg_fb;                 dc6 = 0 dc r_lt_acc;
  tel
```

At the beginning of the code we declare 9 imported nodes, one for each functional block (we only show 3 declarations here for more conciseness). After that we define the node FCS which takes 4 inputs (a_angle, y_acc, e_angle and z_acc) and returns 2 outputs (a_order and e_order). We also declare a set of local variables which correspond to the variables exchanged between the nodes. The set of equations between **let** and **tel** defines how outputs and local variables are computed from inputs and how imported nodes communicate. To specify the "don't care" communications accordingly to the syntax, we add 6 auxiliary variables ($dc1$ to $dc6$).

Since the language does not include over-sampling or sub-sampling operators (such as `when` or `current`), all the flows are on the same clock (the base logical time). Therefore we do not provide any clock calculus. Mixing sampling operators and *"don't care"* will be studied in future work. All the flows are well initialised because the delay operator (`fby`) includes an initialisation value.

2.2   Kahn's Semantics

We provide a Kahn's semantics [8] for our language, which details the sequence of values corresponding to flow expressions. We introduce the following grammar to represent such sequences:

$$E ::= \{x_1, \ldots, x_n\} \qquad s ::= E.s$$

E is a set of values. $E.s$ denotes the sequence whose head value is non deterministically chosen among the values in E and whose tail is s. We abusively write $v.s$ instead of $\{v\}.s$ to denote a flow whose first value is deterministic. Finally, we define:

$$< E_1.s_1| \ldots |E_n.s_n > = \cup_{1 \leq i \leq n} E_i. < s_1| \ldots |s_n >$$

For any operator $\diamond$, $\diamond^\#(p_1, \ldots, p_n) = s$ means that the operator $\diamond$ applied to parameters $p_1, \ldots, p_n$ produces the sequence s. Let $\prod_{i=1}^{n} E_i = E_1 \times \ldots \times E_n$ denote the cartesian product of the sets E_i. The semantics of flow expressions is given with:

$$cst^\# \qquad\qquad = cst.cst^\#$$

$$imp^\#(E_1.s_1, \ldots, E_m.s_m) = \cup_{t \in \prod_{i=1}^{m} E_i} \{imp(t)\}.imp^\#(s_1, \ldots, s_m)$$

$$\mathtt{fby}^\#(cst, s) \qquad\qquad = cst.s^\#$$

$$\mathtt{dc}^\#(cst, s) \qquad\qquad = < \mathtt{fby}^\#(cst, s)|s^\# >$$

1. The first rule describes the constant: it simply produces a flow that always has the same value.

2. The second rule is the call of an imported node. At each step of the sequence, we may take as input for the node any combination of the non deterministic values of its inputs (any tuple in the cartesian product of the possible head values of each input) and then we apply the imported node to each combination. In other words, we simply apply an imported node point-by-point on the sequence of values of its inputs.
3. The third rule is for the fby operator. It simply concatenates the initialisation value to the flow, thus delaying each value of the input flow by one reaction.
4. The last rule is for the dc operator. It introduces non-determinism by stating that the dc operator can either be replaced by a fby or by the identity.

Example 2. We illustrate the semantics in an example where the imported node *plus* simply computes the addition of the two inputs.

```
imported node plus (i1,i2) returns (o);
node ex (i) returns (o)
var v1, v2;
let
    v1 = 0 dc i;
    v2 = 1 fby v1;
    o = plus(v1, v2);
tel
```

i	5	3	7	...
v_1	$\{0,5\}$	$\{5,3\}$	$\{3,7\}$	
v_2	$\{1\}$	$\{0,5\}$	$\{5,3\}$	
o	$\{1,6\}$	$\{3,5,8,10\}$	$\{6,8,10,12\}$	

2.3 Latency Requirements

Let $x \xrightarrow{0} x'$ denote that the variable x' immediately depends on the variable x. Similarly, $x \xrightarrow{1} x'$ denotes a delayed dependency and $x \xrightarrow{?} x'$ a "don't care" dependency. Let $x \to x' \overset{def}{\Leftrightarrow} x \xrightarrow{0} x' \vee x \xrightarrow{1} x' \vee x \xrightarrow{?} x'$. Let $Var_0(e)$ denote the variables that appear free in e and not as an argument of a fby or a dc, $Var_1(e)$ those that are an argument of a fby and $Var_?(e)$ those argument of a dc. Given a program p and $c \in \{0,1,?\}$, we have $x \xrightarrow{c} x'$ in p iff there is an equation $io = e$ in p such that $x' \in io$ and $x \in Var_c(e)$.

Definition 1 (Functional chain). *A functional chain* $(x_1, \ldots, x_n)$ *is a list of flow variables such that* $\forall 1 \le i < n$, $x_i \to x_{i+1}$.

Example 3. Let us consider again the program ex of example 2. There are two chains from the input i to the output o: $L = (i, v_1, v_2, o)$ and $L' = (i, v_1, o)$.

The latency of a functional chain is the number of delays of the chain. Latency constraints impose a bound on this number and are in most cases maximum latency constraints, i.e. constraints of the form $Lat(x_1 \ldots x_n) < k$, where $k \in \mathbb{N}^*$ and $(x_1 \ldots x_n)$ is a functional chain. Our approach can however support constraints where $<$ is replaced by any other comparison operator. In a program, latency constraints are specified using the keyword req.

Example 4. The flight control system specified in example 1 contains several chains. The requirements on those mentioned in the introduction are:

```
req (z_acc, o_z_acc, d2, dc2, r_a_angle, a_order) < 1; --L2
req (p_order, r_lt_acc, dc6, r_a_angle, a_order) < 4; --L3
```

3   Concretisation of an Abstract Program

We propose a compilation scheme in two steps: a) Translate the specification
into a standard deterministic synchronous data-flow program; b) Apply a synchronous compiler. The second step is well studied [7] and is out of the scope of
this paper. This section describes the first step, which consists in choosing one
program among the different deterministic synchronous programs which semantics is included in the semantics of the original non deterministic program. The
compiler performs a *purely syntactic* translation that replaces each "don't care"
operator either by a direct communication or by a delayed communication.

3.1   Instance Space

Non deterministic programs are called *abstract* programs, while deterministic
ones are called *concrete* programs.

Definition 2. *A system (or a program) is said* concrete *if and only if it contains
no* dc *operations, otherwise it is* abstract.

Example 5. The abstract program ex given in example 2 corresponds to several
concrete versions. If the "don't care" operator is syntactically translated into
either the identity or the fby operator, there are 2 solutions (ex1 and ex2). A
more complex solution (not supported in our approach) would be to interleave
direct and delayed communications (for instance, ex3).

```
node ex1 (i) returns (o)        node ex2 (i) returns (o)
var v1, v2;                     var v1, v2;
let                             let
   v1 = i;                         v1 = 0 fby i;
   v2 = 1 fby v1;                  v2 = 1 fby v1;
   o = plus(v1, v2);               o = plus(v1, v2);
tel                             tel
```

```
node ex3 (i) returns (o)
var v1, v2, j;
let
   j = true fby (not j);
   v1 = if j then i
           else (0 fby i);
   v2 = 1 fby v1;
   o = plus(v1, v2);
tel
```

Let *sys* denote an abstract system. Let $\text{dc}(sys) = \{dc_1, \ldots, dc_n\}$ denote the
ordered set of dc operators in *sys* (we take the chronological apparition order
of the operators in the set of equations). Let $p = (dc_i \mapsto \text{fby})sys$ denote the
program p resulting of the substitution of operator dc_i by a fby operator in *sys*.
Similarly, $(dc_i \mapsto id)sys$ denotes the substitution of dc_i by the identity operator
and $(dc_x \mapsto op, \ldots, dc_y \mapsto op)sys$ denotes the program resulting of the set of
substitutions $dc_x \mapsto op, \ldots, dc_y \mapsto op$ (where op is either fby or the identity).

Definition 3 (Instance). *Let p be a concrete system and sys be an abstract
program such that* $\text{dc}(sys) = \{dc_1, \ldots, dc_n\}$. *$p$ is an instance of sys iff there
exists a set of substitutions $dc_1 \mapsto op_1, \ldots, dc_n \mapsto op_n$ such that:*

$$p = (dc_1 \mapsto op_1, \ldots, dc_n \mapsto op_n)sys$$

*In the following, $sys[b_1, \ldots, b_n]$ denotes the instance $p = (sub_1, \ldots, sub_n)sys$
such that:*

$$\begin{cases} sub_i = dc_i \mapsto id & \text{if } b_i = 0 \\ sub_i = dc_i \mapsto \text{fby} & \text{if } b_i = 1 \end{cases}$$

Example 6. The program ex has two instances as shown in example 5, with ex1=ex[0] and ex2=ex[1].

Let us denote by $\mathcal{I}(sys)$ the set of instances of the system $sys(dc_1, \ldots, dc_n)$. We define the relation $\sqsubseteq_{sys}$ between instances of sys as follows:

Definition 4. *Let $p = sys[n_1, \ldots, n_m]$ and $p' = sys[n_1', \ldots, n_m']$ be two instances of sys:*

$$p \sqsubseteq_{sys} p' \overset{def}{\iff} \forall i \leq m, n_i' \leq n_i$$

In other words, dc communications are "more immediate" in p' than in p.

Proposition 1. *$(\mathcal{I}(sys), \sqsubseteq_{sys})$ is a finite lattice in which the top element is $sys[0, \ldots, 0]$ (all dc communications are immediate) and the bottom element is $sys[1, \ldots, 1]$ (all dc communications are delayed).*

This is a very classical example of a Boolean lattice. We use a Hasse diagram to represent the lattice $(\mathcal{I}(sys), \sqsubseteq_{sys})$. In such a diagram, each element of $\mathcal{I}(sys)$ is a vertex and there is an upward edge from s to s' whenever $s \sqsubseteq s'$ and there is no s'' such that $s \sqsubseteq s'' \sqsubseteq s'$. Notice that $(\mathcal{I}(sys), \sqsubseteq_{sys})$ is a n-dimensional hypercube.

Example 7. The instance space of the simplified flight control system $FCS(dc1, dc2, dc3, dc4, dc5, dc6)$ is described by the 6-dimensional hypercube:

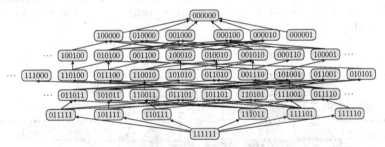

3.2   Valid Instance Space

Only a subset of the instances of an abstract program are valid. We say that an instance p of sys is *valid* if and only if 1) p is causal and 2) p satisfies all the latency requirements of the system. Part 1) ensures that the instance is implementable (by checking that the instance does not contain an data-dependency cycle). However, not all implementable instances satisfy latency requirements, thus we also need to check 2).

Respecting latency requirements. Let us first define formally the latency of a functional chain.

Definition 5. *Let sys be a system and $(x_1, \ldots, x_n)$ be a functional chain of sys. The latency of the chain in sys is defined inductively as:*

$$Lat_{sys}(x_1,\ldots,x_n) = \begin{cases} 1 + Lat_{sys}(x_1,\ldots,x_{n-1}) & \text{if } x_{n-1} \xrightarrow{1} x_n \\ Lat_{sys}(x_1,\ldots,x_{n-1}) & \text{if } x_{n-1} \xrightarrow{0} x_n \text{ or } x_{n-1} \xrightarrow{?} x_n \end{cases}$$

with $Lat_{sys}() = 0$, where $()$ is the empty functional chain.

Example 8. For program ex and the chain $L = (i, v_1, v_2, o)$, $Lat_{ex}(L) = Lat_{ex1}(L) = 1$ and $Lat_{ex2}(L) = 2$.

We say that dc_i *is involved in* C if there exists two variables x, x' in C such that $x \xrightarrow{?} x'$ and dc_i is the dc operator between x and x'. The following proposition details how the latency of a chain is computed for a given instance.

Proposition 2. *Let* $sys(dc_1,\ldots,dc_n)$ *be an abstract system, let* C *be a functional chain of sys and let* $p = sys[b_1,\ldots,b_n]$ *be an instance of sys. We have*

1. $Lat_p(C) = \sum_{j=1}^{l} b_{i_j} + Lat_{sys}(C)$, *where the operators* dc_{i_j} *are those involved in* C, $l \le n$ *and for all* i_j, $1 \le i_j \le n$.
2. *If* p' *is another instance such that* $p \sqsubseteq p'$: $Lat_p(C) < k \implies Lat_{p'}(C) < k$

This proposition allows us to partition the instance space into two sets: the instances satisfying the requirements and those which do not.

Example 9. The flight control system Figure 1 has to satisfy the requirement $R = Lat(z\_acc, o\_z\_acc, d2, dc2, r\_a\_angle, a\_order) < 1$. The partitioning is depicted below.

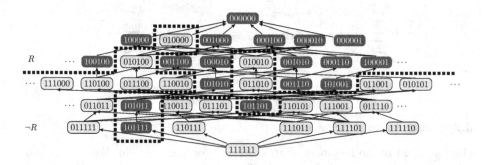

Causality. A program is causal if it does not contain instantaneous data-dependency cycles. A non-causal program must be rejected because we cannot find a computation order that satisfies all data-dependencies. As a consequence, in a concrete program data-dependency cycles are allowed only if they contain a fby.

Definition 6. *The functional chain* $C = (x_1,\ldots,x_n,x_1)$ *is a dc-cycle iff:*

$$\exists i, 1 \le i \le n, x_i \xrightarrow{?} x_{(i \bmod n)+1}$$

Example 10. The following program contains a cycle where a `dc` is involved:

```
imported node n1 (i1,i2) returns (o);
node causal (i) returns (o)
var v1;
let
  o = n1(i,v1);
  v1 = 0 dc o;
tel
```

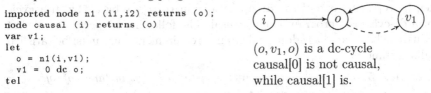

(o, v_1, o) is a dc-cycle
causal[0] is not causal,
while causal[1] is.

Definition 7. *Let* $sys(dc_1, \ldots, dc_n)$ *be an abstract system.*

1. *sys is* strongly causal *if all its instances are causal.*
2. *sys is* weakly causal *if sys admits at least one causal instance.*
3. *sys is* non-causal *if it admits no causal instance.*

Example 11. The program **ex** of example 2 is strongly causal since there is no cycle in the data dependency graph. **causal** of example 10 is weakly causal.

Proposition 3. *Let* $sys(dc_1, \ldots, dc_n)$ *be an abstract system,*

1. *If sys is strongly causal, then sys is also weakly causal.*
2. *sys is strongly causal if and only if* $sys[0, \ldots, 0]$ *is causal.*
3. *sys is weakly causal if and only if* $sys[1, \ldots, 1]$ *is causal.*

Proposition 4. *Let* $sys(dc_1, \ldots, dc_n)$ *be an abstract system. Let* p *and* p' *be two instances of sys such that* $p \sqsubseteq p'$. *Then if* p' *is causal, so is* p.

Proof. If $p \sqsubseteq p'$, for all equations $io = e$, we have $Var_1^{p'}(e) \subseteq Var_1^p(e)$. Thus, the dependency graph of p is a sub graph of the one of p'. If p' is causal, it means that the dependency graph of p' is acyclic and so is any subgraph.

As a consequence, the Hasse diagram of a system can be partitioned into two sets: a "south" partition which contains the causal instances of *sys* and a "north" partition which contains the non causal instances of *sys*.

Example 12. If we consider again the flight control system Figure 1, the graph of instances of this system can be partitioned as shown below. As a result, the set of valid instances of the abstract program is the intersection of the causal instances with the black instances in figure of example 9. There are 4 valid instances: 101111, 101011, 101010, 101101.

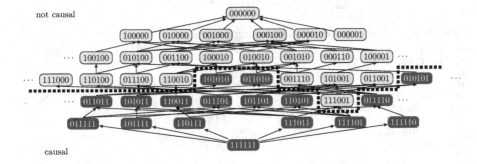

If a cycle is a dc-cycle, it is possible to find an instance p where this cycle is broken by replacing one of the dc operations in the cycle by a fby. If a cycle is not a dc-cycle the program is not causal. The following property shows that causality can be treated as additional latency requirements that must be satisfied by valid instances:

Proposition 5. *Let sys be an abstract system, p be an instance of sys, $C = (x_1, \ldots, x_n, x_1)$ be a dc-cycle in sys:*

$$C \text{ is a cycle in } p \Leftrightarrow Lat_p(C) = 0.$$

3.3 Generation of Valid Instances

Finding a valid instance p of $sys(dc_1, \ldots, dc_n)$ consists in finding a valuation $sys[b_1, \ldots, b_n]$ which satisfies the latency constraints explicitly specified in the node definition and the constraints generated by the causality analysis. If there exists several solutions, we arbitrarily choose one among them (there is no notion of "better" solution). In this section, we show that we can solve this problem by translating it into a pseudo-Boolean problem, which enables us to reuse existing solvers, such as SAT4J [9] for instance.

Let sys be a system with several latency requirements of the form $L = Lat(C) \sim k$ (where $\sim \in \{<, >\}$). According to proposition 2, an instance p of sys satisfies L if and only if:

$$\sum_{j=1}^{l} b_{i_j} \sim k - Lat_{sys}(C)$$

where dc_{i_j} are the dc operators involved in the chain $(x_{i_1}, \ldots, x_{i_l})$ and $b_{i_j} \in \{0, 1\}$. Thus, the set of latency constraints can be translated into a conjunction of linear pseudo-Boolean constraints of this form. The variables of the pseudo-Boolean problem are the b_{i_j} and $k - Lat_{sys}(C)$ can be considered as a constant as it does not depend on instance p.

The causality analysis can also be translated into pseudo-Boolean constraints. We enumerate the elementary cycles of the form $C = (x_{i_1}, \ldots, x_{i_m}, x_{i_1})$ of the data-dependency graph of sys using a classic cycle detection algorithm such as that of Tarjan [18]. According to proposition 5, a cycle C will be avoided (broken) if and only if:

$$\sum_{j=1}^{l} b_{i_j} + Lat_{sys}(x_{i_1}, \ldots, x_{i_m}, x_{i_1}) > 0$$

Example 13. Let us consider the following program:

```
node trad (i) returns (o1,o2)
req (i,v1,v2,v3,o2) < 3;
var v1, v2, v3;
let
    o1 = n1(i,v1);
    v1 = 0 dc o1; --dc1
    v2 = 0 dc v1; --dc2
    v3 = 0 fby v2;
    o2 = n2(v2);
tel
```

The set of constraints is

$$\begin{cases} b1 + b2 + 1 < 3 \\ b1 > 0 \end{cases}$$

3.4 Implementation

To implement the valid instance search, we could proceed as follows:

1. Translate latency constraints into pseudo-Boolean (PB) constraints;
2. For each cycle, add a PB constraint to break the cycle;
3. Solve the whole set of PB constraints.

However, the enumeration of the cycles of a graph is a problem with exponential time-complexity (even though the complexity of Tarjan's algorithm is close to polynomial when the number of cycles is small). Thus, instead we use an iterative process, described in Algorithm 1: we ask the PB-solver for a solution, if the solution is non-causal we add a PB constraint to break a cycle and iterate. With this solution, we do not enumerate all cycles, because breaking one cycle often breaks several other cycles. Experiments suggest that we actually only perform a polynomial number of iterations (even in worst cases), but this remains a conjecture that needs to be proved in future works.

Algorithm 1. Implementation of the valid instance search

Translate latency constraints into pseudo-Boolean constraints.
Check the causality for non-dc cycles only[1].
while The PB-solver finds a solution to the constraints **do**
    if The solution is not-causal **then**
        Add a PB constraint to break the first cycle we find
    else
        We have found a valid instance, return the solution.
    end if
end while

We have implemented an OCaml prototype, which translates a specification with partial delays into a valid synchronous program. The compilation process is shown in Figure 2. The compiler first takes an abstract program and generates the corresponding pseudo-Boolean problem. The problem is then solved using the solver SAT4J [9]. There may be several iterations between the solver and the compiler so that the compiler checks the causality of the solution returned by the solver. Finally, the compiler produces the valid instance corresponding to the final solution returned by the solver.

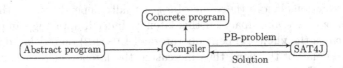

Fig. 2. The compilation process

We have experimented the compiler on several examples and in particular an avionic application similar to the one presented in [2]. It is made up of 3994 imported nodes and 16186 variables. We made the experiments by duplicating all the variables with a "don't care" variable. If we do not specify any latency requirements, the compiler produces the trivial solution where all dc are replaced by a fby. We then generate some latency requirements to have an overview of the performance of the compiler. The time needed to parse the file is about 1 second. The experiments were made on a Linux machine with 4 GB of memory. We make 10 different benchmarks on each point. These first results are very promising because they show that the method scales well on a representative case study.

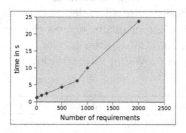

4   Conclusion and Perspectives

In this paper we have presented an extension of a synchronous data-flow language with a new operator (dc), which enables to specify communications that can either be immediate or delayed. We also introduced the possibility to specify latency requirements. We have detailled how a high level specification containing dc can be translated into a classic synchronous program without dc, taking latency and causality constraints into account.

There are several open questions and future works. First, experiments show that we should ease the specification of latency requirement. For instance we could introduce some kind of pattern matching, e.g. to compute all functional chains matching with (i,*,v,*,o).

Second, we need to study the problem complexity when considering only latency requirements of the form $Lat(\mathcal{C}) \leq k$. In that case, we have a conjection of slighly less general constraints of the form $\Sigma a_j \leq k$ and $\Sigma a_j > 0$.

The third perspective concerns the extension with sampling operators. If we define the exact latency of a functionnal chain $(x_1, \ldots, x_m)$ as the maximum number of reactions before the value of x_m actually depends on x_1, then sampling operators have an impact on this latency. Indeed, applying sampling operators (such as the when/current operators of LUSTRE) on a delayed flow can increase the delay of the flow, thus increasing the latency of the chains it belongs to. The effect of general Boolean sampling operators on latencies is hard to analyse: latencies may fluctuate with the sampling condition and even be unpredictable if the condition is an input flow. Instead, we could focus on more restrictive sampling operators that can be analysed more efficiently, such as the *strictly periodic clock* sampling operators of PRELUDE [16]. On the contrary to Boolean sampling operators, latencies should be constant and computable fully statically.

Acknowledgment. The authors would like to thank Jean-Louis Colaço for his careful analysis and help for improving this work.

References

1. Benveniste, A., Caspi, P., Edwards, S.A., Halbwachs, N., Le Guernic, P., de Simone, R.: The synchronous languages 12 years later. Proceedings of the IEEE 91(1), 64–83 (2003)
2. Boniol, F., Hladik, P.-E., Pagetti, C., Aspro, F., Jégu, V.: A Framework for Distributing Real-Time Functions. In: Cassez, F., Jard, C. (eds.) FORMATS 2008. LNCS, vol. 5215, pp. 155–169. Springer, Heidelberg (2008)
3. Cottet, F., Delacroix, J., Kaiser, C., Mammeri, Z.: Scheduling in real-time systems. John Wiley & Sons (October 2002)
4. Dormoy, F.-X.: Scade 6 a model based solution for safety critical software development. In: Embedded Real-Time Systems Conference, ERTS 2008 (2008)
5. Feiler, P.H., Gluch, D.P., Hudak, J.J.: The architecture analysis & design language (AADL): An introduction. Technical Report CMU/SEI-2006-TN-011, Software Engineering Institute, Carnegie Mellon University (February 2006)
6. Halbwachs, N., Lagnier, F., Ratel, C.: Programming and verifying real-time systems by means of the synchronous data-flow language lustre. IEEE Trans. Software Eng. 18(9), 785–793 (1992)
7. Halbwachs, N., Raymond, P., Ratel, C.: Generating Efficient Code from Data-Flow Programs. In: Małuszyński, J., Wirsing, M. (eds.) PLILP 1991. LNCS, vol. 528, pp. 207–218. Springer, Heidelberg (1991)
8. Kahn, G.: The semantics of simple language for parallel programming. In: IFIP Congress, pp. 471–475 (1974)
9. Le Berre, D., Parrain, A.: The sat4j library, release 2.2 system description. Journal on Satisfiability, Boolean Modeling and Computation 7, 59–64 (2010)
10. Leiserson, C.E., Saxe, J.B.: Optimizing synchronous systems. In: 22nd Annual Symposium on Foundations of Computer Science, SFCS 1981, pp. 23–36. IEEE (1981)
11. Mallet, F., DeAntoni, J., André, C., de Simone, R.: The clock constraint specification language for building timed causality models. Innovations in Systems and Software Engineering 6, 99–106 (2010), doi:10.1007/s11334-009-0109-0
12. Maraninchi, F., Halbwachs, N.: Compositional Semantics of Non-Deterministic Synchronous Languages. In: Riis Nielson, H. (ed.) ESOP 1996. LNCS, vol. 1058, pp. 235–249. Springer, Heidelberg (1996)
13. OMG. A UML profile for MARTE. Technical report, Object Management Group, Inc. (2007)
14. OMG. Systems modeling language. Technical report, Object Management Group, Inc. (2010)

15. O'Neil, T.W., Tongsima, S., Sha, E.H.-M.: Optimal scheduling of data-flow graphs using extended retiming. In: Proceedings of the ISCA 12th International Conference on Parallel and Distributed Computing Systems, pp. 292–297 (1999)
16. Pagetti, C., Forget, J., Boniol, F., Cordovilla, M., Lesens, D.: Multi-task implementation of multi-periodic synchronous programs. Discrete Event Dynamic Systems 21(3), 307–338 (2011)
17. Pouzet, M.: Lucid Synchrone, version 3. Tutorial and reference manual. Université Paris-Sud, LRI (2006)
18. Tarjan, R.E.: Enumeration of the elementary circuits of a directed graph. SIAM J. Comput. 2(3), 211–216 (1973)

Concurrent Test Generation Using Concolic Multi-trace Analysis

Niloofar Razavi[1,2], Franjo Ivančić[1], Vineet Kahlon[1], and Aarti Gupta[1]

[1] NEC Laboratories America
[2] University of Toronto

Abstract. Discovering concurrency bugs is inherently hard due to the nondeterminism in multi-thread scheduling. Predictive analysis techniques have been successfully used to find such bugs by observing given test runs, and then searching for other interesting thread interleavings. For sequential code, concolic execution techniques have been used successfully to generate interesting test inputs to increase structural code coverage such as branch or statement coverage. In this paper, we propose the use of a concolic multi-trace analysis (CMTA) to efficiently increase code coverage in concurrent programs. We have implemented CMTA, and show encouraging results for some interesting benchmark programs.

1 Introduction

Given the omnipresence of software in today's society, there is a great need to develop technologies that target effective verification technologies for software. In industry, software testing and coverage-based metrics are still the predominant techniques to find correctness and performance issues in software systems. Recently, there has been extensive interest in both sequential test generation methods as well as predictive testing for concurrent programs. This paper seeks to extend test input generation methods used in sequential programs with predictive analysis for the concurrent setting.

Sequential Concolic Execution. In the past decade, there has been extensive interest in *concolic execution* for automatically generating tests to increase path coverage of sequential programs [2,8,19]. These techniques combine symbolic execution for path exploration with powerful satisfiability modulo theory (SMT) solvers [4,5] to compute inputs to previously unexplored branches or paths. To allow for a scalable and complete branch or path exploration, these techniques generally fall back upon concrete values observed during execution to handle non-linear computations or calls to external library functions, for which no good symbolic representation is available. The term concolic execution captures the combination of concrete and symbolic path exploration [19].

Predictive Analysis for Concurrency. Discovering concurrency bugs – often called *Heisenbugs*[15] – is inherently hard due to the nondeterminism in multi-thread scheduling. One approach to discover concurrency bugs is based on systematic testing using stateless model checking [7,15]. Another popular approach uses predictive analysis techniques (see, for example, [3,23,24]). In predictive analysis, concurrency bugs are targeted by first observing multi-threaded execution traces *on a given test input*. Assume that the observed execution trace did not violate any embedded checks for concurrency

R. Jhala and A. Igarashi (Eds.): APLAS 2012, LNCS 7705, pp. 239–255, 2012.

issues, such as assertions, NULL pointer dereferences, deadlocks, or data races. Predictive analysis then tries to statically find a feasible permutation of the concurrent events of the observed trace, such that the permuted trace violates some property.

Concolic Multi-trace Analysis. This paper addresses the test generation problem for concurrent multi-threaded programs. We are primarily concerned with generating tests that will increase structural coverage of such programs. Thus, we are not necessarily interested in covering all possible thread interleavings unless this would increase structural coverage as well. However, having generated a set of relevant test inputs, it is always possible to perform a full predictive analysis as discussed above for each such test input. For sake of brevity, we do not further discuss this extension.

We are interested in exploiting *interesting def-use pairs*, where a definition (def) represents a write of a shared variable in some thread, and a use represents a read of that variable in some other thread. We are interested to search over the space of such def-use pairs – however, in practice, this may not scale very well even with partial order reduction based on conflicting accesses. We exploit the fact that many different tests (inputs or schedules) may already be available or are easy to generate. By observing already available test runs for various writes to shared variables, we are then able to select parts of previously observed tests, and interject them into other tests to target previously unseen def-use pairs, thereby leading to new interesting concurrent program behaviors. In the following, we will call previously observed multi-threaded execution fragments that end in a write to a shared variable as *interlopers*.

Given this intuition, we have to address two issues: (1) How to generate an interesting set of test inputs and thread schedules to start with, if none is provided; and (2) how to efficiently search for feasible interlopers that may result in new relevant def-use pairs. In this work, we focus on branch coverage. We are interested in def-use pairs that lead to previously uncovered branches. To address the first question, we rely on sequential test generation methods – i.e., we generate inputs preventing context switching. To address the second question, we develop the concolic multi-trace analysis described below.

This paper utilizes the fact that state-of-the-art sequential test generation methods are generally able to quickly cover a large part of the program in terms of branches even for concurrent programs. Indeed, the branches of the concurrent program that are not covered using sequential methods alone are often due to *interesting* synchronizations between threads of the concurrent program that are worth exploring deeper. By focusing on such branches after all *sequentially coverable* branches are reached, we are able to explore synchronization related branches. Like predictive analysis, we look for alternate interleavings of observed events, but in *multiple traces*, not a single trace. Furthermore, we use a concolic approach to also generate alternate test inputs that can cover a branch or a target path. Thus, we try to cover branches or paths by generating appropriate SMT queries where the solver tries to find both a particular thread schedule and a required test input. Finally, note that in an *active testing framework* [9], many runtime bugs can be encoded as branches that we try to cover as part of structural code coverage.

Overview of the Approach. Our high-level test input generation method is outlined in Figure 1. We alternate between sequential test generation methods and our novel *concolic multi-trace analysis (CMTA)* described shortly. We use sequential test generation

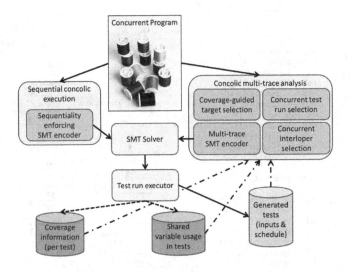

Fig. 1. Overview of test generation procedure

methods as long as they are able to increase coverage on individual threads. In our case, we adapted the concolic execution tool CREST [1] as the test input generator. Upon coverage saturation, we use CMTA to generate new test inputs and thread schedules to cover previously uncovered branches in one of the threads. After generating new test inputs and thread schedules using CMTA, we then try to extend these new tests using sequential test generation again. This means, we follow the generated test in terms of inputs and schedule up to the previously uncovered branch in some thread T_i. Then, given that a new branch in thread T_i was covered, we try to further explore potentially other previously uncovered parts of the program by exploring continuations of the test only along the thread T_i, i.e. without allowing additional context switches.

We use concolic multi-trace analysis (CMTA) to find a new thread schedule *and* new test inputs to cover a previously unreached branch. First, we select a target branch of interest, and corresponding traces that have been previously observed to come *close* to the target branch. Note that each previously observed trace has a given test input and thread schedule that it followed. As shown in Figure 1, we also remember for each test run which statements and branches in each thread are traversed, as well as the shared variables that are written to during the test. Assume that the uncovered branch depends on some set of shared variables S. Generally, the test condition may not be in terms of shared variables, but by intra-thread value tracing, we can obtain S. We then choose candidate *interloper trace segments* from the set of so-far obtained traces, such that the interloper trace segments result in a shared variable state over S that satisfies the condition on the target branch. Note, that these interloper segments may contain executions of multiple threads. We can apply filtering heuristics to choose an *appropriate* interloper segment to insert into one of the runs that came close to the target branch. Then, we formulate an SMT problem that tries to find a viable test input and thread schedule of the modified original run, which also contains the chosen interloper segment.

```
#define ADD 0              void func(int action){
#define STOP 1             m1if (action == ADD) {
pthread_t t1, t2;          m2:    int status = -1;
int pendingIO = 1;         m3:    if(!stoppingFlag){
bool stopped = false;      m4:       pendingIO++;
bool stoppingFlag =        m5:       status = 0;
      false;                      }
bool stoppingEvent =       m6:    if (status==0) {
      false;               m7:       if (stopped)
int ac1, ac2;              m8:          assert(false);
                           m9:          //do actual work
                                 }
main(int* arg) {           m10:   pendingIO–;
  ac1 = arg[0];                   ...
  ac2 = arg[1];            n2: }else if(action==STOP){
  pthread_create(&t1,      n3:    stoppingFlag = true;
      func, &ac1);         n4:    pendingIO–;
  pthread_create(&t2,      n5:    if (pendingIO == 0)
      func,&ac2);          n6:       stoppingEvent=true;
  pthread_join(t1);        n7:    assume(stoppingEvent);
  pthread_join(t2);        n8:    stopped = true;
}                                }
                           }
```

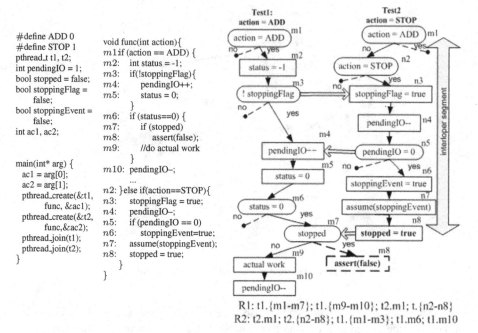

R1: t1.{m1-m7}; t1.{m9-m10}; t2.m1; t.{n2-n8}
R2: t2.m1; t2.{n2-n8}; t1.{m1-m3}; t1.m6; t1.m10

Fig. 2. A test driver for testing Bluetooth driver (from [16]). Test1 and Test2 are two tests generated in sequential testing of each thread.

Motivating Example. We illustrate the main steps of our procedure using the following example. Figure 2 shows a test driver for a simplified version of a Bluetooth driver (from [16]). Function func gets an input, named action, which defines whether the operating system wants to perform I/O in the driver (action = ADD) or to stop the device (action = STOP). The test driver consists of two threads calling func concurrently with their own inputs. There are four shared variables: pendingIO, stoppingFlag, stoppingEvent, and stopped. The variable pendingIO is initialized to 1 and keeps track of the number of concurrently executing threads in the driver. The boolean variable stoppingFlag is initialized to false and will be set to true to signal the closing of the device. New threads are not supposed to enter the driver once stoppingFlag is set to true. Variable stoppingEvent is initialized to false, and will be set to true after pendingIO becomes zero. Finally, stopped is initialized to false and the thread stopping the driver sets it to true after it is established that there are no other threads running in the driver. Threads that perform I/O in the driver expect stopped to be false (assertion at line m8) after entering the driver.

Suppose sequential concolic testing of each thread generates two tests, Test1 and Test2, in which action is set to ADD and STOP, respectively. Figure 2 shows the paths taken in the control flow graph of function func under these two tests (for now, ignore the arrows between the graphs). So far, we cannot cover the assertion at line m8 since the corresponding if-branch at line m7 is not covered, i.e., stopped is always false at m7. Our concurrent test generation approach attempts to find appropriate inputs and thread schedules to cover the if-branch at line $m7$. Suppose that with the sequential tests ac1 = ADD and ac2 = STOP, we get two runs of the program: R1, in which thread t1 is executed sequentially before thread t2, and R2 in which t2 is executed before t1.

We now pick a run reaching the if-statement at $m7$ – assume R1 in this case – and look for a variable that affects the condition of the if-statement (i.e., stopped). Next, we pick a different run which assigns a value to it – assume R2 in this case. Then, we search for an interloper segment from R2, that has an assignment to stopped as its last event, and that can be inserted before the read from stopped in the corresponding if-statement in R1. To make it insertable, we require that the location of t2 in R1 at the insertion point is the same as the location at the beginning of the interloper segment. (This is necessary, but not sufficient.) Since t2 is always at $m1$ in R1 before the if-statement, the interloper segment is selected as shown in the figure. Then, a multi-trace predictive analysis is performed to symbolically encode a set of feasible runs, where the interloper segment is inserted in R1 and the if-branch at line $m7$ is taken. The encoding is detailed in Section 4.2. We use a state-of-the-art SMT solver [5] to find solutions to such queries. Each solution corresponds to a thread schedule and a test input.

Our test generation approach covers the if-branch at line $m7$ (and the assertion violation). It generates inputs ac1=ADD and ac2=STOP and a schedule where the statements at $m3$, $n5$, and $n8$ are executed before statements at $n3$, $m4$, and $m7$, respectively, to ensure the if-branches at $m3$, $n5$, and $m7$ will be taken. The arrows between the two sequential paths in Figure 2 represent these orderings in the predicted run.

Contributions. This paper makes the following novel contributions:

☐ We try to increase structural code coverage for concurrent programs by generating new test inputs and thread schedules that are extensions/compositions of previously observed test runs. We look for *uses* (variable reads) of shared variables that lead to previously uncovered code parts, and then find appropriate *defs* (variable writes) in some other test runs that may feasibly be intertwined.

☐ To do so, we formulate the intertwining of multiple multi-threaded runs as an SMT problem, in a manner similar to concolic execution with predictive analysis to simultaneously consider alternate test inputs and thread schedules.

☐ Unlike previous extensions of concolic execution to concurrent programs based on global program structure, our approach targets branch coverage on the code of each individual thread. We believe this is inherently more scalable. Our search is guided by selection heuristics, providing a *relatively complete predictive* exploration in the limit (which we want to avoid in practice).

☐ We implemented the technique in a test generation tool to generate tests and schedules for concurrent programs. We show that the technique can successfully generate interesting tests, thus increasing structural code coverage.

Paper Outline. Next, we present some preliminaries. Section 3 shows how we utilize sequential concolic test generation. Then, we present how we use the generated sequential tests to improve branch coverage using concurrent test generation in Section 4. In Section 5, we discuss a theoretical extension to achieve *relative completeness* in prediction from observed test runs. Section 6 presents additional related work. In Section 7, encouraging experimental evidence of the proposed approach are discussed.

2 Preliminaries

2.1 Programs and Execution Traces

A *concurrent program* has a finite set of *threads* and a finite set SV of *shared variables*. Each thread T_i, where $1 \leq i \leq k$, has a finite set of *local variables* LV_i. Let $Tid = \{1, \ldots, k\}$ be the set of thread indices and $V_i = SV \cup LV_i$, where $1 \leq i \leq k$, be the set of variables accessible in T_i. Each thread T_i executes a set of program statements. Each program statement has a unique identifier and can be of one of the following forms:

- $(\mathsf{assume}(c), asgn)$ is the atomic *guarded assignment*, where
  - $asgn$ is a set of assignments, each of the form $v := exp$, where $v \in V_i$ is a variable and exp is an expression over V_i.
  - $\mathsf{assume}(c)$ means the conditional expression c over V_i must be true for the assignments in $asgn$ to execute.
- $\mathsf{assert}(c)$ is the assertion action. The conditional expression c over V_i must be true when the event is executed; otherwise, an error is raised.

The guarded assignment $(\mathsf{assume}(c), asgn)$ may have the following variants: (1) when $c = \mathsf{true}$, it can represent normal assignments; (2) when the assignment set is empty, $\mathsf{assume}(c)$ itself can represent the then-branch of an `if(c)`-statement, while $\mathsf{assume}(\neg c)$ can represent the else-branch; and (3) with both guard and assignments, it can represent an atomic *check-and-set*, which is the foundation for synchronization primitives. In particular, we precisely capture the semantics of all synchronization primitives in the standard *PThreads* library. For example, acquiring lock lk in thread T_i is modeled as $(\mathsf{assume}(lk = 0), \{lk := i\})$, where i is the thread id; and acquiring the counting semaphore se is modeled as $(\mathsf{assume}(se > 0), \{se := se - 1\})$.

Let $stmtIds$ represent the set of statement identifiers in the program. We assume that each statement is executed atomically. We refer to the execution of statements as *events*. An *event* $e \in \rho$ is a tuple $\langle tid, loc \rangle$, where $tid \in Tid$ is a thread index, $loc = \langle stmtId, instId \rangle$ represents the location of thread T_i in which $stmtId \in stmtIds$ is the identifier of the statement and $instId$ represents its thread-local instance identifier. The instance identifiers are used to distinguish different occurrences of the same statement in a trace, i.e., within a loop or from different calling contexts. A *symbolic execution trace* of a program is a finite sequence of unique events $\rho = e_1 \ldots e_n$.

2.2 Concurrent Trace Programs

The semantics of CTPs is defined using state transition systems. Let $V = \bigcup_{i=1}^{k} LV_i \cup SV$, be the set of variables and Val be a set of values. A *state* is a map $s : V \to Val$ assigning a value to each variable. We use $s[v]$ and $s[exp]$ to denote variable and expression values in state s. A *state transition* $s \xrightarrow{e} s'$ exists, where s, s' are states and e is an event in thread T_i, $1 \leq i \leq k$, iff $e = \langle i, loc \rangle$ and one of these conditions holds:

- $loc.stmtId$ is a statement of form $(\mathsf{assume}(c), asgn)$, $s[c]$ is true, and for each assignment $v := exp$ in $asgn$, $s'[v] = s[exp]$ holds; s and s' agree on other variables. Note, that if $s[c]$ is false, the transition does not exist (i.e., execution is blocked).

- $loc.stmtId$ is the identifier of a statement of form assert(c) and $s[c]$ is true. When $s[c]$ is false, an attempt to execute event e raises an error.

Let $\rho = e_1 \ldots e_n$ be a symbolic execution trace of a concurrent program P, defining a total event order. From ρ we derive a partial order called the concurrent trace program (CTP).

Definition 1. *A concurrent trace program of ρ is a partially ordered set $CTP_\rho = (T, \sqsubseteq)$ such that $T = \{e \mid e \in \rho\}$ is a set of events, and $\sqsubseteq$ is a partial order, where for any $e_i, e_j \in T$, $e_i \sqsubseteq e_j$ iff $tid(e_i) = tid(e_j)$ and $i < j$ (in ρ, event e_i appears before e_j).*

A CTP_ρ orders events from the same thread by their execution order in ρ; events from different threads are not *explicitly* ordered. Any linearization of this partial order is a schedule of events in ρ. Let $\rho' = e'_1 \ldots e'_n$ be a linearization of CTP_ρ. ρ' is said to be a *feasible linearization* iff there exist states $s_0, \ldots, s_n$ such that, s_0 is the initial state of the program and for all $i = 1, \ldots, n$ there exists a transition $s_{i-1} \xrightarrow{e'_i} s_i$.

2.3 Symbolic Predictive Analysis Using CTPs

Given an execution trace ρ, a model CTP_ρ is derived to *symbolically* check all its feasible linearizations. For this, a formula Φ_{CTP_ρ} is created such that Φ_{CTP_ρ} is satisfiable iff there exists a feasible linearization of CTP_ρ.

CSSA Encoding. The SMT encoding is based on transforming a CTP into a concurrent static single assignment (CSSA) form [13]. The CSSA form has the property that each variable is defined exactly once. A *definition* of variable v is an event that modifies v, and a *use* is an event when v appears in an expression. The transformation consists of (1) renaming variables that have more than one definition, (2) adding ϕ-functions at merge points of if-statements to handle multiple thread-local definitions, and (3) adding π-functions before shared variable uses to represent the confluence of multiple definitions in different threads.

From CSSA to Φ_{CTP_ρ}. Each event e is assigned a fresh integer variable $\mathcal{O}(e)$ denoting its execution time. Let $HB(e, e')$ denote that e happens before e'. In the SMT formula, $HB(e, e')$ is implemented as a logical constraint: $\mathcal{O}(e) < \mathcal{O}(e')$.

A path condition $g(e)$ is defined for all events e in CTP such that e is executed iff $g(e)$ is true. The predecessor of an event e is the edge immediately preceding e in the graph. The path condition is defined as follows: If t is the first event in the CTP (at the entry of the main thread), let $g(e) :=$ true. Otherwise, let $e_1, \ldots, e_k$ be the predecessors of e, and $g_{in} := \bigvee_{i=1}^{k} g(e_i)$: if the statement of e contains $assume(c)$, then $g(e) := c \wedge g_{in}$; otherwise, $g(e) := g_{in}$.

$\Phi_{CTP_\rho} = \Phi_{CTP_\rho}^{PO} \wedge \Phi_{CTP_\rho}^{ST} \wedge \Phi_{CTP_\rho}^{\pi}$ is constructed as follows ($\Phi_{CTP_\rho}^{PO} = \Phi_{CTP_\rho}^{ST} = \Phi_{CTP_\rho}^{\pi} =$ true initially).

1. **Program Order:** For each non-initial event $e \in CTP_\rho$ and each predecessor e' of e in the CTP, let $\Phi_{CTP_\rho}^{PO} := \Phi_{CTP_\rho}^{PO} \wedge HB(e', e)$.
2. **Statements:** For each event $e \in CTP_\rho$, if the corresponding statement of e has $lval := exp$, let $\Phi_{CTP_\rho}^{ST} := \Phi_{CTP_\rho}^{ST} \wedge (g(e) \rightarrow (lval = exp))$. If e contains $assert(c)$, let $\Phi_{CTP_\rho}^{ST} := \Phi_{CTP_\rho}^{ST} \wedge (g(e) \rightarrow c)$.

3. π-**Functions:** For each $w \leftarrow \pi(v_1, \ldots, v_k)$, defined in e, let e_i be the event that defines v_i, let $\Phi^{\pi}_{CTP_\rho} := \Phi^{\pi}_{CTP_\rho} \wedge \bigvee_{i=1}^{k} [(w = v_i) \wedge g(e_i) \wedge HB(e_i, e) \wedge$
$$\bigwedge_{j=1, j \neq i}^{k} (HB(e_j, e_i) \vee HB(e, e_j)))].$$
Intuitively, the π-function evaluates to v_i iff it chooses the i-th definition in the π-set. Having chosen v_i, all other definitions occur before e_i or after the use of v_i.

3   Sequential Test Generation

Our goal is to achieve high branch coverage on each thread. For that, we first consider each thread separately and try to cover as many branches as possible using traditional concolic testing [1,8]. Then, we try to cover the uncovered branches by our proposed concurrent test generation technique. The intuition behind this approach is that many bugs in concurrent programs are sequential bugs that do not relate to any specific interleavings of concurrent execution of the programs.[1] The idea is to catch those bugs by sequential testing, which is cheaper than concurrent testing, without requiring to consider the interleaving space. Then, concurrent test generation aims to cover the remaining uncovered branches by exploring the input space and the interleaving space simultaneously to find a combination that would cause the branch to be taken.

In order to perform sequential testing of a concurrent program, we first execute the program with a set of random inputs, I, to obtain a concurrent trace of the program (represented by ρ). Then, we focus on sequential testing of each thread T_i at a time. Based on the observed trace, we generate a trace ρ', which represents a sequential execution of T_i, by enforcing a set of ordering constraints between the events of different threads in ρ. These constraints ensure that in ρ': (1) thread T_i is created, and (2) thread T_i is executed sequentially and without any interference from other threads (if possible) after it is created until it is completed. To do so, we generate happens-before relations on the events of ρ to enforce the schedule to be the same as ρ until thread T_i is created, and then to enforce all of the events of other threads (after T_i is created) to happen after the last event of T_i. In cases where the complete sequential execution of T_i is not possible due to some synchronization, we stick to the corresponding orderings between the events of different threads in ρ to let T_i complete.

For sequential testing of thread T_i, we apply traditional concolic testing starting with input set, I, and following the schedule implied by ρ' until T_i is completed. Traditional concolic testing then performs a DFS and collects a set of path constraints corresponding to the inner-most uncovered branch in T_i. A satisfiable solution for these constraints provides a set of inputs for the next round in concolic testing.

4   Concurrent Test Generation

4.1   Test Generation Algorithm

Assume that there is a branch in thread T_i which cannot be covered by sequential testing. Suppose that there is a run, represented by run, that hits the conditional statement corresponding to the uncovered branch. Also, suppose that x is a shared variable whose

---

[1] Similar observations were made by others as well [12].

```
concurrentTestGeneration (branchSet, runSet) begin
1:      br = selectBranch (branchSet)
2:      runChoices = subset of runs in runSet that hit br
3:      while (runChoices ≠ ∅) do
4:          run = extract a run from runChoices
5:          aVarSet = set of variables whose value affect the condition of br in run
6:          while (aVarSet ≠ ∅) do
7:              aVar = extract an affecting variable from aVarSet
8:              < w, r > = last write/read of aVar in run just before br
9:              foreach event e such that w < e < r do
10:                 gLoc = global location in run at e
11:                 segmentSet = findInterloperSegments (gLoc, aVar, runSet)
12:                 while (segmentSet ≠ ∅) do
13:                     segment = extract a segment from segmentSet
14:                     constraints = multiTraceAnalysis (run, br, w, r, segment, gLoc)
15:                     call SMT solver to generate input/schedule for constraints
16:                     if (constraints is satisfiable) then
17:                         return input/schedule solution
```

Fig. 3. Concurrent Test Generation Algorithm

value affects the condition. The main idea of our concurrent test generation is to generate schedule/inputs in which the last write to x before the branch in run is overwritten by another write to x which will cause the branch to be taken. To that end, we find an interloper segment from a run (could be different from run), with a write to x, that could be "soundly" inserted after the last write to x in run and search for possible inputs that will cause the branch to be taken after the segment is inserted in run.

Figure 3 shows the proposed algorithm for concurrent test generation. It gets as input a set of successful runs of the program, $runSet$, and a set $branchSet$ of branches that are left uncovered during sequential testing. Initially, $runSet$ mostly contains sequential runs, but over time it accumulates multi-threaded executions as well.

First, an uncovered branch is selected by selectBranch as the target to be covered. selectBranch uses heuristics to select a branch, e.g. the depth of the branch in the CFG, number of failures in targeting to cover the branch, etc. Then, for the selected branch, we pick a set of runs ($runChoices$) from $runSet$ that hit the branch condition. Obviously, the branch condition is $false$ in all of these runs. In lines 3-17, we iterate over the runs in $runChoices$ until we find an appropriate segment and corresponding inputs that would likely cause the branch to be taken after the segment is inserted in the run. At line 4, we pick a run run from $runChoices$ and then find the set $aVarSet$ of shared variables whose values affect the branch condition by performing a traditional def-use analysis on run. In lines 6-17, we go over these variables to find a segment containing a write to the selected variable that can be inserted after the last write to the variable in run. For an affecting variable $aVar$, let $< w, r >$ be a pair of write/read events where w represents the last write event to $aVar$ before the branch and r represents the read event reading the value of $aVar$ just before the branch in run. In fact, the write to $aVar$ in the segment can be inserted anywhere between w and r in run.

The interloper segments should be selected in such a way that they could be inserted soundly in run. At a minimum, threads executing in the segment should be at the same

```
findInterloperSegment (gLoc, aVar, runSet) begin
```
1:    $segmentSet = \emptyset$
2:    $runChoices$ = set of runs in $runSet$ that write to $aVar$
3:    **while** $(runChoices \neq \emptyset)$ **do**
4:        run = extract a run from $runChoices$
5:        $candidateWrites$ = set of all writes to $aVar$ in run
6:        **foreach** $(w' \in candidateWrites)$ **do**
7:            $segment = \emptyset$, $segment$.push(w')
8:            loc = global location in run at w'
9:            $threadSet = w'$.tId, $e' = w'$
10:           **while** $(gLoc|_{threadSet} \neq loc|_{threadSet}$ && e' is not the first event in $run)$ **do**
11:               e' = preceeding event of e' in run
12:               loc = global location in run at e'
13:               **if** $(w'$ causally depends on $e')$ **then**
14:                   $segment$.push(e'), $threadSet = threadSet \cup e'$.tId
15:           **if** $(gLoc|_{threadSet} = loc|_{threadSet})$ **then**
16:               $segmentSet = segmentSet \cup segment$
17:    **return** $segmentSet$;

Fig. 4. Algorithm for Finding Interloper Segments

locations as they are at the insertion point in run. We define a global location as a tuple $< loc_1, loc_2, ... >$ where loc_i is the location of thread T_i. Recall that a location contains both the statement identifier as well as an instance identifier. Given a run, the global location can be computed at each point by looking at the last event of each thread in the run before that point. In lines 9-17, we go over the global locations at an event e, such that $w < e < r$, where $<$ represents the order of the events in run, and try to find an appropriate set of interloper candidates. Given a global location $gLoc$, an affecting variable $aVar$, and a set of runs $runSet$, algorithm findInterloperSegments returns a set of segments from $runSet$ that can be inserted soundly (and not necessarily atomically) at any point with global location $gLoc$. All segments end with a write to the shared variable $aVar$. We discuss how findInterloperSegments works in the next paragraph. In lines 12-17, we go over the interloper segments and call the multi-trace predictive analysis engine which encodes the set of all feasible runs of the program that result from inserting a specific segment at $gLoc$ in run as a set of constraints (see Section 4.2). Then, an SMT solver is used over the concolic execution to search for inputs and a schedule that would cause the branch to be taken. If such inputs/schedule exist, then we stop the search and execute the program with the found inputs according to the corresponding schedule which guarantees the branch to be taken.

Figure 4 presents the algorithm for finding interlopers from a set of given runs $runSet$ based on a global location $gLoc$ and an affecting variable $aVar$. We consider the set of all runs in which there is at least one write to $aVar$ (line 2). For each run, we iterate over the set of writes to $aVar$ and find candidate segments containing a write as their last event while starting at a global location consistent with $gLoc$. To that end, for a selected write to $aVar$, we perform a static backward analysis in the corresponding run, until we reach a $gLoc$-consistent location. Note that some threads may be active in the run without causally affecting the write to $aVar$. Requiring the location of such threads to match with $gLoc$ is too restrictive and could miss useful segments. Therefore, as we go backward in the run, we add events to the segment only if the selected write is causally dependent on the event. We keep track of the threads corresponding to such events, represented by $threadSet$. At each location loc in the run, we check whether the projection of global location loc to the threads in $threadSet$ is equal to the projection of global location $gLoc$ to this set of threads; i.e. $gLoc|_{threadSet} = loc|_{threadSet}$. If this check passes, the segment is added to the candidate segment set.

Figure 5 depicts the backward analysis performed on the multi-threaded Run2 that leads to a candidate write at w' to the shared variable x. This write is chosen because we want to control the value read at r in Run1, since it may lead us to a target branch depicted by the if-statement. We have kept this step quite light-weight, choosing to match only relevant thread locations. In general, additional global state or path invariants, when available or easily computable, can also be used to filter the candidates.

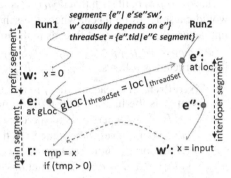

Fig. 5. Finding feasible interloper segments

4.2 Multi-trace Predictive Analysis with Input Generation

Given a run run, containing an uncovered branch br with the affecting read r, an interloper segment seg with a candidate write w, and a global location $gLoc$ in run representing the insertion point, we symbolically encode a set of feasible runs, in which the schedule is the same as in run until reaching $gLoc$ and then the interloper segment is inserted (not necessarily atomically) at $gLoc$ in a way that r is guaranteed to read the value written by w. The inputs of the program are treated symbolically allowing us to use SMT solvers [4,5] to simultaneously search for inputs and a schedule that would cause br to be taken. We call the event sequence in run before the insertion point the *prefix segment* and the events after the insertion point and before br the *main segment*.

CMTA is based on the $CTPs$ of the main and the interloper segments, which already represent program inputs symbolically. Let CTP_{main} and CTP_{int} denote the $CTPs$ of the main and interloper segments, respectively. Note that the algorithm in Figure 4 ensures that the location of each thread in the interloper segment is the same at the beginning of both segments. Therefore, threads in the interloper segment should have a maximum common prefix of locations in both CTP_{main} and CTP_{int}; i.e. $\forall\, T_i\; in\; CTP_{int} \exists\, k : \forall_{j \leq k} j\; CTP_{main}|_{T_i}[j].loc = CTP_{int}|_{T_i}[j].loc$. The threads may then diverge after this prefix in the segments. To avoid duplication when inserting the interloper segment in the main segment, it should be ensured that each thread is at each location at most once in the predicted run. Let $de_{T_i}^{main}$ and $de_{T_i}^{int}$ represent the first event of thread T_i in CTP_{main} and CTP_{int} at which $de_{T_i}^{main}.loc \neq de_{T_i}^{int}.loc$, respectively. Since the segments diverge after $de_{T_i}^{main}$ and $de_{T_i}^{int}$, this means that for each thread after this point we should consider events either from the main segment or from the interloper segment. This will be enforced using *indicator bits* (see below, item 6).

Suppose that E^{main} and E^{int} represent the set of events in the main and interloper segments, respectively. Note that not all of these events may be required for prediction. Indeed, certain events may be inconsistent with each other, if they originated from diverging runs. Therefore, for each event $e_i \in E^{main} \cup E^{int}$ we consider an *indicator bit* b_{e_i} whose value determines whether the event is required to happen before the branch in the predicted run or not. Based on the given run and an interloper segment, a formula Φ_{MCTP} is built such that Φ_{MCTP} is satisfiable iff there exist inputs/schedule that would cause br to be taken, where the schedule follows the prefix segment and then interleaves the execution of threads in the main and interloper segments.

$$\Phi_{MCTP} = \Phi_{MCTP}^{FP} \wedge \Phi_{MCTP}^{PO} \wedge \Phi_{MCTP}^{ST} \wedge \Phi_{MCTP}^{\pi} \wedge \Phi_{MCTP}^{BR} \wedge \Phi_{MCTP}^{AWR} \wedge \Phi_{MCTP}^{Ind}$$

is constructed as follows ($\Phi_{MCTP}^{FP} = \Phi_{MCTP}^{\pi} = \Phi_{MCTP}^{Ind} = true$ initially).

- **Fixed Prefix:** For each event e_i in the prefix segment:
  - if e_i is the first event in run, do nothing. Otherwise, $\Phi_{MCTP}^{FP} = \Phi_{MCTP}^{FP} \wedge HB(e_i', e_i)$ where e_i' is the predecessor of e_i in the prefix segment. This keeps the order of events the same as in the prefix segment.
  - if the corresponding statement of e_i has $lval := exp$, let $\Phi_{MCTP}^{FP} = \Phi_{MCTP}^{FP} \wedge g(e_i) \wedge (lval = exp)$. If e_i contains $assert(c)$, let $\Phi_{MCTP}^{FP} = \Phi_{MCTP}^{FP} \wedge g(e_i) \wedge (g(e_i) \to c)$. Note that $g(e_i)$ is required to be true in any case.
- **Inserting Interloper Segment in Suffix:**
  1. **Program Order:** $\Phi_{MCTP}^{PO} = \Phi_{CTP_{main}}^{PO} \wedge \Phi_{CTP_{int}}^{PO}$.
  2. **Statements:** $\Phi_{MCTP}^{ST} = \Phi_{CTP_{main}}^{ST} \wedge \Phi_{CTP_{int}}^{ST}$.
  3. **π-Functions:** Define a new π-function for each shared variable use in $E^{main} \cup E^{int} \setminus \{r\}$ to include definitions in both run and the interloper segment. Then, as in standard CTPs, for each $w \leftarrow \pi(v_1, \ldots, v_k)$, defined in $e \in E^{main} \cup E^{int} \setminus \{r\}$, let e_i be the event that defines v_i, let $\Phi_{MCTP}^{\pi} = \Phi_{MCTP}^{\pi} \wedge \bigvee_{i=1}^{k}[(w = v_i) \wedge g(e_i) \wedge HB(e_i, e) \wedge \bigwedge_{j=1, j \neq i}^{k}(HB(e_j, e_i) \vee HB(e, e_j))]$.
  4. **Target Branch:** Suppose that $(assume(c), \emptyset)$ is the uncovered branch statement. In fact, the branch event e_{br} in run relates to a statement $(assume(\neg c), \emptyset)$ representing the other branch of the corresponding conditional statement. Let $\Phi_{MCTP}^{BR} = g(e_{br}) = c \wedge g(e')$ where e' is the predecessor of e_{br}.
  5. **Affecting Write/Read Matching:** Let W_{aVar} represent all the write events to $aVar \in E^{main} \cup E^{int} \setminus \{w\}$. Then, $\Phi_{MCTP}^{AWR} = HB(w, r) \wedge \bigwedge_{e_i \in W_{aVar}} (HB(e_i, r) \vee HB(w, e_i))$.
  6. **Indicator Bits:** For each event e_i in $E^{main} \cup E^{int}$
     - $\Phi_{MCTP}^{Ind} := \Phi_{MCTP}^{Ind} \wedge (b_{e_i} \to g(e_i)) \wedge (b_{e_i} \to HB(e_i, e_{br})) \wedge (\neg(b_{e_i}) \to HB(e_{br}, e_i))$
     - If e_i belongs to thread T_i, let e_j be the predecessor of e_i in T_i. Then, $\Phi_{MCTP}^{Ind} = \Phi_{MCTP}^{Ind} \wedge (b_{e_i} \to b_{e_j})$
     - For each active thread T_i in the interloper segment: $\Phi_{MCTP}^{Ind} = \Phi_{MCTP}^{Ind} \wedge (b_{de_{T_i}^{main}} \to \neg(b_{de_{T_i}^{int}})) \wedge (b_{de_{T_i}^{int}} \to \neg(b_{de_{T_i}^{main}}))$.

5 Relative Completeness

In Section 4, we formulated a procedure to insert an interloper segment with the goal of forcing the execution of a target branch br. Towards that end, we started by identifying a tuple of the form $\langle w, r \rangle$, where w and r are the last write and read events, respectively, for a variable affecting the valuation of *br*. In general, however, to cover all partial orders induced by shared variable accesses in different threads, we need to explore a potential insertion of interlopers between each tuple $\langle w', r' \rangle$, where w' and r' are the definition and use, respectively, of a shared variable *sh*, say, occurring along a def-use chain leading to a variable impacting the valuation of *br*. This is because any change to the value of *sh* between events w' and r' propagates to *br* potentially affecting it.

Motivated by the above discussion, let *Tup* be the set of all tuples of the form $\langle w', r' \rangle$, where w' and r' are the definition and use, respectively, of a shared variable occurring along a def-use chain leading to a variable impacting the valuation of *br*. We then modify our test generation algorithm from Figure 3 as follows. We add an outer loop that enumerates each subset *Tup'* of *Tup*. Then, as discussed above, each def-use tuple in this subset is a candidate for interloper insertion. This is accomplished by identifying an event e_{tup} for each $tup \in Tup'$ where an interloper can be inserted. As before the interloper can be identified via a call to findInterloperSegments. The constraints for the SMT solver need to be modified to ensure consistency for the simultaneous insertion of all $|Tup'|$ interlopers.

Note that the above modification will explore only those partial orders that are generated by shared variable accesses occurring in the set of runs *runSet*. This is why this procedure only guarantees *relative completeness*, i.e., with respect to the set *runSet*. This is similar to other predictive and concolic techniques that are biased towards observed test runs. In general, the dynamic tests can be supplemented by static analysis. However, in the limit, this procedure may not scale due to an explosion in the number of runs that may be generated. In the future, we plan to investigate prioritization schemes over the set of interleavings that need to be explored in order to excite a given branch.

6 Related Work

Prediction-based testing has emerged as a promising approach in concurrent program testing. Based on program executions these approaches predict other possible runs which violate a certain property, by encoding the set of feasible runs symbolically [17,25], or by using static and dynamic analysis techniques [3,6,11,24]. In fact, all of these approaches keep the inputs of the program fixed and explore the interleaving space according to a *single* observed run at a time. In contrast, in our concolic testing approach we explore the input space and interleaving space simultaneously. Furthermore, our prediction approach goes beyond a single run and performs analysis over information observed in different runs.

With respect to automatic test input and thread schedule generation for concurrent programs, Sen et al. presented an extension of sequential concolic execution to concurrent programs [18,20]. In contrast to these efforts, we focus on branch coverage of individual threads and avoid reasoning in the product state-space as much as possible. Furthermore, we leverage sequential test generation modularly on individual threads to enhance scalability.

Other efforts have also focused on (*def-use*) of shared variables in concurrent programs. Shi et al. used invariants based on def-use for bug detection and error diagnosis [22]. Hong et al. developed heuristics to increase *synchronization coverage* of statement pairs [10]. A notion called predecessor set (*pset*) based on conflicts was used

Table 1. Experimental results (avg.: average, br: branches, cov.: covered, il.: interlopers)

Bench-mark	# of inputs	# of threads	LOC	Thread	# of br.	Sequential Testing			Concurrent Testing						
						# of tests	cov. br.	time in s	# of tests	cov. br.	time in s	bug found	# br. w/ il.	avg. #il.	% of cov. br. seq.→conc.
Bluetooth	3	2	88	each	12	2	7	0.6	4	5	1.3	yes	3	1	58→100
Apache1s	1	2	253	each	8	4	7	2.9	1	1	8.2	yes	1	2	87→100
Apache1	3	2	640	each	22	6	16	10.4	2	2	332	yes	2	2	72→81
Apache2s	2	2	268	each	10	3	7	1.9	2	2	5.4	yes	3	1	70→90
Apache2	3	2	864	each	22	4	15	8.9	1	1	81	yes	3	2	68→73
ctrace1	1-fixed	2	1466	T1	64	1	35	17.7	1	3	341	yes	8	2.3	54→59
				T2	22	1	14	11.5	0	0	9.0				64→64
ctrace2	1-fixed	2	1523	T1	114	1	67	17.7	1	14	447	yes	3	5	59→71
				T2	22	1	14	11.5	0	0	9.0				64→64
splay	1-fixed	2	1013	T1	16	1	5	4.9	3	7	90	no	3	2.3	33→75
				T2	16	1	11	10.6	1	1	75	bug			69→75
aget	1-fixed	2	680	each	18	1	12	121	1	1	179	yes	2	1	66→72

by Yu and Narayanasamy for runtime failure avoidance [27], and by Wang et al. for coverage-guided testing [26]. However, none of these approaches targeted structural coverage or provided input test generation. Our notion of interloper segments is related to work by Shacham et al. [21], where they consider testing linearizability of concurrent collection operations by interleaving operations from an adversarial environment, and the search is guided to interleave non-commutative simple operations. In contrast, our interloper segments may contain multiple threads that generate a different value of interest, and we use SMT solvers to find feasible interlopers. Finally, at a high level, our main insight to separate sequential coverage and leverage it for concurrent programs is similar to the insight by Joshi et al. [12], that many bugs in concurrent programs can be found by sequential analysis. Their goal, however, was to improve the usability of concurrent bug finding tools by filtering away bugs that can be reproduced sequentially.

7   Experiments

We implemented the concurrent test generation (described in Section 4) and applied it on a benchmark suite of 9 concurrent programs. We used CREST [1] for the sequential test generation part. Experiments were performed on a Linux server with 3GB memory.

Bluetooth is the version of the motivating example shown in Figure 2. Apache1 and Apache2 are programs corresponding to two bugs in APACHE FTP server from *BugBench* [14]. Apache1s and Apache2s are simplified versions of Apache1 and Apache2, respectively, where we removed parts of the code that were immaterial to branches with respect to shared variables. ctrace is a fast, lightweight trace/debug C library. ctrace1 and ctrace2 are two test drivers using this library, which contain some data races. splay is a program built using a C library implementing several tree structures. Finally, aget is a multi-threaded download accelerator.

Table 1 presents the experimental results for concurrent test generation. It reports numbers (i.e. total number of branches, number of generated tests, covered branches and the corresponding time) for both sequential and concurrent tests. Note that we report the number of "structurally different" branches, i.e. branches in the CFG, when we refer to the number of branches. The table also presents how much the branch coverage increased using CMTA, and for how many branches we found potential interloper segments, as well as the average number of interlopers for each such branch.

According to Table 1, concurrent test generation is successful in increasing the structural coverage over sequential test generation. For example, in case of `splay`, branch coverage is increased from 33% to 80%. Note that many uncovered branches have interlopers, and often a few additional concurrent tests can cover multiple branches. The experiments show that our test generation algorithm is effective in finding bugs also – even though this was not the immediate goal. This suggests that branches that cannot be covered by purely sequential testing are good candidates to look for interesting synchronization patterns – including bugs. All of the bugs found in the benchmark suite were revealed by covering an un-covered branch in concurrent test generation. Furthermore, our overall approach is reasonably fast in practice. This is largely due to the fact that we initially rely on the strength of concolic testing techniques to cover most branches sequentially, and our concurrent test generation is effective in finding interloper segments to cover target branches.

Some programs in our benchmark suite have fixed inputs. For example, `aget` expects a URL as input which we fixed for testing purposes. Therefore, the number of sequential concolic tests is one. However, concurrent test generation targets exploring uncovered parts. Note that this is different than predictive analysis (for which the inputs are fixed as well) as concurrent test generation aims to increase the structural coverage while predictive analysis explores the permutations of events of a single observed run.

We investigated why our method was only able to cover 59% and 64% of the branches in `ctrace` using the `ctrace1` test driver. The remaining branches were either not coverable by the driver of `ctrace1`, or were branches related to sanity checks. Such sanity checks include checks on system calls, such as whether a file-operation succeeded or not. Since our test execution was not providing any mock environment, such as for the file system, these sanity checks were not reachable.

To analyze the scalability of our SMT-based approach, we increased the number of threads in `Apache2` from 2 to 15. The average number of accesses to shared variables (that is, excluding thread-local events) for 15 threads reached over 500. Despite the large number of events in an execution with 15 threads, the test generation approach finished within 14 minutes, showing the scalability of the SMT-based CMTA. In this example, increasing the number of threads did not affect branch coverage.

To investigate the need for automated test input generation, we also ran our in-house dynamic partial order reduction (DPOR) [7] tool FUSION [25] on these benchmarks (see Table 2). FUSION finds concurrency bugs such as data races, but does not report on coverage. Therefore, we highlight whether the *known bugs* in

Table 2. Comparison with FUSION

Bench-mark	FUSION on fixed inputs			FUSION on generated inputs			New approach using CMTA	
	Runs	Time	bug found	Runs	Time	bug found	Tests	Time
Bluetooth	423	27s	no	33	4s	yes	6	2s
Apache1s	35	9s	no	2	1s	yes	5	11s
Apache1	399	3m4s	no	2	1s	yes	8	5m42s
Apache2s	126	2m2s	no	2	1s	yes	5	7s
Apache2	5974	23m50s	no	2	2s	yes	5	1m30s
ctrace1	did not finish			did not finish			3	5m58s
ctrace2	did not finish			did not finish			3	8m4s
splay	30	27s	no bug	N/A (no inputs)			6	3m0s
aget	6	43s	yes	N/A (no inputs)			2	5m0s

the benchmarks are discovered or not. For most benchmarks, our new approach needed to generate new test inputs and not just find alternate thread schedules. Thus, we also present the performance after we provided the generated *bug-triggering* input to FUSION. As can be seen, DPOR alone can spend substantial analysis time in searching for alternative thread interleavings without finding the known bugs, as in the case of Apache2. However, once the generated bug-triggering input was provided to FUSION, it generally performed well to find the bug of interest. This suggests that separating test input generation from the analysis of thread scheduling related issues is a promising testing strategy.

References

1. Burnim, J., Sen, K.: Heuristics for scalable dynamic test generation. In: ASE. IEEE (2008)
2. Cadar, C., Dunbar, D., Engler, D.R.: KLEE: Unassisted and automatic generation of high-coverage tests for complex systems programs. In: OSDI. USENIX Association (2008)
3. Chen, F., Serbanuta, T.F., Roşu, G.: JPredictor: A predictive runtime analysis tool for Java. In: ICSE, pp. 221–230 (2008)
4. de Moura, L., Bjørner, N.: Z3: An Efficient SMT Solver. In: Ramakrishnan, C.R., Rehof, J. (eds.) TACAS 2008. LNCS, vol. 4963, pp. 337–340. Springer, Heidelberg (2008)
5. Dutertre, B., de Moura, L.: A Fast Linear-Arithmetic Solver for DPLL(T). In: Ball, T., Jones, R.B. (eds.) CAV 2006. LNCS, vol. 4144, pp. 81–94. Springer, Heidelberg (2006)
6. Farzan, A., Madhusudan, P., Sorrentino, F.: Meta-analysis for Atomicity Violations under Nested Locking. In: Bouajjani, A., Maler, O. (eds.) CAV 2009. LNCS, vol. 5643, pp. 248–262. Springer, Heidelberg (2009)
7. Flanagan, C., Godefroid, P.: Dynamic partial-order reduction for model checking software. In: POPL. ACM (2005)
8. Godefroid, P., Klarlund, N., Sen, K.: DART: Directed automated random testing. In: PLDI, pp. 213–223 (2005)
9. Godefroid, P., Levin, M.Y., Molnar, D.A.: Active property checking. In: EMSOFT (2008)
10. Hong, S., Ahn, J., Park, S., Kim, M., Harrold, M.J.: Testing concurrent programs to achieve high synchronization coverage. In: ISSTA, pp. 210–220. ACM (2012)
11. Huang, J., Zhang, C.: Persuasive prediction of concurrency access anomalies. In: ISSTA, pp. 144–154 (2011)
12. Joshi, S., Lahiri, S.K., Lal, A.: Underspecified harnesses and interleaved bugs. In: POPL, pp. 19–30. ACM (2012)
13. Lee, J., Padua, D.A., Midkiff, S.P.: Basic compiler algorithms for parallel programs. In: PPOPP. ACM (1999)
14. Lu, S., Li, Z., Qin, F., Tan, L., Zhou, P., Zhou, Y.: BugBench: Benchmarks for evaluating bug detection tools. In: Workshop on the Evaluation of Software Defect Detection Tools (2005)
15. Musuvathi, M., Qadeer, S.: CHESS: Systematic Stress Testing of Concurrent Software. In: Puebla, G. (ed.) LOPSTR 2006. LNCS, vol. 4407, pp. 15–16. Springer, Heidelberg (2007)
16. Qadeer, S., Wu, D.: KISS: Keep it simple and sequential. In: PLDI. ACM (2004)
17. Said, M., Wang, C., Yang, Z., Sakallah, K.: Generating Data Race Witnesses by an SMT-Based Analysis. In: Bobaru, M., Havelund, K., Holzmann, G.J., Joshi, R. (eds.) NFM 2011. LNCS, vol. 6617, pp. 313–327. Springer, Heidelberg (2011)
18. Sen, K.: Scalable automated methods for dynamic program analysis (2006)
19. Sen, K., Marinov, D., Agha, G.: CUTE: A concolic unit testing engine for C. In: ESEC/FSE. ACM (2005)

20. Sen, K., Roşu, G., Agha, G.: Detecting Errors in Multithreaded Programs by Generalized Predictive Analysis of Executions. In: Steffen, M., Zavattaro, G. (eds.) FMOODS 2005. LNCS, vol. 3535, pp. 211–226. Springer, Heidelberg (2005)
21. Shacham, O., Bronson, N., Aiken, A., Sagiv, M., Vechev, M., Yahav, E.: Testing atomicity of composed concurrent operations. SIGPLAN Not. 46(10), 51–64 (2011)
22. Shi, Y., Park, S., Yin, Z., Lu, S., Zhou, Y., Chen, W., Zheng, W.: Do I use the wrong definition? DeFuse: Definition-use invariants for detecting concurrency and sequential bugs. In: OOPSLA (2010)
23. Smaragdakis, Y., Evans, J., Sadowski, C., Yi, J., Flanagan, C.: Sound predictive race detection in polynomial time. In: POPL. ACM (2012)
24. Sorrentino, F., Farzan, A., Madhusudan, P.: PENELOPE: Weaving threads to expose atomicity violations. In: FSE, pp. 37–46 (2010)
25. Wang, C., Kundu, S., Ganai, M., Gupta, A.: Symbolic Predictive Analysis for Concurrent Programs. In: Cavalcanti, A., Dams, D.R. (eds.) FM 2009. LNCS, vol. 5850, pp. 256–272. Springer, Heidelberg (2009)
26. Wang, C., Said, M., Gupta, A.: Coverage guided systematic concurrency testing. In: ICSE. ACM (2011)
27. Yu, J., Narayanasamy, S.: A case for an interleaving constrained shared-memory multiprocessor. In: ISCA (2009)

Java Bytecode Instrumentation Made Easy: The DiSL Framework for Dynamic Program Analysis

Lukáš Marek[1], Yudi Zheng[2], Danilo Ansaloni[3], Aibek Sarimbekov[3],
Walter Binder[3], Petr Tůma[1], and Zhengwei Qi[2]

[1] Charles University, Czech Republic
{lukas.marek,petr.tuma}@d3s.mff.cuni.cz
[2] Shanghai Jiao Tong University, China
{zheng.yudi,qizhwei}@sjtu.edu.cn
[3] University of Lugano, Switzerland
{danilo.ansaloni,aibek.sarimbekov,walter.binder}@usi.ch

Abstract. Many software development tools (e.g., profilers, debuggers, testing tools) and frameworks (e.g., aspect weavers) are based on bytecode instrumentation techniques. While there are many low-level bytecode manipulation libraries that support the development of such tools and frameworks, they typically provide only low-level abstractions and require detailed knowledge of the Java Virtual Machine. In addition, they often lack the necessary infrastructure for load-time instrumentation with complete bytecode coverage to ensure that each method with a bytecode representation gets instrumented. In this paper we give an introduction to DiSL, a domain-specific aspect language and framework for bytecode instrumentation that reconciles high expressiveness of the language, high level of abstraction, and efficiency of the generated code. We illustrate the strengths of DiSL with a concrete analysis as a case study. The DiSL framework is open-source and has been successfully used in several research projects.

Keywords: Bytecode instrumentation, aspect-oriented programming, domain-specific languages, Java Virtual Machine.

1 Introduction

Java bytecode instrumentation is widely used for implementing dynamic program analysis tools and frameworks. It is supported by a variety of rather low-level bytecode manipulation libraries, such as ASM[1], BCEL[2], Soot [9], ShrikeBT[3], or Javassist [2,3]; the latter also provides a source-level API. Mainstream aspect-oriented programming (AOP) languages such as AspectJ [4] offer a convenient pointcut/advice model that allows expressing certain instrumentations in a concise manner; for this reason, some researchers have implemented dynamic program analysis tools with AOP, such as DJProf [7]. Unfortunately, mainstream

---

[1] http://asm.ow2.org/
[2] http://commons.apache.org/bcel/
[3] http://wala.sourceforge.net/wiki/index.php/Shrike_technical_overview

R. Jhala and A. Igarashi (Eds.): APLAS 2012, LNCS 7705, pp. 256–263, 2012.

AOP languages severely limit instrumentation flexibility, making it impossible to implement some relevant instrumentations. In addition, the high-level programming model results in some overhead, as the implementation of some language features is expensive.

DiSL [5, 10] is a new domain-specific language and framework for Java bytecode instrumentation. DiSL is inspired by AOP, but in contrast to mainstream AOP languages, it features an open join point model where any region of bytecodes can be selected as a *join point* (i.e., code location to be instrumented). DiSL reconciles high-level language constructs resulting in concise instrumentations, high expressiveness (i.e., any instrumentation can be expressed in DiSL), and efficiency of the inserted instrumentation code. Thanks to the pointcut/advice model adopted by DiSL, instrumentations are similarly compact as aspects written in AspectJ. However, in contrast to AspectJ, DiSL does not restrict the code locations that can be instrumented, and the code generated by DiSL avoids expensive operations (such as object allocations that are not visible to the programmer). Furthermore, DiSL supports instrumentations with *complete bytecode coverage* [6] out-of-the-box and tries to avoid structural modifications of classes that would be visible through reflection and could break the instrumented code.

In this paper we give a tutorial-style introduction to DiSL programming, helping the developers of dynamic program analysis tools to get started with DiSL. Due to the limited space, we only cover the basic features of DiSL; for a discussion of the design, we refer to [5]. Section 2 introduces the DiSL framework using an evolving program analysis example and pointing out the advantages of DiSL. Section 3 describes the instrumentation process with DiSL. Finally, Section 4 concludes.

2   DiSL by Example

A common example of a dynamic program analysis tool is a method execution time profiler, which usually instruments the method entry and exit join points and introduces storage for timestamps. We describe the main features of DiSL by gradually developing the instrumentation for such a profiler.

2.1   Method Execution Time Profiler

Each DiSL instrumentation is defined through methods declared in standard Java classes. Each method—called *snippet* in DiSL terminology—is annotated so as to specify the join points where the code of the snippet shall be inlined.[4]

In the first version of our execution time profiler, we only output the entry and exit time of each executed method. As illustrated in Figure 1, the first snippet prints the entry time and the second snippet prints the exit time. The @Before annotation on the first snippet directs the framework to inline the snippet before each marked region of bytecodes (representing a join point); the use of the @After

---

[4] The name of the method is not constrained and can be arbitrarily chosen by the programmer.

```
public class SimpleProfiler {
  @Before(marker=BodyMarker.class)
  static void onMethodEntry() {
    System.out.println("Method entry " + System.nanoTime());
  }
  @After(marker=BodyMarker.class)
  static void onMethodExit() {
    System.out.println("Method exit " + System.nanoTime());
  }
}
```

Fig. 1. Instrumenting method entry and exit

```
public class SimpleProfiler {
  @SyntheticLocal
  static long entryTime;

  @Before(marker=BodyMarker.class)
  static void onMethodEntry() {
    entryTime = System.nanoTime();
  }
  @After(marker=BodyMarker.class)
  static void onMethodExit() {
    System.out.println("Method duration " + (System.nanoTime() - entryTime));
  }
}
```

Fig. 2. Data passing with a synthetic local variable

annotation places the second snippet after (both normal and abnormal) exit of each marked region.

The marked bytecode regions are specified with the *marker* parameter of the annotation. In our example, *BodyMarker* marks the whole method (or constructor) body. The resulting instrumentation thus prints a timestamp upon method entry and exit. DiSL provides a library of markers (e.g., *BasicBlockMarker*, *BytecodeMarker*) for intercepting many common bytecode patterns. For special use cases, DiSL allows the programmer to define custom markers intercepting user-defined bytecode sequences.

The elapsed wall-clock time from method entry to method exit can be computed in the after snippet. To perform the computation, the timestamp of method entry has to be passed from the before snippet to the after snippet. Whereas in traditional AOP languages this would be handled using the around advice, DiSL supports data passing between snippets using *synthetic local variables* [1]. Synthetic local variables are static fields annotated as *@SyntheticLocal*. The variables have the scope of a method activation and can be accessed by all snippets that are inlined in the method; that is, they become local variables on the stack. Synthetic local variables are initialized to the default value of their declared type (e.g., 0, false, null). Figure 2 illustrates the use of a synthetic local variable named *entryTime* for computing the method execution time.

```
@After(marker=BodyMarker.class)
static void onMethodExit(MethodStaticContext msc) {
  System.out.println(msc.thisMethodFullName() + " duration "
    + (System.nanoTime() - entryTime));
}
```

Fig. 3. Accessing the method name through static context

The output of the profiler should also contain the name of each profiled method. The information about the instrumented class, method, and bytecode region can be obtained through special *static context interfaces*. Static context interfaces that provide the desired information can be declared as arguments to the snippet, in any order. At instrumentation time, DiSL replaces calls to these interfaces with the corresponding static context information. This implementation choice improves the efficiency of the resulting tools, since static context information is computed at instrumentation time rather than at runtime.

In our example, we are interested in the predefined static context *MethodStaticContext*, which provides the method name, signature, and modifiers (among other static data about the intercepted method and its enclosing class). Figure 3 refines the after snippet of Figure 2 to access the fully qualified name of the instrumented method.

DiSL provides a set of commonly used static context interfaces. The DiSL programmer may also define custom static context interfaces to perform additional static analysis at instrumentation time or to access information not directly provided by DiSL.

2.2 Profiler with Stack Trace

Another extension to our example provides the stack trace of each profiled method. There are several ways to obtain the stack trace information in Java, such as calling the *getStackTrace()* method from *java.lang.Thread*. However, frequent calls to this method may be expensive.

As an alternative approach, DiSL allows programmers to obtain stack trace information using instrumentation. The algorithm to reify the call stack is simple. Upon method entry, the method name is pushed onto a thread-local shadow call stack. Upon method exit, the method name is popped off the shadow call stack.

Figure 4 shows two additional snippets for call stack reification. Each thread maintains its shadow call stack, referenced by the thread-local variable *cs*.[5] In our example, *cs* is initialized for each thread in the before snippet. The shadow call stack can be accessed from all snippets using *cs*; for example, it could be included in the profiler's output.

To make sure all snippets observe the shadow call stack in a consistent state, the two snippets for call stack reification have to be inserted in a correct order relative to the other snippets. DiSL allows the programmer to specify the order in

---

[5] DiSL offers a particularly efficient implementation of thread-local variables with the *@ThreadLocal* annotation.

```
@ThreadLocal
static Stack<String> cs; // call stack

@Before(marker=BodyMarker.class, order=1000)
static void enterCS(MethodStaticContext msc) {
  if (cs == null) { cs = new Stack<String>(); }
  cs.push(msc.thisMethodFullName());
}
@After(marker=BodyMarker.class, order=1000)
static void exitCS() {
  cs.pop();
}
```

Fig. 4. Call stack reification

```
@After(marker=BodyMarker.class)
static void onMethodExit(MethodStaticContext msc, DynamicContext dc) {
  int identityHC = System.identityHashCode(dc.getThis());
  ...
}
```

Fig. 5. Accessing dynamic context information

which snippets matching the same join point should be inlined as a non-negative integer in the snippet annotation. The smaller this number, the closer to the join point the snippet is inlined. In our profiler, the time measurement snippets and the stack reification snippets match the same join point (i.e., method entry, resp. exit). We assign a high order value (1000) to the call stack reification snippets and keep the lower default order value (100) of the snippets for time measurement.[6] Consequently, the callee name is pushed onto the shadow call stack before the entry time is measured, and the exit time is measured before the callee name is popped off the stack.

2.3 Profiling Object Instances

Our next extension addresses situations where the dependency of the method execution time on the identity of the called object instance is of interest. Figure 5 refines the after snippet of Figure 2 by computing the identity hash code of the object instance on which the intercepted method has been called.

The instrumentation in Figure 5 uses a *dynamic context interface* (i.e., *DynamicContext*) to get a reference to the current object instance. Similar to the static context interfaces, the dynamic context interfaces are also passed to the snippets as method arguments. Unlike the static context information, which is resolved at instrumentation time, calls to the dynamic context interface are replaced with code that obtains the required dynamic information at runtime. Besides the reference used in the example, DiSL provides access to other dynamic context information including the local variables, method arguments, and values on the operand stack.

---

[6] If snippet ordering is used, it is recommended to override the value in all snippets for improved readability.

```
public class LoopGuard {
  @GuardMethod
  public static boolean methodContainsLoop() {
    ... // Loop detection based on control flow analysis
  }
}
```

Fig. 6. Loop guard skeleton

```
@Before(marker=BodyMarker.class, guard=LoopGuard.class)
static void onMethodEntry() { ... }
@After(marker=BodyMarker.class, guard=LoopGuard.class)
static void onMethodExit(...) { ... }
```

Fig. 7. Time measurement snippets with loop guard

2.4 Profiling Only Methods with Loops

Often, it is useful to restrict the instrumentation to certain methods. For example, one may want to profile only the execution of methods that contain loops, as methods containing repetitions are likely to contribute more to the overall execution time.

DiSL allows programmers to restrict an instrumentation using the *guard* construct. A guard is a user-defined condition evaluated during instrumentation. This condition determines whether a snippet matching a particular join point is inlined or not.

The signature of a guard restricting the instrumentation only to methods containing loops is shown in Figure 6. The guard is a Java class where one method must carry the *@GuardMethod* annotation. The *methodContainsLoop* guard method implements the detection of a loop in a method (not shown, a loop detector based on control flow analysis is included as part of DiSL).

The loop guard is associated with a snippet using the *guard* annotation parameter, as illustrated in Figure 7. Note that the loop guard is not used in the snippets for stack reification, since we want to maintain complete stack trace information without omitting the stack frames of methods that do not contain any loops.

3   The Instrumentation Process with DiSL

The DiSL framework supports deployment of instrumentations, sanity checking, and debugging. To reduce perturbation of the observed application and facilitate complete bytecode coverage, the DiSL engine can run in a separate Java Virtual Machine (JVM); a native JVMTI agent within the observed application's JVM sends all loaded classes (starting with *java.lang.Object*) to the DiSL engine for load-time instrumentation. Alternatively, the DiSL engine offers an offline mode for static bytecode instrumentation.

Complete bytecode coverage introduces additional issues. Before the main method of an application is called, the JVM executes bootstrap code. Executing the inserted instrumentation during bootstrap may crash the JVM. Furthermore, if the inserted instrumentation uses the Java class library that is itself instrumented, infinite recursion can occur. DiSL solves these issues with the help of polymorphic bytecode instrumentation [6], which allows resorting to unmodified code during bootstrap and during execution of the inlined snippets.

Instrumentation code inserted by DiSL is intended only for application observation, it should never alter the observed application's control flow. DiSL has been carefully designed to prevent the insertion of any code that could change the control flow. It can automatically insert code intercepting all exceptions originating from the snippets, reporting an error if an exception is thrown (and not handled) by the inserted code regions. Once the instrumentation has reached production-level quality, this exception checking can be turned off to reduce overhead.

To ease debugging, DiSL also supports dumping of the unmodified and instrumented classes.

4 Conclusion

This paper gives an introduction to DiSL, a domain-specific aspect language and framework for bytecode instrumentation. DiSL eases the development of instrumentation-based dynamic program analysis tools without restricting the join points that can be instrumented. Instrumentation code to be inserted is specified in the form of snippets, that is, annotated Java methods. Snippets have access to comprehensive static and dynamic context information. By default, the DiSL framework instruments every method that has a bytecode representation, including methods in the Java class library and in dynamically generated code.

The design of DiSL rules out two types of errors that are often made when resorting to low-level bytecode manipulation techniques. First, as snippets are Java code that is compiled, the bytecode within each snippet is guaranteed to be valid. Second, snippets cannot tamper with local variables and stack locations used by the instrumented base program. Nonetheless, the DiSL programmer needs to be aware of the semantics of individual bytecodes in order to correctly access the desired context information. It is possible to write incorrect instrumentations that result in instrumented classes failing bytecode verification. Hence, we are developing advanced checkers for DiSL in our ongoing research.

DiSL offers a unique combination of a high-level pointcut/advice model with the flexibility and detailed control of low-level bytecode instrumentation. As such, it is a valuable tool for the programming language and software engineering communities—both in academia and in industry—that can reduce the effort needed for developing new dynamic analysis tools and instrumentation-based programming frameworks. DiSL may also serve as a framework for implementing higher-level analysis or aspect languages. DiSL is available open-source[7] and has already been used in several projects, such as for building a toolchain for workload characterization [8].

---

[7] http://disl.ow2.org

Acknowledgments. The research presented in this paper has been supported by the Swiss National Science Foundation (project CRSII2_136225), by the European Commission (Seventh Framework Programme grant 287746), by the Czech Science Foundation (projects GACR P202/10/J042 and GACR 201/09/H057), by Charles University institutional funding SVV-2012-265312, by a Sino-Swiss Science and Technology Cooperation (SSTC) Institutional Partnership (project IP04–092010), by the National Natural Science Foundation of China (project 61073151), and by the Science and Technology Commission of Shanghai Municipality (project 11530700500).

References

1. Binder, W., Ansaloni, D., Villazón, A., Moret, P.: Flexible and efficient profiling with aspect-oriented programming. Concurrency and Computation: Practice and Experience 23(15), 1749–1773 (2011)
2. Chiba, S., Nishizawa, M.: An Easy-to-Use Toolkit for Efficient Java Bytecode Translators. In: Pfenning, F., Macko, M. (eds.) GPCE 2003. LNCS, vol. 2830, pp. 364–376. Springer, Heidelberg (2003)
3. Chiba, S.: Load-Time Structural Reflection in Java. In: Bertino, E. (ed.) ECOOP 2000. LNCS, vol. 1850, pp. 313–336. Springer, Heidelberg (2000)
4. Kiczales, G., Lamping, J., Menhdhekar, A., Maeda, C., Lopes, C., Loingtier, J.M., Irwin, J.: Aspect-Oriented Programming. In: Aksit, M., Auletta, V. (eds.) ECOOP 1997. LNCS, vol. 1241, pp. 220–242. Springer, Heidelberg (1997)
5. Marek, L., Villazón, A., Zheng, Y., Ansaloni, D., Binder, W., Qi, Z.: DiSL: a domain-specific language for bytecode instrumentation. In: AOSD 2012: Proceedings of the 11th International Conference on Aspect-Oriented Software Development, pp. 239–250 (2012)
6. Moret, P., Binder, W., Tanter, É.: Polymorphic bytecode instrumentation. In: AOSD 2011: Proceedings of the 10th International Conference on Aspect-Oriented Software Development, pp. 129–140 (2011)
7. Pearce, D.J., Webster, M., Berry, R., Kelly, P.H.J.: Profiling with AspectJ. Software: Practice and Experience 37(7), 747–777 (2007)
8. Sewe, A., Mezini, M., Sarimbekov, A., Ansaloni, D., Binder, W., Ricci, N., Guyer, S.Z.: new Scala() instanceof Java: A comparison of the memory behaviour of Java and Scala programs. In: ISMM 2012: Proceedings of the International Symposium on Memory Management. pp. 97–108 (2012)
9. Vallée-Rai, R., Gagnon, E., Hendren, L., Lam, P., Pominville, P., Sundaresan, V.: Optimizing Java Bytecode Using the Soot Framework: Is It Feasible? In: Watt, D.A. (ed.) CC 2000. LNCS, vol. 1781, pp. 18–34. Springer, Heidelberg (2000)
10. Zheng, Y., Ansaloni, D., Marek, L., Sewe, A., Binder, W., Villazón, A., Tuma, P., Qi, Z., Mezini, M.: Turbo DiSL: Partial Evaluation for High-Level Bytecode Instrumentation. In: Furia, C.A., Nanz, S. (eds.) TOOLS 2012. LNCS, vol. 7304, pp. 353–368. Springer, Heidelberg (2012)

Indexed Realizability for Bounded-Time Programming with References and Type Fixpoints[*]

Aloïs Brunel[1] and Antoine Madet[2]

[1] Laboratoire d'Informatique de Paris-Nord, Université Paris 13
[2] Univ Paris Diderot, Sorbonne Paris Cité,
PPS, UMR 7126, CNRS, F-75205 Paris, France

Abstract. The field of implicit complexity has recently produced several bounded-complexity programming languages. This kind of language allows to implement exactly the functions belonging to a certain complexity class. We present a realizability semantics for a higher-order functional language based on a fragment of linear logic called **LAL** which characterizes the complexity class **PTIME**. This language features recursive types and higher-order store. Our realizability is based on biorthogonality, indexing and is quantitative. This last feature enables us not only to derive a semantical proof of termination, but also to give bounds on the number of computational steps of typed programs.

1 Introduction

Implicit Computational Complexity — This research field aims at providing machine-independent characterizations of complexity classes (such as polynomial time or logspace functions). One approach is to use type systems based on linear logic to control the complexity of higher-order functional programs. In particular, the so-called light logics (*e.g.* **LLL** [7], **SLL** [10]) have led to various type systems for the λ-calculus guaranteeing that a well-typed term has a bounded complexity [3]. These logics introduce the modalities '!' (read *bang*) and '§' (read *paragraph*). By a fine control of the nesting of these modalities, which is called the *depth*, the duplication of data can be made explicit and the complexity of programs can be tamed. This framework has been recently extended to a higher-order process calculus [6] and a functional language with recursive definitions [19]. Also, Amadio and Madet have proposed [15] a multi-threaded λ-calculus with higher-order store that enjoys an elementary time termination.

Quantitative Realizability — Starting from Kleene, the concept of realizability has been introduced in different forms and has been shown very useful to

---

[*] Work partially supported by the Future and Emerging Technologies (FET) programme within the Seventh Framework Programme for Research of the European Commission, under FET-Open grant number: 243881 (project CerCo).

R. Jhala and A. Igarashi (Eds.): APLAS 2012, LNCS 7705, pp. 264–279, 2012.

build models of computational systems. In a series of works [13,12], Dal Lago and Hofmann have shown how to extend Kleene realizability with quantitative informations in order to interpret subsystems of linear logic with restricted complexity. The idea behind Dal Lago and Hofmann's work is to consider bounded-time programs as realizers, where bounds are represented by elements of a *resource monoid*. In [5] the first author has shown how this quantitative extension fits well in a biorthogonality based framework (namely Krivine's classical realizability [9]) and how it relates to the notion of forcing.

Step-Indexing — In order to give a semantical account of features like recursive or reference types, one has to face troublesome circularity issues. To solve this problem, Appel and McAllester [2] have proposed step-indexed models. The idea is to define the interpretation of a type as a predicate on terms indexed by numbers. Informally, a term t belongs to the interpretation of a type τ with the index $k \in \mathbb{N}$ if when t is executed for k steps, it satisfies the predicate associated to τ. Then, it is possible to define by induction on the index k the interpretation of recursive or reference types. Step-indexing has been related to Gödel-Löb logic and the *later* operator $\triangleright$ [17].

Contributions — In this paper, we present a typed λ-calculus called $\lambda_{\mathrm{LAL}}^{\mathrm{Reg},\mu}$ whose functional core is based on the light logic **LAL** [3]. We extend it with recursive types and higher-order store. Even in presence of these features, every program typable in $\lambda_{\mathrm{LAL}}^{\mathrm{Reg},\mu}$ terminates in polynomial time. To prove termination in bounded-time, we propose a new quantitative realizability semantics with the following features:

- It is biorthogonality based, which permits a simple presentation and allows the possibility to interpret control operators (though it is only discussed informally in the conclusion of this paper).
- It is indexed, which permits to interpret higher-order store and recursive types. The particularity is that our model is indexed by depths (the nesting of modalities) instead of computational steps (like in step-indexing).

To our knowledge, this is the first semantics presenting at the same time quantitative, indexed and biorthogonality features.

Outline — Section 2 introduces the language $\lambda_{\mathrm{LAL}}^{\mathrm{Reg},\mu}$ and its type system. In Section 3, we introduce the indexed quantitative realizability. It is then used to obtain a semantic model for $\lambda_{\mathrm{LAL}}^{\mathrm{Reg},\mu}$, which in turn implies termination in polynomial time of typed programs. Finally, we mention related works in Section 4 and in Section 5 we discuss future research directions and conclude.

2 The Language

This section presents the language $\lambda_{\mathrm{LAL}}^{\mathrm{Reg},\mu}$ and its type system. Before going into details, we give some intuitions on the modalities and explain how we deal with side-effects with the notion of *region*.

On Modalities — The functional core of the language is an affine λ-calculus which means that λ-abstractions can use their argument at most once. To provide some duplication power, we introduce two modal constructors '!' and '§' that originate from **LAL**. Values of the shape $!V$ and $\S V$ can then be destructed against specific let! and let §-expressions.

On Regions — Following a standard practice in effect systems [14], the state of a program is abstracted into a finite set of regions where each region may represents several dynamically allocated values. Then, side-effects are produced by read and write operations on these regions. As noted by Amadio [1], the reduction rules of an abstract language with regions can be formalized such that they simulate the reduction rules of a concrete language with dynamic allocation. Working at the abstract level of regions allows to encompass several interaction mechanisms like references and channels (for the latter, the language should dispose of concurrency constructs). Moreover, termination in polynomial time of the language with regions entails termination in polynomial time of the language with dynamic allocation since the simulation preserves the number of reduction steps. Finally, we find it easier to give a semantic model of a type system with regions instead of dynamic locations.

How these modalities relate to polynomial time and how regions simulate dynamic locations is further explained in Section 2.2.

2.1   Syntax and Operational Semantics

The syntax of the language is the following:

$$
\begin{array}{lll}
Values & V ::= x \mid \lambda x.M \mid r \mid () \mid !V \mid \S V \\
Terms & M ::= V \mid M_1 M_2 \mid !M \mid \S M \mid \mathsf{get}(r) \mid \mathsf{set}(r, V) \\
& \quad\;\; \mathsf{let}\; !x = V \;\mathsf{in}\; M \mid \mathsf{let}\; \S x = V \;\mathsf{in}\; M
\end{array}
$$

We suppose having a countable set of variables denoted $x, y, \ldots$ and of regions denoted by the letters $r, r', \ldots$. The terminal value *unit* is denoted by (). Modal terms and modal values are built with the unary constructors ! and § and are destructed by the respective let! and let §-expressions. The terms $\mathsf{get}(r)$ and $\mathsf{set}(r, V)$ are respectively used to read a value from a region r and to assign a value V to a region r. We denote by $M[N/x]$ the term M in which each free occurrence of x has been substituted by N.

The operational semantics of the language is presented in the form of an abstract machine. We first define the configurations of the abstract machine:

$$
\begin{array}{lll}
Environments & E ::= \diamond \mid V \cdot E \mid M \odot E \mid ! \cdot E \mid \S \cdot E \\
Stores & S ::= r \Leftarrow V \mid S_1 \uplus S_2 \\
Configurations & C ::= \langle M, E, S \rangle
\end{array}
$$

Programs are intended to be executed with a right-to-left call-by-value strategy. Hence, an environment E is either an empty frame $\diamond$, a stack of frames to evaluate on the left of a value $(V \cdot E)$, on the right of a term $(M \odot E)$ or in-depth of a term $(! \cdot E$ and $\S \cdot E)$. Finally, a store S is a multiset of region assignments $r \Leftarrow V$. A configuration of the abstract machine is executed according to the following rules:

$$\langle \lambda x.M, V \cdot E, S \rangle \longrightarrow \langle M[V/x], E, S \rangle$$
$$\langle MN, E, S \rangle \longrightarrow \langle N, M \odot E, S \rangle$$
$$\langle V, M \odot E, S \rangle \longrightarrow \langle M, V \cdot E, S \rangle$$
$$\langle \dagger M, E, S \rangle \longrightarrow \langle M, \dagger \cdot E, S \rangle \qquad \text{if } M \text{ is not a value}$$
$$\langle V, \dagger \cdot E, S \rangle \longrightarrow \langle \dagger V, E, S \rangle$$
$$\langle \text{let } \dagger x = \dagger V \text{ in } M, E, S \rangle \longrightarrow \langle M[V/x], E, S \rangle$$
$$\langle \text{get}(r), E, (r \Leftarrow V) \uplus S \rangle \longrightarrow \langle V, E, S \rangle$$
$$\langle \text{set}(r, V), E, S \rangle \longrightarrow \langle (), E, (r \Leftarrow V) \uplus S \rangle$$

For the sake of conciseness we wrote $\dagger$ for $\dagger \in \{!, \S\}$. Observe that let $\dagger$-expressions destruct modal values $\dagger V$ and propagate V. Reading a region amounts to *consume* the value from the store and writing to a region amounts to *add* the value to the store. We consider programs up to α-renaming and in the sequel $\longrightarrow^*$ denotes the reflexive and transitive closure of $\longrightarrow$.

Example 1. Here is a function $F = \lambda x.\text{let } !y = x \text{ in } \text{set}(r_1, \S y); \text{set}(r_2, \S y)$ that duplicates its argument and assign it to regions r_1 and r_2. It can be used to duplicate a value from another region r_3 as follows:

$$\langle F\text{get}(r_3), \diamond, r_3 \Leftarrow !V \rangle \longrightarrow^* \langle (), \diamond, (r_1 \Leftarrow \S V) \uplus (r_2 \Leftarrow \S V) \rangle$$

Remark 1. As usual, we can encode the sequential composition $M; N$ by the application $(\lambda x.N)M$ where x does not occur free in N. Thus, the reduction rule $\langle V; M, E, S \rangle \longrightarrow \langle M, E, S \rangle$ can be assumed.

Definition 1. *We define the notation* $\langle M, E, S \rangle \Downarrow^n$ *as the following statement:*

- *The evaluation of* $\langle M, E, S \rangle$ *in the abstract machine terminates.*
- *The number of steps needed by* $\langle M, E, S \rangle$ *to terminate is n.*

2.2 Type System

The light logic **LAL** relies on a *stratification* principle which is at the basis of our type system. We first give an informal explanation of this principle.

On Stratification — Each occurrence of a program can be given a depth which is the number of nested modal constructors for which the occurrence is in scope. Here is an example for the program P where each occurrence is labeled with its depth:

$$P = (\lambda x.\text{let } !y = x \text{ in } \text{set}(r, \S y))!V; \text{get}(r)$$

The depth $d(M)$ of a term M is the maximum depth of its occurrences. The stratification principle is that the depth of every occurrence is preserved by reduction. On the functional side, it can be ensured by these two constraints: (1) if a λ-abstraction occurs at depth d, then the bound variable must occur at depth d; (2) if a let $\dagger$-expression occurs at depth d, then the bound variable must occur at depth $d+1$. These two constraints are respected by the program P and we observe in the following reduction

$$\langle P, \diamond, \emptyset \rangle \longrightarrow^* \langle \mathsf{set}(r, \S V); \mathsf{get}(r), \diamond, \emptyset \rangle$$

that the depth of V is preserved. In order to preserve the depth of occurrences that go through the store, this third constraint is needed: (3) for each region r, $\mathsf{get}(r)$ and $\mathsf{set}(r)$ must occur at a fixed depth d_r. We observe that this is the case of program P where $d_r = 0$. Consequently, the reduction terminates as follows

$$\langle \mathsf{set}(r, \S V); \mathsf{get}(r), \diamond, \emptyset \rangle \longrightarrow^* \langle \mathsf{get}(r), \diamond, r \Leftarrow \S V \rangle \longrightarrow^* \langle \S V, \diamond, \emptyset \rangle$$

where the depth of V is still preserved. Stratification on the functional side has been deeply studied by Terui with the Light Affine λ-calculus [20] and extended to regions by Amadio and the second author [15].

Types and Contexts   —   The syntax of types and contexts is the following:

Types	$A, B, C ::= X \mid \mathsf{Unit} \mid A \multimap B \mid {!}A \mid \S A \mid \mu X.A \mid \mathsf{Reg}_r A$
Variable contexts	$\Gamma, \Delta ::= x_1 : (u_1, A_1), \dots, x_n : (u_n, A_n)$
Region contexts	$R ::= r_1 : (\delta_1, A_1), \dots, r_n : (\delta_n, A_n)$

We have a countable set of type variables $X, X', \dots$. We distinguish the terminal type Unit, the affine functional type $A \multimap B$, the type $!A$ of terms which reduce on a duplicable value, the type $\S A$ of terms containing values that may have been duplicated, recursive types $\mu X.A$ and the type $\mathsf{Reg}_r A$ of terms which reduce to region r that contains values of type A. Hereby types may depend on regions. Following [15], a region context associates a natural number δ_i to each region r_i of a finite set of regions $\{r_1, \dots, r_n\}$ that we write $dom(R)$. Writing $r : (\delta, A)$ means that the region r contains values of type A and that gets and sets on r may only happen at a fixed depth depending on δ. A variable context associates each variable with an usage $u \in \{\lambda, \S, !\}$ which constraints the variable to be bound by a λ-abstraction, a let $\S$-expression or a let $!$-expression respectively. In the sequel we write Γ_u for $x_1 : (u, A_1), \dots, x_n : (u, A_n)$. Writing $x : (u, A)$ means that the variable x ranges on values of type A and can be bound according to u.

Types depend on region names. Therefore, we have to be careful in stating when a type A is well-formed with respect to a region context R, written $R \vdash A$. Informally, the judgment $r_1 : (\delta_1, A_1), \dots, r_n : (\delta_n, A_n) \vdash B$ is well formed provided that: (1) all the region names occurring in the types $A_1, \dots, A_n, B$ belong to the set $\{r_1, \dots, r_n\}$, (2) all types of the shape $\mathsf{Reg}_{r_i} B$ with $i \in \{1, \dots, n\}$ and occurring in the types $A_1, \dots, A_n, B$ are such that $B = A_i$. The judgment $R \vdash \Gamma$

is well-formed if $R \vdash A$ is well-formed for every $x : (u, A) \in \Gamma$. We invite the reader to check in [1] that these judgements can be easily defined.

Typing Rules — A typing judgment takes the form $R; \Gamma \vdash^\delta P : A$ and is indexed by an integer δ. The rules are given in Figure 1. They should entail the following:

- if $x : (\lambda, A) \in \Gamma$ then x occurs at most once and it must be at depth 0 in P,
- if $x : (\S, A) \in \Gamma$ then x occurs at most once and it must be at depth 1 in the scope of a $\S$ constructor in P,
- if $x : (!, A) \in \Gamma$ then x occurs arbitrarily many times and it must be at depth 1 in the scope of a $\dagger$ constructor in P,
- if $r : (\delta', A) \in R$ then $\mathsf{get}(r)$ and $\mathsf{set}(r)$ occur at depth $\delta - \delta'$ in P.

$$
\text{v} \frac{R \vdash}{R; x : (\lambda, A) \vdash^\delta x : A} \quad
\text{u} \frac{R \vdash}{R; - \vdash^\delta () : \mathsf{Unit}} \quad
\text{r} \frac{R \vdash \quad r : (\delta, A) \in R}{R; - \vdash^\delta r : \mathsf{Reg}_r A}
$$

$$
\text{c} \frac{R; \Gamma, x : (!, A), y : (!, A) \vdash^\delta M : B}{R; \Gamma, z : (!, A) \vdash^\delta M[z/x, z/y] : B} \quad
\text{w} \frac{R; \Gamma \vdash^\delta M : B \quad R \vdash \Gamma, x : (u, A)}{R; \Gamma, x : (u, A) \vdash^\delta M : B}
$$

$$
\text{lam} \frac{R; \Gamma, x : (\lambda, A) \vdash^\delta M : B}{R : \Gamma \vdash^\delta \lambda x. M : A \multimap B} \quad
\text{app} \frac{R; \Gamma \vdash^\delta M_1 : A \multimap B \quad R; \Delta \vdash^\delta M_2 : A}{R; \Gamma, \Delta \vdash^\delta M_1 M_2 : B}
$$

$$
\text{!-prom} \frac{R; x : (\lambda, A) \vdash^\delta V : A}{R; x : (!, A) \vdash^{\delta+1} !V : !A} \quad
\text{\S-prom} \frac{R; \Gamma_\lambda, \Delta_\lambda \vdash^\delta M : A}{R; \Gamma_\S, \Delta_! \vdash^{\delta+1} \S M : \S A}
$$

$$
\dagger\text{-elim} \frac{R; \Gamma \vdash^\delta V : \dagger A \quad R; \Delta, x : (\dagger, A) \vdash^\delta M : B}{R; \Gamma, \Delta \vdash^\delta \mathsf{let} \; \dagger x = V \; \mathsf{in} \; M : B} \quad
\text{get} \frac{R; - \vdash^\delta r : \mathsf{Reg}_r A}{R; - \vdash^\delta \mathsf{get}(r) : A}
$$

$$
\text{set} \frac{R; - \vdash^\delta r : \mathsf{Reg}_r A \quad R; \Gamma \vdash^\delta V : A}{R; \Gamma \vdash^\delta \mathsf{set}(r, V) : \mathsf{Unit}} \quad
\text{un/fold} \frac{R; \Gamma \vdash^\delta M : \mu X. A}{R; \Gamma \vdash^\delta M : A[\mu X. A / X]}
$$

Fig. 1. Typing rules

Here are several crucial remarks on the rules:

- In binary rules, we implicitly require that contexts Γ and Δ are disjoint. There are explicit rules (w) and (c) for the weakening and contraction of variables and we may only contract variables with usage '!'. Therefore, λ-abstractions and $\mathsf{let} \S$-expressions can bind at most one occurrence of free variable while $\mathsf{let} !$-expressions can bind several occurrences.

- The rule !-prom entails that $!V$ may contain at most one occurrence of free variable. This is to rule out a term like $Z = \lambda x.\text{let } !y = x$ in $!(\lambda z.yy)$ whose n-th application $(Z \ldots (Z(Z!V)))$ would duplicate 2^n times the value $!V$. To recover some duplication power, the rule §-prom allows a term of the shape $§M$ to contain many occurrences of free variable. On the other hand, let §-expressions cannot bind many occurrences of free variable.
- It is important that the type $§A \multimap !A$ is *not* inhabited, otherwise from a value of the shape $§(\lambda z.yy)$ we can produce a value $!(\lambda z.yy)$ and we loose the subject reduction property for there are two occurrences of y under a bang. Also, the rule !-prom must only applies to values so that the program $\lambda x.\text{let } !y = x$ in $§\text{set}(r, x); !\text{get}(r)$ cannot be given type $§A \multimap !A$.
- The depth δ of a judgment is incremented when we construct a modal term. This allows to count the number of nested modalities and to stratify regions by requiring that the depth of a region matches the depth of the judgment in the rule R.
- For space consideration the rule un/fold can be used upside down.

Definition 2. *We say that a program M is well-typed if a judgment $R; \Gamma \vdash^\delta M : A$ can be derived for some R, Γ and δ such that:*

(1) If $r : (\delta_r, B) \in R$ then $B = §C$.
(2) For every type fixpoint $\mu X.B$ that appears in R, Γ and A, the occurrences of X in B are guarded by (occur under) a modality †.
(3) Every depth index in the derivation is positive. Note that if it is not the case, we can always find $\delta' > \delta$ and R' such that it is true for $R'; \Gamma \vdash^{\delta'} M : A$.

Remark 2. The above three conditions are required to give a well-founded interpretation. The fact that region types can only be guarded by a paragraph is due to properties of the light monoid (see Lemma 2).

The following progress property can be derived as long as the program does not try to read an empty region.

Proposition 1 (Progress). *If $R; \Gamma \vdash^\delta M : A$ then $\langle C, \diamond, \emptyset \rangle \longrightarrow^* \langle V, \diamond, S \rangle$ and $R; \Gamma \vdash^\delta V : A$ and every assigned value in S can be typed.*

Remark 3. A program whose state is partionned into a fixed number of regions can simulate a program with a statically unknown number of dynamic allocations. In fact, there is a typed translation from the language with dynamic locations to the language with regions. Let us consider a small example where for the sake simplicity we do not care about the multiplicity of variables. Here is a program that generates two references à la ML with the same value V:

$$((\lambda f.\lambda x.fx; fx)(\lambda y.\text{ref } y))V$$

A single region r can be used to abstract both references by assigning the type $\text{Reg}_r A$ to the subterm $(\text{ref } y)$. It then suffices to translate $(\text{ref } y)$ into $(\text{set}(r, y); r)$ and observe that the translated program reduces to the configuration

$$\langle r, \diamond, (r \Leftarrow V) \uplus (r \Leftarrow V) \rangle$$

Regions simulate references as long as the values written to regions do not over-write the previous ones. This is the case in our abstract machine, but also, reading a region amounts to consume a value from the region while the values stored in references should be persistent. We note that it is enough to duplicate, use and rewrite the value to the store to simulate this phenomenon.

The goal of the next section is to prove the following theorem

Theorem 1 (Polynomial termination). *There exists a family of polynomials $\{P_d\}_{d\in\mathbb{N}}$ such that if M is well-typed then $\langle M,\diamond,\diamond\rangle$ terminates in at most $P_{d(M)}(size(M))$ steps.*

3 "Indexed" Quantitative Realizability

We now present a biorthogonality-based interpretation of $\lambda_{LAL}^{Reg,\mu}$. Apart from the use of biorthogonality, this interpretation has two particularities:

- First, the realizability model is *quantitative*. A type is interpreted by a set of *weighted realizers* (that is a program together with a store and a quantity bounding its normalization time). This allows to prove complexity properties of programs.
- Secondly, the semantics is *indexed* (or *stratified*), meaning that we interpret a type by a family of sets indexed by $\mathbb{N}$. Moreover the interpretation of a type is defined by double induction, first on the *index n*, and secondly on the *size* of the type. This allows to interpret recursive types and references.

It is worth noticing that while our interpretation is similar to the so-called "step-indexed" models, the meaning of indexes is not (directly) related to the number of computation steps but to the depth of terms (and so our model could be described as a "depth-indexed" model). It is the quantitative part which is used to keep track of the number of computational steps.

3.1 The Light Monoid

The realizability model is parametrized by a *quantitative monoid*, whose elements represent an information about the amount of time needed by a program to terminate.

Definition 3. *A* quantitative monoid *is a structure* $(\mathcal{M}, +, \boldsymbol{0}, \boldsymbol{1}, \leq, \|.\|)$ *where:*

- $(\mathcal{M}, +, \boldsymbol{0}, \leq)$ *is a preordered monoid.*
- $\|.\| : \mathcal{M} \longrightarrow \mathbb{N}$ *is a function such that:*
  - *for every $p, q \in \mathcal{M}$, we have $\|p\| + \|q\| \leq \|p + q\|$.*
  - *Morever, $\|.\|$ is compatible with $\leq$.*
- $\boldsymbol{1} \in \mathcal{M}$ *is such that $1 \leq \|\boldsymbol{1}\|$.*

Example 2. A simple instance of a quantitative monoid is given by the set $\mathbb{N}$ of positive integers, endowed with the usual addition on integers, the elements 0 and 1, and the operation $\|.\|$ defined by $\|n\| = n$.

From now on, we will often denote a quantitative monoid by its carrier $\mathcal{M}$, and we use lower-case consonnes letters $p, q, m, v, \ldots$ to denote its elements. Moreover, $\mathbf{n}$ denotes the element of $\mathcal{M}$ defined as $\underbrace{1 + \cdots + 1}_{n \text{ times}}$.

Remark 4. Here are some intuitions about the previous definition.

- The operation $+$ is used to obtain the resource consumption resulting of the interaction of two programs.
- The elements of $\mathcal{M}$ are abstract quantities, so given such an abstract quantity $p \in \mathcal{M}$, $\|p\|$ provides the *concrete* quantity associated to it.
- The inequality $\forall p, q, \|p\| + \|q\| \leq \|p + q\|$ informally represents the fact that the amount of resource consumed by the interaction of two programs is potentially more important than the total amount of resource used by the two programs alone.

Definition 4. *Given a quantitative monoid, we say that a function $f : \mathcal{M} \longrightarrow \mathcal{M}$ is* sensible *if whenever $p \in \mathcal{M}$ we have $f(p) \leq f(p + 1)$ and $\|f(p)\| \neq \|f(p + 1)\|$. The set of sensible functions on $\mathcal{M}$ is denoted by $\mathcal{M}[.]$.*

We now define the notion of *light monoid*, which will be used to describe the execution time of $\lambda_{\text{LAL}}^{\text{Reg},\mu}$ programs.

Definition 5. *We call* light monoid *a quantitative monoid $\mathcal{M}$ equipped with three sensible functions $!, \S, F : \mathcal{M} \longrightarrow \mathcal{M}$ such that for every $p, q \in \mathcal{M}$, the following properties hold:*

- *There is some p' such that $p \leq p'$ and $\S p' \leq !p$*
- *$\S(p + q) \leq \S p + \S q$*
- *There are p', q' such that $p \leq p'$ and $q \leq q'$, that enjoy $\S p' + \S q' \leq \S(p + q)$*
- *$!p + !p \leq !p + \mathbf{1}$*
- *$!(p + q) \leq F(p) + !q$*

Those inequations will be needed to prove that our realizability interpretation is sound with respect to the typing rules involving the modalities $!$ and $\S$. Such a light monoid exists, as witnessed by the following example and property.

Example 3. We define the structure $(\mathcal{M}_l, +, \mathbf{0}, \mathbf{1}, \leq, \|.\|)$ where

- $\mathcal{M}$ is the set of triples $(n, m, f) \in \mathbb{N} \times \mathbb{N} \times \mathbb{N}^{\mathbb{N}}$ where f is a polynomial.
- $(n, m, f) + (l, k, g) = (n + l, max(m, k), max(f, g))$.
- $\mathbf{0} = (0, 0, x \mapsto 0)$
- $\mathbf{1} = (1, 0, x \mapsto x)$
- $(n, m, f) \leq (l, k, g)$ iff $n \leq l \wedge n + m \leq l + k \wedge f \leq g$
- If $(n, m, f) \in \mathcal{M}$, $\|(n, m, f)\| = n f(m + n)$.

Then $\mathcal{M}_l$ is a quantitative monoid. Moreover, we can define the three following operations $!, \S, F$ on $\mathcal{M}_l$:

- $\S = (n, m, f) \mapsto (n/m, m, x \mapsto x^2 f(x^2))$
- $! = (n, m, f) \mapsto (1, n + m, x \mapsto x^3 f(x^3))$
- $F = (n, m, f) \mapsto (1 + n + m, m, x \mapsto x^3 f(x^3))$

Property 1. The three operations $!, \S$ and F endow $\mathcal{M}_l$ with a structure of light monoid.

Notice that in the monoid $\mathcal{M}_l$, the operations $!, \S$ and F make the degree of the third component of any element of $\mathcal{M}_l$ grow.

3.2   Orthogonality

The main technical tool used to define our model is orthogonality. Whereas it is usually defined as a relation between a program and an environment, in our work it is a relation between weighted programs and weighted environments. From now on, $\mathcal{M}$ denotes a light monoid.

Definition 6.   – *A* weighted term *is a tuple* (M, p) *where M is a term and p an element of $\mathcal{M}$. The set of weighted terms is denoted by $\Lambda_{\mathcal{M}}$.*
  – *A* weighted stack *is a pair* (E, e) *where E is a stack and e an element of $\mathcal{M}[.]$. The set of weighted stacks is denoted by $\Pi_{\mathcal{M}}$.*

We choose a *pole* $\perp\!\!\!\perp \subseteq \mathsf{Conf} \times \mathcal{M}$ as the set of bounded-time terminating weighted configurations:

$$\perp\!\!\!\perp = \{(\langle M, E, S \rangle, p) \mid \langle M, E, S \rangle \Downarrow^n \wedge n \leq \|p\|\}$$

In orthogonality-based models, fixing a pole, also called *observable*, corresponds to choosing a notion of *correct* computation.

Proposition 2. *This pole satisfies some important properties:*

1. *($\leq$-saturation) If* $(\langle M, E, S \rangle, p) \in \perp\!\!\!\perp$ *and* $p \leq q$ *then* $(\langle M, E, S \rangle, q) \in \perp\!\!\!\perp$.
2. *($\longrightarrow$-saturation) If* $(\langle M, E, S \rangle, p) \in \perp\!\!\!\perp$ *and* $\langle M', E, S' \rangle \longrightarrow \langle M, E, S \rangle$ *then* $(\langle M', E', S' \rangle, p + 1) \in \perp\!\!\!\perp$.

The pole induces a notion of orthogonality. In contrast with usual models, since we need to deal with references, the orthogonality relation is parametrized by a set $\mathcal{S}$ of stores.

Definition 7. *The orthogonality relation* $\perp_{\mathcal{S}} \subseteq \Lambda_{\mathcal{M}} \times \Pi_{\mathcal{M}}$ *is defined as:*

$$(M, p) \perp_{\mathcal{S}} (E, e) \text{ iff } \forall (S, s) \in \mathcal{S}, (\langle M, E, S \rangle, e(p + s)) \in \perp\!\!\!\perp$$

This orthogonality relation lifts to sets of weighted terms and weighted stacks. If $X \subseteq \Lambda_{\mathcal{M}}$ *(resp $X \subseteq \Pi_{\mathcal{M}}$),*

$$X^{\perp_s} = \{ (E, e) \in \Pi_{\mathcal{M}} \mid \forall (M, p) \in X, (M, p) \perp_{\mathcal{S}} (E, e) \}$$

$$(\text{resp. } X^{\perp_s} = \{ (M, p) \in \Lambda_{\mathcal{M}} \mid \forall (E, e) \in X, (M, p) \perp_{\mathcal{S}} (E, e) \})$$

The operation $(.)^{\perp s}$ satisfies the usual orthogonality properties.

Lemma 1. *Suppose* $X, Y \subseteq \Lambda_{\mathcal{M}}$ *or* $X, Y \subseteq \Pi_{\mathcal{M}}$:

1. $X \subseteq Y$ *implies* $Y^{\perp s} \subseteq X^{\perp s}$
2. $X \subseteq X^{\perp s \perp s}$
3. $X^{\perp s \perp s \perp s} = X^{\perp s}$

Definition 8. *If* X *is a set of weighted realizers, we define its* $\leq$-*closure* $\overline{X} = \{ (M, p) \mid \exists q \leq p, (M, q) \in X \}$.

Remark 5. Notice that for any S, we have $\overline{X} \subseteq X^{\perp s \perp s}$.

We say that a set $X \subseteq \Lambda_{\mathcal{M}}$ is a S-behavior if $X = X^{\perp s \perp s}$. Finally, we can define the set of S-reducibility candidates. To do that, we first need to extend the language of terms with a new constant

$$M \quad ::= \dots \quad | \quad \maltese$$

This constant comes with no particular reduction rule. It can be seen as a special variable considered as a closed term and is in a sense the dual of the empty stack. Notice that none of the previous constructions are modified. Moreover, at the end of the day, because we only consider typable terms (that do not contain any $\maltese$), $\maltese$ is only a technical intermediate.

Definition 9. *The set of* S-*reducibility candidates, denoted by* CR_S *is the set of* S-*behaviors* X *such that* $(\maltese, \mathbf{0}) \in X \subseteq \{(\diamond, x \mapsto x)\}^{\perp s}$

Remark 6. If $(M, p) \in X$ where X is a S-reducibility candidate and if $(\diamond, \mathbf{0}) \in S$, then $\langle M, \diamond, \diamond \rangle$ terminates in at most $\|p\|$ steps. In fact our notion of reducibility candidate extends the usual notion in the non-quantitative case.

Finally, suppose R is a set of regions and suppose S_R is a set of stores whose domain is restricted to a R. We say that :

$S_R \sqsubseteq S' \Leftrightarrow S'$ contains S_R and if $(S, s) \in S'$ and if we write $S = S^\delta \uplus S''$, then there is a decomposition $s = s' + s''$ such that $(S^\delta, s') \in S_R$, $dom(S'') = \{ r_i \mid \delta_i > \delta \}$ and moreover, if $(S_R, s_R) \in S_R$ then $(S'' \uplus S_R, s'' + s_R) \in S'$.

Remark 7. This quite involved definition will permit to the interpretation of a type to enjoy properties similar to the one called *extension/restriction* in [1]. In other words, given a store, it gives a way to say what substore can be removed safely and what stores can be added to it safely.

3.3 Interpretation of $\lambda_{\mathrm{LAL}}^{\mathrm{Reg}, \mu}$

Using the orthogonality machinery previously defined, we can give an interpretation of $\lambda_{\mathrm{LAL}}^{\mathrm{Reg}, \mu}$ types as reducibility candidates. Suppose R is the following region context:

$$R = r_1 : (\delta_1, \S A_1), \dots, r_n : (\delta_n, \S A_n)$$

We define three indexed sets: the *interpretation* $|R|_\delta$ of the region context R, the *pre-interpretation* $\|R \vdash A\|_\delta$ of a type A and its *interpretation* $|R \vdash A|_\delta^{\mathcal{S}}$ with respect to a set of stores $\mathcal{S}$. These three notions are defined by mutual induction, first on the index δ, and then on the size of the type A.

$$|R|_{=\delta} = \{ \ (S, \sum_{\delta_i=\delta} \sum_{1 \leq j \leq k_i} \S q_j^i) \mid dom(S) = \{ \ r_i \mid r_i : (\delta_i, \S A_i) \in R \wedge \delta_i = \delta \ \}$$
$$\wedge \quad \forall r_i \in dom(S), S(r_i) = \{\S V_1^i, \S V_2^i, \ldots, \S V_{k_i}^i\}$$
$$\wedge \quad \forall j \in [1, k_i], (V_j^i, q_j^i) \in \|R \vdash A_i\|_{\delta_i - 1} \ \}$$

$$|R|_{\delta+1} = \{ \ (S_1 \uplus S_\delta, s_1 + \S s_\delta) \mid (S_1, s_1) \in |R|_{=\delta+1}, (S_\delta, s_\delta) \in |R|_\delta \ \}$$

For convenience, we start the indexing of the interpretation at -1 instead of 0.

$$\|R \vdash A\|_{-1} = \overline{\{(\maltese, 0)\}}$$

For $\delta \geq 0$, we define the pre-interpretation as:

$$\|R \vdash \mathsf{Unit}\|_\delta = \overline{\{((), 0)\}}$$
$$\|R \vdash \mathsf{Reg}_r A\|_\delta = \overline{\{(r, 0)\}}$$
$$\|R \vdash A \multimap B\|_\delta = \overline{\{ \ (\lambda x.M, p) \mid \forall (V, v) \in \|R \vdash A\|_\delta, \forall \mathcal{S}, |R|_\delta \sqsubseteq \mathcal{S}, (M[V/x], p + v) \in |R \vdash B|_\delta^{\mathcal{S}} \ \}}$$
$$\|R \vdash \S A\|_\delta = \overline{\{ \ (\S V, \S v) \mid (V, v) \in \|R \vdash A\|_{\delta-1} \ \}}$$
$$\|R \vdash !A\|_\delta = \overline{\{ \ (!V, !v) \mid (V, v) \in \|R \vdash A\|_{\delta-1} \ \}}$$
$$\|R \vdash \mu X.A\|_\delta = \|R \vdash A[\mu X.A/X]\|_\delta$$

The interpretation of a type with respect to a set $\mathcal{S}$ is just defined as the biorthogonal of the pre-interpretation:

$$|R \vdash A|_\delta^{\mathcal{S}} = \|R \vdash A\|_\delta^{\perp_{\mathcal{S}} \perp_{\mathcal{S}}}$$

Remark 8. Because of the presence of type fixpoints and regions, there are several circularities that could appear in the definition of $\|R \vdash A\|_\delta$. Yet, the interpretation is well defined for the following reasons:

- The type fixpoints $\mu X.A$ we consider are such that every occurrence of X in A is *guarded* by a modality ! or $\S$. But these modalities make the index of the interpretation decrease by one. Hence, $\|R \vdash \mu X.A\|_{\delta+1}$ is well defined as soon as $\|R \vdash \mu X.A\|_\delta$ is.
- To define $\|R \vdash A\|_{\delta+1}$, we need $|R|_{\delta+1}$ to be already defined. But here again, in R each type is guarded by a modality $\S$. This implies that to define $|R|_{\delta+1}$, we only need to know each $\|R \vdash A_i\|_\delta$.

An important point is that the interpretation of a formula A with respect to a region context R and to an index $\delta \in \mathbb{N}$ is a $|R|_\delta$-reducibility candidate (it will be used to prove bounded-time termination).

Proposition 3. *For all $\delta \in \mathbb{N}$ we have $|R \vdash A|_\delta^{|R|_\delta} \in \mathsf{CR}_{|R|_\delta}$.*

Table 1. Inferring a bound from a $\lambda_{LAL}^{Reg,\mu}$ typing judgment

$$\text{v}\frac{}{\vdash^\delta x : 0} \qquad \text{r}\frac{}{\vdash^\delta r : 0} \qquad \text{u}\frac{}{\vdash^\delta () : 0} \qquad \text{get}\frac{}{\vdash^\delta \text{get}(r) : 5}$$

$$\text{set}\frac{\vdash^\delta V : [\![V]\!]}{\vdash^{\delta+1} \text{set}(r, \S V) : \S[\![V]\!] + 1} \qquad \text{fold}\frac{\vdash^\delta M : [\![M]\!]}{\vdash^\delta M : [\![M]\!]} \qquad \text{unfold}\frac{\vdash^\delta M : [\![M]\!]}{\vdash^\delta M : [\![M]\!]}$$

$$\text{c}\frac{x :!, y :! \vdash^\delta M : [\![M]\!]}{z :! \vdash^\delta M[z/x, z/y] : [\![M]\!] + 1} \qquad \text{w}\frac{\vdash^\delta M : [\![M]\!]}{x : \delta \vdash^\delta M : [\![M]\!]}$$

$$\text{lam}\frac{\vdash^\delta M : [\![M]\!]}{\vdash^\delta \lambda x.M : [\![M]\!]} \qquad \text{app}\frac{\vdash^\delta M_1 : [\![M_1]\!] \qquad \vdash^\delta M_2 : [\![M_2]\!]}{\vdash^\delta M_1 M_2 : [\![M_1]\!] + [\![M_2]\!] + 3}$$

$$\text{\S-prom}\frac{\vdash^\delta M : [\![M]\!]}{\vdash^{\delta+1} \S M : \S[\![M]\!] + 4} \qquad \text{\S-elim}\frac{\vdash^\delta V : [\![V]\!] \qquad \Gamma \vdash^\delta M : [\![M]\!]}{\vdash^\delta \text{let } \S x = V \text{ in } M : [\![M]\!] + [\![V]\!] + 3}$$

$$\text{!-prom}\frac{\vdash^\delta M : [\![M]\!]}{\vdash^{\delta+1} !M : F([\![M]\!])} \qquad \text{!-elim}\frac{\vdash^\delta V : [\![V]\!] \qquad \Gamma \vdash^\delta M : [\![M]\!]}{\vdash^\delta \text{let } !x = V \text{ in } M : [\![M]\!] + [\![V]\!] + 3}$$

3.4 Adequacy and Bounded-Time Termination

We now prove the soundness of our model with respect to $\lambda_{LAL}^{Reg,\mu}$ and as a corollary the bounded-time termination theorem. In Table 1 is described how to infer an element of $\mathcal{M}$ from a $\lambda_{LAL}^{Reg,\mu}$ typing judgment: the notation $[\![M]\!]$ corresponds to the element of $\mathcal{M}$ already inferred from the typing judgment of $[\![M]\!]$, and each rule corresponds to the way $[\![M]\!]$ is built.

Definition 10. *We use the notations $\overline{V}$, $\overline{p}$ and $\overline{y}$ to denote respectively a list of values $[V_1, \ldots, V_n]$, a list $[p_1, \ldots, p_n]$ of elements of $\mathcal{M}$ and a list of variables $[y_1, \ldots, y_n]$. If M is a term, we denote by $M[\overline{V}/\overline{y}]$ the term $M[V_1/y_1, \ldots, V_n/y_n]$. If $\overline{p}$ is a list of elements of $\mathcal{M}$ and $\dagger \in \{!, \S\}$, we denote by $\dagger\overline{p}$ the list $[\dagger p_1, \ldots, \dagger p_n]$. We also define $\sum \overline{p}$ to be the sum $\sum_{1 \le i \le n} p_i$.*

If A is a type then we define λA as A itself. Suppose $\Gamma = x_1 : (e_1, A_1), \ldots, x_n : (e_n, A_n)$. Then the notation $(\overline{V}, \overline{p}) \Vdash^\delta \Gamma$ stands for $(W_i, p_i) \in \|R \vdash e_i A_i\|_\delta$ for $1 \le i \le n$ with $W_i = V_i$ if $e_i = \lambda$ and $W_i = \dagger V_i$ if $e_i = \dagger$.

Example 4. If we have $(\overline{V}, \overline{p}) \Vdash^\delta (x_1 : (\lambda, A_1), x_2 : (\S, A_2), x_3 : (!, A_3))$ then $\overline{V} = [V_1, V_2, M_3]$ and $\overline{p} = [p_1, \S p_2, !p_3]$ such that $(V_1, p_1) \in \|R \vdash A_1\|_\delta$, $(\S V_2, \S p_2) \in \|R \vdash \S A_2\|_\delta$ and $(!V_3, !p_3) \in \|R \vdash !A_3\|_\delta$.

Theorem 2 (Adequacy). *Suppose that $R; \Gamma \vdash^\delta M : C$. Let $(\overline{V}, \overline{p}) \Vdash^\delta \Gamma$, Then, for any $\mathcal{S}$ such that $|R|_\delta \sqsubseteq \mathcal{S}$,*

$$(M[\overline{V}/\overline{x}], [\![M]\!] + \sum \overline{p}) \in |R \vdash C|_\delta^\mathcal{S}$$

Moreover, if M is a value, then we have $(M[\overline{V}/\overline{x}], [\![M]\!] + \sum \overline{p}) \in \|R \vdash C\|_\delta$.

Proof. The proof is done by induction on the typing judgment.

One of the inductive cases here is particularly interesting, namely the §-promotion rule. It requires to prove the following lemma.

Lemma 2 (§-prom). *Suppose that for any S such that $|R|_\delta \sqsubseteq S$, $(M, m) \in |R \vdash A|_\delta^S$ holds. Then for any S such that $|R|_{\delta+1} \sqsubseteq S$, we have $(\S M, \S m + 4) \in |R \vdash \S A|_{\delta+1}^S$.*

This case is very important, since it justifies many definitions.

- Its proof crucially relies on the fact that in the definition of the region context interpretation $|R|_\delta$, each value is guarded by a modality § and not by a modality !. Indeed, it requires the monoidality property, which is true for § but not for !: $\forall p, q \in \mathcal{M}, \S(p + q) \leq \S p + \S q$.
- It also relies on the fact that we can consider any set of store S such that $|R|_\delta \sqsubseteq S$, which is also built-in in our interpretation of the linear arrow $\multimap$.

As a corollary of the adequacy theorem, we obtain the announced bounded-time termination theorem for $\lambda_{\text{LAL}}^{\text{Reg}, \mu}$ programs. As we have proved adequacy for *any* choice of a light monoid, we now consider a particular one, that is the light monoid defined in Example 3.

Proof (Termination theorem (Theorem 1)). This theorem is proved using adequacy together with Property 3. Indeed, we know that $\langle M, \diamond, \diamond \rangle$ terminates in at most $\|[\![M]\!]\|$ steps. Now, because we use the light monoid $\mathcal{M}_l$ of Example 3, it is easy to see that only the promotion rules for § and ! make the value of $\|[\![M]\!]\|$ increase significantly: the degree of the third component of $[\![M]\!]$ (which is a polynomial) is bounded by a function of the depth of M. A similar argument is made more precise in [11], for instance.

4 Related Work

Approximation Modality   —   In a series of two papers, Nakano introduced a normalizing intuitionistic type system that features recursive types, which are guarded by a modality • (the approximation modality). Nakano also defines an indexed realizability semantics for this type system. The modality § plays in our work almost the same role as •: it makes the index increase. We claim that when we forget the quantitative part of our model, we obtain a model for a language with guarded references, that can be extended to handle control operators, based on a fragment of Nakano's type system: the only difference is that the • modality does not enjoy digging anymore (in presence of control operators, this principle would break normalization).

Stratified Semantics for Light Logics   —   Several semantics for the "light" logics have been proposed, beginning with fibered phase models [16], a truth-value semantics for **LLL**. We can also mention stratified coherent spaces [4].

These two models are indexed, like ours, but while the indexing is used to achieve completeness with respect to the logic, we use it to interpret fixpoints and references.

Reactive Programming — In [18], Krishnaswami & al. have proposed a type system for a discrete-time reactive programming language that bounds the size of the data flow graph produced by programs. It is based on linear types and a Nakano-style approximation modality, thus bounding space consumption and allowing recursive definitions at the same time. They provide a denotational semantics based on both ultrametric semantics and length spaces. These latter, introduced by Hofmann [8] constitute the starting point of the quantitative realizability presented here.

5 Research Directions

We see several possible directions we plan to explore.

Control Operators — Since we use a biorthogonality-based model, it is natural to extend the language with control operators. Adding the call-cc operator can be done, but it requires to add a modality type ? for *duplicable contexts*. This involves some technical subtleties in the quantitative part, like the symmetrization of the notion of $\mathcal{M}$-contexts. Indeed, in our framework, a $\mathcal{M}$-context can be used to *promote* a weight associated to a term, but with this new ? type, a weight associated to a term would need to be able to promote a weight associated to a stack.

Multithreading — In the original work of Amadio and Madet [15], the language features regions but also multithreading. It is possible to add it to $\lambda_{\mathrm{LAL}}^{\mathrm{Reg},\mu}$ but so far, it seems difficult to adapt the quantitative framework for this extension. It may be possible to adapt the notion of *saturated store* presented in [1], but with a boundedness requirement on it. We plan to explore this direction in the future.

References

1. Amadio, R.M.: On Stratified Regions. In: Hu, Z. (ed.) APLAS 2009. LNCS, vol. 5904, pp. 210–225. Springer, Heidelberg (2009)
2. Appel, A.W., McAllester, D.: An indexed model of recursive types for foundational proof-carrying code. ACM Transactions on Programming Languages and Systems (TOPLAS) 23(5), 657–683 (2001)
3. Asperti, A.: Light affine logic. In: Proceedings of the Thirteenth Annual IEEE Symposium on Logic in Computer Science, pp. 300–308 (1998)
4. Baillot, P.: Stratified coherence spaces: a denotational semantics for light linear logic. Theoretical Computer Science 318(1), 29–55 (2004)
5. Brunel, A.: Quantitative classical realizability (submitted, 2012)

6. Dal Lago, U., Martini, S., Sangiorgi, D.: Light logics and higher-order processes. Electronic Proceedings in Theoretical Computer Science 41 (2010)
7. Girard, J.-Y.: Light Linear Logic. In: Leivant, D. (ed.) LCC 1994. LNCS, vol. 960, pp. 145–176. Springer, Heidelberg (1995)
8. Hofmann, M.: Linear types and non-size-increasing polynomial time computation. Information and Computation 183(1), 57–85 (2003)
9. Krivine, J-L.: Realizability in classical logic. Course notes of a series of lectures given in the University of Marseille (May 2004) (last revision: July 2005), Panoramas et syntheses, Société Mathéematique de France (2005)
10. Lafont, Y.: Soft linear logic and polynomial time. Theoretical Computer Science 318(1-2), 163–180 (2004)
11. Dal Lago, U., Hofmann, M.: Bounded Linear Logic, Revisited. In: Curien, P.-L. (ed.) TLCA 2009. LNCS, vol. 5608, pp. 80–94. Springer, Heidelberg (2009)
12. Dal Lago, U., Hofmann, M.: A semantic proof of polytime soundness of light affine logic. Theory of Computing Systems 46, 673–689 (2010)
13. Dal Lago, U., Hofmann, M.: Realizability models and implicit complexity. Theoretical Computer Science 412(20), 2029–2047 (2011), Girard's Festschrift
14. Lucassen, J.M., Gifford, D.K.: Polymorphic effect systems. In: Proceedings of the 15th ACM SIGPLAN-SIGACT Symposium on Principles of Programming Languages, POPL 1988, pp. 47–57. ACM, New York (1988)
15. Madet, A., Amadio, R.M.: An Elementary Affine λ-Calculus with Multithreading and Side Effects. In: Ong, L. (ed.) TLCA 2011. LNCS, vol. 6690, pp. 138–152. Springer, Heidelberg (2011)
16. Okada, M., Kanovich, M.I., Scedrov, A.: Phase semantics for light linear logic. Theoretical Computer Science 294(3), 525–549 (2003)
17. Nakano, H.: A modality for recursion. In: Proceedings of the 15th Annual IEEE Symposium on Logic in Computer Science, pp. 255–266. IEEE (2000)
18. Benton, N., Krishnaswami, N.R., Hoffmann, J.: Higher-order functional reactive programming in bounded space. In: Proceedings of the 39th Annual ACM SIGPLAN-SIGACT Symposium on Principles of Programming Languages, pp. 45–58. ACM (2012)
19. Baillot, P., Gaboardi, M., Mogbil, V.: A PolyTime Functional Language from Light Linear Logic. In: Gordon, A.D. (ed.) ESOP 2010. LNCS, vol. 6012, pp. 104–124. Springer, Heidelberg (2010)
20. Terui, K.: Light affine lambda calculus and polynomial time strong normalization. Archive for Mathematical Logic 46(3-4), 253–280 (2007)

A New Order-Theoretic Characterisation of the Polytime Computable Functions[*]

Martin Avanzini[1], Naohi Eguchi[2], and Georg Moser[1]

[1] Institute of Computer Science, University of Innsbruck, Austria
{martin.avanzini,georg.moser}@uibk.ac.at
[2] Mathematical Institute, Tohoku University, Japan
eguchi@math.tohoku.ac.jp

Abstract. We propose a new order-theoretic characterisation of the class of polytime computable functions. To this avail we define the *small polynomial path order* (*sPOP** for short). This termination order entails a new syntactic method to analyse the innermost runtime complexity of term rewrite systems fully automatically: for any rewrite system compatible with sPOP* that employs recursion upto depth d, the (innermost) runtime complexity is polynomially bounded of degree d. This bound is tight.

Keywords: Term Rewriting, Implicit Computational Complexity, Runtime Complexity, Polynomial Time Functions.

1 Introduction

In this paper we are concerned with the complexity analysis of term rewrite systems (TRSs for short). Based on a careful investigation into the principle of *predicative recursion* as proposed by Bellantoni and Cook [1] we introduce a new termination order, the *small polynomial path order* (*sPOP** for short). The order sPOP* provides a new characterisation of the class FP of polytime computable functions. Any function f computable by a TRS $\mathcal{R}$ compatible with sPOP* is polytime computable. On the other hand for any polytime computable function f, there exists a TRS $\mathcal{R}_f$ computing f such that $\mathcal{R}$ is compatible with sPOP*. Furthermore sPOP* directly relates the depth of recursion of a given TRS to the polynomial degree of its runtime complexity. More precisely, we call a rewrite system $\mathcal{R}$ *predicative recursive of degree d* if $\mathcal{R}$ is compatible with sPOP* and the depth of recursion of all function symbols in $\mathcal{R}$ is bounded by d (see Section 3 for the formal definition). We establish that any predicative recursive rewrite system of degree d admits runtime complexity in $O(n^d)$.

---

[*] This work is partially supported by FWF (Austrian Science Fund) project I-608-N18 and by a grant of the University of Innsbruck. The second author is supported by a grant from the John Templeton Foundation for the project "Philosophical Frontiers in Reverse Mathematics".

R. Jhala and A. Igarashi (Eds.): APLAS 2012, LNCS 7705, pp. 280–295, 2012.

Thus we obtain a direct correspondence between a syntactic (and easily verifiable) condition of a program and the asymptotic worst-case complexity of the program. In this sense our work is closely related to similar studies in the field of *implicit computational complexity* (*ICC* for short). On the other hand the order sPOP* entails a new syntactic criteria to automatically establish polynomial runtime complexity of a given TRS.

This criteria extends the state of the art in runtime complexity analysis as it is more precise or more efficient than related techniques. Note that the proposed syntactic method to analyse the (innermost) runtime complexity of rewrite systems is fully automatic. For any given TRS, compatibility with sPOP* can be efficiently checked by a machine. Should this check succeed, we get an asymptotic bound on the runtime complexity directly from the parameters of the order. It should perhaps be emphasised that compatibility of a TRS with sPOP* implies termination and thus our complexity analysis technique does not presuppose termination.

In sum, in this work we make the following contributions:

- We propose a new *recursion-theoretic characterisation* B_wsc over binary words of the class FP. We establish that those B_wsc functions that are definable with d nestings of predicative recursion can be computed by predicative recursive TRSs of degree d (cf. Theorem 13). Note that these functions are computable on a register machine operating in time $O(n^d)$.
- We propose the new termination order sPOP*; sPOP* captures the recursion-theoretic principles of the class B_wsc. Thus we obtain a new *order-theoretic characterisation* of the class FP. Moreover, for any predicative recursive TRS of degree d its runtime complexity lies in $O(n^d)$ (cf. Theorem 3). Furthermore this bound is tight, that is, we provide a family of TRSs, delineated by sPOP*, whose runtime complexity is bounded from below by $\Omega(n^d)$, cf. Example 5.
- We extend upon sPOP* by proposing a generalisation of sPOP*, admitting the same properties as above, that allows to handle more general recursion schemes that make use of *parameter substitution* (cf. Theorem 16).
- sPOP* gives rise to a new syntactic method for *polynomial runtime complexity method*. This method is fully automatic. We have implemented the order sPOP* in the *Tyrolean Complexity Tool* TCT, version 1.9, an open source complexity analyser.[1] The experimental evidence obtained indicates the efficiency of the method and the obtained increase in precision.

Related Work. There are several accounts of predicative analysis of recursion in the (ICC) literature. We mention only those related works which are directly comparable to our work. See [2] for an overview on ICC.

Notable the clearest connection of our work is to Marion's *light multiset path order* (*LMPO* for short) [3] and the *polynomial path order* (*POP** for short) [4,5,6]. Both orders form a strict extension of the here proposed order sPOP*, but lack the precision of the latter. Although LMPO characterises FP,

---

[1] Available at http://cl-informatik.uibk.ac.at/software/tct.

the runtime complexity of compatible TRSs is not polynomially bounded in general. POP* induces polynomial runtime complexities, but the obtained complexity certificate is usually very imprecise. In particular, due to the multiset status underlying POP*, for each $d \in \mathbb{N}$ one can form a TRS compatible with POP* that defines only a single function, but whose runtime is bounded from below by n^d.

In Bonfante et. al. [7] restricted classes of polynomial interpretations are studied that can be employed to obtain polynomial upper bounds on the runtime complexity of TRSs. None of the above results are applicable to relate the depth of recursion to the runtime complexity, in the sense mentioned above. We have also drawn motivation from [8] which provides a related fine-grained classification of the polytime computable functions, but which lacks applicability in the context of runtime complexity analysis.

Polynomial complexity analysis is an active research area in rewriting. Starting from [9] interest in this field greatly increased over the last years, see for example [10,11,12,13,14]. This is partly due to the incorporation of a dedicated category for complexity into the annual termination competition (TERMCOMP).[2] However, it is worth emphasising that the most powerful techniques for runtime complexity analysis currently available, basically employ semantic considerations on the rewrite systems, which are notoriously inefficient.

We also want to mention ongoing approaches for the automated analysis of resource usage in programs. Notably, Hoffmann et al. [15] provide an automatic multivariate amortised cost analysis exploiting typing, which extends earlier results on amortised cost analysis. To indicate the applicability of our method we have employed a straightforward (and complexity preserving) transformation of the RAML programs considered in [15] into TRSs. Equipped with sPOP* our complexity analyser TCT can handle all examples from [15] and yields (asymptotically) optimal bounds. Finally Albert et al. [16] present an automated complexity tool for Java Bytecode programs, Alias et al. [17] give a complexity and termination analysis for flowchart programs, and Gulwani et al. [18] as well as Zuleger et al. [19] provide an automated complexity tool for C programs.

Outline. We present the main intuition behind sPOP* and provide an informal account of the technical results obtained.

The order sPOP* essentially embodies the predicative analysis of recursion set forth by Bellantoni and Cook [1]. In [1] a recursion-theoretic characterisation $\mathcal{B}$ of the class of polytime computable functions is proposed. This analysis is connected to the important principle of *tiering* introduced by Simmons [20] and Leivant [21]. The essential idea is that the arguments of a function are separated into *normal* and *safe* arguments (or correspondingly into arguments of different tiers). Building on this work we present a subclass $\mathcal{B}_{\mathsf{wsc}}$ of $\mathcal{B}$. Crucially the class $\mathcal{B}_{\mathsf{wsc}}$ admits only a weak form of composition. Inspired by a result of Handley and Wainer [22], we show that $\mathcal{B}_{\mathsf{wsc}}$ captures the polytime functions. We formulate

---

[2] http://termcomp.uibk.ac.at/.

the class $\mathcal{B}_{\mathsf{wsc}}$ over the set $\{0,1\}^*$ of binary words, where we write ϵ to denote the empty sequence and $S_i(;x)$ to denote the word xi.

The arguments of every function are partitioned into normal and safe ones. Notationally we write $f(t_1,\ldots,t_k\,;t_{k+1},\ldots,t_{k+l})$ where *normal* arguments are to the left, and *safe* arguments to the right of the semicolon. Abbreviate $\boldsymbol{x} = x_1,\ldots,x_k$ and $\boldsymbol{y} = y_1,\ldots,y_l$. The class $\mathcal{B}_{\mathsf{wsc}}$, depicted in Fig. 1, is the smallest class containing certain initial functions and closed under *safe recursion on notation* (**SRN**) and *weak safe composition* (**WSC**). By the weak form of composition only values are ever substituted into normal argument positions.

Initial Functions

$$S_i(;x) = xi \qquad (i = 0,1)$$
$$P(;\epsilon) = \epsilon$$
$$P(;xi) = x \qquad (i = 0,1)$$
$$I_j^{k,l}(\boldsymbol{x}\,;\boldsymbol{y}) = x_j \qquad (j \in \{1,\ldots,k\})$$
$$I_j^{k,l}(\boldsymbol{x}\,;\boldsymbol{y}) = y_{j-k} \qquad (j \in \{k+1,\ldots,l+k\})$$
$$C(;\epsilon,y,z_0,z_1) = y$$
$$C(;xi,y,z_0,z_1) = z_i \qquad (i = 0,1)$$
$$O(\boldsymbol{x}\,;\boldsymbol{y}) = \epsilon$$

Weak Safe Composition
$$f(\boldsymbol{x}\,;\boldsymbol{y}) = h(x_{i_1},\ldots,x_{i_n}\,;\boldsymbol{g}(\boldsymbol{x}\,;\boldsymbol{y}))$$

Safe Recursion on Notation
$$f(\epsilon,\boldsymbol{x}\,;\boldsymbol{y}) = g(\boldsymbol{x}\,;\boldsymbol{y})$$
$$f(zi,\boldsymbol{x}\,;\boldsymbol{y}) = h_i(z,\boldsymbol{x}\,;\boldsymbol{y},f(z,\boldsymbol{x}\,;\boldsymbol{y})) \qquad (i = 0,1)$$

Fig. 1. Defining initial functions and operations for $\mathcal{B}_{\mathsf{wsc}}$

Suppose the definition of a TRS $\mathcal{R}$ is based on the equations in $\mathcal{B}_{\mathsf{wsc}}$. It is not difficult to deduce a precise bound on the runtime complexity of $\mathcal{R}$ by measuring the number of nested applications of safe recursion. In contrast Bellantoni and Cooks definition [1] of $\mathcal{B}$ is obtained from Fig. 1 by replacing weak safe composition with the more liberal scheme of *safe composition* (**SC**): $f(\boldsymbol{x}\,;\boldsymbol{y}) = h(\boldsymbol{i}(\boldsymbol{x}\,;)\,;\boldsymbol{j}(\boldsymbol{x}\,;\boldsymbol{y}))$. Hence in $\mathcal{B}$, normal, that is recursion, parameters can grow and consequently one cannot in general relate the number of nested applications of safe recursion to the runtime complexity of the defined function.

Our central observation is that from the function algebra $\mathcal{B}_{\mathsf{wsc}}$, one can distill a termination argument for the TRS $\mathcal{R}$. With sPOP*, this implicit termination argument is formalised as a termination order.

In order to employ the separation of normal and safe arguments, we fix for each defined symbol in $\mathcal{R}$ a partitioning of argument positions into *normal* and *safe* positions. For constructors we fix (as in $\mathcal{B}_{\mathsf{wsc}}$) that all argument positions are safe. Moreover sPOP* restricts recursion to normal argument. Dual, only safe argument positions allow the substitution of recursive calls. Via the order constraints we can also guarantee that only normal arguments are substituted at normal argument positions. We emphasise that our notion of predicative recursive TRS is more liberal than the class $\mathcal{B}_{\mathsf{wsc}}$. Notably values are not restricted to words, but can be formed from an arbitrary constructors. We allow arbitrary deep right-hand sides, and implicit casting from normal to safe arguments. Still the main principle underlying $\mathcal{B}_{\mathsf{wsc}}$ remains reflected.

The remainder of the paper is organised as follows. After giving some preliminaries, Section 3 introduces the order sPOP*. In Section 4 we prove correctness of sPOP* with respect to runtime complexity analysis. In Section 5 we show that the order is complete for FP, in particular we precisely relate sPOP* to the class $\mathcal{B}_{\mathsf{wsc}}$. In Section 6 we incorporate parameter substitution. Finally in Section 7 we conclude and provide ample experimental evidence. Due to space restrictions some proofs have been omitted. These can be found in the full version [23].

2   Preliminaries

We denote by $\mathbb{N}$ the set of natural numbers $\{0, 1, 2, \dots\}$. For a binary relation R we denote by R^+ the transitive, by R^* the transitive and reflexive closure, and R^n denotes for $n \in \mathbb{N}$ the n-fold composition of of R. We write $a \, R \, b$ for $(a, b) \in R$ and call R *well-founded* if there exists no infinite sequence $a_1 \, R \, a_2 \, R \, a_3 \, R \dots$.

We assume at least nodding acquaintance with the basics of term rewriting [24]. We fix a countably infinite set of *variables* $\mathcal{V}$ and a finite set of *function symbols* $\mathcal{F}$, the *signature*. The set of terms formed from $\mathcal{F}$ and $\mathcal{V}$ is denoted by $\mathcal{T}(\mathcal{F}, \mathcal{V})$. The signature $\mathcal{F}$ contains a distinguished set of *constructors* $\mathcal{C}$, elements of $\mathcal{T}(\mathcal{C}, \mathcal{V})$ are called *values*. Elements of $\mathcal{F}$ that are not constructors are called *defined symbols* and collected in $\mathcal{D}$. For a term t, the *size* of t is denoted by $|t|$ and refers to the number of symbols occurring in t, the depth $\mathsf{dp}(t)$ is given recursively by $\mathsf{dp}(t) = 1$ if $t \in \mathcal{V}$, and $\mathsf{dp}(f(t_1, \dots, t_n)) = 1 + \max\{\mathsf{dp}(t_i) \mid i = 1, \dots, n\}$. Here we employ the convention that the maximum of an empty set is equal to 0. A *rewrite rule* is a pair (l, r) of terms, in notation $l \to r$, such that the *left-hand* side $l = f(l_1, \dots, l_n)$ is not a variable, the *root* f is defined, and all variables appearing in the *right-hand* r occur also in l. A *term rewrite system* (*TRS* for short) $\mathcal{R}$ is a set of rewrite rules.

We adopt *call-by-value* semantics and define the *rewrite relation* $\to_{\mathcal{R}}$ by

$$(i) \; \frac{f(l_1, \dots, l_n) \to r \in \mathcal{R}, \; \sigma : \mathcal{V} \to \mathcal{T}(\mathcal{C}, \mathcal{V})}{f(l_1\sigma, \dots, l_n\sigma) \to_{\mathcal{R}} r\sigma} \quad (ii) \; \frac{s \to_{\mathcal{R}} t}{f(\dots, s, \dots) \to_{\mathcal{R}} f(\dots, t, \dots)}.$$

If $s \to_{\mathcal{R}} t$ we say that s *reduces to* t in one step. For (i) we make various assumptions on $\mathcal{R}$: we suppose that there is exactly one *matching* rule $f(l_1, \dots, l_n) \to r \in \mathcal{R}$; l_i $(i = 1, \dots, n)$ contains no defined symbols; and variables occur only once in $f(l_1, \dots, l_n)$. That is, throughout this paper we fix $\mathcal{R}$ to denote a *completely defined*,[3] *orthogonal constructor* TRS [24]. Furthermore we are only concerned with *innermost* rewriting. Note that orthogonality enforces that our model of computation is deterministic,[4] in particular when $\mathcal{R}$ is *terminating*, i.e. when $\to_{\mathcal{R}}$ is well-founded, the semantics given as follows is well defined. For every n-ary defined symbol $f \in \mathcal{D}$, $\mathcal{R}$ defines a partial function $\llbracket f \rrbracket : \mathcal{T}(\mathcal{C}, \mathcal{V})^n \to \mathcal{T}(\mathcal{C}, \mathcal{V})$

---

[3] The restriction is not necessary, but simplifies our presentation, compare [6].

[4] As in [6] it is possible to adopt nondeterministic semantics, dropping orthogonality.

where

$$[\![f]\!](u_1,\ldots,u_n) := v \quad :\Leftrightarrow \quad \exists v. f(u_1,\ldots,u_n) \to_\mathcal{R} \ldots \to_\mathcal{R} v \text{ with } v \in \mathcal{T}(\mathcal{C},\mathcal{V})$$

and $[\![f]\!](u_1,\ldots,u_n)$ is undefined otherwise.

Following [10] we adopt a unitary cost model. Reductions are of course measured in the size of terms. Let $\mathcal{T_b}(\mathcal{F},\mathcal{V})$ denote the set of *basic* terms $f(u_1,\ldots,u_n)$ where $f \in \mathcal{D}$ and $u_1,\ldots,u_n \in \mathcal{T}(\mathcal{C},\mathcal{V})$. We define the *(innermost) runtime complexity function* $\mathrm{rc}_\mathcal{R} : \mathbb{N} \to \mathbb{N}$ as

$$\mathrm{rc}_\mathcal{R}(n) := \max\{\ell \mid \exists s \in \mathcal{T_b}(\mathcal{F},\mathcal{V}), |s| \leqslant n \text{ and } s = t_0 \to_\mathcal{R} t_1 \to_\mathcal{R} \cdots \to_\mathcal{R} t_\ell\}$$

Hence $\mathrm{rc}_\mathcal{R}(n)$ maximises over the *derivation height* of terms s of size up to n, regarding only basic terms. The latter restriction accounts for the fact that computations start only from basic terms. The runtime complexity function is well-defined if $\mathcal{R}$ is terminating. If $\mathrm{rc}_\mathcal{R}$ is asymptotically bounded from above by a polynomial, we simply say that the runtime of $\mathcal{R}$ is polynomially bounded. In [25,26] it has been shown that the unitary cost model is reasonable: all functions $[\![f]\!]$ computed by $\mathcal{R}$ are computable on a conventional models of computation in time related polynomial to $\mathrm{rc}_\mathcal{R}$. In particular, if the runtime of $\mathcal{R}$ is polynomially bounded then $[\![f]\!]$ is polytime computable on a Turing machine for all $f \in \mathcal{D}$.

We say that a function symbol f is *defined based on* g ($f \dashv_\mathcal{R} g$ for short), if there exists a rewrite rule $f(l_1,\ldots,l_n) \to r \in \mathcal{R}$ where g occurs in r. We call f *recursive* if $f \dashv_\mathcal{R}^+ f$ holds, i.e., is defined based on itself. Noteworthy our notion also captures mutual recursion. Recursive functions are collected in $\mathcal{D}_{\mathsf{rec}}^\geqslant \subseteq \mathcal{D}$. We denote by $\geqslant$ least *preorder*, i.e., reflexive and transitive relation, on $\mathcal{F}$ containing $\dashv_\mathcal{R}$ and where constructors are equivalent, i.e., $c \geqslant d$ for all constructors $c, d \in \mathcal{C}$. The preorder $\geqslant$ is called the *precedence* of $\mathcal{R}$. We denote by $>$ and $\sim$ the usual separation of $\geqslant$ into a proper order $>$ an an equivalence $\sim$. Kindly note that for $f \sim g$, if $g \in \mathcal{C}$ then also $f \in \mathcal{C}$; similar if $g \in \mathcal{D}_{\mathsf{rec}}^\geqslant$ then also $f \in \mathcal{D}_{\mathsf{rec}}^\geqslant$. The *depth of recursion* $\mathrm{rd}(f)$ of $f \in \mathcal{F}$ is defined as follows: let $d = \max\{\mathrm{rd}(g) \mid f > g\}$ be the maximal recursion depth of a function symbol g underlying the definition of f; then $\mathrm{rd}(f) := 1 + d$ if f is recursive, otherwise $\mathrm{rd}(f) := d$.

Example 1. Consider following TRS $\mathcal{R}_{\mathsf{arith}}$, written in predicative notation.

1: $+(0;y) \to y$ 3: $+(\mathsf{s}(x);y) \to \mathsf{s}(+(x;y))$ 5: $\mathsf{f}(x,y;) \to +(x;\times(y,y;))$

2: $\times(0,y;) \to 0$ 4: $\times(\mathsf{s}(x),y;) \to +(y;\times(x,y;))$

The TRS $\mathcal{R}_{\mathsf{arith}}$ follows along the line of $\mathcal{B}_{\mathsf{wsc}}$ from Figure 1. The functions $[\![+]\!]$ and $[\![\times]\!]$ denote addition and multiplication on natural numbers, in particular $[\![f]\!](\mathsf{s}^m(0),\mathsf{s}^n(0)) = \mathsf{s}^r(0)$ where $r = m + n^2$. The precedence is given by $\mathsf{f} > (\times) > (+) > \mathsf{S} \sim 0$ where addition $(+)$ and multiplication $(\times)$ are recursive, but f is not. Conclusively $\mathrm{rd}(+) = 1$, as f is not recursive we have $\mathrm{rd}(\mathsf{f}) = \mathrm{rd}(\times) = 2$.

3   The Small Polynomial Path Order

We arrive at the formal definition of sPOP*. Technically this order is a tamed recursive path order with product status, embodying *predicative analysis* of recursion set forth by Bellantoni and Cook [1]. We assume the arguments of defined symbol are separated into two kinds (by semicolon), normal and safe argument positions, cf. Fig. 1. For constructors we fix that all argument positions are safe. We denote by $>_{\mathsf{spop*}}$ the particular sPOP* based on the precedence $\succsim$ underlying the analysed TRS $\mathcal{R}$ and the aforementioned separation of argument positions.

The order $>_{\mathsf{spop*}}$ relies on some auxiliary relations. First of all, we lift equivalence $\sim$ underlying the precedence $\succsim$ to terms in the obvious way, but additionally disregarding the order on arguments: s and t are *equivalent*, in notation $s \sim t$, if $s = t$, or $s = f(s_1, \ldots, s_n)$ and $t = g(t_1, \ldots, t_n)$ where $f \sim g$ and $s_i \sim t_{\pi(i)}$ for all arguments and some permutation π. *Safe equivalence* $\stackrel{s}{\sim} \subseteq \sim$ takes also the separation of argument positions into account: we additionally require that i is a normal argument position of f if and only if $\pi(i)$ is normal argument position of g. We emphasise that $\sim$ (and consequently $\stackrel{s}{\sim}$) preserves values: if $s \sim t$ and $s \in \mathcal{T}(\mathcal{C}, \mathcal{V})$ then $t \in \mathcal{T}(\mathcal{C}, \mathcal{V})$. We extend the (proper) subterm relation to term equivalence. Consider $s = f(s_1, \ldots, s_k \,; s_{k+1}, \ldots, s_{k+l})$. Then $s \rhd_{/\!\!\sim} t$ if $s_i \unrhd_{/\!\!\sim} t$ for some s_i $(i = 1, \ldots k + l)$, where $\unrhd_{/\!\!\sim} = \sim \cup \rhd_{/\!\!\sim}$. Further $s \rhd^n_{/\!\!\sim} t$ if $s_i \unrhd_{/\!\!\sim} t$ for some *normal* argument position $(i = 1, \ldots, k)$.

Definition 2. *Let s and t be terms such that $s = f(s_1, \ldots, s_k \,; s_{k+1}, \ldots, s_{k+l})$. Then $s >_{\mathsf{spop*}} t$ if one of the following alternatives holds.*

1. *$s_i \succsim_{\mathsf{spop*}} t$ for some argument s_i of s.*
2. *$f \in \mathcal{D}$, $t = g(t_1, \ldots, t_m \,; t_{m+1}, \ldots, t_{m+n})$ where $f > g$ and the following holds:*
   - *$s \rhd^n_{/\!\!\sim} t_j$ for all normal arguments $t_1, \ldots, t_m$;*
   - *$s >_{\mathsf{spop*}} t_j$ for all safe arguments $t_{m+1}, \ldots, t_{m+n}$;*
   - *t contains at most one (recursive) function symbols g with $f \sim g$.*
3. *$f \in \mathcal{D}^{\succsim}_{\mathsf{rec}}$, $t = g(t_1, \ldots, t_k \,; t_{k+1}, \ldots, t_{k+l})$ where $f \sim g$ and the following holds:*
   - *$\langle s_1, \ldots, s_k \rangle >_{\mathsf{spop*}} \langle t_{\pi(1)}, \ldots, t_{\pi(k)} \rangle$ for some permutation π on $\{1, \ldots, k\}$;*
   - *$\langle s_{k+1}, \ldots, s_{k+l} \rangle \succsim_{\mathsf{spop*}} \langle t_{\tau(k+1)}, \ldots, t_{\tau(k+l)} \rangle$ for some permutation τ on $\{k+1, \ldots, k+l\}$.*

Here $s \succsim_{\mathsf{spop*}} t$ denotes that either $s \stackrel{s}{\sim} t$ or $s >_{\mathsf{spop*}} t$ holds. In the last clause we use $>_{\mathsf{spop*}}$ also for the extension of $>_{\mathsf{spop*}}$ to products: $\langle s_1, \ldots, s_n \rangle \succsim_{\mathsf{spop*}} \langle t_1, \ldots, t_n \rangle$ means $s_i \succsim_{\mathsf{spop*}} t_i$ for all $i = 1, \ldots, n$, and $\langle s_1, \ldots, s_n \rangle >_{\mathsf{spop*}} \langle t_1, \ldots, t_n \rangle$ indicates that additionally $s_{i_0} >_{\mathsf{spop*}} t_{i_0}$ holds for at least one $i_0 \in \{1, \ldots, n\}$.

We say that the TRS $\mathcal{R}$ is *compatible* with $>_{\mathsf{spop*}}$ if rules are *oriented* from left to right: $l >_{\mathsf{spop*}} r$ for all rules $l \to r \in \mathcal{R}$. As sPOP* forms a restriction of the recursive path order, compatiblity with sPOP* implies termination. Furthermore we call the TRS $\mathcal{R}$ *predicative recursive (of degree d)* if $\mathcal{R}$ is compatible with an instance of sPOP* and the maximal recursion depth $\mathsf{rd}(f)$ of $f \in \mathcal{F}$ is d.

We write $>^{(i)}_{\mathsf{spop*}}$ to refer to the ith case in Definition 2. Consider the orientation of a rule $f(l_1, \ldots, l_n) \to r \in \mathcal{R}$. The case $>^{(2)}_{\mathsf{spop*}}$ is intended to capture functions

f defined by weak safe composition (**WSC**), compare Fig. 1 on page 283. In particular the use of $\triangleright^n_{\sim}$ allows only the substitution of normal arguments of f in normal argument positions of g. The last restriction put onto $>^{(2)}_{\text{spop}*}$ is used to prohibit multiple recursive calls. Finally, $>^{(3)}_{\text{spop}*}$ accounts for recursive calls, in combination with $>^{(2)}_{\text{spop}*}$ we capture safe recursion (**SRN**). The next theorem provides our main result.

Theorem 3. *Let $\mathcal{R}$ be a predicative recursive TRS of degree d. Then the innermost derivation height of any basic term $f(\boldsymbol{u};\boldsymbol{v})$ is bounded by a polynomial of degree $\text{rd}(f)$ in the sum of the depths of normal arguments $\boldsymbol{u}$. In particular, the innermost runtime complexity of $\mathcal{R}$ is bounded by a polynomial of degree d.*

The admittedly technical proof is postponed to the next section. We finish this section with an informal account of Definition 2 in our running example.

Example 4. We show that the TRS $\mathcal{R}_{\text{arith}}$ depicted in Example 1 is predicative recursive. Recall that the precedence underlying $\mathcal{R}_{\text{arith}}$ is given by $f > (\times) > (+) > S \sim 0$, and that $\mathcal{D}^{\geqslant}_{\text{rec}} = \{(\times),(+)\}$. The degree of recursion of $\mathcal{R}_{\text{arith}}$ is thus 2.

The case $>^{(1)}_{\text{spop}*}$ is standard in recursive path orders and allows the treatment of projections as in rules 1 and 2. We have $+(0;y) >^{(1)}_{\text{spop}*} y$ using $y \approx y$ and likewise $\times(0,y;) >^{(1)}_{\text{spop}*} 0$ using $0 \approx 0$. Observe that rule 5 defining f by composition is oriented by $>^{(2)}_{\text{spop}*}$ only: $f(x,y;) >^{(2)}_{\text{spop}*} +(x;\times(y,y;))$ as $f > +$, $f(x,y;) \triangleright^n_{\sim} x$, i.e., x occurs as a normal argument of f, and recursively $f(x,y;) >^{(2)}_{\text{spop}*} \times(y,y;)$, using $f > (\times)$ and $f(x,y;) \triangleright^n_{\sim} y$ (twice).

Finally, consider the recursive cases of addition (rule 3) and multiplication (rule 4). These can be oriented by a combination of $>^{(2)}_{\text{spop}*}$ and $>^{(3)}_{\text{spop}*}$, we exemplify this on rule 4: $\times(s(x),y;) >^{(2)}_{\text{spop}*} +(y;\times(x,y;))$ simplifies using $(\times) > (+)$ to $\times(s(x),y;) \triangleright^n_{\sim} y$ and $\times(s(x),y;) >_{\text{spop}*} \times(x,y;)$. As $(\times) \in \mathcal{D}^{\geqslant}_{\text{rec}}$, using $>^{(3)}_{\text{spop}*}$ the constraint reduces to $\langle s(x),y\rangle >_{\text{spop}*} \langle x,y\rangle$ (which follows as $s(x) >^{(1)}_{\text{spop}*} x$ and $y \approx y$) and $\langle\rangle \geqslant_{\text{spop}*} \langle\rangle$. The careful reader might ask why both arguments position of $(\times)$ are normal. Clearly the former constraint dictates that the first position is normal. By similar reasoning the orientation $+(s(x);y) >_{\text{spop}*} s(+(x;y))$ of rule 3 dictates that the first argument position of $(+)$ is normal. As the second argument to multiplication is substituted into the normal argument position of addition, $\times(s(x),y;) \triangleright^n_{\sim} y$ correctly propagates that y is a recursion parameter. Reconsidering the orientation of rule 5 defining f, $\triangleright^n_{\sim}$ propagates that f takes only normal arguments.

We conclude that $\mathcal{R}_{\text{arith}}$ is predicative recursive, with degree 2. By Theorem 3 runtime of $\mathcal{R}_{\text{arith}}$ is thus bounded by a quadratic polynomial.

As a consequence of our main theorem, any predicative recursive (and orthogonal) TRS $\mathcal{R}$ of degree d computes a function from FP, compare [26]. These functions are even computable on a register machine operating in time $O(n^d)$, provided $\mathcal{R}$ computes functions over a word algebra [23,27]. The latter restriction allows storing values in registers without significant encoding overhead. We emphasise also that the bound provided in Theorem 3 is tight in the sense that for any d we can define a predicative TRS $\mathcal{R}_d$ of degree d admitting runtime complexity $\Omega(n^d)$.

Example 5. We define a family of TRSs $\mathcal{R}_i$ ($i \in \mathbb{N}$) inductively as follows: $\mathcal{R}_0 :=$ $\{f_0(x;) \to a\}$ and $\mathcal{R}_{i+1}$ extends $\mathcal{R}_i$ by the rules

$$f_{i+1}(x;) \to g_{i+1}(x,x;) \qquad g_{i+1}(s(x),y;) \to b(;f_i(y;),g_{i+1}(x,y;)) .$$

Let $d \in \mathbb{N}$. It is easy to see that $\mathcal{R}_d$ is predicative recursive (with underlying precedence $f_d > g_d > f_{d-1} > g_{d-1} > \ldots > f_0 > a \sim b$). As only g_i ($i = 1, \ldots, d$) are recursive, the recursion depth of $\mathcal{R}_d$ is d.

But also the runtime complexity of $\mathcal{R}_d$ is in $\Omega(n^d)$: For $d = 0$ this is immediate. Otherwise, consider the term $f_{d+1}(s^n(a))$ ($n \in \mathbb{N}$) which reduces to $g_{d+1}(s^n(a),s^n(a);)$ in one step. As the latter iterates $f_d(s^n(a))$ for n times, the lower bound is established by inductive reasoning.

4   Soundness

We now show that sPOP* is correct, i.e., we prove Theorem 3. Let $\mathcal{R}$ denote a predicative recursive TRS. Our proof makes use of a variety of ingredients. In Definition 7 we define *predicative interpretations* S that flatten terms to *sequences of terms*, separating safe from normal arguments. In Definition 8 we introduce a family of orders $(\blacktriangleright_\ell)_{\ell \in \mathbb{N}}$ on sequences of terms. The definition of $\blacktriangleright_\ell$ (for fixed ℓ) does not explicitly mention predicative notions and is conceptually simpler than $>_{\text{spop}*}$. In Lemma 11 we show that predicative interpretations S embeds rewrite steps into $\blacktriangleright_\ell$:

$$
\begin{array}{ccccccc}
s & \to_{\mathcal{R}} & s_1 & \to_{\mathcal{R}} & \cdots & \to_{\mathcal{R}} & s_\ell \\
\downarrow & & \downarrow & & & & \downarrow \\
\mathsf{S}(s) & \blacktriangleright_\ell & \mathsf{S}(s_1) & \blacktriangleright_\ell & \cdots & \blacktriangleright_\ell & \mathsf{S}(s_\ell)
\end{array}
$$

Consequently the derivation height of s is bounded by the length of $\blacktriangleright_\ell$ descending sequences, which in turn can be bounded sufficiently whenever s is basic (cf. Theorem 10).

Consider a step $C[f(u\sigma;v\sigma)] \to_{\mathcal{R}} C[r\sigma] = t$. Due to the limitations imposed by $>_{\text{spop}*}$, it is not difficult to see that if $r\sigma$ is not a value itself, then at least all normal arguments are values. We capture this observation in the set $\mathcal{T}_b^\to$, defined as the least set such that (i) $\mathcal{T}(\mathcal{C}, \mathcal{V}) \subseteq \mathcal{T}_b^\to$, and (ii) if $f \in \mathcal{F}$, $v \subseteq \mathcal{T}(\mathcal{C}, \mathcal{V})$ and $t \subseteq \mathcal{T}_b^\to$ then $f(v;t) \in \mathcal{T}_b^\to$. This set is closed under rewriting.

Lemma 6. *Let $\mathcal{R}$ be a completely defined TRS compatible with $>_{\text{spop}*}$. If $s \in \mathcal{T}_b^\to$ and $s \to_{\mathcal{R}} t$ then $t \in \mathcal{T}_b^\to$.*

Since $\mathcal{T}_b^\to$ contains in particular all basic terms, it follows that the runtime complexity function $\mathrm{rc}_{\mathcal{R}}$ depends only on terms from $\mathcal{T}_b^\to$. The *predicative interpretation* S maps terms from $\mathcal{T}_b^\to$ to *sequences* of *normalised* terms by separating normal from safe arguments. We sometimes write f_n for the symbol f if it occurs in a normalised term. If f has k normal arguments, then f_n has arity k. To denote sequences of terms, we use a fresh variadic function symbol $\circ$. Here variadic means that the arity of $\circ$ is finite but arbitrary. We always write $[a_1 \cdots a_n]$ for $\circ(a_1,\ldots,a_n)$, and if we write $f(a_1,\ldots,a_n)$ then $f \neq \circ$. We denote by T^* the set of *sequences* $[t_1 \cdots t_n]$ of normalised terms $t_1,\ldots,t_n$. We lift terms equivalence to sequences by disregarding order of elements: $[s_1 \cdots s_n] \sim [t_1 \cdots t_n]$ if $s_i \sim t_{\pi(i)}$ for all $i = 1,\ldots,n$ and some permutation π on $\{1,\ldots,n\}$. We define *concatenation* as $[s_1 \cdots s_n] \frown [t_1 \cdots t_n] := [s_1 \cdots s_n \, t_1 \cdots t_m]$, and extend it to terms by identifying terms t with the singleton sequences $[t]$, for instance $s \frown t = [s\, t]$.

Definition 7. *We define the* predicative interpretation S *for all* $t \in \mathcal{T}_b^{\rightarrow}$ *as follows. If* $t \in \mathcal{T}(\mathcal{C},\mathcal{V})$, *then* $\mathsf{S}(t) := [\,]$. *Otherwise*

$$\mathsf{S}(f(t_1,\ldots,t_k \,; t_{k+1},\ldots,t_{k+l})) := [\, f_\mathsf{n}(t_1,\ldots,t_k)\,] \frown \mathsf{S}(t_{k+1}) \frown \cdots \frown \mathsf{S}(t_{k+l})\,.$$

We define the *small polynomial path order on sequences* T^*. As these serve a purely technical reason, it suffices to represent the order via finite approximations $\blacktriangleright_\ell$ (compare also [4]). The parameter $\ell \in \mathbb{N}$ controls the width of terms and sequences.

Definition 8. *Let* $\geqslant$ *denote a precedence. For all* $\ell \geqslant 1$ *we define* $\blacktriangleright_\ell$ *on terms and sequences of terms inductively such that:*

1. $f(s_1,\ldots,s_n) \blacktriangleright_\ell g(t_1,\ldots,t_m)$ *if* $f \in \mathcal{D}$, $f > g$ *and the following conditions hold:*
   - $f(s_1,\ldots,s_n) \rhd\!\!/_{\!-} t_j$ *for all* $j = 1,\ldots,m$;
   - $m \leqslant \ell$.
2. $f(s_1,\ldots,s_n) \blacktriangleright_\ell g(t_1,\ldots,t_n)$ *if* $f \in \mathcal{D}_{\mathsf{rec}}^{\geqslant}$, $f \sim g$ *and for some permutation* π *on* $\{1,\ldots,n\}$: $\langle s_1,\ldots,s_n \rangle \rhd\!\!/_{\!-} \langle t_{\pi(1)},\ldots,t_{\pi(n)} \rangle$.
3. $f(s_1,\ldots,s_n) \blacktriangleright_\ell [t_1 \cdots t_m]$ *if the following conditions hold:*
   - $f(s_1,\ldots,s_n) \blacktriangleright_\ell t_j$ *for all* $j = 1,\ldots,m$;
   - *at most one element* t_j *($j \in \{1,\ldots,m\}$) contains a symbols* g *with* $f \sim g$;
   - $m \leqslant \ell$.
4. $[s_1 \cdots s_n] \blacktriangleright_\ell [t_1 \cdots t_m]$ *if there exists terms or sequences* b_i *($i = 1,\ldots,n$) such that:*
   - $[t_1 \cdots t_m]$ *is equivalent to* $b_1 \frown \cdots \frown b_n$;
   - $s_i \blacktriangleright_\ell b_i$ *for all* $i = 1,\ldots,n$;
   - $s_{i_0} \blacktriangleright_\ell b_{i_0}$ *for at least one* $i_0 \in \{1,\ldots,n\}$.

Here $a \blacktriangleright_\ell b$ denotes that either $a \sim b$ or $a \blacktriangleright_\ell b$ holds, and $\rhd\!\!/_{\!-}$ is also used for its extension to products: $\langle s_1,\ldots,s_n \rangle \rhd\!\!/_{\!-} \langle t_i,\ldots,t_n \rangle$ if $s_i \trianglerighteq\!\!/_{\!-} t_i$ for all $i = 1,\ldots,n$, and $s_{i_0} \rhd\!\!/_{\!-} t_{i_0}$ for at least one $i_0 \in \{1,\ldots,n\}$.

The next lemma collects some facts about the order $\blacktriangleright_\ell$:

Lemma 9. *For all* $\ell \geqslant 1$, *(i)* $\blacktriangleright_\ell \subseteq \blacktriangleright_{\ell+1}$, *(ii)* $\sim \cdot \blacktriangleright_\ell \cdot \sim \subseteq \blacktriangleright_\ell$, *and (iii)* $a \blacktriangleright_\ell b$ *implies* $a \frown c \blacktriangleright_\ell b \frown c$.

Let $\ell \geqslant 1$. The function $\mathsf{G}_\ell : \mathsf{T}^*(\mathcal{F}) \to \mathbb{N}$ measures the length of $\blacktriangleright_\ell$ descending sequence: $\mathsf{G}_\ell(a) := \max\{m \mid a \blacktriangleright_\ell a_1 \blacktriangleright_\ell \cdots \blacktriangleright_\ell a_m\}$. Theorem 10 binds $\mathsf{G}_\ell(s)$ for (normalised) basic terms s sufficiently.

Theorem 10. *Let* $f \in \mathcal{D}$. *Then* $\mathsf{G}_\ell(f_\mathsf{n}(u_1, \ldots, u_k)) \leqslant c \cdot n^{\mathsf{rd}(f)}$ *for all values* $u_1, \ldots, u_k$, *where* $n := \sum_{i=1}^k \mathsf{dp}(u_i)$. *The constant* $c \in \mathbb{N}$ *depends only on* f *and* ℓ.

The remaining missing piece in our reasoning is to show that predicative interpretations *embed* innermost rewrite steps into $\blacktriangleright_\ell$, where ℓ depends only on the considered TRS $\mathcal{R}$.

Lemma 11. *Let* $\mathcal{R}$ *denote a predicative recursive TRS and let* ℓ *be the maximal size of a right-hand side in* $\mathcal{R}$. *If* $s \in \mathcal{T}_\mathsf{b}^\rightarrow$ *and* $s \rightarrow_\mathcal{R} t$ *then* $\mathsf{S}(s) \blacktriangleright_\ell \mathsf{S}(t)$.

Putting things together, we arrive at the proof of the main theorem.

Proof (of Theorem 3). Let $\mathcal{R}$ denote a predicative recursive TRS. We prove the existence of a constant $c \in \mathbb{N}$ such that for all values $\boldsymbol{u}, \boldsymbol{v}$, the derivation height of $f(\boldsymbol{u}; \boldsymbol{v})$ is bounded by $c \cdot n^{\mathsf{rd}(f)}$, where n is the sum of the depths of normal arguments $\boldsymbol{u}$.

Consider a derivation $f(\boldsymbol{u}; \boldsymbol{v}) \rightarrow_\mathcal{R} t_1 \rightarrow_\mathcal{R} \cdots \rightarrow_\mathcal{R} t_n$. Let $i \in \{0, \ldots, n-1\}$. By Lemma 6 it follows that $t_i \in \mathcal{T}_\mathsf{b}^\rightarrow$, and consequently $\mathsf{S}(t_i) \blacktriangleright_\ell \mathsf{S}(t_{i+1})$ due to Lemma 11. So in particular the length n is bounded by the length of $\blacktriangleright_\ell$ descending sequences starting from $\mathsf{S}(f(\boldsymbol{u}; \boldsymbol{v})) = [f_\mathsf{n}(\boldsymbol{u})]$. One verifies that $\mathsf{G}_\ell([f_\mathsf{n}(\boldsymbol{u})]) = \mathsf{G}_\ell(f_\mathsf{n}(\boldsymbol{u}))$. Thus Theorem 10 gives the constant $c \in \mathbb{N}$ as desired.

5   Completeness Results

In this section we show that sPOP* is complete for FP. Indeed, we can even show a stronger result. Let f be a function from $\mathcal{B}_\mathsf{wsc}$ that makes only use of d nestings of safe recursion on notation, then there exists a predicative recursive TRS $\mathcal{R}_f$ of degree d that computes the function f.

By definition $\mathcal{B}_\mathsf{wsc} \subseteq \mathcal{B}$ for Bellantoni and Cooks predicative recursive characterisation $\mathcal{B}$ of FP given in [1]. Concerning the converse inclusion, the following Theorem states that the class $\mathcal{B}_\mathsf{wsc}$ is large enough to capture *all* the polytime computable functions. Here $\mathcal{B}_\mathsf{wsc}^{k,l}$ refers to the subclass of $\mathcal{B}_\mathsf{wsc}$ with k normal and l safe argument positions.

Theorem 12. *Every polynomial time computable function belongs to* $\bigcup_{k \in \mathbb{N}} \mathcal{B}_\mathsf{wsc}^{k,0}$.

One can show this fact by following the proof of Theorem 3.7 in [22], where the unary variant of $\mathcal{B}_\mathsf{wsc}$ is defined and the inclusion corresponding to Theorem 12 is shown, cf. [23].

Theorem 13. *For any* $\mathcal{B}_\mathsf{wsc}$-*function* f *there exists an orthogonal TRS* $\mathcal{R}_f$ *that is predicative recursive of degree* d, *where* d *equals the maximal number of nested application of* (**SRN**) *in the definition of* f.

The completeness of sPOP* for the polytime computable functions is an immediate consequence of Theorem 12 and Theorem 13. The witnessing TRS $\mathcal{R}_f$ for $f \in \mathcal{B}_\mathsf{wsc}$ in Theorem 13 is obtained via a term rewriting characterisation of the class $\mathcal{B}_{\mathsf{wsc}}$ depicted in Fig. 1 on page 283. The term rewriting characterisation expresses the definition of $\mathcal{B}_{\mathsf{wsc}}$ as an *infinite* TRS $\mathcal{R}_{\mathcal{B}_{\mathsf{wsc}}}$.

We define a one-to-one correspondence between functions from $\mathcal{B}_{\mathsf{wsc}}$ and the set of function symbols for $\mathcal{R}_{\mathcal{B}_{\mathsf{wsc}}}$ as follows. Constructor symbols ϵ, S_0 and S_1 are used to denote binary words.

The function symbols P, $\mathsf{I}_j^{k,l}$, C and $\mathsf{O}^{k,l}$ correspond respectively to the initial functions P, $I_j^{k,l}$, C and $O^{k,l}$ of $\mathcal{B}_{\mathsf{wsc}}$. The symbol $\mathsf{SUB}[\mathsf{h}, i_1, \ldots, i_n, \mathbf{g}]$ is used to denote the function obtained by composing functions h and $\mathbf{g}$ according to the schema of (**WSC**). Finally, the function symbol $\mathsf{SRN}[\mathsf{g}, \mathsf{h}_0, \mathsf{h}_1]$ corresponds to the function defined by safe recursion on notation from g, h_0 and h_1 in accordance to the schema (**SRN**).

With this correspondence, $\mathcal{R}_{\mathcal{B}_{\mathsf{wsc}}}$ is obtained by orienting the equations in Fig. 1 from left to right. It is easy to see that $\mathcal{R}_{\mathcal{B}_{\mathsf{wsc}}}$ is a constructor TRS. Further $\mathcal{R}_{\mathcal{B}_{\mathsf{wsc}}}$ is orthogonal, thus any finite restriction $\mathcal{R}_f \subseteq \mathcal{R}_{\mathcal{B}_{\mathsf{wsc}}}$ is confluent.

Proof (of Theorem 13). Let f be a function coming from $\mathcal{B}_{\mathsf{wsc}}$. By induction according to the definition of f in $\mathcal{B}_{\mathsf{wsc}}$ we show the existence of a TRS $\mathcal{R}_f$ and a precedence $\succsim_f$ such that

1. $\mathcal{R}_f$ is a finite restriction of $\mathcal{R}_{\mathcal{B}_{\mathsf{wsc}}}$,
2. $\mathcal{R}_f$ contains the rule(s) defining the function symbol f corresponding to f,
3. $\mathcal{R}_f$ is compatible with $>_{\mathsf{spop}*}$ induced by $\succsim_f$,
4. f is maximal in the precedence $\succsim_f$ underlying $\mathcal{R}_f$, and
5. the depth of recursion $\mathsf{rd}(\mathsf{f})$ equals the maximal number of nested application of (**SRN**) in the definition of f in $\mathcal{B}_{\mathsf{wsc}}$.

The assertion of the theorem follows from Condition (1), (3)) and (5). To exemplify the construction we consider the step case that f is defined from some functions $g, h_0, h_1 \in \mathcal{B}_{\mathsf{wsc}}$ by the schema (**SRN**). By induction hypothesis we can find witnessing TRSs $\mathcal{R}_g, \mathcal{R}_{h_0}, \mathcal{R}_{h_1}$ and witnessing precedences $\succsim_g, \succsim_{h_0}, \succsim_{h_1}$ respectively for g, h_0, h_1. Extend the set of function symbols by a new recursive symbol $\mathsf{f} :\equiv \mathsf{SRN}[\mathsf{g}, \mathsf{h}_0, \mathsf{h}_1]$. Let $\mathcal{R}_f$ be the TRS consisting of $\mathcal{R}_g, \mathcal{R}_{h_0}, \mathcal{R}_{h_1}$ and the following three rules:

$$\mathsf{f}(\epsilon, \boldsymbol{x}; \boldsymbol{y}) \to \mathsf{g}(\boldsymbol{x}; \boldsymbol{y}) \qquad \mathsf{f}(\mathsf{S}_i(; x), \boldsymbol{x}; \boldsymbol{y}) \to \mathsf{h}_i(z, \boldsymbol{x}; \boldsymbol{y}, \mathsf{f}(z, \boldsymbol{x}; \boldsymbol{y})) \quad (i = 0, 1) \, .$$

Define the precedence $\succsim_f$ extending $\succsim_g \cup \succsim_{h_0} \cup \succsim_{h_1}$ by f $\sim$ f and f $>$ g' for any g' $\in \{\mathsf{g}, \mathsf{h}_0, \mathsf{h}_1\}$. Note that the union $\succsim_g \cup \succsim_{h_0} \cup \succsim_{h_1}$ is still a precedence. This can be seen as follows. Assume that both $\mathsf{f}_0 > \mathsf{f}_1$ and $\mathsf{f}_1 > \mathsf{f}_0$ hold for some symbols f_0 and f_1. Then by definition $\mathsf{f}_0 \equiv \mathcal{O}_0[\cdots \mathsf{f}_1 \cdots]$ and $\mathsf{f}_1 \equiv \mathcal{O}_1[\cdots \mathsf{f}_0 \cdots]$ for some operations $\mathcal{O}_0, \mathcal{O}_1 \in \{\mathsf{SUB}, \mathsf{SRN}\}$. This means that the function corresponding to f_0 is defined by either (**WSC**) or (**SRN**) via the function corresponding to f_1 and vice versa, but these contradict. Let $>_{\mathsf{spop}*}$ be the sPOP* induced by $\succsim_f$. Then it is easy to check that $\mathcal{R}_f$ enjoys Condition (1) and (2).

In order to show Condition (3), it suffices to orient the three new rules by $>_{\mathsf{spop}*}$. For the first rule, $\mathsf{f}(\epsilon, \boldsymbol{x}; \boldsymbol{y}) >_{\mathsf{spop}*}^{(2)} \mathsf{g}(\boldsymbol{x}; \boldsymbol{y})$ holds by the definition of $\succsim_f$. For the remaining two rules we only orient the case $i = 0$. Since f is a recursive symbol and $S_0(;z) >^{(1)}_{\mathsf{spop}*} z$ holds, $f(S_0(;z), \boldsymbol{x}; \boldsymbol{y}) >^{(3)}_{\mathsf{spop}*} f(z, \boldsymbol{x}; \boldsymbol{y}))$ holds. This together with the definition of the precedence $\succeq_f$ allows us to conclude $f(S_0(;z), \boldsymbol{x}; \boldsymbol{y}) >^{(2)}_{\mathsf{spop}*} h_0(z, \boldsymbol{x}; \boldsymbol{y}, f(z, \boldsymbol{x}; \boldsymbol{y}))$.

Consider Condition (4). For each $g' \in \{g, h_0, h_1\}$, g' is maximal in the precedence $\succeq_{g'}$ by induction hypothesis for g'. Hence by the definition of $\succeq_f$, f is maximal in $\succeq_f$.

It remains to show Condition (5). Since f is a recursive symbol $\mathsf{rd}(f) = 1 + \max\{\mathsf{rd}(g), \mathsf{rd}(h_0), \mathsf{rd}(h_1)\}$. Without loss of generality let us suppose $\mathsf{rd}(g) = \max\{\mathsf{rd}(g), \mathsf{rd}(h_0), \mathsf{rd}(h_1)\}$. Then by induction hypothesis for g, $\mathsf{rd}(g)$ equals the maximal number of nested application of (**SRN**) in the definition of g in $\mathcal{B}_{\mathsf{wsc}}$. Hence $\mathsf{rd}(f) = 1 + \mathsf{rd}(g)$ equals the one in the definition of f in $\mathcal{B}_{\mathsf{wsc}}$.

6   A Non-trivial Closure Property of the Polytime Functions

Bellantoni already observed that his definition of FP is closed under safe recursion on notation with *parameter substitution*. Here a function f is defined from functions g, h_0, h_1 and $\boldsymbol{p}$ by

$$
\begin{aligned}
f(\epsilon, \boldsymbol{x}; \boldsymbol{y}) &= g(\boldsymbol{x}; \boldsymbol{y}) \\
f(zi, \boldsymbol{x}; \boldsymbol{y}) &= h_i(z, \boldsymbol{x}; \boldsymbol{y}, f(z, \boldsymbol{x}; \boldsymbol{p}(z, \boldsymbol{x}; \boldsymbol{y}))) \qquad (i = 0, 1) .
\end{aligned}
\qquad \textbf{(SRN}_{\textbf{PS}}\textbf{)}
$$

We introduce *small polynomial path order with parameter substitution* ($sPOP^*_{PS}$ for short), that extends clause $>^{(3)}_{\mathsf{spop}*}$ to account for the schema (**SRN$_{\mathbf{PS}}$**).

Definition 14. *Let s and t be terms such that* $s = f(s_1, \ldots, s_k; s_{k+1}, \ldots, s_{k+l})$. *Then* $s >_{\mathsf{spop}^*_{\mathsf{ps}}} t$ *if one of the following alternatives holds.*

1. $s_i \succeq_{\mathsf{spop}^*_{\mathsf{ps}}} t$ *for some argument* s_i *of s.*
2. $f \in \mathcal{D}$, $t = g(t_1, \ldots, t_m; t_{m+1}, \ldots, t_{m+n})$ *where* $f > g$ *and the following holds:*
   - $s \rhd^n_{\_} t_j$ *for all normal arguments* $t_1, \ldots, t_m$;
   - $s >_{\mathsf{spop}^*_{\mathsf{ps}}} t_j$ *for all safe arguments* $t_{m+1}, \ldots, t_{m+n}$;
   - *t contains at most one (recursive) function symbols g with* $f \sim g$.
3. $f \in \mathcal{D}^{\geqslant}_{\mathsf{rec}}$, $t = g(t_1, \ldots, t_k; t_{k+1}, \ldots, t_{k+l})$ *where* $f \sim g$ *and the following holds:*
   - $\langle s_1, \ldots, s_k \rangle >_{\mathsf{spop}^*_{\mathsf{ps}}} \langle t_{\pi(1)}, \ldots, t_{\pi(k)} \rangle$ *for some permutation* π *on* $\{1, \ldots, k\}$;
   - $s >_{\mathsf{spop}^*_{\mathsf{ps}}} t_j$ *for all safe arguments* t_j;
   - *arguments* $t_1, \ldots, t_{k+l}$ *contain no (recursive) symbols g with* $f \sim g$.

Here $s \succeq_{\mathsf{spop}^*_{\mathsf{ps}}} t$ *denotes that either* $s \stackrel{*}{\sim} t$ *or* $s >_{\mathsf{spop}^*_{\mathsf{ps}}} t$. *In the last clause, we use* $>_{\mathsf{spop}^*_{\mathsf{ps}}}$ *also for the product extension of* $>_{\mathsf{spop}^*_{\mathsf{ps}}}$ *(modulo permutation).*

We adapt the notion of predicative recursive TRS of degree d to sPOP$^*_{PS}$ in the obvious way. Parameter substitution extends the analytical power of sPOP* significantly. In particular, sPOP* can handle tail recursion as in the following example.

Example 15. The TRS $\mathcal{R}_{\mathsf{rev}}$ consists of the three rules

$$\mathsf{rev}(xs;) \to \mathsf{rev}_{\mathsf{tl}}(xs;[\,]) \quad \mathsf{rev}_{\mathsf{tl}}([\,];ys) \to ys \quad \mathsf{rev}_{\mathsf{tl}}(x:xs;ys) \to \mathsf{rev}_{\mathsf{tl}}(xs;x:ys)$$

reverses lists formed from the constructors $[\,]$ and $(:)$. Then $\mathcal{R}_{\mathsf{rev}}$ is compatible with $>_{\mathsf{spop}^*_{\mathsf{ps}}}$, but due to the last rule not with $>_{\mathsf{spop}^*}$.

Still sPOP$^*_{\mathsf{PS}}$ induces polynomially bounded runtime complexity in the sense of Theorem 3. As a consequence of the next theorem, the runtime of $\mathcal{R}_{\mathsf{rev}}$ is inferred to be linear.

Theorem 16. *Let $\mathcal{R}$ be a predicative recursive TRS of degree d (with respect to Definition 14). Then the innermost derivation height of any basic term $f(\boldsymbol{u};\boldsymbol{v})$ is bounded by a polynomial of degree $\mathsf{rd}(f)$ in the sum of the depths of normal arguments $\boldsymbol{u}$. In particular, the innermost runtime complexity of $\mathcal{R}$ is bounded by a polynomial of degree d.*

Corollary 17. *The class $\mathcal{B}_{\mathsf{wsc}}$ is closed under safe recursion on notation with parameter substitution. More precisely, for any functions $g, h_0, h_1, \boldsymbol{p} \in \mathcal{B}_{\mathsf{wsc}}$, there exists a unique polytime computable function f such that $f(\epsilon, \boldsymbol{x};\boldsymbol{y}) = g(\boldsymbol{x};\boldsymbol{y})$ and $f(zi, \boldsymbol{x};\boldsymbol{y}) = h_i(z, \boldsymbol{x};\boldsymbol{y}, f(z, \boldsymbol{x}, \boldsymbol{p}(z, \boldsymbol{x};\boldsymbol{y})))$ for each $i = 0, 1$.*

Furthermore sPOP$^*_{\mathsf{PS}}$ is complete for the polytime computable functions. To state a stronger completeness result, we extend the class $\mathcal{B}_{\mathsf{wsc}}$ to a class $\mathcal{B}_{\mathsf{wsc+ps}}$ that is also closed under the scheme (**SRN$_{\mathsf{PS}}$**). Then sPOP$^*_{\mathsf{PS}}$ is complete for $\mathcal{B}_{\mathsf{wsc+ps}}$ in the sense of Theorem 13.

Theorem 18. *For any $\mathcal{B}_{\mathsf{wsc+ps}}$-function f there exists a confluent TRS $\mathcal{R}_f$ that is predicative recursive of degree d (with respect to Definition 14), where d equals the maximal number of nested application of (**SRN$_{\mathsf{PS}}$**) in the definition of f.*

7 Conclusion

We propose a new order, the small polynomial path order sPOP*. Based on sPOP*, we delineate a class of rewrite systems, dubbed systems of predicative recursion of degree d, such that for rewrite systems in this class we obtain that the runtime complexity lies in $O(n^d)$. This termination order induces a new order-theoretic characterisation of the class of polytime computable functions. This order-theoretic characterisation enables a fine-grained control of the complexity of functions in relation to the number of nested applications of recursion.

Moreover, sPOP* gives rise to a new, fully automatic, syntactic method for polynomial runtime complexity analysis. We performed experiments on the relative power of sPOP* (respectively sPOP$^*_{\mathsf{PS}}$) with respect to LMPO [3] and POP* [5]. We selected two test-suites: test-suite TC constitutes of 597 terminating constructor TRSs and test-suite TCO, containing 290 examples, resulting from restricting test-suite TC to orthogonal systems.[5] On the larger

---

[5] The test-suites are taken from the Termination Problem Database (TPDB), version 8.0; http://termcomp.uibk.ac.at.

benchmark TC, LMPO proves an exponential bound on a subset of 57 examples. For four examples this bound is indeed tight, out of the remaining POP* can verify polynomially bounded runtime complexity on 43 examples. 39 examples of these can also be handled with sPOP* and for all these examples the runtime complexity is at most cubic. Thus sPOP* brings about a significant increase in precision, which accompanied with only minor decrease in power. This assessment remains true, if we consider the smaller benchmark set TCO. $sPOP^*_{PS}$ increases the analytic power of POP* on test-suite TC from 39 to 54 examples, from the 15 new examples 13 cannot be handled by any other technique.[6]

To test the applicability of sPOP* in the context of program analysis, we have employed a straightforward (and complexity preserving) transformation of RAML programs considered in [15] into TRSs. In Table 2 we present the performance of TCT on this test-suite. Equipped with $sPOP^*_{PS}$ our complexity analyser TCT can handle all examples in [15] and all but 5 of the RAML test-suite [28]. This is a noteworthy performance as the transforma-

	TCT	TCT/$sPOP^*_{PS}$
$O(n)$	3\ 2.84	3\ 3.65
$O(n^2)$	14\ 13.78	15\ 14.70
$O(n^3)$	15\ 38.80	16\ 39.68
unknown	6\ 36.41	5\ 41.94

Fig. 2. Empirical Evaluation on translated RAML sources

tion from RAML programs to TRSs used amounts to a straightforward (almost naive) program transformation.Furthermore the dedicated prototype crucially exploits the fact that RAML programs are typed. On the other hand TCT works on standard, that is untyped, TRSs.

References

1. Bellantoni, S., Cook, S.: A new Recursion-Theoretic Characterization of the Polytime Functions. CC 2(2), 97–110 (1992)
2. Baillot, P., Marion, J.Y., Rocca, S.R.D.: Guest Editorial: Special Issue on Implicit Computational Complexity. TOCL 10(4) (2009)
3. Marion, J.Y.: Analysing the Implicit Complexity of Programs. IC 183, 2–18 (2003)
4. Arai, T., Moser, G.: Proofs of Termination of Rewrite Systems for Polytime Functions. In: Sarukkai, S., Sen, S. (eds.) FSTTCS 2005. LNCS, vol. 3821, pp. 529–540. Springer, Heidelberg (2005)
5. Avanzini, M., Moser, G.: Complexity Analysis by Rewriting. In: Garrigue, J., Hermenegildo, M.V. (eds.) FLOPS 2008. LNCS, vol. 4989, pp. 130–146. Springer, Heidelberg (2008)
6. Avanzini, M., Moser, G.: Polynomial Path Orders: A Maximal Model. CoRR cs/CC/1209.3793 (2012), http://www.arxiv.org/
7. Bonfante, G., Cichon, A., Marion, J.Y., Touzet, H.: Algorithms with Polynomial Interpretation Termination Proof. JFP 11(1), 33–53 (2001)
8. Marion, J.Y.: On Tiered Small Jump Operators. LMCS 5(1) (2009)
9. Moser, G., Schnabl, A.: Proving Quadratic Derivational Complexities Using Context Dependent Interpretations. In: Voronkov, A. (ed.) RTA 2008. LNCS, vol. 5117, pp. 276–290. Springer, Heidelberg (2008)

---

[6] Full experimental evidence is provided under
http://cl-informatik.uibk.ac.at/software/tct/experiments/spopstar.

10. Hirokawa, N., Moser, G.: Automated Complexity Analysis Based on the Dependency Pair Method. In: Armando, A., Baumgartner, P., Dowek, G. (eds.) IJCAR 2008. LNCS (LNAI), vol. 5195, pp. 364–379. Springer, Heidelberg (2008)
11. Zankl, H., Korp, M.: Modular Complexity Analysis via Relative Complexity. In: Proc. of 21st RTA. LIPIcs, vol. 6, pp. 385–400 (2010)
12. Noschinski, L., Emmes, F., Giesl, J.: A Dependency Pair Framework for Innermost Complexity Analysis of Term Rewrite Systems. In: Bjørner, N., Sofronie-Stokkermans, V. (eds.) CADE 2011. LNCS (LNAI), vol. 6803, pp. 422–438. Springer, Heidelberg (2011)
13. Hirokawa, N., Moser, G.: Automated Complexity Analysis Based on the Dependency Pair Method. CoRR abs/1102.3129 (2011) (submitted)
14. Middeldorp, A., Moser, G., Neurauter, F., Waldmann, J., Zankl, H.: Joint Spectral Radius Theory for Automated Complexity Analysis of Rewrite Systems. In: Winkler, F. (ed.) CAI 2011. LNCS, vol. 6742, pp. 1–20. Springer, Heidelberg (2011)
15. Hoffmann, J., Aehlig, K., Hofmann, M.: Multivariate Amortized Resource Analysis. In: Proc. of 38th POPL, pp. 357–370. ACM (2011)
16. Albert, E., Arenas, P., Genaim, S., Gómez-Zamalloa, M., Puebla, G., Ramírez, D., Román, G., Zanardini, D.: Termination and Cost Analysis with COSTA and its User Interfaces. ENTCS 258(1), 109–121 (2009)
17. Alias, C., Darte, A., Feautrier, P., Gonnord, L.: Multi-dimensional Rankings, Program Termination, and Complexity Bounds of Flowchart Programs. In: Cousot, R., Martel, M. (eds.) SAS 2010. LNCS, vol. 6337, pp. 117–133. Springer, Heidelberg (2010)
18. Gulwani, S., Mehra, K., Chilimbi, T.: SPEED: Precise and Efficient Static Estimation of Program Computational Complexity. In: Proc. of 36th POPL, pp. 127–139. ACM (2009)
19. Zuleger, F., Gulwani, S., Sinn, M., Veith, H.: Bound Analysis of Imperative Programs with the Size-Change Abstraction. In: Yahav, E. (ed.) SAS 2011. LNCS, vol. 6887, pp. 280–297. Springer, Heidelberg (2011)
20. Simmons, H.: The Realm of Primitive Recursion. AML 27, 177–188 (1988)
21. Leivant, D.: A Foundational Delineation of Computational Feasiblity. In: Proc. of 6th LICS, pp. 2–11. IEEE Computer Society (1991)
22. Handley, W.G., Wainer, S.S.: Complexity of Primitive Recursion. In: Computational Logic. NATO ASI Series F: Computer and Systems Science, vol. 165, pp. 273–300 (1999)
23. Avanzini, M., Eguchi, N., Moser, G.: A New Order-theoretic Characterisation of the Polytime Computable Functions. CoRR cs/CC/1201.2553 (2012), http://www.arxiv.org/
24. Baader, F., Nipkow, T.: Term Rewriting and All That. Cambridge University Press (1998)
25. Dal Lago, U., Martini, S.: On Constructor Rewrite Systems and the Lambda-Calculus. In: Albers, S., Marchetti-Spaccamela, A., Matias, Y., Nikoletseas, S., Thomas, W. (eds.) ICALP 2009, Part II. LNCS, vol. 5556, pp. 163–174. Springer, Heidelberg (2009)
26. Avanzini, M., Moser, G.: Closing the Gap Between Runtime Complexity and Polytime Computability. In: Proc. of 21st RTA. LIPIcs, vol. 6, pp. 33–48 (2010)
27. Avanzini, M., Eguchi, N., Moser, G.: On a Correspondence between Predicative Recursion and Register Machines. In: Proc. of 12th WST, pp. 15–19 (2012), http://cl-informatik.uibk.ac.at/users/georg/events/wst2012/
28. Hoffmann, J., Aehlig, K., Hofmann, M.: Resource Aware ML. In: Madhusudan, P., Seshia, S.A. (eds.) CAV 2012. LNCS, vol. 7358, pp. 781–786. Springer, Heidelberg (2012)

A Dynamic Interpretation of the CPS Hierarchy

Marek Materzok and Dariusz Biernacki

University of Wrocław, Wrocław, Poland

Abstract. The CPS hierarchy of control operators $shift_i/reset_i$ of Danvy and Filinski is a natural generalization of the $shift$ and $reset$ static control operators that allow for abstracting delimited control in a structured and CPS-guided manner. In this article we show that a dynamic variant of $shift/reset$, known as $shift_0/reset_0$, where the discipline of static access to the stack of delimited continuations is relaxed, can fully express the CPS hierarchy. This result demonstrates the expressive power of $shift_0/reset_0$ and it offers a new perspective on practical applications of the CPS hierarchy.

1 Introduction

In the recent years delimited continuations have been recognized as an important concept in the landscape of eager functional programming, with new theoretical [1,12], practical [10,13], and implementational [11,14] advances in the field. Of the numerous control operators for delimited continuations, the so-called static control operators $shift$ and $reset$ introduced by Danvy and Filinski in their seminal work [8] occupy a special position, primarily due to the fact that their definition has been based on the well-known concept of the continuation-passing style (CPS). As such, $shift$ and $reset$ have solid semantic foundations [2,8], they are fundamentally related to other computational effects [9] and their use is guided by CPS [2,8].

The hierarchy of control operators $shift_i/reset_i$ [8] is a generalization of $shift/reset$ that has been defined in terms of the CPS hierarchy which in turn is obtained by iterated CPS translations. The idea is that the operator $shift_i$ can access and abstract the context up to the dynamically nearest enclosing control delimiter $reset_j$ with $i \leq j$. The primary goal for considering the hierarchy is layering nested computational effects [8,7] as well as expressing computations in hierarchical structures [2]. Recently, Biernacka et al. have proposed a framework for studying typed control operators in the CPS hierarchy [3], where more flexible than $shift_i/reset_i$ hierarchical control operators have been considered.

While the static delimited-control operators are often the choice for theoreticians and practitioners, it has been observed already in Danvy and Filinski's pioneering article [8], that there is an interesting dynamic variant of $shift$ and $reset$, nowadays known as $shift_0$ and $reset_0$ [16], that allows to inspect the stack of delimited contexts arbitrarily deep. In our previous work [15] we have presented a study of $shift_0$ and $reset_0$ in which we employed a type-and-effect system with subtyping in order to faithfully describe the interaction between terms and layered contexts. Interestingly enough, simple and elegant CPS translations for $shift_0$ and $reset_0$, in both untyped and typed version, have been given.

R. Jhala and A. Igarashi (Eds.): APLAS 2012, LNCS 7705, pp. 296–311, 2012.
© Springer-Verlag Berlin Heidelberg 2012

Since $shift_0$ and $reset_0$ can explore and manipulate the stack of contexts quite arbitrarily, the natural question of their relation to the CPS hierarchy arises. In this work we answer this question by showing that $shift_0$ and $reset_0$ can fully express the CPS hierarchy. To this end, we formally relate their operational semantics, CPS translations and type systems. Furthermore, we show some typical examples of programming in the CPS hierarchy implemented in terms of $shift_0/reset_0$ and an example that goes beyond the CPS hierarchy.

On one hand, the results we present exhibit a considerable expressive power of $shift_0$ and $reset_0$. On the other hand, they provide a new perspective on the practice and theory of the CPS hierarchy, with possible reasoning principles and implementation techniques for the hierarchy in terms of $shift_0$ and $reset_0$.

The rest of the article is structured as follows. In Section 2, we present the syntax, operational semantics, CPS translation and type system for the calculus $\lambda_\$$ that is a variant of λ_{S_0}—a calculus for $shift_0/reset_0$ [15]. In Section 3, we recall the syntax, operational semantics, CPS translation and type system for the calculus $\lambda^H_{\leftarrow}$—a calculus for the CPS hierarchy, as defined in [3]. In Section 4, we provide a translation from $\lambda^H_{\leftarrow}$ to $\lambda_\$$ and we prove soundness of this translation w.r.t. CPS translations, type systems, reduction semantics, and abstract machines. In Section 5, we consider some programming examples that illustrate the use of $shift_0$ and $reset_0$ in typical applications of the CPS hierarchy. Finally, in Section 6 we conclude.

Theorems presented in this paper are machine-checked with the Twelf theorem prover. The proofs can be accessed at http://www.tilk.eu/shift0/.

2 The Calculus λ_{S_0} and Its Variant $\lambda_\$$

In this section, we present the syntax, reduction semantics, abstract machine, CPS translation and type system of the calculus $\lambda_\$$ that is a variant of λ_{S_0} introduced in [15].

2.1 Introducing $Shift_0/Dollar$

The calculus λ_{S_0} is an extension of the call-by-value lambda calculus with a control delimiter $reset_0$ ($\langle\rangle$) that delimits contexts and a control operator $shift_0$ (S_0) that captures delimited contexts. In this work we introduce a new control operator, called $dollar$ ($\$$). This operator is a generalization of the $reset_0$ operator and its variant has been discussed by Kiselyov and Shan [12].[1] It generalizes $reset_0$ in the sense that, while $\langle e\rangle$ intuitively means 'run e with a new, empty, context on the context stack', the expression $e_1 \$ e_2$ means 'evaluate e_1, then run e_2 with the result of evaluating e_1 pushed on the context stack'. Despite this difference, $dollar$ is equally expressive as $reset_0$, in both typed and untyped settings. The former one can obviously macro-express the latter as follows:

$$\overline{\langle e\rangle} = (\lambda x.x) \$ \overline{e}$$

---

[1] The $dollar$ of [12] syntactically allows only coterms (which describe contexts) to be pushed on the context stack. In our language, we do not distinguish between terms and coterms and thus allow any function to be pushed as a context on the context stack.

The latter macro-expresses the former in a more complicated way:

$$\overline{e_1 \$ e_2} = (\lambda k.\langle(\lambda x.\mathcal{S}_0 z.k\, x)\, \overline{e_2}\rangle)\, \overline{e_1}$$

We can read the expression above as follows. First, evaluate e_1 and bind the resulting value to the variable k (we are using the call-by-value semantics.) Then run e_2 in a new context—and after the evaluation finishes, remove the delimiter and call k with the resulting value.

Even though $reset_0$ and *dollar* are equally expressive, we believe that using the little-studied *dollar* operator, rather than the well-known $reset_0$, is justified. The reason is that the translations which express the $shift_k/reset_k$ operators of the CPS hierarchy using $reset_0/dollar$ rely on the semantics of *dollar*; replacing *dollar* with $reset_0$ would result in a clumsy and awkward translation. This will become clear in the main part of the article. The *dollar* operator also has several interesting properties which make it worth studying; in particular, it is, in a sense, the inverse of the $shift_0$ operator.

2.2 Syntax and Semantics of $\lambda_\$$

In this section we formally describe the syntax and reduction semantics of the $\lambda_\$$ language. We introduce the following syntactic categories of terms, values, evaluation contexts and context stacks (called *trails* in this work):

terms	$e ::= x \mid \lambda x.e \mid e\,e \mid e\,\$\,e \mid \mathcal{S}_0 x.e$
values	$v ::= \lambda x.e$
contexts	$K ::= \bullet \mid K\,e \mid v\,K \mid K\,\$\,e$
closed contexts	$\hat{K} ::= v\$K$
trails	$T ::= \square \mid \hat{K} \cdot T$

Additionally, we use $\langle e \rangle$ as a shorthand for $(\lambda x.x)\,\$\,e$. Metavariables $x, y, f, g, \ldots$ range over variables.

Closed contexts are evaluation contexts terminated at the bottom with a *dollar*. For the purpose of easier manipulation of closed contexts, we introduce the following short-hands:

$$(v\$K)\,e = v\$(K\,e) \qquad v'\,(v\$K) = v\$(v'\,K) \qquad (v\$K)\,\$\,e = v\$(K\,\$\,e)$$

We also define $\hat{\bullet}$ to mean $(\lambda x.x)\$\bullet$.

Evaluation contexts and trails are represented inside-out. This is formalized with the following definition of plugging terms inside contexts and trails:

$$\bullet[e] = e \qquad\qquad (v\$K)[e] = v\,\$\,K[e]$$
$$(K\,e')[e] = K[e\,e']$$
$$(v\,K)[e] = K[v\,e] \qquad\qquad \square[e] = e$$
$$(K\,\$\,e')[e] = K[e\,\$\,e'] \qquad (\hat{K} \cdot T)[e] = T[\hat{K}[e]]$$

We define the operation of appending two evaluation contexts as follows:

$$K@\bullet = K \qquad\qquad K@(v\,K') = v\,(K@K')$$
$$K@(K'\,e) = (K@K')\,e \qquad K@(K'\,\$\,e) = (K@K')\,\$\,e$$

$$\langle \lambda x.e, \hat{K} \cdot T \rangle_e \Rightarrow \langle \hat{K}, \lambda x.e, T \rangle_a \qquad \langle \hat{K} \, \$ \, e, v, T \rangle_a \Rightarrow \langle e, (v\$\bullet) \cdot \hat{K} \cdot T \rangle_e$$
$$\langle \hat{K}', \hat{K} \cdot T \rangle_e \Rightarrow \langle \hat{K}, \hat{K}', T \rangle_a \qquad \langle \hat{K} \, e, v, T \rangle_a \Rightarrow \langle e, (v \, \hat{K}) \cdot T \rangle_e$$
$$\langle e_1 \, e_2, \hat{K} \cdot T \rangle_e \Rightarrow \langle e_1, (\hat{K} \, e_2) \cdot T \rangle_e \qquad \langle \hat{K}' \, \hat{K}, v, T \rangle_a \Rightarrow \langle \hat{K}', v, \hat{K} \cdot T \rangle_a$$
$$\langle \mathcal{S}_0 f.e, \hat{K} \cdot T \rangle_e \Rightarrow \langle e[\hat{K}/f], T \rangle_e \qquad \langle (\lambda x.e) \, \hat{K}, v, T \rangle_a \Rightarrow \langle e[v/x], \hat{K} \cdot T \rangle_e$$
$$\langle e_1 \, \$ \, e_2, \hat{K} \cdot T \rangle_e \Rightarrow \langle e_1, (\hat{K} \, \$ \, e_2) \cdot T \rangle_e \qquad \langle (\lambda x.e)\$\bullet, v, T \rangle_a \Rightarrow \langle e[v/x], T \rangle_e$$
$$\langle \hat{K}\$\bullet, v, T \rangle_a \Rightarrow \langle \hat{K}, v, T \rangle_a$$

Fig. 1. Abstract machine for $\lambda_\$$

The operation of appending a closed context to an evaluation context is defined as $(v\$K) @ K' = v\$(K @ K')$.

We have three contraction rules:

$$(\lambda x.e) \, v \rightsquigarrow e[v/x] \qquad (\beta_v)$$
$$v' \, \$ \, v \rightsquigarrow v' \, v \qquad (\$_v)$$
$$\hat{K}[\mathcal{S}_0 f.e] \rightsquigarrow e[\lambda x.\hat{K}[x]/f] \quad (\$/\mathcal{S}_0)$$

The first one is the familiar call-by-value beta-reduction. The second one is a generalization of the $\langle v \rangle \rightsquigarrow v$ rule used in $\lambda_{\mathcal{S}_0}$. Indeed, when we interpret $\langle v \rangle$ in $\lambda_\$$ as a shorthand for $(\lambda x.x) \, \$ \, v$, we have $\langle v \rangle = (\lambda x.x) \, \$ \, v \rightsquigarrow (\lambda x.x) \, v \rightsquigarrow v$. The last rule describes how the *shift$_0$* operator captures the nearest enclosing context (with the delimiting *dollar*) and reifies it as a function.

Finally, we define the reduction relation:

$$K[T[e]] \to K[T[e']] \text{ iff } e \rightsquigarrow e'$$

The semantics defined above satisfies the following unique-decomposition property: for every closed $\lambda_\$$ term e, either it is a value, or it is a stuck term of the form $K[\mathcal{S}_0 f.e]$, or it can be uniquely decomposed into a context K, a trail T and a term e' such that $e = K[T[e']]$ and there exists a term e'' such that $e' \rightsquigarrow e''$.

2.3 The Abstract Machine for $\lambda_\$$

The abstract machine for $\lambda_\$$ (with values including closed contexts) is defined in Fig. 1. It is very similar to the abstract machine for $\lambda_{\mathcal{S}_0}$, as defined in [5] and [15]. The difference comes from the fact that the (closed) evaluation contexts of $\lambda_\$$ are delimited with a *dollar*. This means that empty contexts are not really empty, but contain a terminating value, which needs to be called. That is why instead of the following transition from the abstract machine for $\lambda_{\mathcal{S}_0}$:

$$\langle \bullet, v, K \cdot T \rangle_a \Rightarrow \langle K, v, T \rangle_a$$

we have the following two for $\lambda_\$$:

$$\langle (\lambda x.e)\$\bullet, v, T \rangle_a \Rightarrow \langle e[v/x], T \rangle_e$$
$$\langle \hat{K}\$\bullet, v, T \rangle_a \Rightarrow \langle \hat{K}, v, T \rangle_a$$

$$\bar{x} = \lambda k.k\,x$$
$$\overline{\lambda x.e} = \lambda k.k\,(\lambda x.\bar{e})$$
$$\overline{e_1\,e_2} = \lambda k.\overline{e_1}\,(\lambda v_1.\overline{e_2}\,(\lambda v_2.v_1\,v_2\,k))$$

$$\overline{S_0 x.e} = \lambda x.\bar{e}$$
$$\overline{e_1\,\$\,e_2} = \lambda k.\overline{e_1}\,(\lambda v_1.\overline{e_2}\,v_1\,k)$$

Fig. 2. CPS translation for $\lambda_\$$ (untyped)

$$\frac{\tau \le \tau' \quad \sigma \le \sigma'}{\tau\,\sigma \le \tau'\,\sigma'} \qquad \frac{}{\alpha \le \alpha} \qquad \frac{\tau_1' \le \tau_1 \quad \tau_2\,\sigma \le \tau_2'\,\sigma'}{\tau_1 \xrightarrow{\sigma} \tau_2 \le \tau_1' \xrightarrow{\sigma'} \tau_2'}$$

$$\frac{}{\epsilon \le \epsilon} \qquad \frac{\tau\,\sigma \le \tau'\,\sigma'}{\epsilon \le [\tau\,\sigma]\,\tau'\,\sigma'} \qquad \frac{\tau_1'\,\sigma_1' \le \tau_1\,\sigma_1 \quad \tau_2\,\sigma_2 \le \tau_2'\,\sigma_2'}{[\tau_1\,\sigma_1]\,\tau_2\,\sigma_2 \le [\tau_1'\,\sigma_1']\,\tau_2'\,\sigma_2'}$$

$$\frac{}{\Gamma, x:\tau_1 \vdash x:\tau_1}\ \text{VAR} \qquad \frac{\Gamma \vdash e:\tau\,\sigma \quad \tau\,\sigma \le \tau'\,\sigma'}{\Gamma \vdash e:\tau'\,\sigma'}\ \text{SUB} \qquad \frac{\Gamma, x:\tau_1 \vdash e:\tau_2\,\sigma}{\Gamma \vdash \lambda x.e:\tau_1 \xrightarrow{\sigma} \tau_2}\ \text{ABS}$$

$$\frac{\Gamma, x:\tau_1 \xrightarrow{\sigma} \tau_2 \vdash e:\tau_3\,\sigma'}{\Gamma \vdash S_0 x.e:\tau_1\,[\tau_2\,\sigma]\,\tau_3\,\sigma'}\ \text{SFT} \qquad \frac{\Gamma \vdash e_1:\tau_1 \xrightarrow{\sigma} \tau_2 \quad \Gamma \vdash e_2:\tau_1}{\Gamma \vdash e_1\,e_2:\tau_2\,\sigma}\ \text{PAPP}$$

$$\frac{\Gamma \vdash e_1:\tau_1 \xrightarrow{[\tau_4'\,\sigma_4']\,\tau_3'\,\sigma_3'} \tau_2\,[\tau_2'\,\sigma_2']\,\tau_1'\,\sigma_1' \quad \Gamma \vdash e_2:\tau_1\,[\tau_3'\,\sigma_3']\,\tau_2'\,\sigma_2'}{\Gamma \vdash e_1\,e_2:\tau_2\,[\tau_4'\,\sigma_4']\,\tau_1'\,\sigma_1'}\ \text{APP}$$

$$\frac{\Gamma \vdash e_1:\tau_1 \xrightarrow{\sigma} \tau_2 \quad \Gamma \vdash e_2:\tau_1\,[\tau_2\,\sigma]\,\tau_3\,\sigma'}{\Gamma \vdash e_1\,\$\,e_2:\tau_3\,\sigma'}\ \text{PDOL}$$

$$\frac{\Gamma \vdash e_1:\tau_1 \xrightarrow{\sigma} \tau_2\,[\tau_2'\,\sigma_2']\,\tau_1'\,\sigma_1' \quad \Gamma \vdash e_2:\tau_1\,[\tau_2\,\sigma]\,\tau_3\,[\tau_3'\,\sigma_3']\,\tau_2'\,\sigma_2'}{\Gamma \vdash e_1\,\$\,e_2:\tau_3\,[\tau_3'\,\sigma_3']\,\tau_1'\,\sigma_1'}\ \text{DOL}$$

Fig. 3. The type system for $\lambda_\$$ (with subtyping)

2.4 The CPS Translation for $\lambda_\$$

The CPS translation is defined in Fig. 2. It is very similar to the untyped translation for λ_{S_0}, defined in [15]. The translation for the *reset*$_0$ operator in the original translation is as follows:

$$\overline{\langle e \rangle} = \bar{e}\,(\lambda x.\lambda k.k\,x)$$

In $\lambda_\$$, the translation of $\langle e \rangle = (\lambda x.x)\,\$\,e$ is as follows:

$$\overline{(\lambda x.x)\,\$\,e} = \lambda k.(\lambda k.k\,(\lambda x.\lambda k.k\,x))\,(\lambda v.\bar{e}\,v\,k) =_{\beta\eta} \bar{e}\,(\lambda x.\lambda k.k\,x)$$

2.5 The Type System for $\lambda_\$$

We introduce the syntactic categories of types and effect annotations:

$$\begin{aligned} types \qquad & \tau ::= \alpha \mid \tau \xrightarrow{\sigma} \tau \\ annotations \qquad & \sigma ::= \epsilon \mid [\tau\,\sigma]\,\tau\,\sigma \end{aligned}$$

The type system is shown in Fig. 3. Effect annotations have no meaning by themselves; they should be understood together with types they annotate. The typing judgment $\Gamma \vdash e : \tau'_1 [\tau_1 \sigma_1] \tau'_2 \ldots \tau'_n [\tau_n \sigma_n] \tau$ (we omit ϵ for brevity) can be read as follows: 'the term e in a typing context Γ evaluates to a value of type τ when plugged in a trail of contexts of types $\tau'_1 \xrightarrow{\sigma_1} \tau_1, \ldots, \tau'_n \xrightarrow{\sigma_n} \tau_n$'. The judgment $\Gamma \vdash e : \tau$ means 'the term e in a typing context Γ evaluates to a value of type τ without observable control effects'. Function types also have effect annotations, which can be thought to be associated with the return type.

We made two changes to the type system presented in [15]:

1. The rule for pure application has been generalized. This modification does not change the theory, because both cases of the new rule (with σ empty or non-empty) are derivable using the original rules. Yet some proofs are easier with the new rule.
2. The typing rule for $reset_0$ has been replaced with two rules for $. When we take $\langle e \rangle = (\lambda x.x) \, \$ \, e$, the original rule for $reset_0$ can be derived from them.

This means that the type system in Fig. 3 is a conservative extension of the original type system for $shift_0/reset_0$.

3   The CPS Hierarchy—The Calculus $\lambda^H_{\hookleftarrow}$

For the purpose of formalizing the connection between $shift_0/reset_0$ and the CPS hierarchy, for our second language we use the hierarchy of flexible delimited-control operators, as defined in the article by Biernacka et al. [3]. The main reason is that it has a very expressive type system, defined in the same article, which we relate to the type system of $\lambda_\$$. The language expresses the original CPS hierarchy, as defined in [8], so the results still hold for the original hierarchy.

In this section, we define the syntax, reduction semantics, abstract machine, CPS translation and type system of $\lambda^H_{\hookleftarrow}$. We try to keep the description succinct; more detailed description can be found in [3].

3.1   Syntax and Semantics of $\lambda^H_{\hookleftarrow}$

We define the syntactic categories of terms, values, coterms (which represent evaluation contexts), evaluation contexts and programs:

terms	$e ::= x \mid \lambda x.e \mid e \, e \mid \langle e \rangle_i \mid \mathcal{S}_i k_1 \ldots k_i.e \mid (h_1, \ldots, h_i) \hookleftarrow_i e$
values	$v ::= \lambda x.e$
coterms	$h_i ::= k_i \mid E_i$
level 1 contexts	$E_1 ::= \bullet_1 \mid E_1 \, e \mid v \, E_1 \mid (E_1, \ldots, E_i) \hookleftarrow_i E_1$
level > 1 contexts	$E_i ::= \bullet_i \mid E_i.E_{i-1}$
level n programs	$p ::= \langle e, E_1, \ldots, E_{n+1} \rangle$

$$\langle \lambda x.e, E_1, \ldots, E_{n+1} \rangle_e \Rightarrow \langle \lambda x.e, E_1, \ldots, E_{n+1} \rangle_a$$
$$\langle e_1 e_2, E_1, \ldots, E_{n+1} \rangle_e \Rightarrow \langle e_1, E_1 e_2, E_2, \ldots, E_{n+1} \rangle_e$$
$$\langle (E'_1, \ldots, E'_i) \hookleftarrow_i e, E_1, \ldots, E_{n+1} \rangle_e \Rightarrow \langle e, (E'_1, \ldots, E'_i) \hookleftarrow_i E_1, E_2, \ldots, E_{n+1} \rangle_e$$
$$\langle \langle e \rangle_i, E_1, \ldots, E_{n+1} \rangle_e \Rightarrow \langle e, \bullet_1, \ldots, \bullet_i, E_{i+1}.(E_i.\ldots.(E_2.E_1)),$$
$$E_{i+2}, \ldots, E_{n+1} \rangle_e$$
$$\langle \mathcal{S}_i k_1, \ldots, k_i.e, E_1, \ldots, E_{n+1} \rangle_e \Rightarrow \langle e[E_1/k_1] \ldots [E_i/k_i], \bullet_1, \ldots, \bullet_i,$$
$$E_{i+1}, \ldots, E_{n+1} \rangle_e$$
$$\langle v, E_1 e_2, E_2, \ldots, E_{n+1} \rangle_a \Rightarrow \langle e_2, v E_1, E_2, \ldots, E_{n+1} \rangle_e$$
$$\langle v, (\lambda x.e) E_1, E_2, \ldots, E_{n+1} \rangle_a \Rightarrow \langle e[v/x], E_1, E_2, \ldots, E_{n+1} \rangle_e$$
$$\langle v, (E'_1, \ldots, E'_i) \hookleftarrow_i E_1, E_2, \ldots, E_{n+1} \rangle_a \Rightarrow \langle v, E'_1, \ldots, E'_i, E_{i+1}.(E_i.\ldots.(E_2.E_1)),$$
$$E_{i+2}, \ldots, E_{n+1} \rangle_a$$
$$\langle v, \bullet_i, E_{i+1}, \ldots, E_{n+1} \rangle_a \Rightarrow \langle v, E_{i+1}, \ldots, E_{n+1} \rangle_a$$
$$\langle v, E_i.(E_{i-1}.\ldots.(E_2.E_1)), E_{i+1}, \ldots, E_{n+1} \rangle_a \Rightarrow \langle v, E_1, E_2, \ldots, E_{n+1} \rangle_a$$

Fig. 4. Abstract machine for $\lambda^H_{\hookleftarrow}$

Plugging terms inside evaluation contexts is defined as follows:

$$\bullet_i[e] = e$$
$$(E_1 e')[e] = E_1[e e']$$
$$(v E_1)[e] = E_1[v e]$$
$$((E'_1, \ldots, E'_i) \hookleftarrow_i E_1)[e] = E_1[(E_1, \ldots, E_i) \hookleftarrow_i e]$$
$$(E_i.E_{i-1})[e] = E_i[\langle E_{i-1}[e] \rangle_{i-1}]$$

The syntactic category of programs exists for the purpose of defining the reduction semantics. The *plug* function defined below reconstructs the term represented by a given program tuple:

$$plug \langle e, E_1 e', E_2, \ldots, E_{n+1} \rangle = plug \langle e e', E_1, E_2, \ldots, E_{n+1} \rangle$$
$$plug \langle e, v E_1, E_2, \ldots, E_{n+1} \rangle = plug \langle v e, E_1, E_2, \ldots, E_{n+1} \rangle$$
$$plug \langle e, (E'_1, \ldots, E'_i) \hookleftarrow_i E_1, E_2, \ldots, E_{n+1} \rangle = plug \langle (E'_1, \ldots, E'_i) \hookleftarrow_i e,$$
$$E_1, E_2, \ldots, E_{n+1} \rangle$$
$$plug \langle e, \bullet_1, \ldots, \bullet_i, E_{i+1}.(E_i.\ldots.(E_2.E_1)),$$
$$E_{i+2}, \ldots, E_{n+1} \rangle = plug \langle \langle e \rangle_i, E_1, \ldots, E_{n+1} \rangle$$
$$plug \langle e, \bullet_1, \ldots, \bullet_{n+1} \rangle = \langle e \rangle_n$$

Finally, we define the reduction semantics as follows:

$$\langle (\lambda x.e) v, E_1, \ldots, E_{n+1} \rangle \rightarrow \langle e[v/x], E_1, \ldots, E_{n+1} \rangle$$
$$\langle \mathcal{S}_i k_1 \ldots k_i.e, E_1, \ldots, E_{n+1} \rangle \rightarrow \langle e[E_1/k_1] \ldots [E_i/k_i], \bullet_1, \ldots, \bullet_i,$$
$$E_{i+1}, \ldots E_{n+1} \rangle$$
$$\langle \langle v \rangle_i, E_1, \ldots, E_{n+1} \rangle \rightarrow \langle v, E_1, \ldots, E_{n+1} \rangle$$
$$\langle (E'_1, \ldots, E'_i) \hookleftarrow_i v, E_1, \ldots, E_{n+1} \rangle \rightarrow \langle v, E'_1, \ldots, E'_i, E_{i+1}.(E_i.\ldots.(E_2.E_1)),$$
$$E_{i+2}, \ldots E_{n+1} \rangle$$

3.2 The Abstract Machine for $\lambda^H_{\hookleftarrow}$

The abstract machine is defined in Fig. 4.

$$\overline{x} = \lambda k.k\,x$$
$$\overline{\lambda x.e} = \lambda k.k\,(\lambda x.\overline{e})$$
$$\overline{\langle e \rangle_i} = \lambda k_1.\ldots.\lambda k_{i+1}.\overline{e}\,\theta\,.^{i}.\,\theta$$
$$(\lambda v.k_1\,v\,k_2\,\ldots\,k_{i+1})$$
$$\overline{S_i k_1 \ldots k_i.e} = \lambda k_1.\ldots.\lambda k_i.\overline{e}\,\theta\,.^{i}.\,\theta$$
$$\overline{(h_1,\ldots,h_i) \hookleftarrow_i e} = \lambda k.\overline{e}\,(\lambda v.\lambda k_2.\ldots.\lambda k_{i+1}.\overline{h_1}\,v\,\overline{h_2}\,\ldots\,\overline{h_i}$$
$$(\lambda w.k\,w\,k_2\,\ldots\,k_{i+1}))$$
$$\overline{k} = k$$
$$\overline{\bullet_i} = \theta$$
$$\overline{E_1\,e} = \lambda v.\overline{e}\,(\lambda w.v\,w\,\overline{E_1})$$
$$\overline{v\,E_1} = \lambda w.v^*\,w\,\overline{E_1}$$
$$\overline{(E_1,\ldots,E_i) \hookleftarrow_i E_1'} = \lambda v.\lambda k_2.\ldots.\lambda k_{i+1}.\overline{E_1}\,v\,\overline{E_2}\,\ldots\,\overline{E_i}$$
$$(\lambda w.\overline{E_1'}\,w\,k_2\,\ldots\,k_{i+1})$$
$$\overline{E_i.E_{i-1}} = \lambda v.\overline{E_{i-1}}\,v\,\overline{E_i}$$

$$(\lambda x.e)^* = \lambda x.\overline{e}$$

where $\theta = \lambda x.\lambda k.k\,x$

Fig. 5. CPS translation for $\lambda_{\hookleftarrow}^{\mathrm{H}}$ (eta-reduced)

3.3   The CPS Translation for $\lambda_{\hookleftarrow}^{\mathrm{H}}$

The CPS translation is defined in Fig. 5. It is presented in eta-reduced form. The translated terms can be eta-expanded back to the form presented in [3].

3.4   The Type System for $\lambda_{\hookleftarrow}^{\mathrm{H}}$

We introduce the syntactic categories of types and context types:

types	$\tau ::= \alpha \mid \tau \to [\delta_1, \ldots, \delta_{n+1}]$
level $\leq n$ context types	$\delta_i ::= \tau \rhd \delta_{i+1} \rhd \ldots \rhd \delta_{n+1}$
level $n + 1$ context types	$\delta_{n+1} ::= \neg\tau$

The type system for terms is defined in Fig. 6. For lack of space, we omit the typing rules for coterms (they do not introduce any new essential concepts). The entire type system can be found in [3].

4   Relating $\lambda_\$$ to $\lambda_{\hookleftarrow}^{\mathrm{H}}$

In this section we relate the CPS translations, type systems, abstract machines, and reduction semantics of $\lambda_\$$ and $\lambda_{\hookleftarrow}^{\mathrm{H}}$. This is the main section of the article.

4.1   CPS Translations

We present in Fig. 7 a translation from $\lambda_{\hookleftarrow}^{\mathrm{H}}$ to $\lambda_\$$. The translation represents the control operators of the CPS hierarchy with *shift₀/dollar*, and refunctionalizes the evaluation contexts present in the reduction semantics of $\lambda_{\hookleftarrow}^{\mathrm{H}}$. We arrived at this translation by trying to match the CPS translations of $\lambda_{\hookleftarrow}^{\mathrm{H}}$ and $\lambda_\$$ and to capture the operational meaning of the CPS hierarchy's control operators:

$$\Gamma, x : \tau; \Delta \vdash_n x : \tau \triangleright \delta_2 \ldots \triangleright \delta_{n+1}, \delta_2 \ldots \delta_{n+1}$$

$$\frac{\Gamma, x : \tau; \Delta \vdash_n e : \delta_1', \ldots \delta_{n+1}'}{\Gamma; \Delta \vdash_n \lambda x.e : (\tau \to [\delta_1' \ldots \delta_{n+1}']) \triangleright \delta_2 \ldots \triangleright \delta_{n+1}, \delta_2 \ldots \delta_{n+1}}$$

$$\frac{\Gamma; \Delta \vdash_n e_0 : (\tau \to [\delta_1 \ldots \delta_{n+1}]) \triangleright \delta_2'' \ldots \triangleright \delta_{n+1}'', \delta_2' \ldots \delta_{n+1}' \qquad \Gamma; \Delta \vdash_n e_1 : \tau \triangleright \delta_2 \ldots \triangleright \delta_{n+1}, \delta_2'' \ldots \delta_{n+1}''}{\Gamma; \Delta \vdash_n e_0 e_1 : \delta_1, \delta_2' \ldots \delta_{n+1}'}$$

$$\frac{\mathcal{I}_1(\delta_1') \quad \ldots \quad \mathcal{I}_i(\delta_i') \quad \Gamma; \Delta \vdash_n e : \delta_1' \ldots \delta_i', (\tau \triangleright \delta_{i+2} \ldots \triangleright \delta_{n+1}), \delta_{i+2}' \ldots \delta_{n+1}'}{\Gamma; \Delta \vdash_n \langle e \rangle_i : \tau \triangleright \delta_2 \ldots \triangleright \delta_{n+1}, \delta_2 \ldots \delta_{i+1}, \delta_{i+2}' \ldots \delta_{n+1}'}$$

$$\frac{\mathcal{I}_1(\delta_1') \quad \ldots \quad \mathcal{I}_i(\delta_i') \quad \Gamma; \Delta, k_1 : \delta_1, \ldots, k_i : \delta_i \vdash_n e : \delta_1' \ldots \delta_i', \delta_{i+1} \ldots \delta_{n+1}}{\Gamma; \Delta \vdash_n \mathcal{S}_i k_1 \ldots k_i.e : \delta_1, \delta_2 \ldots \delta_{n+1}}$$

$$\frac{\delta_1 = \tau \triangleright \delta_2 \ldots \triangleright \delta_{n+1} \qquad \delta_{i+1} = \tau' \triangleright \delta_{i+2}' \ldots \triangleright \delta_{n+1}'}{\Gamma; \Delta \vdash_n h_1 : \delta_1 \qquad \ldots \qquad \Gamma; \Delta \vdash_n h_i : \delta_i}{\Gamma; \Delta \vdash_n e : \tau \triangleright \delta_2'' \triangleright \ldots \triangleright \delta_{i+1}'' \triangleright \delta_{i+2} \triangleright \ldots \triangleright \delta_{n+1}, \delta_2', \ldots \delta_{n+1}'}{\Gamma; \Delta \vdash_n (h_1 \ldots h_i) \hookleftarrow_i e : \tau' \triangleright \delta_2'' \triangleright \ldots \triangleright \delta_{i+1}'' \triangleright \delta_{i+2} \triangleright \ldots \triangleright \delta_{n+1}, \delta_2' \ldots \delta_{n+1}'}$$

$$\mathcal{I}_i(\delta_i) := \exists \tau, \delta_{i+2}, \ldots, \delta_{n+1}.\delta_i = \tau \triangleright (\tau \triangleright \delta_{i+2} \triangleright \ldots \triangleright \delta_{n+1}) \triangleright \delta_{i+2} \triangleright \ldots \triangleright \delta_{n+1}$$

Fig. 6. The type system for level n $\lambda_{\hookleftarrow}^{H}$ terms

- The operator $\langle e \rangle_n$ affects only the top $n + 1$ contexts. It resets the top n contexts, and pushes the original contexts down to the $n + 1$-th context. We can achieve that in $\lambda_{\$}$ by first capturing the $n + 1$ contexts by using the *shift₀* operator $n + 1$ times, pushing the extended $n + 1$-th context using $, and then pushing the empty context using *reset₀* n times.
- The operator $(k_1, \ldots, k_n) \hookleftarrow_n e$ works very similar to $\langle e \rangle_n$, only instead of resetting the top n contexts, it replaces them with the given contexts $k_1, \ldots, k_n$. In $\lambda_{\$}$, instead of pushing empty contexts, we push the given contexts using $.
- The operator $\mathcal{S}_n k_1 \ldots k_n.e$ affects only the top n contexts. It captures them and replaces them by empty contexts. We can achieve that in $\lambda_{\$}$ by using the *shift₀* operator n times, and then using *reset₀* n times.

We have the following theorem:

Theorem 1. *For every term e in $\lambda_{\hookleftarrow}^{H}$, we have $\overline{e} =_{\beta\eta} \overline{\llbracket e \rrbracket}$.*

Proof. By induction and simple calculation. It is easy to see that following hold:

$$\frac{}{(\lambda x.e) \, \$ \, e' =_{\beta\eta} \overline{e'} \, (\lambda x.\overline{e})} \qquad \frac{}{x \, \$ \, e =_{\beta\eta} \overline{e} \, x}$$

$$\frac{}{\langle e \rangle =_{\beta\eta} \overline{e} \, \theta} \qquad \frac{}{k_n \, \$ \, \ldots \, \$ \, k_1 \, \$ \, x =_{\beta\eta} k_1 \, x \, k_2 \, \ldots \, k_n}$$

With these, showing the theorem is straightforward.

$$[\![x]\!] = x$$
$$[\![e_1\, e_2]\!] = [\![e_1]\!]\, [\![e_2]\!]$$
$$[\![\lambda x.e]\!] = \lambda x.[\![e]\!]$$
$$[\![\langle e \rangle_i]\!] = \mathcal{S}_0 f_1.\ldots.\mathcal{S}_0 f_{i+1}.(\lambda x.f_{i+1}\,\$\,\ldots\,\$\,f_1\,\$\,x)\,\$\,\langle .\,\vdots\,.\langle [\![e]\!]\rangle\ldots\rangle$$
$$[\![(h_1,\ldots,h_i) \hookleftarrow_i e]\!] = \mathcal{S}_0 f_1.\ldots.\mathcal{S}_0 f_{i+1}.(\lambda x.f_{i+1}\,\$\,\ldots\,\$\,f_1\,\$\,x)\,\$$$
$$[\![h_i]\!]_i\,\$\,\ldots\,\$\,[\![h_1]\!]_1\,\$\,[\![e]\!]$$
$$[\![\mathcal{S}_i k_1 \ldots k_i.e]\!] = \mathcal{S}_0 k_1.\ldots.\mathcal{S}_0 k_i.\langle .\,\vdots\,.\langle [\![e]\!]\rangle\ldots\rangle$$
$$[\![k_i]\!]_i = k_i$$
$$[\![E_i]\!]_i = \lambda x.(\lambda y.[\![E_i]\!]_i^c(y))\,\$\,x$$
$$[\![\bullet_i]\!]_i^c(x) = \langle x \rangle$$
$$[\![E_1\, e]\!]_i^c(x) = [\![E_1]\!]_i^c(x\, [\![e]\!])$$
$$[\![v\, E_1]\!]_i^c(x) = [\![E_1]\!]_i^c([\![v]\!]\, x)$$
$$[\![(E_1,\ldots,E_i) \hookleftarrow_i E_1']\!]_i^c(x) = [\![E_1']\!]_i^c((\lambda y.\mathcal{S}_0 f_1.\ldots.\mathcal{S}_0 f_{i+1}.(\lambda z.f_{i+1}\,\$\,\ldots\,\$\,f_1\,\$\,z)\,\$$$
$$[\![E_i]\!]_n\,\$\,\ldots\,\$\,[\![E_1]\!]_1\,\$\,y)\,x)$$
$$[\![E_i.E_{i-1}]\!]_i^c(x) = (\lambda y.[\![E_i]\!]_i^c(y))\,\$\,[\![E_{i-1}]\!]_{i-1}^c(x)$$
$$[\![\langle e, E_1, E_2, \ldots, E_{n+1} \rangle]\!] = (\lambda x.[\![E_n]\!]_{n+1}^c(x))\,\$\,\ldots\,\$\,(\lambda x.[\![E_1]\!]_1^c(x))\,\$\,[\![e]\!]$$

Fig. 7. Translation of $\lambda_{\hookleftarrow}^{\mathrm{H}}$ to $\lambda_{\$}$

4.2 Type Systems

We use the following convention:

$$\tau' \to (\tau\, \sigma) = \tau' \xrightarrow{\sigma} \tau$$

I.e. annotating the type on the right side of the function arrow means the same as annotating the function arrow. Also, we define the operation of appending a function type and an annotated type as follows:

$$(\tau_1 \xrightarrow{\sigma} \tau_2)\, @\, \tau'\, \sigma' = \tau_1\, [\tau_2\, \sigma]\, \tau'\, \sigma'$$

The meaning of this definition comes from the fact that annotated types describe types of the individual contexts on a trail.

We define the translation from $\lambda_{\hookleftarrow}^{\mathrm{H}}$ types to $\lambda_{\$}$ types as follows:

$$[\![\alpha]\!] = \alpha$$
$$[\![S \to [C_1,\ldots,C_{n+1}]]\!] = [\![S]\!] \to [\![C_1,\ldots,C_{n+1}]\!]$$
$$[\![C_i,\ldots,C_n,\neg S]\!] = [\![C_i]\!]\, @\, \ldots\, @\, [\![C_n]\!]\, @\, [\![S]\!]$$
$$[\![S \rhd C_{i+1} \rhd \ldots \rhd C_{n+1}]\!] = [\![S]\!] \to [\![C_{i+1},\ldots,C_{n+1}]\!]$$

Theorem 2. *If* $\Gamma \vdash_n e : C_1,\ldots,C_{n+1}$ *in* $\lambda_{\hookleftarrow}^{\mathrm{H}}$, *then* $[\![\Gamma]\!] \vdash [\![e]\!] : [\![C_1,\ldots,C_{n+1}]\!]$ *in* $\lambda_{\$}$.

Proof. Cases for variables and lambda abstractions are trivial and follow from the fact that for every τ, τ' and σ, $\tau' \leq \tau' [\tau\, \sigma]\, \tau\, \sigma$.

4.3 Reduction Semantics

The reduction semantics of $\lambda_{\hookleftarrow}^{\mathrm{H}}$ and $\lambda_{\$}$ cannot be related directly. The reason is that in the $\lambda_{\hookleftarrow}^{\mathrm{H}}$ language, evaluation 'goes straight through' the $\langle e \rangle_i$ operators, but their translation to $\lambda_{\$}$ has operational meaning. E.g., the term $\langle (\lambda x.x)\,(\lambda x.x) \rangle_1$ reduces in one step

$$[\![x]\!] = x$$
$$[\![e_1\, e_2]\!] = [\![e_1]\!]\, [\![e_2]\!]$$
$$[\![\lambda x.e]\!] = \lambda x.[\![e]\!]$$
$$[\![\langle e \rangle_i]\!] = S_0 f_1.\ldots.S_0 f_{i+1}.(\lambda x.f_{i+1}\,\$\,\ldots\,\$\,f_1\,\$\,x)\,\$\,\langle\,.\,{:}\,.\langle[\![e]\!]\rangle\,\ldots\rangle$$
$$[\![(k_1,\ldots,k_n) \hookleftarrow_i e]\!] = S_0 f_1.\ldots.S_0 f_{i+1}.(\lambda x.f_{i+1}\,\$\,\ldots\,\$\,f_1\,\$\,x)\,\$$$
$$[\![k_i]\!]_i\,\$\,\ldots\,\$\,[\![k_1]\!]_1\,\$\,[\![e]\!]$$
$$[\![S_i k_1 \ldots k_i.e]\!] = S_0 k_1.\ldots.S_0 k_i.\langle\,.\,{:}\,.\langle[\![e]\!]\rangle\,\ldots\rangle$$

$$[\![k]\!]_i = k$$
$$[\![E_i]\!]_i = [\![E_i]\!]_i^c$$

$$[\![\bullet_i]\!]_i^c = \hat{\bullet}$$
$$[\![E_1\, e]\!]_i^c = [\![E_1]\!]_i^c\, [\![e]\!]$$
$$[\![v\, E_1]\!]_i^c = [\![v]\!]\, [\![E_1]\!]_i^c$$
$$[\![(E_1,\ldots,E_i) \hookleftarrow_i E_1']\!]_i^c = (\lambda y.S_0 f_1.\ldots.S_0 f_{i+1}.(\lambda z.f_{i+1}\,\$\,\ldots\,\$\,f_1\,\$\,z)\,\$$$
$$[\![E_i]\!]_i\,\$\,\ldots\,\$\,[\![E_1]\!]_1\,\$\,y)\,[\![E_1']\!]_i^c$$
$$[\![E_i.(E_{i-1}.(\ldots E_{j+1}.E_j))]\!]_i^c = (\lambda x.[\![E_i]\!]_i^c\,\$\,[\![E_{i-1}]\!]_{i-1}^c\,\$\,\ldots\,\$\,[\![E_{j+1}]\!]_{j+1}^c\,\$\,[\![E_j]\!]_j^c\,\$\,x)\,\$\bullet$$

$$[\![\langle e, E_k, E_{k+1},\ldots,E_{n+1}\rangle_e]\!] = \langle[\![e]\!], [\![E_k]\!]_k^c \cdot [\![E_{k+1}]\!]_{k+1}^c \cdot \ldots \cdot [\![E_{n+1}]\!]_n^c \cdot \hat{\bullet}\rangle_e$$
$$[\![\langle v, E_k, E_{k+1},\ldots,E_{n+1}\rangle_a]\!] = \langle[\![v]\!], [\![E_k]\!]_k^c \cdot [\![E_{k+1}]\!]_{k+1}^c \cdot \ldots \cdot [\![E_{n+1}]\!]_n^c \cdot \hat{\bullet}\rangle_a$$

Fig. 8. Translation of $\lambda_{\hookleftarrow}^{H}$ to $\lambda_\$$ (abstract machines)

to $\langle \lambda x.x \rangle_1$, whereas evaluation of the translated program $\langle\langle(\lambda x.x)\,(\lambda x.x)\rangle_1, \bullet_1, \bullet_2\rangle$ proceeds as follows:

$$(\lambda x.\langle x\rangle)\,\$\,(\lambda x.\langle x\rangle)\,\$\,S_0 f_1.S_0 f_2.(\lambda x.f_2\,\$\,f_1\,\$\,x)\,\$\,\langle(\lambda x.x)\,(\lambda x.x)\rangle$$
$$\rightarrow^* (\lambda x.(\lambda x.(\lambda x.\langle x\rangle)\,\$\,x)\,(\lambda x.(\lambda x.\langle x\rangle)\,\$\,x)\,\$\,x)\,\$\,\langle\lambda x.x\rangle$$
$$\neq (\lambda x.\langle x\rangle)\,\$\,(\lambda x.\langle x\rangle)\,\$\,S_0 f_1.S_0 f_2.(\lambda x.f_2\,\$\,f_1\,\$\,x)\,\$\,\langle\lambda x.x\rangle$$

Interestingly, using a refocused [4] version of the $\lambda_{\hookleftarrow}^{H}$ reduction semantics eliminates this discrepancy.

We present below how another $\lambda_{\hookleftarrow}^{H}$ term evaluates:

$$\langle S_1 k.(k) \hookleftarrow_1 \lambda x.x \rangle_1 \rightarrow \langle(\bullet_1) \hookleftarrow_1 \lambda x.x\rangle_1 \rightarrow \langle\langle\lambda x.x\rangle_1\rangle_1$$

Its translation evaluates as follows:

$$(\lambda x.\langle x\rangle)\,\$\,(\lambda x.\langle x\rangle)\,\$\,S_0 k.\langle S_0 k_1.S_0 k_2.(\lambda x.k_2\,\$\,k_1\,\$\,x)\,\$\,k\,\$\,\lambda x.x\rangle$$
$$\rightarrow^* (\lambda x.\langle x\rangle)\,\$\,\langle S_0 k_1.S_0 k_2.(\lambda x.k_2\,\$\,k_1\,\$\,x)\,\$\,(\lambda x.(\lambda x.\langle x\rangle)\,\$\,x)\,\$\,\lambda x.x\rangle$$
$$\rightarrow^* ((\lambda x.(\lambda x.\langle x\rangle)\,\$\,x)\,\$\,(\lambda x.\langle x\rangle)\,\$\,x)\,\$\,(\lambda x.(\lambda x.\langle x\rangle)\,\$\,x)\,\$\,\lambda x.x$$

We see that the terms representing the evaluation contexts get more and more complicated. This is because in the reduction semantics for $\lambda_\$$, removing a context from the trail and then pushing it back is not the same as just leaving it there:

$$v\,\$\,S_0 k.k\,\$\,e \rightarrow (\lambda x.v\,\$\,x)\,\$\,e \neq v\,\$\,e$$

However, it is easy to see that $\overline{(\lambda x.v\,\$\,x)\,\$\,e} =_{\beta\eta} \overline{v\,\$\,e}$. What is more, we have:

$$\overline{(\lambda x.\hat{K}[x])\,\$\,e} =_{\beta\eta} \overline{\hat{K}[e]}.$$

Let us define $\approx$ as the smallest congruence containing $(\lambda x.\hat{E}[x])\,\$\,e \approx \hat{E}[e]$. Then, if we define the relation of reduction modulo this congruence:

$$e_1 \to^{\approx} e_2 \text{ iff exists } e_1', e_2' \text{ such that } e_1 \approx e_1' \to e_2' \approx e_2,$$

we obtain the following theorem:

Theorem 3. *Suppose that* $\langle e, E_1, \ldots, E_{n+1}\rangle \rightsquigarrow \langle e', E_1', \ldots, E_{n+1}'\rangle$. *Then we have* $[\![\langle e, E_1, \ldots, E_{n+1}\rangle]\!] \to^{\approx *} [\![\langle e', E_1', \ldots, E_{n+1}'\rangle]\!]$.

Another way to resolve this discrepancy is to change the reduction semantics so as not to refunctionalize the closed contexts on capture, and expand them when on the left side of the *dollar*:

$$\hat{K}\,v \rightsquigarrow \hat{K}[v] \qquad \hat{K}[\mathcal{S}_0 f.e] \rightsquigarrow e[\hat{K}/f] \qquad \hat{K}\,\$\,e \rightsquigarrow \hat{K}[e]$$

4.4 Abstract Machines

Relating the abstract machines for the two languages requires a modified translation from $\lambda_{\hookleftarrow}^{H}$ to $\lambda_{\$}$. The idea behind the translation is that we want to 'emulate' the behavior of the control operators of $\lambda_{\hookleftarrow}^{H}$ (as most clearly described by the abstract machine in Fig. 4) by step-by-step manipulation of the trail. The translation, as presented in Fig. 8, differs from the previous one in that it does not refunctionalize the evaluation contexts, translating them to closed contexts of $\lambda_{\$}$.

There is a minor mismatch between the abstract machines of $\lambda_{\hookleftarrow}^{H}$ and $\lambda_{\$}$. The reason is that shifting a context from the trail and then pushing it back with $\$$ alters the trail to a different, but observationally indistinguishable state:

$$\langle \mathcal{S}_0 x.x\,\$\,e, \hat{K}\cdot\hat{K}'\cdot T\rangle_{\mathrm{e}} \Rightarrow \langle \hat{K}\,\$\,e, \hat{K}'\cdot T\rangle_{\mathrm{e}} \Rightarrow^* \langle \hat{K}'\,\$\,e, \hat{K}, T\rangle_{\mathrm{a}} \Rightarrow \langle e, (\hat{K}\$\bullet)\cdot\hat{K}'\cdot T\rangle_{\mathrm{e}}$$

To abstract this detail away, let us define $\approx$ to be a family of congruences defined for $\lambda_{\$}$ expressions, contexts, closed contexts and abstract machines, containing $\hat{K}\$\hat{K}' \approx \hat{K}@\hat{K}'$. We get the following theorem:

Theorem 4. *For every two* $\lambda_{\hookleftarrow}^{H}$ *abstract machine configurations* $m_1 \Rightarrow^* m_2$, *then there exists a* $\lambda_{\$}$ *machine configuration* m *such that* $[\![m_1]\!] \Rightarrow^* m \approx [\![m_2]\!]$ *in* $\lambda_{\$}$.

Because the abstract machine for $\lambda_{\hookleftarrow}^{H}$ uses $n+1$ evaluation contexts for the n-th level of the hierarchy, we need to enclose the translated program in $n+1$ *resets* to match the initial configurations of the machines: $[\![e]\!]_n = \langle {}^{n+1}_{\cdots}\langle[\![e]\!]\rangle \ldots\rangle$. Thus, we have:

$$\langle[\![e]\!]_n, \hat{\bullet}\rangle_{\mathrm{e}} \Rightarrow^* \langle[\![e]\!], \hat{\bullet}\cdot{}^{n+2}_{\cdots}\cdot\hat{\bullet}\rangle_{\mathrm{e}} = [\![\langle e, \bullet_1, \ldots, \bullet_{n+1}\rangle_{\mathrm{e}}]\!]$$

5 Examples

In this section we show example programs to display the correspondence between $\lambda_{\hookleftarrow}^{H}$ and $\lambda_{\$}$. The programming languages used are straightforward extensions of $\lambda_{\hookleftarrow}^{H}$ and $\lambda_{\$}$ to an ML-like language.

fail $() = S_1 k_s.()$ fail $() = S_0 k_s.()$
amb $a\ b = S_1 k_s.(k_s) \hookleftarrow_1 a; (k_s) \hookleftarrow_1 b$ amb $a\ b = S_0 k_s.k_s\ a; k_s\ b$
emit $a = S_2 k_s k_f.a :: (k_s, k_f) \hookleftarrow_2 ()$ emit $a = S_0 k_s.S_0 k_f.a :: (k_f\ \$\ k_s\ ())$
run $f = \langle\langle \text{emit}\,(f\,())\rangle_1; []\rangle_2$ run $f = \langle\langle \text{emit}\,(f\,())\rangle; []\rangle$

Fig. 9. Implementation of *amb* and *emit* in $\lambda^{\text{H}}_{\hookleftarrow}$ (left) and $\lambda_\$$ (right)

5.1 Nondeterminism

One of the classic applications of the CPS hierarchy is an implementation of Mc-Carthy's *amb* non-deterministic choice operator, together with a function for returning results of the non-deterministic computation [8]. The implementation uses two levels of the CPS hierarchy, where the two continuations operate as the success and failure continuations. It is shown in Fig. 9, on the left.

- The *fail* function shifts the success continuation, leaving only the failure continuation to be evaluated.
- The ambiguous choice *amb* operator first shifts the success continuation, and evaluates it twice with the two possible return values. The sequence gets pushed to the failure continuation.
- The *emit* function shifts both the success and failure continuations, adds a new value to the result list, and restores the shifted continuations. The emitted value is pushed to the third continuation.
- The *run* function resets two levels of continuations, freeing them to be used as the success and failure continuations. It then initializes the failure continuation to return the empty list, and the success continuation to emit the final value. Then it calls the body of the backtracking computation.

A program using these functions to solve the n-queens problem is shown in Fig. 10. The functions can be translated to $\lambda_\$$ using the translation of Fig. 7:

$$\text{fail}\,() = S_0 k_s.\langle()\rangle$$
$$\text{amb}\,a\ b = S_0 k_s.\langle S_0 k_1.S_0 k_2.(\lambda x.k_2\ \$\ k_1\ \$\ x)\ \$\ k_s\ \$\ a\ ;$$
$$S_0 k_1.S_0 k_2.(\lambda x.k_2\ \$\ k_1\ \$\ x)\ \$\ k_s\ \$\ b\rangle$$
$$\text{emit}\,a = S_0 k_s.S_0 k_f.\langle\langle a ::$$
$$S_0 k_1.S_0 k_2.S_0 k_3.(\lambda x.k_3\ \$\ k_2\ \$\ k_1\ \$\ x)\ \$\ k_f\ \$\ k_s\ \$\ ()\rangle\rangle$$
$$\text{run}\,f = S_0 k_1.S_0 k_2.S_0 k_3.(\lambda x.k_3\ \$\ k_2\ \$\ x)\ \$$$
$$\langle\langle S_0 k_1.S_0 k_2.(\lambda x.k_2\ \$\ k_1\ \$\ x)\ \$\ \langle\text{emit}\,(f\,())\rangle; []\rangle\rangle$$

The translation follows exactly the semantics of the original functions, but are needlessly complicated by the code ensuring that the appropriate contexts end up on the right positions on the context stack. If we relax those requirements, we can reimplement the four functions in a very similar form to the original definitions (Fig. 9, right).

Even though the definitions are similar, the semantics of this new implementation is very different. We demonstrate this below using abstract machine runs of the $\lambda^{\text{H}}_{\hookleftarrow}$ and $\lambda_\$$ versions of the *fail* and *emit* functions. It's easy to check the other two.

```
ambList [] = fail ()
ambList (h :: t) = amb h (ambList t)

nQueens n = let f 0 l = l
                f k l = let ok _ _ [] = true
                        ok v x (h :: t) =
                            v ≠ h and k + v − 1 ≠ x + h and
                            k − v − 1 ≠ x − h and ok v (x + 1) t
                    in let v = ambList [0..n − 1]
                    in if ok v k l
                        then f (k − 1) (v :: l)
                        else fail ()
          in run (λ().f n [])
```

Fig. 10. Example: solving the n-queens problem

- The *fail* function in $\lambda_{\hookleftarrow}^{\mathrm{H}}$ replaces the success continuation with the empty context, which is then activated before the failure continuation:

$$\langle S_1 k_s.(), E_s, E_f, E_3 \rangle_e \Rightarrow \langle (), \bullet_1, E_f, E_3 \rangle_e \Rightarrow \langle (), \bullet_1, E_f, E_3 \rangle_a \Rightarrow \langle (), E_f, E_3 \rangle_a$$

In $\lambda_\$$, the success continuation is removed, the failure continuation is run directly:

$$\langle S_0 k_s.(), \hat{K}_s \cdot \hat{K}_f \cdot T \rangle_e \Rightarrow \langle (), \hat{K}_f \cdot T \rangle_e \Rightarrow \langle \hat{K}_f, (), T \rangle_a$$

- The *emit* function in $\lambda_{\hookleftarrow}^{\mathrm{H}}$ resets the top two contexts when capturing the success and failure continuations, and these empty contexts are pushed to the third context, along with the emitted value, when restoring the success and failure continuations:

$$\langle S_2 k_s k_f.a :: (k_s, k_f) \hookleftarrow_2 (), E_s, E_f, E_3 \rangle_e \Rightarrow \langle a :: (E_s, E_f) \hookleftarrow_2 (), \bullet_1, \bullet_2, E_3 \rangle_e$$
$$\Rightarrow \langle (E_s, E_f) \hookleftarrow_2 (), a :: \bullet_1, \bullet_2, E_3 \rangle_e \Rightarrow^* \langle (), E_s, E_f, E_3.(\bullet_2.(a :: \bullet_1))) \rangle_a$$

In $\lambda_\$$, the emitted value is placed directly on the third context:

$$\langle S_0 k_s.S_0 k_f.a :: (k_f \$ k_s ()), \hat{K}_s \cdot \hat{K}_f \cdot \hat{K} \cdot T \rangle_e$$
$$\Rightarrow^* \langle a :: (\hat{K}_f \$ \hat{K}_s ()), \hat{K} \cdot T \rangle_e \Rightarrow \langle \hat{K}_f \$ \hat{K}_s (), (a :: \hat{K}) \cdot T \rangle_e$$
$$\Rightarrow \langle \hat{K}_s (), (\hat{K}_f \$\bullet) \cdot (a :: \hat{K}) \cdot T \rangle_e \Rightarrow^* \langle \hat{K}_s, (), (\hat{K}_f \$\bullet) \cdot (a :: \hat{K}) \cdot T \rangle_a$$

5.2 Sorting

In this section we show that there are programs in $\lambda_\$$ which can use an arbitrary number of contexts on the context stack, and therefore an analogous program with direct correspondence between the trail and the layered contexts cannot be written in the CPS hierarchy directly.[2] This would hold even for a hierarchy with no maximum level, because a program in the CPS hierarchy can access only a finite number of layers.

---

[2] The $\lambda_{\hookleftarrow}^{\mathrm{H}}$ language can macro-express $\lambda_\$$, because it contains the ordinary *shift/reset* operators, which were shown to be able to macro-express λ_{S_0} [15,16]. However, such a simulation would not lead to a program of a structure resembling the one presented in Fig. 11.

csort $l =$ let insert $a =$
　　let cinsert $k = S_0 f$.case f [] of
　　　　[] $\to \langle\langle a :: k\,()\rangle\rangle$
　　　　$[b] \to$ if $a < b$ then cinsert $(\lambda x.f \$ k\,x)$ else $f \$ \langle a :: k\,()\rangle$
　　　　in $S_0 k$. cinsert k
　　in $\langle\langle$ foldr $(\lambda x.\lambda l'.$ insert $x; l'\,)$ [] $l\,\rangle\rangle$

Fig. 11. Example: insertion sort on the context stack

The example program, shown in Fig. 11, implements the insertion sort algorithm which uses the context stack to store and manipulate the output list. The main idea is that each element of the output list is contained inside a separate context on the context stack. The empty context marks the end of the output list. The algorithm runs the *insert* helper function for each element of the input list, and then returns [] to finally construct the result. The *insert* function shifts contexts from the context stack until it finds the right place for the element being inserted. Then it puts the element there in a new context and puts back the contexts it shifted.

The program uses $n + 2$ contexts on the context stack, where n is the size of the input list. So it cannot be typed using the type system in Fig. 3.

6   Conclusion and Future Work

We have made and formalized an observation that the delimited-control operators $shift_0$ and $reset_0$ are expressive enough to encode the control operators in the original CPS hierarchy. We have also shown that in programming practice, $shift_0$ and $reset_0$ can do the job of the CPS hierarchy and more. These results demonstrate a considerable expressive power of $shift_0$ and $reset_0$ on one hand. On the other hand, they open a possibility of using the presented translations, e.g., for implementing the hierarchy in terms of any implementation of $shift_0$ and $reset_0$.

Another step in the programme of investigating $shift_0$ and $reset_0$ is a realistic implementation on top of an existing language such as Scala, using the selective CPS translation we have devised in our previous work [15] along with Scala type annotations. Of more theoretical importance, we plan to build a behavioral theory for $shift_0$ and $reset_0$ following recent developments of the second author and Lenglet [6]. We are also in the course of constructing axiomatizations of $shift_0$ and $reset_0$ that are sound and complete with respect to the CPS translations (typed and untyped).

Acknowledgments. We thank Małgorzata Biernacka and the anonymous reviewers for valuable comments. This work has been funded by the Polish National Science Center, DEC-2011/03/B/ST6/00348.

References

1. Biernacka, M., Biernacki, D.: Context-based proofs of termination for typed delimited-control operators. In: López-Fraguas, F.J. (ed.) Proceedings of the 11th ACM-SIGPLAN International Conference on Principles and Practice of Declarative Programming, PPDP 2009, Coimbra, Portugal. ACM Press (September 2009)

2. Biernacka, M., Biernacki, D., Danvy, O.: An operational foundation for delimited continuations in the CPS hierarchy. Logical Methods in Computer Science 1(2:5), 1–39 (2005)
3. Biernacka, M., Biernacki, D., Lenglet, S.: Typing control operators in the CPS hierarchy. In: Hanus, M. (ed.) Proceedings of the 13th ACM-SIGPLAN International Conference on Principles and Practice of Declarative Programming, PPDP 2011, Odense, Denmark. ACM Press (July 2011)
4. Biernacka, M., Danvy, O.: A syntactic correspondence between context-sensitive calculi and abstract machines. Theoretical Computer Science 375(1-3), 76–108 (2007)
5. Biernacki, D., Danvy, O., Millikin, K.: A dynamic continuation-passing style for dynamic delimited continuations. Technical Report BRICS RS-06-15, DAIMI, Department of Computer Science, Aarhus University, Aarhus, Denmark (October 2006)
6. Biernacki, D., Lenglet, S.: Applicative Bisimulations for Delimited-Control Operators. In: Birkedal, L. (ed.) FOSSACS 2012. LNCS, vol. 7213, pp. 119–134. Springer, Heidelberg (2012)
7. Calvès, C.: Complexity and Implementation of Nominal Algorithms. PhD thesis, King's College London, London, England (2010)
8. Danvy, O., Filinski, A.: Abstracting control. In: Wand, M. (ed.) Proceedings of the 1990 ACM Conference on Lisp and Functional Programming, Nice, France, pp. 151–160. ACM Press (June 1990)
9. Filinski, A.: Representing monads. In: Boehm, H.J. (ed.) Proceedings of the Twenty-First Annual ACM Symposium on Principles of Programming Languages, Portland, Oregon, pp. 446–457. ACM Press (January 1994)
10. Kameyama, Y., Kiselyov, O., Shan, C.: Shifting the stage: Staging with delimited control. In: Puebla, G., Vidal, G. (eds.) Proceedings of the 2009 ACM SIGPLAN Symposium on Partial Evaluation and Semantics-Based Program Manipulation, PEPM 2009, Savannah, GA, pp. 111–120. ACM Press (January 2009)
11. Kiselyov, O.: Delimited Control in OCaml, Abstractly and Concretely: System Description. In: Blume, M., Kobayashi, N., Vidal, G. (eds.) FLOPS 2010. LNCS, vol. 6009, pp. 304–320. Springer, Heidelberg (2010)
12. Kiselyov, O., Shan, C.: A Substructural Type System for Delimited Continuations. In: Ronchi Della Rocca, S. (ed.) TLCA 2007. LNCS, vol. 4583, pp. 223–239. Springer, Heidelberg (2007)
13. Kiselyov, O., Shan, C.: Embedded Probabilistic Programming. In: Taha, W.M. (ed.) DSL 2009. LNCS, vol. 5658, pp. 360–384. Springer, Heidelberg (2009)
14. Masuko, M., Asai, K.: Direct implementation of shift and reset in the MinCaml compiler. In: Rossberg, A. (ed.) Proceedings of the ACM SIGPLAN Workshop on ML, ML 2009, Edinburgh, UK, pp. 49–60 (August 2009)
15. Materzok, M., Biernacki, D.: Subtyping delimited continuations. In: Danvy, O. (ed.) Proceedings of the 2011 ACM SIGPLAN International Conference on Functional Programming, ICFP 2011, Tokyo, Japan, pp. 81–93. ACM Press (September 2011)
16. Shan, C.: A static simulation of dynamic delimited control. Higher-Order and Symbolic Computation 20(4), 371–401 (2007)

Scalable Formal Machine Models

Greg Morrisett

Harvard University
greg@eecs.harvard.edu

Abstract. In the past few years, we have seen machine-checked proofs of relatively large software systems, including compilers and micro-kernels. But like all formal arguments, the assurance gained by these mechanical proofs is only as good as the models we construct of the underlying machine. I will argue that how we construct and validate these models is of vital importance for the research community. In particular, I propose that we develop domain-specific languages (DSLs) for describing the semantics of machines, and build interpretations of these DSLs in our respective proof-development systems. This will allow us to factor out and re-use machine semantics for everything from software to hardware.

1 Overview

Thirty years ago, the idea that we might build a real software component, such as a compiler, and construct a machine-checked proof that it was correct, was still a dream. There were some examples, such as the work of Milner and Weyrauch [1], yet those systems tended to be small examples for toy architectures.

In the intervening decades, the community has made great progress: Automated deduction techniques (e.g., SAT solvers and SMT provers) have improved tremendously. Proof development systems including ACL2, Coq, HOL, Isabelle, NuPRL, and PVS have become more powerful, more scalable, and much easier to use. At the same time, our need for strong assurance in safety and security-critical software systems has grown, driving down the cost of proofs relative to the benefits. These factors, amongst others, have led to shining examples of *usable*, real-world software components with detailed proofs of correctness, such as Leroy's CompCert compiler [2] or Klein et al's seL4 micro-kernel [3]. The size and complexity of these artificats has led to a new kind of "proof engineering" where careful design is needed to ensure not only that the proofs can be done, but that they can be maintained as the software systems evolve.

Stepping back, what does it mean to prove a compiler or operating system correct? In each case, we must define a formal semantics for the software component (e.g., the dialect of C supported by CompCert or the API provided by seL4) as well as the underlying machine on which the software is intended to execute. Developing these semantic models takes substantial effort, akin to building an interpreter for a programming language or architecture. For the toy languages and machines of the past, this was not difficult, but for realistic languages (e.g., Java) and architectures (e.g., the x86), constructing a full semantic specification demands an almost overwhelming amount of detail.

R. Jhala and A. Igarashi (Eds.): APLAS 2012, LNCS 7705, pp. 312–314, 2012.

These specifications are so big, that we are sure to get some details wrong, suggesting three things: First, we should avoid building lots of different, incomplete, and incompatible specifications (one for each research project) and instead work together to build robust models for important systems that transcend proof-development environments. Second, the design of our semantic models must support (efficient) execution so that we can test our models against real-world implementations. Finally, these models must be carefully constructed so that we can update them, whether due to a bug or natural evolution, and yet insulate, to the best of our ability, the proofs from these updates.

As an example of some work towards these goals, I will describe an on-going project that my colleague Gang Tan and I have been pursuing on formal models of instruction set architectures. Our primary goal is to build certified tools for enforcing security policies on x86 machine code, including Software Fault Isolation [4], Control-Flow Isolation [5], and variants of Typed Assembly Language [6]. To do so, we require a formal model of the syntax and semantics of x86 code, and while fragments of such models exist, none of them had enough detail that we could directly use them. Furthermore, some of the fragments were coded in ACL2, others in Isabelle, and others in Coq.

Consequently, we started to build a new model of the x86. Our design was broken into two major stages, one addressing decoding and the other addressing execution. Both stages were designed around domain-specific languages (DSLs) inspired by work on re-targeting compilers [7,8,9]. One DSL is used to describe the decoder and is similar to other parsing generators, but unlike say Yacc, comes equipped with a formal semantics that makes it easy to reason compositionally and declaratively about the relation between concrete and abstract syntax. Furthermore, it is carefully designed to support extraction of an efficient, table-driven parser. The execution stage of our x86 model is described via translation to a simple, RISC-like register transfer language. This RTL language is itself parameterized by a notion of machine state and comes equipped with an operational semantics, as well as other tools needed for both symbolic reasoning as well as validation.

Using these tools, we have constructed a semantic model for a significant fragment of the x86 (all of the integer and most of the floating-point instructions), and as described in a previous paper, used the model to prove the correctness of a tool for enforcing software fault isolation [10]. As expected, our model had (and probably still has) a number of bugs, but the ability to extract an executable model for testing has proved invaluable. Furthermore, we believe the modular design makes it relatively easy to add new features to the model, such as support for multiple-cores or alternative instruction sets. Finally, we have found the approach to describing behavior, based largely on translation to a small, orthogonal target language, works well for other kinds of machines, including the abstract machines used for high-level languages.

Nevertheless, in hindsight, there are many design decisions that we got wrong. For instance, we used a deep-embedding of our DSLs into Coq, taking advantage of features such as modules and dependent types that other proof assistants may lack. Consequently, it is not clear how to "port" our specifications to other environments. As another example, we followed the design of compiler-based RTLs a little too closely and used an imperative representation for the intermediate code, when a functional representation makes both execution and symbolic reasoning easier.

References

1. Milner, R., Weyhrauch, R.: Proving compiler correctness in a mechanized logic. In: Proceedings of the 7th Annual Machine Intelligence Workshop. Machine Intelligence, vol. 7, pp. 51–72. Edinburgh University Press (1972)
2. Leroy, X.: Formal verification of a realistic compiler. Commun. of the ACM 52(7), 107–115 (2009)
3. Klein, G., Elphinstone, K., Heiser, G., Andronick, J., Cock, D., Derrin, P., Elkaduwe, D., Engelhardt, K., Kolanski, R., Norrish, M., Sewell, T., Tuch, H., Winwood, S.: sel4: formal verification of an os kernel. In: Proceedings of the ACM SIGOPS 22nd Symposium on Operating Systems Principles, SOSP 2009, pp. 207–220. ACM, New York (2009)
4. Wahbe, R., Lucco, S., Anderson, T.E., Graham, S.L.: Efficient software-based fault isolation. In: Proc. of the 14th ACM Symp. on Operating Systems Principles, SOSP 1993, pp. 203–216. ACM (1993)
5. Abadi, M., Budiu, M., Erlingsson, U., Ligatti, J.: Control-flow integrity. In: Proc. of the 12th ACM Conf. on Computer and Commun. Security, CCS 2005, pp. 340–353. ACM (2005)
6. Morrisett, G., Walker, D., Crary, K., Glew, N.: From System F to typed assembly language. In: Proc. of the 25th ACM SIGPLAN-SIGACT Symp. on Principles of Programming Languages, POPL 1998, pp. 85–97. ACM (1998)
7. Ramsey, N., Fernandez, M.F.: Specifying representations of machine instructions. ACM Trans. Program. Lang. Syst. 19(3), 492–524 (1997)
8. Ramsey, N., Davidson, J.W.: Machine Descriptions to Build Tools for Embedded Systems. In: Müller, F., Bestavros, A. (eds.) LCTES 1998. LNCS, vol. 1474, pp. 176–192. Springer, Heidelberg (1998)
9. Dias, J., Ramsey, N.: Automatically generating instruction selectors using declarative machine descriptions. In: Proc. of the 37th ACM SIGPLAN-SIGACT Symp. on Principles of Programming Languages, POPL 2010, pp. 403–416. ACM (2010)
10. Morrisett, G., Tan, G., Tassarotti, J., Tristan, J.B., Gan, E.: Rocksalt: better, faster, stronger sfi for the x86. In: Proceedings of the 33rd ACM SIGPLAN Conference on Programming Language Design and Implementation, PLDI 2012, pp. 395–404. ACM, New York (2012)

Modular Verification of Concurrent Thread Management

Yu Guo[1], Xinyu Feng[1], Zhong Shao[2], and Peizhi Shi[1]

[1] University of Science and Technology of China
{guoyu,xyfeng}@ustc.edu.cn, sea10197@mail.ustc.edu.cn
[2] Yale University
zhong.shao@yale.edu

Abstract. Thread management is an essential functionality in OS kernels. However, verification of thread management remains a challenge, due to two conflicting requirements: on the one hand, a thread manager—operating below the thread abstraction layer–should hide its implementation details and be verified independently from the threads being managed; on the other hand, the thread management code in many real-world systems is concurrent, which might be executed by the threads being managed, so it seems inappropriate to abstract threads away in the verification of thread managers. Previous approaches on kernel verification view thread managers as sequential code, thus cannot be applied to thread management in realistic kernels. In this paper, we propose a novel two-layer framework to verify concurrent thread management. We choose a lower abstraction level than the previous approaches, where we abstract away the context switch routine only, and allow the rest of the thread management code to run concurrently in the upper level. We also treat thread management data as abstract resources so that threads in the environment can be specified in assertions and be reasoned about in a proof system similar to concurrent separation logic.

1 Introduction

Thread scheduling in modern operating systems provides the functionality of virtualizing processors: when a thread is waiting for an event, it gives the control of the processor to another thread to create the illusion that each thread has its own processor.

Inside a kernel, a thread manager supervises all threads in the system by manipulating data structures called thread control blocks (TCBs). A TCB is used to record important information about a thread, such as the machine context (or processor state), the thread identifier, the status description, the location and size of the stack, the priority for scheduling, and the entry point of thread code. The TCBs are often implemented using data structures such as queues for ready and waiting threads. Clearly, modifying thread queues and TCBs would drastically change the behaviors of threads. Therefore, a correct implementation of thread management is crucial for guaranteeing the whole system safety. Unfortunately, modular verification of real-world thread management code remains a big challenge today.

The challenge comes from two apparently conflicting goals which we want to achieve at the same time: abstraction (for modular verification) and efficiency (for real-world

R. Jhala and A. Igarashi (Eds.): APLAS 2012, LNCS 7705, pp. 315–331, 2012.
© Springer-Verlag Berlin Heidelberg 2012

usability). On the one hand, TCBs, thread queues, and the thread scheduler are specifics used to implement threads so they should sit at a lower abstraction layer. It is natural to abstract them away from threads, and to verify threads and the thread scheduler separately at different abstraction layers. Previous work has shown it is extremely difficult to verify them together in one logic system [15]. On the other hand, in many real-world systems such as Linux-2.6.10 [12] and FreeBSD-5.2 [13], the thread scheduler code itself is also *concurrent* in the sense that there may be multiple threads in the system running the scheduler at the same time. For instance, when a thread invokes a thread scheduler routine (*e.g.*, cleaning up dead threads, load balancing, or thread scheduling) and traverses the thread queue, it may be preempted by other threads who may call the same routine and traverse the queue too. Also, in some systems [12,1] the thread scheduling itself is implemented as a separate thread that runs concurrently with other threads. In these cases, we need to verify thread schedulers in a "multi-threaded" logic, taking threads into account instead of abstracting them away.

Earlier work on thread scheduling verification fails to achieve the two goals at the same time. Ni *et al.* [15] verified both the thread switch and the threads in one logic [14], which treats thread return addresses as first-class code pointers. Although their method may support concurrent thread schedulers in real systems, it loses the abstraction of threads completely, and makes the logic and specifications too complex for practical use. Recent work [3,6] adopts two-layer verification frameworks to verify concurrent kernels. Kernel code is divided into two layers: sequential code in the lower layer and concurrent in the upper layer. In their frameworks, they put the code manipulating TCBs (*e.g.*, thread schedulers) in the low layer, and hide the TCBs of threads in the upper layer so that the threads cannot modify them. Then they use sequential program logics to verify thread management code. However, this approach is not usable for many realistic kernels where thread managers themselves are concurrent and the threads are allowed to modify the TCBs. Other work on OS verification [11,9] only supports non-reentrant kernels, *i.e.*, there is only one thread running in the kernel at any time.

In this paper, we propose a more natural framework to verify concurrent thread managers. Our framework follows the two-layer approach, so concurrent code at the upper layer can be verified modularly with thread abstractions. However, the abstraction level of our framework is much lower than previous frameworks [3,6]. The majority of the code manipulating thread queues and TCBs is put in the upper layer and can be verified as concurrent code. Our framework successfully achieves both verification goals: it not only allows abstraction and modular verification, but also supports concurrency in real-world thread management.

Our work is based on previous work on thread scheduler verification, but makes the following new contributions:

- We introduce a fine-grained abstraction in our two-layer verification framework. The abstraction protects only a small part of sensitive data in TCBs, and at the same time allows multiple threads to modify other part of TCBs safely. Our division of the two abstraction layers is consistent with many real systems. It is more natural and can support more realistic thread managers than previous work.
- In the upper layer, we introduce the idea of treating *threads as resources*. The abstract thread resources can be specified explicitly in the assertion language, and

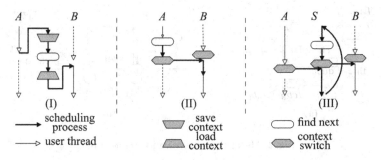

Fig. 1. Three patterns of scheduling

their use by concurrent programs can be reasoned about modularly following concurrent separation logic (CSL) [16]. By enforcing the invariant that the abstract resource is consistent with the concrete thread meta data, we can ensure the safety of the accesses over TCBs and thread queues inside threads.

- Because of the fine-grained abstraction of our approach, the semantics of thread scheduling do not have to be hardwired in the logic. Therefore, our framework can be used to verify various implementation patterns of thread management. We show how to verify the three common patterns of thread scheduling in realistic OS kernels (while previous two-layer frameworks [3,6] can only verify one of them).
- In our extended TR [7], we also use our framework to verify thread schedulers with hardware interrupts, scheduling over multiprocessor with load-balancing, and a set of other thread management routines such as thread creation, join and termination.

The rest of this paper is organized as follows: we first introduce a simplified abstract machine model for the higher-layer of our framework in Sec. 3; to show our main idea, we propose in Sec. 4 our proof system for concurrent thread scheduling code over the abstract machine. We show how to verify two prototypes of schedulers based on context switch in Sec. 5. We compare with related work in Sec. 6, and then conclude.

2   Challenges and Our Approach

In this section, we illustrate the challenges of verifying code of thread scheduling by showing three patterns of schedulers and discuss the verification issues. Then we informally explain the basic ideas of our approach.

2.1   Three Patterns of Thread Scheduling

By deciding which thread to run next, the thread scheduler is responsible for best utilizing the system and makes multiple threads run concurrently. The scheduling process consists of the following steps: selecting which thread to run next in a thread queue by modifying TCBs, saving the context data of the current thread, and loading the context data of the next thread. Context data is the state of the processor. By saving and loading context data, the processor can run in multiple control flows, *i.e.*, threads. Usually, context data can be saved on stacks or TCBs (we assume in this paper that context

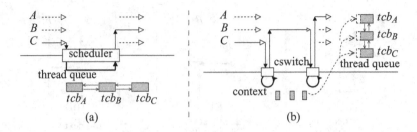

Fig. 2. Abstraction in verification framework

data is saved in TCBs for the brevity of presentation). There are various ways to implement thread schedulers. In Fig. 1 we show three common implementation patterns, all modeled from real systems.

Pattern (I) is popular among embedded OS kernels (*e.g.,* FreeRTOS) and some microkernels (*e.g.,* Minix [8] and Exokernel [2]). The scheduler in this pattern is invoked by function calls or interrupts. Thereafter, the scheduling is done in the following steps: (1) saving the current context data, (2) finding the next thread, and (3) loading the context data of the next thread (and switching to it implicitly through function return).

In pattern (II), the scheduling process is a function with the following steps: (1) finding the next thread firstly, (2) performing context switch (saving the current context data, loading the next one, and jumping to the next thread immediately), (3) and running the remaining code of the function when the control is switched back from other threads. This pattern is modeled from some mainstream monolithic kernels (*e.g.,* Linux [12], and FreeBSD). Some embedded kernels (*e.g.,* RTEMS and uClinux) adopt it too. Note that both the involved threads should be allowed to access the thread queue and TCBs when calling the scheduler.

Pattern (III) uses a separate thread, called *scheduler thread*, to do scheduling. One thread may perform scheduling by doing context switch to the scheduler thread. The scheduler thread is a big infinite loop: finding the next thread; performing context switch to the next thread; and looping after return. This pattern can be seen in the GNU-pth thread library, MIT-xv6 kernel, L4::Ka, *etc.*. Similar to pattern (II), all involved threads in this pattern should be allowed to access the TCB of the scheduler thread and the thread queue.

2.2   Challenges

As we can see from the patterns in Fig. 1, the control flow in the scheduling process is very complicated. Threads switch back and forth via manipulating the thread queues and TCBs. It is very natural to share TCBs and the thread queue among threads in order to support all these scheduling patterns. On the other hand, it is important to ensure that the TCBs are accessed in the right way. The system would go wrong if, for instance, a thread erased the context data of another by mistake, or put a dead thread back into the ready thread queue.

To guarantee the safety of the scheduling process, we must fulfill two requirements:

(1) No thread can incorrectly modify the context data in TCBs.

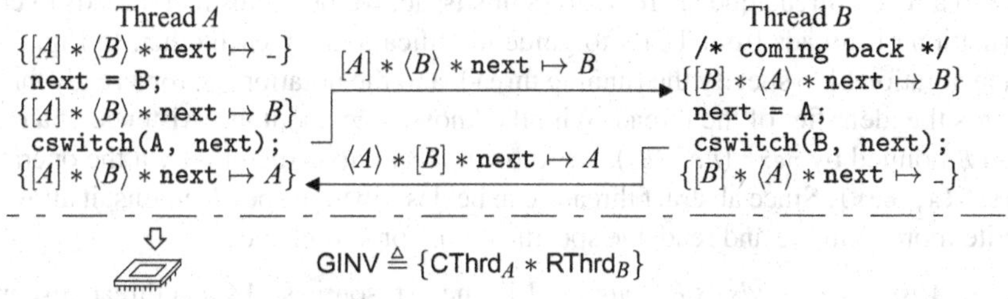

Fig. 3. Abstract thread res. vs. concrete thread res.

(2) The scheduler should know the status of each thread in the thread queues and decide which to run next.

To satisfy the requirement (1), some previous work [3,6] adopts a two-layer-based approach and protects the TCBs through *abstraction*, where the TCBs are simply hidden from kernel threads and become inaccessible. This approach can be used to verify schedulers of pattern (I), for which we show the abstraction line in Fig. 2 (a). Threads above the line cannot modify TCBs, while the scheduler is below this line and has full access to them. The lower-layer scheduler provides an abstract interface to the verification of concurrent thread code at the upper layer. Since it modifies the TCBs in the scheduling time only, we can view the scheduler as a sequential function which does not belong to any thread and can be verified by a conventional Hoare-style logic. However, this approach cannot verify the other two patterns, nor does it fulfill the requirement (2) for concurrent schedulers, where the TCBs are manipulated concurrently (not sequentially as in pattern (I)) and should be known by threads. That is, we cannot completely hide the TCBs from the upper-layer concurrent threads for patterns (II) and (III).

2.3 Our Approach

If we inspect the TCB data carefully, we can see that only a small part of the data is crucial to thread behaviors and cannot be accessed concurrently. It is unnecessary to access it concurrently either. The data includes the machine context data and the stack location. We call them *safety-critical* values. Some values can be modified concurrently, but their correctness is still important to the safety of the kernel, *e.g.,* the pointers organizing thread queues and the status field belong to this kind of values. Other values of TCBs have nothing to do with the safety of the kernel and can be modified concurrently definitely, *e.g.,* the name of a thread or debug information.

Lowering the Abstraction Level. To protect the safety critical part of TCBs, we lower the abstraction line, as shown in Fig. 2 (b). In our framework, the safety-critical data of TCBs is under the abstraction line and hidden from threads. The corresponding operations such as context saving, loading and switching are abstracted away from threads too, with only interfaces exposed to the upper layer. The other part of TCBs are lifted above this line, which can be accessed by concurrent threads.

Building Abstract Threads. We still need to ensure the concurrent accesses of non-safety-critical TCB data are correct. For instance, we cannot allow a dead thread to be put onto a ready thread queue. To address this issue, we build abstract threads to carry information of threads from TCBs to guide modifications by each other. In Fig. 3, we use the notation $[t]$ to specify the running thread, and the notation $\langle t \rangle$, for a ready thread. Here t is the identifier of the thread. With the knowledge about the existence of a ready thread B pointed by next (*i.e.*, $\langle B \rangle$), we know it is safe to switch to it via the operation cswitch(A,next). Since abstract threads can be described in specifications, it allows us to write more intuitive and readable specifications for kernel code.

Treating Abstract Threads as Resources. Like heap resources, abstract thread resources can be either local or shared. We can do *ownership transfers* on thread resources. When context switches, one thread will transfer some of the abstract thread resources (shared) along with the shared memory to the next thread. As shown in Fig. 3, when thread A context switches to thread B, the notation $[A]$ will be changed to $\langle A \rangle$ after context saving; $\langle A \rangle$ and $\langle B \rangle$ are transferred to the thread B along with the shared memory resource next; then $\langle B \rangle$ will be changed to $[B]$ after context loading. With transferred thread resources, thread B will know there is a ready thread A to switch to. Therefore, by treating abstract threads as resources, we find a simple and natural way to specify and reason about context switches. We design a proof system similar to CSL for modular verification with the support of ownership transfers on thread resources.

Defining Concrete Thread Resources. To establish the soundness of our proof system, we must ensure that the abstract threads can be reified by concrete threads. The concrete representation of abstract threads, including stack, TCBs *etc.*, can be defined globally. In Fig. 3, suppose that thread A is running, we ensure that there are two blocks of resources in the system. One of them is the running thread CThrd_A and the other is a ready thread RThrd_B. They correspond to the abstract threads $[A]$ and $\langle B \rangle$ in the assertions of thread A. We use the concrete thread resources to specify the global invariant of the machine, which allows us to prove the soundness of our proof system.

3 Machine Model

In this section, we define a two-layer machine model. The physical machine we use is similar to realistic hardware, where no concept of thread exists. Based on it, we define an abstract machine with logical *abstract threads*, whose meta-data is abstracted into a thread pool. Moreover, the operation of context switch is abstracted as a primitive abstract instruction.

Physical machine. The formal definition of the physical machine is shown in Fig. 4 (left side). A machine configuration $\mathbb{W}$ consists of a code block $\mathbb{C}$, a memory block $\mathbb{M}$, a register file $\mathbb{R}$ and a program counter pc. The machine has 6 general registers. Some common instructions are defined to write programs in this paper. Their meanings, as well as the operational semantics, follow the conventions. For simplicity, we omit many realistic hardware details, *e.g.*, address alignment and bits-arithmetic.

Abstract machine. The abstract machine is shown in Fig. 4 (right side), where threads are introduced at this level. It is more intuitive to build a proof system (Sec. 4) to verify concurrent kernel code at this level. A thread pool P is a partial mapping from thread

(PhyMach)	$\mathbb{W}$	::=	$(\mathbb{C},\mathbb{M},\mathbb{R},pc)$
(PhyCode)	$\mathbb{C}$	::=	$\{f : i\}^*$
(PhyMem)	$\mathbb{M}$	::=	$\{l : w\}^*$ $(l=4n)$
(PhyRegFile)	$\mathbb{R}$	::=	$\{r : w\}^*$
(Register)	r	::=	$v0 \mid a0 \mid a1 \mid a2 \mid sp \mid ra$
(Instruction)	i	::=	$add\ r_d,\ r_s \mid addi\ r_d,\ w$
			$\mid mov\ r_d,\ r_s \mid movi\ r_d,\ w$
			$\mid lw\ r_t,\ w(r_s) \mid sw\ r_t,\ w(r_s)$
			$\mid jmp\ f \mid call\ f \mid ret$
			$\mid subi\ r_d,\ w \mid bz\ r_t,\ f$

(AbsMach)	W	::=	(C,S,pc)
(State)	S	::=	(M,R,P)
(AbsCode)	C	::=	$\{f : c\}^*$
(Mem)	M	::=	$\{l : w\}^*$
(RegFile)	R	::=	$\{r : w\}^*$
(TID)	t	::=	w
(Pool)	P	::=	$\{t : T\}^*$
(Thrd)	T	::=	$run \mid (rdy,R)$
(AbsInstr)	c	::=	$cswitch \mid i$
(TIDList)	L	::=	$t :: L \mid nil$

Fig. 4. Physical and abstract machine models

IDs t to abstract threads T. Each abstract thread has a tag specifying its status, which is either running (*run*) or ready (*rdy*). Each ready thread has a copy of saved register file as its machine context data. The abstract instructions include an abstract operation of context switch (cswitch) and other physical machine instructions defined on the left. We model the operational semantics using the step transition relation $W \longmapsto W'$ defined in Fig. 5. The abstract instruction cswitch requires two thread IDs passed as arguments in a0 and a1, one of which is tagged by *run* and the other is taged by *rdy* in the thread pool. After cswitch, the two abstract threads exchange tags, and the control of processor is passed from the old thread to the new one. The registers of old thread are saved in the source abstract thread and the registers in the destination thread are loaded into machine state. Except for cswitch, the state transitions of other instructions are similar to those of the physical machine.

Machine translation. In our proof system, once a program is proved safe at the abstract machine level, it should be proved safe as well at the physical machine level. We define a relation between abstract machine with physical machine (in the TR). The code block at the abstract machine level is extended with the code of implementation of context switch, and the abstract instruction cswitch is translated to a call instruction that invokes the implementation code of context switch. The memory block at the abstract machine level is translated to physical memory block by being merged with the memory where context data is stored. By the translation, it can be proved that any safe program over the abstract machine is safe over the physical machine.

4   Proof System

In this section, we extend the assertion language of CSL to specify the thread resources, and propose a small proof system supporting verification of concurrent code with modification of TCBs at the assembly level.

	$((M,R,P),\texttt{pc}) \overset{c}{\hookrightarrow} ((M',R',P'),\texttt{pc}')$
if c =	then
i	$((M,R),\texttt{pc}) \overset{i}{\hookrightarrow} ((M',R'),\texttt{pc}') \wedge P = P'$
cswitch	$\exists R'', P''. M = M' \wedge R'' = R\{\texttt{ra} : \texttt{pc}+1\} \wedge t = R(\texttt{a0})$
	$\wedge t' = R(\texttt{a1}) \wedge \texttt{pc}' = R'(\texttt{ra})$
	$\wedge P = \{t : run, \ t' : (rdy, R')\} \uplus P''$
	$\wedge P' = \{t : (rdy, R''), \ t' : run\} \uplus P''$
	R and R' is complete.

	$((M,R),\texttt{pc}) \overset{i}{\hookrightarrow} ((M',R'),\texttt{pc}')$
if i =	then
add r_d, r_s	$M' = M \wedge R' = R\{r_d : R(r_d) + R(r_s)\} \wedge \texttt{pc}' = \texttt{pc}+1$
call f	$M' = M \wedge R' = R\{\texttt{ra} : \texttt{pc}+1\} \wedge \texttt{pc}' = \texttt{f}$
jmp f	$M' = M \wedge R' = R \wedge \texttt{pc}' = \texttt{f}$
ret	$M' = M \wedge R' = R \wedge \texttt{pc}' = R(\texttt{ra})$

$$\frac{C(\texttt{pc}) = c \quad (S,\texttt{pc}) \overset{c}{\hookrightarrow} (S',\texttt{pc}')}{(C,S,\texttt{pc}) \longmapsto (C,S',\texttt{pc}')}$$

Fig. 5. Operational semantics of abstract machine

4.1 Assertion Language and Code Specification

We use p and q as assertion variables, which are predicates over machine states. The assertion constructs, adapted from separation logic [17], are *shallowly embedded* in the meta language , as shown in Fig. 6. In our assertion language, there are two special assertion constructs for abstract threads. One of them is $\langle t \rangle$ specifying a ready thread and the other is $[t]$ specifying a current running thread. Since threads are explicit resources in the abstract machine, their machine context data (values in registers) are preserved across context switch. Hence the resources of registers shouldn't be shared. We explicitly mark a pure assertion by $\natural$, which forbids an assertion specifying resources. An unary notation $(\diamond p)$ mark an assertion p that only specifies shared resources but no thread local resources (*e.g.*, registers). Registers are also treated as resources, and $r \mapsto w$ specifies a register with the value of w. The notation $r_1, \dots, r_n \mapsto w_1, \dots, w_n$ is a compact form for multiple registers.

We borrow the idea from SCAP [4] and use a (p,g) pair to specify instructions at assembly-level. The pre-condition p describes the state before the first instruction of an instruction sequence, while the action g describes the actions done by the whole instruction sequence. In the proof system, each instruction is associated with a (p,g) pair, where g describes the actions from this instruction to the end of the current function. For all instructions in C, their (p,g) pairs are put in Ψ, a global mapping from labels to specifications. The specification form (p,g) is different from the traditional pre-condition and post-condition, which are both assertions and related by auxiliary variables. We can still use a notation to specify instructions in the traditional style,

$$
\begin{aligned}
\text{true} \quad &\triangleq \quad \lambda(M,R,P).\,\text{True}\\
\text{false} \quad &\triangleq \quad \lambda(M,R,P).\,\text{False}\\
\text{emp} \quad &\triangleq \quad \lambda(M,R,P).\,M=\{\cdot\}\wedge R=\{\cdot\}\wedge P=\{\cdot\}\\
p*q \quad &\triangleq \quad \lambda(M,R,P).\,\exists M_1,M_2,R_1,R_2,P_1,P_2.\,M=M_1\uplus M_2\wedge R=R_1\uplus R_2\wedge P=P_1\uplus P_2\\
&\qquad\qquad \wedge\, p\,(M_1,R_1,P_1)\wedge q\,(M_2,R_2,P_2)\\
p-\!\!*q \quad &\triangleq \quad \lambda(M,R,P).\,\forall M_1,R_1,P_1,M',R',P'.\,(M'=M_1\uplus M\wedge R'=R_1\uplus R\wedge P'=P_1\uplus P)\\
&\qquad\qquad \rightarrow p\,(M_1,R_1,P_1)\rightarrow q\,(M',R',P')\\
p\wedge\!\!\!\wedge q \quad &\triangleq \quad \lambda S.\,(p\,S)\wedge(q\,S)\\
p\vee\!\!\!\vee q \quad &\triangleq \quad \lambda S.\,(p\,S)\vee(q\,S)\\
\exists v.\,p \quad &\triangleq \quad \lambda S.\,\exists v.\,p\,S\\
\sharp p \quad &\triangleq \quad \lambda(M,R,P).\,p\wedge M=\{\cdot\}\wedge R=\{\cdot\}\wedge P=\{\cdot\}\\
\diamond p \quad &\triangleq \quad \lambda(M,R,P).\,p\,(M,R,P)\wedge R=\{\cdot\}\\
r\mapsto w \quad &\triangleq \quad \lambda(M,R,P).\,R=\{r:w\}\wedge M=\{\cdot\}\wedge P=\{\cdot\}\\
r\hookrightarrow w \quad &\triangleq \quad \lambda(M,R,P).\,\exists R'.\,R=\{r:w\}\uplus R'\\
1\mapsto w \quad &\triangleq \quad \lambda(M,R,P).\,M=\{1:w\}\wedge 1\neq\text{NULL}\wedge R=\{\cdot\}\wedge P=\{\cdot\}\\
[t] \quad &\triangleq \quad \lambda(M,R,P).\,P=\{t:run\}\wedge t\neq\text{NULL}\wedge M=\{\cdot\}\wedge R=\{\cdot\}\\
\langle t\rangle \quad &\triangleq \quad \lambda(M,R,P).\,P=\{t:(rdy,\_)\}\wedge t\neq\text{NULL}\wedge M=\{\cdot\}\wedge R=\{\cdot\}
\end{aligned}
$$

Fig. 6. Definition of selected assertion constructs

$$
\left\{\begin{matrix}p\\q\end{matrix}\right\}^{(v_1,\dots,v_n)} \triangleq (\lambda S.\,\exists v_1,\dots,v_n.\,(p(v_1,\dots,v_n)*\text{true})\,S,
$$
$$
\lambda S,S'.\,\forall p'.\forall v_1,\dots,v_n.\,(p(v_1,\dots,v_n)*p')\,S\rightarrow(q(v_1,\dots,v_n)*p')\,S')
$$

where p is the pre-condition of instructions, q is the post-condition, and $v_1,\dots,v_n$ are auxiliary variables occurring in the precondition and the postcondition. We define a binary operator for composing two pairs into one.

$$
(p,g)\triangleright(p',g') \triangleq (\lambda S.\,p\,S\wedge(\forall S'.\,g\,S\,S'\rightarrow p'\,S'),
$$
$$
\lambda S,S''.\,p\,S\rightarrow(\exists S'.\,g\,S\,S'\wedge g'\,S'\,S''))
$$

If an instruction sequence satisfies (p,g) and the following instruction sequence satisfies (p',g'), then the composed instruction sequence would satisfy $(p,g)\triangleright(p',g')$. The weakening relation between two pairs is defined as below:

$$
(p,g)\Rightarrow(p',g') \triangleq \forall S.\,p\,S\rightarrow p'\,S\wedge(\forall S'.\,g'\,S\,S'\rightarrow g\,S\,S')
$$

i.e., the precondition p be stronger than p' and the action g be weaker than g'.

$$
\begin{aligned}
\text{(Assert)}\;\; p,q \;\;&::= \;\; \text{true}\,|\,\text{false}\,|\,\text{emp}\,|\,p*q\,|\,p-\!\!*q\,|\,p\wedge\!\!\!\wedge q\,|\,p\vee\!\!\!\vee q\,|\,\exists v.\,p\,|\,1\mapsto w\\
&\quad\;\;|\,[t]\,|\,\langle t\rangle\,|\,\sharp p\,|\,\diamond p\,|\,r\mapsto w\,|\,r\hookrightarrow w\\
\text{(Action)}\;\; g \;\;&\in \;\; \text{State}\rightarrow\text{State}\rightarrow\text{Prop}\\
\text{(Spec)}\;\; \Psi \;\;&::= \;\; \{f:(p,g)\}^*
\end{aligned}
$$

4.2 Invariant for Shared Resources and Inference Rules

As mentioned previously, our proof system draws ideas of ownership transfer from CSL. By defining invariants for shared resources, our proof system ensures safe operations of TCBs.

Unlike the invariant in concurrent separation logic, the invariant of shared resources defined in our proof system is parameterized by two thread IDs: $I(t_s, t_d)$. Briefly, the invariant describes the shared resources before context switch with the direction from the thread t_s to t_d. One of the benefits of parameters is that the invariant is thread-specific.

Like the abstract invariant I in CSL, the invariant $I(t_s, t_d)$ is abstract and can be instantiated to concrete definitions to verify various programs, as long as the instantiation satisfies the requirement of being *precise* [17].

Precisely, the invariant $I(t_s, t_d)$ describes the shared resources when the context switch is invoked from the thread t_s to the thread t_d, but *excluding the resources of the two threads*. Since the control flow from one thread to another is *deterministic* by context switch, every two threads may negotiate a particular invariant that is different from pairs of other threads. We can define different assertions (of shared resources) which depend on the source and the destination threads of a context switch. This is quite different from concurrent code at user-level, where a context switch is non-deterministic and the scheduling algorithm is abstracted away.

The judgment for instructions in our proof system is of the following form: $\Psi, I \vdash \{(p, g)\}$ pc : c, where Ψ and I are given as specifications. The judgement states that an instruction sequence, started with c at the label of pc and ended with a ret, satisfies specification (p, g) under Ψ and I. Some selected inference rules for instructions are shown in Fig. 7.

In the rule of (ADD), the premise says that the specification (p, g) implies the action of the add instruction composed with the specification of the next instruction, $\Psi(\text{pc}+1)$. The action of add instruction is that if the destination register r_d contains the value of w_1, and the source register r_s contains the value of w_2, then after the instruction, r_d will contain the sum of w_1 and w_2, while r_s will remain unchanged.

Functions are reasoned with the rules of (CALL) and (RET). The (CALL) rule says that the specification (p, g) implies the action that is composed by (1) the action of instruction call, (2) the specification of the *function* invoked $\Psi(\mathbf{f})$, (3) the action of instruction ret, and (4) the specification of the next instruction $\Psi(\text{pc}+1)$. The (RET) rule says that the specification (p, g) implies an empty action, which means the actions of the current function should be fulfilled.

The most important rule is (CSW). The precondition of cswitch requires the following resources: the current thread resource, the registers a0 containing the current thread ID t and a1 containing the destination thread ID t', and the shared resource satisfying the invariant $\diamond I(t, t')$. After return from context switch, the current thread will own the shared resources (satisfying $\diamond I(t'', t)$ for some t'') again.

4.3 Invariant of Global Resources and Soundness

Each abstract thread corresponds to the part of global resources representing the concrete resources allocated for this thread. For example, for an abstract thread $\langle t \rangle$, there

$$(p,g) \Rightarrow \left\{ \begin{array}{l} (\mathbf{r}_d \mapsto w1) * (\mathbf{r}_s \mapsto w2) \\ (\mathbf{r}_d \mapsto w1{+}w2) * (\mathbf{r}_s \mapsto w_2) \end{array} \right\}^{(w1,w2)} \triangleright \Psi(\text{pc}+1)$$
$$\overline{\Psi,I \vdash \{(p,g)\}\ \text{pc} : \text{add } \mathbf{r}_d, \mathbf{r}_s} \quad \text{(ADD)}$$

$$(p,g) \Rightarrow \left\{ \begin{array}{l} \mathbf{ra} \mapsto \_ \\ \mathbf{ra} \mapsto \text{pc}+1 \end{array} \right\} \triangleright \Psi(\mathbf{f}) \triangleright \left\{ \begin{array}{l} \mathbf{ra} \mapsto \text{pc}+1 \\ \mathbf{ra} \mapsto \_ \end{array} \right\} \triangleright \Psi(\text{pc}+1)$$
$$\overline{\Psi,I \vdash \{(p,g)\}\ \text{pc} : \text{call } \mathbf{f}} \quad \text{(CALL)}$$

$$\frac{(p,g) \Rightarrow \left\{ \begin{array}{l} \text{emp} \\ \text{emp} \end{array} \right\}}{\Psi,I \vdash \{(p,g)\}\ \text{pc} : \text{ret}} \ \text{(RET)} \qquad \frac{(p,g) \Rightarrow \Psi(\mathbf{f})}{\Psi,I \vdash \{(p,g)\}\ \text{pc} : \text{jmp } \mathbf{f}} \ \text{(JMP)}$$

$$(p,g) \Rightarrow \left\{ \begin{array}{l} [t] * (\mathtt{a0},\mathtt{a1},\mathbf{ra} \mapsto t,t',\_) * \langle t' \rangle * \diamond I(t,t') \\ [t] * (\mathtt{a0},\mathtt{a1},\mathbf{ra} \mapsto t,t',\_) * \exists t''. \langle t'' \rangle * \diamond I(t'',t) \end{array} \right\}^{(t,t')} \triangleright \Psi(\text{pc}+1)$$
$$\overline{\Psi,I \vdash \{(p,g)\}\ \text{pc} : \text{cswitch}} \quad \text{(CSW)}$$

Fig. 7. Inference rules (selected)

exist resources of its TCB, stack, and private resources. Therefore, all resources can be divided into parts and each of them is associated to one thread. The global invariant GINV, defined in Fig. 8, describes the partition of all resources globally. The invariant is the key for proving the soundness theorem of our proof system.

First, for each thread, we define a predicate Cont to specify its resources and control flow, i.e. the *continuation* of this thread. The first parameter n of this predicate specifies the number of functions nested in the thread's control flow. If n is equal to zero, it means that the thread is running in the topmost function, which is required to be an infinite loop and cannot return. If the number n is greater than zero, the predicate says that there is a specification (p,g) in Ψ at pc, such that the resources of the thread satisfies p; and g guarantees that the thread will continue to satisfy Cont recursively after it returns to the address *retaddr*.

The concrete resources of a *running thread* are specified by a continuation Cont with an additional condition, the running thread owns all registers. The parameter pc points to the next instruction the thread is going to run. Here we use an abbreviation $\lfloor R \rfloor$ to denote the resources of all registers, except that the value in $\mathbf{ra}$ is of no interest.

For a *ready thread* (or a runnable thread), its concrete resources are defined by separating implication $-\!*$: if given (1) the resources of saved machine context $\lfloor R \rfloor$, (2) the abstract resource of itself $[t]$, (3) another ready thread t' and (4) shared resources specified by $\diamond I(t',t)$, the resources of the ready thread can be transformed into the resources of a running thread. Its thread ID is specified by the second parameter of RThrd, and the third parameter is the machine context data saved in its TCB. Please note that the program counter of a ready thread is saved into the register $\mathbf{ra}$.

The whole machine state can be partitioned, and each part is owned by one thread, which is either running or ready. Thus, the global invariant GINV is defined in the form of separating conjunction by CThrd and RThrd. The structure of GINV is isomorphic to the thread pool P: the abstract running thread is mapped to the resource specified by

$$\lfloor R \rfloor \quad \triangleq (\mathtt{ra} \mapsto \_) * (\mathtt{v0} \mapsto R(\mathtt{v0})) * (\mathtt{sp} \mapsto R(\mathtt{sp}))$$
$$* (\mathtt{a0} \mapsto R(\mathtt{a0})) * (\mathtt{a1} \mapsto R(\mathtt{a1})) * (\mathtt{a2} \mapsto R(\mathtt{a2}))$$

$$\mathsf{Cont}(n{+}1, \Psi, \mathtt{pc}) \triangleq \lambda S.\, \Psi(\mathtt{pc}) = (p, g) \wedge (p\ S)$$
$$\wedge (\forall S'.\, g\ S\ S' \to (\exists\, retaddr.\, (\mathtt{ra} \hookrightarrow retaddr) \wedge \mathsf{Cont}(n, \Psi, retaddr))\ S')$$

$$\mathsf{Cont}(0, \Psi, \mathtt{pc}) \triangleq \lambda S.\, \Psi(\mathtt{pc}) = (p, g) \wedge (p\ S) \wedge (\forall S'.\, g\ S\ S' \to \mathsf{False})$$

$$\mathsf{CThrd}(\Psi, t, \mathtt{pc}) \triangleq \exists n.\, \mathsf{Cont}(n, \Psi, \mathtt{pc}) \wedge ([t] * \exists R.\, \lfloor R \rfloor * \mathsf{true})$$

$$\mathsf{RThrd}(\Psi, t, R) \triangleq \lfloor R \rfloor * [t] * \exists t'.\, \langle t' \rangle * \diamond I(t', t) -\!\!* \mathsf{CThrd}(\Psi, t, R(\mathtt{ra}))$$

$$\mathsf{GINV}(\Psi, P, \mathtt{pc}) \triangleq \mathsf{CThrd}(\Psi, t, \mathtt{pc}) * \mathsf{RThrd}(\Psi, t_0, R_0) * \cdots * \mathsf{RThrd}(\Psi, t_n, R_n)$$
$$\text{where } P = \{t : run,\ t_0 : (rdy, R_0),\ \ldots,\ t_n : (rdy, R_n)\}$$

Fig. 8. Concrete threads and the global invariant

```
struct tcb {                | void schedule_p2()
  struct context ctxt;      | {
  struct tcb *prev;         |   struct tcb *old, *new;
  struct tcb *next;         |   old = cur;
};                          |   new = deq(&rq);
struct queue {              |   if (new == NULL) return;
  struct tcb *head;         |   enq(&rq, old);
  struct tcb *tail;         |   cur = new;
};                          |   cswitch(old,new);
struct tcb *cur;            |   return;
struct queue rq;            | }
```

Fig. 9. Pseudo C code for schedule_p2()

CThrd; an abstract ready thread is mapped to a resource specified by RThrd. Note that GINV requires that there be one and only one running abstract thread, since the physical machine has only one single processor. Our proof system ensures that the machine state always satisfies the global invariant, $(\mathsf{GINV}(\Psi, P, \mathtt{pc})\ (M, R, P))$.

The soundness property of our proof system states that any program that is well-formed in our proof system will run safely on the abstract machine. The property can be proved by the global invariant GINV, which always holds through machine execution. We can first prove that if every machine configuration satisfies GINV, it can run forward for one step. And we can also prove that if a machine configuration (satisfying GINV) can proceed, the next machine configuration will also satisfy GINV. Hence by the invariant GINV, the soundness theorem of our proof system can be proved. The proof of the soundness theorem has been formalized in Coq [7].

5 Verification Cases

In this section, we show how to use the proof system to verify two schedulers of pattern (II) and (III) shown in Fig. 1. We give the code written in pseudo C to explain the programs and their specifications. The corresponding assembly code and selected assertions of the two schedulers are shown in Fig. 10.

Scheduler as Function. The scheduler function schedule_p2() (see Fig. 9) follows the process discussed in Sec. 2. The functions deq() and enq() are used to remove and insert nodes in thread queues. The main task of the scheduler is to choose a candidate from the thread queue and then perform context switch from the current thread to the candidate. There are two global variables, cur and rq. The variable cur points to the TCB of the running thread; rq points to the thread queue containing TCBs of all other runnable (ready) threads.

The notation $t \overset{field}{\longmapsto} w$ specifies a named field in the structure. The notation ptcb(t) specifies a part of TCB including the fields of next and prev. The predicate RQ(q,L) specifies a doubly linked list as a thread queue pointed to by q, where L is a list of thread IDs of the thread queue. We also use $\langle L \rangle$ as an abbreviation for $\langle t_0 \rangle * \langle t_1 \rangle * \cdots * \langle t_n \rangle$, if L is $t_0 :: t_1 :: \cdots :: t_n ::$ nil, and use $1 \mapsto {}^{(n)}\_$ to specify n continuous memory cells.

$$
\begin{aligned}
1 \overset{field}{\longmapsto} w &\triangleq (l + \textit{offset of the field in the struct}) \mapsto w \\
\text{ptcb}(t) &\triangleq (t \overset{prev}{\longmapsto} \_) * (t \overset{next}{\longmapsto} \_) \\
\text{RQseg}(pv, tl, t, \text{nil}) &\triangleq (t \overset{prev}{\longmapsto} pv) * \exists t'. (t \overset{next}{\longmapsto} \text{NULL}) * \natural(t = tl) \\
\text{RQseg}(pv, tl, t, t' :: L') &\triangleq (t \overset{prev}{\longmapsto} pv) * (t \overset{next}{\longmapsto} t') * \text{RQseg}(t, tl, t', L') \\
\text{RQ}(q, \text{nil}) &\triangleq (q \overset{head}{\longmapsto} \text{NULL}) * (q \overset{tail}{\longmapsto} \text{NULL}) \\
\text{RQ}(q, t :: L) &\triangleq \exists pv. \exists tl. (q \overset{head}{\longmapsto} t) * (q \overset{tail}{\longmapsto} tl) * \text{RQseg}(pv, tl, t, L) \\
\text{K}(bp, n, w_0 :: w_1 :: \ldots :: w_m :: \text{nil}) &\triangleq \exists sp. (\text{sp} \mapsto sp) * \natural(sp = bp + 4n) * (bp \mapsto {}^{(n)}\_) \\
&\quad * (sp \mapsto w_0) * (sp + 4 \mapsto w_1) * \cdots * (sp + 4m \mapsto w_m) \\
\text{K}(bp, n) &\triangleq \text{K}(bp, n, \text{nil})
\end{aligned}
$$

The specification of schedule_p2() is shown below:

$$
\left\{
\begin{aligned}
&[t] * \text{ptcb}(t) * (\text{cur} \mapsto t) * \exists L. \text{RQ}(\text{rq}, L) * \langle L \rangle * (\text{ra} \mapsto ret) \\
&\qquad\qquad\qquad\qquad * \text{K}(bp, 20) * (\text{v0}, \text{a0}, \text{a1} \mapsto \_, \_, \_) \\
&[t] * \text{ptcb}(t) * (\text{cur} \mapsto t) * \exists L. \text{RQ}(\text{rq}, L) * \langle L \rangle * (\text{ra} \mapsto ret) \\
&\qquad\qquad\qquad\qquad * \text{K}(bp, 20) * (\text{v0}, \text{a0}, \text{a1} \mapsto \_, \_, \_)
\end{aligned}
\right\}^{(t, ret, bp)}
$$

Here we use a notation K($bp, n, w :: w' :: \cdots$) to describe a stack frame. The first parameter bp is the base address of a stack frame. The second parameter n is the size of unused space (number of words). And the third parameter is a list of words, representing the values on stack top down, that is, the leftmost value in the list is the topmost value in the stack frame. If the stack frame is empty, we omit the third parameter.

The abstract invariant I is instantiated to a concrete definition specifying the shared resources *before* and *after* context switch for this implementation of scheduler.

$$
I(t, t') \triangleq \text{ptcb}(t') * (\text{cur} \mapsto t') * \exists L. \text{RQ}(\text{rq}, t :: L) * \langle L \rangle
$$

schedule_p2:

$\{[t] * \text{ptcb}(t) * (\text{cur} \mapsto t) * \exists L.\text{RQ}(\text{rq}, L)$
$* \langle L \rangle * (\text{a0}, \text{a1}, \text{v0}, \text{ra} \mapsto \_, \_, \_, ret)$
$* \text{K}(bp, 20)\}$

```
        subi    sp,     12
        sw      ra,     8(sp)
        movi    a0,     cur
        lw      v0,     0(a0)
        sw      v0,     0(sp)
```

$\{[t] * \text{ptcb}(t) * (\text{cur} \mapsto t) * \exists L.\text{RQ}(\text{rq}, L)$
$* \langle L \rangle * (\text{a0}, \text{a1}, \text{v0}, \text{ra} \mapsto \text{cur}, \_, t, \_)$
$* \text{K}(bp, 17, t :: \_ :: ret :: \text{nil})\}$

```
        movi    a0,     rq
        call    deq
        bz      v0,     Ls_ret
```

$\{[t] * \text{ptcb}(t) * \langle t' \rangle * \text{ptcb}(t') * \exists L.\text{RQ}(\text{rq}, L)$
$* \langle L \rangle * (\text{a0}, \text{a1}, \text{v0}, \text{ra} \mapsto \text{rq}, \_, t', \_)$
$* \text{K}(bp, 17, t :: \_ :: ret :: \text{nil}) * (\text{cur} \mapsto t)\}$

```
        sw      v0,     4(sp)
        lw      a1,     0(sp)
        call    enq
```

$\{[t] * \langle t' \rangle * \text{ptcb}(t') * \exists L.\text{RQ}(\text{rq}, t :: L) * \langle L \rangle$
$* (\text{a0}, \text{a1}, \text{v0}, \text{ra} \mapsto \text{rq}, t, 0, \_)$
$* \text{K}(bp, 17, t :: t' :: ret :: \text{nil}) * (\text{cur} \mapsto t)\}$

```
        lw      a1,     4(sp)
        movi    a0,     cur
        sw      a1,     0(a0)
        lw      a0,     0(sp)
```

$\{[t] * \langle t' \rangle * \exists L.\text{RQ}(\text{rq}, t :: L) * \langle L \rangle * \text{ptcb}(t')$
$* (\text{a0}, \text{a1}, \text{v0}, \text{ra} \mapsto t, t', 0, \_)$
$* \text{K}(bp, 17, t :: t' :: ret :: \text{nil}) * (\text{cur} \mapsto t')\}$

```
        cswitch
```

$\{[t] * \text{ptcb}(t) * \exists t''.\langle t'' \rangle * \exists L.\text{RQ}(\text{rq}, t'' :: L)$
$* \langle L \rangle * (\text{a0}, \text{a1}, \text{v0}, \text{ra} \mapsto t, t', \_, \_)$
$* \text{K}(bp, 17, t :: \_ :: ret :: \text{nil}) * (\text{cur} \mapsto t)\}$

Ls_ret:

```
        lw      ra,     8(sp)
        addi    sp,     12
```

$\{[t] * \text{ptcb}(t) * (\text{cur} \mapsto t) * \exists L.\text{RQ}(\text{rq}, L)$
$* \langle L \rangle * (\text{a0}, \text{a1}, \text{v0}, \text{ra} \mapsto \_, \_, \_, ret)$
$* \text{K}(bp, 20)\}$

```
        ret
```

schedth:

$\{[\text{sched}] * (\text{cur} \mapsto \_) * \exists L.\text{RQ}(\text{rq}, L) * \langle L \rangle$
$* (\text{a0}, \text{a1}, \text{v0}, \text{ra} \mapsto \_, \_, \_, \_)$
$* \exists bp.\text{K}(bp, 10)\}$

```
        movi    a0,     rq
        call    deq
        bz      v0,     schedth
        movi    a2,     cur
        sw      v0,     0(a2)
        mov     a1,     v0
        lw      a0,     sched
```

$\{[\text{sched}] * \langle t' \rangle * (\text{cur} \mapsto t') * \text{ptcb}(t')$
$* \exists L.\text{RQ}(\text{rq}, L) * \langle L \rangle$
$* (\text{a0}, \text{a1}, \text{v0}, \text{ra} \mapsto \text{sched}, t', \_, \_)$
$* \exists bp.\text{K}(bp, 10)\}$

```
        cswitch
```

$\{[\text{sched}] * \exists t''.\langle t'' \rangle * \text{ptcb}(t'') * (\text{cur} \mapsto t'')$
$* \exists L.\text{RQ}(\text{rq}, L) * \langle L \rangle * \exists bp.\text{K}(bp, 10)$
$* (\text{a0}, \text{a1}, \text{v0}, \text{ra} \mapsto \text{sched}, \_, \_, \_)\}$

```
        movi    a0,     rq
        lw      a1,     0(a2)
        call    enq
        jmp     schedth
```

schedule_p3:

$\{[t] * \text{ptcb}(t) * \langle \text{sched} \rangle * (\text{cur} \mapsto t)$
$* (\text{a0}, \text{a1}, \text{ra} \mapsto \_, \_, ret) * \text{K}(bp, 10)\}$

```
        subi    sp,     4
        sw      ra,     0(sp)
        movi    a1,     cur
        lw      a0,     0(a1)
        movi    a1,     sched
```

$\{[t] * \text{ptcb}(t) * \langle \text{sched} \rangle * (\text{cur} \mapsto t)$
$* (\text{a0}, \text{a1}, \text{ra} \mapsto t, \text{sched}, ret) * \text{K}(bp, 9, ret)\}$

```
        cswitch
```

$\{[t] * \text{ptcb}(t) * \langle \text{sched} \rangle * (\text{cur} \mapsto t)$
$* (\text{a0}, \text{a1}, \text{ra} \mapsto \_, \_, ret) * \text{K}(bp, 9, ret)\}$

```
        lw      ra,     0(sp)
        addi    sp,     4
```

$\{[t] * \text{ptcb}(t) * \langle \text{sched} \rangle * (\text{cur} \mapsto t)$
$* (\text{a0}, \text{a1}, \text{ra} \mapsto \_, \_, ret) * \text{K}(bp, 10)\}$

```
        ret
```

Fig. 10. Verification of schedule_p2(), schedth() and schedule_p3()

```
struct tcb sched;        |   schedth()
struct tcb *cur;         |   {
struct queue rq;         |     while(1){
schedule_p3()            |       cur = deq(&rq);
{                        |       cswitch(&sched, cur);
  cswitch(cur,&sched);   |       enq(&rq, cur);
  return;                |     }
}                        |   }
```

Fig. 11. Pseudo C code for `schedule_p3()`

Scheduler as a separated thread. A scheduler in the pattern (III) is implemented as a separated thread (see Fig. 11), which does scheduling jobs in an infinite loop. A global variable `sched` is added to represent the TCB of the scheduler thread. A stub function `schedule_p3()` can be invoked by other threads to do scheduling. As shown below, the specification of `schedule_p3()` function is different from the one of `schedule_p2()`. The schedule function in this implementation doesn't own the thread queue, which is owned by the scheduler thread $\langle$sched$\rangle$ instead since all of the operations over the thread queue are put into the separated thread.

$$\left\{ \begin{array}{l} [t] * \mathsf{ptcb}(t) * (\mathsf{cur} \mapsto t) * \langle\mathsf{sched}\rangle * (\mathsf{a0,a1,ra} \mapsto \_,\_,ret) * \mathsf{K}(bp,10) \\ [t] * \mathsf{ptcb}(t) * (\mathsf{cur} \mapsto t) * \langle\mathsf{sched}\rangle * (\mathsf{a0,a1,ra} \mapsto \_,\_,ret) * \mathsf{K}(bp,10) \end{array} \right\}^{(t,bp,ret)}$$

The specification of `schedth()` function is shown below:

$$\left\{ \begin{array}{l} [\mathsf{sched}] * (\mathsf{cur} \mapsto \_) * \exists L.\mathsf{RQ}(\mathsf{rq},L) * \langle L\rangle \\ \qquad\qquad\qquad * (\mathsf{a0,a1,a2,v0,ra} \mapsto \_,\_,\_,\_,\_) * \exists bp.\mathsf{K}(bp,10) \\ \mathsf{false} \end{array} \right\}$$

Since the ready thread queue is only owned by the scheduler thread, it does not need to be shared by other threads and occur in the invariant for the shared resources, I:

$$I(t,t') \triangleq (\sharp(t'=\mathsf{sched}) * (\mathsf{cur} \mapsto t) * \mathsf{ptcb}(t)) \mathbb{W} (\sharp(t=\mathsf{sched}) * (\mathsf{cur} \mapsto t') * \mathsf{ptcb}(t'))$$

The invariant $I(t,t')$ is defined by two cases on the direction of context switch: if the destination thread is the scheduler thread, $I(t,t')$ requires that the value in `cur` be equal to the ID of the source thread, t; or if the source thread is the scheduler thread, $I(t,t')$ requires that the value in `cur` be equal to the ID of the destination thread.

6 Related Work and Conclusions

Gotsman and Yang [6] proposed a two-layer framework to verify schedulers. The proof system in the lower-layer is for verifying code manipulating TCBs, while the upper-layer is for verifying the rest concurrent code of the kernel. Since thread queues and TCBs are hidden from the upper-layer, one thread could not have any knowledge of the others, thus their proof system is unable to verify the scheduling pattern of II and III.

Similar to our assertion RThrd($\cdots$), they introduced a primitive predicate *Process*(G) to relate TCBs in the lower-layer with threads in the upper-layer, but there is no counterpart of $\langle t \rangle$ in their framework.

Feng *et al.* also verified a kernel prototype [3] in a two-layer framework. Code manipulating TCBs needs to be verified in the lower-layer of their framework. The TCBs are connected with actual threads in the upper layer by an interpretation function of their framework. Our use of global invariant is similar to their use of the interpretation function. In the upper-layer, information of threads is completely hidden. Thus, their framework also fails to support the verification of the scheduler pattern of II and III.

Ni *et al.* verified a small thread manager with a logic system [15,14] supporting modular reasoning about code including embedded code pointers. In their logic, however, there is no abstraction of threads. Multithreaded programs are seen as sequential interleaving of pieces of code in low-level continuation passing style. Therefore, TCBs with embedded code pointers can be treated as normal data. But since the reasoning level is too low without any abstraction, TCBs have to be specified by over-complicated logic expressions and then it is very difficult to apply their method to realistic code.

Klein *et al.* verified a micro-kernel, seL4 [11], where the kernel code runs sequentially. Thus they used a sequential proof system to verify most of the kernel code. The scheduling pattern of seL4 is similar to our pattern I, but they trusted the code doing context saving and loading, and left it unverified. Since they do not verify user processes upon the kernel, they need not relate TCBs in the kernel with actual user processes.

Gargano *et al.* used a framework CVM [5] to build verified kernels in the Verisoft project. CVM is a computational model for concurrent user processes, which interleave through a micro-kernel. Starostin and Tsyban presented a formal approach [18] to reason about context switch between user processes. The context switch code and proofs are integrated in a framework for building verified kernels (CVM) [10]. Their framework keeps a global invariant, *weak consistency*, to relate TCBs in the kernel with user processes outside the kernel. Since the kernel itself is sequential, their process scheduling follows pattern I. The other two patterns cannot be verified.

In this paper, we proposed a novel approach to verify concurrent thread management code, which allows multiple threads to modify their own thread control blocks. The assertions of the code and inference rules of the proof system are straightforward and easy to follow. Moreover, it can be easily extended to support other kernel features (e.g., preemptive scheduling, multi-core systems, synchronizations) and to be practically applied to realistic OS code.

Acknowledgements. We thank anonymous referees for suggestions and comments on an earlier version of this paper. Yu Guo, Xinyu Feng and Peizhi Shi are supported in part by grants from National Natural Science Foundation of China (Nos. 61073040, 61202052 and 61229201), the Fundamental Research Funds for the Central Universities (Nos. WK0110000018 and WK0110000025), and Program for New Century Excellent Talents in Universities (NCET). Zhong Shao is supported in part by DARPA under agreement numbers FA8750-10-2-0254 and FA8750-12-2-0293, and by NSF grants CNS-0910670, CNS-0915888, and CNS-1065451. Any opinions, findings, and conclusions contained in this document are those of the authors and do not reflect the views of these agencies.

References

1. Engelschall, R.S.: Portable multithreading: the signal stack trick for user-space thread creation. In: Proc. of ATEC 2000, p. 20. USENIX Association, Berkeley (2000)
2. Engler, D.R., Kaashoek, M.F., O'Toole Jr., J.: Exokernel: an operating system architecture for application-level resource management. In: Proceedings of the 15th ACM Symposium on Operating Systems Principles, SOSP 1995, Copper Mountain Resort, Colorado, pp. 251–266 (December 1995)
3. Feng, X., Shao, Z., Guo, Y., Dong, Y.: Combining Domain-Specific and Foundational Logics to Verify Complete Software Systems. In: Shankar, N., Woodcock, J. (eds.) VSTTE 2008. LNCS, vol. 5295, pp. 54–69. Springer, Heidelberg (2008)
4. Feng, X., Shao, Z., Vaynberg, A., Xiang, S., Ni, Z.: Modular verification of assembly code with stack-based control abstractions. In: Proc. PLDI 2006, pp. 401–414 (June 2006)
5. Gargano, M., Hillebrand, M., Leinenbach, D., Paul, W.: On the Correctness of Operating System Kernels. In: Hurd, J., Melham, T.F. (eds.) TPHOLs 2005. LNCS, vol. 3603, pp. 1–16. Springer, Heidelberg (2005)
6. Gotsman, A., Yang, H.: Modular verification of preemptive os kernels. In: Proc. ICFP 2011, Tokyo, Japan, pp. 404–417. ACM (2011)
7. Guo, Y., Feng, X., Shao, Z., Shi, P.: Modular verification of concurrent thread management (technical report and coq proof) (June 2012), http://kyhcs.ustcsz.edu.cn/~guoyu/sched/
8. Herder, J.N., Bos, H., Gras, B., Homburg, P., Tanenbaum, A.S.: Minix 3: a highly reliable, self-repairing operating system. SIGOPS Oper. Syst. Rev. 40, 80–89 (2006)
9. Hohmuth, M., Tews, H.: The vfiasco approach for a verified operating system. In: Proceedings of the 2nd ECOOP Workshop on Programming Languages and Operating Systems (2005)
10. In der Rieden, T., Tsyban, A.: CVM – A verified framework for microkernel programmers. In: Proc. SSV 2008. Electronic Notes in Theoretical Computer Science, vol. 217C, pp. 151–168. Elsevier Science B.V. (2008)
11. Klein, G., Elphinstone, K., Heiser, G., Andronick, J., Cock, D., Derrin, P., Elkaduwe, D., Engelhardt, K., Kolanski, R., Norrish, M., Sewell, T., Tuch, H., Winwood, S.: seL4: Formal verification of an OS kernel. In: Proc. SOSP 2009, Big Sky, MT, USA, pp. 207–220. ACM (October 2009)
12. Love, R.: Linux Kernel Development, 2nd edn. Novell Press (2005)
13. McKusick, M.K., Neville-Neil, G.V.: The Design and Implementation of the FreeBSD Operating System. Pearson Education (2004)
14. Ni, Z., Shao, Z.: Certified assembly programming with embedded code pointers. In: Proc. POPL 2006, pp. 320–333 (January 2006)
15. Ni, Z., Yu, D., Shao, Z.: Using XCAP to Certify Realistic Systems Code: Machine Context Management. In: Schneider, K., Brandt, J. (eds.) TPHOLs 2007. LNCS, vol. 4732, pp. 189–206. Springer, Heidelberg (2007)
16. O'Hearn, P.W.: Resources, concurrency, and local reasoning. Theor. Comput. Sci. 375(1-3), 271–307 (2007)
17. Reynolds, J.C.: Separation logic: A logic for shared mutable data structures. In: LICS 2002: Proceedings of the 17th Annual IEEE Symposium on Logic in Computer Science, pp. 55–74. IEEE Computer Society, Washington, DC (2002)
18. Starostin, A., Tsyban, A.: Verified Process-Context Switch for C-Programmed Kernels. In: Shankar, N., Woodcock, J. (eds.) VSTTE 2008. LNCS, vol. 5295, pp. 240–254. Springer, Heidelberg (2008)

A Case for Behavior-Preserving Actions in Separation Logic

David Costanzo and Zhong Shao

Yale University

Abstract. Separation Logic is a widely-used tool that allows for local reasoning about imperative programs with pointers. A straightforward definition of this "local reasoning" is that, whenever a program runs safely on some state, adding more state would have no effect on the program's behavior. However, for a mix of technical and historical reasons, local reasoning is defined in a more subtle way, allowing a program to lose some behaviors when extra state is added. In this paper, we propose strengthening local reasoning to match the straightforward definition mentioned above. We argue that such a strengthening does not have any negative effect on the usability of Separation Logic, and we present four examples that illustrate how this strengthening simplifies some of the metatheoretical reasoning regarding Separation Logic. In one example, our change even results in a more powerful metatheory.

1 Introduction

Separation Logic [8,13] is widely used for verifying the correctness of C-like imperative programs [9] that manipulate mutable data structures. It supports *local reasoning* [15]: if we know a program's behavior on some heap, then we can automatically infer something about its behavior on any larger heap. The concept of local reasoning is embodied as a logical inference rule, known as the *frame rule*. The frame rule allows us to extend a specification of a program's execution on a small heap to a specification of execution on a larger heap.

For the purpose of making Separation Logic extensible, it is common practice to abstract over the primitive commands of the programming language being used. By "primitive commands" here, we mean commands that are not defined in terms of other commands. Typical examples of primitive commands include variable assignment $x := E$ and heap update $[E] := E'$. One example of a non-primitive command is $\text{while } B \text{ do } C$.

When we abstract over primitive commands, we need to make sure that we still have a sound logic. Specifically, it is possible for the frame rule to become unsound for certain primitive commands. In order to guarantee that this does not happen, certain "healthiness" conditions are required of primitive commands. We refer to these conditions together as "locality," since they guarantee soundness of the frame rule, and the frame rule is the embodiment of local reasoning.

As one might expect, locality in Separation Logic is defined in such a way that it is *precisely* strong enough to guarantee soundness of the frame rule. In other

R. Jhala and A. Igarashi (Eds.): APLAS 2012, LNCS 7705, pp. 332–349, 2012.
© Springer-Verlag Berlin Heidelberg 2012

words, the frame rule is sound *if and only if* all primitive commands are local. In this paper, we consider a strengthening of locality. Clearly, any strengthening will still guarantee soundness of the frame rule. The tradeoff, then, is that the stronger we make locality, the fewer primitive commands there will be that satisfy locality. We claim that we can strengthen locality to the point where: (1) the usage of the logic is unaffected — specifically, we do not lose the ability to model any primitive commands that are normally modeled in Separation Logic; (2) our strong locality is precisely the property that one would intuitively expect it to be — that the behavior of a program is completely independent from any unused state; and (3) we significantly simplify various technical work in the literature relating to metatheoretical facts about Separation Logic. We refer to our stronger notion of locality as "behavior preservation," because the behavior of a program is preserved when moving from a small state to a larger one.

We justify statement (1) above, that the usage of the logic is unaffected, in Section 3 by demonstrating a version of Separation Logic using the same primitive commands as the standard one presented in [13], for which our strong locality holds. We show that, even though we need to alter the state model of standard Separation Logic, we do not need to change any of the inference rules. We justify the second statement, that our strong locality preserves program behavior, in Section 2. We will also show that the standard, weaker notion of locality is not behavior-preserving. We provide some justification of the third statement, that behavior preservation significantly simplifies Separation Logic metatheory, in Section 5 by considering four specific examples in detail. As a primer, we will say a little bit about each example here.

The first simplification that we show is in regard to *program footprints*, as defined and analyzed in [12]. Informally, a footprint of a program is a set of states such that, given the program's behavior on those states, it is possible to infer all of the program's behavior on all other states. Footprints are useful for giving complete specifications of programs in a concise way. Intuitively, locality should tell us that the set of *smallest safe states*, or states containing the minimal amount of resources required for the program to safely execute, should always be a footprint. However, this is not the case in standard Separation Logic. To quote the authors in [12], the intuition that the smallest safe states should form a footprint "fails due to the subtle nature of the locality condition." We show that in the context of behavior-preserving locality, the set of smallest safe states does indeed form a footprint.

The second simplification regards the theory of data refinement, as defined in [6]. Data refinement is a formalism of the common programming paradigm in which an abstract module, or interface, is implemented by a concrete instantiation. In the context of [6], our programming language consists of a standard one, plus abstract module operations that are guaranteed to satisfy some specification. We wish to show that, given concrete and abstract modules, and a relation relating their equivalent states, any execution of the program that can happen when using the concrete module can also happen when using the abstract one.

We simplify the data refinement theory by eliminating the need for two somewhat unintuitive requirements used in [6], called contents independence and growing relations. Contents independence is a strengthening of locality that is implied by the stronger behavior preservation. A growing relation is a technical requirement guaranteeing that the area of memory used by the abstract module is a subset of that used by the concrete one. It turns out that behavior preservation is strong enough to completely eliminate the need to require growing relations, *without* automatically implying that any relations are growing. Therefore, we can prove refinement between some modules (e.g., ones that use completely disjoint areas of memory) that the system of [6] cannot handle.

Our third metatheoretical simplification is in the context of Relational Separation Logic, defined in [14]. Relational Separation Logic is a tool for reasoning about the relationship between two executions on different programs. In [14], soundness of the relational frame rule is initially shown to be dependent on programs being deterministic. The author presents a reasonable solution for making the frame rule sound in the presence of nondeterminism, but the solution is somewhat unintuitive and, more importantly, a significant chunk of the paper (about 9 pages out of 41) is devoted to developing the technical details of the solution. We show that under the context of behavior preservation, the relational frame rule as initially defined is already sound in the presence of nondeterminism, so that section of the paper is no longer needed.

The fourth simplification is minor, but still worth noting. For technical reasons, the standard definition of locality does not play well with a model in which the total amount of available memory is finite. Separation Logic generally avoids this issue by simply using an infinite space of memory. This works fine, but there may be situations in which we wish to use a model that more closely represents what is actually going on inside our computer. While Separation Logic can be made to work in the presence of finite memory, doing so is not a trivial matter. We will show that under our stronger notion of locality, no special treatment is required for finite-sized models.

All proofs in Sections 3 and 4 have been fully mechanized in the Coq proof assistant [7]. The Coq source files, along with their conversions to pdf, can be found at the link to the technical report for this paper [5].

2   Locality and Behavior Preservation

In standard Separation Logic [8,13,15,4], there are two locality properties, known as Safety Monotonicity and the Frame Property, that together imply soundness of the frame rule. Safety Monotonicity says that any time a program executes safely in a certain state, the same program must also execute safely in any larger state — in other words, unused resources cannot cause a program to crash. The Frame Property says that if a program executes safely on a small state, then any terminating execution of the program on a larger state can be tracked back to some terminating execution on the small state by assuming that the extra added state has no effect and is unchanged. Furthermore, there is a third property, called Termination Monotonicity, that is required whenever we are interested in reasoning about divergence (nontermination). This property says that if a program executes safely and never diverges on a small state, then it cannot diverge on any larger state.

To describe these properties formally, we first formalize the idea of program state. We will describe the theory somewhat informally here; full formal detail will be described later in Section 4. We define states σ to be members of an abstract set Σ. We assume that whenever two states σ_0 and σ_1 are "disjoint," written $\sigma_0 \# \sigma_1$, they can be combined to form the larger state $\sigma_0 \cdot \sigma_1$. Intuitively, two states are disjoint when they occupy disjoint areas of memory.

We represent the semantic meaning of a program C by a binary relation $[\![C]\!]$. We use the common notational convention aRb for a binary relation R to denote $(a, b) \in R$. Intuitively, $\sigma[\![C]\!]\sigma'$ means that, when executing C on initial state σ, it is possible to terminate in state σ'. Note that if σ is related by $[\![C]\!]$ to more than one state, this simply means that C is a nondeterministic program.

We also define two special behaviors bad and div:

- The notation $\sigma[\![C]\!]$bad means that C can crash or get stuck when executed on σ, while
- The notation $\sigma[\![C]\!]$div means that C can diverge (execute forever) when executed on σ.

As a notational convention, we use τ to range over elements of $\Sigma \cup \{\text{bad}, \text{div}\}$. We require that for any state σ and program C, there is always at least one τ such that $\sigma[\![C]\!]\tau$. In other words, every execution must either crash, go on forever, or terminate in some state.

Now we can define the properties described above more formally. Following are definitions of Safety Monotonicity, the Frame Property, and Termination Monotonicity, respectively:

$$1.)\quad \neg\sigma_0[\![C]\!]\text{bad} \wedge \sigma_0 \# \sigma_1 \implies \neg(\sigma_0 \cdot \sigma_1)[\![C]\!]\text{bad}$$
$$2.)\quad \neg\sigma_0[\![C]\!]\text{bad} \wedge (\sigma_0 \cdot \sigma_1)[\![C]\!]\sigma' \implies \exists\sigma_0' . \ \sigma' = \sigma_0' \cdot \sigma_1 \wedge \sigma_0[\![C]\!]\sigma_0'$$
$$3.)\quad \neg\sigma_0[\![C]\!]\text{bad} \wedge \neg\sigma_0[\![C]\!]\text{div} \wedge \sigma_0 \# \sigma_1 \implies \neg(\sigma_0 \cdot \sigma_1)[\![C]\!]\text{div}$$

The standard definition of locality was defined in this way because it is the minimum requirement needed to make the frame rule sound — it is as weak as it can possibly be without breaking the logic. It was not defined to correspond with any intuitive notion of locality. As a result, there are two subtleties in the definition that might seem a bit odd. We will now describe these subtleties and the changes we make to get rid of them. Note that we are not arguing in this section that there is any benefit to changing locality in this way (other than the arguably vacuous benefit of corresponding to our "intuition" of locality) — the benefit will become clear when we discuss how our change simplifies the metatheory in Section 5.

The first subtlety is that Termination Monotonicity only applies in one direction. This means that we could have a program C that runs forever on a state σ, but when we add unused state, we suddenly lose the ability for that infinite execution to occur. We can easily get rid of this subtlety by replacing Termination Monoticity with the following Termination Equivalence property:

$$\neg\sigma_0[\![C]\!]\mathtt{bad} \wedge \sigma_0\#\sigma_1 \implies (\sigma_0[\![C]\!]\mathtt{div} \iff (\sigma_0 \cdot \sigma_1)[\![C]\!]\mathtt{div})$$

The second subtlety is that locality gives us a way of tracking an execution on a large state back to a small one, but it does not allow for the other way around. This means that there can be an execution on a state σ that becomes invalid when we add unused state. This subtlety is a little trickier to remedy than the other. If we think of the Frame Property as really being a "Backwards Frame Property," in the sense that it only works in the direction from large state to small state, then we clearly need to require a corresponding Forwards Frame Property. We would like to say that if C takes σ_0 to σ_0' and we add the unused state σ_1, then C takes $\sigma_0 \cdot \sigma_1$ to $\sigma_0' \cdot \sigma_1$:

$$\sigma_0[\![C]\!]\sigma_0' \wedge \sigma_0\#\sigma_1 \implies (\sigma_0 \cdot \sigma_1)[\![C]\!](\sigma_0' \cdot \sigma_1)$$

Unfortunately, there is no guarantee that $\sigma_0' \cdot \sigma_1$ is defined, as the states might not occupy disjoint areas of memory. In fact, if C causes our initial state to grow, say by allocating memory, then there will always be some σ_1 that is disjoint from σ_0 but not from σ_0' (e.g., take σ_1 to be exactly that allocated memory). Therefore, it seems as if we are doomed to lose behavior in such a situation upon adding unused state.

There is, however, a solution worth considering: we could disallow programs from ever increasing state. In other words, we can require that whenever C takes σ_0 to σ_0', the area of memory occupied by σ_0' must be a subset of that occupied by σ_0. In this way, anything that is disjoint from σ_0 must also be disjoint from σ_0', so we will not lose any behavior. Formally, we express this property as:

$$\sigma_0[\![C]\!]\sigma_0' \implies (\forall \sigma_1 \, . \, \sigma_0\#\sigma_1 \Rightarrow \sigma_0'\#\sigma_1)$$

We can conveniently combine this property with the previous one to express the Forwards Frame Property as the following condition:

$$\sigma_0[\![C]\!]\sigma_0' \wedge \sigma_0\#\sigma_1 \implies \sigma_0'\#\sigma_1 \wedge (\sigma_0 \cdot \sigma_1)[\![C]\!](\sigma_0' \cdot \sigma_1)$$

At first glance, it may seem imprudent to impose this requirement, as it apparently disallows memory allocation. However, it is in fact still possible to model memory allocation — we just have to be a little clever about it. Specifically, we can include a set of memory locations in our state that we designate to be the "free list[1]." When memory is allocated, all allocated cells must be taken from the free list. Contrast this to standard Separation Logic, in which newly-allocated heap cells are taken from outside the state. In the next section, we will show that we can add a free list in this way to the model of Separation Logic without requiring a change to any of the inference rules.

We conclude this section with a brief justification of the term "behavior preservation." Given that C runs safely on a state σ_0, we think of a behavior of C on σ_0 as a particular execution, which can either diverge or terminate at some state

---

[1] The free list is actually a set rather than a list; we use the term "free list" because it is commonly used in the context of memory allocation.

$$E \quad ::= E + E' \mid E - E' \mid E \times E' \mid \ldots \mid -1 \mid 0 \mid 1 \mid \ldots \mid x \mid y \mid \ldots$$
$$B \quad ::= E = E' \mid \mathtt{false} \mid B \Rightarrow B'$$
$$P, Q \quad ::= B \mid \mathtt{false} \mid \mathtt{emp} \mid E \mapsto E' \mid P \Rightarrow Q \mid \forall x.P \mid P * Q$$
$$C \quad ::= \mathtt{skip} \mid x := E \mid x := [E] \mid [E] := E'$$
$$\mid x := \mathtt{cons}(E_1, \ldots, E_n) \mid \mathtt{free}(E) \mid C; C'$$
$$\mid \mathtt{if}\, B \,\mathtt{then}\, C \,\mathtt{else}\, C' \mid \mathtt{while}\, B \,\mathtt{do}\, C$$

Fig. 1. Assertion and Program Syntax

σ_0'. The Forwards Frame Property tells us that execution on a larger state $\sigma_0 \cdot \sigma_1$ simulates execution on the smaller state σ_0, while the Backwards (standard) Frame Property says that execution on the smaller state simulates execution on the larger one. Since standard locality only requires simulation in one direction, it is possible for a program to have fewer valid executions, or behaviors, when executing on $\sigma_0 \cdot \sigma_1$ as opposed to just σ_0. Our stronger locality disallows this from happening, enforcing a bisimulation under which all behaviors are preserved when extra resources are added.

3   Impact on a Concrete Separation Logic

We will now present one possible RAM model that enforces our stronger notion of locality without affecting the inference rules of standard Separation Logic. In the standard model of [13], a program state consists of two components: a variable store and a heap. When new memory is allocated, the memory is "magically" added to the heap. As shown in Section 2, we cannot allow allocation to increase the program state in this way. Instead, we will include an explicit free list, or a set of memory locations available for allocation, inside of the program state. Thus a state is now is a triple (s, h, f) consisting of a store, a heap, and a free list, with the heap and free list occupying disjoint areas of memory. Newly-allocated memory will always come from the free list, while deallocated memory goes back into the free list. Since the standard formulation of Separation Logic assumes that memory is infinite and hence that allocation never fails, we similarly require that the free list be infinite. More specifically, we require that there is some location n such that all locations above n are in the free list.

Formally, states are defined as follows:

$$\text{Var } V \triangleq \{x, y, z, \ldots\} \quad \text{Store } S \triangleq V \to \mathbb{Z} \quad \text{Heap } H \triangleq \mathbb{N} \xrightarrow{\text{fin}} \mathbb{Z}$$

$$\text{Free List } F \triangleq \{N \in \mathcal{P}(\mathbb{N}) \mid \exists n . \forall k \geq n . k \in N\}$$

$$\text{State } \Sigma \triangleq \{(s, h, f) \in S \times H \times F \mid \mathrm{dom}(h) \cap f = \emptyset\}$$

As a point of clarification, we are not claiming here that including the free list in the state model is a novel idea. Other systems (e.g., [12]) have made use of a very similar idea. The two novel contributions that we will show in this section are: (1) that a state model which includes an explicit free list can provide a behavior-preserving semantics, and (2) that the corresponding program logic can be made to be completely backwards-compatible with standard Separation Logic (meaning that any valid Separation Logic derivation is also a valid derivation in our logic).

Assertion syntax and program syntax are given in Figure 1, and are exactly the same as in the standard model for Separation Logic.

Our satisfaction judgement $(s, h, f) \models P$ for an assertion P is defined by ignoring the free list and only considering whether (s, h) satisfies P. Our definition of $(s, h) \models P$ is identical to that of standard Separation Logic.

The small-step operational semantics for our machine is defined as $\sigma, C \longrightarrow \sigma', C'$ and is straightforward; the full details can be found in the extended TR. The most interesting aspects are the rules for allocation and deallocation, since they make use of the free list. $x := \mathrm{cons}(E_1, \ldots, E_n)$ allocates a nondeterministically-chosen contiguous block of n heap cells from the free list, while $\mathrm{free}(E)$ puts the single heap cell pointed to by E back onto the free list. None of the operations make use of any memory existing outside the program state — this is the key for obtaining behavior-preservation.

To see how out state model fits into the structure defined in Section 2, we need to define the state combination operator. Given two states $\sigma_1 = (s_1, h_1, f_1)$ and $\sigma_2 = (s_2, h_2, f_2)$, the combined state $\sigma_1 \cdot \sigma_2$ is equal to $(s_1, h_1 \uplus h_2, f_1)$ if $s_1 = s_2$, $f_1 = f_2$, and the domains of h_1 and h_2 are disjoint; otherwise, the combination is undefined. Note that this combined state satisfies the requisite condition $\mathrm{dom}(h_1 \uplus h_2) \cap f_1 = \emptyset$ because h_1, h_2, and f_1 are pairwise disjoint by assumption. The most important aspect of this definition of state combination is that we can never change the free list when adding extra resources. This guarantees behavior preservation of the nondeterministic memory allocator because the allocator's set of possible behaviors is precisely defined by the free list.

In order to formally compare our logic to "standard" Separation Logic, we need to provide the standard version of the small-step operational semantics, denoted as $(s, h), C \rightsquigarrow (s', h'), C'$. This semantics does not have explicit free lists in the states, but instead treats all locations outside the domain of h as free. We formalize this semantics in the extended TR, and prove the following relationship between the two operational semantics:

$$(s, h), C \overset{n}{\rightsquigarrow} (s', h'), C' \iff \exists f, f' \,.\, (s, h, f), C \overset{n}{\longrightarrow} (s', h', f'), C'$$

The inference rules in the form $\vdash \{P\} C \{Q\}$ for our logic are same as those used in standard Separation Logic. In the extended TR, we state all the inference rules and prove that our logic is both sound and complete; therefore, behavior preservation does not cause any complications in the usage of Separation Logic. Any specification that can be proved using the standard model can also be proved using our model. Also in the TR, we prove that our model enjoys the stronger, behavior-preserving notion of locality described in Sec 2.

Even though our logic works exactly the same as standard Separation Logic, our underlying model now has this free list within the state. Therefore, if we so desire, we could define additional assertions and inference rules allowing for more precise reasoning involving the free list. One idea is to have a separate, free list section of assertions in which we write, for example, $E * \texttt{true}$ to claim that E is a part of the free list. Then the axiom for $\texttt{free}$ would look like:

$$\{E \mapsto -; \texttt{true}\} \, \texttt{free}(E) \, \{\texttt{emp}; E * \texttt{true}\}$$

4   The Abstract Logic

In order to clearly explain how our stronger notion of locality resolves the metatheoretical issues described in Section 1, we will first formally describe how our locality fits into a context similar to that of Abstract Separation Logic [4]. With a minor amount of work, the logic of Section 3 can be molded into a particular instance of the abstract logic presented here.

We define a *separation algebra* to be a set of states Σ, along with a partial associative and commutative operator $\cdot : \Sigma \to \Sigma \rightharpoonup \Sigma$. The disjointness relation $\sigma_0 \# \sigma_1$ holds iff $\sigma_0 \cdot \sigma_1$ is defined, and the substate relation $\sigma_0 \preceq \sigma_1$ holds iff there is some σ_0' such that $\sigma_0 \cdot \sigma_0' = \sigma_1$. A particular element of Σ is designated as a unit state, denoted u, with the property that for any σ, $\sigma \# u$ and $\sigma \cdot u = \sigma$. We require the $\cdot$ operator to be cancellative, meaning that $\sigma \cdot \sigma_0 = \sigma \cdot \sigma_1 \Rightarrow \sigma_0 = \sigma_1$.

An *action* is a set of pairs of type $\Sigma \cup \{\texttt{bad}, \texttt{div}\} \times \Sigma \cup \{\texttt{bad}, \texttt{div}\}$. We require the following two properties: (1) actions always relate $\texttt{bad}$ to $\texttt{bad}$ and $\texttt{div}$ to $\texttt{div}$, and never relate $\texttt{bad}$ or $\texttt{div}$ to anything else; and (2) actions are total, in the sense that for any τ, there exists some τ' such that $\tau A \tau'$ (recall from Section 2 that we use τ to range over elements of $\Sigma \cup \{\texttt{bad}, \texttt{div}\}$). Note that these two requirements are preserved over the standard composition of relations, as well as over both finitary and infinite unions. We write $\texttt{Id}$ to represent the identity action $\{(\tau, \tau) \mid \tau \in \Sigma \cup \{\texttt{bad}, \texttt{div}\}\}$.

Note that it is more standard in the literature to have the domain of actions range only over Σ — we use $\Sigma \cup \{\texttt{bad}, \texttt{div}\}$ here because it has the pleasant effect of making $[\![C_1; C_2]\!]$ correspond precisely to standard composition. Intuitively, once an execution goes wrong, it continues to go wrong, and once an execution diverges, it continues to diverge.

A *local action* is an action A that satisfies the following four properties, which respectively correspond to Safety Monotonicity, Termination Equivalence, the Forwards Frame Property, and the Backwards Frame Property from Section 2:

1.) $\neg \sigma_0 A \texttt{bad} \wedge \sigma_0 \# \sigma_1 \implies \neg (\sigma_0 \cdot \sigma_1) A \texttt{bad}$

2.) $\neg \sigma_0 A \texttt{bad} \wedge \sigma_0 \# \sigma_1 \implies (\sigma_0 A \texttt{div} \iff (\sigma_0 \cdot \sigma_1) A \texttt{div})$

3.) $\sigma_0 A \sigma_0' \wedge \sigma_0 \# \sigma_1 \implies \sigma_0' \# \sigma_1 \wedge (\sigma_0 \cdot \sigma_1) A (\sigma_0' \cdot \sigma_1)$

4.) $\neg \sigma_0 A \texttt{bad} \wedge (\sigma_0 \cdot \sigma_1) A \sigma' \implies \exists \sigma_0' . \, \sigma' = \sigma_0' \cdot \sigma_1 \wedge \sigma_0 A \sigma_0'$

We denote the set of all local actions by **LocAct**. We now show that the set of local actions is closed under composition and (possibly infinite) union. We use the notation $A_1; A_2$ to denote composition, and $\bigcup \mathcal{A}$ to denote union (where $\mathcal{A}$ is a possibly infinite set of actions). The formal definitions of these operations

$$C ::= c \mid C_1; C_2 \mid C_1 + C_2 \mid C^*$$

$$\forall c . [\![c]\!] \in \textbf{LocAct} \qquad\qquad [\![C_1; C_2]\!] \triangleq [\![C_1]\!]; [\![C_2]\!]$$

$$[\![C_1 + C_2]\!] \triangleq [\![C_1]\!] \cup [\![C_2]\!] \qquad\qquad [\![C^*]\!] \triangleq \bigcup_{n \in \mathbb{N}} [\![C]\!]^n$$

$$[\![C]\!]^0 \triangleq \text{Id} \qquad\qquad [\![C]\!]^{n+1} \triangleq [\![C]\!]; [\![C]\!]^n$$

Fig. 2. Command Definition and Denotational Semantics

follow. Note that we require that $\mathcal{A}$ be non-empty. This is necessary because $\bigcup \emptyset$ is $\emptyset$, which is not a valid action. Unless otherwise stated, whenever we write $\bigcup \mathcal{A}$, there will always be an implicit assumption that $\mathcal{A} \neq \emptyset$.

$$\tau A_1; A_2 \tau' \iff \exists \tau'' . \tau A_1 \tau'' \wedge \tau'' A_2 \tau'$$

$$\tau \bigcup \mathcal{A} \tau' \iff \exists A \in \mathcal{A} . \tau A \tau' \qquad (\mathcal{A} \neq \emptyset)$$

Lemma 1. *If A_1 and A_2 are local actions, then $A_1; A_2$ is a local action.*

Lemma 2. *If every A in the set $\mathcal{A}$ is a local action, then $\bigcup \mathcal{A}$ is a local action.*

Figure 2 defines our abstract program syntax and semantics. The language consists of primitive commands, sequencing ($C_1; C_2$), nondeterministic choice ($C_1 + C_2$), and finite iteration (C^*). The semantics of primitive commands are abstracted — the only requirement is that they are local actions. Therefore, from the two previous lemmas and the trivial fact that Id is a local action, it is clear that the semantics of *every* program is a local action.

Note that in our concrete language used if statements and while loops. As shownin [4], it is possible to represent if and while constructs with finite iteration and nondeterministic choice by including a primitive command assume(B), which does nothing if the boolean expression B is true, and diverges otherwise.

Now that we have defined the interpretation of programs as local actions, we can talk about the meaning of a triple $\{P\} C \{Q\}$. We define an assertion P to be a set of states, and we say that a state σ satisfies P iff $\sigma \in P$. We can then define the separating conjunction as follows:

$$P * Q \triangleq \{\sigma \in \Sigma \mid \exists \sigma_0 \in P, \sigma_1 \in Q . \sigma = \sigma_0 \cdot \sigma_1\}$$

Given an assignment of primitive commands to local actions, we say that a triple is valid, written $\models \{P\} C \{Q\}$, just when the following two properties hold for all states σ and σ':

$$1.) \ \sigma \in P \implies \neg \sigma [\![C]\!] \text{bad}$$
$$2.) \ \sigma \in P \wedge \sigma [\![C]\!] \sigma' \implies \sigma' \in Q$$

$$\frac{\neg\sigma[\![c]\!]\mathsf{bad}}{\vdash \{\{\sigma\}\}\, c\, \{\{\sigma' \mid \sigma[\![c]\!]\sigma'\}\}} \text{ (PRIM)} \qquad \frac{\vdash \{P\}\, C_1\, \{Q\} \qquad \vdash \{Q\}\, C_2\, \{R\}}{\vdash \{P\}\, C_1;C_2\, \{R\}} \text{ (SEQ)}$$

$$\frac{\vdash \{P\}\, C_1\, \{Q\} \qquad \vdash \{P\}\, C_2\, \{Q\}}{\vdash \{P\}\, C_1 + C_2\, \{Q\}} \text{ (PLUS)} \qquad \frac{\vdash \{P\}\, C\, \{P\}}{\vdash \{P\}\, C^*\, \{P\}} \text{ (STAR)}$$

$$\frac{\vdash \{P\}\, C\, \{Q\}}{\vdash \{P * R\}\, C\, \{Q * R\}} \text{ (FRAME)} \qquad \frac{P' \subseteq P \qquad \vdash \{P\}\, C\, \{Q\} \qquad Q \subseteq Q'}{\vdash \{P'\}\, C\, \{Q'\}} \text{ (CONSEQ)}$$

$$\frac{\forall i \in I\,.\, \vdash \{P_i\}\, C\, \{Q_i\}}{\vdash \{\bigcup P_i\}\, C\, \{\bigcup Q_i\}} \text{ (DISJ)} \qquad \frac{\forall i \in I\,.\, \vdash \{P_i\}\, C\, \{Q_i\} \qquad I \neq \emptyset}{\vdash \{\bigcap P_i\}\, C\, \{\bigcap Q_i\}} \text{ (CONJ)}$$

Fig. 3. Inference Rules

The inference rules of the logic are given in Figure 3. Note that we are taking a significant presentation shortcut here in the inference rule for primitive commands. Specifically, we assume that we know the exact local action $[\![c]\!]$ of each primitive command c. This assumption makes sense when we define our own primitive commands, as we do in the logic of Section 3. However, in a more general setting, we might be provided with an opaque function along with a specification (precondition and postcondition) for the function. Since the function is opaque, we must consider it to be a primitive command in the abstract setting. Yet we do not know how it is implemented, so we do not know its precise local action. In [4], the authors provide a method for inferring a "best" local action from the function's specification. With a decent amount of technical development, we can do something similar here, using our stronger definition of locality. These details can be found in the technical report [5].

Given this assumption, we prove soundness and completeness of our abstract logic. The details of the proof can be found in our Coq implementation [5].

Theorem 1 (Soundness and Completeness).

$$\vdash \{P\}\, C\, \{Q\} \iff \models \{P\}\, C\, \{Q\}$$

5   Simplifying Separation Logic Metatheory

Now that we have an abstracted formalism of our behavior-preserving local actions, we will resolve each of the four metatheoretical issues described in Sec 1.

5.1   Footprints and Smallest Safe States

Consider a situation in which we are handed a program C along with a specification of what this program does. The specification consists of a set of axioms; each axiom has the form $\{P\}\, C\, \{Q\}$ for some precondition P and postcondition

Q. A common question to ask would be: is this specification *complete*? In other words, if the triple $\models \{P\} C \{Q\}$ is valid for some P and Q, then is it possible to derive $\vdash \{P\} C \{Q\}$ from the provided specification?

In standard Separation Logic, it can be extremely difficult to answer this question. In [12], the authors conduct an in-depth study of various conditions and circumstances under which it is possible to prove that certain specifications are complete. However, in the general case, there is no easy way to prove this.

We can show that under our assumption of behavior preservation, there is a very easy way to guarantee that a specification is complete. In particular, a specification that describes the exact behavior of C on all of its *smallest safe states* is always complete. Formally, a smallest safe state is a state σ such that $\neg \sigma [\![C]\!]$bad and, for all $\sigma' \prec \sigma$, $\sigma' [\![C]\!]$bad.

To see that such a specification may not be complete in standard Separation Logic, we borrow an example from [12]. Consider the program C, defined as $x := \mathtt{cons}(0); \mathtt{free}(x)$. This program simply allocates a single cell and then frees it. Under the standard model, the smallest safe states are those of the form $(s, \emptyset)$ for any store s. For simplicity, assume that the only variables in the store are x and y. Define the specification to be the infinite set of triples that have the following form, for any a, b in $\mathbb{Z}$, and any a' in $\mathbb{N}$:

$$\{x = a \wedge y = b \wedge \mathtt{emp}\} \, C \, \{x = a' \wedge y = b \wedge \mathtt{emp}\}$$

Note that a' must be in $\mathbb{N}$ because only valid unallocated memory addresses can be assigned into x. It should be clear that this specification describes the exact behavior on all smallest safe states of C. Now we claim that the following triple is valid, but there is no way to derive it from the specification.

$$\{x = a \wedge y = b \wedge y \mapsto -\} \, C \, \{x = a' \wedge y = b \wedge y \mapsto - \wedge a' \neq b\}$$

The triple is clearly valid because a' must be a memory address that was initially unallocated, while address b was initially allocated. Nevertheless, there will not be any way to derive this triple, even if we come up with new assertion syntax or inference rules. The behavior of C on the larger state is different from the behavior on the small one, but there is no way to recover this fact once we make C opaque. It can be shown (see [12]) that if we add triples of the above form to our specification, then we will obtain a complete specification for C. Yet there is no straightforward way to see that such a specification is complete.

We will now formally prove that, in our system, there is a canonical form for complete specification. We first note that we will need to assume that our set of states is well-founded with respect to the substate relation (i.e., there is no infinite strictly-decreasing chain of states). This assumption is true for most standard models of Separation Logic, and furthermore, there is no reason to intuitively believe that the smallest safe states should be able to provide a complete specification when the assumption is not true.

We say that a specification Ψ is *complete for C* if, whenever $\models \{P\} C \{Q\}$ is valid, the triple $\vdash \{P\} C \{Q\}$ is derivable using only the inference rules that are not specific to the structure of C (i.e., the frame, consequence, disjunction, and conjunction rules), plus the following axiom rule:

$$\frac{\{P\}\,C\,\{Q\} \in \Psi}{\vdash \{P\}\,C\,\{Q\}}$$

For any σ, let $\sigma[\![C]\!]$ denote the set of all σ' such that $\sigma[\![C]\!]\sigma'$. For any set of states S, we define a *canonical specification on* S as the set of triples of the form $\{\{\sigma\}\}\,C\,\{\sigma[\![C]\!]\}$ for any state $\sigma \in S$. If there exists a canonical specification on S that is complete for C, then we say that S forms a *footprint* for C. We can then prove the following theorem (see the extended TR):

Theorem 2. *For any program C, the set of all smallest safe states of C forms a footprint for C.*

Note that while this theorem guarantees that the canonical specification is complete, we may not actually be able to write down the specification simply because the assertion language is not expressive enough. This would be the case for the behavior-preserving nondeterministic memory allocator if we used the assertion language presented in Section 3. We could, however, express canonical specifications in that system by extending the assertion language to talk about the free list (as briefly discussed at the end of Section 3).

5.2   Data Refinement

In [6], the goal is to formalize the concept of having a concrete module correctly implement an abstract one, within the context of Separation Logic. Specifically, the authors prove that as long as a client program "behaves nicely," any execution of the program using the concrete module can be tracked to a corresponding execution using the abstract module. The client states in the corresponding executions are identical, so the proof shows that a well-behaved client cannot tell the difference between the concrete and abstract modules.

To get their proof to work out, the authors require two somewhat odd properties to hold. The first is called *contents independence*, and is an extra condition on top of the standard locality conditions. The second is called a *growing relation* — it refers to the relation connecting a state of the abstract module to its logically equivalent state(s) in the concrete module. All relations connecting the abstract and concrete modules in this way are required to be growing, which means that the domain of memory used by the abstract state must be a subset of that used by the concrete state. This is a somewhat unintuitive and restrictive requirement which is needed for purely technical reasons. We will show that behavior preservation completely eliminates the need for both contents independence and growing relations.

We now provide a formal setting for the data refinement theory. This formal setting is similar to the one in [6], but we will make some minor alterations to simplify the presentation. The programming language is defined as:

$$C \;::=\; \texttt{skip} \mid c \mid \texttt{m} \mid C_1 ; C_2 \mid \texttt{if } B \texttt{ then } C_1 \texttt{ else } C_2$$
$$\mid \texttt{while } B \texttt{ do } C$$

c is a primitive command (sometimes referred to as "client operation" in this context). m is a *module command* taken from an abstracted set **MOp** (e.g., a memory manager might implement the two module commands cons and free).

The abstracted client and module commands are assumed to have a semantics mapping them to particular local actions. We of course use our behavior-preserving notion of "local" here, whereas in [6], the authors use the three properties of safety monotonicity, the (backwards) frame property, and a new property called contents independence. It is trivial to show that behavior preservation implies contents independence, as contents independence is essentially a forwards frame property that can only be applied under special circumstances.

A *module* is a pair (p, η) representing a particular implementation of the module commands in **MOp**; the state predicate p describes the module's *invariant* (e.g., that a valid free list is stored starting at a location pointed to by a particular head pointer), while η is a function mapping each module command to a particular local action. The predicate p is required to be *precise* [11], meaning that no state can have more than one substate satisfying p (if a state σ does have a substate satisfying p, then we refer to that uniquely-defined state as σ_p). Additionally, all module operations are required to preserve the invariant p:

$$\neg\sigma(\eta\text{m})\text{bad} \wedge \sigma \in p * \text{true} \wedge \sigma(\eta\text{m})\sigma' \implies \sigma' \in p * \text{true}$$

We define a big-step operational semantics parameterized by a module (p, η). This semantics is fundamentally the same as the one defined in [6]; the extended TR contains the full details. The only aspect that is important to mention here is that the semantics is equipped with a special kind of faulting called "access violation." Intuitively, an access violation occurs when a client operation's execution depends on the module's portion of memory. More formally, it occurs when the client operation executes safely on a state where the module's memory is present (i.e., a state satisfying $p * \text{true}$), but faults when that memory is removed from the state.

The main theorem that we get out of this setup is a refinement simulation between a program being run in the presence of an abstract module (p, η), and the same program being run in the presence of a concrete module (q, μ) that implements the same module commands (i.e., $\lfloor \eta \rfloor = \lfloor \mu \rfloor$, where the floor notation indicates domain). Suppose we have a binary relation R relating states of the abstract module to those of the concrete module. For example, if our modules are memory managers, then R might relate a particular set of memory locations available for allocation to all lists containing that set of locations in some order. To represent that R relates abstract module states to concrete module states, we require that whenever $\sigma_1 R \sigma_2$, $\sigma_1 \in p$ and $\sigma_2 \in q$. Given this relation R, we can make use of the separating conjunction of Relational Separation Logic [14] and write $R * \text{Id}$ to indicate the relation relating any two states of the form $\sigma_p \cdot \sigma_c$ and $\sigma_q \cdot \sigma_c$, where $\sigma_p R \sigma_q$.

Now, for any module (p, η), let $C[(p, \eta)]$ be notation for the program C whose semantics have (p, η) filled in for the parameter module. Then our main theorem says that, if $\eta(f)$ simulates $\mu(f)$ under relation $R * \text{Id}$ for all $f \in \lfloor \eta \rfloor$, then for any program C, $C[(p, \eta)]$ also simulates $C[(q, \mu)]$ under relation $R * \mathtt{Id}$. More formally, say that C_1 simulates C_2 under relation R (written $R; C_2 \subseteq C_1; R$) when, for all σ_1, σ_2 such that $\sigma_1 R \sigma_2$:

1.) $\sigma_1 [\![C_1]\!] \mathtt{bad} \iff \sigma_2 [\![C_2]\!] \mathtt{bad}$,   and

2.) $\neg \sigma_1 [\![C_1]\!] \mathtt{bad} \implies (\forall \sigma_2' . \sigma_2 [\![C_2]\!] \sigma_2' \Rightarrow \exists \sigma_1' . \sigma_1 [\![C_1]\!] \sigma_1' \wedge \sigma_1' R \sigma_2')$

Theorem 3. *Suppose we have modules (p, η) and (q, μ) with $\lfloor \eta \rfloor = \lfloor \mu \rfloor$ and a refinement relation R as described above, such that $R * \mathtt{Id}; \mu(f) \subseteq \eta(f); R * \mathtt{Id}$ for all $f \in \lfloor \eta \rfloor$. Then, for any program C, $R * \mathtt{Id}; C[(q, \mu)] \subseteq C[(p, \eta)]; R * \mathtt{Id}$.*

While the full proof can be found in the extended TR, we will semi-formally describe here the one case that highlights why behavior preservation eliminates the need for contents independence and growing relations: when C is simply a client command c. We wish to prove that $C[(p, \eta)]$ simulates $C[(q, \mu)]$, so suppose we have related states σ_1 and σ_2, and executing c on σ_2 results in σ_2'. Since σ_1 and σ_2 are related by $R * \mathtt{Id}$, we have that $\sigma_1 = \sigma_p \cdot \sigma_c$ and $\sigma_2 = \sigma_q \cdot \sigma_c$. We know that (1) $\sigma_q \cdot \sigma_c \overset{c}{\to} \sigma_2'$, (2) c is local, and (3) c runs safely on σ_c because the client operation's execution must be independent of the module state σ_q; thus the backwards frame property tells us that $\sigma_2' = \sigma_q \cdot \sigma_c'$ and $\sigma_c \overset{c}{\to} \sigma_c'$. Now, if c is behavior-preserving, then we can simply apply the forwards frame property, framing on the state σ_p, to get that $\sigma_p \# \sigma_c'$ and $\sigma_p \cdot \sigma_c \overset{c}{\to} \sigma_p \cdot \sigma_c'$, completing the proof for this case. However, without behavior preservation, contents independence and growing relations are used in [6] to finish the proof. Specifically, because we know that $\sigma_q \cdot \sigma_c \overset{c}{\to} \sigma_q \cdot \sigma_c'$ and that c runs safely on σ_c, contents independence says that $\sigma \cdot \sigma_c \overset{c}{\to} \sigma \cdot \sigma_c'$ for any σ whose domain is a subset of the domain of σ_q. Therefore, we can choose $\sigma = \sigma_p$ because R is a growing relation.

5.3   Relational Separation Logic

Relational Separation Logic [14] allows for simple reasoning about the relationship between two executions. Instead of deriving triples $\{P\} C \{Q\}$, a user of the logic derives *quadruples* of the form:

$$\{R\} \begin{array}{c} C \\ \ \\ C' \end{array} \{S\}$$

R and S are binary relations on states, rather than unary predicates. Semantically, a quadruple says that if we execute the two programs in states that are related by R, then both executions are safe, and any termination states will be related by S. Furthermore, we want to be able to use this logic to prove program equivalence, so we also require that initial states related by R have the same divergence behavior. Formally, we say that the above quadruple is valid if, for any states σ_1, σ_2, σ_1', σ_2':

$$1.)\ \sigma_1 R \sigma_2 \implies \neg \sigma_1 [\![C]\!] \text{bad} \wedge \neg \sigma_2 [\![C']\!] \text{bad}$$
$$2.)\ \sigma_1 R \sigma_2 \implies (\sigma_1 [\![C]\!] \text{div} \iff \sigma_2 [\![C']\!] \text{div})$$
$$3.)\ \sigma_1 R \sigma_2 \wedge \sigma_1 [\![C]\!] \sigma_1' \wedge \sigma_2 [\![C']\!] \sigma_2' \implies \sigma_1' S \sigma_2'$$

Relational Separation Logic extends the separating conjunction to work for relations, breaking related states into disjoint, correspondingly-related pieces:

$$\sigma_1 (R * S) \sigma_2 \iff \exists\, \sigma_{1r},\, \sigma_{1s},\, \sigma_{2r},\, \sigma_{2s}\,.$$
$$\sigma_1 = \sigma_{1r} \cdot \sigma_{1s} \wedge \sigma_2 = \sigma_{2r} \cdot \sigma_{2s} \wedge \sigma_{1r} R \sigma_{2r} \wedge \sigma_{1s} S \sigma_{2s}$$

Just as Separation Logic has a frame rule for enabling local reasoning, Relational Separation Logic has a frame rule with the same purpose. This frame rule says that, given that we can derive the quadruple above involving R, S, C, and C', we can also derive the following quadruple for any relation T:

$$\{R * T\} \begin{array}{c} C \\ {} \\ C' \end{array} \{S * T\}$$

In [14], it is shown that the frame rule is sound when all programs are deterministic but it is unsound if nondeterministic programs are allowed, so this frame rule cannot be used when we have a nondeterministic memory allocator.

To deal with nondeterministic programs, a solution is proposed in [14], in which the interpretation of quadruples is strengthened. The new interpretation for a quadruple containing R, S, C, and C' is that, for any σ_1, σ_2, σ_1', σ_2', σ, σ':

$$1.)\ \sigma_1 R \sigma_2 \implies \neg \sigma_1 [\![C]\!] \text{bad} \wedge \neg \sigma_2 [\![C']\!] \text{bad}$$
$$2.)\ \sigma_1 R \sigma_2 \wedge \sigma_1 \# \sigma \wedge \sigma_2 \# \sigma' \implies ((\sigma_1 \cdot \sigma)[\![C]\!] \text{div} \iff (\sigma_2 \cdot \sigma')[\![C']\!] \text{div})$$
$$3.)\ \sigma_1 R \sigma_2 \wedge \sigma_1 [\![C]\!] \sigma_1' \wedge \sigma_2 [\![C']\!] \sigma_2' \implies \sigma_1' S \sigma_2'$$

Note that this interpretation is the same as before, except that the second property is strengthened to say that divergence behavior must be equivalent not only on the initial states, but also on any larger states. It can be shown that the frame rule becomes sound under this stronger interpretation of quadruples.

In our behavior-preserving setting, it is possible to use the simpler interpretation of quadruples without breaking soundness of the frame rule. We could prove this by directly proving frame rule soundness, but instead we will take a shorter route in which we show that, when actions are behavior-preserving, a quadruple is valid under the first interpretation above if and only if it is valid under the second interpretation — i.e., the two interpretations are the same in our setting. Since the frame rule is sound under the second interpretation, this implies that it will also be sound under the first interpretation.

Clearly, validity under the second interpretation implies validity under the first, since it is a direct strengthening. To prove the inverse, suppose we have a quadruple (involving R, S, C, and C') that is valid under the first interpretation. Properties 1 and 3 of the second interpretation are identical to those of the first, so all we need to show is that Property 2 holds. Suppose that $\sigma_1 R \sigma_2$, $\sigma_1 \# \sigma$, and $\sigma_2 \# \sigma'$. By Property 1 of the first interpretation, we know that $\neg \sigma_1 [\![C]\!] \text{bad}$ and $\neg \sigma_2 [\![C']\!] \text{bad}$. Therefore, Termination Equivalence tells us that $\sigma_1 [\![C]\!] \text{div} \iff (\sigma_1 \cdot \sigma) [\![C]\!] \text{div}$, and that $\sigma_2 [\![C']\!] \text{div} \iff (\sigma_2 \cdot \sigma') [\![C']\!] \text{div}$. Furthermore, we know by Property 2 of the first interpretation that $\sigma_1 [\![C]\!] \text{div} \iff \sigma_2 [\![C']\!] \text{div}$. Hence we obtain our desired result.

In case the reader is curious, the reason that the frame rule under the first interpretation is sound when all programs are deterministic is simply that determinism (along with standard locality) implies Termination Equivalence. A proof of this can be found in the extended TR.

5.4   Finite Memory

Since standard locality allows the program state to increase during execution, it does not play nicely with a model in which memory is finite. Consider any command that grows the program state in some way. Such a command is safe on the empty state but, if we extend this empty state to the larger state consisting of all available memory, then the command becomes unsafe. Hence such a command violates Safety Monotonicity.

There is one commonly-used solution for supporting finite memory without enforcing behavior preservation: say that, instead of faulting on the state consisting of all of memory, a state-growing command diverges. Furthermore, to satisfy Termination Monotonicity, we also need to allow the command to diverge on *any* state. The downside of this solution, therefore, is that it is only reasonable when we are not interested in the termination behavior of programs.

When behavior preservation is enforced, we no longer have any issues with finite memory models because program state cannot increase during execution. The initial state is obviously contained within the finite memory, so all states reachable through execution must also be contained within memory.

6   Related Work and Conclusions

The definition of locality (or local action), which enables the frame rule, plays a critical role in Separation Logic [8,13,15]. Almost all versions of Separation Logic — including their concurrent [3,10,4], higher-order [2], and relational [14] variants, as well as mechanized implementation (e.g., [1]) — have always used the same locality definition that matches the well-known Safety and Termination Monotonicity properties and the Frame Property [15].

In this paper, we argued a case for strengthening the definition of locality to enforce *behavior preservation*. This means that the behavior of a program when executed on a small state is identical to the behavior when executed on a larger state — put another way, excess, unused state cannot have any effect on program behavior. We showed that this change can be made to have no effect on the usage of Separation Logic, and we gave multiple examples of how it simplifies reasoning about metatheoretical properties.

Determinism Constancy. One related work that calls for comparison is the property of "Determinism Constancy" presented by Raza and Gardner [12], which is also a strengthening of locality. While they use a slightly different notion of action than we do, it can be shown that Determinism Constancy, when translated into our context (and ignoring divergence behaviors), is logically equivalent to:

$$\sigma_0 \llbracket C \rrbracket \sigma_0' \wedge \sigma_0' \# \sigma_1 \implies \sigma_0 \# \sigma_1 \wedge (\sigma_0 \cdot \sigma_1) \llbracket C \rrbracket (\sigma_0' \cdot \sigma_1)$$

For comparison, we repeat our Forwards Frame Property here:

$$\sigma_0 \llbracket C \rrbracket \sigma_0' \wedge \sigma_0 \# \sigma_1 \implies \sigma_0' \# \sigma_1 \wedge (\sigma_0 \cdot \sigma_1) \llbracket C \rrbracket (\sigma_0' \cdot \sigma_1)$$

While our strengthening of locality prevents programs from increasing state during execution, Determinism Constancy prevents programs from *decreasing* state. The authors use Determinism Constancy to prove the same property regarding footprints that we proved in Section 5.1. Note that, while behavior preservation does not imply Determinism Constancy, our concrete logic of Section 3 does have the property since it never decreases state (we chose to have the `free` command put the deallocated cell back onto the free list, rather than get rid of it entirely).

While Determinism Constancy is strong enough to prove the footprint property, it does not provide behavior preservation — an execution on a small state can still become invalid on a larger state. Thus it will not, for example, help in resolving the dilemma of growing relations in the data refinement theory. Due to the lack of behavior preservation, we do not expect the property to have a significant impact on the metatheory as a whole. Note, however, that there does not seem to be any harm in using *both* behavior preservation and Determinism Constancy. The two properties together enforce that the area of memory accessible to a program be constant throughout execution.

Module Reasoning. Besides our discussion of data refinement in Section 5.2, there has been some previous work on reasoning about modules and their implementations. In [11], a "Hypothetical Frame Rule" is used to allow modular reasoning when a module's implementation is hidden from the rest of the code. In [2], a higher-order frame rule is used to allow reasoning in a higher-order language with hidden module or function code. However, neither of these works discuss relational reasoning between different modules. We are not aware of any relational logic for reasoning about modules.

Acknowledgements. We thank Xinyu Feng and anonymous referees for suggestions and comments on an earlier version of this paper. This material is based on research sponsored by DARPA under agreement numbers FA8750-10-2-0254 and FA8750-12-2-0293, and by NSF grants CNS-0910670, CNS-0915888, and CNS-1065451. The U.S. Government is authorized to reproduce and distribute reprints for Governmental purposes notwithstanding any copyright notation thereon. The views and conclusions contained herein are those of the

authors and should not be interpreted as necessarily representing the official
policies or endorsements, either expressed or implied, of these agencies.

References

1. Appel, A.W., Blazy, S.: Separation Logic for Small-Step Cminor. In: Schneider, K.,
   Brandt, J. (eds.) TPHOLs 2007. LNCS, vol. 4732, pp. 5–21. Springer, Heidelberg
   (2007)
2. Birkedal, L., Torp-Smith, N., Yang, H.: Semantics of separation-logic typing and
   higher-order frame rules. In: Proc. 20th IEEE Symp. on Logic in Computer Science,
   pp. 260–269 (2005)
3. Brookes, S.: A Semantics for Concurrent Separation Logic. In: Gardner, P.,
   Yoshida, N. (eds.) CONCUR 2004. LNCS, vol. 3170, pp. 16–34. Springer, Heidelberg (2004)
4. Calcagno, C., O'Hearn, P.W., Yang, H.: Local action and abstract separation logic.
   In: 22nd Annual IEEE Symposium on Logic in Computer Science, LICS 2007,
   pp. 366–378 (July 2007)
5. Costanzo, D., Shao, Z.: A case for behavior-preserving actions in separation logic.
   Technical report, Dept. of Computer Science, Yale University, New Haven, CT
   (June 2012), http://flint.cs.yale.edu/publications/bpsl.html
6. Filipovic, I., O'Hearn, P.W., Torp-Smith, N., Yang, H.: Blaming the client: on data
   refinement in the presence of pointers. Formal Asp. Comput. 22(5), 547–583 (2010)
7. Huet, G., Paulin-Mohring, C., et al.: The Coq proof assistant reference manual.
   The Coq release v6.3.1 (May 2000)
8. Ishtiaq, S., O'Hearn, P.W.: BI as an assertion language for mutable data structures. In: Proc. 28th ACM Symposium on Principles of Programming Languages,
   pp. 14–26 (January 2001)
9. Kernighan, B.W., Ritchie, D.M.: The C Programming Language, 2nd edn. Prentice
   Hall (1988)
10. O'Hearn, P.W.: Resources, Concurrency and Local Reasoning. In: Gardner, P.,
    Yoshida, N. (eds.) CONCUR 2004. LNCS, vol. 3170, pp. 49–67. Springer, Heidel-
    berg (2004)
11. O'Hearn, P.W., Yang, H., Reynolds, J.C.: Separation and information hiding. ACM
    Trans. Program. Lang. Syst. 31(3), 1–50 (2009)
12. Raza, M., Gardner, P.: Footprints in local reasoning. Journal of Logical Methods
    in Computer Science 5(2) (2009)
13. Reynolds, J.C.: Separation logic: A logic for shared mutable data structures. In:
    Proc. 17th IEEE Symp. on Logic in Computer Science, pp. 55–74 (July 2002)
14. Yang, H.: Relational separation logic. Theor. Comput. Sci. 375(1-3), 308–334 (2007)
15. Yang, H., O'Hearn, P.W.: A Semantic Basis for Local Reasoning. In: Nielsen, M.,
    Engberg, U. (eds.) FOSSACS 2002. LNCS, vol. 2303, pp. 402–416. Springer, Hei-
    delberg (2002)

A Generic Cyclic Theorem Prover

James Brotherston[1], Nikos Gorogiannis[1], and Rasmus L. Petersen[2]

[1] Dept. of Computer Science, University College London
[2] Microsoft Research Cambridge

Abstract. We describe the design and implementation of an automated theorem prover realising a fully general notion of *cyclic proof*. Our tool, called CYCLIST, is able to construct proofs obeying a very general cycle scheme in which leaves may be linked to any other matching node in the proof, and to verify the general, global infinitary condition on such proof objects ensuring their soundness. CYCLIST is based on a new, generic theory of cyclic proofs that can be instantiated to a wide variety of logics. We have developed three such concrete instantiations, based on: (a) first-order logic with inductive definitions; (b) entailments of pure separation logic; and (c) Hoare-style termination proofs for pointer programs. Experiments run on these instantiations indicate that CYCLIST offers significant potential as a future platform for inductive theorem proving.

1 Introduction

In program analysis, *inductive definitions* are essential for specifying the shape of complex data structures held in memory. Thus automated reasoning about such definitions, a.k.a. *inductive theorem proving*, is a key activity supporting program verification. Unfortunately, the explicit induction rules employed in standard inductive proofs pose considerable problems for proof search [10]. *Cyclic proof* has been recently proposed as an alternative to traditional proof by explicit induction for fixed point logics. In contrast to standard proofs, which are simply derivation trees, a cyclic proof is a derivation tree with "back-links" (see Figure 1), subject to a global soundness condition ensuring that the proof can be read as a proof by *infinite descent* à la Fermat [5]. This allows explicit induction rules to be dropped in favour of simple unfolding or "case split" rules.

Cyclic proof systems seem to have first arisen in computer science as tableaux for the propositional modal μ-calculus [23]. Since then, cyclic proof systems have been proposed for a number of applications, including: first-order μ-calculus [22]; verifying properties of concurrent processes [20]; first-order logic with inductive definitions [4,9], bunched logic [6]; and termination of pointer programs [7]. However, despite the fairly rich variety of formal cyclic proof systems, automated tools implementing these formal systems remain very thin on the ground.

In this paper we describe the design and implementation of a new cyclic theorem prover, called CYCLIST, based on a generic theory of cyclic proofs and instantiable to a wide variety of logical systems. We have implemented three concrete instantiations of CYCLIST: (a) a system for a fragment of first-order

R. Jhala and A. Igarashi (Eds.): APLAS 2012, LNCS 7705, pp. 350–367, 2012.

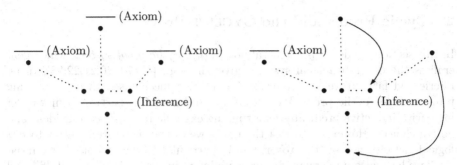

Fig. 1. Left: a typical proof structured as a finite tree, with the parent-child relation between nodes (•) given by a set of inference rules. Right: a typical *cyclic pre-proof*, structured as a tree proof with "back-links" between nodes (shown as arrows).

logic with inductive definitions, based on the formal system in [4]; (b) a system for entailment in separation logic, extending the one in [8]; and (c) a Hoare-style system for termination of pointer programs using separation logic, based on [7].

In Section 2, we give our general cyclic proof framework and, in parallel, discuss our implementation of CYCLIST using its instantiation (a) to first-order logic as a running example.

As above, cyclic proofs can be generally characterised as derivation trees with back-links ("pre-proofs") obeying a global, infinitary soundness condition qualifying them as *bona fide* cyclic proofs. The soundness condition states that every infinite path in the pre-proof must possess a syntactic *trace* that "progresses" infinitely often; informally, a trace can be thought of as a well-founded measure and its progress points to strict decreases in this measure. Our generic theory formalises this characterisation of cyclic proofs, which is entirely independent of the choice of any particular logical formalism.

There are two main technical obstacles to implementation of cyclic proof, both stemming from the structural complexity of cyclic proofs compared to standard proofs. First, the prover must be able to form back-links in the derivation tree. This inevitably leads to a *global* view of proofs, rather than one localised to the current subgoal as in most theorem provers. Second, the prover must be able to check whether or not a given pre-proof satisfies the general soundness condition. Our approach to both difficulties is described in Section 2.

Section 3 briefly describes our instantiations (b) and (c) of CYCLIST to separation logic frameworks. Then, in Section 4, we examine some of the issues pertaining to automated proof search in CYCLIST, and report on our experimental evaluation of the prover's performance in all three instantiations. Particular issues for cyclic proof search include looking for potential back-links in the proof, and deciding when to invoke the (potentially expensive) soundness check. Other issues, such as the priority ordering of rules and the conjecture / application of appropriate lemmas during a proof, are features of inductive theorem proving in general. Finally, Section 5 compares our contribution with related work, and Section 6 outlines directions for future work.

The theoretical framework on cyclic proofs in Section 2 is based on its earlier presentation in the first author's PhD thesis [5].

2   Cyclic Proofs and the CYCLIST Prover

In this section we develop a general notion of a *cyclic proof system*, which generalises the concrete formal systems given in, e.g., [4,6,7,8,20,21,22,23]. In an interleaved fashion we also describe CYCLIST, a mechanised theorem proving framework for cyclic proof. We use its instantiation CYCLIST$_{FO}$ to first-order logic with inductive predicates as a running example to illustrate our ideas and design choices. However, most of the issues we discuss here are relevant to *any* logical instantiation of the prover, and in particular to the two other instantiations we have also implemented: pure entailment in separation logic (cf. [8]) and termination of pointer programs based on separation logic (cf. [7]). In order to avoid overwhelming the reader with technical details, we intentionally elide some finer points of our implementation to begin with, and introduce these gradually as we go along.

2.1   Implementation Platform

The core of CYCLIST is an OCaml functor parameterised over a user-defined datatype that describes the desired logic and its basic rules of inference. The functor provides functions for proof search and basic manipulation of cyclic proofs. CYCLIST also provides an OCaml interface to a custom model checker in C++ that checks the soundness of cyclic proofs.

In contrast to e.g. [8], we decided against implementing CYCLIST inside a theorem prover such as Isabelle or HOL Light. This is because the structural machinery of cyclic proof cannot be straightforwardly represented inside a tool employing a standard, tree-like internal notion of proof. Consequently, as in [8], a *deep embedding* of cyclic proof systems would be necessary, whereby cyclic proofs are represented as explicit datatypes, and reasoned about using functions defined over those datatypes. In addition to its technical difficulty, this approach negates most of the advantages of using a trusted theorem prover, as correctness depends fundamentally on the (unproven) correctness of the deep embedding as well as the correctness of the external soundness checker. Thus we gain implementation efficiency at relatively little expense of confidence by working directly in OCaml.

2.2   Sequents and Inference Rules

First, we assume a set S of objects, corresponding to the '•'s in Figure 1 and called *sequents*, from which our proofs will be built. Next we assume a set R of *proof rules* which are each of the form:

$$\frac{S_1 \ldots S_n}{S} \ (R)$$

where $n \geq 0$ and $S, S_1, \ldots, S_n$ are sequents. S is called the *conclusion* of rule (R) and $S_1, \ldots, S_n$ its *premises*; a rule with no premises is called an *axiom*. (Strictly speaking, the rules are usually understood as rule schemata, where parts of sequents may act as parameters.) A *derivation tree* is then, as usual, a tree each of whose nodes v is labelled with a sequent $S(v)$, and the rule $R(v)$ of which it is the conclusion, in such a way as to respect the proof rules.

CYCLIST expects a user-defined type for sequents, and for inference rules, each of which reduces a given conclusion sequent to a list of premises. However, because rules are really *rule schemata*, a rule may have multiple different applications to a sequent. To support this, rules in CYCLIST return a *list* of lists of premises, corresponding to the results of all possible applications of the rule to the sequent. In particular, axioms always return a list of empty lists of premises.

In CYCLIST$_{FO}$, we define a type for negation-free $\forall\exists$-sequents in disjunctive normal form, built from first-order formulas with equality and disequality, function terms and inductively defined predicates. It is straightforward to define standard rules and axioms for handling equalities, contradiction, simplification, quantifiers and conjunction / disjunction.

2.3 Inductive Predicates and Unfolding Rules

Inductive predicates are specified by a set of *inductive rules* each of the form $F \Rightarrow Pt$, where P is an inductive predicate, $\mathbf{t}$ is a tuple of appropriately many terms and F is a formula (subject to certain restrictions to ensure monotonicity of the definitions).

Example 1. We can define a "natural number" predicate N, mutually defined "even / odd" predicates E and O, and a ternary "addition" predicate Add (where $Add(x, y, z)$ should be read as "$x + y = z$") via the following inductive rules:

$$\Rightarrow N0 \qquad \Rightarrow E0 \qquad Ny \Rightarrow Add(0, y, y)$$
$$Nx \Rightarrow Nsx \qquad Ox \Rightarrow Esx \qquad Add(x, y, z) \Rightarrow Add(sx, y, sz)$$
$$Ex \Rightarrow Osx$$

where 0 is a constant symbol and s is a unary function symbol, understood as the usual zero and "successor" function in Peano arithmetic respectively. □

Given a set of inductive rules, CYCLIST$_{FO}$ generates rules for unfolding inductive predicates on the right and left of sequents. As usual, the right-unfolding rules for a predicate P are just sequent versions of the inductive rules introducing P.

Example 2. Applying the right-unfolding rule corresponding to $Nx \Rightarrow Nsx$ from Example 1 to the conclusion sequent $F \vdash Nsy, Nssz$[1] yields:

$$\frac{\left[[F \vdash Ny, Nssz] \; ; \; [F \vdash Nsy, Nsz] \right]}{F \vdash Nsy, Nssz} \; (R_N)$$

Note the bracketing indicating the two possible applications of this rule (we use ';' to separate list items), each resulting in a single premise sequent. □

---

[1] As usual in sequent calculi, comma corresponds to ∧ in the LHS and ∨ in the RHS.

The left-unfolding rule for an inductive predicate can be seen as a *case distinction* principle that replaces an inductive predicate in the left of a conclusion sequent with a premise for every clause of its definition.

Example 3. Applying the left-unfolding rule for the predicate E given in Example 1 to the conclusion sequent $Ey \vdash G$ yields the following:

$$\frac{[\,[\,y = 0 \vdash G \,;\, y = sz, Oz \vdash G\,]\,]}{Ey \vdash G} (L_E)$$

where z is a fresh variable. Observe that, in this case, there is only one possible application of the rule which results in two premises. □

2.4   Cyclic Proofs and the Forming of Back-Links

We first define cyclic pre-proofs below. Here, a leaf of a derivation tree is called *open* if it is not the conclusion of an axiom, i.e. if $R(v)$ is undefined.

Definition 1 (Pre-proof). A *pre-proof* of a sequent S is a pair $(\mathcal{D}, \mathcal{L})$, where $\mathcal{D}$ is a finite derivation tree whose root is labelled by S, and $\mathcal{L}$ is a *back-link function* assigning to every open leaf ℓ of $\mathcal{D}$ a node $\mathcal{L}(\ell)$ of $\mathcal{D}$ such that $S(\mathcal{L}(\ell)) = S(\ell)$.

  Any pre-proof $\mathcal{P} = (\mathcal{D}, \mathcal{L})$ can be understood as a graph by identifying each open leaf ℓ of $\mathcal{D}$ with $\mathcal{L}(\ell)$. A *path* in $\mathcal{P}$ is an infinite sequence v_i of nodes of $\mathcal{P}$ such that for every i, either (y_i, y_{i+1}) is an edge in $\mathcal{D}$, or $\mathcal{L}(v_i) = v_{i+1}$.

According to Definition 1, a back-link in a cyclic pre-proof is formed by assigning to a leaf ℓ in the derivation tree another node $\mathcal{L}(\ell)$ such that $S(\ell) = S(\mathcal{L}(\ell))$. CYCLIST relaxes this strict requirement slightly and permits back-links between a leaf node S_1 and any other node S_2 such that a user-defined *matching function* returns true, given S_1, S_2 as arguments.[2]

  In CYCLIST$_{\text{FO}}$, we use the following matching function: S_1 matches S_2 if S_1 is derivable from S_2 using only weakening and substitution principles.

Example 4. In CYCLIST$_{\text{FO}}$, the sequent S_1 below matches S_2 because there is a derivation of S_1 from S_2 using weakening and substitution principles, as follows:

$$\frac{\dfrac{\mathbf{S_2}:\;\; Oy \vdash Ny}{Osz \vdash Nsz}\text{(Subst)}}{\mathbf{S_1}:\;\; Osz, Essz, Ez \vdash Nsz, Ny}\text{(Weak)}$$

Thus a leaf labelled by S_1 can be back-linked to any node labelled by S_2. □

---

[2] One could also simply include a rule allowing one to conclude S_1 from S_2 whenever S_1 matches S_2, but our treatment is typically more convenient for proof search.

2.5   Defining the Trace Pair Function

To qualify as a *bona fide* proof, a cyclic pre-proof must satisfy a global soundness condition, defined using the notion of a *trace* along a path in a pre-proof.

Definition 2 (Trace). Let $\mathcal{T}$ be a set of *trace values*. A *trace pair function* is a function $\delta : (\mathcal{S} \times \mathcal{R} \times \mathcal{S}) \to \mathrm{Pow}((\mathcal{T} \times \mathcal{T} \times \{0,1\}))$ (where $\mathrm{Pow}(-)$ is powerset) such that for any $S, S' \in \mathcal{S}$ and $R \in \mathcal{R}$, the set $\delta(S, R, S')$ is finite (and computable). If $(\alpha, \alpha', n) \in \delta(S, R, S')$ for some $n \in \{0,1\}$ then (α, α') is said to be a *trace pair* for (S, R, S'), and if $n = 1$ then (α, α') is said to be a *progressing trace pair*.

Now let $\pi = (v_i)_{i \geq 0}$ be a path in a pre-proof $\mathcal{P}$. A *trace following* π is a sequence $\tau = (\alpha_i)_{i \geq 0}$ such that, for all $i \geq 0$, (α_i, α_{i+1}) is a trace pair for $(S(v_i), R(v_i), S(v_{i+1}))$. If infinitely many of these (α_i, α_{i+1}) are progressing trace pairs, then τ is said to be *infinitely progressing*.

Since we are only interested in traces following paths in a pre-proof, we may assume for simplicity that the domain of a trace pair function δ, written $\mathrm{dom}(\delta)$, is restricted to triples (S, R, S') such that S is the conclusion of an instance of the rule R and S' is one of the premises of that instance. Given such a δ, the tuple $(\mathcal{S}, \mathcal{R}, \mathcal{T}, \delta)$ is then called a *cyclic proof system*.

In order to facilitate checking the global soundness condition, CYCLIST requires pre-proofs to carry information about trace pairs. According to Defn. 2, a *trace pair function* δ takes as input a sequent S, the rule R applied to it and one of the premises S' obtained as a result, and returns the sets of associated *progressing* and *non-progressing* trace pairs. Intuitively, a progressing trace pair identifies a measure that becomes strictly smaller when moving from S to S' under the application of R, while a non-progressing trace pair identifies a measure that at least does not increase. (Defn. 5 below will make precise the correspondence between trace pairs and measures.)

In CYCLIST$_{FO}$, we adopt the notion of trace from [4,5]. There, trace values are atomic formulas of the form Pt occurring on the left of sequents, where P is an inductive predicate. Then (Pt, Qt') is a progressing trace pair on (S, R, S') if R is a left-unfolding rule, Pt is the formula in S being unfolded and Qt' is obtained in S' by unfolding Pt. (Pt, Qt') is a non-progressing trace pair if Pt and Qt' occur on the left of S and S' respectively and $Pt \equiv Qt'$, where the equivalence is equality modulo any substitution applied by the rule R.

To implement this notion in CYCLIST$_{FO}$, each atomic formula Pt in the left of a sequent is annotated with a natural number, called its *tag*. Then for any conclusion sequent S and rule R we use these tags to attach to each premise S' the lists of progressing and non-progressing trace pairs associated with (S, R, S'). Similarly, matching functions are also required to return lists of (usually non-progressing) trace pairs for matching sequents.

Example 5. The following example shows how the premises of an instance of (L_E) are extended with lists of progressing and non-progressing trace pairs (in that order), where the numeric subscripts on atomic formulas are tags:

$$\frac{[\,[\,(N_1x, y = 0 \vdash G, [], [(1,1)]) \;;\; (N_1x, y = sz, O_3z \vdash G, [(2,3)], [(1,1)])\,]\,]}{N_1x, E_2y \vdash G} \,(L_E)$$

Thus, in the right hand premise, the first list indicates that $(2,3)$, denoting the formulas E_2y in the conclusion and O_3y in the premise, is a progressing trace pair, and the second list indicates that $(1,1)$, denoting the formulas N_1x occurring in both conclusion and premise, is a non-progressing trace pair. The left hand premise is similar, except that there are no progressing trace pairs. □

2.6   Soundness of Cyclic Proofs and Decision Procedures

It is clear that a pre-proof may not be sound, e.g., a sequent back-linked to itself. The following definition captures a sufficient condition of soundness.

Definition 3 (Cyclic proof). A pre-proof $\mathcal{P}$ in a cyclic proof system is said to be a *(cyclic) proof* if, for every infinite path $(v_i)_{i \geq 0}$ in $\mathcal{P}$, there is a tail of the path, $\pi = (v_i)_{i \geq n}$, such that there is an infinitely progressing trace following π.

Our trace-based condition qualifying pre-proofs as proofs follows the one by Sprenger and Dam [21], who showed that their trace condition for the first-order μ-calculus subsumed a number of previous formulations by others. Analogous trace conditions were adopted for other logics in [4,6,7]. Sprenger and Dam also established that their trace condition was decidable, a result we extend to the generic notion of trace given by Defn. 2.

Theorem 4 (Decidability of soundness condition). *In any cyclic proof system* $(\mathcal{S}, \mathcal{R}, \mathcal{T}, \delta)$ *it is decidable whether or not a pre-proof is a cyclic proof.*

Proof. (Sketch) From a given pre-proof $\mathcal{P}$ we construct two Büchi automata over strings of nodes of $\mathcal{P}$. The *path automaton* $\mathcal{A}_{Path}$ simply accepts all infinite paths in $\mathcal{P}$. The *trace automaton* $\mathcal{A}_{Trace}$ accepts all infinite paths in $\mathcal{P}$ such that an infinitely progressing trace exists on some tail of the path. $\mathcal{P}$ is then a proof if and only if $\mathcal{A}_{Trace}$ accepts all strings accepted by $\mathcal{A}_{Path}$. We are then done since inclusion between the languages of Büchi automata is known to be decidable. The full details appear as Appendix A of [5]. □

Checking that a pre-proof $\mathcal{P}$ satisfies the soundness condition on cyclic proofs (Defn. 3) amounts to checking language inclusion between two Büchi automata $\mathcal{A}_{Path}$ and $\mathcal{A}_{Trace}$ constructed from $\mathcal{P}$ (see the proof of Theorem 4). We implement this check as a function that, given a CYCLIST pre-proof, constructs the two automata and then uses a model checker to decide language inclusion.

We use *transition-labelled* Büchi automata [11] in constructing $\mathcal{A}_{Path}$ and $\mathcal{A}_{Trace}$, as they allow the most succinct representation. We represent such an automaton as a directed graph with labelled edges, where (u, v, l, n) with $n \in \{0, 1\}$ describes an edge from u to v accepting the label l. The automaton accepts any infinite string of labels such that edges with $n = 1$ are visited infinitely often. The path automaton $\mathcal{A}_{Path}$ accepts all infinite paths in $\mathcal{P}$, and thus it has an edge $(u, v, v, 1)$ for every edge (u, v) of $\mathcal{P}$ (viewing $\mathcal{P}$ as a graph in the obvious way). The trace automaton $\mathcal{A}_{Trace}$ is more complicated, and built using both the node identifiers of $\mathcal{P}$ and the trace pair information attached to rule instances as described above. Essentially, $\mathcal{A}_{Trace}$ accepts any infinite path through $\mathcal{P}$ that eventually (a) is decorated with trace values that agree with the trace pair function and (b) goes through a progressing trace pair infinitely often. Thus, in particular, $\mathcal{A}_{Trace}$ contains an edge $((u, \alpha_1), (v, \alpha_2), v, n)$ whenever (u, v) is an edge of $\mathcal{P}$ and (α_1, α_2) is a trace pair annotating the corresponding rule instance in $\mathcal{P}$, with $n = 1$ if (α_1, α_2) is progressing and $n = 0$ otherwise. For full details of the construction, see Appendix A of [5].

Our model checker is built using Spot [13], an open-source C++ library for building custom, on-the-fly model checkers. We also provide an OCaml interface between CYCLIST and the model-checking C++ code.

Checking inclusion between Büchi automata is computationally expensive, as it entails complementing one of the automata, which can lead to an explosion in the number of states [15]. Thus readers may wonder whether the general infinitary soundness condition on cyclic proofs ought to be discarded in favour of a stronger but simpler condition. The following (admittedly artificial) example is intended to show that a fairly complex proof condition is in fact needed.

Example 6. Define a binary predicate R via the following inductive rules:

$$\Rightarrow R(0, y) \qquad R(x, 0) \Rightarrow R(sx, 0) \qquad R(ssx, y) \Rightarrow R(sx, sy)$$

The following is a cyclic proof of the sequent $Nx, Ny \vdash R(x, y)$, where N is the natural number predicate defined in Example 1 (for brevity, we omit applications of equality rules, contraction and weakening):

$$
\cfrac{
  \cfrac{\vdash R(0, y)}{\ }(R_R) \qquad
  \cfrac{
    \cfrac{
      \cfrac{(*)\ \overline{Nx}, N\underline{y} \vdash R(x, y)}{\overline{Nx'}, \underline{N0} \vdash R(x', 0)}(\text{Subst})
    }{\overline{Nx'}, \underline{N0} \vdash R(sx', 0)}(R_R)
    \qquad
    \cfrac{
      \cfrac{
        \cfrac{(*)\ Nx, N\underline{y} \vdash R(x, y)}{Nssx', N\underline{y'} \vdash R(ssx', y')}(\text{Subst})
      }{Nx', Ny' \vdash R(ssx', y')}(\text{Cut})
    }{
      \cfrac{Nx', Ny' \vdash R(sx', sy')}{\ }(R_R)
    }(L_N)
  }{\overline{Nx'}, N\underline{y} \vdash R(sx', y)}
}{(*)\ \overline{Nx}, N\underline{y} \vdash R(x, y)}(L_N)
$$

where we suppress the easy proof that $Nx' \vdash Nssx'$ in the instance of (Cut) on the right hand branch. The leaves marked (*) are both back-linked to the root.

To see that this pre-proof is in fact a cyclic proof, we must show that any infinite path π has a tail on which an infinitely progressing trace exists. There are two cases to consider. First, if π has a tail consisting entirely of repetitions of the left-hand loop, then we can form a trace following this tail given by the overlined formulas, which progresses (infinitely often) at the first application of (L_N). Otherwise, π must traverse the right-hand loop infinitely often (and might also traverse the left-hand loop infinitely often). In that case, we can form a trace following π given by the underlined formulas, which progresses (infinitely often) at the second application of (L_N). $\square$

CYCLIST$_{\text{FO}}$ is in fact capable of proving the above example. We note that the overlapping of cycles in this example is essentially unavoidable, and that we are forced to select different traces for the left-hand cycle depending on the order in which these overlapping cycles are traversed. Thus, the proof condition cannot be restated in this case as a simpler property to be satisfied by each cycle individually. However, this proof does satisfy Brotherston's condition of having a "trace manifold", which is stated in terms of connected sets of cycles [4,5].

2.7   Soundness of Cyclic Proof Systems

Although our implementation of cyclic proof naturally deals only with the syntactic notion of provability given by Defn. 3, we shall nevertheless outline here how soundness of a cyclic proof system may be established. We assume a set $\mathcal{I}$ of *interpretations* of sequents, which are functions from $\mathcal{S}$ into {true, false}; we write $I \models S$ to mean $I(S) = \text{true}$. S is called *valid* if $I \models S$ for all $I \in \mathcal{I}$.

Definition 5 (Ordinal trace function). An *ordinal trace function* for a cyclic proof system $(\mathcal{S}, \mathcal{R}, \mathcal{T}, \delta)$ and interpretations $\mathcal{I}$ is a function $\sigma : (\mathcal{T} \times \mathcal{I}) \to \mathcal{O}$, where $\mathcal{O}$ is an initial segment of the ordinals, satisfying the following conditions for all $I \in \mathcal{I}$ and $S \in \mathcal{S}$:

$$\text{if } I \not\models S \text{ then } \exists S' \in \mathcal{S}, R \in \mathcal{R}, I' \in \mathcal{I}.$$
$$I' \not\models S' \text{ and } (S, R, S') \in \text{dom}(\delta) \text{ and}$$
$$\text{if } (\alpha, \alpha', n) \in \delta(S, R, S') \text{ then } \begin{cases} \sigma(\alpha', I') \leq \sigma(\alpha, I) & \text{if } n = 0 \\ \sigma(\alpha', I') < \sigma(\alpha, I) & \text{if } n = 1 \end{cases}$$

We note that the existence of an ordinal trace function subsumes local soundness of the proof rules, because of the requirement in Definition 5 that falsifiability of the conclusion of a rule implies falsifiability of one of its premises.

   In the case of first-order logic, it is well known that an inductive predicate P can be generated semantically via a chain of ordinal-indexed *approximants* $(P^\gamma)_{\gamma \geq 0}$. Here, given a suitable interpretation I the ordinal trace function $\sigma(Pt, I)$ returns the smallest γ such that $I \models P^\gamma t$. See e.g. [5,4,9] for details.

Theorem 6 (Soundness). *Suppose there exists an ordinal trace function for* $(\mathcal{S}, \mathcal{R}, \mathcal{T}, \delta)$ *and* $\mathcal{I}$. *Then, if* S *has a cyclic proof, then* S *is valid.*

Proof. (Sketch) Let $\mathcal{P}$ be a cyclic proof of S, and suppose for contradiction that $I \not\models S$. Using local soundness of the rules, we can construct an infinite path $\pi = (v_j)_{j \geq 0}$ in $\mathcal{P}$ and an infinite sequence $(I_j)_{j \geq 0}$ of interpretations such that $I_j \not\models S(v_j)$ for all $j \geq 0$. Since $\mathcal{P}$ is a cyclic proof, there exists an infinitely progressing trace $(\alpha_j)_{j \geq n}$ following some tail $(v_j)_{j \geq n}$ of π. It follows from

```
applyrule(rule,proof,node) :                          proofsearch(bound,proof,node) :
begin                                                 begin
  result := [];                                         if closed(node) then return proof;
  applications := rule(node);                           if bound=0 then return nil;
  foreach subgoallist in applications do                foreach rule in ruleset do
    (proof',subgoalnodes) :=                               if rule is a matching function then
      replacenode(proof, node, subgoallist, rule);           results := backlink(rule, proof, node);
    result := (proof',subgoalnodes) :: result;          else
  end                                                       results := applyrule(rule, proof, node);
  return result;                                         end
end                                                     foreach (proof', subgoalnodes) in results do
                                                          p' := proof';
backlink (matchfun,proof,node) :                          foreach node' in subgoalnodes do
begin                                                       p' := proofsearch(bound-1,p',node');
  result := [];                                             if p'=nil then break;
  foreach node' in proof do                               end
    if matchfun node node' then                           if p'=nil then return nil else return p';
      proof' := linknode(proof,node,node',matchfun);    end
      if sound(proof') then result := (proof', []) :: result;   end
    end                                               end
  end
  return result;
end
```

Fig. 2. Pseudocode for proof search in CYCLIST

Definition 5 that the sequence $(\sigma(\alpha_j, I_j))_{\alpha \geq n}$ is monotonically decreasing, and strictly decreases infinitely often. This contradicts the well-foundedness of $\mathcal{O}$. $\square$

2.8 Proof Search

Provided with the appropriate descriptions of sequents, inductive definitions and inference rules, CYCLIST instantiates a proof search function, `proofsearch()`, shown in pseudo-code in Figure 2. This function, given a proof, a node within that proof and a maximum recursion depth, performs an iterative depth-first search aiming at closing open nodes in the proof. The global variable "ruleset" provides the ordered list of inference rules and matching functions defined by the user; the functions `replacenode()` and `linknode()` do the requisite graph surgery in order to replace an open node in the proof with either the application of an inference rule or a back-link, respectively. Finally, the function `sound()` checks the global soundness of a cyclic proof. The design and trade-offs regarding this algorithm will be further discussed in Section 4.

3 Separation Logic Instantiations of CYCLIST

We briefly present the two instantiations of CYCLIST based on separation logic.

3.1 Separation Logic Entailment Prover

CYCLIST$_{SL}$ is a prover for separation logic similar to the prover in [8]. The syntax (left) and semantics (right) of the $\forall\exists$ DNF-like fragment of separation logic the prover accepts appear below.

$$t ::= x \mid \mathsf{nil}$$
$$\alpha ::= t = t$$
$$\mid t \neq t$$
$$\mid \mathsf{emp}$$
$$\mid t \mapsto \langle t, \dots, t \rangle$$
$$\mid P(t, \dots, t)$$
$$H ::= \alpha \mid H * H$$
$$F ::= H$$
$$\mid F \vee F$$
$$\mid \exists x . F$$

$$s(\mathsf{nil}) \notin \mathrm{dom}(h), \text{ for all } s, h$$
$$s, h \models x = y \text{ iff } s(x) = s(y)$$
$$s, h \models x \neq y \text{ iff } s, h \not\models x = y$$
$$s, h \models \mathsf{emp} \text{ iff } h = \emptyset$$
$$s, h \models a_0 \mapsto \langle a_1, \dots, a_n \rangle \text{ iff } h = \{s(a_0) \mapsto (s(a_1), \dots, s(a_n))\}$$
$$s, h \models H_1 * H_2 \text{ iff } \exists \text{ domain-disjoint } h_1, h_2, \text{ s.t.}$$
$$s, h_1 \models H_1 \text{ and } s, h_2 \models H_2 \text{ and } h = h_1 \circ h_2$$
$$s, h \models F_1 \vee F_2 \text{ iff } s, h \models F_1 \text{ or } s, h \models F_2$$
$$s, h \models \exists x . F \text{ iff } \exists v. \, s[x \mapsto v], h \models H$$

where stacks s are functions from variables to values, heaps h are finite partial maps from addresses to value tuples (where addresses are a subset of values) and $\circ$ is disjoint union. The semantics of inductive predicates are standard [6,7].

Inductive predicates are defined in a manner similar to that in CYCLIST$_{\mathrm{FO}}$. For example, an acyclic, possibly empty, singly-linked list segment is defined as:

$$(a_1 = a_2) \Rightarrow ls(a_1, a_2) \qquad (a_1 \neq a_2) * a_1 \mapsto \langle e_3 \rangle * ls(e_3, a_2) \Rightarrow ls(a_1, a_2)$$

Left- and right-unfolding rules are generated as in CYCLIST$_{\mathrm{FO}}$. Back-linking is also as in CYCLIST$_{\mathrm{FO}}$, except that classical weakening is replaced by the spatial weakening of separation logic, captured by the rule $B \vdash C \Longrightarrow A * B \vdash A * C$.

3.2 Separation Logic Termination Prover

CYCLIST$_{\mathrm{Term}}$ implements a termination prover for heap-manipulating programs in a simple imperative language, the theory of which was presented in [7]. By way of illustrating the programming language, a program that traverses a linked list is as follows.

```
0: if a1=nil goto 3;    1: a1 := a1→next;    2: goto 0;    3: stop.
```

Sequents are of the form $F \vdash_i \downarrow$, where F is a precondition in separation logic as in CYCLIST$_{\mathrm{SL}}$, and i is the line of the program to which the sequent applies. Such a sequent expresses the fact that if execution starts with the program counter set to i at a state satisfying F, then the program will (safely) terminate. For example, the sequent $ls(a_1, \mathsf{nil}) \vdash_0 \downarrow$ means that the above program will terminate if started at line 0 with a heap satisfying $ls(a_1, \mathsf{nil})$.

CYCLIST$_{\mathrm{Term}}$ builds on CYCLIST$_{\mathrm{SL}}$. Additional are rules for the symbolic execution of commands, derived via weakest preconditions. Unfolding rules for inductive predicates are generated in a manner similar to that in CYCLIST$_{\mathrm{SL}}$ apart from the fact that there are no right-unfold rules. Back-linking is also similar to that in CYCLIST$_{\mathrm{SL}}$, except that in CYCLIST$_{\mathrm{Term}}$ the program counters in the sequents must also match (exactly). We note that CYCLIST$_{\mathrm{Term}}$ is not a program analysis as it lacks abstraction capability.

4   Proof Search Issues and Experimental Results

Designing a proof search procedure for a cyclic theorem prover poses some design challenges distinct to those of standard proof search. Here we discuss the main issues, and report on our tests of CYCLIST's proof search performance.

4.1   Global Search Strategy

Non-ancestral back-links, i.e. back-links that point to a sequent which is not an ancestor of the back-link, can significantly reduce the depth of a proof [4]. Thus it is reasonable to conjecture that a breadth-first search might find these shorter proofs, and consequently yield a faster search algorithm than depth-first. Our early experiments overwhelmingly favoured the latter. We conjecture that the high fan-out degree of the search space makes breadth-first search impractical, even though shorter proofs may be found. Also, employing a depth-first strategy will allow some non-ancestral back-links 'to the left' of the current subgoal but also to open subgoals 'to the right' of the current subgoal, thus representing a reasonable compromise. A best-first strategy might perform better and we intend to pursue this question in future work.

4.2   Soundness Checking

Invoking a model checker to check the soundness of a pre-proof can be a costly step during proof search. To mitigate this we employ an abstraction/minimisation heuristic that reduces the size of the proof graphs to be checked by pruning leaf subgoals and composing certain types of successive arcs. In the context of iterative depth-first search we also memoise the results of these checks so as to avoid duplication of effort. This led to an order of magnitude of reduction in the cost of the soundness check, and is reflected in the low proportion of time spent checking soundness in our tests (see Table 1).

4.3   Forming Back-Links

When a partial pre-proof is found to be unsound then we know that it can never form part of a sound, closed proof. Thus we have the choice of either checking soundness once when the proof is closed, or to apply the check eagerly, i.e. every time a back-link is formed. Our tests showed a clear advantage in the eager soundness checking strategy under both depth- and breadth-first search schemes. We conjecture that early elimination of an unsound proof leads to a major reduction of the size of the search space outweighing the cost of frequent soundness checking, especially after our optimisations.

It is known that the set of sequents provable with the use of non-ancestral back-links is equal to that with back-linking restricted to ancestor nodes [4]. This raises the question whether using only ancestral back-links improves performance, due to a smaller number of calls to matching functions and soundness checks. Restricting back-links to ancestral nodes does not speed up the instantiations we provide, but makes some proofs impractical. It seems that the matching functions we use will not fire significantly more often when allowed access to non-ancestral nodes, and thus will not lead to excessive soundness checking.

4.4   Order of Rule Applications

As in most theorem provers, the order in which inference rules/tactics are attempted directly impacts performance. We list here two points specific to cyclic theorem proving. First, when matching functions are computationally cheap, they can be prioritised and attempted early and often, eagerly creating back-links. Used within tactics such as fold-then-match, they can entail a higher computational cost and are thus placed last in the priority order. Second, unfolding rules generally increase the size of sequents, thus have lower priority than other inference rules. In particular, left-unfolding precedes right-unfolding as it introduces progressing trace pairs in the cyclic proof, and, it may (after simplification) enable right-unfolding rules to fire.

4.5   Predicate Folding/Lemma Application

It seems certain that Cut elimination does not hold, in general, for cyclic proof systems. Thus the ability to conjecture and apply lemmas can be crucial to a successful proof, as is the case, e.g., in our Example 6 above. Our instantiations of CYCLIST do not yet permit the application of arbitrary lemmas. Instead, we currently permit only *predicate foldings*, where the lemma applied is essentially an inductive rule. For example, the inductive rule $Add(x, y, z) \Rightarrow Add(sx, y, sx)$ from Example 1 becomes the "folding" lemma $Add(x, y, z) \vdash Add(sx, y, sx)$. We found empirically that this very limited form of lemma application is very useful in quite a number of proofs.

4.6   Limitations

CYCLIST is a young framework aimed at proving theorems with a complex inductive structure. As such, it does not yet utilise the totality of existing know-how on theorem proving, and this entails some limitations.

Focussing on inductive predicates means that function declaration and related equational reasoning facilities are lacking. As a result CYCLIST$_{FO}$ has difficulty dealing with heavily-equational goals, since such goals have to be translated into a predicate-based language resulting in loss of structural information.

Another limitation is that, although we do provide a predicate folding facility as explained above, we have no functionality currently for applying general lemmas, and this restricts the ability of CYCLIST instantiations to prove theorems that must rely on the use of Cut in their proofs.

A well-known example that is unprovable as yet in CYCLIST$_{FO}$ and demonstrates both limitations is the commutativity of addition. In CYCLIST$_{FO}$ this goal can be expressed relationally as $Nx, Ny, Add(x, y, z) \vdash Add(y, x, z)$. This form discourages the use of rewriting techniques guided by the structure of terms. In addition, the cyclic proof of the theorem requires essentially the same lemma, $x + sy = s(x + y)$, as is needed for the standard inductive proof (relationally, this lemma can be stated as $Nx, Ny, Add(x, y, z) \vdash Add(x, sy, sz)$). In standard inductive theorem provers, this lemma would be supplied as a "hint" to the prover, or would be found by an appropriate conjecture mechanism (cf. [16]).

4.7 Experimental Results

The results of tests run on the three instantiations of CYCLIST are summarised in Table 1. All tests were run on a x64 Linux system with an Intel i5 3.33GHz. CYCLIST and all tests are available online at [1].

CYCLIST$_{FO}$. We ran a number of tests with the first-order prover, mainly involving natural number induction. The two most interesting theorems we managed to prove are "the P & Q example" [24], and the sequent appearing in Example 6. Both proofs have a complex inductive structure, multiple cycles and require the use of predicate folding. They are both found in under a second. It is notable that Example 6 uses a lemma ($Nx \vdash Nssx$) that is not an instance of folding (it represents a "double fold"). CYCLIST$_{FO}$ proves this theorem by finding a deeper proof that requires only single folds.

CYCLIST$_{SL}$. The prover was run on the test cases from [8]. Proving time is nearly zero for most, suggesting that CYCLIST$_{SL}$ could be used as a backend for program analysis that automatically handles arbitrary inductive datatypes.

CYCLIST$_{Term}$. We ran the termination checker on a number of small programs including the programs in [7]. Notable are an iterative binary-tree search (program B in Table 1) and the reversal of a frying-pan list (program C, last theorem in Table 1). The authors of [3] report that the MUTANT tool for separation logic, which deals only with lists, fails to prove the latter theorem (under an appropriate precondition). A cyclic termination proof was later presented in [7] where it was painstakingly constructed by hand. CYCLIST$_{Term}$ proves this in under a second. Its proof contains five cycles, all requiring predicate folding.

5 Related Work

There are a few theorem provers employing cyclic proof in some form. The QUODLIBET tool [2], based on first-order logic with inductive datatypes, uses a version of infinite descent to prove inductive theorems whereby a proof node is annotated with a *weight*, which must strictly decrease at back-link sites. Compared to CYCLIST, which is fully automatic, QUODLIBET is intended for semi-interactive proof. An automated cyclic prover for entailments of separation logic, implemented in HOL Light, appeared in [8]. Compared to CYCLIST$_{SL}$, the prover in [8] disallows non-ancestral back-links and uses a restricted soundness condition, which in particular rules out the use of predicate folding. Nguyen and

Table 1. *Upper:* Theorems proved by the instantiations. The column labelled 'Time' is the time taken in milliseconds, 'SC%' is the percentage of time taken by the soundness checks, 'Depth' is the depth of the proof found, 'Nodes' is the number of nodes in the proof and the last column shows the number of calls to the model checker as (calls on unsound proof)/(total calls). *Lower:* The input programs to the termination prover. NB the formulas used for program **C** are loop invariants and as such the program counter in the judgment is set to 1, i.e., a statement in the loop.

Theorem	Time	SC%	Depth	Nodes	Uns./All
$O_1x \vdash Nx$	16	0	5	7	0/1
$E_1x \vee O_2x \vdash Nx$	20	0	6	15	4/6
$E_1x \vee O_1x \vdash Nx$	16	25	4	9	2/4
$N_1x \vdash Ox \vee Ex$	12	0	4	6	0/1
$N_1x \wedge N_2y \vdash Q(x,y)$	512	31	7	13	171/181
$N_1x \vdash Add(x,0,x)$	4	0	3	5	0/1
$N_1x \wedge N_2y \wedge Add_3(x,y,z) \vdash Nz$	24	0	4	6	3/4
$N_1x \wedge N_2y \wedge Add_3(x,y,z) \vdash Add(x,s(y),s(z))$	40	20	5	12	8/9
$N_1x \wedge N_2y \vdash R(x,y)$	560	44	7	26	176/183
$x \mapsto y * RList_1(y,z) \vdash RList(x,z)$	16	0	5	8	0/1
$RList_1(x,y) * RList_2(y,z) \vdash RList(x,z)$	16	0	4	7	0/1
$List_1(x,y) * y \mapsto z \vdash List(x,z)$	8	0	4	6	0/1
$List_1(x,y) * List_2(y,z) \vdash List(x,z)$	8	0	3	5	0/1
$PeList_1(x,y) * y \mapsto z \vdash PeList(x,z)$	12	0	4	6	0/1
$PeList_1(x,y) * PeList_2(y,z) \vdash PeList(x,z)$	12	0	3	4	0/1
$DLL_1(x,y,z,w) \vdash SLL(x,y)$	12	0	3	5	0/1
$DLL_1(x,y,z,w) \vdash BSLL(z,w)$	12	0	4	6	0/1
$DLL_1(x,y,z,w) * DLL_2(a,x,w,b) \vdash DLL(a,y,z,b)$	8	0	3	4	0/1
$ListO_1(x,y) * ListO_2(y,z) \vdash ListE(x,z)$	12	0	5	12	0/1
$ListE_1(x,y) * ListE_2(y,z) \vdash ListE(x,z)$	20	0	5	8	0/1
$ListE_1(x,y) * ListO_2(y,z) \vdash ListO(x,z)$	24	0	5	8	0/1
$BinListFirst_1x \vdash BinTreex$	8	0	4	6	0/1
$BinListSecond_1x \vdash BinTreex$	20	0	4	6	0/1
$BinPath_1(x,z) * BinPath_2(z,y) \vdash BinPath(x,y)$	24	0	3	6	0/2
$BinPath_1(x,y) \vdash BinTreeSeg(x,y)$	16	0	4	8	0/2
$BinTreeSeg_1(x,z) * BinTreeSeg_2(z,y) \vdash BinTreeSeg(x,y)$	12	0	3	6	0/2
$BinTreeSeg_1(x,y) * BinTreey \vdash BinTree(x)$	12	0	3	6	0/2
$x \neq z * x \mapsto y * ls_1(y,z) \vdash ls(x,z)$	0	0	2	2	0/0
$ls_1(x,y) * ls_2(y,\mathrm{nil}) \vdash ls(x,\mathrm{nil})$	16	0	3	4	0/1
$ListE_1(x,y) \vee ListO_1(x,y) \vdash List(x,y)$	16	0	4	9	2/4
A: $ls_1(x,\mathrm{nil}) \vdash_0 \downarrow$	16	0	5	7	0/1
B: $btx \vdash_0 \downarrow$	12	0	6	13	0/2
C: $ls_1(x,\mathrm{nil}) * ls_2(y,\mathrm{nil}) \vdash_1 \downarrow$	52	8	8	10	13/14
D: $y \neq \mathrm{nil} * ls_1(x,\mathrm{nil}) * ls_2(y,\mathrm{nil}) \vdash_0 \downarrow$	2036	16	12	24	197/233
$ls(x,z) * ls(y,\mathrm{nil}) * z \mapsto a * ls(a,z)$ $\vee ls(b,\mathrm{nil}) * z \mapsto b * ls(x,z) * ls(y,z)$					
C: $\vee\, ls(x,\mathrm{nil}) * ls(y,z) * z \mapsto c * ls(c,z) \vdash_1 \downarrow$	124	0	9	39	19/23

A	**B**	**C**	**D**
// List traversal	// Bin. tree search	// List reversal	// List append
0: if x=nil goto 3;	0: if x=nil goto 6;	0: y := nil;	// (one-at-a-time)
1: x := x→next;	1: if * goto 4;	1: if x=nil goto 7;	0: if x=nil goto 10;
2: goto 0;	2: x := x→left ;	2: z := x;	1: z := y→next;
3: stop	3: goto 0 ;	3: x := x→next;	2: if z≠nil goto 8;
	4: x := x→right ;	4: z→next := y;	3: y→next := x;
	5: goto 0 ;	5: y := z;	4: x := x→next;
	6: stop	6: goto 1;	5: y := y→next;
		7: stop	6: y→next := nil;
			7: goto 0;
			8: y := y→next;
			9: goto 0;
			10: stop

Chin [19] provide a separation logic entailment prover using cyclic proof, but which appears to be restricted in at least as many ways as [8].

In summary, the main restrictions on previous cyclic provers are: (a) a single logical setting; (b) ancestral cycle schemes; (c) strong soundness conditions that rule out many proofs; and (d) automated search limited to cut-free proofs. CYCLIST lifts all of these restrictions, albeit only partially in the case of (d).

The "size change principle" for program termination by Lee et al [18] is based on a condition similar to the soundness condition for cyclic proofs: a program terminates if every possible infinite execution in the control flow graph would result in an infinite descent of some well-founded data value. It is plausible that the approach of [18] to termination checking, empirically shown to often be more efficient in practice than a Büchi automata construction [14], would also benefit the soundness checking in CYCLIST. However, in contrast to size-change termination problems, the main problem we face is not in checking the soundness condition, but in discovering the correct candidate pre-proofs.

Finally, there are a number of mature, automated theorem provers employing explicit induction, including ACL2 [17], IsaPlanner [12], LambdaOtter and many others. Unfortunately, most test suites for these provers are largely based on equational reasoning about functions over inductive datatypes, whereas our instantiations of CYCLIST currently only cater for inductively defined predicates, making a direct comparison difficult. These tools will most probably outperform ours on problems requiring extensive rewriting, generalisation or the application of non-trivial lemmas. On the other hand, CYCLIST performs well on small problems requiring complex induction schemes, which are typically problematic for explicit induction (cf. Example 6). Thus we believe that integrating the sophisticated non-inductive features of explicit-induction provers into CYCLIST might yield significant benefits. For example, conjecturing appropriate lemmas (cf. [16]) seems extremely useful in forming back-links during proof search.

6   Conclusions and Future Work

The main contributions of this paper are our generic theory of cyclic proof, its unrestricted implementation in our theorem prover CYCLIST, and the application of CYCLIST to three concrete logical systems, including automated proof search procedures. In particular, we provide the first implementation of the cyclic proof system for program termination proposed in [7]. We believe that CYCLIST represents the first fully general implementation of cyclic proof.

Although CYCLIST is by no means an industrial-strength theorem prover, the results of our experiments to date are nevertheless encouraging. In its various instantiations, the prover is capable of automatically proving theorems with a complex inductive structure, notable Wirth's "P&Q" example, the proof of in-place reversal of a "frying-pan" list from [7], and our own Example 6.

There are obvious directions in which CYCLIST could be improved, both at the generic level (e.g. function definition over datatypes, rewriting support, lemma application and generalisation mechanisms) and in its various instantiations (e.g.

more advanced search strategies for particular logics). There is also the potential for developing new instantiations of CYCLIST to other fixed-point logics, such as the μ-calculus or temporal logics. We warmly encourage the development of such instantiations by interested readers.

References

1. Cyclist framework download, http://www.cs.ucl.ac.uk/staff/ngorogia/
2. Avenhaus, J., Kühler, U., Schmidt-Samoa, T., Wirth, C.-P.: How to Prove Inductive Theorems? QUODLIBET! In: Baader, F. (ed.) CADE-19. LNCS (LNAI), vol. 2741, pp. 328–333. Springer, Heidelberg (2003)
3. Berdine, J., Cook, B., Distefano, D., O'Hearn, P.W.: Automatic Termination Proofs for Programs with Shape-Shifting Heaps. In: Ball, T., Jones, R.B. (eds.) CAV 2006. LNCS, vol. 4144, pp. 386–400. Springer, Heidelberg (2006)
4. Brotherston, J.: Cyclic Proofs for First-Order Logic with Inductive Definitions. In: Beckert, B. (ed.) TABLEAUX 2005. LNCS (LNAI), vol. 3702, pp. 78–92. Springer, Heidelberg (2005)
5. Brotherston, J.: Sequent Calculus Proof Systems for Inductive Definitions. Ph.D. thesis, University of Edinburgh (November 2006)
6. Brotherston, J.: Formalised Inductive Reasoning in the Logic of Bunched Implications. In: Riis Nielson, H., Filé, G. (eds.) SAS 2007. LNCS, vol. 4634, pp. 87–103. Springer, Heidelberg (2007)
7. Brotherston, J., Bornat, R., Calcagno, C.: Cyclic proofs of program termination in separation logic. In: POPL-35, pp. 101–112. ACM (2008)
8. Brotherston, J., Distefano, D., Petersen, R.L.: Automated Cyclic Entailment Proofs in Separation Logic. In: Bjørner, N., Sofronie-Stokkermans, V. (eds.) CADE 2011. LNCS (LNAI), vol. 6803, pp. 131–146. Springer, Heidelberg (2011)
9. Brotherston, J., Simpson, A.: Sequent calculi for induction and infinite descent. Journal of Logic and Computation 21(6), 1177–1216 (2011)
10. Bundy, A.: The automation of proof by mathematical induction. In: Handbook of Automated Reasoning, vol. I, ch. 13, pp. 845–911. Elsevier Science (2001)
11. Couvreur, J.-M.: On-the-fly Verification of Linear Temporal Logic. In: Wing, J., Woodcock, J., Davies, J. (eds.) FM 1999. LNCS, vol. 1708, pp. 253–271. Springer, Heidelberg (1999)
12. Dixon, L., Fleuriot, J.: IsaPlanner: A Prototype Proof Planner in Isabelle. In: Baader, F. (ed.) CADE-19. LNCS (LNAI), vol. 2741, pp. 279–283. Springer, Heidelberg (2003)
13. Duret-Lutz, A., Poitrenaud, D.: Spot: An extensible model checking library using transition-based generalized Büchi automata. In: MASCOTS, pp. 76–83 (2004)
14. Fogarty, S., Vardi, M.Y.: Büchi Complementation and Size-Change Termination. In: Kowalewski, S., Philippou, A. (eds.) TACAS 2009. LNCS, vol. 5505, pp. 16–30. Springer, Heidelberg (2009)
15. Friedgut, E., Kupferman, O., Vardi, M.Y.: Büchi Complementation Made Tighter. In: Wang, F. (ed.) ATVA 2004. LNCS, vol. 3299, pp. 64–78. Springer, Heidelberg (2004)
16. Johansson, M., Dixon, L., Bundy, A.: Conjecture synthesis for inductive theories. Journal of Automated Reasoning 47(3) (October 2011)
17. Kaufmann, M., Manolios, P., Moore, J.S.: Computer-Aided Reasoning: An Approach. Kluwer (2000)

18. Lee, C.S., Jones, N.D., Ben-Amram, A.M.: The size-change principle for program termination. In: POPL-28, pp. 81–92. ACM (2001)
19. Nguyen, H.H., Chin, W.N.: Enhancing Program Verification with Lemmas. In: Gupta, A., Malik, S. (eds.) CAV 2008. LNCS, vol. 5123, pp. 355–369. Springer, Heidelberg (2008)
20. Schöpp, U., Simpson, A.: Verifying Temporal Properties Using Explicit Approximants: Completeness for Context-free Processes. In: Nielsen, M., Engberg, U. (eds.) FOSSACS 2002. LNCS, vol. 2303, pp. 372–386. Springer, Heidelberg (2002)
21. Sprenger, C., Dam, M.: A note on global induction mechanisms in a μ-calculus with explicit approximations. Theor. Informatics and Applications 37, 365–399 (2003)
22. Sprenger, C., Dam, M.: On the Structure of Inductive Reasoning: Circular and Tree-Shaped Proofs in the μ-Calculus. In: Gordon, A.D. (ed.) FOSSACS 2003. LNCS, vol. 2620, pp. 425–440. Springer, Heidelberg (2003)
23. Stirling, C., Walker, D.: Local model checking in the modal μ-calculus. Theoretical Computer Science 89, 161–177 (1991)
24. Wirth, C.P.: Descente infinie + Deduction. Logic J. of the IGPL 12(1), 1–96 (2004)

Decision Procedures
over Sophisticated Fractional Permissions

Le Xuan Bach, Cristian Gherghina*, and Aquinas Hobor**

National University of Singapore

Abstract. Fractional permissions enable sophisticated management of resource accesses in both sequential and concurrent programs. Entailment checkers for formulae that contain fractional permissions must be able to reason about said permissions to verify the entailments. We show how entailment checkers for separation logic with fractional permissions can extract equation systems over fractional shares. We develop a set decision procedures over equations drawn from the sophisticated boolean binary tree fractional permission model developed by Dockins *et al.* [4]. We prove that our procedures are sound and complete and discuss their computational complexity. We explain our implementation and provide benchmarks to help understand its performance in practice. We detail how our implementation has been integrated into the HIP/SLEEK verification toolset. We have machine-checked proofs in Coq.

1 Introduction

Separation logic is fundamentally a logic of resource accounting [13]. Control of some resource (*i.e.*, a cell of memory) allows the owner to take certain actions with that resource. Traditionally, ownership is a binary property, with full ownership associated with complete control (*e.g.*, the ability to read, modify, and deallocate the cell), and empty ownership associated with no control.

Many programs, particularly many concurrent programs, are not easy to verify with such a coarse understanding of access control [2,1]. Fractional permissions track ownership—*i.e.*, access control—at a finer level of granularity. For example, partial ownership might allow for reading, while full ownership might in addition enable writing and deallocation. This access control scheme helps verify concurrent programs that allow multiple threads to share read access to heap cells as long as no thread has write access.

A share model defines the representation for fractions π (*e.g.*, a rational number between 0 and 1) and a three-place join relation $\oplus$ that combines them (*e.g.*, addition, allowed only when the sum is no more than 1). The join relation must satisfy a number of technical properties such as functionality, associativity, and commutativity. The fractional π-ownership of the memory cell ℓ, whose value is currently v, can then be written in separation logic as $\ell \overset{\pi}{\mapsto} v$. When π is full

---

* Supported by MoE Tier-2 grant MOE2009-T2-1-063.
** Supported by a Lee Kuan Yew Postdoctoral Fellowship (T1-251RES0902).

R. Jhala and A. Igarashi (Eds.): APLAS 2012, LNCS 7705, pp. 368–385, 2012.

ownership we simply omit it. We modify the standard separating conjunction $\star$ to respect fraction permissions via the equivalence $\ell \overset{\pi_1 \oplus \pi_2}{\hookrightarrow} v \Leftrightarrow \ell \overset{\pi_1}{\hookrightarrow} v \star \ell \overset{\pi_2}{\hookrightarrow} v$.

Unfortunately, while they are very intuitive, rational numbers are not a good model for fractional ownership. Consider the following attempt at a recursively defined predicate for fractionally-owned binary trees:

$$\mathsf{tree}(\ell, \pi) \equiv (\ell = \mathsf{null} \wedge \mathsf{emp}) \vee (\ell \overset{\pi}{\hookrightarrow} (\ell_l, \ell_r) \star \mathsf{tree}(\ell_l, \pi) \star \mathsf{tree}(\ell_r, \pi)) \quad (1)$$

This tree predicate is obtained directly from the standard recursive predicate for wholly-owned binary trees in separation logic by asserting only π ownership of the root and recursively doing the same for the left and right substructures, and so at first glance looks obviously correct. The problem is that when $\pi \leq 0.5$, then $\mathsf{tree}_\mathbb{Q}$ can describe some non-tree directed acyclic graphs.

Parkinson then developed a share model that avoided this problem, but at the cost of certain other technical shortcomings and a total loss of decidability (even for equality testing) [12]. Decidability is crucial for developing automated tools to reason about separation logic formulae containing fractional permissions. Finally, Dockins *et al.* then developed a tree-share model detailed in §3 that overcame the technical shortcomings in Parkinson's model and in addition enjoyed a decidable test for equality and a computable join relation $\oplus$ [4]. The pleasant theoretical properties of the tree-share model led to its use in the design and soundness proofs of several flavors of concurrent separation logic [7,8], and the basic computability results led to its incorporation in two program verification tools: HIP/SLEEK [11] and Heap-Hop [15].

However, it is one thing to incorporate a technique into a verification tool, and another thing to make it complete enough to work well. Heap-Hop employed a simplistic heuristic to prove entailments involving tree shares [14], and although HIP/SLEEK did better, the techniques were still highly incomplete [9]. Even verifying small programs can require hundreds of share entailment checks, so in practice this incompleteness was a significant barrier to the use of these tools to reason about programs whose verification required fractional shares.

Our work overcomes this barrier. We show how to extract a system of equations over shares from separation logic formulae such that the truth of the system is equivalent to the truth of the share portion of the formulae. This extraction can be done with no knowledge about the underlying model for shares. These systems of equations are then handed to our solver: a standalone library of sound and complete decision procedures over fraction tree shares. Although the worst-case complexity is high, our benchmarks demonstrate that our library is fast enough in practice to be incorporated into practical entailment checkers.

Contributions

- We demonstrate how to extract a system of equations over fractional shares from separation logic formulae (§2).
- We prove that the key problems over these systems are decidable.
- We develop a tool that solves the problems and benchmark its performance.
- We incorporated our tool into the HIP/SLEEK verification toolset.
- Our prototype is available at:
  www.comp.nus.edu.sg/~cristian/projects/prover/shares.html

2   Extracting Shares from Separation Logic Formulae

Program verification tools, such as HIP, usually do not verify programs on their own. Instead, a program verifier usually applies Hoare rules to verify program commands and then emits the associated entailments to separate checkers such as SLEEK. Entailment checkers usually follow in the footsteps of SMT solvers by dividing the input formulae according to the background theories and in turn rely on specialized provers for each theory, *e.g.* Omega for Presberger arithmetic.

We plan to follow the same pattern for fractional shares. The program verifier itself needs to know almost nothing about fractional shares, because it will simply emit entailments over formulae containing such shares to its entailment checker. The entailment checker needs to know a bit more: how to separate share information from formulae into a specialized domain, *i.e.*, systems of equations over shares. The choice of this domain is an important modularity boundary because it allows the entailment prover to treat shares as an abstract type. The entailment checker only knows about certain basic operations such as equality testing, combining, and splitting shares. To check entailments over shares it calls our new backend share prover (detailed in §4).

To demonstrate that the entailment checker can treat the shares abstractly, we defer the share model until §3, and will first outline the extraction of systems of equations over shares from separation logic formulae. Here we will just write χ for share constants; if our domain were rationals between 0 and 1, then an example χ would be 0.25. Our actual domain is more sophisticated and is given in §3, but our point here is that extracting equations over shares can be done without actually knowing the underlying share model.

Entailment checkers are complicated, in part because information discovered in one subdomain can impact another (*e.g.*, alias analysis can affect share constraints). Due to the tight link between heap-specific reasoning and share reasoning, extra share constraints are generated while discharging heap obligations. This information seepage prevents a modular and compositional description of the share constraint generation process. For brevity, we will illustrate share constraint extraction from a core separation logic; interested readers are referred to the description for a richer logic given in [9, §8.4]. Extracting share information from more complex formulae depends on the exact nature of said formulae but usually follows the pattern we give here in a straightforward way; the end result is just larger systems of equations.

The logic formulae we will consider here are of the following form:

$$\Phi := \exists\, v.\kappa \wedge \beta \mid \kappa \wedge \beta \qquad\qquad \kappa := \kappa * \kappa \mid v \xmapsto{\pi} v$$
$$\beta := \beta \wedge \beta \mid v = \pi \mid \pi \oplus \pi = \pi \qquad \pi := v \mid \chi$$

Here, v denotes variables (over shares, locations, and values) and $v \xmapsto{\pi} v$ is the fractional points-to predicate. Obtaining the share equation systems from the entailment $\Phi_a \vdash \Phi_c$ conceptually requires three steps.

First, the formulae are normalized in order to ensure that the heap component does not contain two distinct points-to predicates when the pointers are provably aliased. This reduction step can be described as:

$$v_1 \xmapsto{\pi_1} v_2 * v_3 \xmapsto{\pi_2} v_4 \wedge \beta \xrightarrow{\ \beta \vdash v_1 = v_3\ } \exists \pi_3\,.\, v_1 \xmapsto{\pi_3} v_2 \wedge (\beta \wedge \pi_3 = \pi_1 \oplus \pi_2 \wedge v_2 = v_4)$$

Second, formulae are partitioned based on the domains (*e.g.*, heaps, shares, arithmetics, bags) and all non heap related expressions are floated out of the heap fragment k. Share constants are floated out of the points-to relations by introducing a fresh share variable. Thus $v_1 \overset{\chi}{\mapsto} v_2$ becomes $\exists v'.v_1 \overset{v'}{\mapsto} v_2 \wedge v' = \chi$.

Third, heap related obligations are discharged and any share constraint generated in the process is added to the share constraints previously extracted. SLEEK discharges heap constraints by pairing each points-to predicate $p_c \overset{s_c}{\mapsto} c_c$ in the consequent with a corresponding predicate in the antecedent $p_a \overset{s_a}{\mapsto} c_a$ when $p_a = p_c$. This pairing generates extra proof obligations over both the content of the memory $(c_a = c_c)$ and the shares. For shares, SLEEK considers two possibilities: either the owned share s_a in the antecedent is equal to the one in the consequent $(s_a = s_c)$, or s_a is strictly greater $(\exists s_r \, . \, s_a = s_c \oplus s_r)$. This case split leads to the generation of two proof obligations, with the original entailment succeeding if at least one of the two new obligations is satisfied[1].

Furthermore, it is common for separation logic entailment checkers to also infer a frame or residue—the part of the antecedent not required to prove the consequent. If s_a is larger than s_c, then there exists a non-empty share s_r such that $s_r \oplus s_c = s_a$. This share residue is captured by the instantiation of s_r.

After the heap constraints are discharged, the share relevant portion of the entailment consists of sets of formulae over **non empty** shares with the syntax:

$$\phi ::= \exists v.\phi \mid \phi_1 \wedge \phi_2 \mid \pi_1 \oplus \pi_2 = \pi_3 \mid v_1 = v_2 \mid v = \chi$$

That is, share formulae ϕ contain share variables v, existential binders $\exists$, conjunctions $\wedge$, join facts $\oplus$, equalities between variables, and assignments of variables to constants χ. Unless bound by an existential, variables are assumed to be universally bound, with universals bound before existentials ($\forall\exists$ rather than $\exists\forall$); despite implementing a translation for the feature-rich separation logic for SLEEK [9] we have not needed arbitrary nesting of quantifiers. We will view the share formulae as equation systems Σ, *i.e.* as a pair of sets: (1) a set of equations of the form $a \oplus b = c$ or $v = w$, and (2) a set of existentially quantified variables.

To clarify the interaction between entailment checkers and the share solver, we outline extraction of share equations from two entailments:

$$x \overset{\chi_1}{\mapsto} v_a * x \overset{\chi_2}{\mapsto} v_a \vdash \exists s_c. x \overset{s_c}{\mapsto} v_c \quad \| \quad x \overset{\chi_a}{\mapsto} v_a \vdash x \overset{\chi_c}{\mapsto} v_c$$

First, the two entailments need to be normalized and the shares floated out[2]:

$$x \overset{s_a}{\mapsto} v_a \wedge \chi_1 \oplus \chi_2 = s_a \vdash \exists s_c. x \overset{s_c}{\mapsto} v_c \quad \| \quad x \overset{s_a}{\mapsto} v_a \wedge s_a = \chi_a \vdash \exists s_c. x \overset{s_c}{\mapsto} v_c \wedge s_c = \chi_c$$

Discharging the heap obligations occurs by pairing the $x \overset{s_c}{\mapsto} v_c$ predicate with $x \overset{s_a}{\mapsto} v_a$, which generates the share obligations $s_a = s_c$ or $\exists s_r. s_a = s_c \oplus s_r$. These obligations are combined with the rest of the share constraints, resulting in two share proof obligations for each original entailment.

$$\begin{cases} \chi_1 \oplus \chi_2 = s_a \vdash \exists s_c \quad . \; s_a = s_c \\ \chi_1 \oplus \chi_2 = s_a \vdash \exists s_c, s_r. \; s_c \oplus s_r = s_a \end{cases} \quad \Big\| \quad \begin{cases} s_a = \chi_a \vdash \exists s_c \quad . \; s_c = \chi_c \wedge s_a = s_c \\ s_a = \chi_a \vdash \exists s_c, s_r. \; s_c = \chi_c \wedge s_a = s_c \oplus s_r \end{cases}$$

---

[1] We are almost always able to avoid a serious exponential search by using the search prunings described in [9].

[2] The antecedent $\exists$ is automatically interpreted as a $\forall$ over the entailment using renaming when needed to avoid name clashes.

Although simple, the first original entailment often occurs when verifying a method that requires only read access to a heap location; the existential allows callers to be flexible regarding which specific share of x they have. One technical point is that many separation logics (including those used in HIP/SLEEK, Heap-Hop, and coreStar) only allow *positive* (non-empty) fractional shares over a points-to predicate (the empty share over a points-to is equivalent to $\perp$); thus, the above existential must be restricted to never choose the empty share.

We have now given two examples of extracting share equations from separation logic formulae. Once the translation is finished, a separation logic entailment checker can ask our share prover two questions:

1. (SAT) A *solution* S of Σ is a (finite) mapping from the variables of Σ into tree shares. We say that a solution S satisfies the equation system Σ, written $S \models \Sigma$, when the mapping makes the equations and equalities in Σ true. The SAT query asks if an equation system Σ is satisfiable, *i.e.*, $\exists S.\ S \models \Sigma$? SLEEK uses SAT checks to help prune unfeasible proof searches.
2. (IMPL) Given two systems Σ_a and Σ_c, does Σ_a entail Σ_c?
   That is: $\Sigma_a \vdash \Sigma_c$ iff $\forall S.\ S \models \Sigma_a \Rightarrow S \models \Sigma_c$.

In practice this is sufficient; in §4 we will detail how we answer these questions.

3 Binary Boolean Trees as a Fractional Share Model

Here we briefly explain the tree-share fractional permissions model of Dockins *et al.* [4]. A tree share τ is inductively defined as a binary tree with boolean leaves:

$$\tau ::= \circ \ \mid \ \bullet \ \mid \ \widehat{\tau\ \tau}$$

Here $\circ$ denotes an "empty" leaf while $\bullet$ a "full" leaf. The tree $\circ$ is thus the empty share, and $\bullet$ the full share. There are two "half" shares: $\widehat{\circ\ \bullet}$ and $\widehat{\bullet\ \circ}$, and four "quarter" shares, beginning with $\widehat{\bullet\ \circ\ \circ}$. Notice that the two half shares are not identical; this is a feature, not a bug: this property ensures that the definition of tree from equation (1) really describes fractional trees instead of DAGs.

Notice also that we presented the first quarter share as $\widehat{\bullet\ \circ\ \circ}$ instead of $\widehat{\bullet\ \circ\ \circ\ \circ}$. This is deliberate: the second choice is not a valid share because the tree is not in *canonical form*. A tree is in canonical form when it is in its most compact representation under the inductively-defined equivalence relation $\cong$:

$$\overline{\circ \cong \circ} \qquad \overline{\bullet \cong \bullet} \qquad \overline{\circ \cong \widehat{\circ\ \circ}} \qquad \overline{\bullet \cong \widehat{\bullet\ \bullet}} \qquad \frac{\tau_1 \cong \tau_1' \quad \tau_2 \cong \tau_2'}{\widehat{\tau_1\ \tau_2} \cong \widehat{\tau_1'\ \tau_2'}}$$

The canonical representation is needed to guarantee some of the technical properties described below. Managing the canonicality is a minor performance cost for the computable parts of our system but a major technical hassle in the proofs. Our strategy for this presentation is to gloss over some of these details, folding and unfolding trees into canonical form when required by the narrative. We justify our informalism in the presentation because all of the operations we define on trees have been verified in Coq to respect the canonicality.

Functional:	$x \oplus y = z_1 \;\Rightarrow\; x \oplus y = z_2 \;\Rightarrow\; z_1 = z_2$
Commutative:	$x \oplus y \;=\; y \oplus x$
Associative:	$x \oplus (y \oplus z) \;=\; (x \oplus y) \oplus z$
Cancellative:	$x_1 \oplus y = z \;\Rightarrow\; x_2 \oplus y = z \;\Rightarrow\; x_1 = x_2$
Unit:	$\exists u.\ \forall x.\ x \oplus u = x$
Disjointness:	$x \oplus x = y \;\Rightarrow\; x = y$
Cross split:	$a \oplus b = z \wedge c \oplus d = z \Rightarrow \exists ac, ad, bc, bd.$

$$ac \oplus ad = a \wedge bc \oplus bd = b \wedge ac \oplus bc = c \wedge ad \oplus bd = d$$

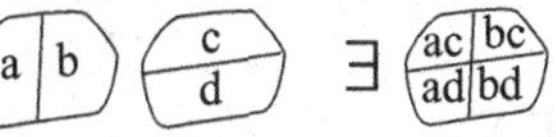

$$\forall \;\boxed{a\,|\,b}\;\;\boxed{\begin{smallmatrix}c\\d\end{smallmatrix}}\;\;\exists\;\boxed{\begin{smallmatrix}ac\,|\,bc\\ad\,|\,bd\end{smallmatrix}}$$

Infinite Splitability: $x \neq \circ \;\Rightarrow\; \exists x_1, x_2.\ x_1 \neq \circ \wedge x_2 \neq \circ \wedge x_1 \oplus x_2 = x$

Fig. 1. Properties of tree shares

The join relation for trees is inductively defined by unfolding both trees to the same shape and joining leafwise using the rules $\circ \oplus \circ = \circ$, $\circ \oplus \bullet = \bullet$, and $\bullet \oplus \circ = \bullet$; afterwards the result is refolded into canonical form as in this example:

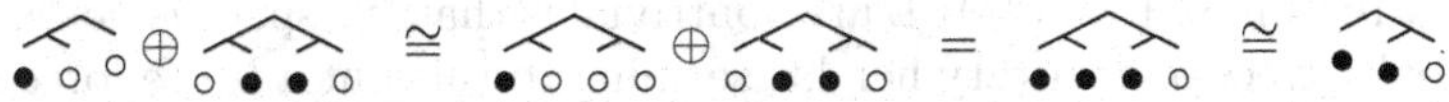

$$\widehat{\bullet_{\circ}{}_{\circ}{}^{\circ}} \oplus \widehat{{}_{\bullet}{}_{\circ}{}_{\bullet}{}_{\circ}} \;\cong\; \widehat{{}_{\bullet}{}_{\circ}{}_{\circ}{}_{\circ}} \oplus \widehat{{}_{\circ}{}_{\bullet}{}_{\bullet}{}_{\circ}} \;=\; \widehat{{}_{\bullet}{}_{\bullet}{}_{\bullet}{}_{\circ}} \;\cong\; \widehat{\bullet_{\bullet}{}_{\circ}}$$

Because $\bullet \oplus \bullet$ is undefined, the join relation on trees is a partial operation. Dockins *et al.* prove that the join relation satisfies a number of useful properties detailed in Figure 1. The tree share model is the only model that simultaneously satisfies Disjointness (forces the **tree** predicate—equation 1— to behave properly), Cross-split (used *e.g.* in settings involving overlapping data structures), and Infinite splittability (to verify divide-and-conquer algorithms). In the domain of tree shares, Disjointness is equivalent to $x \oplus x = y \;\Rightarrow\; x = \circ$; the name Disjointness comes from a related axiom at the level of formulae by Parkinson.

Unfortunately, while the $\oplus$ operation has many nice properties useful for verifying programs, they fall far short of those necessary to permit traditional algebraic techniques like Gaussian elimination. Dockins also defines a kind of multiplicative operation $\bowtie$ between shares used to manage a token counting setting (as opposed to the divide-and-conquer algorithms we can verify), but our decision procedures do not support $\bowtie$ at this time.

4   Decision Procedures over Tree Shares

Here we introduce a decision procedure for discharging tree share proof obligations generated by program verifiers. Recall from §2 that equation systems contain equations of the form $a \oplus b = c$ and $v = w$, plus a list of variables that should be quantified existentially. Moreover, a *solution* S of Σ is a (finite) mapping from the variables of Σ into tree shares. We write $S \models \Sigma$ to mean that the system Σ is satisfied by solution S; the SAT query is then simply $\exists S. S \models \Sigma$. Furthermore, we write $\Sigma_a \vdash \Sigma_c$ to mean that every solution S that satisfies Σ_a also satisfies Σ_c, *i.e.*, $\forall S.\ S \models \Sigma_a \Rightarrow S \models \Sigma_c$; this is exactly the IMPL query.

REDUCE(Σ)
  $\Sigma' = $ SIMPLIFY(Σ)
  If ($|\Sigma'| = 0$)
    Return FORMULA(Σ')
  Else
    $(\Sigma^l, \Sigma^r) = $ DECOMPOSE(Σ')
    $\Phi = $ REDUCE(Σ^l)$\wedge$REDUCE(Σ^r)
    Return Φ

SAT(Σ)
  $\Phi = $ REDUCE(Σ)
  Return SMT_SOLVER(Φ)

REDUCEI(Σ_a, Σ_b)
  $\Sigma'_a = $ SIMPLIFY(Σ_a)
  $\Sigma'_c = $ SIMPLIFY(Σ_c)
  If ($|\Sigma'_a| = 0 \wedge |\Sigma'_c| = 0$)
    Return (FORMULA(Σ'_a), FORMULA(Σ'_c))
  Else
    $(\Sigma^l_a, \Sigma^r_a) = $ DECOMPOSE(Σ'_a)
    $(\Sigma^l_c, \Sigma^r_c) = $ DECOMPOSE(Σ'_c)
    $(\Phi^l_a, \Phi^l_c) = $ REDUCEI(Σ^l_a, Σ^l_c)
    $(\Phi^r_a, \Phi^r_c) = $ REDUCEI(Σ^r_a, Σ^r_c)
    Return($\Phi^l_a \wedge \Phi^r_a, \quad \Phi^l_c \wedge \Phi^r_c$)

IMPL(Σ_a, Σ_c)
  $(\Phi_a, \Phi_c) = $ REDUCEI(Σ_a, Σ_c)
  Return $\neg$ SMT_SOLVER($\Phi_a \wedge \neg\Phi_c$)

Fig. 2. SAT   **Fig. 3.** IMPL

The key reason SAT and IMPL are nontrivial is that the space is dense[3]. That is, there exist trees of arbitrary height, seeming to rule out a brute force search. If we cannot find a solution to Σ at height 5, how do we know that one is not lurking at height 10,000? If we check $\Sigma_a \vdash \Sigma_c$ when the variables are restricted to constants of height 5, how do we know that the entailment will continue to hold when the variables range over constants of arbitrary height?

Our key theoretical insight is that despite the infinite domain, both SAT and IMPL are decidable by searching in the finite subdomain of trees with bounded height. Define the *system height* $|\Sigma|$ as the height of the highest tree constant in Σ or 0 if Σ contains only variables[4]. For solutions S, let $|S|$ be the highest constant in its codomain. In §5, we will prove our key theoretical result: that for both SAT and IMPL queries, if the height of the system(s) of equations is n, then it is sufficient to restrict the search to solutions of height n.

Of course, we do not want to blindly search through an exponentially large space if we can avoid it! Our goal for this section is to describe and prove sound the algorithms for SAT and IMPL given in Figures 2 and 3. The core of our decision procedures are the REDUCE and REDUCEI functions, which use the shape of the tree constants in the system to guide their search. There are four subroutines: SIMPLIFY, DECOMPOSE, FORMULA, and SMT_SOLVER. SMT_SOLVER is just a call into an off-the-shelf SAT/SMT solver; our prototype attaches to both MiniSat and Z3. The other three subroutines are discussed in detail below.

SIMPLIFY. SAT/SMT solvers can require a lot of computation time. Accordingly, SIMPLIFY attempts reduce the size of the problem with a combination of several techniques. First, each equation that contains two or three tree constants

---

[3] This is by design: density is needed to enable the "Infinite Splitability" axiom, which is needed to support the verification of divide-and-conquer algorithms.

[4] Since we are computer scientists, we start counting with 0, so $|\circ| = |\bullet| = 0$.

is simplified into an equality (or $\top/\bot$). To do so, SIMPLIFY sometimes uses the inverse operation of $\oplus$, written $\ominus$, and which satisfies $a \oplus b = c$ iff $c \ominus a = b$. To calculate the (partial) operation $a \ominus b$, unfold a and b to the same shape (just as with $\oplus$); calculate the difference leafwise using the rules $\bullet \ominus \bullet = \circ$, $\bullet \ominus \circ = \bullet$, and $\circ \ominus \circ = \circ$; and then fold the result back into canonical form, $e.g.$,

$$\text{(tree)} \ominus \text{(tree)} \cong \text{(tree)} \ominus \text{(tree)} = \text{(tree)} \cong \text{(tree)}$$

$\ominus$ is needed when one of the constants appears on the RHS of an equation, $e.g.$,[5]

$$\text{(tree)} \oplus a = \text{(tree)} \rightsquigarrow a = \text{(tree)}$$

If an equation reaches a tautology ($e.g.$, $\circ \oplus v = v$) then it is removed; if an equation reaches a contradiction ($e.g.$, $\bullet \oplus \bullet = v$) then we mark the entire system as equivalent to $\bot$. Second, SIMPLIFY will rewrite equalities; $e.g.$, if the equality $v = \chi$ is in the system then SIMPLIFY will substitute χ for v in the remainder of the system. Third, SIMPLIFY uses certain domain-specific knowledge to simplify equations with zero or one tree constant(s), including the following examples:

$$
\begin{aligned}
v_1 \oplus v_2 = \circ &\rightsquigarrow v_1 = \circ \wedge v_2 = \circ & \qquad v_1 \oplus \circ = v_2 &\rightsquigarrow v_1 = v_2 \\
v_1 \oplus \bullet = v_2 &\rightsquigarrow v_1 = \circ \wedge v_2 = \bullet & \qquad v_1 \oplus v_2 = v_1 &\rightsquigarrow v_2 = \circ \\
v_1 \oplus v_1 = v_2 &\rightsquigarrow v_1 = \circ \wedge v_2 = \circ &
\end{aligned}
$$

The result of SIMPLIFY is a new (in practice considerably smaller!) system of equations Σ' that has the same solutions, as expressed by the following Lemma:

Lemma 1. *For all solutions* S, $S \models \Sigma$ *iff* $S \models$ SIMPLIFY(Σ).

We will also need to know that SIMPLIFY does not increase the height of an equation system. To prove this, we need the following fact about $\oplus$ and $\ominus$:

Lemma 2. *If* $a \oplus b = c$ *or* $a \ominus b = c$ *then* $|c| \leq \mathsf{max}(|a|, |b|)$.

Given that fact, it is straightforward to prove the associated fact on SIMPLIFY:

Lemma 3. $|$SIMPLIFY$(\Sigma)| \leq |\Sigma|$

Proper equation systems. An equation system Σ is *proper* when all of the equations and equalities in Σ have no more than one constant. SIMPLIFY(Σ) is always proper, which simplifies some of our upcoming soundness proofs; accordingly, **hereafter we assume that all of our equation systems are proper.**

DECOMPOSE. The heart of our decision procedure is DECOMPOSE, which takes an equation system Σ of height n and produces two independent systems Σ_l and Σ_r with heights at most $n-1$. We decompose equalities and equations as follows:

---

[5] In §4 we use the symbol $\rightsquigarrow$ to indicate a transformation taken by the subroutine currently under discussion, so here it is referring to one of the operations of SIMPLIFY.

$$v \quad \rightsquigarrow \quad (v_l, v_r) \qquad\qquad\qquad\qquad\qquad\qquad\qquad\qquad vars$$

$$\circ \quad \rightsquigarrow \quad (\circ, \circ) \qquad \bullet \quad \rightsquigarrow \quad (\bullet, \bullet) \qquad \widehat{\tau_1 \, \tau_2} \quad \rightsquigarrow \quad (\tau_1, \tau_2) \quad consts$$

$$\left.\begin{array}{l} a \quad \rightsquigarrow \quad (a_l, a_r) \\ b \quad \rightsquigarrow \quad (b_l, b_r) \\ c \quad \rightsquigarrow \quad (c_l, c_r) \end{array}\right\} \quad \begin{array}{l} a \oplus b = c \quad \rightsquigarrow \quad (a_l \oplus b_l = c_l, \; a_r \oplus b_r = c_r) \\[6pt] a = b \qquad \rightsquigarrow \quad (a_l = b_l, \; a_r = b_r) \end{array} \qquad eqs$$

In addition, DECOMPOSE also transforms the list of existentially bound variables so that if v was existentially bound in Σ then v_l is existentially bound in Σ_l and v_r is existentially bound in Σ_r. Fresh variable names are chosen so that the system can determine which "parent" variables are associated with which "child" variables. We write $\hat{x}$ for the parent variable function, e.g., $\hat{v_l} = \hat{v_r} = v$.

The key fact about DECOMPOSE is that the solution of the original system is tightly related to the solutions of the decomposed systems, as follows:

Lemma 4. *Given a system Σ and a solution S such that* DECOMPOSE$(\Sigma) = (\Sigma_l, \Sigma_r)$ *and* DECOMPOSE$(S) = (S_l, S_r)$, *then* $S \models \Sigma$ *iff* $S_l \models \Sigma_l$ *and* $S_r \models \Sigma_r$.

By DECOMPOSE(S) we mean the division of S into two independent solutions:

$$\text{DECOMPOSE}(S) \quad \equiv \quad (\lambda v.\text{DECOMPOSE}(S(\hat{v})).1, \lambda v.\text{DECOMPOSE}(S(\hat{v})).2)$$

Lemma 4 holds because the left and right subtrees of a binary tree are independent from each other. Moreover, DECOMPOSE decreases height:

Lemma 5. *If* DECOMPOSE$(\Sigma) = (\Sigma_l, \Sigma_r)$, *then* $|\Sigma| > \max(|\Sigma_l|, |\Sigma_r|)$ *or we were at height 0 to begin with, i.e.,* $|\Sigma| = |\Sigma_l| = |\Sigma_r| = 0$.

FORMULA. After repeatedly applying DECOMPOSE, $|\Sigma| = 0$, *i.e.*, the embedded constants are only $\circ$ and $\bullet$. Tree constants at height zero have a natural interpretation as booleans, with $\circ$ as $\bot$ and $\bullet$ as $\top$. Likewise, solutions at height zero can be used as valuations (maps from variables to $\top$ and $\bot$) for logic formulae. Accordingly, FORMULA translates the equations and equalities in a system of equations of height zero into logic formulae as follows:

$$\begin{array}{lcl} a \oplus b = c & \rightsquigarrow & (\neg a \wedge \neg b \wedge \neg c) \vee (\neg a \wedge b \wedge c) \vee (a \wedge \neg b \wedge c) \\ a = b & \rightsquigarrow & (\neg a \wedge \neg b) \vee (a \wedge b) \end{array}$$

Each resulting formula is $\wedge$-conjoined together to get a single formula that represents the entire system, as indicated by the following lemma:

Lemma 6. *Let* $|S| = |\Sigma| = 0$ *and* $v_1, \ldots, v_n$ *be the existentially bound variables in* Σ. *Then* $S \models \Sigma$ *iff* $S \models \exists v_1 \ldots \exists v_n.$ FORMULA(Σ)

To connect to a pure SAT solver (*e.g.*, MiniSat) we then compile the existential into a disjunction; *e.g.*, $\exists v.\phi \rightsquigarrow (v{=}\top \wedge \phi) \vee (v{=}\bot \wedge \phi)$. In contrast, SMT solvers such as Z3 can handle existentials over booleans directly.

The proof of Lemma 6 is by simple case analysis, but critics will rightly observe that the hypothesis $|S| = 0$, which is crucial to make the case analysis finite, is in general not true. We will see below how to overcome this difficulty.

SAT. We are almost ready to prove the correctness of the SAT function. The last puzzle piece we need is one of the two major theoretical insights of this paper:

Theorem 1. Σ *is satisfiable if and only if* Σ *can be satisfied with a solution* S *whose height is* $|\Sigma|$, *i.e.,* $\exists S.\ S \models \Sigma$ *iff* $\exists S.\ |S| = |\Sigma| \wedge S \models \Sigma$.

We will defer the proof of Theorem 1 until §5.1; our task in this section is to show how it fits into our correctness proof for SAT, *i.e.,*

Theorem 2. $\mathsf{SAT}(\Sigma) = \top$ *if and only if* Σ *is satisfiable, i.e.,* $\exists S.S \models \Sigma$.

Proof. Given Σ, we call REDUCE and feed the result into the SMT solver, so Theorem 2 depends on REDUCE turning Σ into an equivalent logical formula.

The proof of REDUCE is by (complete) induction on $|\Sigma|$. Both the base case and the inductive case begin by applying applying SIMPLIFY to reach Σ'. By Lemma 1, Σ' is satisfiable iff Σ was satisfiable; moreover, by Lemma 3, $|\Sigma'| \leq |\Sigma|$. After simplification, the base case and the inductive case proceed differently.

In the base case, $|\Sigma'| = 0$ and REDUCE calls FORMULA to produce a logical formula that by Lemma 6 is equivalent to Σ' as long as the solution has height 0. Theorem 1 completes the base case by telling us that testing satisfiability at height 0 is sufficient to determine satisfiability in general.

In the inductive case, we DECOMPOSE Σ' into Σ_l and Σ_r. Lemma 5 tells us that both new systems have lower height, so we can apply the induction hypothesis to verify the recursive call and get two new formulae whose truth are equivalent to Σ^l and Σ^r. Lemma 4 completes the inductive step by telling us that the conjunction of Σ^l and Σ^r is equivalent to Σ'. $\square$

IMPL. We need the second major theoretical insight of this paper to verify IMPL.

Theorem 3. $\Sigma_a \vdash \Sigma_c$ *iff* $\Sigma_a \vdash \Sigma_c$ *for all solutions* S *s.t.* $|S| = |\Sigma_a|$, *i.e.,* $\forall S.\ S \models \Sigma_a \Rightarrow S \models \Sigma_c$ *iff* $\forall S.\ |S| = |\Sigma_a| \Rightarrow S \models \Sigma_a \Rightarrow S \models \Sigma_c$.

We will defer the proof until §5.2; just as we did with Theorem 1 above, our task here is to show how Theorem 3 fits into our correctness proof for IMPL, *i.e.,*

Theorem 4. $\mathsf{IMPL}(\Sigma_a, \Sigma_c)$ *if and only if* $\Sigma_a \vdash \Sigma_c$, *i.e.,* $\forall S.\ S \models \Sigma_a \Rightarrow S \models \Sigma_c$.

Proof. The major effort is proving that REDUCEI correctly transforms Σ_a and Σ_c into equivalent logical formulae Φ_a and Φ_c such that $\Sigma_a \vdash \Sigma_c$ iff $\Phi_a \Rightarrow \Phi_c$; afterwards we simply use the standard SAT/SMT solver trick of converting a validity check for $\Phi_a \Rightarrow \Phi_c$ into an **unsatisfiability** check for $\Phi_a \wedge \neg\Phi_c$.

The proof of REDUCEI is largely in parallel with the proof of REDUCE in Theorem 2. We proceed by complete induction, this time on $\max(|\Sigma_a|, |\Sigma_c|)$. Again the base and inductive cases begin in the same way. We apply SIMPLIFY to reach Σ'_a and Σ'_c and again use Lemma 1 to guarantee that $\Sigma'_a \vdash \Sigma'_c$ iff $\Sigma_a \vdash \Sigma_c$; Lemma 3 ensures that $\max(|\Sigma'_a|, |\Sigma'_c|) \leq \max(|\Sigma_a|, |\Sigma_c|)$.

After simplification, the base and inductive cases diverge. In the base case, $\max(|\Sigma'_a|, |\Sigma'_c|) = 0$ and we call FORMULA to reach two logical formulae, the first equivalent to Σ'_a and the second equivalent to Σ'_c, as long as the solutions are of height zero (Lemma 6). Theorem 3 completes the base case by observing that it is sufficient to check only the solutions of height $|\Sigma'_a|$, *i.e.* zero.

In the inductive case, we DECOMPOSE Σ'_a and Σ'_c into Σ^1_a, etc., decreasing the maximum of their heights (Lemma 5), and thus letting us use the induction hypothesis for the recursive calls. Afterwards, we have four formulae (Φ^1_a, etc.); we then conjoin both antecedents and both consequents using Lemma 4. □

Optimizations. The algorithms presented in figures 2 and 3 get the job done but yield far from optimal performance. Our prototype incorporates a number of additional optimizations including. Optimizations during SAT include dropping equalities after substitution and a lazier on-demand version of DECOMPOSE. In addition to utilizing the lazier version of DECOMPOSE, optimizations during IMPL include dropping existentials from the antecedent, substituting equalities from the antecedent into the consequent, and stopping decomposition when the antecedent has reached height zero and performing a SAT check on the antecedent if the consequent has not also reached height zero. Several optimizations require some additional theoretical insight; *e.g.*, the last requires the following:

Lemma 7. *Let S be a solution of Σ. Then $|S| \geq |\Sigma|$.*

Proof. Recall that we assume that Σ is proper, *i.e.*, each equation has at most one constant. If $|\Sigma| = 0$, we are done. Otherwise, by definition of $|\Sigma| = n$, there must be an equation σ containing a constant χ with height n. Since $S \models \Sigma$ we know that $S \models \sigma$. Assume both variables v_1 and $v_2 \in \sigma$ have height lower than n in S (*i.e.*, $\max(|S(v_1)|, |S(v_2)|) < |\chi|$). By Lemma 2 we also know that $|\chi| \leq \max(|S(v_1)|, |S(v_2)|)$, so by transitivity we have $|\chi| < |\chi|$, a contradiction. Accordingly, at least one of the variables v_i must have had height at least n. □

Unsurprisingly, the actual code used in the prototype is much more complicated than the algorithms presented above, and accordingly is much harder to verify. For future work we would like to develop a verified implementation.

Complexity. One might wonder what complexity class SAT and IMPL belong to. Tree-SAT when restricted to systems of height zero is already NP-COMPLETE.

Proof. We can use the following clause-by-clause reduction from 3-SAT, in which new variables (X, Y, Z, M, and N) are chosen fresh for each disjunctive clause:

$$
\begin{aligned}
A \vee B \vee C &\rightsquigarrow (A \oplus X = \bullet) \wedge (X \oplus Y = Z) \wedge (B \oplus M = Z) \wedge (M \oplus N = C) \\
\neg A \vee B \vee C &\rightsquigarrow (A \oplus X = Y) \wedge (B \oplus Z = Y) \wedge (Z \oplus M = C) \\
\neg A \vee \neg B \vee C &\rightsquigarrow (A \oplus X = Y) \wedge (B \oplus Z = M) \wedge (C \oplus X = M) \\
\neg A \vee \neg B \vee \neg C &\rightsquigarrow (A \oplus X = Y) \wedge (B \oplus Z = M) \wedge (X \oplus Z = C)
\end{aligned}
$$

The clause on the LHS is satisfiable iff the clause on the RHS is satisfiable. □

We hypothesize that tree-SAT on systems of arbitrary height is still "only" NP-COMPLETE because our SAT algorithm seems to scale the formulae polynomially with the description of the system. Going a bit further onto a limb, we further hypothesize that tree-IMPL is no worse than NP^{NP}-COMPLETE. Happily, as we show in §7, performance seems to be adequate in practice.

5 Sufficiency of Finite Search over Tree Shares

The SAT and IMPL algorithms presented in §4 are basically doing a shape-guided search through a finite domain. Our key theoretical insight is that a finite search is sufficient, as formalized in the statement of Theorems 1 and 3 in §4. Our next task is to prove these theorems, which is the focus of the remainder of this section. The most technical parts—Lemmas 8 and 10—have been mechanically verified in Coq. The remaining proofs have been carefully checked on paper.

5.1 The Sufficiency of Finite Search for SAT

We begin by explaining two related operations given a tree τ and natural n: left rounding, written $\lfloor \overset{\leftarrow}{\tau} \rfloor_n$; and right rounding, written $\lfloor \overset{\rightarrow}{\tau} \rfloor_n$. Because of the canonical form for tree shares, their associated formal definitions are somewhat unpleasant, but informally what is going on is simple. First, the tree τ is unfolded to height n. Second, we shrink the height of the tree by uniformly choosing the left (respectively, right) leaf from each pair of leaves at height n. Finally, we refold the resulting tree back into canonical form.

For illustration, here we left and right round the tree $\bullet \circ \bullet \circ \bullet$ to height 3. To help visually track what is going on, we have highlighted the left leaf in each pair with the color red and the right leaf in each pair with the color blue.

Lemma 8 (Properties of $\lfloor \overset{\leftarrow}{\tau} \rfloor_n$ and $\lfloor \overset{\rightarrow}{\tau} \rfloor_n$)

1. If $n > |\tau|$ then $\lfloor \overset{\leftarrow}{\tau} \rfloor_n = \lfloor \overset{\rightarrow}{\tau} \rfloor_n = \tau$

2. If $n = |\tau|$, $\tau_l = \lfloor \overset{\leftarrow}{\tau} \rfloor_n$, and $\tau_r = \lfloor \overset{\rightarrow}{\tau} \rfloor_n$ then $\max(|\tau_l|, |\tau_r|) < n$

3. If $\tau_1 \oplus \tau_2 = \tau_3$ and $n = \max(|\tau_1|, |\tau_2|, |\tau_3|)$, then $\lfloor \overset{\leftarrow}{\tau_1} \rfloor_n \oplus \lfloor \overset{\leftarrow}{\tau_2} \rfloor_n = \lfloor \overset{\leftarrow}{\tau_3} \rfloor_n$ and $\lfloor \overset{\rightarrow}{\tau_1} \rfloor_n \oplus \lfloor \overset{\rightarrow}{\tau_2} \rfloor_n = \lfloor \overset{\rightarrow}{\tau_3} \rfloor_n$

Proved in Coq. Lemma 8 states (1) that $\lfloor \overset{\leftarrow}{\tau} \rfloor_n$ and $\lfloor \overset{\rightarrow}{\tau} \rfloor_n$ do not affect τ if $n > |\tau|$; and (2) will decrease the height if $n = |t|$. Most importantly, (3) $\lfloor \overset{\leftarrow}{\tau} \rfloor_n$ and $\lfloor \overset{\rightarrow}{\tau} \rfloor_n$ preserve the join relation when n is the height of the equation.

We extend $\lfloor \overset{\leftarrow}{\cdot} \rfloor_n$ and $\lfloor \overset{\rightarrow}{\cdot} \rfloor_n$ to work over solutions S pointwise as follows:

$$\lfloor \overset{\leftarrow}{S} \rfloor_n \equiv \lambda v. \lfloor \overset{\leftarrow}{S(v)} \rfloor_n \qquad \lfloor \vec{S} \rfloor_n \equiv \lambda v. \lfloor \overset{\rightarrow}{S(v)} \rfloor_n$$

The key point of the rounding functions is given by the next lemma, a corollary of lemma 8 after using a solution S to instantiate variables in a system Σ.

Lemma 9. *Let* $S \models \Sigma$, $n = |S| > |\Sigma|$, $S_l = \lfloor \overleftarrow{S} \rfloor_n$, *and* $S_r = \lfloor \overrightarrow{S} \rfloor_n$. *Then* $S_l \models \Sigma$, $S_r \models \Sigma$, *and* $\max(|S_l|, |S_r|) < n$.

The key to this lemma is that since we are rounding only at a height $n > |\Sigma|$, all of the constants in Σ are unchanged. Only the variables in S with height greater than $|\Sigma|$ are modified, but their new values are also solutions for Σ. With the preliminaries out of the way, we are finally ready to prove Theorem 1.

Theorem 1. Σ *is satisfiable if and only if* Σ *can be satisfied with a solution* S *whose height is* $|\Sigma|$, *i.e.,* $\exists S.\ S \models \Sigma$ *iff* $\exists S.\ |S| = |\Sigma| \wedge S \models \Sigma$.

Proof. $\Leftarrow$: Immediate. $\Rightarrow$: Suppose $S \models \Sigma$. By Lemma 7, we have $|S| \geq |\Sigma|$, i.e., $|S| = |\Sigma| + n$ for some n. We proceed by strong induction on n. If $n = 0$ we are done. Otherwise, by Lemma 9 we know that $S_l = \lfloor \overleftarrow{S} \rfloor_{|\Sigma|+n}$ satisfies Σ and $|S_l| < |S|$, letting us apply the induction hypothesis. □

5.2 The Sufficiency of Finite Search for IMPL

IMPL is more complicated than SAT due to the contravariance. Suppose we have computationally checked that all solutions S of height $|\Sigma_a|$ that satisfy Σ_a also satisfy Σ_c. Now suppose that $S \models \Sigma_a$ for some S such that $|S| = |\Sigma_a| + 1$, and we wish to know if $S \models \Sigma_c$. Lemma 9 tells us that $\lfloor \overleftarrow{S} \rfloor_{|\Sigma_a|+1} \models \Sigma_a$. Our computational verification then tells us that $\lfloor \overleftarrow{S} \rfloor_{|\Sigma_a|+1} \models \Sigma_c$, but then we are stuck: on its own, $\lfloor \overleftarrow{S} \rfloor_{|\Sigma_a|+1} \models \Sigma_c$ is too weak to prove $S \models \Sigma_c$.

The root of the problem is that $\lfloor \overleftarrow{\tau} \rfloor_n$ does not contain enough information about the original because half of the leaves are removed. Fortunately, the leaves that were dropped when we round left are exactly the leaves that are kept when we round right, and vice versa. We can define a third operation, written $\tau_l \bigtriangledown_n \tau_r$ and pronounced "average", that recombines the rounded trees back into the original. Just as was the case with the rounding functions, although the formal definition of $\tau_l \bigtriangledown_n \tau_r$ is somewhat unpleasant due to the necessity of managing the canonical forms, the core idea is straightforward. First, τ_l and τ_r are unfolded to height $n - 1$. Second, each leaf in τ_l is paired with its corresponding leaf in τ_r. Finally, the resulting tree is folded back into canonical form.

We illustrate with another example, highlighting again with red and blue:

Lemma 10 (Properties of $\tau_l \bigtriangledown_n \tau_r$)

1. *If* $n > |\tau|$ *then* $\tau \bigtriangledown_n \tau = \tau$.
2. *If* $n \geq |\tau|$, *then* $\lfloor \overleftarrow{\tau} \rfloor_n \bigtriangledown_n \lfloor \overrightarrow{\tau} \rfloor_n = \tau$.
3. *If* $n > \max(|\tau_1|, |\tau_2|, |\tau_3|, |\tau_1'|, |\tau_2'|, |\tau_3'|)$, $\tau_1 \oplus \tau_2 = \tau_3$, *and* $\tau_1' \oplus \tau_2' = \tau_3'$, *then* $(\tau_1 \bigtriangledown_n \tau_1') \oplus (\tau_2 \bigtriangledown_n \tau_2') = (\tau_3 \bigtriangledown_n \tau_3')$.

Proved in Coq. The key points are (1) τ is an identity with itself, (2) $\bigtriangledown_n$ is the inverse of $\lfloor \overleftarrow{\tau} \rfloor_n$ and $\lfloor \overrightarrow{\tau} \rfloor_n$, and (3) $\bigtriangledown_n$ preserves the join operation $\oplus$.

Given a system Σ, Lemma 10 contains the facts we need to prove that the ∇_n-combination of two solutions S_l and S_r as defined below is also a solution.

$$S_l \nabla_n S_r \equiv \lambda v.\ S_l(v) \nabla_n S_r(v)$$

Lemma 11 (Properties of $S_l \nabla_n S_r$)

1. For all S, if $n \geq |S|$ then $\lfloor \overleftarrow{S} \rfloor_n \nabla_n \lfloor \overrightarrow{S} \rfloor_n = S$.
2. Let S_l, S_r be solutions of Σ and $n > \max(|S_l|, |S_r|)$. Then $S = S_l \nabla_n S_r$ is a solution of Σ.

Direct from Lemma 10. We are now ready to attack the main IMPL theorem.

Theorem 3. $\Sigma_a \vdash \Sigma_c$ iff $\Sigma_a \vdash \Sigma_c$ for all solutions S s.t. $|S| = |\Sigma_a|$, i.e., $\forall S.\ S \models \Sigma_a \Rightarrow S \models \Sigma_c$ iff $\forall S.\ |S| = |\Sigma_a| \Rightarrow S \models \Sigma_a \Rightarrow S \models \Sigma_c$.

Proof. $\Rightarrow$: Immediate. $\Leftarrow$: We apply complete induction, starting from $|\Sigma_a|$, on the height of solutions S of Σ_a. The base case ($|S| = |\Sigma_a|$) is immediate. For the inductive case, we know $S \models \Sigma_a$ and that all solutions S' of Σ_a such that $|S'| < |S|$ are also solutions of Σ_c. By Lemma 9, we know that $\lfloor \overleftarrow{S} \rfloor_{|S|}$ and $\lfloor \overrightarrow{S} \rfloor_{|S|}$ are both solutions to Σ_a with lower heights. The induction hypothesis yields that $\lfloor \overleftarrow{S} \rfloor_{|S|}$ and $\lfloor \overrightarrow{S} \rfloor_{|S|}$ are also both solutions of Σ_c. Lemma 11 completes the proof by telling us that $\lfloor \overleftarrow{S} \rfloor_{|S|} \nabla_{|S|} \lfloor \overrightarrow{S} \rfloor_{|S|} = S$ is also a solution of Σ_c. $\square$

6 Handling Non-zeros

For fear of cluttering the presentation we omitted showing how to restrict a variable to non-zero shares in SAT and IMPL queries.

However, our methods are able to handle this detail: each system of equations also contains a list of "non-zero" variables. This list is taken into account when constructing the first-order boolean formula: for each non-zero variable, an extra disjunctive clause over all the decompositions of that variable is generated. This forces at least one of the boolean variables corresponding to the initial non-zero variable to be true in each solution. In the tree domain, this clause ensures that the non-zero variable has at least one $\bullet$ leaf.

The full algorithms have an extra call to the NON_ZERO function, which returns a conjunction of the clauses encoding the non-zero disjunctions (not shown: sometimes we need to lift existentials to the top level). To force a variable v to be strictly positive at least one of the variables decomposed from v needs to be true (*i.e.*, the tree value has at least one.$\bullet$ leaf). If v_i is the set of variables obtained from decomposing v then positivity is encoded by $\bigvee_i v_i$.

```
SAT(Σ)                          IMPL(Σₐ, Σ_c)
  Φ = REDUCE(Σ)                   (Φₐ, Φ_c) = REDUCEI(Σₐ, Σ_c)
  Φ_r = Φ ∧ NON_ZERO(Σ)           Φ'ₐ = Φₐ ∧ NON_ZERO(Σ₁)
  Return SMT_SOLVER(Φ_r)          Φ'_c = Φ_c ∧ NON_ZERO(Σ₂)
                                  Return ¬ SMT_SOLVER(Φ'ₐ ∧ ¬Φ'_c)
```

Because these *non-zero* constraints relate otherwise disjoint equation subsystems to each other, it is not obvious how to verify each subsystem independently, which is why we produce one large boolean formula rather than many small ones.

Furthermore, the non-zero set forces extra system decompositions. To illustrate this point, observe that the equation $v_1 \oplus v_2 = \bullet$ has no solution of depth 0 in which both v_1 and v_2 are non-empty. However, decomposing the system once will yield the system: $v_1^l \oplus v_2^l = \bullet \wedge v_1^r \oplus v_2^r = \bullet$ with two possible solutions $(v_1^l = \circ; v_1^r = \bullet; v_2^l = \bullet; v_2^r = \circ)$ and $(v_1^l = \bullet; v_1^r = \circ; v_2^l = \circ; v_2^r = \bullet)$ which translate into $(v_1 = \widehat{\circ \, \bullet}; v_2 = \widehat{\bullet \, \circ})$ and $(v_1 = \widehat{\bullet \, \circ}; v_2 = \widehat{\circ \, \bullet})$. We have proved that for each non-zero variable, $\lceil log_2(n) \rceil$ is an upper bound on the number of extra decompositions, where n is the total number of variables. In practice we do not need to decompose nearly that much, and we have not noticed a meaningful performance cost. We speculate that we avoid most of the cost of the additional decompositions because the extra variables are often handled by some of the fast simplification rules we have incorporated into our tool.

7   Solver Implementation

Here we discuss some implementation issues. Our prototype is an OCaml library that implements (an optimized version of) the algorithms from §4 to resolve the SAT and IMPL queries issued by an entailment checker such as SLEEK.

Architecture. Our library contains four modules with clearly delimited interfaces so that each component can be independently used and improved:

1. An implementation of tree shares that exposes basic operations like equality testing, tree constructors, the join operation, and left/right projection.
2. The core: which reduces equation systems to boolean satisfiability. The bulk of the core module translates equation systems into boolean formulas via an optimized version of the procedures given in §4. As we will see, a considerable number of queries reduce to tautologies after repeated simplification/decomposition and can thus be discharged without the SAT/SMT solver. If we are not that lucky, then the system is reduced to a list of existentially quantified variables, a list of variables that must be strictly positive, and a list of join facts over booleans of the form $v_1 \oplus v_2 = (\bullet|v_3)$.
3. The backend: tasked with interfacing with the SAT/SMT solver: translating the output format from the core to the input format of the SAT/SMT solver and retrieving the result. Our backend is quite lightweight so changing the underlying solver is a breeze. We provide backends to MiniSat [5] and Z3 [3]; each add some final solver-specific optimizations.
4. A frontend: although the prover can be used as an OCaml library, we believe users may also want to query it as a standalone program. We provide a module for parsing input files and calling the core module.

Evaluation A: SLEEK embedding. Our OCaml library is designed to be easily incorporated into a general verification system. Accordingly, we tested our implementation by incorporating it into the SLEEK separation logic entailment prover and comparing its performance with our previous attempt at a share prover [9, §8.1]. That prover attempted to find solution by iteratively bounding the range of variables and trying to reach a fixed point; for example from $\widehat{\circ}_\bullet \oplus x = y$ it would deduce $\circ \leq x \leq \widehat{\bullet}_\circ$ and $\widehat{\circ}_\bullet \leq y$. The resulting highly incomplete solver was unable to prove most entailments containing more than one share variable, even for many extremely simple examples such as $v_1 \oplus v_2 = v_3 \vdash v_2 \oplus v_1 = v_3$.

We denote the implementation of the method presented here as ShP (Share Prover), and use BndP (Bound Prover) for the previous prover and present our results in Table 1. In the first column, we name our tests, which are broken into three test groups. The next five columns deal with the SAT queries generated by the tests, and the final five columns with the IMPL queries.

The first two test groups were developed for BndP in [9] and so the share problems they generate are not particularly difficult. The first four tests verify increasingly precise properties of a short (32-line) concurrent program in HIP, which calls SLEEK, which then calls BndP/ShP. In either case, the number of calls is the same and is given in the column labeled "call no."; *e.g.*, barrier-weak requires 116 SAT checks and 222 IMPL checks.

The columns labeled "BndP (ms)" contain the cumulative time in milliseconds to run the BndP checker on all the queries in the associated test, *e.g.*, barrier-weak spends 0.4ms to verify 116 SAT problems and 2.1ms to verify 222 IMPL checks. BndP may be highly incomplete, but at least it is *rapidly* highly incomplete. The columns labeled "ShP" contain the cumulative time in milliseconds to run the ShP checker, *e.g.*, barrier-weak spends 610ms verifying 116 SAT problems and 650ms verifying 222 IMPL problems. Obviously this is quite a bit slower, but part of the context is that the rest of HIP/SLEEK is approximately 3,000ms on each of the first four tests—in other words, ShP, although much slower than BndP, is still considerably faster than the rest of HIP/SLEEK.

The remaining columns shed some light on what is going on; "SAT no." gives the number of queries that ShP actually submitted to the underlying SAT solver. For example, barrier-weak submitted 73 out of 116 queries to the underlying solver for SAT and 42 out of 222 queries to the underlying solver for IMPL; the remaining 43+180 queries were solved during simplification/decomposition. Finally "SAT (ms)" gives the total amount of time spent in the underlying SAT solver itself; in every case this is the dominant timing factor. While it is not surprising that the SAT solver takes a certain amount of time to work its mojo, we suspect that most of the time is actually spent with process startup/teardown and hypothesize that performance would improve considerably with some clever systems engineering. Of course, another way to improve the timings in practice is to run BndP first and only resort to ShP when BndP gets confused.

Tests five through nine were also developed for BndP, but bypass HIP to test certain parts of SLEEK directly. Observe that when the underlying solver is not called, ShP is quite fast, although still considerably slower than BndP.

Table 1. Experimental timing results

test	SAT					IMPL				
	call no.	BndP (ms)	ShP (ms)	SAT no.	SAT (ms)	call no.	BndP (ms)	ShP (ms)	SAT no.	SAT (ms)
barrier-weak	116	0.4	610	73	530	222	2.1	650	42	450
barrier-strong	116	0.6	660	73	510	222	2.2	788	42	460
barrier-paper	116	0.7	664	73	510	216	2.2	757	42	460
barrier-paper-ex	114	0.8	605	71	520	212	2.3	610	40	430
fractions	63	0.1	0.1	0	0	89	0.1	110	11	110
fractions1	11	0.1	0.1	0	0	15	0.1	31.3	3	30
barrier	68	0.1	0.9	0	0	174	1.2	3.9	0	0
barrier3	36	0.2	0.1	0	0	92	0.2	2.2	0	0
barrier4	59	0.1	0.7	0	0	140	0.9	2.4	0	0
read_ops	14	FAIL	210	14	208	27	FAIL	317	9	150
construct	4	FAIL	70	4	65	17	FAIL	880	17	270
join_ent	3	FAIL	70	3	30	3	FAIL	50	3	48

On the other hand, even if the total time is reasonable, what is the point of advocating a slower prover unless it can verify things the faster prover cannot? The tenth test tries to verify a simple 25-line **sequential** program whose verification uses fractional shares; we write FAIL to indicate that BndP is unable to verify the queries. Finally, the eleventh and twelfth tests bypass HIP and instruct SLEEK to check entailments that BndP is unable to help verify.

For brevity, we report here the timings obtained only with the Z3 backend. Usually, choice of backend does not make much difference, but in a few cases, *e.g.* read_ops and join_ent, choosing MiniSat can degrade the performance by a factor of 10. We leave the investigation of this behavior for future work.

Evaluation B: Standalone. While verifying programs, and their associated separation logic entailments is really the main goal, it is not so easy to casually develop HIP and SLEEK input files that exercise share provers aggressively. We designed a benchmark of 53 SAT and 50 IMPLY queries, many of which we specifically designed to stress a share prover in various tricky ways, including heavily skewed tree constants, evil mixes of non-zero variables, deep heterogenous tree constants, numerous unconstrained variables, and a number of others.

ShP solved the entire test suite in 1.4s; 24 SAT checks and 18 IMPL checks reached the underlying solver. BndP could solve fewer than 10% of the queries.

8   Related and Future Work

Simpler fractional permissions are used in a variety of logics [2,1] and verification tools [10]. Their use is by no means restricted to separation logic as indicated by their use in CHALICE [6]. Despite the simpler domain, and associated loss of useful technical properties, we could find no completeness claims in the literate. It is our hope that other program verification tools will decide to incorporate more sophisticated share models now that they can use our solver.

In the future we would like to improve the performance of our tool by trying to mix the sound but incomplete bounds-based method [9] with the techniques described here; make a number of performance-related engineering enhancements, integrate the ⋈ operation, and develop a mechanically-verified implementation.

9 Conclusion

We have shown how to extract a system of equations over a sophisticated fractional share model from separation logic formulae. We have developed a solver for the equation systems and proven that the associated problems are decidable. We have integrated our solver into the HIP/SLEEK verification toolset and benchmarked its performance to show that the system is usable in practice.

References

1. Bornat, R., Calcagno, C., O'Hearn, P., Parkinson, M.: Permission accounting in separation logic. In: POPL, pp. 259–270 (2005)
2. Boyland, J.: Checking Interference with Fractional Permissions. In: Cousot, R. (ed.) SAS 2003. LNCS, vol. 2694, pp. 55–72. Springer, Heidelberg (2003)
3. de Moura, L., Bjørner, N.: Z3: An Efficient SMT Solver. In: Ramakrishnan, C.R., Rehof, J. (eds.) TACAS 2008. LNCS, vol. 4963, pp. 337–340. Springer, Heidelberg (2008)
4. Dockins, R., Hobor, A., Appel, A.W.: A Fresh Look at Separation Algebras and Share Accounting. In: Hu, Z. (ed.) APLAS 2009. LNCS, vol. 5904, pp. 161–177. Springer, Heidelberg (2009)
5. Eén, N., Sörensson, N.: An Extensible SAT-solver. In: Giunchiglia, E., Tacchella, A. (eds.) SAT 2003. LNCS, vol. 2919, pp. 502–518. Springer, Heidelberg (2004)
6. Heule, S., Leino, K.R.M., Müller, P., Summers, A.J.: Fractional permissions without the fractions. In: FTfJP (2011)
7. Hobor, A.: Oracle Semantics. PhD thesis, Princeton University, Department of Computer Science, Princeton, NJ (October 2008)
8. Hobor, A., Gherghina, C.: Barriers in Concurrent Separation Logic. In: Barthe, G. (ed.) ESOP 2011. LNCS, vol. 6602, pp. 276–296. Springer, Heidelberg (2011)
9. Hobor, A., Gherghina, C.: Barriers in concurrent separation logic: Now with tool support! Logical Methods in Computer Science 8(2) (2012)
10. Jacobs, B., Smans, J., Philippaerts, P., Vogels, F., Penninckx, W., Piessens, F.: VeriFast: A Powerful, Sound, Predictable, Fast Verifier for C and Java. In: Bobaru, M., Havelund, K., Holzmann, G.J., Joshi, R. (eds.) NFM 2011. LNCS, vol. 6617, pp. 41–55. Springer, Heidelberg (2011)
11. Nguyen, H.H., David, C., Qin, S., Chin, W.N.: Automated Verification of Shape and Size Properties Via Separation Logic. In: Cook, B., Podelski, A. (eds.) VMCAI 2007. LNCS, vol. 4349, pp. 251–266. Springer, Heidelberg (2007)
12. Parkinson, M.: Local Reasoning for Java. PhD thesis. University of Cambridge (2005)
13. Reynolds, J.C.: Separation logic: A logic for shared mutable data structures. In: LICS, pp. 55–74 (2002)
14. Villard, J.: Personal communication (2012)
15. Villard, J., Lozes, É., Calcagno, C.: Tracking Heaps That Hop with Heap-Hop. In: Esparza, J., Majumdar, R. (eds.) TACAS 2010. LNCS, vol. 6015, pp. 275–279. Springer, Heidelberg (2010)

Mechanized Semantics for Compiler Verification

Xavier Leroy

INRIA Paris-Rocquencourt
xavier.leroy@inria.fr

Abstract. The formal verification of compilers and related programming tools depends crucially on the availability of appropriate mechanized semantics for the source, intermediate and target languages. In this invited talk, I review various forms of operational semantics and their mechanization, based on my experience with the formal verification of the CompCert C compiler.

What does this program do, exactly? What is this program transformation or analysis supposed to do, exactly? Formal semantics is the art of providing mathematically-precise answers to these questions. It is a prerequisite to the verification of individual programs, and also to the specification (let alone verification) of programs that operate over other programs, such as static analyzers, program provers, code generators, and optimizing compilers.

Fundamental questions rarely have unique answers. Indeed, a great many different styles of semantics have been explored over the last 50 years, ranging from denotational to axiomatic to operational. In some application areas, *de facto* standards of semantics have emerged, such as labeled transition systems for concurrency, following Milner's seminal work on CCS and the π-calculus [1,2], and small-step reduction semantics in the type systems community, following Wright and Felleisen's preservation-and-progress pattern for type soundness proofs [3].

The landscape of programming languages research evolves quickly, renewing interest in other forms of semantics. For example, mechanization—formalizing semantics "on machine" with the help of interactive theorem provers, rather than "on paper"—is becoming standard practice in our field. The POPLmark challenge [4] showed that elementary semantic tools such as capture-avoiding substitution can be difficult to mechanize. On the other hand, the power of proof assistants makes it easier to work with semantic styles that are difficult to get right on paper, such as step-indexed logical relations [5] or definitional interpreters [6].

Another evolution worth noting is to formalize "real world" languages, such as C and Javascript, and to prove semantic properties that go beyond type safety, such as semantic preservation for a code generation or optimization algorithm. The reduction-based semantics that work so well to prove type safety for small languages such as IMP, Mini-ML or Featherweight Java can "burst at the seams" when applied to big, messy languages such as C. Likewise, relating the executions of two programs, before and after a code transformation, is fundamentally more

R. Jhala and A. Igarashi (Eds.): APLAS 2012, LNCS 7705, pp. 386–388, 2012.

difficult than showing the preservation of a typing invariant throughout the execution of a single program.

In this talk, I survey some of these issues based on my personal experience with the formal verification of the CompCert C compiler [7]. As part of this effort, S. Blazy and I had to give mechanized semantics to 14 languages: a very large subset of ANSI C as the source language, assembly for the ARM, PowerPC and x86 machine architectures as target languages, and 10 intermediate languages that bridge the semantic gap between the source and target languages. This semantic engineering is a large part of the CompCert effort, first because these semantics appear prominently in the statement of compiler correctness that we prove, second because we had to change these semantics in essential ways throughout the development of CompCert, in order to prove stronger correctness statements and to accommodate progressively bigger subsets of ANSI C.

The first verifications were conducted against natural (big-step) semantics for the source language and most of the intermediate languages; only the target assembly language was in pure transition (small-step) style [8,9]. Natural semantics lived up to its name, resulting in relatively straightforward specifications for our languages, and helping us discover the main insights of the semantic preservation proofs. However, we quickly hit limitations of natural semantics, such as its inability to describe nonterminating executions.

The second iteration of CompCert, therefore, uses a combination of small-step transition semantics with explicit call stack for most of the intermediate languages [10], and of *coinductive big-step semantics* for the source language and the first intermediate languages. Coinductive big-step semantics, as introduced by Grall and Leroy [11], enable divergence to be described by coinductive inference rules that follow the structure of executions, like natural semantics does for termination.

We then wanted to account for unstructured control (the **goto** statement) and nondeterministic evaluation order of C, and also to make provisions for a future extension towards shared-memory concurrency—many features where big-step semantics is not appropriate. We therefore switched to small-step, labeled transition semantics for the source and intermediate languages with structured control. We found reduction semantics in the style of MiniML or Featherweight Java inadequate for compiler proofs, but succeeded in using *continuation-based semantics* as introduced by Appel and Blazy [12]. These semantics carefully separate the current sub-command under execution from the execution context in which it appears, with the context being represented "inside-out" as a continuation term. This style of operational semantics is reminiscent not only of the CEK abstract machine [13], but also of polarization and focusing in proof theory and in λ-calculus [14,15]

CompCert's journey through the landscape of operational semantics has been rather tortuous, but led to the discovery of original forms of operational semantics along the way. Are we at the end of the path? It depends on the language features we would like to model in the future. For instance, giving semantics to program fragments (compilation units) and reasoning about separate compilation and linking probably requires more compositional reasoning principles based on logical relations, in the style of Benton and Hur [16]. In all likelihood, the large-scale formal verification of compilers and static analyzer, as well as other emerging applications of semantics, will keep challenging the state of the art in semantics and exposing the need for new approaches and mechanizations.

References

1. Milner, R.: Communication and Concurrency. Prentice-Hall (1990)
2. Milner, R.: Communicating and Mobile Systems: the pi-Calculus. Cambridge University Press (1999)
3. Wright, A.K., Felleisen, M.: A syntactic approach to type soundness. Information and Computation 115(1), 38–94 (1994)
4. Aydemir, B.E., Charguéraud, A., Pierce, B.C., Pollack, R., Weirich, S.: Engineering formal metatheory. In: 35th Symposium Principles of Programming Languages, pp. 3–15. ACM Press (2008)
5. Appel, A.W., McAllester, D.A.: An indexed model of recursive types for foundational proof-carrying code. ACM Transactions on Programming Languages and Systems 23(5), 657–683 (2001)
6. Danielsson, N.A.: Operational semantics using the partiality monad. In: International Conference on Functional Programming 2012, pp. 127–138. ACM Press (2012)
7. Leroy, X.: Formal verification of a realistic compiler. Communications of the ACM 52(7), 107–115 (2009)
8. Leroy, X.: Formal certification of a compiler back-end, or: programming a compiler with a proof assistant. In: 33rd Symposium Principles of Programming Languages, pp. 42–54. ACM Press (2006)
9. Blazy, S., Dargaye, Z., Leroy, X.: Formal Verification of a C Compiler Front-End. In: Misra, J., Nipkow, T., Sekerinski, E. (eds.) FM 2006. LNCS, vol. 4085, pp. 460–475. Springer, Heidelberg (2006)
10. Leroy, X.: A formally verified compiler back-end. Journal of Automated Reasoning 43(4), 363–446 (2009)
11. Leroy, X., Grall, H.: Coinductive big-step operational semantics. Information and Computation 207(2), 284–304 (2009)
12. Appel, A.W., Blazy, S.: Separation Logic for Small-Step Cminor. In: Schneider, K., Brandt, J. (eds.) TPHOLs 2007. LNCS, vol. 4732, pp. 5–21. Springer, Heidelberg (2007)
13. Felleisen, M., Friedman, D.P.: Control operators, the SECD machine and the λ-calculus. In: Formal Description of Programming Concepts III, pp. 131–141. North-Holland (1986)
14. Liang, C., Miller, D.: Focusing and polarization in linear, intuitionistic, and classical logics. Theoretical Computer Science 410(46), 4747–4768 (2009)
15. Curien, P.L., Munch-Maccagnoni, G.: The Duality of Computation under Focus. In: Calude, C.S., Sassone, V. (eds.) TCS 2010. IFIP AICT, vol. 323, pp. 165–181. Springer, Heidelberg (2010)
16. Benton, N., Hur, C.K.: Biorthogonality, step-indexing and compiler correctness. In: International Conference on Functional Programming 2009, pp. 97–108. ACM Press (2009)

Author Index